D0371396

New Hampshire

New Hampshire

Christina Tree & Christine Hamm

 The Countryman Press ✳ Woodstock, Vermont

We welcome your comments and suggestions. Please contact Explorer's Guide Editor, The Countryman Press, P.O. Box 748, Woodstock, Vermont 05091 or e-mail countrymanpress@wwnorton.com.

Copyright © 1991, 1994, 1996 by Christina Tree and Peter Randall
Copyright © 1999, 2002, 2006 by Christina Tree and Christine Hamm

Sixth Edition

ISBN-10 0-88150-620-6
ISBN-13 978-0-88150-620-4
ISSN 1538-8409

Maps by XNR Productions, © 2006 The Countryman Press
Book design by Bodenweber Design
Text composition by PerfecType, Nashville, TN
Cover photograph of Tamworth, NH, by Robert J. Kozlow

Published by The Countryman Press, P.O. Box 748, Woodstock, Vermont 05091

Distributed by W. W. Norton & Company, Inc., 500 Fifth Avenue, New York, NY 10110

Printed in the United States of America

10 9 8 7 6 5 4 3 2 1

DEDICATION

For William A. Davis
　　　　　—Christina Tree

For Tessie, Ellen, and Roger, whose extra eyes have
made these explorations an excellent adventure.
　　　　　—Christine Hamm

EXPLORE WITH US!

Welcome to the most widely used and comprehensive travel guide to the Granite State. As we have expanded our guide in response to the increase in ways to explore New Hampshire, we have also been increasingly selective, making recommendations based on years of conscientious research. All inclusions—attractions, inns, and restaurants—are chosen on the basis of personal experience, not paid advertising.

The following points will help to get you started on your way.

WHAT'S WHERE

In the beginning of the book you'll find an alphabetical listing of highlights and important information that you may want to reference quickly.

LODGING

Prices: Please don't hold us or the respective innkeepers responsible for the rates listed as of press time in 2006. Some changes are inevitable. The state **rooms and meals tax is 8 percent** as of this writing, but that also may change. The following codes are used to specify: **EP:** lodging only; **MAP:** lodging, breakfast, and dinner; **B&B:** lodging and breakfast; **AP:** lodging and three meals.

RESTAURANTS

In most sections, please note a distinction between *Dining Out* and *Eating Out*. Restaurants in the *Eating Out* group are generally inexpensive.

KEY TO SYMBOLS

⌾ The wedding ring symbol denotes properties that specialize in weddings.

🐾 The special value symbol appears next to lodging and restaurants that combine quality and moderate prices.

🐾 The pet symbol appears next to lodgings that accept pets (usually with prior notice).

🧸 The kids alert symbol appears next to lodgings, restaurants, activities, and shops of special appeal to youngsters.

♿ The wheelchair symbol appears next to lodgings, restaurants, and attractions that are partially or completely handicapped accessible.

We would appreciate your comments and corrections about places you visit or know well in the state. Please address your correspondence to Explorer's Guide Editor, The Countryman Press, P.O. Box 748, Woodstock, VT 05091. You can also e-mail Chris Tree: ctree@traveltree.net.

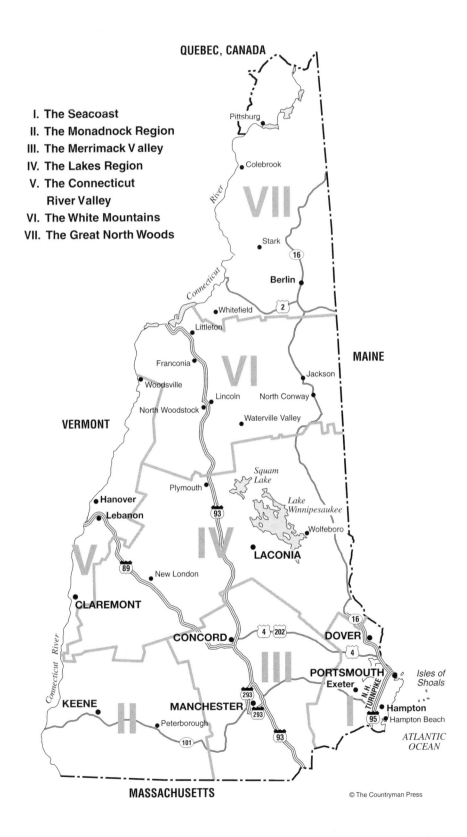

QUEBEC, CANADA

I. The Seacoast
II. The Monadnock Region
III. The Merrimack Valley
IV. The Lakes Region
V. The Connecticut
   River Valley
VI. The White Mountains
VII. The Great North Woods

Pittsburg

Colebrook

VII

Stark

16

Berlin

Whitefield

Littleton

2

Franconia

Woodsville

VI

Jackson

Lincoln

North Conway

North Woodstock

Waterville Valley

MAINE

VERMONT

Squam
Lake

Plymouth

Lake
Winnipesaukee

Hanover

Wolfeboro

Lebanon

93

V

IV

LACONIA

89

New London

CLAREMONT

Concord
River

DOVER

16

4

CONCORD

4   202

III

PORTSMOUTH

Isles of
Shoals

Exeter

KEENE

II

MANCHESTER

293

N.H.
TURNPIKE

Hampton

101

Peterborough

293

95

Hampton Beach

93

ATLANTIC
OCEAN

MASSACHUSETTS

© The Countryman Press

CONTENTS

7   The Great North Woods

INTRODUCTION

In the 19th century fine scenery, fresh air, and a flourishing work ethic brought thousands of tourists to New Hampshire. Ever since artist Thomas Cole first visited the Granite State in 1827, his pictures and those of a host of followers brought the landscape that Cole called "a union of the picturesque, the sublime, and the magnificent" to the attention of the world. Mark Twain, who summered in the Monadnock region, reported that "the atmosphere of the New Hampshire highlands is exceptionally bracing and stimulating, and a fine aid to hard and continuous work." Visitors came to see for themselves.

With the improvement of roads and the coming of the railroads, the fame of the region spread. As the eastern seaboard became more and more urbanized, the country atmosphere of New Hampshire's farms and villages offered a step back in time that was only a short train ride away.

At the same time, small country households throughout the state were opening their doors to guests and major entrepreneurs were investing in the new business of tourism. By the turn of the 20th century, the Granite State had become the most heavily touristed spot in New England, with a greater concentration of grand resort hotels in New Hampshire's White Mountains than anywhere else in America. Travelers flocked to hundreds of these wooden hotels, built to accommodate city dwellers who wanted a sanitized version of the wilderness, a kind of eastern dude ranch in which families could ride in the relative comfort of a stagecoach to view the Flume, Echo Lake, and the Old Man of the Mountain. In late afternoon parents and grandparents could retire to a rocking chair, sip a glass of claret, and view the peaks of the Presidentials from the cloister of a sweeping, colonnaded porch. This curious mix of wilderness and civility made the area an ideal destination. Most tourists stayed at one hotel for a week, a month, or for the entire summer season. Far enough away but not so dangerously distant as the still wild-seeming West, the towering waterfalls, emerald hills, and placid ponds of New Hampshire offered an escape to another world.

In the early part of the 20th century, the automobile changed this vacation pattern. As travelers gained more mobility, the large establishments with all their amenities for a full "season" closed. Many of the big, wooden hotels were destroyed by fire, while others were razed, unable to compete with the more economical cabin colonies and, later, motels. For New Hampshire there was a real decline in accommodations. This situation changed dramatically during the 1980s and '90s, however, when the state experienced an explosion of new lodgings. The proliferation of inviting places to stay—all around the state, not just along tried-and-true tourist routes—inspired us to attempt to bring the entire state into focus.

This book is intended for New Hampshire residents and visitors alike. No other portrait of the state gathers so much practical information between two covers. All listings in this book are free; there is no paid advertising.

Each chapter focuses on a different region. It begins with a verbal snapshot of the landscape and historical background. Sources of information, how to get around, and descriptions of everything to see and do, from winter sports to places to swim and picnic, follow. Then come capsule descriptions of places to stay. Our focus is on inns and bed & breakfasts, because we feel that the Mobil and AAA guides do a fine job with motels. We have personally visited more than 90 percent of the lodgings included (the other 10 percent have been highly recommended). We generally include prices because categories like "moderate" and "expensive" can be misleading, depending on what they include. Please allow for inflation. Most lodging places add the 8 percent New Hampshire room and meals tax (a small percentage include it in the price), and some also add a service charge; be sure to inquire. After lodging come critiques of local upscale restaurants (*Dining Out*) and more casual options (*Eating Out*). We also describe shops worth seeking out and the special events of that area.

New Hampshire's recent upswing in lodging options is particularly noticeable along the seacoast, where visitors can now linger long enough in and around historic Portsmouth to sample the region's many fine restaurants, theaters, museums, boat excursions, and beaches. It's equally noteworthy in the Monadnock region, which remains pristine ironically because it's too near Boston to be generally viewed as a place to stay the night. So it happens that despite its exceptional beauty, its great hiking and biking, and the quality of its inns and B&Bs (which give guests access to the swimming holes that are off-limits to day-trippers), it remains low-key and relatively pristine.

Lake Winnipesaukee, the state's largest lake, remains the popular tourist destination that it's been for more than a century. Still, there are quiet corners such as Squam Lake and the hills around Center Sandwich. Wolfeboro is home to America's first summer resort.

In the region we call the Western Lakes—because it harbors so many lakes, not just Sunapee—widely scattered lodging places offer access to swimming, sailing, summer theater, fine dining, and hiking up such mountains as Sunapee, Kearsarge, and Cardigan.

The Upper Valley region—recently designated one of America's Scenic Byways—includes towns scattered along both the Vermont and New Hampshire banks of the Connecticut River for some 20 miles north and south of Dartmouth College. Here you can enjoy a picnic and chamber music concert on the lawns of the Saint-Gaudens National Site in Cornish, New Hampshire, overlooking Mount Ascutney in Vermont. The country's longest covered bridge links the two. Esssentially rural, this is also one of New England's most sophisticated corridors, with outstanding museums, dining, and lodging.

The White Mountains form a ragged line, beginning near the Connecticut River with Mount Moosilauke and marching diagonally northeast across New Hampshire. We begin by describing the Western Whites, a rugged region largely within the White Mountain National Forest. It includes Loon Mountain and Waterville Valley, both founded as ski areas but now full-fledged year-round resorts, especially good bets for families, offering varied activities and condo-based lodging. This region also includes dramatic Franconia Notch and the old resort communities of Franconia, Sugar Hill, and Bethlehem.

Mount Washington, literally the high point of New England, has been New Hampshire's top tourist attraction for more than 150 years. Accessible by cog railway and car or "stage" as well as by spectacular hiking trails from all directions, it remains magnificent and untamed. This region has loomed large on the national ski map since the birth of alpine skiing. It presently offers a choice of half a dozen varied ski resorts and hundreds of miles of outstanding cross-country trails. During summer and fall it is a mecca for hikers and technical climbers as well as a great family destination, offering an easy entrée both to natural and human-made attractions. It also represents one of New Hampshire's largest concentration of lodging places, complemented by a wide range of dining spots and a wide variety of outlet shopping. We call the foothills of the White Mountains, just south of this area, the Mount Washington Gateway region. It's spotted with small lakes, inviting country roads and villages, and some exceptional places to stay.

The least touristed section of the state is the Great North Woods, the vast forested area that includes the northern White Mountains, the headwaters of the Connecticut River, and the mighty Androscoggin. Here moose graze beside the roads, and you can find wilderness campsites and fall asleep to the call of loons. You can also stay in The Balsams and the newly reopened Mountain View Grand Resort and Spa, two surviving grand hotels, or in a surprisingly wide choice of sporting camps and lodges.

Those visitors who scoot on by the urban communities along the Merrimack Valley in southern New Hampshire miss what those who live in the state consider some of its most popular destinations. Several well-marked sights are well worth the short detours off I-93. In addition to a suddenly thriving downtown with excellent restaurants and bistros, Manchester offers the superb Currier Museum of Art, tours of a residence designed by Frank Lloyd Wright, and the Millyard Museum, which chronicles what was once the world's largest mill community. There's also the Verizon Center, frequent host to a galaxy of such big-name stars as Elton John and Bette Midler, as well as the Manchester Monarchs hockey team. Concord's state capitol building is the oldest in the nation still in use, and the Museum of New Hampshire History across the street offers a superb introduction to the state. The city also boasts the state-of-the-art Christa McAuliffe Planetarium and the updated Capitol Center for the Arts; it too featuring big-name entertainers. In contrast, a quick dip off the highway reveals that many of the surrounding towns are as picturesque as any in New England.

One author of this book is a "visitor," the other a longtime resident. Chris Tree has explored the Granite State for more than 30 years as a travel writer whose New England stories appear regularly in the *Boston Globe* Sunday travel section. She is the author of *How New England Happened* (a historical guide to the region) and of the *Explorer's Guides* to Maine, Vermont, and the Berkshire Hills and Pioneer Valley.

Christine Hamm moved in 1972 to Hopkinton, New Hampshire, where she now lives in one of the state's classic white-clapboard villages within earshot of a Paul Revere bell. In addition to many years of writing for the *Concord Monitor's* arts and entertainment section, Chris has contributed articles to the *New York Post*, *Yankee Magazine's New England Travel Guide*, and numerous statewide publications. She is currently a member of the New Hampshire State Legislature.

The authors wish to thank Peter Randall, original coauthor of the book, who contributed hugely to its first two editions. We also owe thanks to numerous local chambers of commerce, innkeepers, and friends who helped provide and check information for the book.

For help with the "Great North Woods" chapter, Chris Tree wants to thank Dick Mallion of Whitefield, and Jackie Corrigon of Gorham. For help with the Mount Washington Valleys, she is indebted to Rob Burbank of the AMC and to Marti Mayne; for help with the Connecticut River Valley, to Debbie Albee, Kay and Peter Shumway, Susie Klein, and Susan Brown; for the Western Whites, to Jayne O'Conner, Mike and Meri Hern, and Bonnie MacPherson. Thanks especially to Steve Smith of Lincoln for his meticulous help with copy, maps, and images as well as book recommendations, and to former *Boston Globe* travel editor Bill Davis, her long-suffering husband, who cheered her on over icy winter roads and returned alone in summer to reupdate the Mount Washington Valley.

Chris Hamm wants to acknowledge those chamber of commerce staff members who helped lighten the load with their editorial comments and enthusiasm for the project. She extends particular thanks to chamber members Carolyn O'Brien and Tim Sink from Concord, Kristin Sawyer and Carol Bitov from Dover, Tina Collins from Hampton, Jane Natches from Manchester, Mary-Ellen Marcouillier from Nashua, and Kendra Frangos from Portsmouth. Others who were particularly helpful along the way include Paul Cossette at the New Hampton Visitors Center, Jayme and Laura Simoes of Louis Karno Communications, Mariaelena Koopman of the Inn at Christian Shore in Portsmouth, Rob Pinkham of the Cliff Lodge in Bristol, Bill Webb of the Inn on Golden Pond in Holderness, Rae Andrews and Cindy Foster of the Squam Lake Inn in Holderness, Jacqueline Caserta of the Inn at Valley Farms in Walpole, Robert Short of the Hancock Inn, Carol Beckwith of the Ashburn House in Fitzwilliam, Steve Hodges of the Highland Lake Inn in Andover, and Victoria Cimino of the New Hampshire Department of Travel and Tourism.

Thanks especially to our editors, Jennifer Thompson and Laura Jorstad, and to Kermit Hummel at The Countryman Press, for their support and patience.

WHAT'S WHERE IN NEW HAMPSHIRE

AREA CODE 603 covers all of New Hampshire.

AGRICULTURAL FAIRS New Hampshire boasts a baker's dozen summer and fall country fairs. Part of the social fabric of the 19th century, and still popular today, the country fair is the place where farm families meet their friends and exhibit their best home-canned and fresh vegetables, livestock, and handwork such as quilts, baked goods, and needlework. Horse and cattle pulling, 4-H competitions, horse shows, and woodsmen's competitions are joined by midways, food stalls, and exhibits of farm imple-

ments, home furnishings, and a host of other items. The New Hampshire's Rural Heritage pamphlet from the **New Hampshire Department of Agriculture** (603-271-3551; www .nhfarms.com) lists the dates and locations of all fairs. These events are also mentioned in the *Special Events* sections of this book. The largest fair is Deerfield, held annually in fall, but other popular fairs include Hopkinton and Lancaster, both held on Labor Day weekend; Cheshire Fair in Swanzey, held in early August; and Sandwich, on Columbus Day weekend. Additionally, many local towns and organizations hold annual 1-day fairs. Check with local chambers of commerce for exact dates.

AIR SERVICE Manchester Airport (603-624-6539; www.flymanchester .com) is northern New England's major gateway with connections to all parts of the country and Canada. It's served by United Airlines, US Airways and US Airways Express, Continental, Air Canada, Delta Air Lines, Comair, Independence Air, Northwest Airlines, and Southwest Airlines; also by national rental car companies, limo servcies, taxis, and bus lines. **Lebanon Municipal Airport** (603-298-8878), just off I-89 in West Lebanon, is served by US Airways Express to New York's LaGuardia Airport. Boston's **Logan International Airport** (www.massport.com/logan) and the **Portland (Maine) International Jetport** (www.portlandjetport.org) are also major gateways for New Hampshire. In addition, the state offers 20 airfields without scheduled service. Flying schools are located at Berlin, Claremont, Concord, Hampton, Jaffrey, Keene, Laconia, Lebanon, Manchester, Nashua, Rochester, Whitefield, and Wolfeboro. For details contact the **New Hampshire Division of Aeronautics** (603-271-2551), 65 Airport Rd., Concord 03301.

AMTRAK After many years without servcice, New Hampshire now has daily service to New York and Montreal, albeit on the **Vermonter** (1-800-872-7245; www.amtrak.com), which stops at Claremont and White River Junction, Vt.

ANTIQUARIAN BOOKSHOPS It's hard to resist a good old book, and New Hampshire has enough dealers in used, rare, and antiquarian books to keep any bibliophile busy. Among the specialty dealers are shops selling first editions and books related to espionage, gardening, the White Mountains, hot-air ballooning, and women's studies. Members of the **New Hampshire Antiquarian Booksellers Association** are listed at www.nhaba .org; a brochure version of the listing can be found at most antiquarian bookstores.

ANTIQUES The **New Hampshire Antiques Dealers Association**

(P.O. Box 2033, Hampton 03843; www.nhada.org). From the seacoast to the mountains and from the Lakes region to the Monadnock region, there are dealers in nearly every community, and the diversity of items offered equals any to be found in New England. Perhaps the largest concentration of shops is along Rt. 4 in Northwood and Epsom, but Concord, and environs has nearly as many shops. Meredith, Center Harbor, and Center Sandwich also have many shops, as do Hillsboro, Peterborough, Fitzwilliam, and Rt. 1 in the seacoast area. The association's annual show is held in early August in Manchester.

APPALACHIAN MOUNTAIN CLUB Founded (www.outdoors.org) in 1876 to blaze and map hiking trails through the White Mountains, the AMC was a crucial lobbying group for the passage of the Weeks Act. Today it continues to support environmental causes and cater to hikers, maintaining hundreds of miles of trails and feeding and sheltering hikers in a chain of eight "high huts" in the White Mountains, each a day's hike apart. **Pinkham Notch Camp** in Gorham, a comfortable complex at the eastern base of Mount Washington, and the appealing new

AMC

Highland Center in Crawford Notch at the western base of Mount Washington are the venues for a wide variety of year-round workshops in subjects ranging from nature drawing to North Country literature as well as camping, cross-country skiing, snowshoeing, and mountaineering. The AMC also maintains a hostel-like camping and lodging facility at Mount Cardigan, runs shuttle buses for hikers in the White Mountains, and much more. Their guidebooks (see *Canoeing and Kayaking* and *Hiking*) remain the best of their kind. For more information contact AMC headquarters at 5 Joy St., Boston, MA 02108 (617-536-0636).

APPLE AND FRUIT PICKING New Hampshire has many orchards and farms where you can pick your own apples, pears, peaches, and berries, and press cider. The vegetable- and fruit-picking season begins in early summer, while apples and other tree fruits ripen as fall begins. Many orchards have weekend festivals with fresh-baked apple pies, doughnuts and cider, pumpkins, tractor-pulled wagon rides, music, and other activities aimed at making a perfect family outing. Don't forget to visit the orchards in spring when the trees are blossoming. From the **New Hampshire Department of Agriculture** (603-271-3788; www.nhfarms.com), request the Experience Rural New Hampshire and Harvest New Hampshire pamphlets.

ART MUSEUMS AND GALLERIES New Hampshire's two major art museums are the **Currier Museum of Art** (www.currier.org) in Manchester and the **Hood Museum of Art** (www.hoodmuseum.dartmouth.edu)

at Dartmouth College. The Currier's collection includes some outstanding 19th- and 20th-century European and American works, and the museum is a departure point for tours to the Zimmerman House, designed by Frank Lloyd Wright. The Hood Museum's permanent collection ranges from some outstanding ancient Assyrian bas-reliefs to Picasso and Frank Stella. Both museums stage changing exhibits. (See "The Manchester/Nashua Area" and "Upper Valley Towns" for descriptions of each museum.)

BANDS Town bands are still popular in New Hampshire, and many hold summer concerts in outdoor bandstands. Schedules change yearly, so check with local chambers of commerce. Conway, North Conway, Alton, Wolfeboro, Exeter, Hopkinton, and Hampton Beach are among the places with regular band concerts. The Temple Band claims to be the oldest town band in the country.

BED & BREAKFASTS B&Bs appear under their own listing within the *Lodging* section of each chapter. We don't list every one, but we checked out every B&B we could find. Our selection ranges from from two-guest-room private homes to ski lodges to elegant mansions with up to a dozen rooms but serving only breakfast. B&B rates in this book are for two people (unless otherwise specified); single rates are somewhat lower.

BICYCLING The Monadnock region is particularly popular with touring bikes (see "Peterborough" for rentals). For mountain biking check Waterville Valley and Loon Mountain in "The Western Whites"; Mount Sunapee and Gunstock in "The Lakes Region"; Great Glen Trails; and Attitash Bear Peak in Bartlett. Other popular venues include **Bear Brook State Park** in Allentown (603-485-9874), **Pawtuckaway State Park** in Raymond (603-895-3031), and **Pisgah State Park** in Winchester (603-239-8153). Maps for the White Mountain National Forest can be obtained by calling 603-528-8721. The **Granite State Wheelmen** (www.granitestate wheelmen.org) schedule frequent rides throughout the state for resident bicycling enthusiasts. Request copies of New Hampshire Regional Bicycle Maps from the Department of Transportation (603-271-1668; www .nhbikeped.com).

BIRDING **Pondicherry National Wildlife Refuge** in Whitefield, with its Big and Little Cherry Ponds and extensive wetland, is well known to New England birders. More than 234 species have been recorded here. It's also a haven for butterflies, dragonflies, and moose; the adjacent grasslands around the Whitefield Airport are a prime birding area as well. Another favorite venue is coastal Rt. 1A from Seabrook to New Castle, which provides numerous ocean, harbor, and salt-marsh vantage points for observing shorebirds and sea fowl of all types, as well as various ducks and larger wading birds, especially in summer when snowy egrets, great and little blue herons, glossy ibises, and black-crowned night herons are common. Umbagog Lake, described in "Northern White Mountains," has nesting eagles and ospreys, loons, and other freshwater birds. In the course of the book we have described many of the more than 40 properties maintained by the **Audubon Society of**

New Hampshire (603-224-9909; www.nhaudubon.org). Regional Audubon chapters offer bird walks throughout the year. Audubon House, the society's headquarters (3 Silk Rd., Concord, just off I-89, Exit 2), includes an information center and Audubon Nature Store and walking trails around Great Turkey Pond.

BOATING New Hampshire law requires all boats used in fresh water to be registered, a formality that most marinas can provide. Otherwise contact the **New Hampshire Department of Safety, Motor Vehicle Division** (603-271-2251.www.nh.gov), Hazen Dr., Concord. In the Lake Winnipesaukee area, contact the **Safety Services Marine Division** (603-293-2037), Rt. 11, Glendale. Boats used in tidal waters must be registered with the U.S. Coast Guard. Contact the **USCG Portsmouth Harbor Station** (603-436-0171), New Castle 03854 or the **New Hampshire Port Authority** (603-436-8500; www.portofnyh.org). Also see *Canoeing and Kayaking*. Request the excellent New Hampshire Boating & Fishing Public Access Map from the **New Hampshire Fish and Game Department** (603-271-2224; www.wildlife.state.nh.us).

BOOKS The **Mountain Wanderer Map & Book Store** in Lincoln (1-800-745-2707; www.mountain wanderer.com) is devoted to New Hampshire maps and guidebooks; author-owner Steve Smith, himself an authority on the state's history, hiking, and snowshoeing, offers the following recommendations:

For a general history of the state, try *The Granite State—New Hampshire: An Illustrated History*, by

Ronald Jager & Grace Jager (American Historical Press). Michael J. Caduto's *A Time Before New Hampshire* (University Press of New England) is a fascinating chronicle of the state's geological origins and the life of its Native American peoples. *It Happened in New Hampshire*, by Stillman Rogers (Globe Pequot Press), describes 31 landmark events in the state's history, and *The New Hampshire Century*, edited by Felice Belman and Mike Pride (University Press of New England), is an illustrated account of 100 people who shaped the state during the 20th century. *Classic New Hampshire*, by Linda Landry (University Press of New England), profiles 15 unique New Hampshire institutions. The recently reissued *New Hampshire Architecture: An Illustrated Guide*, by Bryant F. Tolles Jr. (University Press of New England), is an invaluable guide to the rich architectural heritage of the state. *The White Mountains: Alps of New England*, by Randall H. Bennett (Arcadia Publishing), is an excellent history of that region. Out-of-print classics that may be available at your local library or through interlibrary loan include *New Hampshire*, by Elting and Elizabeth Morison, Jere Daniell's *Colonial New Hampshire: A History*, and *New Hampshire: Portrait of the Land and Its People*. Peter Randall's *New Hampshire: A Living Landscape* (University Press of New England) is a collection of panoramic photographs. The photographs of Dick Hamilton, the recently retired "Mr. White Mountains," are displayed in *New Hampshire: Scenes and Seasons* (New England Press).

The *New Hampshire Atlas & Gazetteer* (DeLorme) has topographic maps that cover the entire state, plus detailed maps of all major communi-

ties. The most detailed maps for the state are found in the *New Hampshire Road Atlas* (Jimapco). The waterproof New Hampshire Outdoor Travel Map (Topaz Maps) is a useful resource. The Appalachian Mountain Club publishes the definitive guidebooks to outdoor recreation in New Hampshire (1-800-262-4455; www.outdoors.org). Also be sure to check with independent bookstores, most of which have strong local book sections and may carry titles unavailable elsewhere.

BUS SERVICE **Concord Trailways** (1-800-639-3317; www.concordtrailways.com) serves the Merrimack Valley and north on the one hand to the Lake Winnipesaukee region, and on the other to Franconia, North Conway, and Jackson in the White Mountains and north to Berlin. Its Dartmouth Coach offers frequent service among Hanover, Boston, and the Logan International Airport. **Vermont Transit** (1-800-552-8737; www.vttransit.com) stops in Keene, Concord, Manchester, Nashua, and Portsmouth en route from to and from Boston.

CAMPGROUNDS New Hampshire camping opportunities range from primitive sites with few amenities to full-service areas with water and sewer hookups, electricity, TV, stores, recreation buildings, playgrounds, swimming pools, and boat launching. The most complete information is available from the **New Hampshire Campground Owners' Association** (603-846-5511; www.ucampnh.com), Box 320, Twin Mountain 03595. Its 80-page directory lists private and state campgrounds. The **New Hampshire State Park** (wwww.nhstate parks.org) campgrounds operate on a first-come, first-served basis and by reservation (accepted at least 1 week in advance for a minimum 2-night stay; 3 nights on major weekends) between mid-May and Columbus Day. Call 603-271-3628 Jan.–Oct., weekdays 9–4 (see www .nhstateparks.com).

The **White Mountain National Forest** (WMNF) operates 23 campgrounds ranging in size from 7 to 176 sites. No electrical, water, or sewer connections, no camp stores, no playgrounds. Toilets, water, tables, and fireplaces are provided. The sites were designed for tent camping, although trailers and RVs can be accommodated. Most of the campgrounds are open mid-May–mid-Oct., with a few opening earlier and closing later; several are open all winter, though the roads are not plowed. The daily fees range $18–20 per site, first come, first served. Where indicated below, reservations are accepted. The reservation service (1-877-444-6777; ReserveUSA.com) operates Mar.– Sep., Mon.–Fri. noon–9 PM, weekends noon–5, and costs $9 in addition to the camping fee. Reservations may be made 120 days before arrival, but 10 days before arrival is the minimum time. For details about specific campgrounds see "White Mountain National Forest" and the entry at the end of this chapter.

CANOEING AND KAYAKING New Hampshire offers many miles of flatwater and whitewater canoeing opportunities. The Androscoggin, Connecticut, Saco, and Merrimack rivers are the most popular waters for canoeing, but there are many other smaller rivers as well. Many folks also like to paddle the numerous lakes and ponds. Since spring runoffs have an

impact on the degree of paddling difficulty, make sure you know what your river offers before heading downstream. The best source of information is the *AMC River Guide: New Hampshire and Vermont*, published by the Appalachian Mountain Club, 5 Joy St., Boston, MA 02108. Also see *Canoe Camping Vermont and New Hampshire Rivers* (Backcountry Publications). Contact the **Merrimack River Watershed Council** (603-224-8322) in Concord for information on the Merrimack River. Canoe and kayak rentals have, happily, become too numerous to list here. Check every chapter. Outstanding outfitters include **North Star Livery** (www .kayak-canoe.com), in Cornish, which will shuttle patrons to put-ins farther up the Connecticut River and to campsites in Wilgus State Park on the Vermont bank; and **Northern Waters Outfitters** (www.beoutside .com) in Errol.

CHILDREN, ESPECIALLY FOR Throughout the book, the 𝒮 symbol indicates restaurants, lodgings, and attractions that are appropriate for children and families. Although it is technically a science museum in Vermont (just across the bridge from Hanover, N.H.), the **Montshire Museum of Science** (www .montshire.org) in Norwich (see "Upper Valley Towns") gets our vote for the most stimulating children's museum, both inside and out. The **White Mountain Attractions** add up to the state's single largest family-geared magnet. With members ranging from the excursion vessel M/S *Mount Washington* on Lake Winnipesaukee to the gondola at **Wildcat Mountain**, from natural phenomena like **Lost River** (in North Woodstock) to theme parks like **Story Land** (in Glen) and **Six Gun City** and **Santa's Village** (both in Jefferson), this is a highly organized promotional association with a helpful visitors center just off Exit 32, I-93, in North Woodstock. Phone 603-745-8720 or 1-800-FIND-MTS; www.visitwhitemountains.com, or e-mail them at info@visitwhite mountains.com.

CHILDREN'S SUMMER CAMPS More than 100 summer camps are located in New Hampshire. For a free brochure contact the **New Hampshire Camp Directors' Association** (1-800-549-2267; www.nhcamps.org), P.O. Box 501, Farmington 03835.

CHRISTMAS TREES Plantation-grown New Hampshire Christmas trees are perfect for the holidays. The trees are grown to be harvested at about 10 years of age. Some growers allow you to come early in the season to tag your own tree, which you can cut at a later time; others allow choose-and-cut only in December. Contact the **Department of Agriculture** (603-271-3551; www.nhfarms.com).

COLLEGES AND UNIVERSITIES Higher-education opportunities range from 2-year schools to the highly regarded University of New Hampshire and Dartmouth College. For information contact the **New Hampshire College and University Council** (603-669-3432; www.nh cuc.org), 2321 Elm St., Manchester 03104.

CONSERVATION GROUPS Elsewhere in this section, see the **Appalachian Mountain Club,** the **Society for the Protection of New Hampshire Forests** (SPNHF), and the **Audubon**

Society of New Hampshire (under *Birding*). The **Nature Conservancy** (603-224-5853; www.nature.org), a national organization with state holdings, publishes its own list.

COVERED BRIDGES New Hampshire harbors 64 covered bridges. These are marked on the official state highway map, and we have tried to describe them within each chapter. The country's longest covered bridge connects Cornish with Windsor, Vermont (technically the New Hampshire line runs to the Vermont shore, so it's all in New Hampshire). The state's oldest authenticated covered bridge (1827) links Haverhill and Bath. The Swanzey area near Keene (see "Peterborough, Keene") boasts the state's greatest concentration of covered bridges: five within little more than a dozen miles.

CRAFTS The **League of New Hampshire Craftsmen** (603-224-3375; www.nhcrafts.org), with headquarters at 205 N. Main St., Concord 03301, is one of the country's oldest, most effective statewide craft groups. It maintains eight shops displaying work by members and sponsors the outstanding annual **Craftsmen's Fair** in early August at Mount Sunapee State Park in Newbury. In the Monadnock region the **Sharon Arts Center** in Peterborough offers destination crafts shopping.

CRUISES New Hampshire has many trips available, from the ocean to the lakes. The two most popular cruises are the M/V *Thomas Laighton* (Isles of Shoals Steamship Company), which sails several times daily from Portsmouth to the offshore Isles of Shoals, and the M/S *Mount Washington* on

Robert J. Kozlow

Lake Winnipesaukee. Squam Lake has two small boat cruises, and Lake Sunapee has several as well. For details see *To Do—Boat Excursions* in the relevant chapters.

EMERGENCIES The statewide emergency number is 1-800-525-5555; **911** also now covers the state.

EVENTS The *Official New Hampshire Guidebook* (see *Information*) lists current events, and in each chapter we have listed special events that occur year after year (see *Special Events*). From May through mid-September, you can phone 1-800-258-3608 for a recording of upcoming events. Special events are also listed on the state's visitors information web site (www .visitnh.gov); agricultural fairs and festivals are listed at www.nhfarms.com.

FACTORY OUTLETS New Hampshire charges no sales tax. Its best-known shopping mecca is **North Conway**, with more than 200 shops, discount stores, and factory outlets. North Hampton also has a large outlet shopping complex, but seacoast shoppers also drive across the Piscataqua River to Kittery, Maine, where outlets line Rt. 1. In the Winnipesaukee area more than 50 outlets are grouped in the **Lakes Region Factory Stores** just off I-93, Exit 20, at **Tilton**.

FARM STANDS AND FARMER'S MARKETS One day each week, mainly from late June through Columbus Day, 34 New Hampshire towns host farmer's markets, gatherings of farmers and craftspeople, frequently musicians too. The day for each differs but can easily be checked by contacting the **New Hampshire Department of Agriculture** (603-271-3788; www.nhfarms.com or www.agriculture .nh.gov. The web site also has lists of farm stands. Both directories are available in pamphlet form.

FISHING Freshwater fishing requires a license for anyone age 12 and older. Some 450 sporting goods and country stores sell licenses or you can buy one online from the **New Hampshire Fish and Game Department** (603-271-3211; www.nhfg.net), 11 Hazen Dr., Concord. Request a copy of the New Hampshire Boating and Fishing Public Access Map. No license is required for saltwater fishing. Party boats leave several times daily from April until October from docks at Rye, Hampton, and Seabrook harbors. Most of these boats have full tackle for rent. Fishing guides and outfitters are listed in the "Great North Woods" chapters.

FOLIAGE Color first appears on hillsides in the North Country in mid-September, and by the end of that month Franconia, Crawford, and Pinkham Notches are usually spectacular. The colors spread south and through lower elevations during the first 2 weeks in October. Columbus Day weekend is traditionally the time New England residents come "leaf-peeping," and it's the period we suggest you avoid, if possible. At least avoid the traditional foliage routes—the Kancamagus Highway, Rt. 3 through Franconia Notch, and Rt. 16 to North Conway—on those 3 days. Come a week earlier instead and try to get off the road entirely. This is prime hiking weather—no bugs. The state maintains a **Fall Foliage Hotline** (1-800-258-3608) with "conditions" updated regularly; their web site keeps a visual tab on what's going on: www.visitnh.gov. Weekend lodging reservations are advised well in advance for this period.

GOLF We describe golf courses as they appear region by region. They are also listed in the *Official New Hampshire Guidebook* (see *Information*).

HANDICAPPED ACCESS Throughout this book, the wheelchair symbol &. indicates restaurants, lodgings, and attractions that are handicapped accessible.

HIGH HUTS OF THE WHITE MOUN-TAINS The most unusual lodging opportunities in the state are found in the White Mountains, where the Appalachian Mountain Club operates eight full-service high-mountain huts. Generally the huts are open from June through Labor Day, but several

Kim Grant

welcome hikers through September and two are open all year on a self-serve, caretaker basis. Guests hike to the huts, most of which are located a day's walk apart so that you can walk for several days and stay in a different hut each night. You sleep in coed bunk rooms equipped with mattresses and blankets. Meals are huge and varied. Reservations are required. A shuttle service allows you to park at the trailhead for one hut, then ride back to your vehicle after your hike. Contact the **Appalachian Mountain Club Pinkham Notch Camp** (603-466-2727 for overnight or workshop reservations; www.outdoors.org). See "Mount Washington."

HIKING New Hampshire offers the most diverse hiking in New England. The **White Mountain National Forest** alone has some 1,200 miles of hiking trails, and there are additional miles in state parks. A long, difficult section of the **Appalachian Trail**

Loon Mountain Resort

cuts through New Hampshire, entering the state near Hanover, crossing the highest peaks, including Mount Washington, and exiting along the rugged Mahoosuc Range on the Maine border. The White Mountains is the most popular hiking area, and the many trails offer easy to challenging routes. The most spectacular climbs are on the Franconia Ridge and over the Presidential Range, which includes **Mount Washington,** at 6,288 feet the highest peak in the Northeast. Although relatively low compared with the Rockies, Mount Washington records the worst weather for any surface station outside the polar regions. Hikers are urged to use caution and to consult weather forecasts before venturing onto the exposed areas above tree line. More than 110 people have died on Mount Washington, some of them in summer when caught unprepared by sudden, extreme changes in weather conditions. For current conditions at the top check www.mountwashington.org.

The **Appalachian Mountain Club** (603-466-2727; www.outdoors.org) offers hikers year-round meals, lodging, equipment, and workshops at both its Pinkham Notch and its Highland Center facilities. The White Mountain National Forest desk at the **White Mountains Gateway Visitors Center** (603-745-3816) in North Woodstock offers daily weather updates.

Mount Monadnock in southern New Hampshire is one of the most heavily climbed peaks in the world, and **Kearsarge** in central New Hampshire offers a relatively easy walk to its summit and 360-degree views. Several lower mountains in the Lake Winnipesaukee area are easily climbed. **Mount Major**, in particular, is easy and has a fine view across the lake. These hikes are described elsewhere in this book, but for more details one of the following books is recommended. The *AMC White Mountain Guide* has the most comprehensive trail information available for hiking anywhere in New Hampshire, but also see *50 Hikes in the White Mountains*, *50 More Hikes in New Hampshire*, *Waterfalls of the White Mountains*, and *Ponds and Lakes of the White Mountains* (all Countryman Press).

HISTORIC MUSEUMS, HOMES, AND SITES Most New Hampshire communities have historical societies, and throughout the state many historic buildings and sites are open to the public; most are listed in this guide. The **Association of Historical Societies of New Hampshire** (www .historicalsociety.org) offers an online guide to town historical societies, including open hours and admission fees. The largest concentration of historical houses is in Portsmouth, home of **Strawbery Banke** (www.straw berybanke.org) and eight other houses open to the public. Along New Hampshire highways, roadside markers

RUSSELL COLBATH HOUSE HISTORIC SITE ON THE KANCAMAGUS HIGHWAY

Bill Davis

recount short tidbits of local history. *New Hampshire Architecture* (University Press of New England) is a fine guide to historical and significant buildings. The New Hampshire Historical Society's **Museum of New Hampshire History** (603-226-3189; www.nhhistory.org) in Concord (see "The Merrimack Valley") is well worth checking out, as are the New Hampshire State House (the nation's oldest state capitol in which a legislature still meets in its original chambers) and Manchester's **Millyard Museum** (www.manchesterhistoric .org), which offers a glimpse into the area's onetime predominance as the world's leading textile center. The state's other major historical museum is **Canterbury Shaker Village** (www .shakers.org) in the same chapter. Many more are described as they appear regionally.

HONEY More than 200 members of the New Hampshire Beekeepers Association (www.nhbeekeepers.org) have hives throughout the state, and their honey is usually for sale at farmer's markets, some country stores, and roadside stands.

HORSEBACK RIDING Rising insurance costs are narrowing trail-riding options, but you can still ride a horse through the woods at several places in the state, including **Rocky Ridge Ranch** in the Waterville Valley area, the **Gunstock Cobble Mountain Stables** in Gilford, **PemiValley Excursions** just past the Hobo Rail-Road in Lincoln, **Loon Mountain** in the Western Whites, the **Mount Washington Hotel**, **Farm by the River**, and **Black Mountain** (see "Mount Washington and Its Valleys").

INFORMATION

We describe regional information sources at the head of each chapter. The **New Hampshire Division of Travel & Tourism Development** maintains a toll-free hotline (1-800-258-3608) with recorded info, varying with the season; or check their web site at www.visitnh.gov. You can also call (603-271-2665; 1-800-386-4664) or write to the office for a copy of the *Official New Hampshire Guidebook* and a highway map. The guidebook includes year-round listings of the basics: golf courses, alpine and cross-country ski areas, covered bridges, scenic drives, events, fish and game rules, state parks, and state liquor stores. It also includes paid dining and lodging listings. Maps and pamphlets are available in the state's 17 full-service highway rest areas. Three are open 24 hours a day: Hooksett (I-93 northbound and southbound) and Seabrook (northbound on I-95). The department also offers a seasonal events guide.

HUNTING New Hampshire has long been a popular state for hunting. Licenses are required and are available from some 450 sporting goods and country stores, or online from the **New Hampshire Fish and Game Department** (603-271-3421; www .nhfg.net), 11 Hazen Dr., Concord 03301.

ICE CREAM It's hard to beat **Annabelle's Ice Cream**, located on Ceres Street in Portsmouth, open from spring through late fall. Another popular homemade brand of ice cream is served at **Lagos' Lone Oak Dairy Bars** on old Rt. 16 in Rochester and Rt. 1 in Rye. In the Lake Winnipesaukee region **Kellerhaus** is the big name, while **Sandwich Creamery** is the insider's pick. **Beech Hill Farm,** just off Rts. 9, 202, and 103 between Concord and Hopkinton, has been owned by the Kimball family since 1776. The old dairy farm remains the place to go for a scoop of history along with make-your-own sundaes. If you happen to be in North Haverhill, don't pass up **Mountain Scoops**.

Christina Tree

MOUNTAIN SCOOPS, NORTH HAVERILL

LAKES Central New Hampshire is open, rolling country, spotted with lakes. **Winnipesaukee** is by far the state's largest, most visitor-oriented lake, and it is surrounded by smaller lakes: **Winnisquam**, **Squam**, **Wentworth**, **Ossipee**. Traditionally this has been New Hampshire's Lakes region, but we've added the Western Lakes because there are so many west of I-93 as well: **Sunapee** and **Newfound** for starters; **Little Sunapee**, **Massasecum**, **Pleasant**, **Highland**, and **Webster** when you start looking for places to swim. Outdoorsmen are also well aware of the grand expanses of **Umbagog Lake** and the **Connecticut Lakes** in New Hampshire's Great North Woods. *Ponds and Lakes of the White Mountains* by Steve B. Smith (Countryman Press) describes more than 100 lakes and ponds, "from wayside to wilderness," including many bodies of water hidden deep in the woods (with detailed directions on finding them).

LIBRARIES Every New Hampshire city and town has a public library, and there are many college and private libraries as well. On the seacoast, the **Portsmouth Public Library** and the **Portsmouth Athenaeum** and the **Exeter Public Library** and **Exeter Historical Society** are centers for regional history and genealogical research. The **University of New Hampshire's Dimond Library** has an extensive New Hampshire special collections section and all of the resources you would expect to find in a major educational institution. In Concord the **State Library**—with its relatively new Political Library (www .politicallibrary.org) devoted to New Hampshire's half-century history as host to the first-in-the-nation primary—and the **New Hampshire Historical Society**, located side by side on Park Street, are centers for New Hampshire research. **Peterborough's Public Library** was the first in New Hampshire, and it and the nearby **Peterborough Historical Society library** have important regional collections. In Keene the **Historical Society of Cheshire County Archive Center** and the **Keene State Library** are the best sources for local research. **Baker Library at Dartmouth College** is one of the finest institutions in the East. Among its many resources is an extensive White Mountains collection.

LOTTERY New Hampshire's is the oldest legal lottery (nhlottery.org) in the country. Since 1964 it has funded more than $930 million to local education.

MAGAZINES AND NEWSPAPERS The *New Hampshire Union Leader* (www.theunionleader.com) is the only statewide daily, and its strong conservative editorial policy has made it well known throughout the country. It is the best source of statewide news, but there are also dailies in Portsmouth, Dover, Laconia, Conway, Claremont, Lebanon, Keene, Nashua, and Concord. Many of the larger towns also have weekly newspapers. An alternative Manchester/Nashua weekly, *The Hippo Press* (www.hippopress.com), is reputed to have the state's second highest circulation.

MAPLE SUGARING When cool nights and warm days during late February through April start the sap running in maple trees, maple syrup producers fire up their evaporators to begin making the sweet natural treat. Most producers welcome visitors and many offer tours, sugar-on-snow parties, and breakfast (pancakes with maple syrup, of course). For a list of maple

Robert J. Kozlow

syrup producers, contact the **New Hampshire Maple Producers** (603-225-3757; www.nhmapleproducers.com). During Maple Weekend, usually the last weekend in March, more than 50 sugarhouses hold open house and stage special events.

MOOSE The state's largest animal is becoming more common and is often seen along roadsides, especially in the mountainous northern half of the state. Stay very alert when driving, since moose may unexpectedly walk into the road without looking. The state has recorded nearly 200 vehicle–moose collisions. A colorful annual **North Country Moose Festival**, based in the town of Colebrook, is staged annually the last weekend in August. See the "Great North Woods" introduction for a full description of this noble beast. The state's most popular organized moose tours are based in Gorham, described in "Northern White Mountains."

MOUNTAINTOPS The summits of some New Hampshire mountains are more popular than others mainly because they offer better views, great hiking trails, or ways to ride to the top. The most popular, of course, is Mount Washington, at 6,288 feet the highest peak in the Northeast. The **Mount Washington Auto Road** (www.mt-washington.com) is an 8-mile graded road on which you can drive your own car or opt for a "stage"; in winter modified vans also offer rides a ways up the mountain. The **Mount Washington Cog Railway** (www.thecog.com), the world's oldest mountain-climbing railway, is still steam powered, carrying passengers all the way to the summit in-season and a portion of the way

up—permitting them to ski or snow-shoe down—in winter. Across Rt. 16 from Mount Washington, the **Wildcat Mountain gondolas** whisk you to the top of that wooded peak for a spectacular view of the Presidential Range, and at **Attitash** in Bartlett you can ride to the top of the mountain on the chairlift; slide down the curving, bowed, 0.75-mile **Alpine Slide** on a self-controlled sled; then cool off in the Aquaboggin Waterslide. At the **Loon Mountain Skyride** gondolas hoist you to a summit complete with cafeteria, cave walk, and hiking trails. Both here and at **Mount Sunapee** (where a chairlift hoists you to the summit), cookout-style suppers are offered throughout summer. The **Cannon Mountain Tramway** in Franconia offers its riders a view of the Franconia Range, the state's second highest group of mountains. Although not a mountaintop, **Castle in the Clouds** (Rt. 109, Moultonborough) gives nonhikers the best view of Lake Winnipesaukee. For purist hikers **Mount Lafayette** is the favored summit in Franconia Notch. **Mount Moosilauke**, westernmost of the White Mountains, is also a spectacular summit. Lower mountains can nonetheless provide worthy views: **Mount Chocorua** rises beside Rt. 16 in Tamworth; although only 3,400 feet high, it is a challenging hike with a great vista from its summit. **Mount Major** (Rt. 11, Alton) and **Mount Kearsarge** in Warner offer easy walks to relatively open summits. **Mount Monadnock** dominates the view throughout southwestern New Hampshire, but if you're not up to the hike, drive to the top of nearby **Pack Monadnock** (Miller State Park), Rt. 101, Peterborough. For those who like a challenge, the **Appalachian Moun-**

tain Club has an informal Four Thousand Footer Club; become a member by climbing all 48 New Hampshire mountains higher than 4,000 feet in elevation. The peaks are listed in the *AMC White Mountain Guide*. Some rugged folks have climbed all 48 in winter; others have done them all twice, or with their dogs, or some other unique way.

MUSEUMS The **New Hampshire Farm Museum** (www.farmmuseum .org) in Milton tells the history of farming in the state. The **Montshire Museum of Science** (www.mont shire.org) in Norwich, Vermont (just across the river from Hanover, New Hampshire, where it began), is the most highly regarded science museum in northern New England, worth a stop for inquiring minds of all ages. The **Mount Kearsarge Indian Museum** (www.indianmuseum.org) in Warner is also well worth checking out. We have described the state's historical museums and houses region by region. **Canterbury Shaker Museum** (www.shakers.org) in Canterbury (see "The Concord Area") is an outstanding museum village. Also see *Art Museums and Galleries* and *Children, Especially For*.

MUSIC Music festivals are described under *Entertainment* and/or *Special Events* in each chapter. Check out the **New Hampshire Music Festival** (www.nhmf.org) in Center Harbor, year-round performances at the **North Country Center for the Arts** in Lincoln, summer concerts at the **Great Waters Music Festival** in Wolfeboro (www.greatwaters.org), **Meadowbrook Farm** (www.meadow brookfarm.net) in Gilford, the **Prescott Park Festival** in Portsmouth,

the **Mount Washington Valley Arts Festival**, and the **Cochecho Arts Festival** in Dover. The Monadnock region is a traditional center for outstanding classical music; **Monadnock Music** is a series of two dozen summer concerts, operas, and orchestra performances (many of them free) staged in town halls, churches, and schools, and the **Apple Hill Chamber Players** in Nelson offers free faculty concerts. Band music is another sound of summer in New Hampshire. The **Temple Band**, also based in the Monadnock region, claims to be the oldest town band in the country. **Saint-Gaudens National Historic Site** (www.nps.gov/saga) in Cornish is the setting for a series of free Sunday-afternoon concerts. It's a glorious setting with Mount Ascutney in the background and picnic-packing patrons spread out across the estate's wide lawn.

NATIONAL PUBLIC RADIO Check out www.nhpr.org for an overview of what's offered. New Hampshire Public Radio is good and getting better all the time. For (FM) commercial-free news and music turn to 103.9 in Portsmouth, 89.1 in Concord and southern New Hampshire, 90.3 in Nashua, 104.3 in Dover, 91.3 in the Upper Valley, 90.7 in the Monadnock region, 99.5 in Jackson, and 107.1 in Berlin. You can also pick up Vermont Public Radio (VPR) at 89.5 in the western part of the state, and WGBH (Boston Public Radio) at 89.7 as you near the Massachusetts border.

PARKS The **New Hampshire Division of Parks and Recreation** (603-271-3556; www.nhstateparks.org) is one of the oldest and best state park systems in the country. There are nearly 50 parks with activities that include swimming, fishing, picnicking, camping, and hiking. A map/guide to the parks and campgrounds is available at most rest areas. Also check out the privately maintained, very helpful site www.nhstateparks.com. Almost all cities and towns have parks, many of which include tennis courts open to the public. Also see *Campgrounds*.

PETS, TRAVELING WITH The dog paw symbol 🐾 indicates lodgings that accept pets as of press time in 2006. Most require prior notice and a reservation; many also require an additional fee. But don't take our word for it; always call ahead to confirm an establishment's policy when traveling with your pet.

RAIL EXCURSIONS The **Mount Washington Cog Railway** (www .thecog.com), the country's oldest railroad excursion, takes nonhikers on a steam locomotive trip to the top of the highest mountain in the Northeast (see "Mount Washington and Its Valleys"). Less hair-raising but just as appealing is the **Conway Scenic Railroad** (www.conwayscenic.com), which journeys through historic Crawford Notch. Also see the **Hobo Railroad** (www.hoborr.com) in Lincoln and the **Winnipesaukee Railroad** based in Weirs Beach.

RENTAL COTTAGES, CONDOMINIUMS Cottages are particularly plentiful and available in the **Lake Winnipesaukee** and **Western Lakes** areas (contact the local chambers). Condominiums at the state's self-contained ski resorts like Waterville Valley, Loon Mountain, Cranmore, and Attitash Bear Peak are good-value family summer rentals, with golf,

horseback riding, hiking, and a variety of other activities. The **Mount Washington Valley Chamber of Commerce** (603-356-3171; 1-800-367-3364) also keeps year-round tabs on condominiums and other family lodging. In the seacoast region, contact the **Hampton Beach Chamber of Commerce** (603-926-8718; 1-800-GET-A-TAN) for information about condo and cottage rentals.

ROCKHOUNDING Ruggles Mine in Grafton (see "The Western Lakes") is said to offer 150 kinds of minerals and gemstones. Commercial production of mica began here in 1803, and it's an eerie, interesting place that has gotten many a rockhound hooked.

SALES TAX New Hampshire has no sales tax, making it a destination for shoppers from throughout the Northeast.

SKIING, CROSS-COUNTRY New Hampshire offers more than 1,300 km of trails. The **Jackson Ski Touring Foundation** (www.jacksonxc.org) is the state's largest, with 154 km of varied trails including a run down the backside of Wildcat Mountain (accessible from the alpine summit via a

Kim Grant

single ride on its gondola). Three of the state's surviving grand hotels offer substantial touring systems: **The Balsams Wilderness** (www.thebalsams .com) up in Dixville Notch with 95 km has reliable snow cover as well as grooming; **Bretton Woods Nordic Ski Center** (www.bretton-woods.com) features a run from the top of its alpine area and a total of 100 km of trails as well as a full-service center; and **Mountain View** (www.mountainviewgrand.com) in Whitefield offers 27 km. The **Mount Washington Valley Ski Touring & Snowshoe Center** (www.cross countryskinh.com) has another 65 km, while the **Appalachian Mountain Club** (www.outdoors.org) in Pinkham Notch and at the **Highland Center** in Crawford Notch offers cross-country workshops and guided tours on national forest trails. **Great Glen Trails Outdoor Center** (www.great glentrails.com) in Pinkham Notch boasts 50 km of trails as well as a run down the lower portion of the auto road.

Farther south both **Loon Mountain** and **Waterville Valley** offer cross-country centers that tie into national forest trails. **NorskCross Country Ski and Winter Sports Center** (www.skinorsk.com) in New London offers 30 km in central New Hampshire, and **Windblown Ski Touring Center** (www.windblown .info) with 40 km in New Ipswich is favored by Bostonians; it's high, handy, and quite beautiful. The New Hampshire **cross-country snow report** line is 1-800-887-5464. The centers are described region by region within this book. Information on all these and all the state's ski-touring centers is available from **Ski New Hampshire** (www.skinh.com).

Waterville Valley

SKIING, DOWNHILL New Hampshire boasts 17 major downhill ski areas and one of the world's largest concentrations of snowmaking. The quality of the snowmaking varies, but most of the state's alpine slopes are now dependably white from Christmas through Easter. **Ski New Hampshire** (www.skinh.com) is the prime source for all areas, big and small. On weekends the proximity to Boston puts Granite State lifts at a real premium, but on weekdays they tend to be empty. **Cannon Mountain** (www .cannonmt.com) in Franconia Notch—home of the **New England Ski Museum** (www.skimuseum .org)—offers some of the most challenging skiing around. **Loon Mountain** (www.loonmt.com) in Lincoln and **Waterville Valley** (www.water ville.com), also in "The Western Whites," are major self-contained, condo-based resorts, both under the same ownership as **Cranmore Mountain Resort** (www.cranmore .com), one of the country's oldest ski hills, right in the village of North

Conway. **Attitash** (www.attitash.com), **Wildcat Mountain** (www.skiwildcat .com), and **Bretton Woods Mountain Resort** (www.brettonwoods .com) are all major ski mountains described in "Mount Washington and Its Valleys." **Mount Sunapee Ski Resort** (www.mountsunapee.com) in "The Western Lakes," a state-owned resort now leased to and expanded by the owners of Okemo Mountain in Vermont and Crested Butte in Colorado, has a growing clientele. **Crotched Mountain** (www.crotched mountain.com) is smaller but newly revived and within an hour's drive of Boston in the Monadnock region, while **Pat's Peak** in Henniker (www .patspeak.com) is one of the most accessible and challenging areas in southern New England. Among half a dozen other small but beloved mountains, **Ragged Mountain Resort** (www.raggedmountainresort.com) in Danbury in the Lakes region stands out thanks to recent improvements in lifts, lodge, and trails.

SLED DOG RACES The world championships are in Laconia in February, but earlier in the winter there are local races in Tamworth and Meredith. Snow conditions often determine whether or not races are held. The New Hampshire–based **New England Sled Dog Club** (www .nesdc.org) was founded in 1924.

SNOWMOBILING Some 6,800 miles of trails are maintained by the 115 local clubs that are members of the **New Hampshire Snowmobile Association** (603-224-8906; www .nhsa.com). Large portions of the White Mountain National Forest are off-limits to snowmobiling, but most state parks do permit off-road vehi-

cles on marked trails. For a current map of the 24 long-distance snowmobile corridor trails and regulations as well as rental outlets, contact the **New Hampshire Bureau of Trails** (603-271-3254; www.nhtrails.org); for trail reports check out www.nhtrails .org. Given its reliable snow cover, the Great North Woods area is a favorite destination; winter lodging and dining options have increased in response to the demand.

SOCIETY FOR THE PROTECTION OF NEW HAMPSHIRE FORESTS (SPNHF) Founded in 1901 to fight the systematic leveling of the state's forests by lumber firms, SPNHF was instrumental in securing passage of the 1911 Weeks Act, authorizing (for the first time) the federal purchase of lands to create national forests. One direct result is the 800,000-acre White Mountain National Forest. The group is also largely responsible for Mount Monadnock's current public status, and it now holds more than 60 properties for public use that total more than 20,000 acres. Many are described within this book, especially within the Monadnock region, which harbors a large percentage. Stop by SPNHF headquarters (603-224-9945; www .spnhf.org) in East Concord (just off I-93, Exit 15) to obtain a copy of the society's *Lands Map & Guide* to its properties. If you are a hiker, angler, or cross-country skier, this is a valuable key to real treasure.

SUMMER THEATER New Hampshire offers some outstanding summer theater. The **Barnstormers** in Tamworth, the **Peterborough Players** in Peterborough, and the **New London Barn Playhouse** in New London all rank among New England's oldest, best-respected "straw hat" theaters. The **Weathervane Theatre** in Whitefield, the **Lakes Region Theater** in Meredith, the **Hopkins Center** at Dartmouth College in Hanover, the **Arts Center at Brickyard Pond** in Keene, and the **Prescott Art Festival** in Portsmouth also stage lively summer productions. See *Entertainment* for each region.

TRAILS, LONG-DISTANCE New Hampshire from the road is beautiful, but unless you see its panoramas from a high hiking trail, you miss its real magnificence. Long-distance hiking trails now crisscross the state. The longest, most spectacular, and most famous, the **Appalachian Trail**, cuts diagonally across the White Mountains, entering the state in Hanover on the west and traversing Franconia Notch, Mount Washington, and Pinkham Notch on its way into Maine. Detailed maps and guides as well as a free pamphlet guide, The Appalachian Trail in New Hampshire

and the White Mountains, are available from the **Appalachian Mountain Club** (www.outdoors.org). The **Metacomet Trail**, running 14 miles south from Little Monadnock; the **Wapack Trail**, which heads south along ridges from North Pack Monadnock; the **Monadnock-Sunapee Trail**, a 47-mile footpath; and the 75-mile emerald necklace of hiking trails known as the **Sunapee-Ragged-Kearsarge Greenway** (www.srkg .com), are also well mapped. (Also see *Hiking* within each region.) The newest long-distance trail links existing paths, railbeds, and logging roads into one continuous trail from Bartlett down in the Mount Washington Valley to the Canadian border in Pittsburg. See www.cohostrail.org for details.

WATERFALLS The White Mountains have the best waterfalls to view. All are described in *Waterfalls of the White Mountains* (Countryman Press), which lists 30 trips to some 100 waterfalls.

Robert J. Kozlow

WHITE MOUNTAIN NATIONAL FOREST (WMNF) The 800,000-acre **White Mountain National Forest** (www.fs.fed.us/r9/white) runs through the middle of New Hampshire from east to west. The largest national forest in the East, it is managed for multiple-use activities including lumbering as well as recreation. The **White Mountains Gateway Visitors Center** in Lincoln (I-93, Exit 32)— open year-round, daily 8:30–5:30, until 6:30 July–Columbus Day— includes interactive displays about wildlife-watching and the history and mandate of the White Mountain National Forest. A staffed WMNF desk here (603-745-3816) is stocked with hiking, biking, and cross-country maps, as well as information about biking trails, fishing, and camping. It's also a source for the **recreation passes now required within the forest**. This is a great location, handy both to the 34-mile long east–west **Kancamagus National Scenic By-**way through the heart of the national forest and to Franconia Notch with its many trails, just to the north.

Information is also available from the following: **WMNF headquarters** (603-528-8721), 719 Main St., Laconia 03246. Contact them, especially in the off-season, for details on campgrounds, fishing, hiking, and other activities. **WMNF Saco Ranger Station** (603-447-5448), 33 Kancamagus Scenic Byway just off Rt. 16, Conway. Hours vary depending on season. **WMNF Androscoggin Ranger Station** (603-466-2713), 300 Glen Rd., Gorham. WMNF **Ammonoosuc Ranger Station** (603-869-2626), 660 Trudeau Rd., off Rt. 302, Bethlehem. Hours vary depending on season. **WMNF Evans Notch Visitor Center** (207-824-2134), 18 Mayville Rd., Bethel, Me. Hours vary depending on season. **WMNF Pemigewasset Ranger District** (603-536-1310), Rt. 175, Plymouth.

The Seacoast 1

Robert J. Kozlow

INTRODUCTION

With only 18 miles of oceanfront, New Hampshire's seacoast is often overlooked by visitors, who are more impressed with neighboring Maine's more than 2,500 miles of coastline. In its small coastal area, however, New Hampshire has more than enough historical sites, beaches, restaurants, and events and attractions to keep her guests busy for many days and returning again and again for more.

At opposite ends of the seacoast are Portsmouth and Hampton Beach, near to each other in mileage but much farther apart in ambience and style.

Settled in 1630, Portsmouth was the colonial capital and an important seaport during the Georgian and Federal eras, periods that have given the city its distinctive architectural character. With fine inns and restaurants, a number of original and restored historical houses open to the public, theater, dance, music, and a superb waterfront park, Portsmouth is New Hampshire's most delightful and interesting city, loved and appreciated by its residents and visitors alike.

Hampton Beach has been one of New England's most popular seaside resorts since the development of the electric trolley at the turn of the 20th century. Too bad the trolleys don't operate anymore, since the automobile traffic, especially on weekends, is one long snarl. Sand and sun, pizza and fried dough, and lively entertainment characterize Hampton Beach, where more than 200,000 people can be found on a summer holiday weekend. For many people, a week at Hampton Beach has been an annual family tradition for half a century or more.

Between these two extremes are mostly small towns (with populations ranging from less than 1,000 up to to 12,000) with white churches, town commons, Colonial architecture, and an ambience that is attracting many new residents and straining the capacity of these towns to manage the growth that has characterized this area since the end of World War II. Onetime Pease Air Force Base is now an industrial park and airport. The seacoast's superb location and abundant educational, cultural, physical, and human resources seem to be more than adequate to continue the region's reputation as one of the top places in the country to live and work (and vacation).

GUIDANCE Greater Portsmouth Chamber of Commerce (603-436-1118; www .portsmouthchamber.org), 500 Market St., Box 239, Portsmouth, NH 03802-0239,

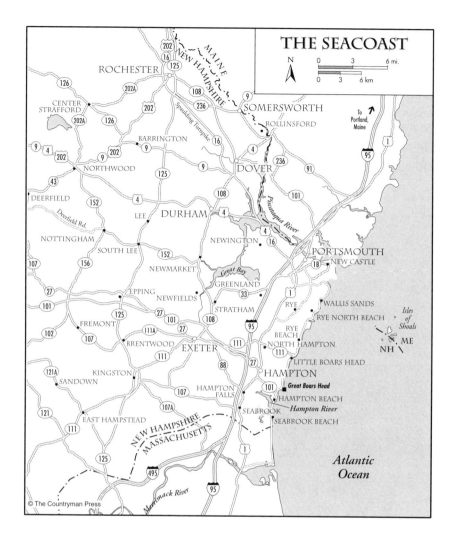

publishes the region's most comprehensive, year-round visitors guide and stocks a wealth of information on local history, attractions, accommodations, dining, and shopping.

GETTING THERE *By plane:* Boston's Logan Airport, Portland's Jetport, and the Manchester Airport are each an hour's drive from the seacoast.

By car: I-95, the state's first superhighway, built in the 1950s, bisects the seacoast, connecting New Hampshire to the seacoast regions of Massachusetts and Maine. From the west, Rts. 4 and 101 connect the seacoast with the central regions of the state, while Rt. 16 is the road from the mountains.

By bus: **Greyhound Bus Lines** (603-436-0163; www.greyhound.com) stops daily in Portsmouth's Market Square, connecting the seacoast with nationwide

bus service. **Coach Company** (603-431-0163; 1-800-874-3377; www.coachco
.com) has twice-daily trips to Boston. **C&J Trailways** (603-431-2424; 603-742-
2990; www.cjtrailways.com) provides many trips daily, connecting Logan Airport
and downtown Boston with Dover, Durham, and Portsmouth (Pease), N.H.;
Newburyport, Ma.; and Portland, Me. **Hampton Shuttle** (603-659-9853; outside New Hampshire, 1-800-225-6426), a reservation-only shuttle service, makes
eight trips daily from Hampton, Exeter, and Seabrook to Logan Airport.

By train: **Amtrak** 1-800-USA-RAIL; www.amtrakdowneaster.com). Slide down
the Maine and New Hampshire coasts with ease on the Downeaster, a com-
muter train that links Portland and Boston. The train runs year-round. On the
seacoast it stops at Dover, Durham, and Exeter.

PORTSMOUTH AND VICINITY

For more than 300 years the seacoast's largest community has been influenced by its maritime location. "We came to fish," announced Portsmouth's first residents in 1630, but shortly the community (first called Strawbery Banke) became a center for the mast trade, supplying long, straight timbers for the Royal Navy. Portsmouth's captains and crews soon roamed the entire world in locally built vessels, hauling cargoes to and from New England, the Caribbean, Europe, and the Far East. In the years before and after the Revolutionary War, wealthy captains and merchants built many of the fine homes and commercial buildings that characterize Portsmouth today.

Unhappy with the demands of the British government, Portsmouth residents were quick to voice opposition to the Crown. Before Paul Revere rode to Lexington and Concord, he first galloped to Portsmouth, warning the patriots to raid nearby Fort William and Mary (now Fort Constitution) and to remove the gunpowder before the British came from Boston to strengthen the undermanned fort. John Paul Jones lived in Portsmouth while overseeing the construction of two major warships during the Revolution. Built on the banks of the Piscataqua River were 28 clippers, unrivaled in construction, beauty, and speed as they hauled passengers and merchandise around the world.

The Portsmouth Naval Shipyard, founded in 1800, has long been associated with submarines, turning out 100 vessels to aid the Allied cause in World War II. Portsmouth's red and green tugboats symbolize the city's current maritime activity. Oil tankers and bulk cargo vessels continue to ply the river, halting traffic as they pass through bridges, creating a bustle of activity now missing from so many other old New England seaports, which have lost their commercial ship traffic.

The result of this 300-year maritime heritage is present in the city's architecture; in its active waterfront, which is used for international, commercial, and recreational boating; and in the many cultural activities that involve its riverfront location. Once an old swabbie town, complete with rundown bars and a decaying city center and surrounding neighborhoods, Portsmouth has been transformed

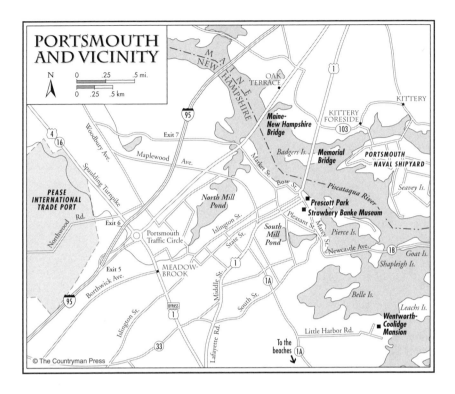

PORTSMOUTH AND VICINITY

N
0   .25   .5 mi.
0   .25   .5 km

© The Countryman Press

into an exciting city as its residents have begun to appreciate its historical traditions and classic architecture. Portsmouth's renaissance continues, fueled by fine restaurants (the best north of Boston, and some would say "including" Boston), inns, music, dance, theater, and, seemingly, a festival every month of the year.

The Piscataqua River, one of the fastest-flowing navigable rivers in the world, separates New Castle, Portsmouth, and Newington, New Hampshire, from Kittery and Eliot, Maine. It is crossed by three main bridges. The lowest is Memorial Bridge, near the center of town, which raises its draw many times daily for commercial and recreational vessels. Residents and visitors alike usually stop to watch as the little tugs shepherd huge oceangoing vessels past this bridge. Next upstream is the Sarah Mildred Long Bridge, once the busiest bridge for motor vehicles but no longer now that the I-95 bridge just upriver carries most of the through traffic. The Piscataqua drains Great Bay, a large, relatively shallow tidal bay known for its wildlife and winter ice fishing.

GUIDANCE **Greater Portsmouth Chamber of Commerce** (603-436-1118; www.portsmouthchamber.org), 500 Market St., Box 239, Portsmouth, NH 03802-0239. A busy and active promoter of local tourism, the chamber has a year-round information center on Market St., a short walk west of downtown. It serves Portsmouth and adjacent communities on both sides of the Piscataqua River. There is also a summer information kiosk in Market Square.

GETTING AROUND *By taxi:* **Portsmouth Taxi** (603-430-1222) is available by phone.

By bus: **COAST** (Cooperative Alliance for Seacoast Transportation) (603-743-5777; www.coastbus.org), the local bus transportation, connects Portsmouth and major outlying shopping centers with Durham, Dover, Newmarket, Rochester, and Somersworth, N.H., and Berwick, Me. A main stop is in Market Square. Fares range from 75¢ to $1.75; children under 5 ride free.

By car: When traveling on I-95, take Exit 7, Market St., which leads directly downtown, past the Chamber of Commerce Information Center to Market Square.

PARKING Although Portsmouth's traffic is no worse than any other city's, it does have limited on-street parking, and its meter attendants will often issue a ticket within moments of your parking meter's expiration. Metered parking (daily except Sun.) is limited to 2 hours, so seek out the 50¢ per hour parking garage, situated just off Market Square in the middle of town, or the large lot off Pleasant Street, adjacent to the South Mill Pond. All of Portsmouth's points of interest and finest restaurants are within an easy walk of both places. Portsmouth is best enjoyed on foot anyway.

MEDICAL EMERGENCY **Portsmouth Regional Hospital** (603-436-5110; 1-800-685-8282), 333 Borthwick Ave., Portsmouth. The hospital offers 24-hour emergency walk-in service.

Careplus Ambulance Service (1-800-633-3590).

✳ Villages

Portsmouth is surrounded by four small towns: Newington, Greenland, New Castle, and Rye. **Newington**, upriver from Portsmouth, is the commercial and industrial center of the region. It has two major shopping malls and many other shops, plus a large power plant, oil storage tanks, and other industries. Most of this commercial-industrial complex is located between the river and the Spaulding Turnpike (Rt. 4/16). The residential area and village are south of the turnpike, by the former Pease Air Force Base, whose construction in the 1950s cut the town of Newington in half. **Greenland** is south of Newington, another residential town with a

NORTH CHURCH AND TROLLEY, DOWNTOWN PORTSMOUTH

Tom Cocchiaro, courtesy of the Greater Portsmouth Champber of Commerce picturesque village green. East along the Piscataqua is the small island village of **New Castle**. Winding, narrow streets lined with 18th- and 19th-century homes combine to give New Castle the appearance of a town unchanged since the turn of the 20th century. The historic Wentworth-by-the-Sea Hotel recalls the area's maritime glory and, along with the adjacent large marina, keeps the town's tourist image alive. Next to New Castle is the largest of the four towns, **Rye**, once a popular summer retreat when it had several large hotels. Those old structures are gone now, and its summer residents live in oceanfront cottages. Several of the finest residential developments have been built in Rye, and it is a popular address for many seacoast executives. Rt. 1A along the coast of Rye is a fine bike route, passing several state parks, restaurants, and a few motels.

Also not to be missed is the **Isles of Shoals**, a historic, nine-island group about 10 miles off the coast and visible from Rt. 1A. Summer ferry service provides tours around the islands and a 3-hour stopover on **Star Island**.

✴ To See

St. John's Episcopal Church (603-436-8283; www.stjohnsnh.org), 101 Chapel St., Portsmouth. Open Sun. and other times by applying at the church office in the adjacent building. Built in 1732, this church is a prominent city landmark located beside the river. Its classic interior has wall paintings, religious objects, and interesting plaques. Its adjacent 1754 graveyard is the resting place of many of the city's colonial leaders, including Benning Wentworth, royal governor 1741–1766.

Little Harbor Chapel (603-436-4902), Little Harbor Rd., Portsmouth. Tucked behind tall pines and a crop of rhododendrons, this 1902 redbrick, Colonial Revival chapel is a charming site on the road to the Wentworth-Coolidge Mansion.

Newington Historical Society (603-649-7420), Nimble Hill Rd., Newington. Open Thu. 2–4 PM in July and Aug. The Old Parsonage, built in 1710, has local artifacts and a special children's room with antique toys. Across the street is the 1712 Old Meetinghouse, in continuous use since that time but structurally altered, and nearby is the Langdon Library, with an extensive genealogical collection.

Albacore Park (603-436-3680), 600 Market St., Portsmouth. Take Exit 7 off I-95, drive 0.2 mile east, and turn right off Market St. Open daily 9:30–5, Memorial Day–Columbus Day; 9:30–3:30 every day but Tue. and Wed. the rest of the year. Closed Jan. 3–Feb. 12. $5 adults, $4 over 60, $2 ages 7–17; under 7 free. Tour the USS *Albacore*, an important experimental submarine built in the 1950s at the nearby Portsmouth Naval Shipyard. Once the world's fastest submarine, this 55-person vessel was used for 20 years as the design model for the contemporary U.S. nuclear fleet. The tour includes a memorial park and gardens, a short film, a picnic area, a gift shop, and the submarine.

Portsmouth Harbor Lighthouse (603-431-9155; www.portsmouthharborlight house.org), off Rt. 1B adjacent to Fort Constitution and the U.S. Coast Guard Station, New Castle. Also known as Fort Point Lighthouse, New Castle Lighthouse and Fort Constitution Lighthouse, this was the first light station north of Boston in the American colonies. Today's 48-foot tower was built in 1877. A preservation organization offers tours one Sunday a month 11–3, May–Oct. Call for dates.

Portsmouth Athenaeum (603-431-2538), 9 Market Square, Portsmouth. Research library open Tue. and Thu. 1–4, Sat. 10–4, and by appointment. Reading Room open to the public for tours Thu. 1–4. Free. This three-story brick Federal building, with its four white pilasters, is the architectural anchor for Market Square. Built in 1805, after one of Portsmouth's disastrous fires, the building has, since 1823, been the home of the Athenaeum, a private library and museum. Genealogy, maritime history, biographies, and Civil War memorabilia are among its important holdings. Throughout the building are fully rigged ship models, half models, and paintings.

Redhook Ale Brewery (603-430-8600), 35 Corporate Dr., Pease International Tradeport, Portsmouth. Open daily. Founded in Seattle in 1981, the Redhook Brewery was an innovator in America's craft beer movement. Its Portsmouth facility has Bavarian-inspired rooflines. Inside, the equipment is state of the art. Brewery tours $1. Gift shop.

Star Island (603-430-6272; www.starisland.org), Isles of Shoals. One of the nine Isles of Shoals off the coast of Portsmouth, Star Island has an eclectic history that includes sojourns by pirates, writers, fishermen, artists, and naturalists. Today the old Oceanic Hotel offers summer conferences and retreats sponsored by the Unitarian Universalist Church. Day-trippers, arriving by chartered or private boat, are welcome to explore the circa-1800 stone chapel, visit an exhibit of poet Celia Thaxter memorabilia, or sit and enjoy the view from the sprawling hotel porch. There's a snack bar, bookstore, and gift shop, plus, plenty of sea air, windswept scenery, wildflower paths, and inspiring picnic opportunities.

Strawbery Banke (603-433-1100; www.strawberybanke.org), ticket office off Marcy St., Portsmouth. Open May–Oct., daily 10–5 daily, Sun. noon–5; Nov. 1–Apr. 30, Thu.–Sat. 10–2, Sun. noon–2. In the early 1960s the 10-acre site that is now this nationally known and respected restoration was supposed to be razed for an urban renewal project. Local protests stopped the demolition, saving more than 30 historically significant buildings. The museum now has 42 buildings, including several moved to this site to protect them from demolition elsewhere in the city. Most of the buildings are on their original foundations, which makes this a unique project compared with other historical restorations composed of

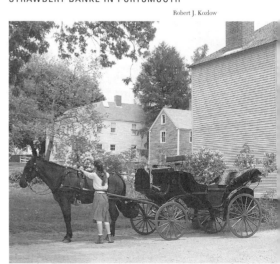

STRAWBERY BANKE IN PORTSMOUTH

Robert J. Kozlow

new re-creations or buildings assembled from many places. As the location of Portsmouth's first settlement in 1630 and a residential area until the early 1960s, Strawbery Banke reflects the living 300-year history of this neighborhood, not just one era. Furnished houses have rooms reflecting life from the 17th through the mid–20th centuries, depicting a variety of lifestyles, from wealthy merchants and professional people to sea captains, poor widows, and ordinary working families. Other houses have exhibits, displays, and craftspeople who offer their work for sale. The December candlelight stroll is a popular holiday attraction, and there are other special events throughout the year, including militia musters, horticulture and fabric workshops, and small-craft displays—the latter complementing the institution's wooden boat shop. Extensive 18th- and 19th-century gardens enhance the grounds. The **Museum Shop**, offering books and gifts, is open year-round. The **Café on the Banke** (603-436-8803), one of the city's best spots for gourmet sandwiches, soups, and light meals, is on the grounds.

Also see *Green Space*.

HISTORIC HOMES Beginning at the kiosk in Market Square, knowledgeable **Portsmouth Harbor trail guides** (603-436-1118) offer a wealth of background about the city's early settlers, patriots, ship captains, and industrialists on regularly scheduled tours June–mid-Oct., Mon. and Thu.–Sat. at 10:30 AM and 5:30 PM, Sun. at 1:30 PM. $8 adults, $5 ages 8–14. There is also a trail guide and map, available for $2 from many area shops and hotels, which highlights three different routes through the city's waterfront and downtown.

John Paul Jones House (603-436-8420), Middle and State sts., Portsmouth. Open mid-May–mid-Oct., 11–4 every day but Wed. Tours begin on the hour, last tour at 4 PM. $6 adults, $2.50 ages 6–14. The museum house of the Portsmouth Historical Society, this home was the residence of Captain John Paul Jones when he lived in Portsmouth overseeing the construction of two Revolutionary War frigates, the *Ranger* and the *America*. A traditional Georgian house, built in 1758, it has furnished period rooms and a small museum.

Governor John Langdon Memorial (603-436-3205; www.spnea.org/visit/homes/landon.htm), 143 Pleasant St., Portsmouth. Open June–Oct. Tours on the hour Fri.–Sun. 11–4. Admission $6. One of New England's finest Georgian mansions, this house was built in 1784 by John Langdon, a wealthy merchant who was an important figure in the Revolution and later a U.S. senator and governor of New Hampshire. George Washington was entertained in this house, which is now owned by the Society for the Preservation of New England Antiquities. Extensive gardens are behind the house.

Moffat-Ladd House (603-436-8221; www.whipple.org), 154 Market St., Portsmouth. Open mid-June–mid-Oct., Mon.–Sat. 11–5, Sun. 1–5. Guided tours. $5 adults, $1 children. Built in 1763, this house was the residence of wealthy 18th-century shipowners and merchants and is furnished in that period to reflect the family's lifestyle. William Whipple, a signer of the Declaration of Independence, lived here. Its great hall is a masterpiece of detailed woodworking. Internationally famous gardens fill the backyard, and don't miss the summerlong book sale in the carriage house. Owned by the Society of Colonial Dames.

Rundlet-May House (603-436-3205; www.spnea.org), Middle St., Portsmouth. Open first Sat. of every month, June–Oct. Guided tours on the hour. Twilight tours in Aug. $6 adults. Built in 1807, this Federal mansion remained in the builder's family until just a few years ago, when it was acquired by the Society for the Preservation of New England Antiquities. Although it has many fine Federal pieces built especially for the house, it does reflect the continuous ownership of successive generations of a family who valued the original features of the house and adapted their lifestyle with an appreciation for the past. The stable is impressive, as are the extensive gardens and grounds, which retain much of their original layout.

Warner House (603-436-5909; www.warnerhouse.org), 150 Daniel St., Portsmouth. Open early June–Oct., Mon.–Sat. 11–4, Sun. noon–4. $5 per adult. The finest New England example of an 18th-century, urban brick dwelling, this house was built in 1716 and, during its early years, was the home of leading merchants and officials of the royal provincial government. It has outstanding murals painted on the staircase walls, splendid paneling, and period furnishings. Benjamin Franklin is said to have installed the lightning rod on the west wall. Owned by the Warner House Association.

Wentworth-Gardner and Tobias Lear Houses (603-436-4406; www .seacoastnh.com), Gardner and Mechanic sts., Portsmouth. The Wentworth-Gardner House is open mid-June–mid-Oct., Tue.–Sun. 1–4; the Lear House is open Wed. 1–4. $5 adults, $2 children. Built in 1760, the Wentworth-Gardner House is one of the most perfect examples of Georgian architecture found in America. Built by Elizabeth (Rindge) and Mark Hunking Wentworth as a gift to their son Thomas (brother of the last royal governor), its exquisite carving took 14 months to complete. At one time the Metropolitan Museum planned to move it to New York's Central Park; then a group of Portsmouth citizens repurchased the building, and restored and furnished it as it is today. Adjacent is the **Tobias**

THE WENTWORTH-COOLIDGE MANSION

Kim Grant

Lear House, built in 1740, the childhood home of George Washington's private secretary. The president enjoyed tea in the parlor in 1789. Both houses are owned by the Wentworth-Gardner and Tobias Lear Houses Association.

Richard Jackson House (603-436-3205), 76 Northwest St., Portsmouth. Open the first Sat. of every month June–mid-Oct. Tours on the hour 1–4. Admission $6. This is New Hampshire's oldest house, built in 1664 with later additions. It has few furnishings and is of interest primarily for its 17th-century architectural details. It is most picturesque in May when its apple orchard is in bloom. Owned by the Society for the Preservation of New England Antiquities.

Wentworth-Coolidge Mansion Historic Site (603-436-6607), Little Harbor Rd. (off Rt. 1A), Portsmouth. Open mid-May–mid-Oct.,Wed.–Sat. 10–3, Sun. noon–4. Admission fee. Owned by the state, this rambling 40-room mansion is one of the most interesting and historic buildings in New Hampshire. It was the home of Royal Governor Benning Wentworth, whose term from 1741 until 1766 was the longest of any royal governor in America. Council meetings were held in an ornately paneled room overlooking the channel between Portsmouth and Little Harbors. Its lilacs, which bloom in late May, are said to be the first planted in America. Although the house is not furnished, its extensive woodwork is an exquisite display of the prowess of Portsmouth craftsmen of the period.

FOR FAMILIES ✪ **Water Country** (603-427-1111; www.watercountry.com), Rt. 1, 3 miles south of Exit 5 off Rt. 95, Portsmouth. Open mid-June–Labor Day. Open July 1–mid-Aug. 9:30–7; otherwise 10–5 or 6. Called New England's largest water park, this complex has multiple large water slides, a huge wave pool, a Racing Rapids ride and plunge, plus an Adventure River ride, bumper boats, fountains, and a kiddie pool. One admission covers all day for all rides; tube and boat rentals are additional.

✪ **The Children's Museum of Portsmouth** (603-436-3853; www.childrens -museum.org), 280 Marcy St., Portsmouth. Open Tue.–Sat. 10–5, Sun. 1–5. Also open Mon. during the summer and school vacation weeks. Closed some holidays. $6 adults and children, $5 seniors; members and children under 1 free. Children under 12 must be accompanied by an adult. While plans are afoot for this museum to move to the old armory building in Dover, it is currently housed in an old meetinghouse in Portsmouth's historic South End, a colorful site, exciting for children of all ages. Many of the museum's exhibits reflect the area's maritime heritage. Kids can explore the yellow submarine, ride in the lobster fishing boat, or climb inside a human-sized kaleidoscope to see unending reflections of themselves. There are many other hands-on exhibits, changing displays, and organized activities.

✪ **Seacoast Science Center** (603-436-8043; www.seacntr.org), Rt. 1A at Odiorne State Park, 570 Ocean Blvd., Rye. Open all year, 10–5. $3 adults, $1 ages 3–12; under 3 free. A facility of the Audubon Society of New Hampshire, this environmental center is right on the rocky shore and offers marine exhibits and aquariums, a museum shop, children's workshops, tidepooling and marsh walks, and occasional lectures.

✔ **Prescott Park** (603-436-2848), Marcy St., Portsmouth. Located directly across from Strawbery Banke, this city park offers lovely gardens and an annual arts festival with a full schedule of attractions late May–mid-Oct. Locals and tourists alike fill the lawn with blankets and picnics to enjoy jazz concerts, Broadway musicals, and Shakespeare under the stars. Admission is free, although a $5 donation is suggested.

HISTORIC CEMETERIES **North Cemetery**, Maplewood Ave., Portsmouth. Dating from 1753, this cemetery holds the remains of prominent people from the Revolutionary War to the War of 1812. Diverse headstones reveal the skill of early stonecutters.

Point of Graves Cemetery, off Marcy St., Portsmouth. Adjacent to Prescott Park, this old cemetery was established in 1671. Although most of the oldest stones have sunk from sight, many old and uniquely carved stones remain.

✳ To Do

BOAT EXCURSIONS ✔ **Isles of Shoals Steamship Company** (603-431-5500; 1-800-441-4620; www.islesofshoals.com), Barker Wharf, 315 Market St., Portsmouth 03801. Open daily mid-June–Labor Day; special fall schedule until Oct. 30. This is the Isles of Shoals ferry, hauling passengers and freight to Star Island and providing one of New England's finest narrated tours. The 90-foot *Thomas Laighton* is a replica of a turn-of-the-20th-century steamship, the type of vessel used when the islands were the leading New England summer colony, attracting the era's most famous artists, writers, poets, and musicians. The boat docks at Star Island, home of the Star Island Conference Center, a summer religious institution meeting here since the turn of the 20th century. Some morning trips allow passengers to leave the *Laighton* for a stopover, returning to the mainland in the late afternoon. Buy tickets early—they sometimes sell out. Bring your picnic lunch and camera. Since the *Laighton* is the supply line for the conference center, delivering food, drinking water, supplies, mail, and oil for the island's generators, it operates rain or shine. The trip to the islands takes about an hour; the round trip, about 3 hours. In addition to the daily Isles of Shoals cruises, the *Laighton* is used for dinner cruises, including clambakes and big-band dance cruises. The 71-foot *Oceanic* is used for whale-watching (an all-day, offshore trip), special lighthouse cruises, the nightly sunset cruise to the islands, and weekend cocktail and dance cruises. Reservations may be made by phone or online. Parking at the dock is $3 per vehicle.

✔ **Portsmouth Harbor Cruises** (603-436-8084; 1-800-776-0915; www.portsmouthharbor.com), Ceres St. Dock, Portsmouth. Open mid-May–Oct. The 49-passenger *Heritage* offers a variety of narrated cruises, which, depending on the tide and the season, tour the harbor and wend down the Piscataqua, past the two lighthouses, around New Castle Island, through Little Harbor, and back to the dock. Several trips circle the Isles of Shoals, and fall foliage trips travel the winding rivers and expanse of Great Bay. Our favorite is the 5:45 sunset cruise—no narration, just a cool drink and a quiet ride after a hot summer day. Several trips regularly sell out, so buy tickets early. Also available is a large sailboat for single-day or overnight charters.

Island Cruises Inc. (603-964-6446; www.ryeharborcruises.com), Rye Harbor State Marina, Rt. 1A, Ocean Blvd., Rye. Open weekends in spring and fall, daily late June–late Aug. *Uncle Oscar*, a 20-passenger Maine-built lobster boat, ferries folks on a 1-hour lobster trip, a 2-hour tour of the Isles of Shoals, or a 3-hour trip with a stopover and the possibility of eating dinner at the Oceanic Hotel on Star Island. Since Rye Harbor is the closest mainland port to the islands, fares are a little less than from Portsmouth.

Tug Alley Too (603-430-9556; www.tugboatalley.com), 2 Ceres St., Portsmouth. *Tommie the Tugboat*, aka *Tug Alley Too*, is available for charter excursions of Portsmouth Harbor and the Piscataqua River. Pack your own picnic or skippers Bob and Natalie Hassold (who own the retail shop Tugboat Alley) will provide one. They'll also provide a justice of the peace in case you want to get married or renew your vows while cruisin' down the river. Accommodates up to six passengers.

✔ **Granite State Whale Watch** (603-964-5545; 603-382-6743; www.whales-rye .com), Rye Harbor State Marina, Rt. 1A, Box 232, Rye. Open daily mid-June–Labor Day; weekend whale-watches May, June, Sep., and Oct. Ride the 150-person-capacity *Granite State* for a 6-hour whale-watch or a 2-hour cruise around the Isles of Shoals.

Atlantic Fishing and Whalewatching (603-964-5220; 1-800-WHALE-NH; www.atlanticwhalewatch.com), Rye Harbor Marina, Rt. 1A, Box 678, Rye. Open weekends mid-Apr.–May for all-day fishing; daily through Labor Day weekend for whale-watch tours and half-day fishing excursions; reduced schedule through mid-Oct. The speedy, 70-foot *Atlantic Queen II* is designed for all-weather ocean fishing. Offshore trips seek cod, cusk, pollack, haddock, mackerel, striped bass, and bluefish. Marine biologists from the Blue Ocean Society for Marine Conservation serve as naturalists. Reservations strongly recommended.

Portsmouth Kayak Adventures (603-559-1000; www.portsmouthkayak.com), Witch Cove Marina, 185 Wentworth Rd., Portsmouth. Certified guides are available to instruct paddlers in the basics of the sport and escort them to the Piscataqua River Basin and its tributaries. The area is rich in nautical history and natural beauty, a favorite spot for great blue herons—sometimes even harbor seals.

Portsmouth Rent & Ride (603-43306777; www.portsmouthrentandride.com), 37 Hanover St., Suite 2, Portsmouth. Open daily 9–5 though times may vary with the season. This outdoor recreation outfitter rents and sells bikes, kayaks, snowshoes, cross-country skis, and all-terrain skates. Guided tours available.

Saboutime Sailing, LLC (207-475-6248; www.saboutimesailing.com), Pepperell Cove Town Dock, Kittery Point, Me. (just across Memorial Bridge from downtown Portsmouth). Open mid-May–mid-Oct., Mon.–Sat. Three-hour morning or afternoon sails are $25 adult, $15 ages 5–12. Evening cruises are $5 more for adults. A range of lessons and customized tours are also available.

Amaryllis **Sailing** (603-205-0630; www.sailamaryllis.com), Badgers Island Marina, Portsmouth Harbor. This 45-foot luxury catamaran can accommodate up to six passengers for a day sail, sunset dinner cruise, or offshore B&B charter to the

Isles of Shoals. If desired, guests can join the crew to help hoist and trim the sails. Reservations recommended.

FARMER'S MARKET **Farmer's Market** (603-778-6003; www.seacoastgrowers .org), Parrott Ave., Portsmouth. June–mid-Oct., Sat. 9–1. Fresh, locally grown veggies and fruits in-season, home-baked goods, and crafts. Seacoast Growers' Association. Also markets in Dover, Durham, Exeter, Hampton, Kingston, and Stratham.

GOLF **Breakfast Hill Golf Club** (603-426-5001; www.breakfasthill.com), 339 Breakfast Hill Rd., Greenland. The seacoast's newest 18-hole championship public golf course on 170 acres of rolling fairways and contoured greens. Pro shop, driving range, practice green, and snack bar with outdoor deck.

Pease Golf Club (603-433-1331; www.peasedev.org), 200 Grafton Rd., Portsmouth. A 27-hole regulation course open to the public daily spring–Nov. Tee times available 7 days in advance. Pro shop, cafeteria, golf and pull cart rentals, and driving and practice ranges.

Portsmouth Country Club (603-436-9719), Country Club Dr. (off Rt. 101 south of Portsmouth), Greenland. Open mid-Apr.–mid-Nov. Designed by Robert Trent Jones; 18 holes, the longest course in New Hampshire, with several holes sited on the shores of Great Bay. Cart rentals, full bar and food service, and pro shop. Call for starting times.

WALKING TOURS **Art 'Round Town** (603-431-4230; www.artroundtown .org), 136 State St., Portsmouth. A gallery walk of 10 local art spaces, more than 100 artists. May–Dec., the second Fri. of the month, 5–8 PM. Sponsored by the New Hampshire Art Association–Robert Levy Gallery.

Portsmouth Black Heritage Trail (603-431-2768; www.seacoastnh.com/ blackhistory; www.friendsofthepearl.org). A self-guided walking tour of 24 sites relating the story of early African Americans and their descendants in this port city. Tour brochures are available at the Strawbery Banke Museum Visitor Center, across Marcy Street from the start of the trail in Prescott Park, as well as at the Strawbery Banke Museum Shop and the Greater Portsmouth Chamber of Commerce, Market Street Extension.

✳ Green Space

PARKS 🐾 ✐ **Prescott Park**, Marcy St., Portsmouth. Open year-round. Marcy Street was once an area of bawdy houses, bars, and run-down businesses. The Prescott sisters, who were born in this section of the city, inherited millions of dollars and sought to clean up the waterfront by creating a park, which they gave to the city. Supported by a substantial trust fund, the park is famous for its beautiful gardens, but it also includes boat wharves, an amphitheater, picnic areas, sculpture, fountains, and the historic 1705 Sheafe Warehouse with exhibits. During the summer it is the location of the daily Prescott Park Arts Festival (donation requested), offering outdoor summer theater, varied musical performances, an art exhibit, and children's theater and art programs. At the eastern end of the park, cross the bridge to adjacent Pierce Island, home of the state's commercial fishing pier, and walk out to Four Tree Island, a picnic ground nearly in the middle of the river.

🌸 **Urban Forestry Center** (603-431-6774), Elywn Rd., off Rt. 1 south of Portsmouth. Open year-round; summer 8–8, winter 8–4; office hours Mon.–Fri. 8–4. Free. Bordering tidal Sagamore Creek, this site has nature trails, herb gardens, hiking, cross-country skiing, and snowshoeing, and offers environmental programs throughout the year.

🌸 ⚓ **Fort Constitution**, off Rt. 1A, New Castle. Open year-round 10–5. Turn in at the U.S. Coast Guard Station and park where indicated. Free. This historic site was first used for fortifications in the early 1600s, but today it reflects the Revolutionary and Civil War periods. In December 1774, after being alerted by Paul Revere, local patriots raided what was then called Fort William and Mary, overwhelmed its few defenders, and removed its powder and some weapons before British warships from Boston could reinforce the garrison. This is considered to be the first overt act against the king and predated the war's outbreak by some 4 months. The powder was used against the British at the battle of Bunker Hill. The last royal governor, John Wentworth, and his family fled their home in the city and remained in the fort before leaving the rebellious province. Restored and maintained by the state, the fort's entrance portcullis reflects the colonial period, while the fortifications along the water date from the Civil War, although there were no battles here. Adjacent to the fort is the picturesque and still-important Fort Point lighthouse, and just offshore is the Whaleback lighthouse. Ten miles at sea the Isles of Shoals are visible.

Fort Stark, Wild Rose Lane, off Rt. 1A, New Castle. Open May–Oct., weekends and holidays 10–5. Free. To protect the important Portsmouth Naval Shipyard during World War II, the military occupied several points at the mouth of the river. One was Fort Foster, across the river from Fort Constitution, and Fort Stark was another. Although used as a fort from 1746, the site today reflects its World War II service.

⚓ **New Castle Great Common**, Rt. 1A, New Castle. Open year-round; a small fee is charged to nonresidents during summer. Another World War II site, this was Camp Langdon, an army base. It was acquired by the town of New Castle as a recreation area and the site for a new office complex. There are restrooms, picnic tables, a small beach, and a pier for fishing. Overlooking the mouth of the river and its two lighthouses, this area is one of the scenic highlights along the coast.

⚓ ♿ **Odiorne Point State Park** (603-436-7406), Rt. 1A, Rye. Open year-round; a park fee is charged in the main season, June–Sep. This 137-acre oceanfront park is the site of the first settlement in New Hampshire in 1623. Later, fine mansions were built here; then the site was taken over during World War II and named Fort Dearborn, with huge guns placed in concrete bunkers. As a park it has handicapped-accessible nature trails, a boat-launching ramp, picnic tables, and a fine nature center—open late June–late Aug.—operated by the University

RYE HARBOR

of New Hampshire. The center has exhibits and offers varied daily nature programs using the park, its nearby marsh, and the ocean's intertidal zone. No swimming. Also see the Seacoast Science Center in *For Families*.

Rye Harbor State Park and Marina (603-436-5294), Rt. 1A, Rye. Open year-round; a fee is charged in the summer season for the park and boat launching. New Hampshire's smallest state park, this jewel occupies an ocean point just south of Rye Harbor. It has picnic tables, a playground, a jetty for fishing, a view of the picturesque harbor, and cooling ocean breezes on hot summer days. Around the corner is the **Rye Harbor State Marina** with a launching ramp and wharves, where you can buy tickets for deep-sea fishing, whale-watches, or sightseeing boat rides.

BEACHES **Wallis Sands State Park** (603-436-9404), Rt. 1A, Rye. Open weekends mid-May–late June, then daily until Labor Day. A large, sandy beach with lifeguards, restrooms, parking, and a snack bar. Fee charged.

Jenness State Beach, Rt. 1A, Rye. Another large, sandy beach with lifeguards, restrooms, and parking meters. A snack bar is across the street.

New Castle State Park, Rt. 1A, New Castle. Grills, parking, restrooms, sandy beach. Fee charged.

✳ Lodging

RESORT **Wentworth by the Sea** (603-422-7322; www.wentworth.com), 588 Wentworth Rd., New Castle 03854. One of New Hampshire's historic "Grand Hotels." In 1905 this seaside superstructure was the site of the peace talks that ended the Russo-Japanese War. Although it once hosted socialites, film stars, and presidents, in recent years the formerly opulent hotel had grown faded and stood empty until 2003, when the Marriott Hotel chain invested millions to perform a miracle. Perched high

THE SPECTACULAR EXTERIOR OF WENTWORTH BY THE SEA IN NEW CASTLE

atop a bluff overlooking the Atlantic Ocean, the hotel, originally built in 1874, now boasts 161 rooms, two restaurants, lavish gardens, indoor and outdoor pools, state-of-the-art meeting space, and a full-service spa. There's also golf, tennis, and a marina for guests who arrive by "yacht" available at the nearby Wentworth-by-the-Sea Country Club. Call for rates.

BED & BREAKFASTS **The Arbor Inn** (603-431-7010; www.arborinn.com), 400 Brackett Rd., Rye 03870. Located within walking distance of Wallis Sands Beach, this reproduction Colonial offers all the comforts of home and then some. You can rent the luxuriously furnished, four-bedroom house for $3,000 per week in June and Sep.; $3,500 in July and Aug. The rest of the year it's a B&B with rooms available for $95–185 per couple. Gourmet breakfast.

Bow Street Inn (603-431-7760; www.bowstreetinn.com), 121 Bow St., Portsmouth 03801. Open all year. Overlooking the waterfront, this converted brick brewery has a cosmopolitan feel with the Seacoast Repertory Theatre on the main floor; the inn is an elevator's ride above. Only 2 of the 10 rooms have river views, but all have a queen-sized brass bed, private bath, phone, cable TV, and air-conditioning. The harbor-view rooms are mini suites. Just a short walk to all of the city's sights and fine dining. Continental breakfast with fresh-baked items. $99–175, depending on season and accommodations.

The Governor's House (603-427-5140; www.governors-house.com), 32 Miller Ave., Portsmouth 03801. Once the home of a former New Hampshire governor, this stately Colonial Revival home offers four guest rooms, each with private bath, queen-sized bed, cable TV and DVD player, air-conditioning, and high-speed Internet access. There's an outdoor hot tub, lighted tennis court, library and game room, all within a 10-minute walk from downtown. Or you can catch the coast trolley at the door. The $165–245 rate (depending on season and accommodations) includes pampering—Italian linens and robes, evening wine and cheese, and a continental breakfast with fresh fruit and freshly baked breads served in your room, on the porch, or in the handsome dining room. Massages and tennis lessons available for an additional fee.

The Inn at Christian Shore (603-431-6770; www.portsmouthnh.com), 335 Maplewood Ave., Portsmouth 03801. Open year-round. Mariaelena Koopman is a gracious and cosmopolitan innkeeper who has traveled the world to assemble an eclectic mix of art and antiques shown off to advantage in this lovely, in-town Federal house. A B&B since 1979, the inn has five comfortable, individually furnished rooms, all with private bath, air-conditioning, and TV. Koopman's unerring eye for arrangements makes her collection of African baskets, pre-Columbian ceramics, Malaysian textiles, Argentine silver, and old and new art seem right at home. A full breakfast and afternoon tea are served in a charming dining room with a roaring fire, brass candelabra, and exposed old beams—or, when weather permits, outside in a tree-shaded garden. Rates are $100–120, June–Oct. and holidays; $95–100, the rest of the year.

The Inn at Strawbery Banke (603-436-7242; 1-800-428-3933; www .innatstrawberybanke.com), 314 Court St., Portsmouth 03801. Around the corner from Strawbery Banke and two blocks from Market Square, Sarah Glover O'Donnell's homey B&B has location, location, location! It also boasts seven bright, comfortable rooms that meander through the circa-1800 home and a more recent addition. All have updated private bath. Some rooms have queen-sized beds; others, a queen and a single.

Upstairs and down, common rooms offer TV and travel books. A skylit breakfast room overlooks gardens, a strawberry patch, and bird feeders, assuring a sunny start to your day. Full breakfast. Rates are $135–140 high season, $100–105 off-season.

Martin Hill Inn (603-436-2287), 404 Islington St., Portsmouth 03801. Open year-round. Superfriendly innkeepers Jane and Paul Harnden have invested the city's first B&B with their love of antiques and their talent for gardening. From the street this yellow-clapboard inn with its white picket fence looks cheery and chic. Inside, the elegance of early Portsmouth comes alive. Adjacent 1820 and 1850 houses are joined by a brick garden path overlooking a courtyard and water garden. The main inn has three guest rooms with period furnishings and canopy or four-poster beds. The Guest House has four rooms, three of which are suites, one with an attached sunroom. All rooms have private bath, air-conditioning, writing tables, sofa, or separate sitting area. A no-smoking inn. Full breakfast is served in the elegant, mahogany-furnished dining room. Rates are $98–155, depending on the room and season.

Portsmouth Harbor Inn & Spa (207-439-4040; www.innatports mouth.com), 6 Water St., Kittery, ME 03904. While not technically in Portsmouth (or even New Hampshire), this inn offers a pleasing alternative within maybe not a stone's throw, but at least catapult distance from downtown Portsmouth. Just across Memorial Bridge, the 1879 redbrick Victorian looks back at Portsmouth Harbor. Five luxurious rooms, each with private bath, feature period antiques and modern amenities. A full-service day spa is available in a restored barn connected to the inn. Rates, ranging $170–220, include a full gourmet breakfast.

Sise Inn (603-433-1200; 1-800-267-0525), 40 Court St., Portsmouth 03801. Open year-round. An easy walk from Portsmouth's "happening" Market Square, the Sise Inn offers hotel amenities in a handsomely restored Victorian stick-style home and addition. The 34 rooms, including several suites, have private bath, mostly queen-sized beds, TV, VCR, telephone, alarm clock, radio, table, and comfortable chairs. Many also have CD player and whirlpool baths; one, a skylight and private staircase. With several meeting rooms, the inn was designed for the business traveler, but vacationers are welcome to share the Victorian luxury as well. A light breakfast is served. Rates are $189–269 in summer and foliage season, $119–189 the rest of the year.

Rock Ledge Manor (603-431-1413; www.rockledgemanor.com), 1413 Ocean Blvd. (Rt. 1A), Rye 03870. Open all year; reservations requested. On a knoll overlooking the ocean with views from each room to the Isles of Shoals, this picturesque white-shingled Victorian "cottage" has three rooms, each with private bath, queen bed, and air-conditioning. The upstairs suite also has a pull-out sofa in an adjoining room. After breakfast, relax on the veranda overlooking the sea. A 5-minute walk to the beach; 10 minutes by car to Portsmouth. There's good biking from the door. A nonsmoking inn. Rooms are $150 May–Oct., $125 the rest of the year. The suite is $200 in-season, $175 Nov.–May.

Downtown on Market Street (Exit 7 off I-95) is the full-service Sheraton Harborside Portsmouth Hotel and Conference Center (603-431-2300) with 205 rooms, restaurant, and lounge, within walking distance of everything.

Additional accommodations are available in nearby Kittery and Eliot, Me., just across Memorial Bridge. In addition to **Portsmouth Harbor Inn & Spa** listed above, these include **Enchanted Nights B&B** (207-439-1489) in Kittery, and **Farmstead Bed and Breakfast** (207-748-3145; www .farmstead.qpg.com) in Eliot.

MOTELS Portsmouth is well supplied with motels, most of which are located on Rt. 1 south of the city and at the traffic circle intersection of I-95, Rt. 1 bypass, and Rt. 4/16 (Spaulding Turnpike). Among these are the **Anchorage Inn** (603-431-8111), **Comfort Inn** (603-433-3338), **Courtyard by Marriott** (603-436-2121), **Hampton Inn** (603-431-6111), **Holiday Inn** (603-431-8000), **Wren's Nest Village Inn** (603-436-2481), and **Howard Johnson Hotel** (603-436-7600).

❋ **Where to Eat**

Portsmouth is famous for its numerous quality restaurants, the best collection of fine dining north of Boston. Several of the top restaurants are located in the Old Harbor area where Bow, Ceres, and Market streets intersect. Here six-story warehouses, the largest structures north of Boston when built in the early 1800s, have been remodeled as restaurants and shops. A treat for summer and early-fall visitors are the five outdoor decks located here on the waterfront, open for lunch and late into the evening (until the legal closing for serving liquor). Everything from snacks to sandwiches and full dinners is available on the decks. View the tugboats and watch large oceangoing ships pass, seemingly within an arm's length.

DINING OUT ♿ **43° North Kitchen and Wine Bar** (603-430-0225; www .fortythreenorth.com), 75 Pleasant St., Portsmouth. Open Mon.–Sat. for dinner at 5. Reservations strongly encouraged. European ambience, a stellar wine selection (served by the glass and half bottle, too), and an ambitious menu combine to attract an upscale crowd to this small, well-proportioned bistro just a short block off bustling Market Square. The star of the attractive room is the wine bar tucked in a corner, which you can see from most tables. The menu here changes frequently; expect to find dishes borrowing from Asian, Italian, and French cuisines. Appetizers are served tapas style and include small plates of duck spring rolls drizzled in tamari, pan-seared rock shrimp, and blue point oysters topped with creamy Gorgonzola and crispy pancetta. The main-course selection usually features meats, seafood, and pasta such as tuna, quail, wild mushroom ravioli (for vegetarians), elk, and flatiron steak. Vintages are carefully chosen, and you can be assured of a perfect match— these folks know their food and wine. Entrées $18–26, appetizers $7.50–11.

Anthony Alberto's Ristorante Italiano (603-436-4000; www.anthony albertos.com), 59 Penhallow St., Portsmouth. Dinner daily from 5; closed Sun. in summer. Tucked along a picturesque side street, this romantic basement restaurant features elegantly prepared northern and southern Italian cuisine in a grottolike setting. The pastas are homemade, with interesting selections such as pappardelle with braised rabbit, fettuccine with shrimp, or cappellini topped with scallops and prosciutto; the antipasti and entrées are a mix of creative and classic specialties. Olive-marinated filet mignon, grilled rack of lamb, and seared salmon with beet-encrusted scallops are among the good choices. Fresh seafood specials change daily. Entrées $18.95–26.95.

Bananas Bar & Grill (603-431-5795; www.bananasbarandgrill.com), 172 Hanover St., Portsmouth. Open Tue.–Sat. 11:15 AM–last call, Sun. 9 AM–10 PM. Kitchen closes at 9 PM Sun., 10 PM the rest of the week. The curved second-story window with its green neon palm trees and yellow bananas makes this place hard to miss, but it's a good measure of what's inside. The only restaurant in town with regular dance music, a disc jockey comes by Tue.–Sat. at 9 PM to keep this place swinging and swaying. Burgers, pizza, pasta, barbecue, seafood. Moderate prices.

Blue Mermaid (603-427-2583; www .bluemermaid.com), The Hill, Portsmouth. Open all year, daily at 11:30 AM for lunch and dinner. This eclectic and lively restaurant offers a diverse, flavorful menu that covers the globe. The kitchen pays homage to its coastal proximity with appetizers such as lobster and corn chowder or a Caesar salad topped with grilled shrimp; this trend carries over to the main dishes where you can take your pick from a variety of seafood and have it tossed on the wood grill. Land-based dishes are easy to come by, too: Barbecued ribs, lamb on a skewer, and pad Thai make ordering a challenge for the daring diner. Light eaters can order from the small tapas-style menu—it features the likes of yucca fritta with cilantro adobo or a lobster quesadilla—and interesting side dishes such as plantains also pop up here and there. Eating here is definitely a unique adventure, and you may also be treated to an evening of live music if you visit on the weekend. Entrées $13.95–19.95.

Café Mirabelle and La Crêperie (603-430-9301; www.cafemirabelle .com), 64 Bridge St., Portsmouth. Open Wed.–Sun. for dinner from 5:15. A cozy place with many plants and large windows, this restaurant offers authentic country French dining (the chef-owner hails from France) in a romantic setting. Entrées are $17.95–22.95. Desserts are equally French—profiteroles, mousses, soufflés, clafoutis, and crème brûlée.

The Carriage House (603-964-8251; www.carriagehouserye.com), 2263 Ocean Blvd., Rye Beach. Open daily at 5 PM, Sunday brunch 11–3. Built as a restaurant in the 1920s, the Carriage House has been a favorite gourmet eatery for two decades, offering quality Continental cuisine at reasonable prices. Specialties might include a Madras curry of the day; a navarin of lobster pan-roasted with big juicy sea scallops and vegetables and flamed with Pernod; or the frutti di mare fra diavolo, which features shrimp, scallops, mussels, squid, and fish all sautéed in Chablis, garlic, and lemon and tossed with spicy marinara sauce—then served over linguine! There are several pasta entrées, salmon poached with Chablis in parchment, sole Oscar, roast duckling, and steaks. Many selections offer both

large and small portions. Entrées $14.50–28.95.

Chiangmai Thai Restaurant (603-433-1289), 128 Penhallow St., Portsmouth. Dinner Tue.–Sun., 5–close. An extensive menu of authentic Thai cooking with curries and both hot and spicy dishes. Chicken, seafood, and vegetarian entrées are featured; some entrées allow you to create your own meal. Tasty Thai spring rolls and hot-and-sour soups highlight the appetizers. Appetizers from $3.25; entrées $10.95–17.50 (for lychee duck).

The Dolphin Striker (603-431-5222; www.dolphinstriker.com), 15 Bow St., Portsmouth. Lunch 11:30–2, dinner 5–9:30. On the waterfront in a restored warehouse, this is an old favorite with a new menu that features creatively prepared seafood and such innovative specialties as grilled andouille sausage with apple-braised red cabbage, and grilled beef tenderloin topped with a roasted chili, balsamic syrup, and chipotle sauce. On the lower level is the **Spring Hill Tavern**, offering entertainment amid a collection of memorabilia that celebrates the city's maritime heritage. Entrées $17–28.

Jumpin' Jay's Fish Café (603-766-FISH; www.jumpinjays.com), 150 Congress St., Portsmouth. Open Mon.–Thu. 5:30–9:30 PM, Fri. and Sat. 5–10, Sun. 5–9. The red-snapper-painted walls lined with contemporary fish prints set the mood for this casually hip fish house. Often there are people lined up around the corner waiting to catch the fun. You have a choice of 10 catches of the day served with your choice of a half dozen sauces, ranging from $18.50–23.50. Raw bar, hot and cold appetizers, salads, and several fish and pasta dishes round out the menu.

The Library (603-431-5202; www .libraryrestaurant.com), 401 State St., Portsmouth. Open for lunch Mon.–Sat. 11:30–3, dinner Sun.–Thu. 5–9:30, Fri. and Sat. until 10. Sunday brunch 11:30–3. The dark paneled walls and ceilings of the old Rockingham Hotel, once Portsmouth's finest hostelry, give this restaurant its name. The menu features steaks plus traditional favorites with contemporary flair. Salmon Benedict is a Sunday brunch favorite. In the English-style pub, the hotel's original front desk makes an impressive backdrop for a nightcap or cigar. $30 for a 16-ounce steak; $20 for 8 ounces.

Lindbergh's Crossing (603-431-0887), 29 Ceres St., Portsmouth. Open daily 5:30–9:30 PM. Brick walls and understated elegance in both food and atmosphere at this bistro and wine bar. The menu, with its French country roots, reaches beyond to Spain and North Africa for inspiration. Order tapas—say, fresh figs and roasted almonds in a carrot emulsion for $5.50—or go for a larger first course of tender braised baby octopus with Tunisian tomato salad for $10. Whichever, be sure to leave room for an entrée, maybe a seafood tagine ($25) or peppered veal strip steak with housemade spinach gnocchi and chanterelle cream sauce ($26).

& **The Metro** (603-436-0521; www .themetrorestaurant.com), 20 Old High St., Portsmouth. Open for lunch 11:30–2:30, dinner 5:30–9:30 Mon.–Thu.; 5–10 Fri. and Sat.; closed Sun. Located just off Market Square, this is one of the city's most elegant restaurants, with rich paneling and a brass rail in the bar . . . . *très* belle

epoque. An updated menu features Maine crabcakes and smoked salmon carpaccio for appetizers; pan-seared diver scallops with a champagne tarragon sauce served with black tobiko caviar, rack of lamb à la Provençal with ratatouille, fresh seafood swimming in a leek, fennel, and tomato broth, and choice beef or lobster specials as entrées. Handicapped accessible, parking adjacent. Entrées $18–28. Fri. and Sat. are jazz nights, no cover charge.

Oar House (603-436-4025; www .portsmouthnh.com), 55 Ceres St., Portsmouth. Lunch Mon.–Sat. 11:30–3, Sunday brunch until 3:30; dinner Mon.–Sat. 5–9:30. Valet parking. Located in a remodeled warehouse, this is another longtime favorite on the waterfront and our choice for chowder. Seafood is featured and varies from bouillabaisse and baked stuffed lobster to broiled scallops and Oar House Delight, a sautéed combination of shrimp, scallops, and fresh fish topped with sour cream and crumbs baked in the oven. Sirloin with peppercorn sauce, rack of lamb, and a chef's chicken, varied daily, are also offered. The Oar House deck, open Memorial Day–early autumn, is our favorite for picturesque riverside relaxing and dining. Entrées $20–34.

Pesce Blue (603-430-7766; www .pesceblue.com), 103 Congress St., Portsmouth. Open for lunch Mon.–Fri. 11:45–2, dinner daily 5–9:30, Fri. and Sat. until 10. Seasonal patio dining. The loftlike ceilings, chrome bar, and sleek blue mosaic tiles add up to a cool urban look much appreciated by the regional media. Those coming north from Boston also appreciate the prices. While Pesce Blue is hardly cheap, some say the same meal would be three times the price an hour away. Seafood is the passion here. Sauces are subtle to bring out the ocean flavor. Grilled yellowfin tuna with crispy English pea risotto cake, pea tendrils, peperoncino oil, and wasabi caviar at $26.50 is a good example of the crisp, fresh, California-inspired menu.

Portsmouth Gas Light Company (603-431-9122; www.portsmouthgas light.com), 64 Market St. (or enter through Attrezzi), Portsmouth. Open Sun.–Wed. 11 AM–10 PM, Thu.–Sat. until 11 PM. The upstairs nightclub is open Thu.–Sat. 9 PM–1 AM. Breakfast and lunch served 8 AM–noon in the main dining room on weekends. After a long, costly renovation, the Gas Light is back, illuminating the downtown restaurant scene with a trinity of dining and entertainment opportunities—brick-oven pizza downstairs, where you can get an all-you-can-eat lunch pizza buffet for $6.50 on weekdays; an upscale dining room with exposed brick, lighted alabaster bar, and a bistro menu on the main floor; and upstairs, a nonsmoking nightclub that offers a multicolored light show, circular bar, music, and dancing for the 21–35 age group.

Radici Ristorante (603-373-6464; www.radicirestaurant.com), 142 Congress St., Portsmouth. Open Mon.–Thu. 5:30–9:30 PM, Fri.–Sat. 5–10, Sun. 5–9. Rated one of the top 10 restaurants north of Boston by the *Boston Globe*, which called it "classy but not unfriendly or too upscale." *Radici* means "roots," and here that means Italian carried to the next generation. Well-priced house specialties include grilled New York sirloin with a balsamic demiglaze, and gremolata served with a Gorgonzola polenta pie over an arugula mixed green salad for $17; or try osso buco (braised veal shanks) with shallots and wild mushrooms served with herbed potatoes and vegetable in a Madeira demiglaze for $19.

Sake Japanese Restaurant (603-431-1822), 141 Congress St., Portsmouth. Open Mon.–Thu. 11:30 AM–10 PM, Fri.–Sat. 11:30–11, Sun. 12:30–10. A large, modern, open room with a long sushi bar and lots of sushi selections. Luncheon and dinner specials include mushi mono (fresh fish fillets steamed with scallion and ginger soy sauce), tepan yaki (chunks of seafood and meat with seasonal vegetables and noodles in a light sauce), and yaki zakana (lightly seasoned broiled fish with citrus dipping sauce), as well as the more traditional tempura and teriyaki. Prices are moderate.

Sakura (603-431-2721; www.ports mouthnh.com), 40 Pleasant St., Portsmouth. Lunch Tue.–Fri. 11:30–2:30, dinner weekdays and Sun. 5–9, Fri. and Sat. until 10:30. Fine Japanese dining with a long sushi bar where you can watch the chefs prepare creative and tasty portions of sushi and sashimi. We like the dinner box (the meal is actually served in a portioned box) with miso soup, rice, salad, and a choice of two portions of sushi, sashimi, tempura, teriyaki, and other specialties. Although fish is featured, there is beef and chicken teriyaki and sukiyaki (slices of beef and vegetables with soup and rice). For a special occasion, try "Heaven"—12 pieces of sushi and two rolls with 10 pieces of sashimi. Japanese beer, sake, and plum wine also served. Entrées $12–22, dinner box $13.50, sushi bar selections from $13.

Saunders at Rye Harbor (603-964-6466; www.saundersatryeharbor.com), off Rt. 1A at Rye Harbor, Rye. Open all year, daily from noon. This well-known restaurant started in the 1920s selling fish from the dock. The specialty is lobster (boiled, baked, or broiled stuffed) served fresh from saltwater tanks, but the diverse menu also includes chicken with lemon and herbs, Saunders jambalaya (lobster, crab, scallops, shrimp, sausage, vegetables, and Creole sauce over rice), a variety of fresh fish, and land 'n' sea (prime rib with shrimp, scallops, or sautéed lobster). Saunders's deck overlooking picturesque Rye Harbor is one of the best spots on the seacoast for a relaxing lunch or beverage. Pianist on Fri. and Sat. evenings. Dinner prices $15–25.95; lobster dishes, including lobster cooked with ginger and macadamia nuts, at market price.

Victory Restaurant and Bar (603-766-0960; www.96statestreet.com), 96 State St., Portsmouth. Open Tue.–Sat. 5:30–9:30 PM. A handsome new restaurant with old brick, marine prints, white pillar candles, black Windsor chairs, and polished wood set the stage for equally fine, no-nonsense dining. Seafood includes roasted wild king salmon with herb mustard crust, sorrel crème fraîche, lentils, and roasted beet vinaigrette for $21. A New York strip steak with bordelaise sauce is $27.

The Wellington Room (603-431-2989; www.thewellingtonroom.com), upstairs at 67 Bow St., Portsmouth. Open for tea Wed.–Sun. 3:30–5, for dinner Wed.–Fri. 5–9, Sat. 5–9:30, Sun. 4–9. Chef-owner David G. Robinson, one of 50 Master Chefs in the world, has realized a dream in this small, second-floor restaurant overlooking the harbor. After paying his dues in kitchens in Washington, DC, and the Boston area, he's brought his careful attention to cuisine to his own elegant but casual dining room. The afternoon tea idea, with the possibility of scones, tea sandwiches, and pastries, is making a splash. The dinner menu is classic French country, artfully prepared. Robinson is also happy to honor special requests. Entrées $16–26.

EATING OUT **The Blue Claw** (603-427-2529; www.theblueclaw.com), 58 Ceres St., Portsmouth. Open daily, weather permitting, from 11 AM. Not exactly inexpensive but less upscale than some of its neighbors, this waterfront restaurant features a large deck with a view of the harbor and tugboat landing. It specializes in lobster rolls and steamed lobster dinners, prices subject to change with the market. Redhook beer-battered shrimp or fish-and-chips, with your choice of a side dish, are more consistent at $13.99. Take-out available.

Celebrity Sandwich (603-433-7009; hotline for daily specials, 603-433-2277; www.portsmouthnh.com), 171 Islington St., Portsmouth. Open Mon.–Fri. 10–6; Sat. 11–3. More than 100 sandwiches, each named for a different celebrity, served in an art deco dining room. Box lunches, soups, salads, and desserts too. Eat in or take out. All sandwiches $5.25 whole, $3.25 half.

Currents (603-427-5427; www.currentsbistro.com), 23 Market St., Portsmouth. Open Mon.–Fri. 11–3, Sat. 11:30–2:30 for lunch; Wed.–Sat. 5–9 for dinner; Sun. 8–2 for brunch; and Sat. 8–11:30 for breakfast. A

Mediterranean bistro offering full-service dining or yummy take-out soups, salads, and sandwiches.

The Ferry Landing (603-431-5510; www.ferrylanding@portsmouthnh .com), 10 Ceres St., Portsmouth. Open Apr. 15–Sep., daily from 11:30 AM. Light seafood dishes of many varieties, sandwiches, chowder, and burgers are served in this 100-year-old building, which was the original ferry landing before the bridges were built. Hanging out over the river, right beside the tugboats, the place is mostly a deck. It is always busy (especially the bar on weekends) during its summer season. Lobster roll $16.95; in the rough $20.95.

✐ **Friendly Toast** (603-430-2154), 121 Congress St., Portsmouth. Open Mon.–Thu. 7 AM–noon; Fri. and Sat. open 24 hours; Sun. 7 AM–9 PM. This popular kitsch-a-thon features great breakfasts and lunches that scream *diversity*. Pick from unusual combinations like orange French toast, green eggs and ham, Almond Joy pancakes (buttermilk pancakes with chocolate chips, coconut, and almonds), omelets, egg scrambles, and a whopping list of sides including Cuban beans, vegetarian "soysage," and home fries. Lunch is slightly tamer, and you can get old-time faves like BLTs, club sandwiches, and grilled cheese sandwiches along with late-20th-century newcomers such as hummus or nachos. Be prepared for wait staff sporting unique tattoos, piercings, and a *doin'-my-own-thing* attitude. The room appears to have been furnished by a *Leave It to Beaver* set decorator gone bad, with Formica tables and clown paintings clashing with folk art touches. Most items $3.25–7.

Geno's Chowder and Sandwich Shop (603-427-2070), 177 Mechanic St., Portsmouth. Open Mon.–Fri., 8:30 AM–4 PM, Sat. until 3 PM. Good food is its own reward—fresh lobster rolls, New England chowders, and homemade desserts—and the waterfront deck view is there to remind you that before it was a tourist destination, Portsmouth was indeed a port city.

Gilley's Diner (603-744-2321), 149 Fleet St., Portsmouth. Open 11:30 AM–2:30 AM. An urban legend for sure, this diner managed to accumulate 5,000 unpaid parking tickets before it was moved in the1970s from its original location in Market Square. The original truck is still attached but going nowhere. Burgers, hot dogs, chili, fries, and beer.

The Ice House (603-431-3086), Wentworth Rd., Rye. Open for lunch and dinner. A popular local take-out and eat-in place since 1952. The decor, recently redone, features bleached knotty-pine walls hung with license plates. The extensive menu has hot and cold sandwiches, burgers, chicken, and all kinds of fish—baked, broiled, and fried.

Me & Ollie's Café (603-436-7777), 10 Pleasant St., Market Square, Portsmouth. Open daily 7 AM–8 PM. Great central location makes this a good stop for a satisfying sandwich, either traditional or grilled panini. Half sandwich and cup of soup (all vegetarian) or small salad runs $6.25. No wonder they call it "Honest Food."

Muddy River Smokehouse (603-430-9582; info@muddyriver.com), 21 Congress St., Portsmouth. Open Sun.–Thu. 11 AM–9:30 PM; Fri. and Sat. nights until 10:30. Just what it sounds like, a barbecue and blues joint, voted "Best in the State" by *New Hampshire Magazine* readers. Forget pretension. With barnboard on the walls and paper towels on the tables, this is all about down-and-dirty eating. Ribs, pulled pork, chili, Tex-Mex, and all-around backwoods grub. Moderate.

Poco's Bow Street Cantina (603-431-5967; www.portsmouthnh.com), 37 Bow St., Portsmouth. Open daily 11:30 AM–9 PM, Fri. and Sat. until 11. A popular Mexican restaurant with big bay windows overlooking the tugboats and the river; local art covers the walls. Almost any Mexican item you can imagine is here (sizzling fajitas a specialty), plus Mexican beer, sangria, Cuban drinks, and the best margaritas in the city. The riverside deck opens as early as April and closes when it's too cool to use it (usually mid-October). Sun. brunch served when the deck is closed. Prices range $4.50–19. Lighter menus served in the downstairs bar and on the deck.

The Portsmouth Brewery (603-431-1115), 56 Market St., Portsmouth. Open daily 11:30 AM–12:30 AM. A lively spot best known for its microbrewery, which has been producing the city's signature beers, including Old Brown Dog, Pale Ale, Amber Lager, and Black Cat Stout, since 1991. A downstairs lounge features comfortable seating with a pool table, shuffleboard, and a jukebox. The menu is varied and includes soups, salads, chili, pizza, hot and cold supersandwiches, and nine dinner entrées. Special dishes, changing monthly, might include spicy poached salmon or Thai curry chicken. Inexpensive to moderate. Brewery store on premises.

The Press Room (603-431-5186), 77 Daniel St., Portsmouth. Open 7 nights a week, this Irish-style pub has been the place to go since 1976 for the best jazz, blues, and folk music in the city. Inexpensive, light meals, nachos, pizza, salads, soups, and sandwiches. The food is good and served with draft beer. Tuesday "hoot nights" start at 7:30; see *Entertainment*.

Ray's Seafood Restaurant (603-436-2280), 1677 Ocean Blvd., Rye. Open daily 11:30 AM–closing. For more than 30 years a seacoast favorite specializing in fresh fried seafood, lobsters, and steamers. Dinners and lobsters cooked to go. Moderate.

The Stockpot (603-431-1851), 53 Bow St., Portsmouth. Open daily 11 AM–11:30 PM. This has been a local waterfront favorite since it opened in 1982. Owned by the same folks who operate The Loaf and Ladle in Exeter, the restaurant specializes in homemade soups and desserts, a variety of salads and sandwiches, fresh seafood, and paella (a Spanish dish with chicken, mussels, shrimp, chorizo, and veggies served over rice). Full bar. A small deck, open whenever it's warm enough to use it, offers relaxing dining with views past the tugboats and up the river. Dinner entrées, served between 5 and 10, range $13–18.

LOBSTER Lobsters are a seacoast specialty, and almost every restaurant has a lobster dish. Live or cooked lobsters to go are available at several places. **Sanders Lobster Pound** is the largest local dealer. Their main lobster pound is at 54 Pray St. (603-436-3716; 1-800-235-3716; www.sanders lobster.com), open Mon.–Sat. 8 AM–5 PM, Sun. 10–5; and they own the **Olde Mill Fish Market**

(603-436-4568) nearby at 367 Marcy St., open daily 9–6. The latter shop has all kinds of fresh fish in addition to live or cooked-to-order lobsters. Sanders can ship a mini clambake anywhere in the country.

ICE CREAM AND SNACKS Ceres Bakery (603-436-6518), 51 Penhallow St., Portsmouth. Open 6 AM–5:30 PM, Sat. 7–4, closed Sun. Our favorite bakery. Has the best bran muffins anywhere but also brioches, croissants, cookies, and a host of breads, cakes, and other diet busters. A few mostly vegetarian soups, quiches, and salads are served for lunch; special breakfast and lunch items on Saturday. Many local restaurants serve Ceres Bakery breads.

Breaking New Grounds (603-436-9555), 14 Market Square, Portsmouth. Open daily 6:30 AM–11 PM, midnight in summer. Café Brioche occupied this corner for 20 years before BNG took over in March 2004. The ambience remains easygoing and friendly with breads and sweets, homemade soups, salads, and a variety of sandwiches plus espresso and cappuccino. Especially popular in warm weather, when the outdoor tables and street performers lend a European-plaza atmosphere. Definitely still the center of bustling Market Square.

Annabelle's (603-436-3400), 49 Ceres St., Portsmouth. Open for lunch until late in the evening; closed in winter. Imaginative and tasty handmade ice cream comes from this popular local landmark. Their red, white, and blueberry ice cream even made the White House menu one year for the Fourth of July. Sandwiches and soups are secondary to the sundaes, sodas, banana splits, and hand-scooped cones.

✳ Entertainment

Portsmouth's busiest performance season is Sep.–May, except for the Prescott Park Arts Festival, which features theater and music outdoors July–mid-Aug. The night scene is active all year with nearly a dozen restaurants and lounges offering live music on weekends and several other nights: jazz, blues, big-band, folk, and country music.

Seacoast Repertory Theatre (603-433-4472; 1-800-639-7650; www .seacoastrep.org), 125 Bow St., Portsmouth. Professional theater in the former Theatre-by-the-Sea building. Several different plays are performed Sep.–early June. Also presents youth theater.

The Music Hall (603-436-2400; www.themusichall.org), 28 Chestnut St., Portsmouth. Built in 1878 as a stage theater and, more recently, revised as a movie theater, this restored hall has been acquired by a nonprofit group and offers a variety of dance, theater, and musical performances throughout the year. International classical music, and national entertainment including magic shows, bluegrass, and jazz are among the regular offerings. Also frequent screenings of independent and classic films.

Pontine Movement Theatre (603-436-6660; www.pontine.org), 135 McDonough St., Portsmouth. This nationally known company with guest performers offers four productions between fall and spring but no summer performances.

The Players' Ring (603-436-8123; www.playersring.org), 105 Marcy St., Portsmouth. Attend a variety of theatrical and musical performances at this attractive and historic venue.

The Press Room (603-431-5186), 77 Daniel St., Portsmouth. Open nightly. This Irish-style pub has lots of live music. Acoustic guitar, folk, Irish, blues, and country sounds in an informal atmosphere make this a popular spot with the locals. Often nationally known performers sit in with local favorites.

✳ Selective Shopping

Portsmouth is filled with small shops, especially in the waterfront area bounded by Market, Bow, and Ceres streets. Here rows of mostly Federal-era brick buildings have been remodeled and restored to offer the shopper everything from upscale clothing and antiques to natural foods, candles, secondhand clothing, jewelry, a fine children's shop, and even a Christmas shop. With several of the city's best restaurants and five waterfront decks, this is a busy and lively place until late in the evening—several shops are open until 11.

Attrezzi (603-603-427-1667; www .attrezzinh.com), 78 Market St., Portsmouth. Handsome store featuring cooking, dining, and garden accessories as well as occasional complimentary wine tastings and cooking demonstrations.

Celtic Crossing (603-436-0200; www .celticcrossing.com), 112 Congress St., Portsmouth. Ireland, Scotland, and Wales are the source for an extensive collection of gifts, wedding bands, and Highland kilt attire.

Kittery Outlets (1-888-548-8379; www.thekitteryoutlets.com), Exit 3 off Rt. 95 north, Rt. 1, Kittery, Me. Open Jan. 2–Apr., Sun.–Thu. 10–6, Fri.–Sat. 10–8; May–Jan. 1, Mon.–Sat. 9–8, Sun. 10–6. Just minutes from downtown Portsmouth, this shopping mecca provides visitors with 120 factory outlet stores (Banana Republic, Coach, Coldwater Creek, J. Crew, Harry & David, Waterford Wedgwood, and 114 more), all in a single location.

Lollipop Tree (1-800-842-6691; www.lollipoptree.com), 319 Vaughan St., Portsmouth. Open Mon.–Fri. 8:30–5:30, Sat. 10–1. Gift collections and baskets of salad dressings, grilling sauces, jams, and specialty baking mixes at factory store prices. Daily samplings.

Nahcotta (603-433-1705; www .nahcotta.com), 110 Congress St., Portsmouth. Handcrafted furniture and rotating exhibitions of contemporary paintings by some of the region's up-and-coming artists.

Somnia (603-433-7600; www.somnia .net), 107 Congress St., Portsmouth. Luxurious linens, furnishings, and accessories for bedroom and bath.

Stonewall Kitchen (1-800-207-5267; www.stonewallkitchen.com), 10 Pleasant St., Portsmouth. One of several shops throughout Maine and New Hampshire representing this specialty food label—well known in New England and beyond for fine jams, mustards, sauces, and baking mixes.

Ed Weissman, Antiquarian (603-431- 7575), 110 Chapel St., Portsmouth. Open June–Nov. by appointment only. A careful selection of 18th- and 19th-century furnishings, paintings, and accessories, two blocks from Market Square.

ART GALLERIES **New Hampshire Art Association–Robert Levy Gallery** (603-431-4230), 136 State St., Portsmouth. Open all year, Wed.–Sun. 11–5. Members exhibit oils, watercolors, acrylics, photo-graphs, prints, and sculpture. Also sponsors Art 'Round Town (www.artroundtown.org), a gallery walk of 10 local art spaces, more than 100 artists, 5–8 PM, the second Friday of the month, May–Dec.

Coolidge Center for the Arts (603-436-6607), 375 Little Harbor Rd., Portsmouth. Open Wed.–Sat. 10–4, Sun. 1–5 or by appointment. Located in the Wentworth-Coolidge Mansion, this gallery provides a classical setting for artists to display their work, which changes monthly.

Welcome to My Home Gallery (608-431-8726; www.alanawater colors.com), 58 Cranfield St., Rt. 1B, New Castle. Maddie Alana operates a gallery and studio in her pretty village home. Fine art commissions of sea-scapes, florals, pets, homes, boats, and more, including custom tile painting, since 1986.

BOOKSTORES Two great antiquarian bookshops are located in downtown Portsmouth:

The Book Guild of Portsmouth (603-436-1758), 58 State St., near Strawbery Banke, specializes in mar-itime and local books.

The Portsmouth Book Shop (603-433-4406), 1 Islington St., is located in a historic house and offers local history, travel, literature, maps, and prints.

RiverRun Bookstore (603-431-2100; www.riverrun.booksense.com), 7 Commercial Alley (ground floor). Open Mon.–Sat. 9–8, Sun. until 6. Portsmouth's only downtown full-service bookstore, offering new books as well as fast and easy special orders.

Gulliver's (603-431-5556; www.gul liversbooks.com), 7 Commercial Alley (basement). Open Mon.–Sat. 10–5, Sun. noon–5. Claims to offer every-thing for travel but the tickets, with the largest selection of travel books, maps, globes, language guides, and travel video rentals north of Boston.

✳ Special Events

Summer on the seacoast offers a nearly unlimited number of special events and activities for people of all ages. Check with local chambers of commerce, the Portsmouth Children's Museum, and Strawbery Banke for varied activities.

February: **Annual African-Ameri-can Heritage Festival** (603-929-0654), seacoast-wide. Various organizations sponsor a variety of musical, art, theater, and other events in several seacoast locations. Coordi-nated by the Blues Bank Collective.

April: **New England Blues Confer-ence** (603-929-0654), Portsmouth. Blues workshops, conferences, and concerts.

Early June: **Prescott Park Chowder Festival** (www.artfest.org). For $7 adults or $5 children, sample the city's best restaurant chowders.

Second Saturday in June: **Market Square Day** (603-436-5388; www.pro portsmouth.org). The center of Portsmouth is closed to traffic, and the streets are lined with booths sell-ing food, crafts, and more; as many as four stages provide continuous enter-tainment. More than 30,000 people jam the city for this free event. A pop-ular clambake is held the night before at the Port Authority; purchase tickets in advance.

Mid-June: **Blessing of the Fleet**, Prescott Park. The Piscataqua River's commercial fishing fleet, with all boats decorated, converges for a water parade and traditional blessing for safety at sea.

Early July: **Seacoast Jazz Festival** (www.artfest.org), Prescott Park. The show runs noon–6 PM. Top jazz artists from across the country join local musicians for a musical blast. A $5 donation is requested.

✍ *Early July–late August:* **Prescott Park Arts Festival** (www.artfest.org), on the waterfront, Portsmouth. A daily variety of outdoor theater and musical events beginning late in the afternoon. Come early, bring a picnic basket, and spend a few enjoyable hours at one of New England's most popular summer festivals. A $5 donation is requested. There are also art shows and art classes for kids.

Mid-July: **Bow Street Fair** (603-433-4793). A colorful weekend street fair with music and booths selling food and crafts. Affiliated with the Seacoast Repertory Theatre. **Chautauqua** (603-224-4071; www.nhhc.org), Marcy St. at Strawbery Banke, Portsmouth. History comes alive during this annual 4-day happening, usually the last week in July. The New Hampshire Humanities Council–sponsored event features workshops, reading discussions, musical performances, and reincarnations of historic figures, all under a giant tent.

Mid-August: **Candlelight house tour** (603-436-1118). An evening tour of Portsmouth's historic houses, all lit by candles. **Blues Festival** (603-929-0654; www.bluesbankcollective.org),

Harbor Place, Portsmouth. Blues on an outdoor, waterfront stage, and in several bars, along with a gospel blues church service. Starts at 11 AM and runs until sunset.

Late August: **Prescott Park Folk and Acoustic Festival** (603-436-2848). Seacoast folkies congregate in this spacious and attractive park 3–9 PM to appreciate a variety of folk and world music—Celtic and African drumming among the offerings.

Late September: **Grand Old Portsmouth Brewers' Festival**. This annual Strawbery Banke event celebrates the history of brewing in Portsmouth. **Chili Cook-Off** (www.artfest .org), Prescott Park. Sample the culinary skills of the city's best chili cooks. A $7 donation is requested.

Columbus Day weekend: **Piscataqua Faire** (www.artfest.org), Prescott Park. A Renaissance weekend on the waterfront with food, crafts, and entertainment from a time when knights ruled the day. The first day of the faire runs 10–5, the second 11–4. $6 adults, $4 children. **Building the Sukkah**, a Strawbery Banke Jewish harvest celebration.

Late November and early December: **Candlelight Stroll** (603-433-1100), Strawbery Banke. See Strawbery Banke's historic houses by candlelight.

✍ *December 31:* **First Night** (603-436-5388). A nonalcoholic, family-oriented New Year's Eve celebration held annually in Portsmouth, late afternoon to midnight, with a wide variety of musical performances and other entertainment. Most events are held in downtown churches.

HAMPTON, HAMPTON BEACH, EXETER, AND VICINITY

The two large towns of Hampton and Exeter were founded in 1638, but while Hampton has retained little of its architectural heritage, Exeter's streets are lined with old houses and buildings.

Hampton was mostly a farming town with a small, beachside tourist community until the beginning of the 20th century, when trolley lines connected the town and its beach with the large cities of the Merrimack Valley and cities in Massachusetts and central New Hampshire. The low-cost trolley transportation made the beach an inexpensive and accessible place for urban workers to bring their families for a day or a week. A large casino was built to provide these visitors with games to play, lunches, and ballroom dancing—though not on Sunday. Hampton is now a fast-growing residential community. After World War II the population was about 2,300; now it is 12,000 people, and much of its open space has been developed except for large family holdings west of I-95. Hampton has a small shopping district, a movie complex, and several good restaurants.

Though Hampton village was small, Hampton Beach boomed and became one of the leading family vacation centers in New England. Now, during peak summer weekends, more than 200,000 people jam the beach, nearly covering the long, sandy oceanfront from one end to the other with blankets. Young people seem to predominate, but there are plenty of older folks who would not consider any other place to spend their summer free time. The center of the beach is still the 90-year-old Casino, complete with restaurants, shops, penny arcades, and a nightclub offering nationally known entertainment.

Often overlooked by residents and visitors alike is the Hampton River. Here three family-owned fishing-party businesses have been serving the public for more than 50 years, recently expanding to include whale-watches and some sightseeing cruises. Surrounding the harbor is the state's largest salt marsh, once thought of as a swamp and earmarked to be dredged and filled to create a lagoon-style seasonal home development. Although Hampton Beach development has pushed into the fringes of this 1,300-acre marsh, people now know the importance of the tidal wetlands as a source of nutrients for a wide variety of marine life, and the marshes are protected from development by state and local laws. As a green space, the marsh is used by anglers, boaters, and bird-watchers; it is perhaps the only piece of ground left on the seacoast that still looks today about the way it did when settlers arrived in the 1600s. South of the Hampton River bridge in Seabrook, bordering the marsh, is a recently protected sand dunes natural area.

West of Hampton is Exeter, with a much larger commercial area and one of the country's premier college preparatory schools. Its marvelous architectural diversity reflects its past as the state capital during the American Revolution, as well as its prominence as an industrial and educational center. Today Exeter has about 12,000 people, although its growth has been slower than Hampton's. Several historic houses open to the public date from the Revolution. The falls on the Squamscott River helped power textile mills, giving the community an important economic base.

Phillips Exeter Academy, one of America's leading preparatory schools, has a list of alumni who have achieved the highest levels of prominence in literature, business, and government service. Distinguished visiting lecturers in all fields, who often speak or perform for the public, and a fine art gallery contribute to the cultural and educational atmosphere of the town and the area. Many students from surrounding towns attend the academy as day students. The academy's buildings reflect nearly three centuries of architectural design, contributing to the great diversity of Exeter's cityscape. The academy is in the center of the Front Street Historic District, where the wide variety of architectural styles ranges from colonial residences of the 1700s to 20th-century institutional buildings. Notable are the First Parish Meetinghouse, a variety of Victorian buildings, and the contemporary Phillips Exeter Academy Library designed by Louis Kahn, featured in the recent documentary *My Father, the Architect*.

Historic Rt. 1 bisects the seacoast from south to north. On the Massachusetts border is Seabrook, home of the controversial nuclear power plant, a huge facility that pays most of the town's taxes, giving Seabrook one of the lowest property tax rates in the state. The low property tax, combined with the state's lack of a sales tax, has fueled commercial development in Seabrook; most of the retail shoppers come from heavily taxed Massachusetts. Seabrook Beach is a heavily developed residential area with little public access to the ocean since parking is limited, but many summer homes here are available for weekly rentals.

Seabrook's unplanned growth is in contrast with neighboring Hampton Falls, a residential community whose many farms are now being subdivided into exclusive home developments. North of Hampton along Rt. 1 is North Hampton, also primarily a

BELL TOWER AT PHILLIPS EXETER ACADEMY

residential community but with a large colony of summer mansions along the coast in the section called Little Boars Head.

Adjacent to Exeter, and extending west to the Merrimack Valley, are mostly small towns, once farming communities, now being heavily developed with residential subdivisions. Among these towns are Stratham, Kensington, Epping, Newfields, Brentwood, Fremont, Danville, Hampstead, the Kingstons, and Nottingham. Since New Hampshire has no sales or income taxes, and once had low property taxes, the seacoast-area towns have been rapidly growing into popular bedroom communities for people who work in the Boston area, many of whom grew up in Massachusetts but moved north to escape the congestion of urban life for the peaceful countryside. The attractions of the seacoast and its proximity to metropolitan Boston have made the area a magnet for new residents and for visiting tourists.

GUIDANCE **Hampton Area Chamber of Commerce** (603-926-8718; outside New Hampshire, 1-800-GET-A-TAN; www.hamptonchamber.org), 1 Park Ave., Suite 3G, Hampton 03842. A seasonal information center is open daily at the state park complex in the middle of Hampton Beach. The chamber runs daily summer events at the beach and seasonal programs in Hampton village, and publishes a free accommodations and things-to-do guide.

Exeter Area Chamber of Commerce (603-772-2411; www.exeterarea.org), 120 Water St., Exeter 03833. The chamber offers a Historic Walking Tour brochure as well as Exeter-area gift certificates.

GETTING AROUND *By car:* Rt. 1 (Lafayette Rd.) between Seabrook and Portsmouth is lined with strip development and on summer weekends is especially snarled with traffic. If you want to go to Hampton Beach just to see the sights and the latest bathing suits, we do not recommend the weekend, when traffic entering the beach from I-95 or Rt. 1A south may be backed up for several miles.

By taxi: **Exeter Taxi** (603-778-7778) serves Exeter and offers Logan Airport service.

By trolley: A seasonal trolley service serves Hampton Beach, running the length of Ocean Blvd., with stops in Hampton village and the North Hampton Factory Outlet Center.

By train: **Amtrak** (1-800-USA-RAIL; www.amtrakdowneaster.com) stops in the area with service between Boston, Ma., and Portland, Me.

PARKING Municipal and private parking lots behind Hampton's main beach, just a short walk to the sand, are the best places to park if you are not staying at beach lodgings. The parking meters are part of the state park and are closely monitored, so keep them filled with quarters to avoid an expensive ticket.

MEDICAL EMERGENCY **Exeter Hospital** (603-778-7311), 5 Alumni Dr., Exeter, offers 24-hour emergency walk-in service. **Exeter ambulance:** 603-772-1212. **Hampton ambulance:** 603-926-3315.

Fuller Gardens (603-964-5414; www.fullergardens.org), 10 Willow Ave., Little Boars Head, North Hampton. Open early May–mid-Oct., 10–5:30. One of the few remaining estate gardens of the early 20th century, this beautiful spot was designed in the 1920s for Massachusetts governor Alvin T. Fuller, whose family members still live in many of the surrounding mansions. There is an ever-changing display here as flowers bloom throughout the season. Among the highlights are 1,500 rosebushes, extensive annuals, a Japanese garden, and a conservatory of tropical and desert plants. Nominal fee charged.

𝒮 **The Science and Nature Center at Seabrook Station** (1-800-338-7482), Rt. 1, Seabrook. Open Mar.–Thanksgiving, Mon.–Sat. 10–4, Mon.–Fri. the rest of the year. Free admission. After years of demonstrations, construction delays, lengthy and complex legal proceedings, and the bankruptcy of its prime owner, the Seabrook Nuclear Power Plant began producing power in 1990. The best off-site view of the plant is from Rt. 1A at the Hampton River, where it rises above the marsh on the western shore of the estuary. The center is the plant's educational facility and has a variety of exhibits about electricity, nuclear power, and the environment, especially the nearby marsh habitat, which you can view on a mile-long nature trail.

𝒮 **Tuck Memorial Museum** (603-929-0781; www.hamptonhistoricalsociety.org), 40 Park Ave., Hampton. Open mid-June–mid-Sep., Wed., Fri., and Sun. 1–4. The museum of the Hampton Historical Society has local memorabilia, especially related to early families, the trolley era, and Hampton Beach. Adjacent is the **Hampton Firefighter's Museum** with a hand engine, other equipment, and a district schoolhouse, all restored. Free admission.

Atkinson Historical Society (603-362-4760), 3 Academy Ave., Atkinson. Open Wed. 2–4. The Kimball-Peabody Mansion houses a collection of local artifacts plus extensive genealogical materials.

Exeter Historical Society (603-778-2335; exhissoc@aol.com), 47 Front St., Exeter. Open Tue., Thu., and Sat. 2–4:30. Located in the former 1894 town library, this society has research materials for local history and genealogy, artifacts, photographs, maps, and changing exhibits.

Fremont Historical Society (603-895-4032), 225 South Rd., Rt. 107, Fremont. Open by appointment. The museum was the town library, built in 1894 and measuring only 20 feet by 14 feet. From 1965 until 1981 it was a first-aid society, lending its rural residents hospital equipment.

Hampton Historical Society & Tuck Museum (603-929-0781), 40 Park Ave., Hampton. Call ahead for hours. The adjoining Pine Grove Cemetery, circa 1654, is the oldest public cemetery in the state.

&. **Sandown Historical Society and Museum** (603-887-6100; www.sandownnh.org), Depot Rd., Box 300, Sandown. Open May–Oct., Sat.–Sun. 1–5. Local history and railroad artifacts; wheelchair access plus restrooms, picnic tables, and a nearby public swimming beach.

Stratham Historical Society (603-778-0434; 603-778-1347; www.stratham historicalsociety.org), corner of Portsmouth Ave. and Winnicutt Rd., Stratham. Open Tue. 9–11:30 AM, Thu. 2–4 PM, and the first Sun. of each month 2–4. The former Wiggin Library has recently been acquired by the historical society. Local artifacts and some genealogical materials.

HISTORIC HOMES ✐ **American Independence Museum** (603-772-2622; www .independencemuseum.org), 1 Governor's Lane, Exeter. Open May–Oct., Wed.– Sat. 10–4; last tour at 3. $5 adults, $3 children over 6; under 6 free. Also known as Cincinnati Hall, and one of New Hampshire's most historic buildings, part of this place was constructed in 1721. It served as the state treasury from 1775 to 1789 and as governor's mansion during the 14-year term of John Taylor Gilman. The Gilman family members were political and military leaders during the Revolutionary War, when Exeter served as the revolutionary capital. The house has recently been restored, and its diverse exhibits, including an original Dunlop broadside of the Declaration of Independence, revitalized.

Gilman Garrison House (603-436-3205; www.spnea.org), 12 Water St., Exeter. Open June–Oct., Tue., Thu., Sat., and Sun. noon–5. Fee charged. A portion of this house was constructed of logs in 1660 as a garrison, but most of the building reflects the 18th century with fine paneling, especially in the governor's council meeting room. Owned by the Society for the Preservation of New England Antiquities.

HISTORIC SITES **Fremont Meetinghouse and Hearse House**, Rt. 107, Fremont. Open May 30 and the third Sun. in Aug. or by appointment; inquire locally. Built in 1800, this unique meetinghouse, unaltered since it was built, contains an early choir stall, slave pews, and twin porches. The Hearse House, built in 1849, has a hand engine built in that same year.

Sandown Meeting House (603-887-3946), Fremont Rd., Sandown. Owned by the Old Meeting House Association, this is the finest meetinghouse of its type in New Hampshire, unaltered since it was built in 1774. Its craftsmanship and architectural details are nationally recognized. You can easily imagine our colonial ancestors listening to a fire-and-brimstone sermon from the preacher standing in the wineglass pulpit. Service at 11 AM, second Sun. in Aug. Open by appointment; inquire locally for the caretaker.

Old South Meetinghouse (Rt. 1) and **Boyd School** (Washington St.), Seabrook. School opens the third Sun. in Aug. The old school has exhibits and local artifacts relating to salt-hay farming, shoemaking, and decoys used for bird hunting. The church is open by appointment only; inquire locally. Built in 1758, it has been altered inside.

SCENIC DRIVES Follow Rt. 1B through New Castle, passing by Forts Constitution and Stark, and the Wentworth Hotel. Then connect with Rt. 1A through Rye, North Hampton, and Hampton Beach to the Massachusetts border. The ocean is in view most of the way, and there are several restaurants and beaches, including Jenness Beach State Park just south of the receiving station for the first Atlantic Cable (on Old Beach Road). Coastal marshes and fish houses dot the route. About midway you'll see Little Boars Head, once called the showplace of eastern New Hampshire for its fine seaside mansions. This drive is also popular with bicyclists.

The American Independence Byway is a 29-mile cultural and historic loop that winds through the heart of two of New Hampshire's four original towns— Exeter and Hampton—and Hampton Falls and Kensington, both once part of Hampton. A map and description is available at area tourist centers and attractions, or by calling 603-778-0885.

✷ To Do

Exeter Bandstand. The Exeter Brass Band, the oldest in the country, performs at the bandstand in the center of town Monday nights in July.

Hampton Airfield (603-964-6749; www.hampton-airfield.com), Rt. 1, North Hampton. Open cockpit thrill rides.

✆ **Hampton Beach** is an attraction by itself. The center of activity is the Casino, a historic, rambling complex with arcades, gifts, specialty shops, and the Casino Ballroom, featuring a string of big-name entertainers mid-June–Columbus Day. Adjacent is the Casino Cascade Water Slide. Nearby, along the 0.5-mile business district, is the first seasonal McDonald's plus other fast-food take-outs, more arcades, shops, gift and clothing stores, miniature golf, and bike rentals. Across the street from the Casino are the ocean and the state park complex with the chamber of commerce information center, restrooms, a first-aid room, and the bandstand, which offers free concerts and talent shows throughout the summer. There are fireworks on the Fourth of July and every Wed. night during July and Aug., the heart of the season; but many places are open weekends beginning in Apr., then daily in June. A few of the newer, larger hotels are open year-round, and some have restaurants and lounges.

Hampton Summer Theatre (603-926-2281), Performing Arts Center at Winnacunnet, off Rt. 1, Hampton. A full slate of plays and musicals, performed Wed.–Sat., late June–Aug., by the Artists' Collaborative Theatre of New England (ACT ONE). Also morning shows for young audiences.

Platypus Tours (603-929-4696), west side of Hampton State Park, Hampton Beach. Open May–Oct. 10. Tours start every 90 minutes 9–6, June 29–Labor Day; limited hours rest of season. Amphibious vehicles once owned by the U.S. Coast Guard provide a land-and-sea tour of Hampton Beach's historic homes and landmark buildings. Tickets also available at the Hatch Shell on Ocean Blvd.

Seabrook Greyhound Park (603-474-3065; www.seabrookgreyhoundpark .com), Rt. 107, Seabrook. For a dog-gone good time, spend a day at the races. Live matinee racing Tue.–Sun. 12:35 PM; evening racing (buffet available for $15.95) Fri.–Sat. 7:35 PM. Daily simulcasting. Call for package rates for accommodations, dining, and admission. Free trolley from Hampton Beach.

BOAT EXCURSIONS **Smith and Gilmore Fishing Parties** (603-926-3503; 1-877-272-4005), Rt. 1A, Hampton Harbor, Hampton 03842. All-day fishing on

Wed. and weekends Apr.–Columbus Day; daily half-day trips May–Sep.; night fishing June–Aug.; weekend evening whale-watches July and Aug.; fireworks cruises on Wed. July–Aug. Two modern vessels provide a variety of fishing experiences for this longtime family-operated business. The business also has a bait-and-tackle shop, rowboats to rent for Hampton Harbor flounder fishing, and a restaurant. Family operated since 1929.

Al Gauron Deep Sea Fishing (603-926-2469; 1-800-905-7820; www.deepsea fishing.nh.com; www.whalewatching.nh.com), State Pier, Hampton Beach 03842. All-day fishing, spring–Columbus Day; two half-day trips daily; bluefish trips; night fishing; fireworks cruises on Wed. nights in July and Aug.; evening whale-watches. Four vessels including the 90-foot *Northern Star*. Family owned and operated for half a century.

Eastman's Fishing Fleet (603-474-3461; www.eastmansdocks.com), River St., Rt. 1A, Seabrook. Open Apr.–Oct. Whale-watching July–Aug., daily 1:30–6 PM. $24 adults, $16 children, under 5 free, and a special Mon.–Fri. senior rate for those 62 and above: $18. The oldest of the family-operated fishing businesses on the seacoast. The Lucky Lady fleet has three modern vessels with a variety of fishing forays available and a Wednesday-night fireworks cruise ($14 adult, $12 child) during July and Aug. Tackle-and-bait shops plus a full restaurant and pub with patio dining overlooking the harbor.

Seacoast Kayak Inc. (603-474-1025; www.seacoastkayak.com), Rt. 1A, 210 Ocean Blvd., Seabrook. Open year-round. Sit-on-top or single and double recreational kayaks for half-day, full-day or weekly rentals. Includes life vests and paddles. Cartop carrier systems $3 extra. The harbor offers flatwater paddling through miles of scenic estuaries; more experienced paddlers can head out to sea. Surf kayaks also available.

GOLF **Apple Hill Country Club** (603-642-4414), Rt. 107, East Kingston. Open whenever weather conditions permit; 18 holes, cart rentals, snack bar.

Captain's Cove Adventure Golf (603-926-5011; www.covegolf.com), Rt. 1, 812 Lafayette Rd., Hampton. Open Memorial Day–Labor Day, daily 10–10, weather permitting. An 18-hole mini golf adventure with a nautical theme.

Exeter Country Club (603-772-4752), Jady Hill Rd. (off Portsmouth Ave.), Exeter. Open May–Oct.; 18 holes, cart rentals, full bar, and food service.

✈ **Putt-A-Round Miniature Golf & Railroad** (603-964-GOLF), 178 Lafayette Rd., North Hampton. Open daily in-season, 10–10. Eighteen mini golf holes, train rides, waterfalls, and ice cream.

Sagamore-Hampton Golf Course (603-964-8322), North Rd. (off Ry. 1), North Hampton. Open mid-Apr.–mid-Dec.; 18 holes, no motorized carts allowed, pro shop, light food, and beverages. A busy recreational course, inexpensive.

ORCHARDS, PICK-YOUR-OWN, FARMER'S MARKETS ✈ **Applecrest Farm Orchards** (603-926-3721), Rt. 88, Hampton Falls. Open year-round, but the best times to visit are in May when apple blossoms cover the hillsides and in late summer–fall when apples are harvested. Pick your own apples and enjoy weekend festivals in-season. Also pick your own strawberries, raspberries, and blueberries. Cross-country ski in winter. The Apple Mart and gift shop are open year-round.

Jewell Towne Vineyards (603-394-0600; www.jewelltownevineyards.com), 65 Jewell St., South Hampton. Free tours and complimentary tastings offered May–Dec., weekends 1–5. Now in operation for more than a decade, this is New Hampshire's oldest winery.

Raspberry Farm (603-926-6604), Rt. 84, Hampton Falls. Open the first week in July–Oct. The state's largest grower, with 6.5 miles of rows in which to pick your own blackberries, black raspberries, and raspberries, plus a farm stand with vegetables and baked goods.

Farmer's markets are open Tue. afternoons June–Oct. at Sacred Heart School, Rt. 1, in Hampton, and Thu. afternoons at Swasey Pkwy. in Exeter. Local home-grown vegetables, herbs, flowers, fruits, and plants plus baked goods and crafts.

✴ Green Space

✐ **North Hampton State Beach**, Rt. 1A, North Hampton. A long, sandy beach with lifeguards, parking meters, and restrooms. A small take-out food stand is across the street. For one of the area's most scenic walks, park here, then proceed north past the old fish houses, which are now summer cottages, and a beautiful garden maintained by the Little Boars Head Garden Club. A sidewalk follows the coast for about 2 miles to the Rye Beach Club.

✐ **Hampton Central Beach**, Rt. 1A, Hampton. From the intersection of High St. and Rt. 1A, south through the main section of Hampton Beach, is a state park with lifeguards, metered parking, and restrooms. North of Hampton's Great

HAMPTON BEACH

Robert J. Kozlow

Boars Head the beach is much less crowded, but at high tides has limited sand area. South of Great Boars Head the beach is opposite the business and touristy area. At the main beach are an information center, a first-aid room, and restrooms. Opposite the Ashworth Hotel is the **New Hampshire Marine Memorial**, a large statue and plaque dedicated to state residents in the merchant marine service who were lost at sea during World War II.

✔ **Hampton Beach State Park and Harbor** (603-925-3784), Rt. 1A, Hampton. Fees charged for the beach and boat launching in-season. At the mouth of the Hampton River is this long, sandy beach with some of the state's last oceanfront sand dunes. There is a bathhouse with dressing rooms, restrooms, and snack bar. Twenty RV sites with full hookups are available on a first-come, first-served basis. Across Rt. 1A is the harbor, with a boat-launching ramp and the state pier.

✔ **Swasey Parkway**, off Water St., Exeter. A small park beside the Squamscott River in downtown Exeter. Picnic area and playground. Free concerts on Thursday nights in summer.

✔ **Sandy Point Discovery Center** (603-778-0015; www.greatbay.org), 89 Depot Rd., just off Rt. 101, Stratham. Part of the Great Bay National Estuarine Research Reserve, this new education center is set up primarily for school groups, but it offers great bird-watching on self-guided nature trails through wooded uplands and over a 1,600-foot boardwalk on the tidal marsh. The grounds are available all year during daylight hours. The building, with interpretive exhibits on the ecology of an estuary, is open 10–4 on weekends in May, and Wed.–Sun., June–Oct. There is a launch ramp for cartop boats.

Kingston State Beach, off Rt. 125, Kingston. Open weekends beginning Memorial Day, daily late June–Labor Day. A small state facility on Great Pond, this park has a long, sandy beach, picnic groves, and a bathhouse. Fee charged.

✳ Lodging

Hampton and Hampton Beach offer a nearly unlimited number of rooms for tourists, especially at the beach and along Rt. 1 between Hampton Falls and North Hampton. The Hampton Area Chamber of Commerce provides a guide to most of the motels, but we have listed a few lodgings below. Both Hampton and Seabrook Beaches have numerous cottages to rent by the week, and Hampton also has many condo units. Seabrook Beach is just residential and thus quieter than Hampton, and its beach is uncrowded. For information try **Harris Real Estate** (603-926-3400), **Preston Real Estate** (603-474-3453; 603-926-2604), or **Oceanside Real Estate** (603-926-3542).

BED & BREAKFASTS **Around the Corner B&B** (603-778-0058 or 1-800-443-0344; dday4@mediaone .net), 72 High St., Exeter 03833. Open all year. "Around the corner" from Exeter's main drag, this home is located in a quiet residential neighborhood, a short walk from the historic downtown. The three guest rooms (one with private bath; the other two share a bath) are named for and inspired by the innkeepers' favorite artists: Claude Monet, Winslow Homer, and three generations of Wyeths.

All of the rooms have books about artists and are filled with the artwork of their namesakes. Full breakfast. Donna and Dick Herrmann and Evelyn Shields, innkeepers. $60–85 double, $145 suite with two bedrooms.

The Inn by the Bandstand (603-772-6352; www.innbythebandstand.com), 4 Front St., Exeter 03833. Open all year. This stylish 1809 golden yellow town house, run by Susan Henderson and two amiable golden retrievers, is in downtown Exeter overlooking the historic bandstand, close to movies, restaurants, and shopping. There are nine cleverly decorated rooms, including one honeymoon suite with a Jacuzzi, CD player, kitchenette, and living room, and two other family-style suites. All rooms are furnished with pizzazz, and all have phone with dataport for laptop computers. Working fireplaces and antique canopy or four-poster queen beds (one room with twins) reside harmoniously with more contemporary amenities such as air-conditioning, cable TV, and refrigerator. Coffee, tea, and sherry are available; breakfast is full and described by the owners as "fun." There's also a fax and copier machine on site, and active types can rent kayaks, canoes, or bikes. $129–210 for two; cot $20 extra.

Stillmeadow B&B (603-329-8381; www.stillmeadmeadowbandb.com; lori@stillmeadowbandb.com), 545 Main St., Hampstead 03841. Open all year. This 1850 Greek Revival, Italianate village inn has five chimneys and three staircases. Each of four and a half rooms (one includes a sitting room with a trundle bed) has a private bath. The family suite has two queen beds, a TV, and a refrigerator.

There are formal living and dining rooms, and the cookie jar's always kept full. Not far away is the **Robert Frost Farm** and several other attractions. Expanded continental breakfast. $65–100. Lori Offord, host.

The Victoria Inn (603-929-1437; www.thevictoriainn.com), 430 High St., Hampton 03842. Open year-round. Once the carriage house of former New Hampshire governor George Ashworth, this spacious inn has six guest rooms, all with private bath, air-conditioning and overhead fan, cable TV, and telephone. There are two sitting rooms, one with TV, and a glassed-in porch where a full gourmet breakfast is served. Lovely grounds with a Victorian gazebo, 0.5 mile from the beach. Nicholas and Tara DiTullio, innkeepers. Rates are $75–115; off-season discounts available. Nonsmoking. Children over 10 welcome.

HOTELS & **Ashworth by the Sea** (603-926-6762 or 1-800-345-6736; www.ashworthhotel.com), 295 Ocean Blvd., Hampton 03842. The only full-service oceanfront hotel has been a beach landmark and the finest beach lodging since the early 1900s. With the addition of a modern new wing and remodeling of the original hotel, it is now open year-round. Most of its 105 rooms have queen- or king-sized bed; others have two doubles. Five handicapped-accessible rooms. There is a lounge with nightly entertainment, three restaurants (see *Dining Out*), an indoor pool, and private sundecks overlooking the ocean. Summer rates are $130–275; off-season Oct.–Mar. is $74–250; package rates and discounts for multinight stays.

D. W.'s Oceanside Inn (603-926-3542 or 1-866-OCEAN-SI; info@ oceansideinn.com), 365 Ocean Blvd., Hampton Beach 03842. Open mid-May–mid-Oct. This turn-of-the-20th-century summer home, located across the street from the ocean, has undergone many changes, but its interior has been maintained and tastefully furnished to reflect its Victorian beginnings. Innkeepers Duane "Skip" and Debbie Windemiller have fulfilled their dream of providing a luxurious and restful oceanside escape; returning guests tell them it's a place they dream of the rest of the year. This is not typical Hampton Beach lodging. There are nine rooms, all with private bath, all distinctively decorated, many with antiques and period pieces, including two with canopy bed; a lovely Victorian common room; and two porches. Midsummer rates (late June–Labor Day) are $180–225; off-season, 20 percent less. Discounts for multinight stays. Breakfast included. No smoking.

&. **The Inn of Exeter** (603-772-5901; 1-800-782-8444; www.someplaces different.com), 90 Front St., Exeter 03833. Open year-round. On the campus of Phillips Exeter Academy but no longer owned by the private school, this three-story, Georgian-style inn with restaurant was originally intended to accommodate visiting dignitaries and students' families. Now the inn serves a wide clientele of tourist and business travelers. The 46 rooms and suites are individually decorated with traditional antique and reproduction furnishings. Some have fireplaces; those with views of the back lawn are favorites. There are nice amenities such as complimentary coffee and Danish, or feel particularly civilized with a glass of wine and some quiet conversation by the living room fireplace. Handicapped accessible. The fine restaurant serves three meals daily and an award-winning Sunday brunch (see *Dining Out*). Rates for two: $140–255.

Lamie's Inn & Tavern (603-926-0330 or 1-800-805-5050; www .lamiesinn.com), 490 Lafayette Rd. (corner of Rts. 1 and 27), Hampton 03842. While the old homestead dates to the 1740s, and the inn and tavern to 1928, historic credentials are only part of this inn's draw. Since acquiring the property in 1999, the Higgins family has renovated. Now the 32 rooms offer Colonial styling with 21st-century amenities . . . private bath, phone, air-conditioning, and cable TV with HBO. Rates, May–Sep., are $115 weeknights, $125 per night for the weekend, and $135 Sat. only; lower the rest of the year. There are also theater, dining, golf, and ski packages.

HOUSEKEEPING UNITS ✔ **Seaside Village Resort** (603-964-8204), 1 Ocean Blvd., North Hampton 03862. Open May–Sep., weather permitting. This is the only motel in New Hampshire with lodging right on the beach, with no street to cross. There are 19 units, 13 of which are full housekeeping, and 6 motel units for two to four people. Housekeeping guests bring towels and linens and rent Sat. to Sat. Eight new housekeeping units have a private master bedroom and a loft for the kids; the motel units are rustic but air-conditioned and have refrigerator and access to a galley, grills, and picnic tables. Many of the units are rented by the end of one season for the season to come. Housekeeping units run around $1,000 per week, depending on size and number of guests; motel units around $100 per night for two to three people.

✳ Where to Eat

DINING OUT **Breakers at Ashworth by the Sea** (603-926-6762; 1-800-345-6736; www.ashworthhotel.com), 295 Ocean Blvd., Hampton. Open year-round. Breakfast from 6:30 AM; café lounge 11:45 AM–1 AM; dinner in Ashworth dining room 5–9 PM. A full-service, oceanfront hotel, the Ashworth is a beach landmark, and its restaurant is among the best on the main beach. Several lobster entrées, baked and broiled seafood, and steaks are menu features (dinners from $15.95).

The Inn of Exeter (603-772-5901; 1-800-782-8444; www.someplaces different.com), 90 Front St., Exeter. Open year-round. Lunch Mon.–Fri. 11:30–2, dinner 5–9, Sunday brunch 10–2. The restaurant offers classic New England elegance and a menu that changes with the seasons. For lunch you can get a soup, salad and half-sandwich combo for $5.95; a lobster roll for $12.95. Dinner selections range from fresh seafood to Continental favorites; prices from $17 for Atlantic haddock baked with white wine and sweet butter to $29 for an 8-ounce filet mignon with grilled crimini mushrooms The award-winning Sunday brunch is a local favorite. There's also a lounge with a lighter menu.

Ron's Landing at Rocky Bend (603-929-2122; www.ronslanding .com), 379 Ocean Blvd., Hampton 03843. Open daily for dinner in sum-

mer 4–10, also Sunday brunch 11–3. Winter hours are 4–9, Sun. 11–7. Locals say this is the best place in town for casually elegant dining. Great ocean views, white linens, fresh flowers, and candles. While the menu makes a nod to the inveterate carnivore, this seaside dining room takes advantage of its nearby largesse. Fish lovers can count on lobster, tuna, scallops, sole, and more, prepared with appropriate flair. Entrées between $17.95 and $25.95.

The Old Salt Eating & Drinking Place at Lamie's Inn (603-926-8322; www.oldsaltnh.com), 490 Lafayette Rd., Hampton. Open all year. Breakfast, lunch, then dinner served Mon.–Thu. until 9 PM, Fri.–Sat. until 10; noon–8 on Sun. Founded in 1931, this is one of the oldest restaurants in the area, and when Rt. 1 was the main road between Boston and Portland, the place was open 24 hours a day on major weekends. With huge beams, pine paneling, tavern tables, and a large fireplace, Lamie's has a Colonial atmosphere, but its menu adds a Continental accent to the mostly New England fare. Try fried clams or scallops en brochette (placed on a skewer with scallions and bacon), baked lobster pie or beef au poivre with creamy peppercorn sauce, or Shoal's baked seafood delight (clams casino, scallops, scrod, and stuffed shrimp). Also several veal and pasta dishes, plus lamb, dinner sandwiches, and a variety of soups and salads. Lunch, complete dinner, or à la carte are all inexpensive to moderate. A 32-room motor inn with Colonial decor is attached. Entrées $8.99 for fish-and-chips to $18.99 for surf and turf. Early-bird specials (3–5 PM) are

$10.99 for soup or salad, entrée, and dessert.

Ship to Shore Food and Spirits (603-778-7898; www.ship-to-shore .com), Rt. 108, Newfields. Open Tue.–Sat. for dinner from 5 PM. Constructed by a local shipbuilder in 1792, this half barn (built shorter than it is wide) has been restored and turned into an intriguing, antiques-filled restaurant. The menu ranges from baked shrimp and haddock to roast duckling, barbecued baby back ribs, and broiled seafood. Daily chicken, veal, seafood, and pasta specials. Entrées $16.95–28.95. Occasional special wine and game dinners.

The Tavern at River's Edge (603-772-7393), 163 Water St., Exeter. Open Mon.–Sat. 3–10 PM, for light fare; dinner 5:30–9, Sat. from 5 on. This cozy restaurant in the heart of town offers a particularly interesting appetizer selection (wild mushroom and pear salad, for example) that can double as a light meal. The dinner menu is likewise comprehensive, ranging from vegetarian lasagna to rack of lamb. Moderate to expensive.

The Widow Fletcher's Tavern (603-926-8800), 401 Lafayette Rd., Hampton. Open Mon.–Fri. 4–11, Sat. 11–11, Sunday brunch 11–3. This old in-town home is decorated with eclectic folk art and antiques, based loosely on a British theme. It has a popular lounge and diverse menu. Caesar salad supreme is a meal in itself. Try open-flame Thai shrimp as an appetizer; for an entrée, select shrimp and cheese tortellini, swordfish prepared differently daily, English-cut prime rib, roast duck, or grilled pesto chicken. There are many other seafood, beef, and chicken choices. Inexpensive to moderate.

Zampa (603-679-8772; www.zampa .com), 8 Exeter Rd., Epping 03042. Open Tue.–Sat., 5–9 PM. Young ideas in an old setting. The great-grandson of one of the original owners and his fiancée bring their Italian-influenced culinary proclivities to this early estate. *Zampa* is Italian for the paw prints embedded in the fireplace bricks. Appetizers include Italian rice dumplings with herbed beef, Pecorino cheese, spinach, and tomato sauce. The homemade pasta is fresh daily. Moderate to expensive.

EATING OUT **Abercrombie & Finch** (603-964-9774), 219 Lafayette Rd., North Hampton. Open daily 11:30–9, Sunday brunch 9–1. Locally popular restaurant and lounge with a large menu ranging from salads, soups, and sandwiches to full dinners. Vegetarian entrées, plus steaks, quiche of the day, lobster pie, baked scrod, stir fries, and fried seafoods. Most entrées $8.95–13.95; a 16-ounce prime rib is $20.95; New England Sunday brunch buffet (eggs and omelets cooked to order).

The Baker's Peel (603-778-0910), 231 Water St., Exeter. Open Mon.–Fri. 7 AM–5:30 PM, Sat. until 3 PM. The Old World bakery atmosphere is authentic. Co-owner Suzanne Lovering hails from Switzerland where husband Judson spent several years learning the trade. In addition to scrumptious pastries, stop by for great iced coffee with coffee ice cubes, plus a great selection of reasonably-priced sandwiches, wraps, salads, and soups. The Baker's Peel (a wooden baking paddle) hangs on the wall.

♪ **Blue Moon Natural Foods & Green Earth Café** (603-778-6850), 8 Clifford St., Exeter. Mon.–Fri. 9 AM–7 PM; Sat. 9 AM–5 PM; Sun.

noon–5 PM. Café open for lunch only Mon.–Sat. 11–2:30. Vegetarians and others rejoice at this healthy place offering sandwiches and salads featuring tofu, tuna, egg salads, free-range chicken, and salad specials such as white bean, couscous, and hummus. There are also daily soup specials. On weekday afternoons the store offers heat-your-own meals from Mexican fare to quiche-to-go. Inexpensive.

& **Galley Hatch Restaurant & Pelican Pub** (603-926-6152; www.galley hatch.com), 325 Lafayette Rd., Rt. 1, Hampton. Open daily 11 AM–10 PM, Fri.–Sat. until 11. A large and popular seacoast restaurant with a diverse and reasonably priced menu. Fish, chicken, steaks, pastas, and vegetarian entrées plus pizza, salads, and sandwiches. Breads and pastries are made in the Galley's own bakery, which is open to the public. Two lounges; light meals, special coffees, and desserts served in the lounge until closing. Weekend entertainment. Handicapped accessible. Dinner and movie specials with Hampton Cinema complex next door. Prices are moderate.

Loaf and Ladle, Inc. (603-778-8955), 9 Water St., Exeter. Open Mon.–Sat. 8:30 AM–9 PM, Sun. 9–9. A landmark since 1973, this restaurant has a longtime following. Folks come for the bread (60 different kinds, though not all at one time), which you can also buy by the loaf. Also for sandwiches, soups, chowders, salads, and desserts; everything fresh and homemade, served cafeteria style by cheerful staff. Seating inside and out overlooking the river.

Me & Ollie's Bakery & Café (603-772-4600), 64 Water St., Exeter. Open Mon.–Sat. 8 AM–6:30 PM, Sun. 9–5:30. *Honest Food* is this restaurant's man-

tra. Hearty soups, healthy salads and sandwiches, or grilled panini. Make up your mind over a latte. Its sister café is in downtown Portsmouth.

The Pastry Garden (603-926-3693; www.pastrygarden.net), 836 Lafayette Rd., Hampton. Open Tue.–Fri. 8–6, Sat. 8–3. The name tells says it all. Pastries to order for special occasions or to savor by the slice.

🍴 **Penang and Tokyo Restaurant** (603-778-8388), 97 Water St., Exeter. Open Sun.–Thu. 11:30–10, Fri.–Sat. until 11. Following the odd trend of seacoast-area combination restaurants featuring Malaysian, Chinese, and Japanese (there may even be some Thai in there), this bustling eatery in the heart of Exeter plays host to Phillips Exeter Academy parents, students, families with children, and local business types who don't feel it's a day unless they consume sushi. Don't expect superfriendly service, but do come for the unique Malaysian food, like coconut scallops encrusted with sesame seeds or spicy apple chicken. Everything's well flavored, portions are huge, and the sushi laid out at the sushi bar is nothing if not artful. Prices top out at $25 and usually run $9–15. Look for luncheon specials.

Petey's Summertime Seafood and Bar (603-433-1937), 1323 Ocean Blvd., Rye. Open in-season, 11:30–10. "As good as it gets on paper plates" is what the locals say of this popular seaside spot. Fresh fish, fried and otherwise, is the draw for families, couples, seniors—seemingly the entire East Coast. The chowder, said to be the best on earth, is chocked with seafood, then souped up with real cream and fish stock. Take out, eat in, or compromise by dining on one of the outdoor picnic tables.

Purple Urchin Seaside Café (603-929-0800), 167 Ocean Blvd., Hampton Beach. Seasonal. Patio pub open 11 AM–10 PM; dining room opens at 5 for dinner. Afternoon entertainment Fri.–Sun., 2–6. Laid-back seaside fare with salads, sandwiches, appetizers, handcrafted pizza, and clam chowder served all day. Dinners range from pasta of the day for $13.95 to char-grilled filet mignon for $23.95. Lots of frozen drinks. A dessert alternative is the tiramisu martini rimmed with chocolate syrup.

LOBSTER AND SEAFOOD Fried seafood, chowder, steamed clams, and lobster in the rough are seacoast specialties. Local favorites include the following places:

Brown's Seabrook Lobster Pound (603-474-3331), Rt. 286, Seabrook Beach. Open year-round (weekends mid-Nov.–mid-Apr). Boiled lobster, steamed clams, fried and baked seafood. Its screened dining room is on the marsh beside the Blackwater River—or call ahead for take-out service.

Little Jack's Seafood (603-926-0444), 539 Ocean Blvd., Hampton Beach. Open late spring–Labor Day.

Lobsters are a seacoast trademark. For live or cooked lobsters, try the **New Hampshire Lobster Company** (603-926-3424), located at the Smith and Gilmore Pier at Hampton Harbor, open daily 9 AM–5 PM, summer until 6; or **Al's Seafood** (603-946-9591), Rt. 1, Lafayette Rd., North Hampton, open daily. Al's is a lobster pound and fish market with a small seafood restaurant offering mainly fried seafood, but in warm weather they serve lobster in the rough on a porch.

✳ Selective Shopping

Exeter Fine Crafts (603-778-8282), 61 Water St., Exeter. Open Mon.–Sat. 10–5. More than 200 craft workers, many of them members of the **League of New Hampshire Craftsmen**, supply a wide variety of distinctive handmade items.

Exeter Handkerchief Fabrics and Custom Draperies Co. (603-778-8564), 48 Lincoln St., Exeter. Open Mon.–Sat. 9–5. Long a destination for home sewers, this shop features a huge selection of yard goods, specializing in drapery and upholstery fabric.

✳ Special Events

Summer on the seacoast offers a nearly unlimited number of special events and activities for people of all ages. Check with local chambers of commerce for varied activities.

Mid-May: **Alewife Festival** (603-778-0885), Exeter. Activities and demonstrations focused on the river and its importance to the community. **New Hampshire Towing Association Wrecker Rodeo** (603-926-8717), Hampton Beach State Park. Scores of wreckers parade and compete for prizes. Parade 9 AM on Sun.

Mid-June: **Hobie Cat Regatta** (603-926-8717), Hampton Beach. A weekend of racing just off Hampton Beach makes a colorful spectacle.

Mid- to late June: **Master Sand Sculpting Competition** (603-926-8717). Seven thousand dollars in prize money goes to one of the 12 master sand sculptors who spend a week working and are judged. Past winning sculptures have included a depiction of carpenters building a house and frogs playing at the beach. Each year

250 tons of sand is dumped on the beach for contestants' use.

Late June–early August: **Concerts in the Park** (603-778-0595), Swasey Park, Exeter, every Thu.

July and August: **Hampton Beach fireworks**, every Wed. at 9:30 PM. **Hampton Beach concerts**, every night at 7 and 9:30.

Fourth of July: **Kingston Fair**, Rt. 125, Kingston. A weekend country fair.

Third Saturday of July: **Exeter Revolutionary War Festival**, Exeter. Historic demonstrations, militia encampments, battle reenactments, road race, canoe rally, and lots of family fun.

Late July: **Miss Hampton Beach Pageant**. A serious beauty pageant with evening gown and swimsuit competitions; 2 PM. **Stratham Fair**, Rt.

101, Stratham. A weekend, agricultural country fair with horse and cattle pulling, midway, children's events, fireworks.

✐ *Mid-August:* **Annual Children's Festival** (603-926-8717), Hampton Beach.

September: **Seacoast Seafood Festival** (603-926-8717), Hampton Beach. Held the weekend after Labor Day, this annual gathering offers the chance to sample a variety of seafood prepared by area restaurants.

October: **Fall Festival** (603-772-2411), Exeter. Street vendors, crafts, hay rides, and family fun.

December: **Holiday Open House and Festival of Trees**, (603-772-2411), Exeter. Tree lighting, dozens of decorated trees, hay rides, special late hours for downtown stores.

DOVER, DURHAM, AND VICINITY

Durham is the home of the University of New Hampshire, whose beautiful campus dominates the center of the town. The Paul Creative Arts Center with its galleries, music, dance, theater, and intercollegiate athletics has the most to offer visitors, though these activities tend to happen during the school year, Sep.–May. First settled in 1623, Dover is the oldest continuous settlement in the state and the seventh oldest in the nation. During the past decade, the city has become a model of revitalization, attracting visitors from near and far. Today its historic mills house shops, restaurants, apartments, and offices. The Cochecho River, with its river walk, covered bridge, picnic areas, historic markers, and public boat launch winds through the heart of Dover's downtown.

GUIDANCE Greater Dover Chamber of Commerce (603-742-2218; www.dovernh.org), 299 Central Ave., Dover 03820.

University of New Hampshire main switchboard (603-862-1234) can provide details of various events or direct your questions to the proper office.

GETTING THERE *By car:* From Portsmouth, follow the Spaulding Turnpike (Rts. 4/16) north, then Rt. 4 west for Durham, or remain on the turnpike and take one of the three Dover exits.

By bus: **C&J Trailways** (603-430-1100; www.cjtrailways.com) provides many trips daily connecting Logan Airport and downtown Boston with Dover, Durham, and Portsmouth, N.H.; Newburyport, Ma.; and Portland, Me.

By train: **Amtrak** (800-872-7245; www.amtrak.com). Slide down the Maine and New Hampshire coasts with ease on this short train that heads to Boston. The train runs year-round; one-way fares run about $12–21. On the seacoast the train stops at Dover, Durham, and Exeter.

GETTING AROUND *By bus:* **COAST** (Cooperative Alliance for Seacoast Transportation) (603-743-5777; www.coastbus.org), a local bus transportation network, connects Portsmouth and major outlying shopping centers with Durham, Dover, Newmarket, Rochester, and Somersworth, N.H.; and Berwick, Me.

Wildcat Transit (603-862-2328) makes frequent trips among Dover, Portsmouth, and the University of New Hampshire in Durham.

By boat: **George's Marina** (603-742-9089), 33 Cochecho St., Dover.

MEDICAL EMERGENCY **Wentworth-Douglas Hospital** (603-742-5252; www
.wdhospital.com), 789 Central Ave., Dover, has 24-hour emergency walk-in service. **Dover ambulance: 911. Durham ambulance:** 603-862-1212.

✳ To See

GAME FARM **Little Bay Buffalo Company** (603-868-3300), 50 Langley Rd.,
Durham. Open daily except major holidays 10–5 or dusk. This family-owned and
-operated wildlife estate offers an amazing view—a grand stretch of pastureland
swooping down to a saltwater bay. Add a few dozen buffalo and call it unique.
Sometimes guests can ride across the rolling landscape in a covered wagon
pulled by a vintage Farmall tractor to view the bison as they breed and calve.
Bison meat, bison jerky, and various other bison by-products are available for
sale at the trading post gift shop.

HISTORICAL SOCIETIES AND MUSEUMS **Durham Historical Museum** (603-
868-5436), corner of Main St. and Newmarket Rd., Durham. Open Sep.–May,
Tue. and Thu. 1–3; June–Aug., by appointment only.

Mill Museum (603-231-2600), 100 Main St., Dover. Located in the Cocheco
Millworks in the heart of downtown Dover. Impressive photographic collection
and artifacts documenting Dover's brickyards, and shoe and textile industries.
This city was the site of the first women's strike in the United States.

Lee Historical Society (603-659-5925), Mast Rd., Lee. Open on Lee Fair Day
(the Sat. after Labor Day) and June–Aug., Sat. 9–2. Local artifacts, including
farm tools, household items, and antique photographs, are housed in an old railroad freight station, moved to this site between the town library and the police
station.

Newmarket Historical Society (603-659-7420), Granite St., Newmarket. Open
by appointment and June–Aug., Thu. 2–4. The old Granite School Museum has
old tools and local artifacts plus photographs of Newmarket mills and shoe shops.

Woodman Institute Museum (603-742-1038), 182 Central Ave., Dover. Open
Apr.–Nov., Sun.–Wed. 12:30–4:30. $3 adults, $1 ages 14–18. This three-building
complex is Dover's historical museum. The Woodman House (1818) is a research
library that has galleries and natural history and war-related museum rooms. The
1813 Hale House is a historical museum with period furniture. The Damm Garrison, built in 1675, is a unique building that was used as a home and fortress by
early settlers.

✳ To Do

Cochecho River Tours & Cruises (603-749-1922; 1-866-749-1922; www
.cochechotours.com), George's Marina, 33 Cochecho St., Dover. Open mid-May
to fall. One- to 3-hour tours of the Cochecho and Piscataqua Rivers and the
Great Bay Estuary. A 25-foot pontoon boat allows for a leisurely stroll through
these sometimes shallow waters. Standard tours $14–50. Charters available.

Jenny Thompson Pool and Guppey Park (603-516-6085), Portland Ave., Dover. Dover native Jenny Thompson holds the prize, a dozen Olympic medals, more than any other American in history. Maybe it's the water.

GOLF **Hickory Pond** (603-659-7642; 1-800-658-0065; www.hickorypondinn .com), Rt. 108, Durham. Open spring–early fall. This is a nine-hole, par-3 course. Pro shop. Inexpensive.

Nippo Lake Golf Course (603-664-7616), Province Rd. (off Rt. 126), Barrington. Open Apr.–Nov. Nine holes, cart rentals, full bar and food service year-round; call for starting times on weekends.

Rochester Country Club (603-332-9892), Rt. 125, Gonic. Open mid-Apr.–mid-Nov. Eighteen holes, cart rentals, full bar and food service, and pro shop; call for starting times on weekends.

Rockingham Country Club (603-659-9956), Rt. 108, Newmarket. Open mid-Apr.–mid-Nov. Nine holes, cart rentals, pro shop, full bar and food service; call for starting times on weekends and holidays.

Wadleigh Falls Golf Driving Range (603-659-4444; www.wadleighfallsgolf .com), Rt. 152, Newmarket. Open May 1–fall. Fully lighted family driving range with ice cream stand and gardens in a country setting.

Sunningdale Golf Course (603-742-8056), 301 Green St., Somersworth. Open mid-Apr.–mid-Nov. Nine holes, cart rentals, full bar, and light food.

Granite Fields Golf Club (603-642-9977; www.granitefields.com), Rt. 125, Kingston. Eighteen-hole golf course and driving range.

WALKING TOURS **Dover's Heritage Trails** (603-742-2218), 299 Central Ave., Dover. The chamber of commerce offers a brochure with a series of walking tours exploring Dover's long history.

✴ Green Space

Great Bay National Estuarine Research Reserve (603-868-1095; www .greatbay.org), 37 Concord Rd., Durham. Great Bay, with some 4,500 acres of tidal waters and tidal wetlands and 800 surrounding upland acres, has been designated part of the national estuarine research system. Famous for winter smelt fishing, oystering, and waterfowl, the bay is a unique resource in the midst of the rapidly growing towns of the seacoast. Some 23 rare or endangered species, including bald eagles in winter, depend on the shallow bay as a refuge. It is an important stop for migrating birds of all species. Its status as a research reserve will help continue the scientific studies conducted since 1970 by the University of New Hampshire's Jackson Estuarine Lab on **Adams Point**. From Rt. 108 in Durham, follow Bay Rd. to Adams Point, where there is a launch ramp and a self-guiding nature trail. Return to Bay Rd. and follow it south to Newmarket, an especially scenic drive with views across the bay. Just across the bay from Adams Point is the **Great Bay National Wildlife Refuge** (603-431-7511), part of the Pease International Tradeport. The public is welcome at the **Sandy Point Discovery Center** on Depot Rd., just off Rt. 101 in Stratham (603-778-0015). It's free and open to the public May–Sep. (plus weekends in Oct.), Wed.–Sun. 10–4. Nearby on Rt. 108 in Stratham is **Chapmans Landing**, a launching site with restroom facilities. There is another launch ramp in the middle of **Newmarket** on Rt. 108. Although the bay has a large surface area, its average depth is only 8 feet, making navigation in larger boats a challenge. Some of the Portsmouth tour boats offer fall foliage cruises on the bay and its tributaries. The bay drains through the Piscataqua River, the boundary between Maine and New Hampshire.

✿ **Hilton Park** is located on Dover Point, bisected by the Spaulding Turnpike. It has a boat-launching ramp, picnic tables, outdoor grills, and play area. It is named for Edward Hilton, who acquired a land grant in 1623 from King James of England.

Cochecho River Trail (603-749-4445), Strafford County Farm at County Farm Rd. and County Farm Cross Rd., Dover. An easy 1-mile loop trail that crosses an old floodplain with scenic river vistas and through forests rich with tall pines and ancient oaks. Trail maps and interpretive materials are available at the trailhead.

UNH's Department of Campus Recreation publishes an excellent little booklet of self-guiding hikes on and around the university's sprawling, wooded campus. Call UNH's main switchboard (603-862-1234) or drop by the New England Conference Center (see *Lodging*, below) to pick up a copy of *Running and Walking Routes*.

✳ Lodging

HOTELS ✿ **The New England Conference Center and Hotel** (603-862-2801; 1-800-590-4334; www.newenglandcenter.com), 15 Strafford Ave., UNH, Durham 03824. Located on the University of New Hampshire campus, this contemporary conference center (also open to the public) has 115 guest rooms, 61 of which are located in the newest of the two green, ceramic brick towers that make up the complex. The building, designed by the same architect as the Transamerica Building in San Francisco, echoes the lines of the soaring evergreens around it. All rooms have dramatic views across the campus or into the treetops of this heavily wooded site. They also boast wall-to-wall carpet, air-conditioning, TV, hair dryer, iron and ironing board, and phone. The newer wing has two queen-sized beds in each room. There is daily bus service to Boston's Logan Airport, about an hour away. On campus is a 100,000-square-foot recreation facility, including fitness center, a good way to keep in shape before dining in the Acorns Restaurant and Lounge, which serves breakfast, lunch, and dinner daily (see *Dining Out*). Rates vary seasonally: Nov.–Apr., $104–119; May–Oct., $119–134. There's a $10 charge for children over 12.

The Hotel New Hampshire (603-868-1234; www.hotelnewhampshire.net), 2 Main St., Durham 03824. Located just a short walk from the University of New Hampshire, this hotel with the literary reference to Exeter native John Irving's novel of the same name is Durham's newest lodging property. It offers 68 guest rooms including two luxury suites. Rates include continental breakfast, flat-screen televisions with 70 cable channels, high-speed Internet access, both wired and wireless, complimentary beer and wine in the evenings, and other extras. The hotel also offers a guest computer station, guest laundry, and two meeting rooms. Nonsmoking; the public spaces and some guest rooms are handicapped accessible. Rates vary seasonally: May–Oct., $119, Nov.–Apr., $99.

BED & BREAKFASTS Durham Point B&B (603-868-1162), 1 Sunnyside Dr., Durham 03824. A well-kept new Colonial-style home set back from the road on the way to Durham Point. Philip and Elena Rainville offer two air-conditioned rooms with shared bath at $80 each; a third with private bath goes for $90. Breakfast included.

Hickory Pond Inn and Golf Course (603-659-2227; 1-800-658-0065; www.hickorypondinn.com), Rt. 108 and Stagecoach Rd., Durham 03824. Open all year. In a country location just 2.5 miles from the university campus and midway between Durham and Newmarket, this inn has 18 rooms—10 in the original structure dating back to 1783, 8 more in a newer addition. All have private bath, cable TV, and telephone. A continental breakfast is served in one of two large common areas. Floor-to-ceiling windows overlook a challenging par-3, nine-hole golf course, open to guests and the public. In winter the course turns into a cross-country ski area. Libby and Doug Baker, innkeepers. $69–129.

Highland Farm (603-743-3399; www.highlandfarmbandb.com), 148 County Farm Rd., Dover 03820. Open year-round. This interesting brick Victorian country house is on the outskirts of the city in a unique pastoral setting. There are nature trails for walking or cross-country skiing along the nearby Cochecho River. Four guest rooms, two with private bath; the other rooms share two baths. Beds include a queen-sized with a canopy. Most rooms have a queen-sized bed or two twin beds. Common rooms include a living room, wood-paneled library, sunroom, and dining room. Furnishings are antiques, enhanced by the unusual woodwork and architectural design of this house. Full breakfast. Rates are $90–145 for two.

The Inn at Packers Falls (603-659-5500; 1-866-995-6500; www.dewbandb.com), 191 Packers Falls Rd., Durham 03824. There are five rooms, each with private bath and double or king bed, in this comfortable home owned and operated by retired social science professor, Richard Dewey, and his daughter Marilyn. The front lawn dips down to the Lamprey River, and you can too if you're in the mood for a swim. Children and pets accepted; breakfast included; and rates, at $70-$100 ($20 per extra person), are a bargain for the area.

Three Chimneys Inn (603-868-7800; 1-888-399-9777; www.threechimneysinn.com), 17 Newmarket Rd., Durham 03824. Open all year. Seemingly no expense was spared when Sagamore Hill, Inc., purchased Durham's oldest home in 1997 and transformed it into the area's poshest public lodgings. During three and a half centuries the original 1649 house on a hill has gone through several expansions and incarnations, each time reflecting the owners' rising fortunes. The inn, overlooking its own formal gardens, the Oyster River, and Old Mill Falls, is an easy walk to the University of New Hampshire campus and 10 miles from Portsmouth. The 23 guest rooms—all with private bath, many with gas fireplace—are luxuriously furnished with four-poster beds, Edwardian bed draperies, tapestries, and Oriental rugs. Added comforts include desk, sitting area, and Internet service. Wedding and conference facilities are available for up to 150. Rates ($249 for two in high season, $109 the rest of the year) include a full breakfast served in the Maples dining room (see *Dining Out*). Children over 6 welcome; $25 charge for third person in a room.

&. **The Williams House Inn** (603-750-4200; 1-800-871-4177; www .thewilliamshouseinn.com), 103 Silver St., Dover 03820. Open year-round. Located on a residential street, this gray, mansard-roofed B&B was built in the 1880s by a wealthy leather machine belt manufacturer who spared nothing in the way of Gilded Age elegance. Many of the architectural details, including mahogany, crystal, slate, and Caen stone, were imported from Western Europe, and the craftsmanship of the molded plaster ceilings and hand-painted dining room walls reflects the sumptuousness of the age. Eight rooms (all with private bath) have air-conditioning, telephone, hair dryer and robes, plus cable TV with DVD and a video library to choose from. One downstairs room is handicapped accessible. Its king-sized bed, surrounded by rose silk wall panels and custom crown molding, makes the room truly fit for royalty. The dining and living rooms and the ornate library are comfortable and have fireplaces. Full breakfast. Rates are $109–149 July–Columbus Day weekend; $99–129 the rest of the year.

✳ Where to Eat

DINING OUT The Acorns Restaurant and Lounge (603-862-2815; www.acornsrestaurant.com), 15 Strafford Ave., Durham. Open year-round for breakfast, lunch, and dinner. Dinner is 5–10, Sunday brunch 11–1:30. Part of the New England Conference Center and Hotel, this is one of the most popular restaurants in the region. It's as well known for its fine food as for its distinctive architecture, which features angled walls and huge windows that place diners seemingly in the midst of the surrounding forest. Interesting, well-priced, award-winning menu; also lighter fare. The Sunday brunch, with jazz to accompany, has been called the best in New Hampshire, so be smart—a good idea on a university campus—and reserve ahead.

Blue Latitudes Bar & Grill (603-750-4222; www.bluelatitudes.net), 100 Main St., Suite 102, Dover. Open Tue.–Thu., 11–9 (bar till 10); Fri.–Sat., 11:30–10 (bar till 11); Sun., 10–8. The high wooden ceilings and brick walls recall this restaurant's mill origins but the stylish decor and sophisticated menu are evidence of a new day dawning. The menu breaks tradition with such lunch offerings as South American empanada, and gravlax pumpernickel crostini. For dinner there's three-pepper lamb chops at $22.95, veal Milanese with apple cinnamon compote at $19.95, and a Malaysian stir-fry with tuna strips, wild mushrooms, pineapple, and coconut milk for a dollar less. Sunday brunch, 10–2, features jazz along with everything from two eggs, bacon or sausage, toast, and rosti potatoes for $7 to a lobster scramble with shrimp sauce and vegetable for $15.

Crescent City Bistro & Rum Bar
(603-742-1611), 83 Washington St.,
Dover. Open for dinner till 9 week-
nights, 10 on weekends. The bar goes
until last call, with live music on Tue.
after 9. Who knew there were so
many Cajun wannabes on the New
Hampshire seacoast? The weekly "Fat
Tuesday" bands and weekend live jazz
nights are attracting plenty of Mardi
Gras fans. The atmosphere and menu
are offbeat and fun—bright gold
walls, black-and-white floor tiles, a
copper-wrapped rum bar—plus jambalaya, crawfish étouffée, blackened
redfish, and grilled wild boar chops.
The specialty rum drinks require a
separate menu. *À votre santé!*

Foxfire Grille (603-679-3700; www
.thefoxfiregrille.com), 96 Calef Hwy.,
Rt. 125, Epping. Open Sun.–Thu.
11–2 for lunch, 5–9 for dinner, Fri.
and Sat. until 10. Breakfast served
from 7 on weekends. Opened in 2002
in what was once the local hardware
store, this restaurant has been winning acclaim for its casual feel and
gourmet food. Chef Andrew Robinson once aspired to be a musician;
now he says his art is cooking. For the
full menu, choose the dining room.
Otherwise, you can loll on the deck or
play billiards in the lounge.

Orchard Street Chop Shop (603-
749-0006; www.orchardstreetchop
shop.com), 1 Orchard St. (adjacent to
the municipal parking off the lower
square), Dover. Open daily for lunch
from 11:30, dinner from 5. Reservations recommended for dinner.
Housed in a remodeled 1830s firehouse, this may be the most elegant
example of Dover's dining renaissance. The walls are red, the atmosphere mellow, the menu memorable.
Appetizers range from wild boar

sausage with creamy cabbage slaw
and mustard seed emulsion, to beef
carpaccio with saffron aioli (both $9).
Entrées include free-range chicken,
center-cut veal chop, ahi tuna, and a
wide selection of USDA prime-grade
beef. Continue the indulgence with
fine Napa wines and a Cuban-style
cigar lounge. Upstairs, the "Top of the
Chop," offers a lower-priced lunch
menu.

Three Chimneys Inn (603-868-
7800; 1-888-399-9777; www.three
chimneysinn.com), 17 Newmarket
Rd., Durham. Open year-round with
dinner served nightly from 5. Whether
dining in the formal Georgian-style
room, the granite-walled tavern, or
alfresco on a terrace under an old
English grape arbor, you can count
on style here, both in surroundings
and food. Oysters, chowder, mussels,
smoked salmon crêpes, hazelnut-
crusted chicken livers, and chilled
jumbo shrimp crown the appetizer
menu. The entrées range from pork
shank osso buco with red beans and
rice ($18.95), to stuffed calamari with
sausage and eggplant ($18.95), to beef
tenderloin with lump blue crab meat
and classic béarnaise ($26.95).

EATING OUT **Alexander's Italian
Restaurant** (603-742-2650), 489
Portland Ave. (Rt. 4), Rollinsford.
Tue.–Thu. 11:30–9, Fri. until 10, Sat.
4–10, Sun. noon–8. This popular
restaurant is located just west of
downtown Dover. For antipasti select
red peppers and anchovies or eggplant parmigiana, then try calamari
with linguine in red sauce, octopus
with linguine, or shrimp with garlic
and butter on linguine. Meat entrées
range from veal parmigiana and roast
veal to chicken cacciatore, pork

chops, and New York strip steak. Also pizza (white with Fontina cheese), lasagna, and fettuccine carbonara. Inexpensive.

The Barn Tavern (603-742-1231; www.schoonerhouseinn.com), 17 Portland Ave., Dover. Open daily 11–9 (to 10 on weekends; closed Sun. in winter). This historic waterfront barn overlooking the Cochecho River offers a casual pub atmosphere with reasonably priced sandwiches, salads, pasta dishes, and entrées for lunch and dinner. Full-service bar. Located directly behind the Schooner House Inn, once a sea captain's home, which now offers short-term rental suites.

Café on the Corner (603-742-0314), 478 Central Ave., Dover. Open for breakfast, lunch, and coffee until midnight. A cozy spot that draws most of its clientele from nearby UNH, Café on the Corner features great coffee, sandwiches, soups, and salads as well as Internet access (there's a minimum charge even if you're just quickly checking your e-mail), board games, books, and comfortable seating. It's very friendly, and even if the crowd is younger than you might like, it's open for a bite or a coffee far later than almost anything else in the seacoast area. Try the banana Foster smoothie.

Kelley's Row Restaurant (603-750-7081), 421 Central Ave., Dover. Open 11–10, Sun. until 9. Last call at 12:30. Another of Dover's downtown mill conversions, this one with a patio overlooking the old Cochecho Mill Pond, great for a midsummer meal or drink. The menu features soups, salads, big sandwiches served on a bulkie roll with choice of french fries or pasta salad, and low-carb, low-priced options such as a 6-ounce

haddock fillet, or grilled salmon with salad or vegetable for $9.50.

Newick's Lobster House and Restaurant (603-742-3205; www.newicks.com), 431 Dover Point Rd., Dover. Open daily 11–9, Memorial–Columbus Day; Sun.–Thu. 11–8:30, Fri.–Sat. 11–9 the rest of the year. Fresh fish and lobster right off the boat are the specialties at this large, very popular restaurant overlooking Great Bay. Not fancy dining, but you can have deep-fried (in cholesterol-free vegetable oil) fish of all kinds with combinations of scallops, oysters, haddock, clams, and shrimp. Portions are huge. For those with lighter tastes, try boiled lobsters, steamers, or broiled, baked, or stuffed fish dinners. Also chicken, sandwiches, chowders, and lobster stew. Expect a wait at weekend dinnertimes. $4.50–$20 and above.

Strafford Farms Restaurant (603-743-3045), 58 New Rochester Rd., Rt. 108, Dover. Open Sun.–Thu. 6 AM–9 PM; Fri. and Sat. till 10. Sixty years ago Leo Allen and the Rollins families opened a milk-processing plant, which soon expanded to sell ice cream, and eventually became a full-fledged restaurant serving breakfast, lunch, and dinner. Today, despite its location on a busy strip of fast-food restaurants and chain stores, Strafford Farms continues to offer such homemade, back-on-the-farm specialties as Yankee pot roast, meat loaf, and turkey croquettes. The full menu also includes hot and cold sandwiches, seafood entrées, Black Angus beef, homemade soups, salads, and several Italian dishes. Most are priced under $10. Turkey potpie in a bread bowl with vegetable and roll is $7.25; a 20-ounce prime rib with all the trimmings is $16.95.

Weeks Restaurant (603-749-4673), 1 Locust St., Dover. Open daily 6 AM–2 PM, Sun. 7–1. A treasured local hangout that serves breakfast till closing, along with soup, salads, and sandwiches for lunch.

✳ Entertainment

⚘ **Cochecho Arts Festival** (603-742-2218), Rotary Arts Pavilion, Dover. Open July–late Aug. In the center of Dover beside the Cochecho River is a huge textile mill complex, recently remodeled into a business center. The pavilion is the location for Friday-night, Wednesday-noon, and occasional Sunday-evening concerts featuring a variety of regional music groups. Children's concerts and programs are held Tuesday at noon at the Dover Public Library.

Garrison Players Performances (603-740-0069; 603-450-4ART; www.garrisonplayers.org), Garrison Players Arts Center, Rt. 4, Rollinsford. Year-round community theater group that performs plays, musicals, and revues geared for family audiences.

Mill Pond Center for the Arts (603-868-2068; www.millpondcenter.org), 50 Newmarket Rd., Durham. You'll be amazed at the bounty of performing arts housed in this historic former inn set in the woods. Year-found chamber music, dance, and theater performances. Call for schedules and pricing information.

✳ Selective Shopping

Calef's Country Store (603-664-2231; 1-800-462-2118; www.calefs.com), Rts. 9 and 125, Barrington. Open daily 8–6, Sun. till 5. Since 1869, five generations of Calefs have operated this old-fashioned country store. Penny candy, cheddar cheese, maple syrup, Barbados molasses, jams and jellies, pickles and crackers in the barrel, dried beans for baking, hand-dipped candles, pumpkins in fall, gifts, and more.

The Christmas Dove (1-800-550-3683; www.christmasdove.com), junction of Rts. 125 and 9, Barrington. Open daily 10–5; Nov.–Christmas Eve 10–8. This Dover establishment, which has sister stores in New York, Boston, and Ogunquit, Maine, has been around for more than a quarter century. Trimmings, lights, nutcrackers, candles, and nativities turn the complex into a southerly North Pole, allowing organized shoppers to ho-ho-ho all year. Also stocks seasonal decor, including Halloween.

Cocheco Falls Gallery (603-743-3411), 421 Central Ave., Dover. Open daily 11–5:30; Sat. and Sun. until 5. Owner Cheryl Hoess has accumulated an eclectic mix of new and old artwork, collectibles, jewelry, and furnishings from near and far.

Farmer's Market, Henry Law Park, Dover. Wed. afternoons, June–Oct. Locally grown veggies and fruits, home-baked goods, and crafts.

Flag Hill Winery (603-659-2949; www.flaghillenterprises.com), 0.25 mile off Rt. 155 in Lee. Rolling hills and French hybrid grape vineyards surround this 200-year-old, family-run farm. Wine-tasting bar, vineyard tours, and gift shop, Wed.–Sun., 11–5.

Salmon Falls Stoneware (603-749-1467; www.salmonfallsstoneware.com), the Oak Street Engine House, Dover. Open Mon.–Sat. 8–5, Sun. from 9. Salmon Falls Stoneware has gained a following for its line of cobalt-blue country designs on salt-glazed pottery. The casserole dishes, crocks, dinnerware, mugs, and pie plates are ovenproof, and microwave and dishwasher safe. There's a shop that sells both first-quality items and selected seconds, as well as a studio where you can watch potters at work.

Red's Famous Shoe Barn (603-742-1893), 35 Broadway Rd., Dover. New Hampshire's largest shoe store, featuring more than 100 famous brands at discount prices for the entire family. Open 7 days and 5 nights.

The Sugar Shack (603-868-6636; 1-800-57-MAPLE; www.maplesugar shack.net), 0.5 mile from the Lee traffic circle on Rt. 4W in Barrington. Open Feb.–Dec., Wed.–Sat. 10:30–5:30. All-you-can-eat spring breakfasts begin the last weekend in February and run through Mother's Day. The shop is open for sampling and buying a variety of maple products, many produced on the premises. The maple syrup is finger-lickin' good—naturally!

Tuttle's Red Barn (603-742-4313), Dover Point Rd., Dover. Open daily 10–6. Tuttles have lived on this site since 1632, making this the oldest continuously operating family farm in America. Once just a seasonal farm stand operating from the large, old red barn, it has been expanded as a market and garden center. While the surroundings can no longer be called quiet or country, much of the produce, especially sweet corn, comes from the surrounding fields in-season. There's also good bread and a wide variety of fruits, vegetables, and cheeses.

Wiswall House Antiques (603-659-5106; jmcarter5@comcast.net), 28 Wiswall Rd., Durham. Open Mar.–Dec., Wed.–Sat. 10–5, Sun. afternoon by chance or appointment. Interesting selection of American furnishings, unusual lighting, linens, and more.

✷ Special Events

April: **Seacoat Flower, Home & Garden Show** (603-862-1199), Whittemore Center Arena, 128 Main St., Durham. This popular annual event features landscapers, realtors and remodelers offering valuable home tips, demonstrations, and displays.

May: **Antiques Appraisal Day** (603-742-1038), Woodman Institute, 182 Central Ave., Dover. Bring the family heirlooms. **Lilac Family Fun Festival** (603-332-2577), downtown Rochester. Features games, rides, eating and baking contests, live entertainment.

June: **Somersworth International Children's Day**, an all-day event with four entertainment stages including one for children, a crafts fair, food booths, a hands-on crafts tent for children, and an activities section for children. **Great Cochecho Boat Race** (603-868-1494). Sponsored by the Strafford Rivers Conservancy, this canoe race proves a challenge to all participants and is great fun to watch. **Children's Fishing Derby**, Willow Pond, Dover. **New Hampshire Soap Box Derby** (603-743-4547), Central Ave., Dover. Coasting race for small, gravity-powered cars built by their drivers and assembled within guidelines on size, weight, and cost.

❧ July–August: **Cochecho Arts Festival** (603-742-2218), Rotary Arts Pavilion, Dover. Music and children's programs, several times weekly.

August: **Seacoast Irish Festival** (603-516-6100), Dover Lodge of Elks, Rt. 108, Dover. Features live performances by a variety of Irish bands with food, beer, and fun for all ages.

Early September: **Lee Fair Day**, Mast Rd., Lee. A community fair with exhibits, games, and food.

Mid-September: **Rochester Fair** (603-332-6585), 72 Lafayette St., Rochester. A 10-day fair with a midway, agricultural exhibits, and parimutuel harness racing. **Antique and Classic Car Show**, (603-742-1038), Woodman Institute Museum, Dover. View and vote for your favorite antique autos.

♪ *First Saturday in October:* **Apple Harvest Day** (603-742-2218), Dover. An all-day craft fair with entertainment, food, petting zoo, children's activities, and more.

November: **Holiday Parade** (603-742-2218), Central Ave., Dover. Santa Claus always shows for this traditional holiday parade held on the Sunday following Thanksgiving.

December: **Holiday Home Tour** (603-740-2818), Dover. Self-guided tour of elegant homes decorated for the holidays. **Santa Claus House** (603-740-6435), Cocheco Courtyard, Dover. Thu. and Fri. 5–7 PM, Sun. 1–4. Santa stops by on weekends to listen to kids' Christmas wish lists. **Winter Solstice** (603-740-9700), downtown Dover. Organized by Dover Yoga Studio to celebrate holiday customs around the world.

The Monadnock 2
Region

PETERBOROUGH, KEENE, AND
SURROUNDING VILLAGES

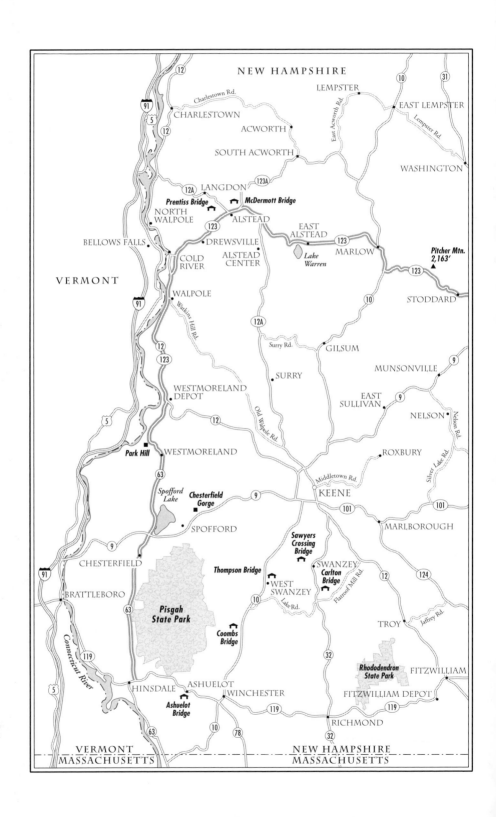

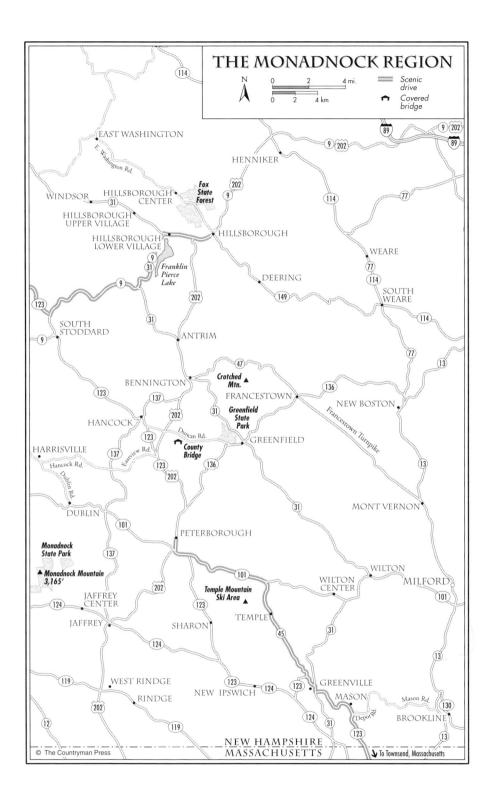

THE MONADNOCK REGION

N

0   2   4 mi.

0   2   4 km

Scenic drive

Covered bridge

114

89

9 202

89

9 202

EAST WASHINGTON

HENNIKER

E. Washington Rd.

202

9

Fox State Forest

WINDSOR

HILLSBOROUGH CENTER

31

114

77

HILLSBOROUGH UPPER VILLAGE

HILLSBOROUGH

WEARE

HILLSBOROUGH LOWER VILLAGE

9

31

Franklin Pierce Lake

DEERING

77

114

9

123

123

202

31

149

SOUTH WEARE

114

SOUTH STODDARD

9

ANTRIM

31

77

13

47

Crotched Mtn.

136

BENNINGTON

123

137

FRANCESTOWN

NEW BOSTON

202

31

Greenfield State Park

HANCOCK

123

Duncan Rd.

Francestown Turnpike

13

HARRISVILLE

137

Eastview Rd.

County Bridge

GREENFIELD

Hancock Rd.

123

136

Dublin Rd.

202

31

MONT VERNON

DUBLIN

101

Monadnock State Park

137

PETERBOROUGH

WILTON

Monadnock Mountain 3,165'

101

WILTON CENTER

MILFORD

JAFFREY CENTER

202

Temple Mountain Ski Area

101

124

123

13

JAFFREY

TEMPLE

31

SHARON

45

124

13

119

WEST RINDGE

123

GREENVILLE

202

RINDGE

NEW IPSWICH

124

123

MASON

Mason Rd.

12

119

124

31

Depot Rd.

BROOKLINE

130

13

NEW HAMPSHIRE

MASSACHUSETTS

123

To Townsend, Massachusetts

© The Countryman Press

PETERBOROUGH, KEENE, AND SURROUNDING VILLAGES

Mount Monadnock towers a dramatic 2,000 feet above the surrounding roll of southwestern New Hampshire. Not only is the mountain visible from up to 50 miles in every direction, but it's also as much a part of the dozens of surrounding towns as the steeples on their meetinghouses. Uplands around the mountain, in turn, rise like a granite island 1,000 feet above the rest of southern New Hampshire. Hardy spruce, fir, and birch are the dominant trees, and the rugged terrain has deflected both developers and interstate highways.

Depending on where you draw the line, the Monadnock region as a whole encompasses some 40 towns, all characterized by narrow roads, quintessential New England villages, and mountain vistas. A region of rushing streams, this entire area was once spotted with small 19th-century mills, and many of these buildings survive. Harrisville, with its two cupola-topped mills graceful as churches, is said to be the country's most perfectly preserved early-19th-century mill village. Larger brick mill buildings in South Peterborough and in Keene now house shops and restaurants, and half a dozen old mills are still producing a wide variety of products: paper, lightbulbs, and matchbooks, for starters.

Mount Monadnock itself spawned the region's tourism industry early in the 19th century. Early settlers had trimmed its lower beard of hardwood and spruce, planting orchards and pasturing sheep between tidy stone walls right up its rocky shoulders. Then they took to burning the summit. The idea was to kill off the wolves, but the effect was to expose the mountain's bald pate. Once this bare spot was created, alpine flora (usually found only on mountains twice as high) took root, and hikers could enjoy not only the high-altitude landscape but also the spectacular view.

"Grand Monadnock" quickly became a famous freak. By 1823 a shed, the Grand Monadnock Hotel, was selling refreshments just below the summit, and a rival, Dinsmore's Comfortable Shantee, opened high on the mountain a few years later. By the 1850s local farmers and innkeepers had blazed trails up every side of Monadnock, and from 100 to 400 people could be found hiking them on any good day.

In the 1850s the mountain inspired works by Henry David Thoreau and Ralph Waldo Emerson, and around the turn of the century Dublin became known as a literary and art colony—writers included Samuel Clemens and Willa Cather; artists included Abbot Thayer, Frank Benson, and Rockwell Kent. In 1908 the MacDowell Colony in Peterborough became one of the country's first formal retreats for musicians, artists, and writers. The region's cultural climate remains rich, expressed through the unusual number of art galleries and musical and theatrical productions.

Most of the 19th-century summer hotels around Mount Monadnock are long gone, but half a dozen of the region's earlier stagecoach taverns survive, and over the past decades a couple of dozen attractive bed & breakfasts have opened. The Monadnock region is thus once more a destination area. But even innkeepers will tell you that a resort area it isn't. Residents take pride in the fact that Mount Monadnock is the world's second most heavily hiked mountain (after Mount Fuji in Japan), but everyone wants to keep the region's roads as delightfully traffic-free as they are.

Mount Monadnock itself is unquestionably the region's spiritual and physical hub—but mountains, after all, divide. There's some rivalry between Keene and Peterborough for recognition as the commercial center of the region. In fact, Mount Monadnock divides the area in two; all roads west of the mountain seem to converge in Keene, while in the hillier area to the east they run to Peterborough.

Keene is the shire town of Cheshire County, home of Keene State College and the place most residents of southwestern New Hampshire come to go to the movies or the hospital or to shop seriously. Far smaller Peterborough prides itself on having "the first tax-supported Free Public Library in the world," on having inspired Thornton Wilder to write *Our Town*, and on serving as home for one of New England's oldest summer theaters. It also offers some unexpectedly fine shopping and dining.

The Monadnock region remains pristine in part because of its location: too near Boston to be generally viewed as a place to spend the night, too far from Manhattan to draw the New Yorkers, who tend to get no farther east than Vermont. So it happens that, despite the region's beauty, its ski and hiking trails, biking routes, and wealth of antiques shops, and the quality of its lodging and dining, prices are relatively and refreshingly low. The only way to truly experience and explore the region, moreover, is to stay at least overnight.

GUIDANCE **Greater Peterborough Chamber of Commerce** (603-924-7234; www.peterboroughchamber.com), P.O. Box 401, Peterborough 03458. Open weekdays 9–5; Sat. in summer and fall, 10–3. The chamber publishes a beautiful 100-page guide to the 20 central and eastern towns in the region, and the walk-in information center at the junction of Rts. 101 and 202 is unusually friendly and helpful.

Greater Keene Chamber of Commerce (603-352-1303; www.keenechamber .com), 48 Central Square, Keene 03431. Open weekdays 9–5. The Keene chamber's easy-to-find, walk-in office is also a source of brochures and detailed information about the western and Connecticut River Valley sides of the region.

GETTING THERE *By air:* **Manchester Airport** (603-624-6539) offers connecting service to the world; see *Air Service* under "What's Where." **Silver Ranch Airpark** (603-532-8870; www.silverranchairpark.com), 190 Turnpike, Jaffrey, accommodates private planes.

By bus: **Vermont Transit Lines** (1-800-451-3292; in Keene, 603-352-1331; www.vermonttransit.com) stops in Keene (Gilbo Ave.), Troy, and Fitzwilliam en route from Boston to Montreal.

GETTING AROUND *By car:* Although the beauty of this region is its winding country roads, it's also worth noting the straightest, quickest routes: **Rt. 101**, which becomes Rt. 9 west of Keene, bisects the region from east to west, linking with Boston via Rts. 101A and 3; by the same token, **Rt. 202** serves as a north–south spine linking I-89 north of Hillsborough with Rt. 2 (via Rt. 140) in Massachusetts. These two high roads cross at the lights in Peterborough, site of the region's prime information center. Rt. 12 also links with Rt. 140 to form an obvious route (the one the bus takes) from Boston via Fitzwilliam and Keene to southern Vermont.

WHEN TO GO Occasionally this high and hilly corner of New Hampshire gets the kind of old-fashioned winter on which its ski areas once thrived. In recent years, however, the snowline has moved north and the alpine areas are gone. More than ever, this is a summer and fall destination.

MEDICAL EMERGENCY **911** covers the entire region. **Cheshire Medical Center and Dartmouth-Hitchcock** (603-354-5400; www.cheshire-med.com), 580 and 590 Court St., Keene. **Monadnock Community Hospital** (603-924-7191), 452 Old St. Rd., Peterborough, has a 24-hour emergency department.

✳ Villages

No other area in New England is as thickly studded with picture-perfect villages— clusters of clapboard and brick buildings around common centers that have changed hardly at all since the mid–19th century. Each has a town clerk, listed with directory assistance, who can furnish further information. See *Scenic Drives* for suggestions on ways to thread these villages together.

Alstead. There are actually three Alsteads (pronounced *AAL-sted*), a grouping of quiet hill towns in the northwestern corner of the region not far from the Connecticut River. From the handsome old white houses and the Congregational church in **East Alstead**, Rt. 123 dips down by Lake Warren and into Mill Hollow, by 18th-century water-powered **Chase's Mill**, and by **Vilas Pool**—an unusual dammed swimming area with an elaborate island picnic spot, complete with carillon. The center of **Alstead** includes a general store and the **Shedd-Porter Memorial Library** (inquire here for the hours of the historical society), a domed, Neoclassical Revival building given by native son John Shedd. Shedd was an associate of Marshall Field, who gave an almost identical library to his

hometown of Conway. Turn left at the library and follow Hill Road up into **Alstead Center**, another hilltop cluster of old homes. The town also boasts
two covered bridges.

Dublin. The flagpole in the middle of the village sits 1,493 feet above sea level,
placed in New Hampshire's highest village center. But the best views (a mile or
so west on Rt. 101) are of Mount Monadnock rising above **Dublin Lake**. Large
old summer homes are sequestered in the greenery around the lake and on
wooded heights that enjoy this view. The original offices of *Yankee Magazine* and
The Old Farmer's Almanac are in the middle of the village, as is the "oldest public library in the United States supported by private funds."

Fitzwilliam. The buildings gathered around this handsome green include an
elegantly steepled town hall, an inviting, double-porched inn, and a number of
pillared and Federal-style homes. One of the latter is now a library, and another
is a friendly historical society called the **Amos J. Blake House** (603-585-7742;
www.fitzwilliam.org/ftblake.htm), open Memorial Day weekend–Labor Day
weekend, 1–5 and some weekends during the fall, or by appointment. Exhibits
include a law office, old-time schoolroom, military room, and a vintage-1779
fire engine.

The **town hall** was first built as a Congregational church in 1816 and then totally rebuilt after lightning struck it the following year. The spire is four tiered: a
belfry above the clock tower, then two octagonal lanterns topped by a steeple
and a weather vane. The facade below is graced by a Palladian window and slender Ionic pillars set in granite blocks quarried right in town. Of course, the bell
was cast by Paul Revere. **Laurel Lake** on the western fringe of town is a
favorite local swimming hole, and **Pinnacle Mountain**, just down the street
from the Fitzwilliam Inn, offers inviting walks in summer and cross-country skiing in winter. **Rhododendron State Park** is on the edge of town.

Francestown. Named for Governor Wentworth's wife, Francestown has an
almost feminine grace. The white-pillared, 1801 meetinghouse stands across
from the old meetinghouse at the head of a street lined on both sides by graceful
Federal-era houses. One of these is now the **George Holmes Bixby Memorial
Library** (603-547-2730), 52 Main St., with wing chairs, Oriental rugs, and a children's story corner that many a passing adult would like an excuse to curl up in;
inquire about the historical collection upstairs. Pick up a guide to local antiques
shops in the **Francestown General Store**. Contra dances are held the second
Saturday of every month in the town hall. **Crotched Mountain** is just up the
road.

Greenfield is best known for its state park, with **Otter Lake** as its centerpiece,
and for the **Crotched Mountain Rehabilitation Center**, which sits high on
the shoulder of the mountain and has spectacular views. The village itself is
appealing. The vintage-1795 **Congregational church** is the oldest meetinghouse in New Hampshire, serving as both a church and a town hall. It stands tall
with maples in front and a graveyard curving up the hill behind. The heart of the
village is **Carbee's Corner**, a store that's been in the same family since 1952,
housed in the mansard-roofed complex across from the church and a source of
penny candy and assorted gifts. The parakeets are a nice touch.

Hancock. The Hancock Inn, one of the oldest continuously operating inns in New England, forms the centerpiece of this village, and **Norway Pond** shimmers on the edge. There's also a green with a bandstand. A number of the aristocratic old homes have been occupied by "summer people" since the mid–19th century. The **Harris Center for Conservation Education** offers guided and unguided walks and workshops.

Harrisville. What excites historians about this pioneer mill village is the uncanny way in which it echoes New England's earliest villages. Here life revolved around the mills instead of the meetinghouse: The mill owner's mansion supplanted the parsonage, and the millpond was the common. What excites most other people about Harrisville is its beauty. This little community of brick and granite and white-trimmed buildings clusters around a millpond and along the steep **Goose Creek Ravine** below. The two mills have cupolas, and the string of wooden workers' houses, "Peanut Row," is tidy. Decades ago when the looms ceased weaving, townspeople worried that the village would become an industrial version of Old Sturbridge Village. Instead, new commercial uses have been found for the old buildings, a few of them appropriately filled by **Harrisville Designs**, founded by John Colony III the year after his family's mill closed. "Wool has been spun here every year since 1790," he notes.

The Hillsboroughs. This town is one of the region's more confusing areas, but it is rewarding once you figure out how it fits together. The oldest part of town, **Hillsborough Center**, is an incredibly photogenic grouping of more than a dozen late-18th- and early-19th-century houses with a church, graveyard, pond, and several open studios. It's up School Street beyond the **Fox State Forest** from **Bridge Village**, a funky mill town with an unusual number of surviving wooden mills along the Contoocook River. Note the "Dutton Twins," two Greek Revival 1850s mansions on Main Street. The **Franklin Pierce Homestead** is in **Hillsboro Lower Village** (continue west on West Main St., which is also Rt. 9, past the Sylvania bulb plant, and turn north on Rt. 31). On the banks of the Contoocook River, **Kemps Truck Museum** is said to hold the biggest collection of Mack trucks in the world. There are also two local swimming holes.

Jaffrey Center. Jaffrey itself is a workaday town, but Jaffrey Center, west on Rt. 124 just east of Mount Monadnock, is a gem. Its centerpiece is a white, steepled meetinghouse built in 1773, the site of the summer lecture series known as the **Amos Fortune Forum Series**. Willa Cather, who spent many summers in attic rooms at the Shattuck Inn writing two of her best-known books—*My Antonia* and *Death Comes to the Archbishop*—is buried in the cemetery here. So are Amos Fortune (1710–1801), an African-born slave who bought his freedom, established a tannery, and left funds for the Jaffrey church and schools, and "Aunt" Hannah Davis (1784–1863), a beloved spinster who made, trademarked, and sold this country's first wooden bandboxes. The **Melville Academy Museum**, Thorndike Pond Rd., Jaffrey Center, a Greek Revival schoolhouse built in 1833, houses an eclectic collection of Jaffrey artifacts and documents (open July and Aug., weekends 2–4). The **Inn at Jaffrey Center** marks the middle of the village. **Jaffrey Chamber of Commerce** (603-532-4549), 7 Main St., offers

10–2. Here you'll find a historical society collection with information about past Jaffrey personalities—including Willa Cather, Amos Fortune, and Hannah Davis—and changing exhibits by local artists. Note *Buddies*, the World War I monument outside, carved from a single block of granite.

Mason. Another picture-perfect cluster of Georgian- and Federal-style homes around a classic Congregational church, complete with horse sheds and linked by stone walls. A historic marker outside one modest old house explains that this was the boyhood home of Samuel Wilson (1766–1844), generally known as "Uncle Sam" because the beef he supplied to the army during the War of 1812 was branded U.S. We were lucky enough to first visit Mason with Elizabeth Orton Jones, illustrator of the Golden Book *Little Red Riding Hood*. Today the house that served as a basis for "Grandmother's House" is **Pickity Place**, an herb farm and restaurant.

Nelson. This quiet gathering of buildings includes 1841 Greek Revival and Gothic Revival churches and an early, plain-faced but acoustically fine town hall that's the site of contra dancing every Monday night.

Stoddard. Sited on a height-of-land that's said to divide the Connecticut and Merrimack River watersheds, Stoddard is known for the fine glass produced in three (long-gone) 19th-century factories. The **Stoddard Historical Society** is open Sun. 2–4 in July and Aug. **Pitcher Mountain**, with a picnic area and trailhead on Rt. 123, is a short hike yielding a spectacular view.

Temple. The common, framed by handsome old homes and a tavern (now the **Birchwood Inn**), is classic. Known for its glasswork in the 18th century, Temple is now known chiefly for its band, founded in 1799.

Wilton Center. Just off Rt. 101, but seemingly many miles away, is a ridgeline of grand old houses ranging from 18th-century to late-19th-century summer homes. Continue through the center of town, and follow signs to the **Frye's Measure Mill** (603-654-6581), a shingled, 19th-century mill, its works still water powered, that turns out Shaker-style boxes. The old Grange hall houses **Andy's Summer Playhouse** (603-654-2613), a performance camp for children 8–18, who stage productions in July and Aug.

❋ To See

Must-see: In contrast to most regions, this one offers no significant "sights" beyond Mount Monadnock itself. The beauty of the villages, the roads that connect them, and the surprises that you'll find along the way—swimming holes, antiques shops, art galleries, summer music, and small-town celebrations—are what this area is about. Peterborough is the most visitor-friendly town, good for dining and shopping.

In Keene

A small city (population: 22,500), Keene serves as shopping hub for a tristate area that includes southeastern Vermont and much of upcountry Massachusetts.

IN PETERBOROUGH

Far smaller than Keene, Peterborough (population: 5,883) serves as the dining, shopping, and entertainment hub of the eastern half of the Monadnock region. Its walkable core is **Depot Square**, a gathering of galleries, shops, and restaurants that also offers parking and riverside picnicking. The former depot itself is now a popular restaurant; the old A&P is a bookstore and café, and the Sharon Arts Center's crafts and art gallery is a destination in itself. The **Peterborough Historical Society, Museum and Archives** (603-924-3235), 19 Grove St. Open year-round Mon.–Fri. 10–4; donations accepted. An unusually large and handsome facility with an intriguing upstairs exhibit of the town's past products—from thermometers to soapstone stoves. Even a quick visit will help fill in the obviously missing buildings along Grove and Main Streets. Note the photos of the big old Tavern Hotel that stood at the head of Grove Street and in the middle of Main Street until 1965, of the depot, and of the Phoenix Cotton Mill that used to stand near the middle of town. A circa-1800 mill house has been preserved behind the museum, as well as an 1824 one-room schoolhouse, open by appointment only. A colonial kitchen can be seen in the museum, and the research library is extensive. Also check out the new **Mariposa Museum of World Culture** in the former Baptist Meeting House, 26 Main St., open in summer and fall, daily noon–4. Exhibits feature folk art, local and worldwide, with many special events. The **Aquarius Fire Museum**, located at the town fire department, houses antique fire engines and equipment.

The most interesting shopping is to be found in the **Colony Mill Marketplace**, but Keene's long **Main Street**, the widest in New England, is well worth exploring. It includes the historic houses described below as well as **Keene State College** buildings like Elliot Hall, worth stepping inside to see the Barry Faulkner mural depicting Keene's **Central Square**. Some first-rate restaurants are clustered around the square itself, site of the high-steepled **United Church of Christ** (built in 1786), the town hall, and the chamber of commerce.

Thorne-Sagendorph Gallery at Keene State College (603-358-2720), Wyman Way off Main St. at Keene State College, Keene. Open during the academic year, daily noon–4, Thu. and Fri. until 7; in summer, open Wed.–Sun. noon–4. A handsome, modern gallery. The permanent collection includes many 19th-century landscapes; there are also changing exhibits.

Historical Society of Cheshire County (603-352-1895), 246 Main St., Keene. Open Mon.–Fri. 9–4, Wed. evening until 9, Sat. 9–noon. An archival center for much of New England that features products once made in the area, including Keene and Stoddard glass. Changing exhibits are often worth checking.

COVERED BRIDGES

The Swanzey area, just south of Keene, boasts one of the densest concentrations of covered bridges east of Madison County. Our favorite is the white, red-roofed **Winchester–Ashuelot**, built in 1864 across the Ashuelot River just off Rt. 119 in Ashuelot. The 1830s **Winchester–Coombs bridge** across the Ashuelot is west of Rt. 10, 0.5 mile southwest of Westport. The 1860s **Swanzey–Slate bridge** across the Ashuelot is east of Rt. 10 at Westport. The 1830s, 155-foot **Swanzey–West Swanzey bridge** across the Ashuelot is east of Rt. 10 at West Swanzey. **Swanzey–Sawyer's Crossing**, rebuilt in 1859, bridges the Ashuelot 1 mile north of Rt. 32 at Swanzey village. The **Swanzey–Carlton bridge** across the South Branch of the Ashuelot River is east of Rt. 32, 0.5 mile south of Swanzey village. **The Swanzey Historical Museum**, Rt. 10 in West Swanzey (open mid-May–foliage season, weekdays 1–5, weekends and holidays 10–5), dispenses maps locating the covered bridges and displays a Concord Coach, an Amoskeag steam fire pumper, and much more. Off by itself 1 mile east of Rt. 202 or 3.5 miles west of Greenfield is the **Hancock–Greenfield bridge**, built in 1937, which spans the Contoocook.

WINCHESTER–ASHUELOT COVERED BRIDGE

Robert J. Kozlow

Horatio Colony House Museum (603-352-0460; www.horatiocolonymuseum
.org), 199 Main St., Keene. Open May–mid-Oct., Wed.–Sun. 11–4; winter hours
by appointment; free. A Federal-era home filled with elegant family furnishings
and souvenirs collected by Horatio and Mary Colony from their extensive travels
throughout the world. Special collections include cribbage boards, walking sticks,
Buddhas, beer steins, paperweights, and thousands of books.

The Wyman Tavern (603-357-3855), 339 Main St., Keene. Open June–Labor
Day, Thu.–Sat. 11–4, or by appointment. Maintained to represent the period
between 1770 and 1820, this was the scene of the first meeting of the trustees of
Dartmouth College under President Eleazar Wheelock in 1770. It was also from
this site that 29 of Keene's Minutemen set out for Lexington in April 1775.

HISTORIC HOUSES **The Barrett Mansion** (603-878-2517), 79 Main St. (Rt.
123), New Ipswich. Open June–mid-Oct., Sat. and Sun. tours hourly 11–4.
$4 adults, $3.50 seniors, $2 ages 12 and under. One of New England's finest
Federal-style, rural mansions, built in 1800 as a wedding gift. The bride's father
is said to have boasted that he would furnish as large a house as the groom's
father could build. Both fathers outdid themselves, and it remained in the family
until 1948. The rich furnishings are mainly Empire and Victorian, and they offer
a sense of the surprisingly early sophistication of this area. Inquire about teas
and other frequent special events. Operated by the Society for the Preservation
of New England Antiquities.

Franklin Pierce Homestead (603-478-3165), 3 miles west of town near the
junction of Rts. 9 and 31, Hillsborough. Open daily in July and Aug., 10–4 PM
Sun. 1–4; otherwise weekends only in June and Sep.; July 4 and Labor Day
10–4. Nominal admission for adults; under 18 free. This is the restored, vintage-
1804 home of the 14th president of the United States (1853–1857), the only one
from New Hampshire. The hip-roofed, twin-chimney house was built in 1804 by
Benjamin Pierce, Franklin's father, two-time New Hampshire governor. It is
beautifully restored to illustrate the gracious home Franklin knew as a boy.

FOR FAMILIES ✒ **Friendly Farm** (603-563-8444; www.friendlyfarm.com), Rt.
101, Dublin. Open daily 10–5 (weather permitting), late May–Labor Day, and
then weekends through mid-Sep. $6 adults, $5.25 children. Operated since 1965
by Allan and Bruce Fox, this 7-acre preserve is filled with barnyard animals: cows,
horses, pigs, goats, sheep, donkeys, chickens, geese, turkeys, rabbits, and a working beehive. Feeding and cuddling welcome. Don't forget your camera. (We
treasure photos of our presently 6-foot, 3-inch son feeding a Friendly Farm
goat when he was still small enough to heft.)

✒ **Stonewall Farm** (603-357-7278; www.stonewallfarm.org), 242 Chesterfield
Rd., Keene. This not-for-profit education center and working farm welcomes visitors on weekdays, 8:30–4:30; call for weekend hours and special programs. Cows
are milked at 4:30 daily, and there are hiking trails, a wetlands boardwalk, and a
learning center. No admission fee.

✒ Also see **Eccardt Farm** (603-495-3157), described under *Scenic Drive* in "The
Western Lakes." Phone the farm for directions from Antrim or Hillsborough.

SCENIC DRIVES **From the Boston area to Peterborough**. Take Rt. 119 to West Townsend and turn right over the bridge up Rt. 123, but at the first fork bear right on the unnumbered road to Mason. Then take Rt. 123 into Greenville, a classic mill village; Rt. 45 to Temple; and Rt. 101 into Peterborough.

Hinsdale to Walpole. Take Rt. 63, a high, rural road, past the entrance to **Pisgah State Park** and on up to the hilltop village of **Chesterfield**. Drive across Rt. 9 (careful: it's a major east–west highway) on up Rt. 63 past **Spofford Lake** and through Westmoreland, another vintage village, then on to **Park Hill**, a showstopper even by Monadnock village standards. Its meetinghouse was built in 1762 and a Paul Revere bell was installed in 1827; handsome early homes frame the hilltop common. At Westmoreland Depot continue north on Rt. 12 until you reach the yellow blinking lights, then go left up the hill into Walpole Village.

Walpole to Hillsborough. Take Rt. 12 to Rt. 123 and drive through **Drewsville** (another village you can fit in a photograph) to Alstead, then on through East Alstead (unless you want to check out the two covered bridges on the way to Acworth) to Marlow, a pretty village by a lake. Be sure to stop at the trailhead for **Pitcher Mountain**, because it's a quick hike to the fire tower for a panoramic view. From here the road plunges down to Stoddard and on to its Mill Village, where two adjacent general stores divide the town. Continue on along Rt. 23 to Rt. 9.

✳ To Do

BALLOONING **The Wings Group Balloon Company** (603-672-0508), 51 Knight St., Milford. Hot-air balloon rides are available in Hillsborough, home of the mid-July Hot Air Balloon Fest, from **George Seymour** (603-464-5053) and **Mary Ann Lappis** (603-478-5666).

BICYCLING The Monadnock region's many miles of back roads and widely scattered lodging places endear it to bicyclists of all abilities.

BOATING **Boat rentals** are available at **Greenfield State Park** (603-547-3497), which also offers a boat launch on Otter Lake and at **Eastern Mountain Sports** (603-924-7231) north of Peterborough on Rt. 202, handy to access points on ponds, lakes, and rivers. **Monadnock Outdoors** (603-924-9832), based at Peterborough Manor, offers guided kayaking and canoeing half- and full-day paddles on local waters.

Public boat landings can also be found (ask locally to find them) in Antrim on Franklin Pierce Lake, Gregg Lake, and Willard Pond; in Bennington on Whittemore Lake; in Dublin on Dublin Lake; in Francestown on Pleasant Pond and Scobie Lake; in Hancock on Norway Pond; in Jaffrey on Frost Pond; and in Rindge on the Contoocook River, Emerson Pond, Grassy Pond, and Pool Pond. A popular canoe route begins in Peterborough, where the Contoocook River crosses under Rt. 202, with a take-out at Powder Mill Pond in Bennington. The Audubon Society of New Hampshire's Willard Pond is rich in water wildlife.

CARRIAGE RIDES, SLEIGH RIDES, HAYRIDES **Inn at East Hill Farm** (603-242-6495), Jaffrey Rd., Troy. Sleigh rides along with cross-country skiing are offered to nonguests; also horseback riding.

Silver Ranch (603-532-7363), Rt. 124, Jaffrey. Carriage rides, hayrides, and sleigh rides are a tradition.

Sleeper Hill Farm (603-478-1100), 20 Severance Rd., Hillsborough. Horseback riding and lessons.

Stonewall Farm (603-357-7278), 243 Chesterfield Rd., Keene. Specializes in groups of 15 or more; hayrides, sleigh rides.

FISHING Anglers have discovered the Contoocook River as a source of cold-water species, especially above Hillsborough and the stretch along Rt. 202 north of Peterborough. The North Branch is stocked with trout.

Hillsborough Trout Farm (603-464-3026), 154 Old Henniker Rd., Hillsborough. Three ponds are stocked with rainbow trout; no license needed, and you can rent a rod or buy bait.

GOLF **Bretwood Golf Course** (603-352-7626; www.bretwoodgolf.com), E. Surry Rd., Keene. Two full-length 18-hole layouts, par 72; driving range, pro shop, golf carts, and snack bar. **Crotched Mountain Golf Club and Resort** (603-588-2000; www.crotchedmountaingolf.com), Rt. 47, Francestown. Eighteen holes, Donald Ross design, par 72. Full pro shop, packages including dining, lodging, and golf school. **Woodbound Inn Resort** (603-532-8341), Woodbound Rd., Jaffrey. Nine holes, rental clubs, par-3 course. **The Shattuck** (603-532-4300; www.sterlinggolf.com), 53 Dublin Rd., Jaffrey. Championship golf at the foot of Mount Monadnock.

GREYHOUND RACING **Hinsdale Greyhound Park** (603-336-5382; 1-800-NH-TRACK; www.hinsdalegreyhound.com), 688 Brattleboro Rd., Rt. 119, Hinsdale. Year-round racing, dining room, and club room.

HIKING Also see *Green Space*.

Crotched Mountain. Three trails lead to this 2,055-foot summit. The start of the Bennington Trail is marked 3 miles north of Greenfield on Rt. 31. The Greenfield Trail starts just beyond the entrance to Crotched Mountain Rehabilitation Center (also on Rt. 31). The Francestown Trail starts beyond the entrance to the former Crotched Mountain Ski Area on Rt. 47.

Harris Center for Conservation Education (603-525-3394); follow signs from Hancock village. A nonprofit land trust and education center with 7 miles of hiking trails, including two mountains with summit views; guided hikes and snowshoeing treks offered on weekends.

Long-distance trails. Hikers are advised to pick up trail maps to the following trails from the Monadnock State Park Ecocenter (see the Mount Monadnock sidebar).

Mount Monadnock (603-532-8862), Monadnock State Park. Marked from Rt. 124, just west of Jaffrey Center. **Monadnock** is reportedly Algonquian for "mountain that stands alone," and in the early 19th century the name spread from this mountain to designate every solitary prominence in the world that rises above its surroundings. To distinguish it from all others, purists now call this mountain "Grand" Monadnock. It acquired its bald summit in the 1820s (see the introduction to this chapter) and has been one of the country's most popular hiking mountains ever since. In 1885 the town of Jaffrey managed to acquire 200 summit acres, and, with the help of the Society for the Protection of New Hampshire Forests (SPNHF), which still owns 3,672 acres, much of the rest of the mountain was gradually acquired. The state park on the western side of the mountain is 900 acres. There are 40 miles of trails and half a dozen varied routes up to the 3,165-foot summit. First-timers, however, are advised to follow either the White Dot or the White Cross Trail from the state park in Jaffrey. Detailed information about the mountain is available at a small museum, the Ecocenter. There are also restrooms, a snack bar, and picnic grounds. The park and its 21-tent campground are open year-round, and 12 miles of marked, cross-country trails are maintained. Admission charge for visitors over age 11. Dogs are not permitted on the trails.

The **Metacomet Trail** is the northernmost 14 miles of a trail that theoretically leads to Meriden, Ct. The two most popular sections are Little Monadnock, accessible from the parking lot at Rhododendron State Park in Fitzwilliam, and Gap Mountain, accessible from trailheads on Rt. 124 west of Jaffrey Center from a spot just east of the Troy town dump. The trail is marked with white rectangles and is famed for its abundance of wild blueberries in July.

Monadnock–Sunapee Trail. The 47-mile, northern continuation of the Metacomet Trail, originally blazed in the 1920s by the SPNHF, was reblazed in the early 1970s by Appalachian Mountain Club volunteers. It descends Mount Monadnock on the Dublin Trail, then cuts across Harrisville, through Nelson village, up and down Dakin and Hodgeman Hills in Stoddard, up Pitcher Mountain (a rewarding stretch to hike from Rt. 123 in Stoddard), and up Hubbard Hill (prime blueberry picking). It then goes up 2,061-foot Jackson Hill, through Washington, and up through successive, high ridges in Pillsbury State Park to Sunapee. Sounds great to us, but since we've never done it, be sure to pick up a detailed trail map from the Ecocenter, which displays a topographic relief map of the entire trail.

Wapack Trail. A 21-mile ridgeline trail with many spectacular views from North Pack Monadnock in Greenfield to Mount Watatic in Massachusetts. The trail crosses roads about every 4 miles. Just west of Miller State Park on Rt. 101, turn right onto Mountain Rd., continue until the road makes a T, and then turn right. After the road turns to gravel, look for a trail to your right. You will see a parking area. A 45-minute climb here yields great views.

Willard Pond, Hancock Village, is a wildlife sanctuary with Bald Mountain on the north, surrounded by large glacial boulders. You can walk around the northern side of the pond and hike to the top of Bald Mountain, from which there is a spectacular view.

SPA **The Grand View Inn & Resort** (603-532-9880; www.thegrandviewinn .com), Rt. 124, 4.5 miles west of Jaffrey, open daily 7 AM–10 PM. Housed in a converted stable, this attractive day spa offers a full menu of services: a variety of massages, herbal, mud, and parafango wraps, as well as a steam room and sauna, great for the day after hiking.

SPECIAL PROGRAMS **Harrisville Designs** (603-827-3996; www.harrisville .com), Harrisville 03450. Open Tue.–Sat., 10–5. The weaving tradition that once shaped the life of this village continues in the Weaving Center, an old brick textile factory overlooking the original millpond. Weekend and multiday weaving workshops, as well as sessions featuring knitting, felting, and other skills, are held throughout the year; some are simply introductions to weaving, others are specialized and advanced courses. The workshops are held in the Weaving Center, and lodging is available in nearby B&Bs as well as the Cheshire Mills Boardinghouse, built in 1850 for transient weavers. Daylong workshops are also offered; request a schedule.

Sharon Arts Center (603-924-7256; www.sharonarts.org), Rt. 123, Sharon. This rebuilt facility is a venue for year-round day, weekend, and multiday courses in drawing and painting, glass, basketmaking, photography, weaving, jewelry, ceramics, and more.

The Old School, 23 Hadley Hwy., Temple 03084. A former brick schoolhouse with long windows now houses this yoga retreat center (founder Robert Moses is widely known in Ashtanga yoga circles), just off the common of a classic Monadnock village. Facilities include the Yoga Hall, a meditation hall in a separate building, and accommodations for 16 guests in dorm-style rooms with a separate bathhouse. The center is also handy to several B&Bs.

SWIMMING Although the region is spotted with clear lakes and ponds, public beaches are jealously held by towns—understandably, given their proximity to Boston. Guests at local inns and B&Bs, of course, have access to local sand and water.

In Alstead: **Vilas Pool**, just off Rt. 123. Open in summer Wed.–Sun. A dammed pool in the Cold River with bathhouse and picnic area. **Lake Warren** has swimming from the public landing.

In Greenfield: **Greenfield State Park** (603-547-3497), off Rt. 136, offers a beach that's mobbed on summer Sundays but not midweek. Modest fee.

In Hillsborough: Options include **Franklin Pierce Lake** (Manhattan Park is just off Rt. 9) and **Beard Brook** (along Beard Rd.), both at the shaded public beach and at the Glean Falls bridge.

In Jaffrey: **Contoocook Lake Beach**, a small but lovely strip of soft sand along Quantum Rd. east of the junction of Rts. 124 and 202 (take Stratton Rd. to Quantum), and **Sciatic Park Beach** on Thorndike Pond near the main entrance to Monadnock State Park are both open to nonresidents; weekend fee.

In Rindge: **Pearly Pond** adjacent to the Franklin Pierce College campus is good for swimming and picnicking.

In Roxbury: **Otter Brook Recreation Area**, Rt. 9, northwest of Keene. A human-made lake with lawns and sandy beach that can fill the bill on a hot day. Fee.

In Spofford: **Spofford Lake**, Rt. 9. Town-run beach.

In Surry: **Surry Mountain Dam and Lake**, Rt. 12A not far north of Keene, offers a sand beach, as well as picnicking. Free.

In Swanzey: **Swanzey Lake** and **Wilson Pond**.

✳ Winter Sports

SLEIGH RIDES See *Carriage Rides, Sleigh Rides, Hayrides*, under *To Do*, above.

DOWNHILL SKIING Crotched Mountain (603-588-3668; www.crotched mountain.com), 615 Francestown Rd., Bennington. A newly reopened family ski area featuring five lifts including two quad chairs, automated snowmaking system, night skiing, and a brand-new 40,000-square-foot lodge with open-style food court and well-equipped, self-serve rental center. Sunday Family Night (4–7 PM) offers ticket, ski rental, and introductory clinic for $25.

CROSS-COUNTRY SKIING Also see *Green Space*.

Windblown (603-878-2869), Rt. 124 west of the village, New Ipswich. Open Thu.–Sun. and holidays. Since 1972 Al and Irene Jenks have been constantly expanding and improving their high, wooded spread that straddles the Wapack Trail. Thanks to the elevation and northerly exposure, this 40-km network frequently has snow when the ground is bare just 10 miles away. There's an unusual variety to the trails: easy loops from the ski shop and around Wildlife Pond; wooded, more difficult trails up on the Wapack; backcountry trails, including a climb to Mount Watatic (1,800 feet high);

WELL-GROOMED TRAILS WIND THROUGH WOODLANDS AT WINDBLOWN CROSS-COUNTRY SKI AREA

and a long, 75-foot-wide, open slope for practicing telemarking. Homemade soups, sandwiches, spiced cider, and home-baked munchies are served at the shop; there's a warming hut and a couple of cabins. Rentals, instruction. Trail fee.

The Inn at East Hill Farm (603-242-6495), Jaffrey Rd., Troy. Some 13 miles of trails meander gently around this property with its great view of Mount Monadnock. Rentals and instruction are offered, and informal meals are available at the inn. A warming hut on the trail, with fireplace and woodstove, serves hot drinks on weekends. Trail fee.

Sargent Center (603-525-3311), Windy Row, Peterborough. A dozen miles of cross-country trails web this 850-acre property maintained by Boston University.

Woodbound Inn (603-532-8341), Jaffrey. Fourteen kilometers of wooded trails; rental equipment. Trail fee.

Mount Monadnock State Park (603-532-8862), Dublin Rd. from Rt. 124, Jaffrey Center. A 12-mile, well-marked but ungroomed system of trails webs the base of the mountain; loops from 1 mile to more than 7 miles. Winter camping is also available. Entrance fee. No dogs allowed.

✳ Green Space

Also see *Hiking* and *Swimming* under *To Do*.

In the Keene area
Bear Den Geological Park, Rt. 10, Gilsum. Look for a large pull-off area on the right (heading north). This is a geologically fascinating area, with glacial potholes, caves, and ledges believed to have once been a denning area for bears.

Cathedral of the Pines (603-899-3300; www.virtualnh.com/cathedralpines), marked from Rt. 119, a few miles east of Rt. 202, Rindge. Open for an Easter sunrise service, then May–Oct., 9–5. Tall pine trees shelter simple wooden benches, and the backdrop of the ridgetop stone altar is Mount Monadnock, rising grandly beyond intervening, heavily wooded hills. The roadside farmhouse and its 400 acres had been the summer home of Douglas and Sibyl Sloane for quite some time before the 1938 hurricane exposed this magnificent view, and their son Sandy picked the site for his future home. When Sandy was shot down over Germany in 1944, his parents dedicated the hilltop "cathedral" to his memory. In 1956 the U.S. Congress recognized it as a national memorial to all American war dead. It's used for frequent nondenominational services and for weddings (performed in the nearby stone Hilltop House in case of rain). On the stone Memorial Bell Tower at the entrance to the pine grove, four bronze bas-reliefs, designed by Norman Rockwell, honor American women. A museum in the basement of the Hilltop House is a mix of religious and military pictures and artifacts, thousands of items donated by visitors from throughout the country. Visitors are welcome to stroll the extensive grounds. Please: No dogs, no smoking, no picnicking (the Annett Wayside Area is a mile up the road). The **Cathedral House Bed & Breakfast** (603-899-6790) caters wedding receptions and is otherwise geared to the many weddings in the adjoining "cathedral." During July and Aug., outdoor organ meditations are scheduled Mon.–Fri. 10–2, weather permitting. Ecumenical services.

Charles L. Pierce Wildlife and Forest Reservation, Stoddard. From Rt. 9 in Stoddard, follow Rt. 123 north approximately 2 miles; turn right at the fire station; cross the bridge. At the junction go straight on a dirt road approximately 1 mile; park in the lot 300 feet beyond the woods road, on the left. The 5-mile Trout-n-Bacon Trail, beginning at a small brook to the left of the road, offers outstanding views from Bacon Ledge and leads to Trout Pond. This is a 3,461-acre preserve with more than 10 miles of hiking trails and woods roads that wind over ridges, through deep forest, and around beaver dams. The Society for the Protection of New Hampshire Forests (SPNHF) also owns the 379-acre Thurston V. Williams Forest and the 157-acre Daniel Upton Forest in Stoddard.

Chesterfield Gorge 603-239-8153), Rt. 9, Chesterfield. Open weekends. Footpaths along the gorge were carved by a stream that cut deep into ledges. The 0.75-mile trail crosses the stream several times, and there are plenty of picnic tables within sound and sight of the rushing water. Volunteers staff the Park Visitor Center, which houses a logging tool collection and displays of local mammals.

Horatio Colony Trust, off Daniels Rd. (take a left 0.5 mile west of the blinking light on Rt. 9), Keene. A 450-acre bird and animal preserve with marked trails through the woods.

Piper Memorial Forest, off Rt. 9, East Sullivan. A 199-acre wooded SPNHF property traversed by a loop trail to the top of Boynton Hill.

Pisgah State Park (603-239-8153), Chesterfield, Hinsdale, Winchester, with entrances off Rts. 9, 10, 63, and 119). A 13,500-acre, largely undeveloped area with pit toilets and old logging trails (good for hiking, hunting, and cross-country skiing), plus ponds to satisfy the adventurous angler. Parking and maps at all six major trailheads. No camping or fires allowed.

Rhododendron State Park (603-239-8153), Rt. 119 west of the village, Fitzwilliam. $3 day-use fee; children 11 and under are free. The wild rhododendrons grow up to 30 feet high and are salted along paths above wildflowers and ferns and under pine trees. It is one of those deeply still and beautiful places. These rhododendrons reach maximum bloom in mid-July. A great place for a picnic.

In the Peterborough and eastern Monadnock area

Fox State Forest (603-464-3453), Center Rd., Hillsborough. Twenty miles of trails within 1,445 acres of woodland. A detailed booklet guide is available from the state's Division of Forests Office in Concord.

Gap Mountain Reservation, Jaffrey. From Troy, follow Rt. 12 south 0.4 mile; turn left onto Quarry Rd.; continue past transmission lines. At a sharp left in the road, a woods road continues straight uphill. Park and hike up the hill. Near the top, trail markers bear left through the woods. Gap Mountain is a favorite with berriers and picnickers. The 1,107-acre preserve includes three peaks, two bays, and a rich variety of plants and wildlife.

Greenfield State Park (603-547-3497), Rt. 136, 1 mile west of Greenfield. Admission $3; children under 11 are free. A 401-acre preserve with 0.5-mile frontage on Otter Lake; 252 tent sites access their own beach. Snowmobiling and cross-country skiing in winter.

The Heald Tract, off Rt. 31 in Wilton. A Society for the Protection of New Hampshire Forests (SPNHF) preserve with fairly flat trails, pond views.

MacDowell Reservoir (603-924-3431), Peterborough. Good for picnicking, boating, and fishing. Maintained by the U.S. Army Corps of Engineers.

McCabe Forest, Antrim. Take Rt. 202 north from Antrim for 0.2 mile; turn right onto Elm St. Extension; turn right to the parking area. This former 192-acre farm has 2 miles of trails, including a fine self-guided interpretive trail, and a variety of wildlife.

Monadnock State Park (603-532-8862), off Rt. 124 or Dublin Rd., west of Jaffrey. In addition to the most-climbed mountain in North America, this park offers 40 miles of New England's most popular trails, as well as 21 tent sites, picnic grounds, a visitors center, a park store, and ski-touring trails. Admission charged; pets not permitted.

Otter Brook Dam and Lake (Roxbury, Keene). There's picnicking and swimming with a sandy beach and lawns at this human-made lake. Free admission.

Pack Monadnock Mountain in Miller State Park (603-924-7433), Rt. 101, 3 miles east of Peterborough. Admission $3; children 11 and under are free. For those who don't feel up to climbing Mount Monadnock, this 2,300-foot-high summit is a must. A 1.5-mile winding, steep, but paved road leads to the top, where there are walking trails, picnic sites, and views of Vermont to the west and (on a good day) Boston skyscrapers to the south. Opened in 1891, this was New Hampshire's first state park.

Pierce Island State Park (Spofford Lake). This 5-acre island, densely wooded with hemlocks, lies less than a mile from the state boat landing. No facilities.

✿ **Shieling Forest**, off Old St. Rd., Peterborough (marked from Rt. 202 north of town). This is one place you can walk your dog. There are 45 acres of tree-covered ridges and valleys, and a forestry learning center.

✳ Lodging

INNS

In and around Keene
✿ **Chesterfield Inn** (603-256-3211; 1-800-365-5515; www.chesterfield inn.com), Rt. 9, West Chesterfield 03466. The original house served as a tavern from 1798 to 1811, but the present facility is a luxurious contemporary country hotel with a large, attractive dining room overlooking sweeping views of the Connecticut River Valley and the Green Mountains of Vermont, a spacious parlor,

and 15 guest rooms scattered between the main house and the Guest House. All rooms have a sitting area, phone, controlled heat or air-conditioning, and optional TV and wet bar; some have working fireplace or Jacuzzi. Innkeepers Phil and Judy Hueber have created a popular dining room (see *Dining Out*) and a comfortable, romantic getaway spot that's well positioned for exploring much of southern Vermont as well as the Monadnock region and Connecticut River Valley. The inn is set back from busy Rt. 9, much closer to Brattleboro, Vermont, than to Keene. $150–250 double ($110, single occupancy weekdays) includes breakfast; $25 higher during foliage season and holiday weekends. Inquire about MAP rates. Pets are accepted with advance permission.

& **E. F. Lane Hotel** (603-357-7070; 1-888-300-5056; www.someplaces different.com), 30 Main St., Keene 03431. Shop till you drop in downtown Keene, then mosey on into what was once Goodnow's, known for a century as the area's finest department store. A member of the Someplace(s) Different hotel chain, this stately 1890 brick and granite structure is now doing a star turn as the city's most luxurious "inn" spot. Its 31 rooms and nine suites vary in size from large to two-story Chairman Suites suitable for a small household. Although no two are alike, each is furnished in elegant period style and is equipped with high-speed Internet access, computer/fax modems, and individual temperature control. Many suites offer whirlpool tub and separate sitting room. The Salmon Chase Bistro (see *Dining Out*) offers a light breakfast buffet, included in the $139–194 room rate. Check for corporate and group rates. Children welcome; wheelchair access.

🐾 ✂ **Inn at East Hill Farm** (603-242-6495; 1-800-242-6495; www .east-hill-farm.com), 460 Monadnock St., Troy 03465. This isn't a fancy place, but over the years (since 1973) David and Sally Adams have created a lively, friendly family resort. The core of the complex is an 1830s inn with a fireplace in its living room and a large dining room in which meals are

served at individual small tables; it's frequently cleared for square dances and other events. In all there are now 70 guest rooms and family units, all with private bath. Facilities include an indoor and two outdoor pools, a lake beach, tennis, shuffleboard, and boats. Water-skiing, horseback riding, and a children's program are also available, and the barn is filled with animals. $90–100 per person plus 15 percent gratuity; children's rates; all three meals are included, and weekly rates are available. Credit cards are accepted but not for gratuities.

Note: At this writing the landmark **Fitzwilliam Inn** in Fitzwilliam is closed, awaiting new ownership.

In and around Peterborough

& **The Hancock Inn** (603-525-3318; 1-800-525-1789; www.hancockinn .com), 33 Main St., Hancock 03449. Built in 1789 and the state's oldest, this inn has a late-19th-century look, thanks to two-story pillars and a mansard roof. We arrived on a midsummer evening and, after a rum punch in the tavern, attended a free concert of classic blues just outside on a picture-perfect village green before returning to the inn's elegant, deep cranberry-colored dining room for dinner. Innkeeper Robert Short offers 15 guest rooms (all with private bath, some with Jacuzzi), with elegantly classic country inn decor: canopy and four-poster beds, handmade quilts, braided and hooked rugs, rockers, wingback chairs, and several fireplaces. One room is decorated with genuine Rufus Porter murals, and authentic 1830s stencil patterns decorate many of the other rooms as well. Both the tavern room, which serves light meals in the evening, and the dining room (see *Dining Out*), are

Robert J. Kozlow

THE HANCOCK INN, ONE OF THE COUNTRY'S OLDEST CONTINUOUSLY OPERATING INNS, FORMS A CENTERPIECE FOR HANCOCK VILLAGE

open to the public. $120–250 double; no smoking, no children under 12.

Inn at Jaffrey Center (603-532-7800; 1-877-510-7019; www.theinn atjaffreycenter.com). Under ownership by Noel and Stephen Pierce and his brother Max Mitchell, this fine old landmark (formerly the Monadnock Inn) has blossomed. The 11 rooms, all upstairs, have been deftly, tastefully decorated in soft, pleasing colors, each different and varying widely in size but all with private bath. The old plumbing has been retained: Claw-foot tubs have been glazed and sinks refitted. Furnishings are a mix of antiques and reproductions. The food is superb, too (see *Dining Out*), but we lament the loss of the parlor, now another dining room. While families are welcome and some guest rooms are quite large (there's also a two-room suite), shared space is limited to the tavern and dining areas. Room rates range $65–150, depending on season. There are also off-peak mid-week specials, with any room $60 per night, first come, first choice (Sun.–Thu. evenings only).

The Grand View Inn & Resort (603-532-9880; www.thegrandview inn.com), 580 Mountain Rd., Jaffrey 03452. The inn itself is a white brick mansion set off in its own 330 acres at the base of Mount Monadnock. The former stables, just below the inn, have been transformed into a spa facility, with a full menu of treatments, and **Churchill's**, a restaurant open to the public (see *Dining Out*). Common space includes formal living and dining rooms, a large screened porch, and a breakfast room. Guest rooms, divided between the mansion and the neighboring "Tom Thumb cottage," are pleasant but we think a bit high for what they are at $100–125 for the three smallest rooms (two with shared bath), $170–175 for the remaining five, and $250 for a suite with a sitting room, fireplace, and bath with Jacuzzi and steam shower. Facilities include a pool, outdoor hot tub, and game and smoking rooms. Weddings are a specialty. Horses can be boarded in the stables across the road.

🍴 **The Birchwood Inn** (603-878-3285; www.thebirchwoodinn.com),

340 Rt. 45, P.O. Box 23, Temple 03084. Henry Thoreau is counted among past guests at this small brick inn, now on the National Register of Historic Places. Built around 1800 in the center of a tiny back-road village, today the inn is owned by two Brits, Andrew and Nick, and their American partner, Trish. Since purchasing the hostelry in 2004, the trio have set about renovating the six guest rooms (five with private bath), furnishing each with authentic items from various English cities. Even the beds, including linens and hangings, have been imported. Downstairs, there's a cheerful pub and a fine little dining room with 1820s murals by Rufus Porter (see *Dining Out*). $74–99 double, breakfast included; single rates also offered.

☀ ✍ **Woodbound Inn** (603-532-8341; 1-800-688-7770; www.wood bound.com), 62 Woodbound Rd., Rindge 03461. A rambling old inn complex set in 200 wooded acres on Contoocook Lake. Owned now by the Kohlmorgan family, it caters to groups and families. More than half of the 44 units are motel style in a newer annex (preferable to rooms in the main inn), and there are 11 lakeside cabins with fireplace. Facilities include a nine-hole par-3 USGA-sanctioned golf course, cross-country ski trails and rentals, and a private beach. Pets permitted in cabins. $99–109 for rooms; cabins run $145–215. Rates include three full meals.

BED & BREAKFASTS

In and around Keene
✍ **Hannah Davis House** (603-585-3344); www.hannahdavishouse.com, 106 Rt. 119, Fitzwilliam 03447. Kaye and Mike Terpstra have turned an

1820s Federal-style house into an outstanding bed & breakfast. Guests enter through a cheery, light- and flower-filled country kitchen and gather in the sitting and breakfast rooms or on the deck overlooking a beaver pond. All three of the upstairs bedrooms have been nicely furnished. Our favorite is Chauncey's Room, with bold colors, a queen-sized, antique iron bed, and a working fireplace. There is also a downstairs suite with a king bed and working wood-burning fireplace. The most sumptuous accommodation (great for a family) is, however, to the rear of the house. Named Popovers, it has a private entrance, deck, vaulted ceiling, and wall of windows overlooking the beaver pond, also a wood-burning fireplace, antique cannonball bed (a queen), and sleeper sofa. The original carriage house is called the Loft, a romantic hideaway with its own entrance, a sitting room with fireplace and a bath downstairs, and a loft-style sleeping area. $80–165 per room includes an extravagant breakfast.

✍ **The Carriage Barn Guest House** (603-357-3812; www.carriage barn.com), 358 Main St., Keene 03431. Dave Rouillard, a retired fifth-grade teacher, is the enthusiastic host of this B&B attached to the back of a large home just past the college on the southern end of Keene's Main St. His librarian wife, Marilee, knows the area well and can direct you to downtown shops, movies, restaurants, and a host of nearby activities. Behind their large home, a converted Civil War–era barn now holds four guest rooms, each with private bath, a large sitting room with TV and phone, and a sunny breakfast room. $65–100 double includes tax as well as a continental "plus" breakfast. Children over 5 are welcome.

🌢 **Darby Brook Farm** (603-835-6624; 347 Hill Rd., Alstead 03602.) Open May–Oct. Alstead is in the little-touristed northwestern corner of the region, handy to canoeing on the Connecticut River; there's also a choice of swimming holes in town. Howard Weeks has summered all his life in this Federal-style house that's been changed little by the three families who have owned it since the 1790s. Weeks has devoted his retirement to maintaining the house and its 10-acre hay field, the apple orchard above the field, and the berry bushes and sizable vegetable garden just behind the house. He also takes care of a few chickens. The two large front rooms share a bath but have working fireplaces, set in their original paneling, and the $40-per-person rate includes tax as well as a full breakfast, served in the elegant old dining room.

Goose Pond Guest House (603-357-4787; www.goosepondguest house.com), E. Surry Rd. (2 miles north of Central Square, past the hospital off Court St., and 0.6 mile before Bretwood Golf Course), Keene 03431. Set on a knoll along a pretty country road, this 15-room vintage-1790 Colonial is a classic. There are three guest rooms, each furnished stylishly in period antiques. One is a suite with its own entrance, fridge, woodstove, and private terrace. Depending on the season, you can hike, swim, or skate at nearby Goose Pond; golf at the 27-hole course next door; or simply amble the surrounding 13 acres. The $85–125 rate for two ($20 for a third person) includes continental breakfast in the formal

dining room. Nonsmoking. Children over 6 are welcome.

⚡ **Green Meadow Nature Escape** (603-835-6580; www.tamarackfarm .com), 561 Rt. 123A, Alstead 03602; mail: Box 215, Alstead 03602. Six generations have owned and operated this family farm. Now Tim and Clare Gowen have decided to "share the beautiful land with others" by opening a bed & breakfast for folks with a hankering to get back to nature. In early spring that means boiling maple syrup; in late summer, harvesting hay. The newly renovated house offers five guest rooms, each with private bath (some with whirlpool) and views of the hills and meadows. For the best view of all, enjoy an afternoon on the deck in the hot tub or, for the more adventuresome, a tube ride down Cold River. The pool is up the hill. Rates, $95–170, include a farm-fresh breakfast—naturally.

⚡ **Inn of the Tartan Fox** (603-357-9308; 1-877-836-4319; www.tartan fox.com), 350 Old Homestead Hwy., Swanzey 03446. Once known as Meademere, this Arts & Crafts–style stone cottage, with its mahogany woodwork and cobblestone fireplace, is an unexpected architectural surprise. Owners Meg Kupiec and Wayne Miller offer four guest rooms, each appointed with Eastlake-era antiques and a signature tartan plaid. Private bathrooms boast heated marble floors. One, which opens onto a terrace, has a shower wide enough for a wheelchair. The four-course breakfast, included in the $90–150 rate (for two), is an elegant affair.

🐾 **Stonewall Farm** (603-478-1947), 235 Windsor Rd., Hillsborough 03244. Halfway between Concord and Keene, this imposing farmhouse is two minutes off Rt. 9 and two centuries off the beaten track. Built in 1785, the house crowns a quiet ridge, looking much the same as it probably did when neighbors Franklin Pierce (the only New Hampshire native to serve as president) and his father, Benjamin, used to come to call. Current owners Skip and Meg Curtis have researched the home's history. Nearly every room has a framed document or photo relating to the past. One summer day when we visited, the house was cool. It was equally inviting in February when the Glenwood stove in the big country kitchen was the obvious congregating spot. The five guest rooms, each with private bath, are pleasant and furnished with antiques, featuring antique linens and quilts. The 6 acres of grounds include walking paths, raspberry bushes, and the possibility of a game of croquet, horseshoes, or volleyball. Meg is a serious cook who throws her all into breakfast, included in $85–175 double. Crated, trained dogs are welcome.

🐾 ❦ **The Maples of Poocham** (603-399-8457; 1-800-659-6810; www.themaplesofpoocham.com), 283 Poocham Rd., Westmoreland 03467. Where's Waldo? Find Larry McFarland's furry golden retriever friend and you'll have found this cozy retreat located on a back road off Rt. 63. When we visited one cold day in February, Waldo beckoned along with a group of hanging lanterns on the porch. In summer you might find an upturned canoe, wicker rockers, and hanging planters. Inside, bright colors and books continue the genial atmosphere. Two upstairs bedrooms share a bath across the hall. Weekdays, there's cereal, muffins,

fruit, and coffee laid out in the dining room; on weekends, owner Larry is around to cook pancakes, eggs, or French toast. He'll also give directions to hiking trails and the nearby heron rookery. Rates range $50–70, depending on season. Pets are welcome with advance notice and deposit.

Ashburn House (603-585-7198; www.ashburnhouse.net), 20 Upper Troy Rd., Fitzwilliam 03447. This lovely inn, just off classic Fitzwilliam common with its many antiques shops, is operated by Carole and Ken Beckwith. Three guest rooms, all with private bath and two with fireplace, are furnished with color and flair, including antiques and artifacts from the innkeepers' travels. There are both formal and informal parlors, one with board games and a piano; the other with TV, VCR, and DVD. The dining room with fireplace and candelabra is the perfect spot for a full Irish- or Yankee-style breakfast, included in the room rate. Rates are $60–95, depending on season. Children welcome.

The Little House (603-585-3023; www.cmfarm.com), 325 Richmond Rd., Fitzwilliam 03447. The Little House is a separate two-story cottage located just past Crescent Moon Farm on a road through the woods between Richmond and Fitzwilliam. Andrew and Sherri Walters have renovated the country Victorian building, adding a slate roof and dormers, Rumford fireplace, wraparound porch overlooking the flower garden, and new 1920s-style kitchen complete with icebox and Glenwood stove. The house, rented by the week or weekend only, is a perfect haven for a private getaway or honeymoon. Rates are $150–170. Fix your own breakfast or ask to have it delivered.

In and around Peterborough

🌸 **Apple Gate B&B** (603-924-6543), 199 Upland Rd., Peterborough 03458. Ken and Dianne Legenhausen's 1832 house sits beside an apple orchard not far from the Sharon Arts Center. It's all very tasteful yet cozy—the double parlor, fireplace, and piano in the living room, and the low-beamed dining room. All four guest rooms, ranging from an inviting single in the back to spacious doubles (one with twin beds), have private bath. Rooms are named for apples (we particularly like the sunny Cortland Room), which also figure in breakfast dishes—like baked apple with spinach pie or baked apple pancakes. Many small touches, like the fridge under the stairs, make guests feel welcome. $75–90 double includes a full candlelit breakfast. No children under 12 and no smoking, please.

🌸 🐾 ✎ **Auk's Nest** (603-878-3443; auksnest@cs.com), 204 East Rd., Temple 03084. Anne Lunt's 1770s Cape sits at the edge of an apple orchard. It's filled with books and antiques, and offers a low-beamed living room with a Rumford fireplace and three guest rooms, two baths. A country breakfast is served in a sunny, stenciled dining room looking out on gardens and an orchard or, in summer, on the screened-in porch overlooking a meadow. Walks, tennis, swimming, and skiing are all within minutes. Both pets and children are welcome by prior arrangement. From $60 single to $135 double, full breakfast included.

🌸 🐾 **Peterborough Manor Bed & Breakfast** (603-924-9832; www .peterboroughmanor.com), 50 Sum-

mer St., Peterborough 03458. Over the years the Harrisons restored this 1890s Victorian mansion, creating a reasonably priced B&B catering to outdoorspeople. The eight rooms, each with private bath, are unusually large and comfortable; most have both a double and a single bed and phone. Some have cable TV. The kitchen is available for those who want to make their own meals, but Peterborough's many dining options are just down the street. Ann comes from an old local innkeeping family and is an avid hiker knowledgeable about local trails and biking routes. She's even authored a guide. Under the name **Monadnock Outdoors**, she offers guided half- and full-day kayak trips. Continental breakfast is included in the $75–85 rate; $10 per extra person. Children over 7 accepted.

Three Maples B&B (603-924-3503; www.threemaples.com), Rt. 123, Sharon 03458. Directly across from the Sharon Art Center, a fine old country home dating in part to 1795, set behind three, century-old sugar maples. Linda and Dan Claff have created an appealing haven with three guest rooms. One downstairs, furnished in white cottage furniture and a brightly quilted bed, has a two-person sauna as well as a bath. Upstairs are two more nicely furnished rooms, one with a four-poster canopy queen and an extra-deep jet tub. The living room and two of the guest rooms feature gas fireplaces. A full breakfast is included in the $80–115 rates.

✎ **The Benjamin Prescott Inn** (603-532-6637; www.benjamin prescottinn.com), Rt. 124, East Jaffrey 03452. This stately, 1850s Greek Revival farmhouse has been meticulously restored. Each of the 10 guest rooms has a private bath and charm of its own, and a few of the rooms, especially the upstairs suite with views out across the fields, are ideal for honeymooners. A downstairs suite with two bedrooms and a sitting room is ideal for families. A full breakfast is served in the large, attractive combination dining room/sitting room. $85–165 double. No children under 12.

Eastern Monadnock region

☀ ✿ ♿ **The Inn at Crotched Mountain** (603-588-6840; www.virtual -cities.com), Mountain Rd., off Rt. 47, Francestown 03043. The 1822 brick farmhouse is now a centerpiece for wooden wings, but it still contains a gracious parlor and two dining rooms. The Pine Room also serves as a small gathering space for guests. The real beauty of this place is its setting at 1,300 feet, high on a ridge with sweeping views. Three of the 13 rooms have working fireplaces, and 8 have private bath. Amenities include a pool, sited to take advantage of the view, tennis courts, and cross-country skiing. $70–140 double, including full breakfast served 8–9; holidays and foliage season, $20 more. Pets $5. Closed Apr. and first 3 weeks of Nov.

✿ ☀ **Stepping Stones Bed & Breakfast** (603-654-9048; 1-888-654-9048; www.steppingstonesbb .com), Bennington Battle Trail, Wilton Center 03086. This remarkable house—flower and sun filled, at once unusually cozy and airy—is hidden away in a bend off a back road that leads to a picture-perfect old village. Guests enter through a skylit kitchen/ sitting room that is one of the most pleasant we know. The three upstairs guest rooms are small but cheerful, one with a queen, one with a double, and one with twin beds, all with hand-

woven rugs and throws and down comforters; all with private bath. A full breakfast is served in the solar garden room, with its many books and plants. There's a fireplace and a weaving room. The gardens are inviting and extensive, reflecting Ann Carlsmith's training and skill in landscape design. "There's no soil so I use a lot of weavers," she explains about the intensity of the front of the house; the back is terraced, graced with several unusual trees, and usually filled with birds. Breakfast is served on the porch or terrace, weather permitting. $75–85 double occupancy; full, imaginative breakfast included. Inquire about the nearby waterfall. Pets and children accepted.

♦ **The Greenfield Inn** (603-547-6327; www.greenfieldinn.com), Greenfield 03047. Vic and Barbara Mangini have turned this Victorian village mansion into a romantic bed & breakfast. There's a woodstove and organ in the parlor, and each of the nine guest rooms has its own name and lacy decor; all rooms are furnished with antiques and 1890s touches. If the Casanova Room with its delicate pink lace spread isn't your style, you can opt for the smaller, less frilly rooms, which are perfectly comfortable (we like Sweet Violet's). All rooms have TV, and there's a "guest pantry" with sodas and munchies. Breakfast is a party, with crystal, china, and Mozart. Rates are $49–79 per room, $149–159 for the suite with a hot tub and Jacuzzi; breakfast is included. Ask about special packages. Children accepted.

Zahn's Alpine Guest House (603-673-2334; 1-888-745-0051; www.inter condesign.com/zahns), Rt. 13 North, P.O. Box 75, Milford 03055. This alpine chalet, located in the woods down a long drive off the main drag between Milford and Mont Vernon, doesn't just look as if it's been transplanted from Bavaria; in a sense, it has. Longtime importers Bud and Anne Zahn had the post-and-beam structure built to European standards with balcony and overhanging roof, then furnished it with a sea container full of antique farm tables, chairs, linens and accessories and European-sized twin beds that can be pushed together to form an oversized double. The Stube, with its massive *Kachelofen* (tile oven), is the heart of the house, a comfortable sitting room/ kitchen where you are encouraged to serve yourself breakfast or even bring in your own supper to reheat in the microwave. Many European guests regard it as a home away from home. Eight rooms, each with private bath, rent for $65 per person single occupancy, $37.50 per person double (tax and breakfast included). A small additional fee provides access to the full health/fitness facilities of nearby Hampshire Hills.

OTHER LODGING ❦ **Crestwood Chapel & Pavilion** (603-239-6393; www.crestwood-e.com), 400 Scofield Mountain Rd., Ashuelot 03441. Location, location—and not just one but many. The entry allée of maples could be in France; the out-of-sight accommodations suggest a tropical paradise; and the view is pure New England. That much, at least, is no surprise, considering that this 200-acre estate sits in the absolute southwest corner of New Hampshire. Owner Gary O'Neal describes the spot atop Scofield Mountain as 1 mile straight up from the covered bridge in the mill village of Ashuelot (pronounced *ash-WHEEL-it*). Because there are no other mountains immediately around, the summit commands a view west across the Connecticut Valley to the Green Mountains of Vermont and south down the Pioneer Valley to the Holyoke Range in Massachusetts. The chapel, occupying the center of the formal grounds, was built by Cyrus Ingersol Scofield, who was the personal chaplain to famous 19th-century evangelist Dwight Moody, founded the schools that are now Northfield Mount Hermon, and built a big (long-vanished) summer hotel in nearby Northfield, Massachusetts. For more than 20 years O'Neal, owner of a mill in Ashuelot, an avid cook, and also a justice of the peace, has been gradually transforming the estate into a retreat geared to weddings and small meetings. His own house includes handsome common spaces and guest rooms; the Pavilion, a marble-floored cottage in the gardens, is its own luxurious retreat, with a vast living room, Jacuzzi, and full kitchen. The chapel has also been expanded to include guest rooms but continues to be a venue for weddings, as are the gardens. The entire compound accommodates just 12. Rates start at $250 per night for the Pavilion, breakfast included. Inquire about rates for groups and for individual rooms.

Naulakha (802-257-7783; www.land marktrustusa.org), c/o The Landmark Trust, 707 Kipling Rd., Dummerston, VT 05301. Just across the river in Brattleboro, with views east across the hills to Mount Monadnock, this house is the one English novelist Rudyard Kipling built in 1893. It is 90 feet long but just 22 feet wide, designed to resemble a ship riding the hillside like a wave. At 26 years old, Kipling was already one of the world's best-known writers, and the two following years that he spent here were among the happiest in his life. Here he wrote *The Jungle Books*. Here the local doctor, James Conland, a former fisherman, inspired him to write *Captains Courageous* and also delivered his two daughters. Kipling's guests included Sir Conan Doyle, who brought with him a pair of Nordic skis, said to be the first in Vermont. The home has been painstakingly restored by the nonprofit Landmark Trust and is available for rent by the week or, sometimes, the night (3-night minimum). More than half the furnishings—including a third-floor pool table—actually belonged to the Kiplings. There are four bedrooms, ample baths (old fixtures, new plumbing), a full kitchen, and 55 acres. Available for a minimum of 3 nights at $250–335 per night or 1 week ($1,150–3,000) depending on the season.

♨ The Jack Daniels Motor Inn (603-924-7548; www.jackdaniels motorinn.com), Rt. 202 north, Peterborough 03458. An attractive 17-room motel, nicely furnished in cherry with all the comforts: climate control, remote control cable, and WiFi access. It's just north of town on busy Rt. 202 but positioned with its side to the road to minimize noise. $87–119, depending on season, number of persons, and day of week. Pets allowed in some rooms.

CAMPGROUNDS **Monadnock State Park** (603-532-8862) offers 21 sites. See *Green Space.*

Greenfield State Park (603-547-3497) offers 252 tent sites, handy to a public beach and nature trails.

Note: Private campground listings are available from the sources listed under *Guidance.*

✳ Where to Eat
DINING OUT

In and around Keene
₺ Luca's Mediterranean Café (603-358-3335), 10 Central Square, Keene. Open for lunch (11:30–2) and dinner (5–9) Mon.–Thu.; Fri. and Sat. 5–10. Also Sun. in summer 5–8 PM. Be prepared for a culinary journey with this menu that translates the flavors of the Mediterranean from simple Italian to elegant French to hearty Moroccan fare. Entrées range from $12.95–16.95. Their signature pasta is rigatoni à la segreta with grapes, artichoke hearts, roasted peppers, and Gorgonzola for $13.95; tilapia with yellow peppers, grape tomatoes, champagne, and cilantro served over Israeli couscous is $16.95. Dine alfresco when weather permits.

₺ Nicola's Trattoria (603-355-5242), 39 Central Square, Keene. Open for dinner Tue.–Sun. 5–9; Fri. and Sat. until 10. With its open kitchen, chef Nicola Bencivenga's handsome trattoria is probably the most elegant, yet cheerful, in town. The reasonably priced dinner menu is studded with pasta dishes like ziti della casa (chicken sautéed in olive oil with broccoli rabe, arugula, and portobello mushrooms) or osso buco (thick veal shank simmered with onions, tomato, carrots, celery, and fresh Italian herbs). Everything is made to order with fresh ingredients, and you can taste it. Reservations are recommended, but walk-ins can usually be accommodated.

One Seventy-Six Main (603-357-3100), 176 Main St., Keene. Open 11:30 AM–10 PM daily; Sat. until 11. Brunch Sat. and Sun. 11–3. Casual gourmet dining, friendly, warm ambience, walls hung with works by local artists, a wide selection of beers on tap and bottled. Features daily specials along with such house favorites as fish-and-chips for $10.95. Entrées, from sesame tofu stir-fry for $15.45 to surf and turf for $23.95, are served all day, along with wraps, sandwiches, soups, and salads.

Sakura (603-358-9902), 601 S. Main St., Keene. Open Tue.–Sat. for lunch (11:30–3) and dinner (4:30–9:30; 10:30 on weekends); Sun. noon–9:30. First-rate Japanese fare: sushi, tempura, donburi, and udon (Japanese noodles). Entrées $9.95–14.95, less at lunch.

&. **Salmon Chase Bistro and Lounge** (603-357-7070; www.some placesdifferent.com), 30 Main St., Keene. Located in the E. F. Lane Hotel, this attractive dining room features traditional and contemporary American cuisine, and is open to the public for lunch (Mon.–Fri. 11:30–2) and dinner (Mon.–Sat. 5–9). In addition to soups and salads, lunch entrées range from $5.95 for a spinach phyllo triangle with salad to $8.95 for beef Burgundy. The dinner menu ranges from vegetarian pasta at $12.95 to a 7-ounce filet mignon served on a Parmesan crouton for $19.95.

&. **Thai Garden** (603-357-4567), 118 Main St., Keene 03431. Open daily 11:30–3 and 5–10 for lunch and dinner. An attractive restaurant that, like its sisters in Boston and the Berkshires, offers a menu that invites exploration. All the traditional Thai soups and noodle dishes are here.

Dinner entrées range from $7.95 for ground chicken mixed with peanut sauce on a bed of lettuce to $15.95 for seafood curry. Moderately priced luncheon specials Reservations accepted.

&. **Tony Clamato's** (603-357-4345), 15 Court Square, Keene. Closed Mon., otherwise open for dinner and beyond, 4:30 PM–1 AM. Italian trattoria decor and menu with pasta specialties like fettuccine alla Siciliana (egg noodles with prosciutto, mushrooms, and peas) and pollo Gamberi Francese (chicken and shrimp in egg batter, sautéed with lemon, butter, and wine sauce). Moderate.

Chesterfield Inn (603-256-3211), Rt. 9, West Chesterfield. Open for dinner every night except Christmas Eve and Christmas Day. Chef Bob Nabstedt has an enviable reputation for imaginative dishes, and the setting is an 18th-century tavern expanded to create one of the most attractive dining areas in the region, with views of Vermont hills. Entrées on a summer menu here might include a pork chop stuffed with spinach, hazelnuts, and apricots with a port wine glaze ($19); filet mignon with shiitake mushroom and whole-grain mustard sauce ($28); or, for those with an eye to eating light, an appetizer crabmeat and papaya salad with a ginger lime sauce ($8). There is a nightly vegetarian entrée as well.

In and around Peterborough
Acqua Bistro (603-924-9905), 18 Depot Square, Peterborough. Open for dinner Tue.–Sat. from 4 PM; Sunday brunch 11–2:30, light snacks 3–5, dinner 5–9. Reservations advised. Chic decor and menu give this restaurant rave reviews. In summer, dine on the expanded patio overlooking the

brook. Dinner entrées might include venison medallions with spring vegetable ragout and herb spaetzle with fresh blackberries in a port wine sauce for $25, or herb-crusted wild king salmon served with jasmine rice, julienne vegetables, and a scallion ginger sauce for $21. There are also a variety of sophisticated stone-baked, thin-crust pizzas for $12–16. In addition to beer and wine, the fully licensed bar offers a variety of specialty drinks and marvy martinis.

Inn at Jaffrey Center (603-532-7800; 1-877-510-7019), 379 Main St., Jaffrey Center. Open for lunch and dinner Mon.–Sat., and for brunch Sun. 10–2. Sunday dinner is seasonal. Known for more than a century as the Monadnock Inn, this classic country hostelry sits at the center of one of the Monadnock region's prettiest villages, minutes from the entrance to Monadnock State Park. Under new ownership, its dining rooms have been expanded and its reputation for fine dining has soared. We certainly can't complain about the lamb shanks, slow braised with garlic and rosemary. Choices range from vegetarian pastas and fish dishes to a mixed grill of rack of lamb and coconut-grilled shrimp with Hunan sauce. Entrées $15–22. There's also an informal tavern.

The Hancock Inn (603-525-3318), Main St., Hancock village. Open for dinner nightly. An 18th-century inn with an award-winning, candlelit, cranberry-colored dining room and a far-ranging menu that usually features grilled rack of lamb and filet mignon and might also include Asian five-spice pomegranate-glazed salmon, or grilled chicken and portobellos stacked with Boursin and served on a twist of angelhair pasta tossed with fresh basil and tomatoes. Entrées are $20–32. A tavern menu that includes brick-oven-baked thin-crust pizza ($10–16) as well as sandwiches and burgers is available, along with the regular menu, in the genuine old tavern.

Del Rossi's Trattoria (603-563-7195; www.delrossi.com), Rt. 137, Dublin. Open for dinner Tue.–Sat. 5–9. Inquire about scheduled music and poetry readings, which draw talent from across the country. David and Elaina Del Rossi have created a genuine Italian trattoria in a pleasant old house just north of Rt. 101. Homemade pastas are a specialty, as are Italian classics like bisteca and scaloppine with penne pasta Alfredo. The menu might also include fresh Wellfleet littleneck clams steamed in a homemade fish broth with chopped shrimp, served on homemade spaghetti. Entrées $14.95–20.95.

Lilly's on the Pond (603-899-3322), Rt. 202, Rindge. Open Tue.–Sat. for lunch and dinner, Sun. 10–8. A restaurant under various names since 1952, this former sawmill turned gristmill and forge hit the culinary map about 10 years ago when the current owners renamed it for the mermaid said to live on the shores of this pond in the 1700s. Dinner might be tequila lime chicken (if you like margaritas, you'll love this dish)—a boneless breast of chicken sautéed with fresh lime, tequila, cilantro, and cream—or veggie phyllo, artichoke hearts in a spinach-ricotta sauce wrapped in phyllo pastry. Entrées $12.95–16.95.

The Birchwood Inn (603-878-3285; www.thebirchwoodinn.com), Rt. 45, Temple. Main restaurant open for dinner Fri. and Sat. year-round by reservation. Tavern is open Wed.–Sun. 5–10:30 and after noon on Sat. and Sun. British-born innkeeper-chefs Andrew and Nick, and their American counterpart Trish, have infused this cozy restaurant and pub with Continental cheer and cuisine. They dub their menu, which includes steak and ale pie and bangers and mash as well as more geographically diverse weekly specials, "a taste of Old England in New England." The charming candlelit dining room is especially noteworthy for its Rufus Porter mural dating to the early 19th century. At around $12.50 per entrée, prices are moderate though perhaps higher than they were when folks first started frequenting this locale shortly after the Revolution.

Churchill's at the Grand View Inn and Resort (603-532-9880; www .thegrandviewinn.com), 580 Mountain Rd. (Rt. 124), west of Jaffrey Center. Open for dinner Thu.–Sat., 6–9:30; reservations required. The à la carte menu features such entrées as carmelized sea scallops with crispy pancella and red onions for $17 and grilled Australian beef tenderloin with wild mushrooms and garlic rosemary reduction for $25. The post-and-beam dining room is designed to maximize the view and to serve as a space for wedding receptions and other special occasions. There's live entertainment on Friday nights.

The Café at Noon Falls (603-924-6818). Rt. 202 south, Peterborough. Open for breakfast and lunch Mon.–Sat. 8:30–4; for dinner Wed.–Sat., 5–9. The premier space in a former mill building, right by the falls. Pleasant any time of year, it's superb in warm-weather months when you can eat on the deck. The food is now above average: soups and sandwiches with freshly made bread, also Thai and Indian specialties. Under the same management as la Bonne Table, a respected local catering service and culinary arts school.

R. A. Gatto's (603-924-5000), 6 School St., Peterborough. Open Tue.–Sat. for lunch and dinner. This attractive space in a former movie house (designed for the original Latacarta) is now a popular spot for lunch and dinner, specializing in seafood, pasta, homemade desserts. The dinner menu ranges from roasted R. T. chokes with penne pasta to grilled swordfish and New York sirloin.

Pearl Restaurant and Oyster Bar (603-924-5225), 1 Jaffrey Rd., Peterborough. Open for dinner daily. Peterborough's newest restaurant entry is making waves for its trendy, elegant decor as well as for its seafood—oysters and otherwise. Appetizers include a shrimp Thai basil salad, Hanoi spring roll, and spicy squid. Entrées have a similarly pan-Asian theme.

Eastern Monadnock region
The French Bistro (603-249-9605; www.thefrenchbistro.com), 15 Elm St., Milford. Open Tue.–Sun. 11:30–2 for lunch, 5–9 for dinner. It may seem unlikely to discover a French bistro in an old southern New Hampshire mill town, but this restaurant is just what its name implies. French-born owner-chef Thierry Navette had won accolades for his culinary skills in major hotels and restaurants in both Europe and North America before purchasing this little red caboose in the fall of 2004. Since then, both locals and tourists have come away dazzled by his menus. Choose from the daily special— say, soft-shell crab with watermelon salad,

or veal kidney with mustard sauce—or from the main menu with dinner entrées ranging $14.95–20.95. The seared duck breast, Magret de Canard, is a definite find—the French consider it better than filet mignon. Somewhat curiously, there's an ice cream stand attached.

Malarkey's at Tory Pines Resort (603-588-2000), Rt. 47, Francestown. Open daily in summer 11 AM–closing; in winter, Wed.–Sun. from 4 PM. There are several eating areas, ranging from casual to formal, in this 1790 mansion, now the centerpiece of a golf-resort development. Dinner entrées range from Kentucky bourbon turkey skewers for $13.95 to pepper-encrusted filet mignon for $21.95. The pub menu features lower-priced sandwiches, salads, and appetizers. There are several function areas, both indoors and out. The large fireplace, flanked by leather couches, is a favorite winter retreat.

Nonni's Italian Eatery (603-464-6766), 17 Main St., Hillsborough. Open for dinner Mon.–Thu. 4–9, Fri.–Sat. until 10; additional Sat. hours 11:30–2:30, and Sun. 11:30–8. Brooklyn-born owner-chef Matthew Mitnitsky began his career working at Balducci's, then graduated from the Culinary Institute of America before earning additional stripes at such upscale eateries as New York's 21 Club and River Café. Now he and his wife have brought a little bit of Italy to downtown Hillsborough with whitewashed walls, a brick pizza oven, handsome wine bar, and authentic Mediterranean cuisine. It's worth making the short loop off Rts. 202/9. Moderate.

✔ **Pickity Place** (603-878-1151; www .pickityplace.com), Nutting Hill Rd., Mason. Open year-round daily for three lunch sittings: 11:30, 12:45, and 2. Reserve ahead because there are just 15 tables in this 200-year-old house. Homegrown herbs are the draw here, and you come for "herbal lunches." The set menu changes each month. When we stopped by, it included roasted garlic-herb soup; wild mushroom strudel with grilled trout over julienned vegetables with cranberry vin blanc; or Mediterranean spinach fettuccine, along with home-baked breads and dessert. Children can have a Little Red Riding Hood basket of sandwiches and fruit; they come to see "Grandmother's bed" in the Red Riding Hood Museum. A five-course luncheon is $14.95 plus tax.

EATING OUT

In and around Keene
The Stage Restaurant (603-357-8339), 30 Central Square, across from the County Courthouse, Keene. Open Tue.–Fri. 11:30 AM–11 PM, Sat. from 8:30 AM; Sun. 8–4. A trendy, family-owned café with a playbill decor and a large menu: burgers, sandwiches, pasta, steaks, and salads. Full bar. Entrées $9.95–15.95. Live jazz on Thursday.

Martino's (603-357-0859), 16 Cypress St., Keene. Open for lunch Mon.–Fri. 11:30–1:30, dinner Mon.–Sat. 5–9. This quiet, comfortable, no-frills Italian restaurant entices local faithfuls to wander off the beaten path down a block from Main Street. The pastas are well priced, and specials such as Tuscan shrimp and veal and artichoke hearts—not to mention the tiramisu and amaretto sponge cake—provide more tempting fare. Beer and wine list.

🦞 ✍ **Timoleon's Restaurant** (603-357-4230), 27 Main St., Keene. Open daily 6 AM–9 PM. This is the kind of place every town once had: a long counter and booths with better-than-average service, deli and club sandwiches, hot sandwiches, salads, fried haddock, and ham steak with a pineapple ring, served with salad, a roll, and potato for $6.95. Like all Keene restaurants, it's now smoke-free, and we're told business has picked up as a result.

Elm City Brewing Co. (603-355-3335), 222 West St., Keene. Open daily for lunch and until 11 PM Mon.–Thu., until midnight on Fri. and Sat.; Sun. 11:30–8:30. In the Colony Mill, a large, attractive brew-pub with its own ales, draft, and a large, varied, and reasonably priced menu.

Lindy's Diner (603-352-4273), Gilbo Ave. just off Main St. across from the bus station, Keene. Open daily 6 AM–8 PM, Fri. until 9. New owners but the same quick and hearty fare that's been a staple of this location for decades. Homemade pies and take-out ice cream.

Casey J's (603-585-9577), junction of Rts. 12 and 119, Fitzwilliam. Open for all three meals, Mon.–Thu. and Sat. 7 AM–8 PM, Fri. until 9; closes on Sun. at 7. The kind of family restaurant every town should have. The rolls, cakes, pies, soups, and lasagna are all homemade, and the hams, turkeys, and roasts are home baked.

Sunflowers Café (603-585-DINE [-3463]; www.sunflowerscatering.com), junction of Rts. 12 and 119, Fitzwilliam. Open Thu.–Mon., 7:30–7:30. Sunday brunch served 10–2. Carolyn Edwards and Carrie Kidd

have been catering large and small events for more than 20 years; now their talents are available on a regular basis at this light, cheery, and well-furnished eatery. Daily specials include sandwiches and wraps, home-made soups, vegetarian selections, plus take-home dinners and special desserts.

Gap Mountain Bakery Café (603-242-3284), on the common, Rt. 12, Troy. Open Tue.–Sat. 8 AM–9 PM, Mon. 8–5, Sun. 10–5. Diane Kellner's cheerful bakery-café is a source of outstanding morning muffins (made with honey), sundry breads, and oat-meal cookies; also distinctly less healthy but addictive chocolate whoopee pies. Subs, great pizzas by the slice, soups, and salads are served at lunch, and gourmet coffees are on tap.

🦞 ✍ **Mt. Pisgah Diner** (603-239-4101), 18 Main St., Winchester. Open Mon.–Fri. for early breakfast through lunch; Sat., breakfast only. An authentic 1930 Worcester diner (#769) that's sparkling clean and pridefully maintained by Joni Otto. The food's not bad, either! We went for the kielbasa omelet but might have sampled sausage gravy over biscuits with two eggs and home fries.

In and around Peterborough
✍ **Aesops Tables at the Toadstool Bookstore** (603-924-1612), 12 Depot Square, Peterborough. Open weekdays 8:30–4, Sat. 10–3. An inviting corner of this outsized bookstore, a former A&P. The blackboard menu lists sandwiches and café fare like bagels, raspberry squares, and Brazilian chocolate cake. There's a play corner for small fry and a choice of gourmet coffees on tap.

Fiddleheads Café (603-525-4432), 28 Main St., Hancock. Open in summer Mon.–Sat. 7 AM–8 PM, Sun. 8–8; in winter, 7–7 during the week, Sun. 8–2. This café in the middle of Hancock village offers gourmet-to-go plus an attractive sitting room designed for patrons to simply read and relax. Sherry Williams offers several daily soups as well as scones and muffins, pizzas and calzones, and coffees and teas. Local art on the walls is for sale.

Brady's American Grill (603-924-9322), Rt. 202 north, Peterborough. Open daily for lunch and dinner. A friendly place with good food: burgers, sandwiches, salads, pasta, and a surprising choice of dinner entrées. Beer and wine served.

Nonies (603-924-3451), 28 Grove St., Peterborough. Open Mon.–Sat. 6 AM–2 PM, Sun. 7 AM–1 PM. Doughnuts made daily, full breakfasts, soups, sandwiches, local gossip.

The Peterborough Diner (603-924-6202), Depot St., Peterborough. Open daily 6 AM–9 PM. A 1950s green-and-yellow diner featuring dependable diner food including homemade soups, pies, daily and nightly specials, beer. Choose the counter or wooden booth.

Twelve Pine (603-924-6140; www.twelvepine.com), Depot Square, Peterborough. Open Mon.–Fri. 8–7, Sat. 9–6, Sun. 9–4. The aroma is a mix of coffee, spices, and baking, which—combined with the array of salads, quiches, calzones, and soups—is something to savor before deciding on any one thing. This former train depot is now filled with delectable deli and baked items, cheeses, and Italian ices; also specialty foods, flowers, fruit, and wine to take home. Small tables are scattered throughout; or dine outside on one of the two porches or the patio—a great place to

THE MT. PISGAH DINER IN WINCHESTER

Christina Tree

people-watch or enjoy the Contoocook River.

Mama Gee's Café at the Harrisville General Store (603-827-3138), 29 Church St., Harrisville. Open Wed.–Sat. 7:30 AM–6 PM, Tue. and Sun. until 4, Mon. 2. Very much a part of this historic mill village, recently reopened with a few staples and more specialty foods, a first-rate deli with soups, salads, and a wide range of "create-your-own-sandwich" ingredients. There are tables and picnic sites by the neighboring millpond.

Side Trax Café (603-547-3491), 1 Slip Rd., Greenfield. Open Thu.–Sat. 7 AM–8 PM, Mon. and Wed. until 2 PM, Sun. from 8 AM; closed Tue. There's always been a coffee shop in Carbee's Corner, and the current owners offer specialty omelets, pancakes, sausage and biscuit, plus multiple variations on eggs Benedict and French toast. The "Engineer's Breakfast," served until noon, features three eggs, a 7-ounce prime rib, home fries, and two pancakes for $9.95. The lunch and dinner menus feature standard, hearty fare to take out or eat in, at moderate prices.

Eastern Monadnock region

Alberto's (603-588-6512). Rt. 31, Bennington. Open daily at 5 PM. A red-sauce Italian place with a big menu that includes 11 kinds of pizza, garlic bread, and 19 Italian dishes like manicotti, lasagna, and chicken cacciatore.

Aspirations (603-465-7176), 25 Proctor Hill Rd., Rt. 130, Hollis. Open Mon.–Fri. 11–4, Sat. 9–3. This cute gray-and-purple-painted cottage attracted our attention when we first noticed it on busy Rt. 130. The owner started with a catering business,

which she's now expanded into a café with seasonal salads, pastas and pizzas, and a bakery with European pastries and homemade breads. Carry out or eat in. The summertime terrace with umbrella tables and a small frog pond is delightful.

The Melting Pot (603-654-5150), 47 Main St., Wilton (across from town hall). Open Wed.–Fri. for lunch 11–2, dinner Wed. and Thu. 5–8, Fri. and Sat. until 8:30. Sun. breakfast 9–1. This storefront restaurant features a purple-and-green color scheme with a high ceiling and batik tablecloths. It also provides a menu that brings in a full house most days it's open. For lunch, there's a variety of pizzas, salads, burgers, and other sandwiches. Moderately priced dinner entrées change weekly. When we were there, the sautéed pork tenderloin ($12.95) was topped with a creamy green peppercorn sauce and was delicious. Beer, wine, and bar drinks.

Milford Diner (603-673-1815), 63 Union Square, Milford. Open daily 6 AM–8 PM. This early-1900s railroad dining car has been the place to eat and greet for Milford residents as well as perennial presidential candidates for years. Ample breakfasts, homemade pies and chowders, terrific turkey sandwiches. The diner flanks the arched stone bridge crossing the Souhegan River, but the best view of the water and stonework is looking through the picture window behind the bar of the **Stonebridge Tavern** (open 11–11) downstairs.

Parker's Maple Barn (603-878-2308; www.parkersmaplebarn.com), 1316 Brookline Rd., Mason. Open from Valentine's Day–Christmas, Mon.–Fri. 8–2, Sat. and Sun. 7–4. The specialty here is obvious—pancakes, waffles,

French toast—whatever conduit you prefer to heap on the maple syrup, which is made on the premises. For lunch, you can continue the theme with maple baked beans or maple BBQ ribs, or break out and order from a selection of soups, salads, sandwiches, and moderately priced entrées. There's a covered bridge, nature walk, and sugarhouse to add to the barnboard-rustic ambience.

Union Street Grill (603-672-4180), 4 Union St., Milford. Open Mon.–Fri., 6–2, Sat. until 1, Sun. until 12:30. After honing his culinary skills at area restaurants, Milford native Kevin Stephens headed home a few years back and opened this cheery restaurant just beyond the center of town. The yellow-and-blue color scheme features a chicken motif, in keeping with the restaurant's specialty omelets. Folks from around the area consider it a good stop for lunch as well.

Caron's Diner (603-464-3575), Hillsborough. Open 5 AM–2 PM for breakfast and lunch, 5–8 PM for dinner; Sun. 7–noon. One of those places that has obviously forgotten what it looks like from the outside—a chrome diner tacked onto a brick extension with a door that looks like it never opens but does, onto the town's gossip center (your coffee cup never gets empty). It's spanking clean and always full, good for freshly made minestrone, meat loaf, or liver and onions; blackboard specials.

✐ **High Tide** (603-464-4202), Rt. 9, Hillsborough. Open Apr.–Columbus Day, daily 11–8. A seasonal fried-fish place with soft serve and a great screened-in dining area.

Sampan Chinese Restaurant and Lounge (603-464-3663), Rt. 9, Hills-

borough. Open daily, in summer 11–10, in winter 11:30–9. The attractive decor suggests the quality of this place, one of the better spots to eat in the area. Dishes are all cooked to order, no MSG.

Tooky Mills Pub (603-464-6700; www.tookymillspub.baweb.com), 9 Depot St., Hillsborough. Named for the mills that used to border the Contoocook River in these parts, this restaurant right on the main drag is open for lunch and dinner daily. Sun.–Thu. 11:30–9, Fri. and Sat. until 10.

SNACKS **Ava Marie's Handmade Chocolates and Ice Cream** (603-924-5993; www.avamariehandmade chocolates.com), 43 Grove St. in the Grove Village Shoppes, Peterborough. No ordinary chocolates these, and we've heard their turtles are "to die for."

German John's Bakery (603-464-5079), 5 West Main St., Hillsborough. Open year-round Wed.–Sat. 9:30–5; also on Sun. and Tue., July–Christmas. Closed Mon. Best known for their authentic German soft pretzels, but the soft sweet almond and raisin are also worth trying. Or sample a slice of kuchen or streusel, then bring home a loaf of bread.

Kimball Farm Ice Cream, Rt. 124 at Silver Ranch, Jaffrey. Open Apr.–Oct., 10 AM–9 PM. A Massachusetts import, but that doesn't make this ice cream any less delicious in every conceivable flavor.

✳ Entertainment

DANCE **Nelson Town Hall** (603-827-3732), Nelson. Show up any Monday at 8 PM at this elegantly simple old building, one of the region's longtime centers for traditional contra dancing. Young or old, with or without a partner, you'll soon be tapping your toes and caught up in a reel. Several Nelson musicians have gained national reputations. Call or check www.ultra net.com/harts/nhdances for information about events throughout the area.

LECTURE AND PERFORMANCE SERIES 🕮 Amos Fortune Forum

Series, Jaffrey Center Meeting House. Ongoing since 1947, the Forum continues the legacy of this fine old venue by providing free speakers from around the area on topics of interest, Friday evenings at 8 in July and Aug.

Monadnock Summer Lyceum (603-924-6245), Unitarian Church, Main St., Peterborough. Originally established in 1828, the Lyceum offers free programs by well-known speakers, often people who live or vacation in the region, every Sunday in July and Aug. at 11 AM.

MUSIC 🕮 ⚫ **Apple Hill Chamber Players** (603-847-3371; 1-800-472-6677; www.applehill.org), Apple Hill Center for Chamber Music, Apple Hill Rd., East Sullivan 03445. The Apple Hill Summer Chamber Music School attracts 275 participants of all ages; inquire about free weekly concerts by faculty (Tue. at 7:30 PM) and students (check current calendar) in June, July, and Aug.; all concerts are in the hilltop Apple Hill Concert Barn. This noted group also performs throughout the country and the world.

Monadnock Music (603-924-7610; 1-800-868-9613; www.monadnock music.org), Box 255, Peterborough 03458. This is a prestigious summer series of some three dozen concerts, operas, and orchestra performances, many of them free, staged by highly professional artists in churches and meetinghouses throughout the region, from the Walpole Unitarian Church to Marlow's Jones Hall, the Unitarian Church in Wilton Center, and the

MONADNOCK MUSIC STAGES DOZENS OF PERFORMANCES THROUGHOUT THE REGION

Jaffrey Center Meeting House. A subscription series is available for those performed at the Town House in Peterborough. Call or send for the current calendar, or check local listings.

The Peterborough Folk Music Society (603-827-2905), P.O. Box 41, Peterborough 03458, features performances by talented new as well as legendary folk musicians. Performances are at the Union Congregational Church, 33 Concord St. (Rt. 202). Call ahead to join in a potluck dinner. Tickets are available by mail or by credit card at www.virtuous.com or at the Toadstool Bookshops in Milford, Keene, and Peterborough. Cash and checks only at the door.

Raylynmor Opera (www.raylynmor .com) Founded in 1995, this company showcases regional talent while performing fully staged operas, sung primarily in English, either at the Colonial Theatre in Keene or at the Peterborough Town House.

🎵 **Temple Band** (603-878-2829), said to be the oldest town band in the country, performs at the Sharon Arts Center, the Jaffrey Bandstand, and a number of scheduled festivities throughout the summer. Past masters of oompah-pah.

🎵 **Jaffrey Bandstand**. Performances Wednesday evenings in summer.

Also see **Del Rossi's Trattoria** under *Dining Out*.

THEATER 🎵 **Andy's Summer Playhouse** (603-654-2613; www.andys summerplayhouse.org), Wilton. An innovative theater program begun 35 years ago to foster creative collaborations between children and professional artists working in a variety of media: performance art, theater, dance, music, puppetry, video, set and lighting design, and playwriting. Frequent performances in July and Aug. in the old Grange Hall in Wilton Center.

The Colonial Theatre (603-352-2033; www.thecolonial.org), 95 Main St., Keene. A majestic, magical old theater featuring big-name performers and Broadway road companies plus a schedule of current and classic films.

The Arts Center on Brickyard Pond at Keene State College in Keene and Franklin Pierce College in Rindge. Both stage musical, theatrical, and dance performances. Check local listings.

Peterborough Players (603-924-7585; www.peterboroughplayers.org), 55 Hadley Rd., Peterborough. Since 1933 this professional group has performed everything from Will Shakespeare to Tom Stoppard. One of New England's better-known summer theaters, presenting five to seven plays, often with well-known Broadway and Hollywood talent, each summer in a renovated, air-conditioned 19th-century barn.

✳ **Selective Shopping**

Few corners of New England are as conducive to finding just what you want while winding around back roads. The area is studded with genuine finds, ranging from unusual crafted items and antiques to exceptional chocolates and cheeses.

ANTIQUARIAN BOOKSHOPS **Eagle Books** (603-357-8721), 19 West St., just off Central Square, Keene. Open

Wed.–Sat. 10–5; 12,000 volumes specializing in WPA writers' project books and New Hampshire town histories.

Homestead Bookshop (603-876-4213), Rt. 101 just east of Marlborough village next to the Marlborough Country Store. Open weekdays 9 AM–5 PM, weekends until 4:30 PM every day but Christmas and Thanksgiving. They stock som 45,000 volumes specializing in juvenile series, town histories, and older fiction.

Hurley Books (603-399-4342), east side of Rt. 12 (just north of Rt. 63), Westmoreland. Open by appointment or chance; 35,000 volumes specializing in religion, farming, and gardening.

Bequaert Old Books (603-585-3448; www.beqbooks.com), 37 Rt. 119 west, Fitzwilliam. Open Apr.–Nov., weekdays 9–5, weekends 11–5. Closed on Wed. In the vintage barn beside their house near the Fitzwilliam village green, the Bequaerts stock some 35,000 titles, including technical books as well as volumes on mountaineering, fiber arts, and cookbooks.

Stone House Antiques & Books (603-363-4866; www.stonehouse antiques.com), junction of Rts. 9 and 63, Chesterfield. This granite house was once a stagecoach stop. Now the double parlors are divided by pocket doors and fitted with shelves offering a variety of used, antiquarian, and rare books.

ANTIQUES Listing the more than 50 antiques stores in the Monadnock region would simply be confusing. Be it said that antiquing is big but composed of many small shops, thickest in the Francestown and Fitzwilliam areas. Free, frequently updated flyers describing these shops and their whereabouts are available locally.

Fitzwilliam Antiques at the junction of Rts. 12 and 119 is one of the oldest, but there are at least half a dozen more dealers in Fitzwilliam alone (pick up a pamphlet guide). In Peterborough, **The Red Chair** (603-924-5953) in Depot Square offers distinctive antiques, accessories, and jewelry featured in national publications and TV shows. In Jaffrey, **Mainly Antiques** (603-532-7015), 27 Main St., is a cozy group shop with an artistic touch featuring French country furniture, linens, books, and folk art. **Antiques at Colony Mill** (603-358-6343) on West St. in Keene represents approximately 75 dealers. **The Mall of New England** at the junction of Old Wilton Rd. and Rt. 34 in Greenville (603-878-0606; www .antiquesandcollectiblesmall.com) provides good hunting grounds for table linens, china, glassware, and silver. Open Wed.–Sun. 9–6. With 200 dealers, **Knotty Pine, Inc.** (603-352-5252), on Rt. 10 west in West Swanzey, claims to be the state's (if not the country's) oldest and largest group shop. *The Directory of New Hampshire Antiques Dealers*, available from most chambers of commerce and antiques shops, lists dozens of dealers in this area.

ART GALLERIES **Sharon Arts Center** (603-924-7878), 30 Grove St., Peterborough. Open Mon.–Sat. 10–5, Sun. noon–5. Truly the "center" and showcase for the best current art and craft work in this creative corner of the state. The combination art and craft gallery, running a block through from Grove St. to Depot Square, displays a wide variety of original art in many media. This is also a great place to shop for quality gifts ranging from toys to jewelry. Workshops and studio space are at the center's original locale in Sharon.

New England Art Exchange (603-355-9906; www.neartexchange.com), 29 Central Square, Keene. Open Mon.–Sat. 11–4:30, or by appointment. Ken Spector and Jane Larmon have been buying and selling fine prints and period paintings from this location since 1989. They specialize in the Cornish Colony and other artist, primarily from the mid–19th to the mid–20th centuries.

Peterborough Fine Art (603-924-7558), Depot Square, Peterborough. Open year-round, Tue.–Sat. noon–5. A serious gallery specializing in 19th- and early-20th-century landscape paintings, especially those of the Dublin Art Colony, also some contemporary work.

Peterborough Art Academy and Gallery (603-924-4488), Depot Square, Peterborough. Regional artists' gallery, children's and adult classes, summer art camp and art supplies.

AUCTIONS **Ed's Country Auction House** (603-899-6654), Rindge (behind Lilly's on the Pond Restaurant), auctions every Sat. year-round.

Richard Withington (603-464-3232), Hillsborough Center. A legend in his own time, Withington holds auctioneer's license #1 in the state of New Hampshire; at age 87 he has gaveled 2,426 auctions, more than anyone around. You can still watch him start the bidding in the lovely field behind his home at frequent sales, June–Columbus Day.

The Cobb's Auctioneers (603-924-6316), 50 Jaffrey Rd. (Rt. 202), Peterborough. Attractive showrooms in the same former mill that houses the café at Noone Falls, a major local auction house.

BOOKSTORES **The Toadstool Bookshops** (603-924-3543), 12 Depot Square, Peterborough, the Colony Mill (603-352-8815), Keene, and Lordens Plaza (603-673-1734) in Milford. Outstanding bookstores with a wide range of general titles, including many regional and art books. Under *Eating Out* note Aesops Tables, a café in the immense Peterborough store (a former A&P).

Also see *Antiquarian Bookshops*.

CRAFTS **Country Artisans** (603-352-6980), 53 Main St., Keene. Offers a wide selection of crafts produced in New England and beyond.

Five Wings Studio (603-585-6682), 67 E. Lake Rd., Fitzwilliam. Susan Link makes and sells her attractive dinnerware—porcelain with an Oriental look—and two stoneware lines. All pieces are formed on a potter's wheel or hand built, bisque fired in a gas kiln and coated with a clear glaze, and then fired again. Hand-cut painted tiles are also a specialty. The way to the studio is west from Fitzwilliam village on Rt. 119 to the Fitzwilliam Depot fire station. The studio is five houses beyond. Terry Silverman (Susan's husband) also creates distinctive pottery flameware at the Pottery Works.

Frye's Measure Mill (603-654-6581), 12 Frye Mill Rd., Wilton. Open Tue.–Sat. 10–5, Sun. noon–5 most of the year. Closed Tue. in winter, except open 7 days a week from the day after Thanksgiving–Dec. 22. The seven-room shop is housed in part of a 19th-century mill that retains its original machinery, some still water powered to make Shaker boxes and woodenware. Quilts and coverlets, salt-glaze pottery, and other country folk art items are also sold. Call for hours of sawmill demonstrations and other activities.

Harrisville Designs (603-827-3996; www.harrisville.com), Harrisville. Open Tue.–Sat. 10–5. Handweaving looms are designed and made here, priced from $700 to $5,000. Check out the new chil-dren's weaving looms and kits. A variety of yarns and weaving accessories are also sold in the Weaving Center, housed in an 1850 brick storehouse by the millpond. Inquire about used looms.

New Hampshire Quilters' Emporium (603-924-2322; www.nhqe.com), 43 Grove St., Peterborough. Open Tue.–Sat. 10–6, Sun. noon–6. A full-service quilt shop offering classes, supplies, and advice.

SUGARING

Maple sugaring season in the Monadnock region is Mar.–mid-Apr., but farmers may not be "boiling" (40 gallons of sap boil down to 1 gallon of syrup) every day, so phone ahead to make sure there's something to see—and something to eat. Most maple producers offer "sugar parties": sugar-on-snow (usually crushed ice these days) and maybe the traditional accompaniment (a pickle). Most sell a variety of maple products year-round. Call the New Hampshire Maple Phone (603-225-3757) or visit www.nhmaple producers.com for an updated report on the season.

Bascom's Sugar House (603-835-6361), Sugar House Rd. between Alstead and Acworth off Rt. 123A. One of the largest maple producers in New England, a huge sugarhouse and warehouse set high on Mount Kingsbury. Visitors are welcome to tour the plant, which uses unusual reverse-osmosis evaporators. Open year-round weekdays and Sat. mornings.

Ben's Sugar Shack (603-924-3177), 83 Webster Hwy., Temple. Ben Fisk gives tours of his sugarhouse and sells syrup, cream, and candy.

Clark's Sugar House (603-835-6863), 14 Currier Rd., Alstead. Award-winning syrup boiled over a wood fire. Maple treats and free tours. Will ship.

Parker's Maple Barn and Sugar House (603-878-2308; www.parkersmaple barn.com), 1316 Brookline Rd., Mason. Big dining barn open Valentine's Day–Christmas, Mon.–Fri. 8–2; Sat. and Sun. 7–4. See *Eating Out.*

Stonewall Farm (603-357-7278; www.stonewallfarm.org), 242 Chesterfield Rd., Keene. Gift shop open year-round. A sap-gathering contest during season features up to 20 teamsters and their draft horse teams; call for dates.

Stuart & John's Sugar House and Pancake Restaurant (603-399-4486), 19 Rt. 63 at the junction of Rt. 12, Westmoreland. Restaurant open weekends spring through fall; syrup available year-round.

North Gallery at Tewksbury's (603-924-3224), 3 Elm Hill Rd., junction of Rts. 101 and 123, Peterborough. Open daily 10–5:30. The floor and gallery of a former barn are filled with a wide assortment of things you never before knew you wanted—mugs, puzzles, toys, and some well-chosen pieces ranging from contemporary and antique/estate jewelry to place mats, furnishings, throws, pottery, and other items of home decor.

Granite Lake Pottery (603-847-9908), Rt. 9, Munsonville. Open year-round, Tue.–Sat. 10–4. Hand-thrown dinnerware and accessories from mugs to lamps and bathroom sinks (the sinks are a specialty).

Hannah Grimes Marketplace (603-352-6862), 46 Main St., Keene. Open Mon.–Sat, 9:30–5:30, Sun. until 4, selling locally made crafts and farm products.

Sharon Arts Center (603-924-7256), Depot Square, Peterborough. (See also *Art Galleries*.) This is the region's leading craft shop, *the* place to pick up a distinctive, handcrafted gift or accessories for your wardrobe and home.

FARMS, PICK-YOUR-OWN, CUT-YOUR-OWN Cut your own Christmas tree at **Farmstead Acres** (603-352-8730 in Westmoreland, **Wright's Tree Farm** (603-352-4033) in Keene, and **Zahn's Berry and Christmas Tree Farm** (603-673-1908), 211 Jennison Rd. in Milford.

Barrett Hill Farm (878-2351), Barrett Hill Rd., Mason. Strawberry fields forever, daily 8–6, from mid-June into July.

High Hopes Orchard (603-399-4305), 582 Glebe Rd., Westmoreland. Raspberries in July, blue-berries in July and Aug., apples in Sep. and Oct., and pumpkins (wagon rides) in Sep. and Oct.; gift shop, cider, homemade pies, apples, dough-nuts, and apple gift packs Aug.–Dec.

Maple Lane Farm (603-352-2329), 220 Gunn Rd., Keene. PYO apples—dwarf trees make it easy. Also cider, pumpkins, and seasonal specialties. Call for times.

Rosaly's Farmstand (603-924-7774; www.rosalysgarden.com), Rt. 123 just south of Rt. 101, Peterborough. Open mid-May–mid-Oct., daily 9–6. Thanks to reader Alexandra Kelly for her recommendation of Rosaly Bass's you-pick flower and herb gardens and farm stand featuring organic vegetables, most grown on the property. Rosaly also sells hand-painted T-shirts, maple syrup, and muffins, cakes, and bean salads on which you can picnic with a view of the fields and Mount Monadnock.

Monadnock Berries (603-242-6417; www.monadnockberries.com), 545 West Hill Rd., Troy. Open mid-July–mid-Sep., daily 8–7. With 9,000 PYO bushes, they offer "berry big" pickins' of blueberries, raspberries, black and red currants, and gooseber-ries, with a spectacular mountain view.

FARM STANDS **Barrett's Green-house and Farm Stand** (603-352-8665), Rt. 32, Swanzey. Bedding plants, perennials, vegetables, pump-kins, produce, and floral bouquets throughout summer and fall.

Butternut Farm (603-673-2963), 483 Federal Hill Rd., Milford. Open July–Sep., daily 8–6. Named for the tree, not the squash, this farm offers a lovely setting to cut your own floral bouquets, with annuals ranging from asters to zinnias. There are also veggies for sale in the barn.

Chauncey Farm (588-2857), 3 Old Concord Rd., Rt. 202, Antrim. Open mid-July–Halloween, 10–6. Cut your own flowers in summer; in fall, come for straw bales, gourds, Indian corn, mums, and sunflowers plus a variety of fall vegetables. A host for the annual Columbus Day weekend Wool Arts Tour.

HERBS **Harvest Thyme Herbs** (603-563-7032; www.harvestthyme.com), 91 Dooe Rd., Dublin. The handsome post-and-beam barn showroom is open mid-Oct.–Dec., 10–5. Herbal baskets, dips, and related gift items.

Pickity Place (603-878-1151), Nutting Hill Rd., Mason. A large herb garden and gift shop, catalog. (Also see *Dining Out* and *Villages*.)

Red Oak Farm (603-585-9052), 487 Royalston Rd., Fitzwilliam. Herb and perennial plants, dried herbs and flowers, wreaths.

Sage Knoll (603-478-5461), 955 E. Washington Rd., Hillsborough. Open Memorial Day–Labor Day, Tue.–Sat. 10–4. Herbs and perennials, specializing in hardy, farm-grown plants, old-fashioned and colonial varieties.

SHOPPING COMPLEXES **Colony Mill Marketplace** (603-357-1240), 222 West St., Keene. Open daily 10–9, Sun. 11–6. This 19th-century brick woolen mill now houses 24 specialty shops, a food court, and the Toadstool Bookshop.

SPECIAL STORES ✿ **Eastern Mountain Sports** (603-924-7231; www .ems.com), 1 Vose Farm Rd., off Rt. 202 north, Peterborough. Open Mon.–Thu. and Sat. 9–6, Fri. 9–8,

Sun. 11–5. Founded in 1967 and specializing in quality and hard-to-find equipment and clothing for backpacking and climbing enthusiasts, EMS now has 50 stores across the country. This is the corporate headquarters and one of the largest stores, one with a discount corner. Pick up a pamphlet guide to hiking and other outdoor sports possibilities in the Monadnock region.

Peterborough Basket Co. (603-371-9020), 130 Grove St. (south of Rt. 101). Open daily 9–5, Sun. 1–5. The showroom is impressive and prices are reasonable, but the real fun of this outlet is the seconds room with its bins of baskets and major markdowns on large items like woven hampers. Basketmaking has been an important industry in Peterborough since the 1850s, and this company traces its origins to 1875.

Joseph's Coat Peace Crafts (603-924-6683), 15 Depot Square, Peterborough. Colorful clothing, jewelry, shawls, alpaca yarn, quilts, puppets, and gifts from around the world.

Miranda's Verandah (603-352-0681), 1 Main St., Keene. Lots of flair in this shop with clothes that run the gamut from funky to fine.

Morgan's Way (603-924-6255), 28 Main St., Peterborough. Area women consider this a destination for fashionable, classic women's clothing.

The Renaissance Room (603-924-7934), Depot Square, Peterborough. Jacqueline Perry owns this boutique featuring high-style clothing and wearable art. It's the place to find that special outfit or accessory for women who don't mind standing out in a crowd.

Steele's, 40 Main St., Peterborough. In business since 1860, the nicest kind of stationery, card, and generally useful supply store.

✳ Special Events

February: Keene's annual **Ice and Snow Fest** features ice sculptures and a carving contest.

May: **Spring concert**, Monadnock Chorus and Orchestra.

⚘ Mid-May: **Children and the Arts Festival**, Peterborough.

June–September: **Peterborough Players Summer Theater**.

Late June: The annual **Rock Swap** in Gilsum (behind the elementary school on Rt. 10) attracts 8,000 to 10,000 mineral buffs.

July–August: **TGIF Summer Music Series** in Depot Park, Peterborough. Also see *Entertainment* for more music, theater, and lecture series.

July–September: **Monadnock Music Concert Series** (see *Entertainment*).

Fourth of July: The most unusual July 4 celebration is perhaps held July 3 in **Greenville**: At midnight all the bells and sirens in town ring and residents parade down Main Street banging pots and pans, leading a parade that includes fire engines, floats, and baby carriages. In **Peterborough** the Fourth is also a gala celebration with a craft fair, music, food, and children's entertainment at the Peterborough Historical Society 10–4. Stoddard's annual **Olde Home Days** includes a tour of some of the town's early homes.

Third week of July: **Fitzwilliam Antiques Fair**, more than 40 dealers.

Third weekend of July: **The Old Homestead**, a pageant/play, is per-

formed in the Potash Bowl, a natural amphitheater in Swanzey. **Balloon Fest and Fair**, Hillsborough. **Monadnock Festival of the Arts**, Peterborough.

August: **Oak Park Festival**, Greenfield. **Medal Day**, MacDowell Colony, Peterborough (a public picnic and open house). **Old Home Days**, Hancock.

September: **Labor Day Festival**, Francestown. Annual **Balloon Festival**, Monadnock Travel Council. Annual **Music Festival** in Keene.

October: Keene's **Pumpkin Festival** has made national news in recent years: Two 40-foot-high scaffold pyramids are erected on Main Street to display more than 1,000 lighted, hand-carved jack-o'-lanterns. **Foliage Festivals** are also held in Francestown and Greenfield. **Antique Auto Show** and **Octoberfest** at Crotched Mountain Foundation. German music, food, and classic cars. Annual **Book Fair**, MacDowell Colony, Peterborough. Also **Peek Into Peterborough**, an annual shopping festival during the "peak" of this Currier and Ives' community's foliage season. Biannual **Monadnock Festival of Quilts**, Monadnock Quilters Guild. **Wool Arts Tour** of farms and crafts studios in the Francestown-Antrim-Hillsborough area.

November: **Monadnock Music Christmas Fair**, South Meadow School, Peterborough.

December: **Christmas teas** at the Sharon Arts Center. **Messiah Festival** at Franklin Pierce College. **Monadnock Chorus Christmas Concert** at Peterborough Town House.

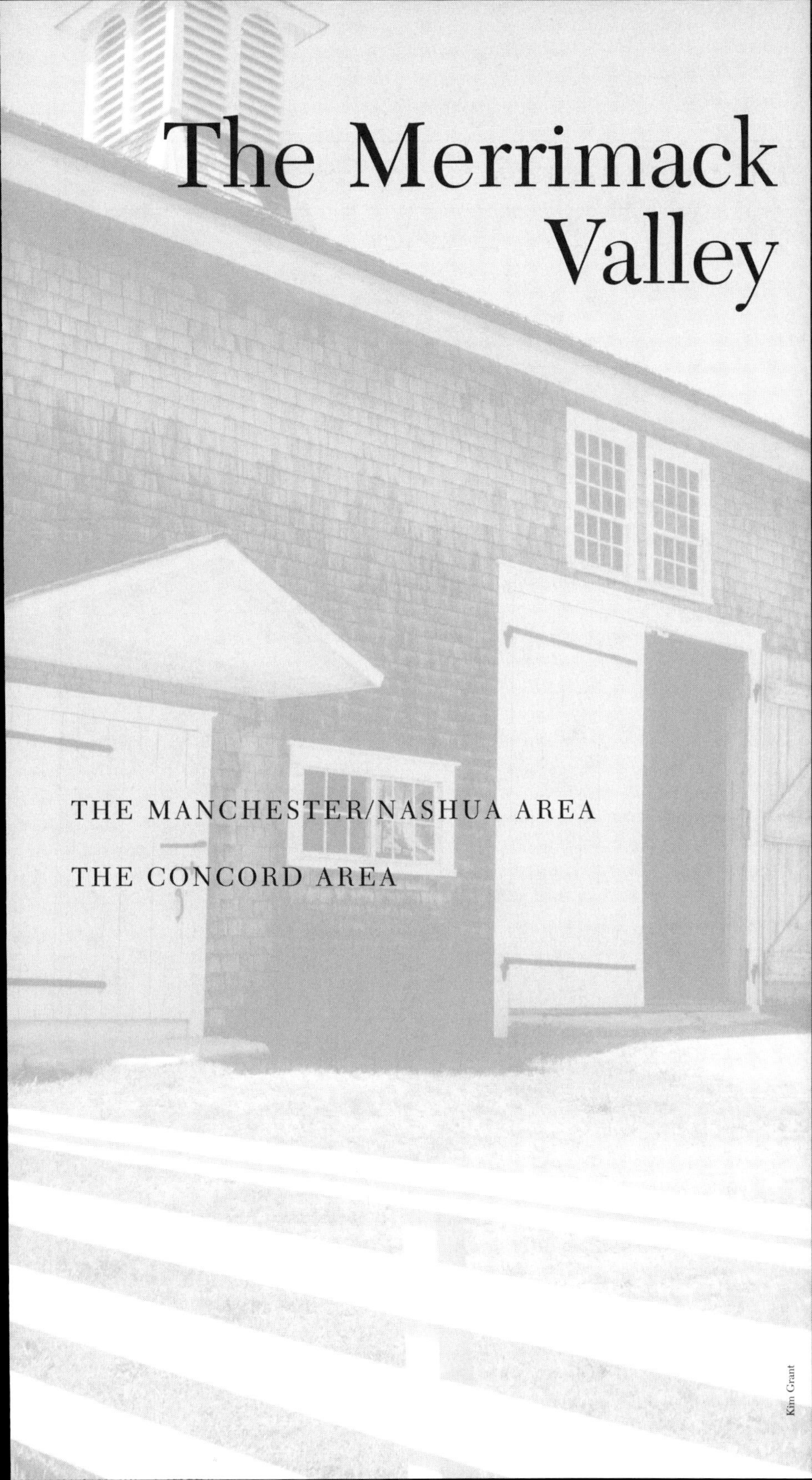

The Merrimack Valley 3

THE MANCHESTER/NASHUA AREA

THE CONCORD AREA

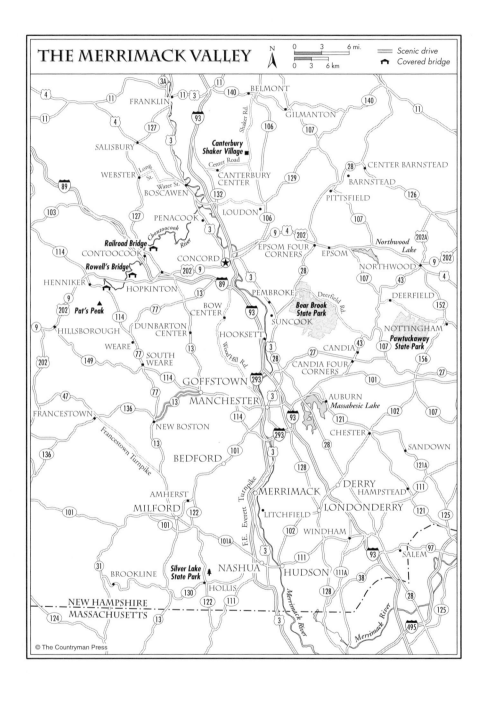

THE MERRIMACK VALLEY

N

| Scenic drive |
| Covered bridge |

0   3   6 mi.
0   3   6 km

4
11
FRANKLIN
3A
11
3
140
BELMONT
11

Shaker Rd.
11
127
93
106
GILMANTON
107
140
11

SALISBURY
3
Canterbury
Shaker Village
28
CENTER BARNSTEAD

WEBSTER
Long St.
Water St.
BOSCAWEN
89
CANTERBURY
CENTER
129
BARNSTEAD
PITTSFIELD
126

103
127
PENACOOK
132
LOUDON
106
107
202A

Railroad Bridge
Chontoocook River
9
4
202
EPSOM FOUR
CORNERS
EPSOM
Northwood
Lake
9
202

114
CONTOOCOOK
CONCORD
NORTHWOOD
107
43
4

Rowell's Bridge
202
9
28
DEERFIELD
152

HENNIKER
HOPKINTON
13
89
PEMBROKE
Deerfield Rd.
9
202
Pat's Peak
114
77
BOW
CENTER
93
Bear Brook
State Park
SUNCOOK
NOTTINGHAM
Pawtuckaway
State Park
107
156
27

9
HILLSBOROUGH
DUNBARTON
CENTER
HOOKSETT
CANDIA
43
101

WEARE
77
SOUTH
WEARE
13
28
CANDIA FOUR
CORNERS
27

202
149
Wood Hill Rd.
3
28

114
GOFFSTOWN
293
AUBURN
Massabesic Lake
102
107

47
136
13
MANCHESTER
3
121
CHESTER
SANDOWN

FRANCESTOWN
136
NEW BOSTON
114
93
293
28
121A

13
101
128
DERRY
HAMPSTEAD
111

BEDFORD
3
MERRIMACK
LONDONDERRY
121
125

AMHERST
MILFORD
122
LITCHFIELD
102
WINDHAM
97
SALEM

101
101
F.E. Everett Turnpike
101A
93
38
28
125

31
BROOKLINE
Silver Lake
State Park
130
NASHUA
HOLLIS
3
111
HUDSON
111A
128

NEW HAMPSHIRE
MASSACHUSETTS
124
13
122
111
Merrimack River
Merrimack River
495

© The Countryman Press

INTRODUCTION

The Merrimack, New England's second longest river, was an early New Hampshire highway, and today it's paralleled by I-93, New Hampshire's north–south transportation spine. One of the state's first settled corridors, the Merrimack Valley has recently been enjoying another migrational rush from hundreds of companies and thousands of families moving north from Massachusetts to take advantage of New Hampshire's tax breaks (no sales or income tax).

Relatively few visitors, however, venture farther into this area than the fast-food chains just off I-93. The very way the highways slice through and around Nashua, Manchester, and Concord does little to encourage exploration. Over recent decades, the southern tier of New Hampshire has become a mecca for Massachusetts émigrés and other expatriates looking for the simple life once exemplified by rural New Hampshire. While tourists see mainly crowded highways and strip malls, those who make this area home know better. Most towns have retained large tracts of conservation land with nature trails and continue to take pride in their old meetinghouses and town halls. Alongside the Rockingham Park mall, Salem continues to boast one of America's most historic racetracks, along with one of its oldest amusement parks (Canobie Lake Park), while Nashua, with a bevy of fine restaurants, is frequently named one of the nation's most livable cities.

Manchester's proud, old, brick shopping streets, its Currier Museum of Art, and its Amoskeag Mills—once the world's largest textile "manufactury"—are rewarding stops. So are Concord's state capitol building, the Museum of New Hampshire History, and the Christa McAuliffe Planetarium. The headquarters for the New Hampshire Audubon Society (just off I-89) and the Society for the Protection of New Hampshire Forests (just off I-93) are also well worth the small detours they require.

Other genuine finds are salted around this little-touristed central New Hampshire corridor. Canterbury Shaker Village, just 15 miles north of Concord, remains a working Shaker community in addition to being one of New England's most interesting museums. "America's Stonehenge" is at Mystery Hill in North Salem. The town of Henniker offers skiing and some fine lodging, dining, and shopping, while Hopkinton village's Main Street, a simple loop between two exits off I-89, presents a picture-perfect slice of early American architecture. There are also numerous state parks with sandy beaches.

THE MANCHESTER/NASHUA AREA

For many visitors to New Hampshire, this area is the gateway. Known to locals as "the Southern Tier," it offers a transition between the more populous, urban areas to the south and the near-wilderness atmosphere of the state's far northern reaches. By blending economic development with respect for its natural assets and historic past, the area's quality of life has become a model for the rest of the country. Perhaps the best example is Nashua, a city of 83,000, twice named *Money Magazine*'s "Best Place to Live in America." The honor is testimony to the city's ability to adapt to change and withstand economic reverses. In the past half century, the Greater Nashua area has moved from mills to microchips. Once a textile manufacturing center, after World War II the community began to reinvent itself, attracting new industries, many of them start-ups by young professionals interested in broadening the reach of the high-tech companies around Boston.

As the state's largest city (the only one with more than 100,000 people), Manchester is also arguably New England's most interesting "mill city," an image the city has recently begun to re-embrace.

When white men first traveled up the Merrimack, they found a large Native American village at Amoskeag Falls. In 1650 the English missionary John Eliot set up one of his "Praying Indian" communities and called it Derryfield. The Native Americans were later displaced by a white settlement early in the 18th century. By 1810 local judge Samuel Blodgett foretold the community's future, suggesting that its name be changed from Derryfield to Manchester, then the world's biggest manufacturing city (in England).

This early American Manchester population was just 615, but Judge Blodgett raised money to build a canal around Amoskeag Falls to enable flat-bottomed boats to glide downstream and onward, via the Middlesex Canal, into Boston. Both the canal and the town's first cotton mill opened in 1809.

It was a group of Boston entrepreneurs, however, who put Manchester on the map. By the 1830s these "Boston Associates" had purchased waterpower rights for the entire length of the Merrimack River and had begun developing a city full of mills in Lowell, Massachusetts, 32 miles downriver from Manchester. Incorporating themselves as the Amoskeag Manufacturing Company, they then bought 15,000 acres around Amoskeag Falls and drew up a master plan for the

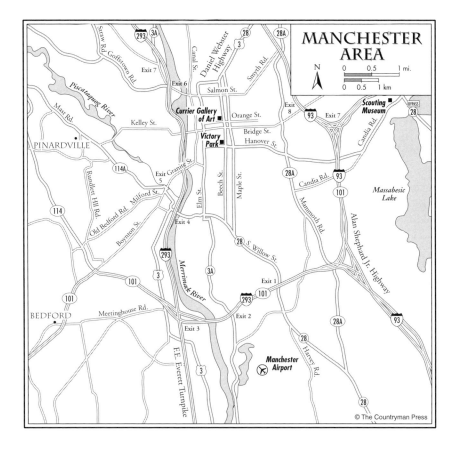

city of Manchester, complete with tree-lined streets, housing, churches, and parks.

Like Lowell, Manchester enjoyed an early utopian period during which "mill girls" lived in well-regulated boardinghouses. It was followed by successive periods of expansion, fueled by waves of foreign immigration. With direct rail connections to Quebec, Manchester attracted predominantly French Canadian workers, but Polish, Greek, and Irish communities were (and are) also substantial.

At its height in the early 20th century, the Amoskeag Manufacturing Company employed 17,000 workers, encompassed 64 mill buildings lining both sides of the Merrimack River for a mile and a half, and contained the world's largest single millyard. Imagine this space filled with the noise and movement of nearly 700,000 spindles and 23,000 looms! Life for workers was unquestionably hard. The tower bells rang each morning at 4:30, and the first call for breakfast was 5:30; the workday began at 6:30, lasting until 7:30 in the evening. But it's a way of life that many workers remember fondly in the oral histories recorded in *Amoskeag: Life and Work in an American Factory-City* by anthropologist Tamara Hareven and photographer Randolph

Langenbach. Based on interviews with thousands of former Amoskeag employees, this interesting book, published in 1978, vividly conveys what it was like to live within Manchester's tightly knit ethnic circles, reinforced by a sense of belonging to a full city of workers united like one family by a single boss.

The Amoskeag Manufacturing Company went bankrupt in 1935, and the following year the mills were shut down. In desperation a group of local businessmen formed Amoskeag Industries, Inc., purchased all the mills for $5 million, and managed to lease and sell mill space to diversified businesses.

"Diversify" has been the city's slogan ever since. Having once experienced complete dependency on one economic source, Manchester now prides itself on the number and variety of its industries and service businesses as well as on its current status as a financial and insurance center. New business and residential buildings rise high above the old mill towers.

Loosely circled by hills and with buildings that rise in tiers above the mills on the eastern bank of the Merrimack, Manchester is an attractive city with a Gothic Revival town hall, handsome 19th-century commercial blocks, the gemlike Palace Theater, and the new 10,000-seat Verizon Wireless Arena featuring such top acts as Bob Dylan and Elton John, as well as the city's own American Ice Hockey League team, the Manchester Monarchs. The Currier Museum of Art, one of the country's outstanding small art museums, is also located here.

GUIDANCE **Greater Manchester Chamber of Commerce** (603-666-6600; www.manchester-chamber.org), 889 Elm St., Manchester 03101. Open 8–5. The chamber office stocks a first-rate Visitors Guide to Greater Manchester.

Manchester Area Convention and Visitors Bureau (603-666-6600; www .manchestercvb.com), 889 Elm St., Manchester 03101. The web site is an excellent resource to the area.

Greater Nashua Chamber of Commerce (603-881-8333; www.nashua chamber.com), 151 Main St., Nashua 03060. Open until 4:30 PM.

Salem, New Hampshire Chamber of Commerce (603-893-3177; www .salemnhchamber.org), 224 N. Broadway, Salem 03079.

GETTING THERE *By bus:* From the **Manchester Transportation Center** (603-668-6133), 119 Canal St., you can get anywhere in the country; Concord Trailways, Vermont Transit Lines, and Peter Pan all stop regularly.

By air: The **Manchester Airport** (603-624-6539) is not only the largest in the state, but also one of the fastest growing in the country. Carriers include United Airlines (1-800-241-6522), US Airways (1-800-428-4322), Continental Express (1-800-525-0280), Delta (1-800-221-1212), Comair Delta (1-800-354-9822), Independence Air (1-800-359-3594), Northwest (1-800-225-2525), Southwest (1-800-435-9792), and Air Canada (1-888-247-2262). There are nonstop flights to Albany, Atlanta, Baltimore, Boston, Chicago, Cincinnati, Cleveland, Detroit, Kansas City, Nashville, New York, Orlando, Philadelphia, Pittsburgh, and Washington DC. Hertz, Budget, Avis, and Thrifty Car Rental are all here and offer free airport transfers. For parking information call 603-641-5444.

By car: The biggest problem with Manchester is finding your way in. It's moated by interstate highways 93 and 293 more effectively than it ever was by canals and mill walls. The simplest access points to downtown are marked from I-293. A handy map, available from the chamber of commerce, pinpoints parking garages, and there are reasonably priced (warning: and well-monitored) meters.

GETTING AROUND **Hudson Bus Lines** (603-424-2446), 22 Pond St., Nashua, offers limousine service between pickup points in Concord, Manchester, Nashua, downtown Boston, and Logan International Airport. City dispatch services are offered by **Town and Country** (603-668-3434), **Yellow Cab** (603-622-0008), and **Executive Airport Service** (603-625-2999).

MEDICAL EMERGENCY **Catholic Medical Center** (603-668-3545), 100 Mac-Gregor St., Manchester.

Dartmouth-Hitchcock Medical Center (603-577-4000; www.dartmouth -hitchcock.org), 591 W. Hollis St., Nashua. Additional branches in Hudson, Merrimack, and Milford.

Elliot Hospital (603-669-5300), 1 Elliot Way, Manchester.

St. Joseph Hospital (603-882-3000; www.stjosephhospital.com), 172 Kinsley St., Nashua.

Southern New Hampshire Medical Center (603-577-2000; www.snhmc.org), 8 Prospect St., Nashua.

✳ To See

MUSEUMS ♿ **Currier Museum of Art** (603-669-6144; www.currier.org), 192 Orange St., Manchester. Open Mon., Wed., Fri., Sun. 11–5, Thu. until 8, Sat. 10–5. $5 adults, $4 seniors or students with ID; under 18, free. Free admission Sat. until 1 PM. This excellent regional museum, already one of New England's finest, received a major bequest in 2001. It offers unexpected treasures: a lovely landscape by Claude Monet; a spooky 1935 Edward Hopper Maine coastal scene

CURRIER MUSEUM OF ART IN MANCHESTER

Currier Museum of Art, Manchester, New Hampshire

Currier Museum of Art, Manchester, New Hampshire. Museum purchase: Currier Funds, 1948.4

AMOSKEAG CANAL, 1948, BY CHARLES SHEELER

titled *The Bootleggers*; a 1940s painting by Sheeler of the Amoskeag mills; and a recently acquired abstract by Mark Rothko. Paintings range from a 13th-century Tuscan Madonna and Child to 20th-century works by Rouault, Picasso, Wyeth, Matisse, and Maxfield Parrish. Silver, pewter, art, glass, textiles, and an extensive collection of early furniture are also displayed. Special exhibits are frequently outstanding. There is a drawing room with interactive arts and crafts projects for children and families, and the café and museum shop have been recently expanded; inquire about frequent lectures and concerts.

The Zimmerman House (603-669-6144; www.currier.org), 201 Myrtle Way. Open year-round except Jan.–Mar. This Usonian home designed in 1950 by Frank Lloyd Wright—his only house open to the public in New England—is also maintained by the Currier. One-hour guided tours are offered by shuttle van from the museum Mon., Thu., and Fri. at 2 PM, Sun. at 1 PM. Special in-depth weekend tours are offered Sat. and Sun. 2:30–4:30. Standard tour is $9 per adult; $6 for seniors, students, and those under 18; this price includes museum admission. The in-depth tour is $15 per adult; $11 for seniors and students (no children under age 7, please). There are also twilight tours on selected Thursday evenings that include refreshments at the museum and classical music performances at the house. Call ahead for handicapped accessibility. The Currier is in a residential neighborhood on the site of the Victorian home of Moody and Hannah Currier, the couple who donated the property and who specified in their will that their house be torn down to make way for the museum. The trick to finding it is to begin at either highway exit from which it's marked (the Amoskeag Bridge exit on Rt. 293 and the Wellington St. exit on I-93), then follow the trail of signs.

Franco-American Centre (603-669-4045; www.francoamericancentrenh.com), 52 Concord St. Open Mon.–Fri. 9–4. Handy to Elm St. and other downtown museums, this is a leading source of information about French culture, heritage, and history in North America. The Beliveau Gallery mounts changing exhibits, primarily by Franco-American artists.

New Hampshire Institute of Art (603-623-0313; www.nhia.edu), 148 Concord St., Manchester. Open Mon., Fri., and Sat. 9–5. Just across Victory Park from the Historical Association, New Hampshire's only independent college of art features changing exhibits of regional and national importance in six galleries. The center also offers lectures and theatrical performances. A gift and art supply shop features handcrafted items.

Currier Museum of Art, Manchester, NH

THE DINING ROOM OF THE FRANK LLOYD WRIGHT–DESIGNED ZIMMERMAN HOUSE

Alva deMars Megan Chapel Art Center, Saint Anselm College (603-641-7470; www.anselm.edu), 100 St. Anselm Dr., Manchester. Changing exhibits by regionally and nationally known artists often coincide with lectures, tours, and concerts.

HISTORICAL MUSEUMS AND SITES ✒ ♿ **Millyard Museum** (603-622-7531; www.manchesterhistoric.org), 225 Commercial St., Mill 3 (corner of Commercial and Pleasant), Manchester. Open Tue.–Sat. 10–4, Sun. noon–4. $6 adults, $5 students and seniors, $2 ages 6–18; under 6 free, with a family maximum of $18. A branch of the Manchester Historic Association, this new museum in former Mill 3 offers a glimpse into what was once the world's largest textile enterprise. Originally conceived as a planned industrial center, the buildings of the former Amoskeag Manufacturing Company still represent one of the country's leading examples of 19th- and early-20th-century industrial architecture. The four- and five-story-high mills stand in two rows along the eastern bank of the river. Built variously from the 1830s to 1910, they look fairly uniform because, as the older mills were expanded, their early distinctive features were blurred. The adjoining blocks lined with tidy, brick mill housing, however, reflect a progression of styles from the 1830s to 1920. The two large mills on the western side of the river were once connected to these by tunnels and bridges. The museum documents the area's history, beginning with a permanent exhibit about the Native Americans who used to catch salmon at Amoskeag Falls. Multimedia exhibits and programs and guided walking tours of the millyard and beyond offer more insights into the social and architectural history of the area. Many of the Amoskeag

Manufacturing Company records, along with city records and family papers, are available in the Henry Fuller Gallery at the museum.

American Credit Union Museum (603-629-1553; www.acumuseum.org), 418–420 Notre Dame Ave., Manchester (main entrance on Armory St.). Open Mon., Wed., and Fri. 10–noon and 1–4. Home of the nation's first credit union, which opened its doors in 1908 to mill workers seeking the American dream. Exhibits, artifacts, and a video present the story of the credit union movement.

Manchester City Hall (603-624-6500; www.ci.manchester.nh.us), 1 City Hall Plaza (west side of Elm St.), Manchester. This Gothic-style structure, built in 1845, houses rotating exhibits by local artists, permanent public exhibits of city paintings and photographs, and the Primary Room with exhibits celebrating New Hampshire's first-in-the-nation primary.

Diocesan Museum (603-624-1729), 140 Laurel St., Manchester. Built in 1896, this historic chapel, once part of the Sisters of Mercy convent, is of interest for its stained-glass windows and marble altars as well as for changing exhibits of religious art and memorabilia.

Sargent Museum of Archaeology (603-627-4802), 1045 Elm St., Suite 303, Manchester. Usually open Tue.–Thu. 9:30–5:30 and other times by appointment, but it's best to call the in advance to be sure. The late Howard R. Sargent, a revered anthropology professor, spent a lifetime collecting Native American and other artifacts from across the continent. His influence ranged far and wide; at the museum's opening in 2001, Steven Tyler, lead singer of Aerosmith, reminisced about finding an arrowhead when he was a kid digging in one of Sargent's excavations. In addition to housing Sargent's collection of artifacts and his 7,000-volume library, the museum serves as a center for field studies, workshops, and lectures focusing on the archaeology, anthropology, and history of New Hampshire and New England. Located in downtown Manchester a few blocks from the soon-to-be-renovated permanent home of the museum in a historic 1841 school building at 88 Lowell Street.

Nashua, New Hampshire's second largest city, has its share of monumental mill buildings along Water and Factory Streets, built by the Nashua Manufacturing Company, which was chartered in 1823 to produce cotton fabric.

Robert Frost Farm (603-432-3091; www.nhstateparks.org/ParksPages/Frost Farm/Frost), 2 miles south of Derry on Rt. 28. Open Memorial Day weekend–mid-June on weekends only, 10–5; mid-June–Labor Day, Tue.–Sat. 10–5, Sun. noon–5; closed Mon. $7 adults, $3 ages 6–17; ages 5 and under and New Hampshire residents over 65, free. Grounds open free at all times. Tours conducted on the hour until 4 PM. This 1880s clapboard house in which the poet lived between 1901 and 1909 is filled with original furnishings. An interpretive nature trail runs through surrounding fields and woods, past the "mending wall." Frost did the bulk of his writing here.

Nashua Historical Society (603-883-0015; www.nashuahistoricalsociety.org), 5 Abbott St., just off Rt. 101A. Open Tue.–Thu. 10–4, Sat. 1–4. The Florence Speare Memorial Museum offers changing exhibits plus a wealth of information regarding Nashua's origins, its evolution into a mill town in the 1800s, and its

continued growth as a leading manufacturing and technological center. The
neighboring Abbot-Spalding House, a fully furnished Federal-era mansion built
by Daniel Abbot, "Father of Nashua" and founder of the city's first cotton mills,
is an extension of the museum. It also contains a library of Nashua history and
materials.

Taylor Up and Down Saw Mill (603-271-2214; http://nh.gov/dred/divisions/
forestandlands/bureaus/communityforestry/taylormill.htm), Island Pond Rd.,
Derry. A 200-year-old, water-powered up-and-down sawmill located on a 71-acre
state forest. The mill operates at about 60 strokes per minute to process logs into
boards. Open usually in spring when the water level is high enough to power it
and approximately every other Saturday, June–Sep. For precise operating times
call the Department of Resources and Economic Development or consult the
web site.

Old Sandown Railroad Museum (603-887-6100), Rt. 121A, 1 Depot Rd.,
Sandown. Open May–Oct., Sat. and Sun. 1–5. Railroad memorabilia, telegraph
equipment, old magazines, posters, photographs, and Civil War letters are
among the exhibits.

Valley Cemetery (603-624-6514; www.valley-cemetery.com), corner of Pine
and Valley streets, Manchester. Walking tours and programs highlight this Victorian garden cemetery, established in 1841; the burial place for many of Manchester's founding families.

FOR FAMILIES ✐ **Amoskeag Fishways** (603-626-3474; www.amoskeagfishways
.org), Amoskeag Dam, 6 Fletcher St. (Exit 6 off I-293), Manchester. Open
Mon.–Sat. 9–5 throughout the year; daily during fish migration season. There's a
fish ladder where you can watch fish returning to spawn in the Merrimack River
during May and June. Year-round educational exhibits highlighting the natural
history of the Merrimack River watershed, include a historic diorama and waterpower displays.

✐ **Canobie Lake Park** (603-893-3506; www.canobie.com), Exit 2, I-93, Salem.
Open Memorial Day–Labor Day, daily noon–10; mid-Apr.–Memorial Day and
Labor Day–late Sep., weekends noon–6. In operation since 1902, this remains
one of the country's finest traditional amusement parks and one of New England's largest. Situated on Canobie Lake and dotted with large old trees, this
well-kept, well-landscaped complex offers more than 40 rides, including a big
roller coaster, extensive Kiddieland, new water park, swimming pool, wild log
flume ride, antique carousel, and excursion boat and mini train ride around the
park. Lots of treats, traditional and otherwise, in more than a dozen food stands.

✐ **Charmingfare Farm** (603-483-5623; www.visitthefarm.com), Rt. 27, Candia.
Open daily mid-May–Columbus Day, 10–4. $9 admission (kids under 1 are free)
includes petting zoo and hayride, weather permitting.

✐ **The Children's Metamorphosis** (603-425-2560; www.childrensmet.org), 6
W. Broadway, Derry. One mile from Exit 4 off I-93. Open Tue.–Sat. 9:30–5, Sun.
1–5, Fri. evening until 8. Admission $5 ($9 per family on Fri. 5–8 PM). Geared to
kids 2–8, there are multiple exhibit areas including a construction site, grocery

store, hospital emergency room, dress-up room, dinosaur area, dentist's office, cave, water play area, and many hands-on exhibits.

⚓ **The Lawrence L. Lee Scouting Museum** (603-669-8919; www.scouting museum.org), Blondin Rd. off Bodwell Rd., Manchester. Open July and Aug., daily 10–4; Sep.–June, Sat. 10–4. Considered the finest collection of Scouting memorabilia and books in the world; exhibits include original drawings and letters of Scouting founder Lord Robert Baden-Powell. The library of 3,000 books and bound periodicals also relates to Scouting.

⚓ **Mystery Hill** (603-893-8300; www.stonehengeusa.com), off Rt. 111, North Salem. Take I-93 Exit 3 and follow Rt. 111 for 5 miles east to Island Pond Rd., then take Haverhill Rd. to the entrance. Open daily except Thanksgiving and Christmas; hours vary by season. Check for current rates. Billed as "America's Stonehenge, one of the largest and possibly the oldest megalithic . . . sites in North America." How and why these intriguing stone formations originated is a mystery, whether built by Native Americans or migrant Europeans, but what's known for sure is that they remain an amazing example of prehistoric astronomical and architectural prowess.

⚓ ♿ **SEE Science Center** (603-669-0400; www.see-sciencecenter.org), 200 Bedford St., Manchester. Open Mon.–Fri. 10–3, Sat. and Sun. noon–5. Housed on two floors of a former textile mill building, this science discovery center allows children of all ages hands-on experience of the principles of electricity, momenturm, sound, light, and other technology. You can walk on the moon, play with giant bubbles and gyroscopes, and see a two-million-piece LEGO replica of the circa-1905 millyard, complete with running water; it's the world's largest LEGO exhibit outside LEGOLAND Park. $5 per person.

SCENIC DRIVES **Goffstown to New Boston**. With its bandstand and country stores, New Boston is an unusually handsome town, and the ride between it and Goffstown is one of the most pleasant around. The road follows the winding Piscataquog River, a good stream for fishing and canoeing. Take Rt. 114 west from Manchester and Rt. 13 to New Boston.

Londonderry. For a glimpse of southern New Hampshire's agricultural past, call the Londonderry town offices at 268B Mammoth Rd., Londonderry, 603-432-1100, ext. 134, to obtain a map for a tour of country roads through blossoms in spring and apples in fall.

✳ To Do

BALLOONING **High 5 Ballooning** (603-893-9643), 4 Joseph St., Derry. Gift certificates available.

Splash & Dash Hot Air Ballooning (603-483-5503), 107 Hook Rd., Candia. Balloon rides offered over Lake Massabesic.

BASEBALL **Holman Stadium** (603-883-2255), 67 Amherst St., Nashua. The Nashua Pride may be a minor-league team (it's part of the Atlantic League of Professional Baseball), but around here it's major summertime fun. Built in

1937, the stadium hosted what is considered the first integrated baseball team in the modern era, when Roy Campanella and Don Newcombe played for the then-Nashua Dodgers in 1946.

BOATING There's public access to the Merrimack River's kayak course from Arms Park in downtown Manchester. Lake Massabesic offers two public launches for sailing, powerboating, and canoeing. The **Merrimack River Watershed Council** (603-626-8828; www.merrimack.org) offers detailed boating maps of the Merrimack River and a series of free trips down southern New Hampshire rivers Apr.–early Oct.

FACTORY TOURS **Anheuser-Busch Brewery** (603-595-1202), 221 Daniel Webster Hwy., Merrimack (between Manchester and Nashua). Tours of the brewery (the brew hall, cold cellars, high-speed packaging operations, and the Budweiser Clydesdales in their Old World–style hamlet), complete with complimentary tastings, are offered May–Dec., daily 10–4 (June–Aug., 9:30–5); Thu.–Mon. 10–4 the rest of the year. The shop where you can buy Budweiser logo merchandise stays open an hour later.

Stonyfield Farm Yogurt Museum (603-437-4040, ext. 3270), 10 Burton Dr., Londonderry. Open Mon.–Sat. 9:30–5. Weekday tours on the hour 10–4. Stonyfield Farm is known for good yogurt and good sense with its environmentally friendly operation. Follow the milk from its arrival at the farm to the end of the line when it emerges as a cup of yogurt. $1.50 per person; children 4 and under free.

GOLF **Bedford Golfland** (603-624-0503), 549 Donald St., Bedford. Year-round driving range and 18-hole miniature golf course. **Apple Hill Golf Course** (603-642-4414), East Kingston. **Atkinson Country Club** (603-362-5681), Atkinson. **Buckmeadow Golf Club** (603-673-7077), Amherst. **Campbell's Scottish Highlands** (603-894-4653), Salem. **Candia Woods Golf Links** (603-483-2307; 1-800-564-4344; www.candiawoods.com), Exit 3, Rt. 101, High St., Candia. Eighteen holes, open to the public, tee times taken 5 days in advance. **Countryside Golf Club** (603-774-5031), Dunbarton. Nine holes. **Derryfield Country Club** (603-669-0235), 625 Mammoth Rd., Manchester. **Granite Fields Golf Club** (603-642-9977; www.granitefields.com), Kingston. **Green Meadow Golf Club** (603-889-1555), Hudson. **Legends Golf & Family Recreation** (603-627-0099), 18 Legends Dr. (behind Wal-Mart), Hooksett. Miniature golf and lighted driving range, along with lessons by a PGA professional and free tips on Wed. night. Also batting cages for baseball and softball. **Londonderry Country Club** (603-432-9789), Londonderry. **Stonebridge Country Club** (603-497-8633), 161 Gorham Pond Rd., Goffstown. Eighteen holes, open to the public.

& **Victorian Park Mini-Golf & Family Entertainment Center** (603-898-1803), 350 N. Broadway, Salem. Open end of Apr.–Halloween, daily 10–10. Victorian-motif ice cream parlor, video arcade, and challenging 18-hole mini golf course.

HOCKEY **Verizon Wireless Arena** (603-644-5000; 603-626-PUCK; 603-626-7825), 555 Elm St., Manchester. The Manchester Monarchs, an affiliate of the

Los Angeles Kings, field this American Hockey League team at New Hampshire's newest and largest sports and entertainment facility. The season lasts mid-Nov.–the first week in Apr.

HORSE RACING Rockingham Park (603-898-2311; www.rockinghampark.com), Rt. 28 and I-93, Salem. New England's first and finest racetrack once played host to such big name thoroughbreds as Seabiscuit. Now the historic track and clubhouse offers live harness racing 4 days a week during summer, and year-round day and night full-card simulcasting from the country's top racetracks throughout the year. Dining at the Sports Club.

MOTORCYCLING EagleRider (603-626-6300; 1-877-736-8431; www.eaglerider .com), 336 Lincoln St., Manchester. As unlikely as it may seem, one of the state's busiest weekends is in June when Harleys crowd most roads heading north toward Weirs Beach and Laconia. If you're a Hog or a wannabe, call the EagleRider motorocycle tourism company at this number to join them.

✳ Green Space

Bear Brook State Park (603-485-9874, 485-9869 for campground), off Rt. 28 in Allenstown. Open daily mid-May–Labor Day; call for other times. Take the Hooksett exit off I-93. Fee. The park has 9,600 heavily forested acres with six lakes, swimming, rental boats, picnicking for up to 1,500 visitors under tall pines, a physical fitness course, nature trails, fishing (Archery Pond is reserved for fly-fishing), and camping with 97 tent sites on Beaver Pond (where the swimming beach is reserved for campers). The Bear Brook Nature Center also has programs, two nature trails, and more than 30 miles of hiking trails in the park with separate routes for ski tourers and snowmobilers in winter. Very crowded on summer weekends but not too bad midweek.

Massabesic Audubon Center (603-668-2045; www.nhaudubon.org/sanctuaries /massabesic.htm), Auburn. Open Tuesday–Sat. 9 AM–5 PM; Sun. noon–5 PM. Free. Miles of scenic trails for hiking, snowshoeing, and skiing. Live animals, osprey viewing, and large nature store with snowshoe and binocular rentals.

Northwood Meadows State Park (603-485-2034), off Rt. 4, Northwood, offers 675 acres of wilderness open year-round. Hiking, picnicking, fishing, nonmotorized boating, snowmobiling, and cross-country skiing, depending on season. Free.

Pawtuckaway State Park (603-895-3031), off Rt. 156, Nottingham. Open weekends only Memorial Day weekend–mid-June, then daily through Columbus Day; call for winter hours. At Raymond, 3.5 miles north of the junction of Rts. 101 and 156. The attraction is a small beach on 803-acre Lake Pawtuckaway, with good swimming, a bathhouse, a 25-acre picnic area, and hiking trails. Rental boats are available; outboard motors are permitted; and the lake is stocked for fishing. Horse Island and Big Island, both accessible to cars, have a total of 170 tent sites, many right on the water; campers have their own boat launch. Trails lead up into the Pawtuckaway Mountains. Both cross-country skiing and snowmobiling are popular here in winter.

Silver Lake State Park (603-465-2342), Rt. 122, Hollis. Open weekends only Memorial Day–mid-June, then daily through Labor Day. Fee. A great beach with a bathhouse, a concession stand, picnic tables, and a diving raft. More than 100 picnic sites are scattered through the pine groves. Summer weekend crowds come from Nashua, but midweek is pleasant.

Clough State Park (603-529-7112), between Rts. 114 and 13, about 5 miles east of Weare. Open weekends only Memorial Day–late June, then daily through Labor Day. Fee. The focus here is 150-acre Everett Lake, created by the U.S. Army Corps of Engineers as a flood-control project. The 50-acre park includes a sandy beach and bathhouses, a picnic grove, and a playground. Motorized boats are not permitted, but there is a boat launch and rental boats are available.

Ponemah Bog (603-224-9909), Amherst. A 100-acre open bog and botanical preserve with boardwalk and trails open year-round.

Mines Fells Park (603-589-3370), Nashua. Part of Nashua's Heritage Trail, the 325-acre park offers wetlands, forests, open fields, and the Nashua River canal for walking, jogging, biking, and cross-country skiing.

✳ Lodging

HOTELS ✧ ♿ **Radisson Hotel Manchester** (603-625-1000; 1-800-333-3333; www.radisson.com/manchester nh), 700 Elm St., Manchester 03101. Originally named The Center of New Hampshire, this hotel, located in the center of downtown near the Verizon Wireless Arena, is the state's major convention venue. Two restaurants, 250 guest rooms (with computer data-port and WiFi Internet access), and garage parking all under one roof. $139–179; group rates and package plans available.

✧ ♿ **The Highlander Inn** (603-625-6426; 1-800-548-9248), 2 Highlander Way, Manchester 03103. A very nice 88-room hotel in a well-landscaped, 33-acre setting with outdoor pool, hot tub, and exercise center, just 2 minutes from the airport. $115–170 for Jacuzzi suites with 24-hour shuttle and discounted airport parking.

✧ ♿ **Wayfarer Inn** (603-622-3766; 1-877-489-3658), 121 S. River Rd., Bedford 03110. A Manchester landmark since the 1960s, this full-service hotel and conference center offers 194 rooms, a health and fitness center with an indoor and outdoor pool, and a restaurant on the historic site of John Goffe's mill. Modern landscaping includes waterfalls and a covered bridge. Free shuttle to Manchester Airport, 4 miles away. Standard room $116, with variable special rates.

INN ✧ ♿ **Bedford Village Inn** (603-472-2001; 1-800-852-1166; www .bedfordvillageinn.com), 2 Olde Bedford Way, Bedford 03110. This is the inn the big-name media folk prefer when they're in town to cover New Hampshire's first-in-the-nation presidential primary. Once a working farm, the circa-1810 dairy barn now offers 12 elegant guest rooms and two apartments. All the rooms are spacious— most equipped with large-screen TV and Jacuzzi—and handsomely decorated with period antiques, custom fabrics, paintings, and Oriental rugs. The complex also includes a patrician-looking Federal home that now houses a restaurant with eight intimate dining rooms and a taproom tavern (see *Dining Out*). Plans are in the works to expand this Four Diamond inn with 36 additional guest suites, an upscale spa facility with a café featuring spa cuisine, and a northern Italian restaurant. Rates, which include breakfast, start at $225 per couple.

BED & BREAKFASTS ♪ **Derryfield Bed & Breakfast** (603-627-2082), 1081 Bridge St. Extension, Manchester 03104. A friendly, gracious B&B in a quiet neighborhood, handy to I-93. The three rooms include an attractive single ($75 per night); a full breakfast is served in the sunny dining room, and guests also have access to the living room (with fireplace and cable TV) and to the pool. $89 per couple.

Ash Street Inn (603-668-9908; www.ashstreetinn.com), 118 Ash St., Manchester 03104-4345. One of Manchester's rambling old Queen Anne houses, this one (circa 1885) is the setting for the Queen City's newest and poshest B&B. In addition to plush queen-sized beds, private bath, and cable TV, the five rooms offer air-conditioning, computer dataport, and voice-mail phone. There's a full breakfast in the dining room, a fireplace in the parlor, and a Rolls-Royce to shuttle you to and from the airport. $139 with breakfast and complimentary shuttle. Packages available that include dining and museum admission. Nonsmoking; no children or pets.

Stephen Clay Homestead (603-483-4096; www.stephenclaybedandbreakfast.com), 193 High St. (Rt. 127 across from the town library), Candia. Just 15 minutes from the Manchester Airport, this classic Colonial home

offers three rooms ranging $98–135 double occupancy. Two have queen beds and nice views of the garden and surrounding small town; the third is a two-room suite and can sleep up to four ($30 per extra adult beyond two). Gourmet breakfast is included in the room rate.

For **camping sites**, see Bear Brook State Park and Pawtuckaway State Park under *Green Space*.

✴ Where to Eat

DINING OUT **Bedford Village Inn** (603-472-2001; 1-800-852-2001; www.bedfordvillageinn.com), 2 Olde Bedford Way, Bedford. Open for breakfast, lunch, and dinner daily; Sun. brunch. This beautifully restored 18th-century house is now a Four Diamond restaurant with a variety of elegant dining rooms. The glassed-in porch has off-white furniture and mint-green carpeting with floral design; another room boasts mahogany paneling. There's also a cheery tavern with its own less expensive menu. Breakfast is a production—specialty omelets and crêpes, plus treats like deep-fried fruit fritters. The seasonally changing dinner menu might include pan-seared jumbo sea scallops served with chive risotto and butternut-apple salad ($27), or veal porterhouse with red wine demiglaze, shallot mashed potatoes, and wilted greens ($29).

Baldwin's on Elm (603-622-5975; www.baldwinsonelm.com), 1105 Elm St., Manchester. Open weekdays for lunch 11:30–2, nightly for dinner 5–9:30, Fri. and Sat. until 10. Closed Sun. The talk of the town since the Verizon Wireless Arena brought new buzz to Elm Street, this restaurant opened in October 2001 with Nathan Baldwin, the former executive chef at the Bedford Village Inn, at the helm. There's a three-course wine-tasting dinner on Mon. for $35. The cosmopolitan menu matches the sleek, contemporary atmosphere with small plates and bowls from $10 for semolina fried calamari on baby greens to larger entrées such as grilled venison chop with roasted corn polenta, chanterelle mushrooms, and red wine sauce for $29.

The Colosseum (603-898-1190), Breckenridge Mall, 264 N. Broadway, Rt. 28, Salem. Open daily except Mon. for dinner from 4 PM (Sat. and Sun. from noon), and Tue.–Fri. for lunch 11:30–3. Popes, politicians, and celebrities have given their blessing to this multi-award-winning restaurant. The extensive menu boasts daily trips to Boston for fresh ingredients and includes a variety of antipasti, pastas, and beef, veal, chicken, and fish dishes at reasonable prices. Among the specialties are pork loin stuffed with provolone, mint, fresh basil, bread crumbs, and garlic, sautéed in a tomato sauce with onions and oregano, for $13.95. A scaloppine of veal sautéed with mushrooms in a sherry sauce with cheese and served with ziti is $18.95.

Cotton (603-622-5488; www .cottonfood.com), 75 Arms Park Dr., Manchester. Open Mon.–Thu. 5–9 PM, Fri. and Sat. until 10, Sun. 4–8. Lunch is served Mon.–Fri. 11:30– 2:30, with a bar menu 2:30–5. Located below Canal St., the bold font and tilted martini glass on the marquee herald the casually sophisticated, slightly 1950s retro look of this trendy bistro in Manchester's historic old mill

complex. Jeffrey Paige, once the chef at Canterbury's Shaker Village, is well known for his innovative dishes and cookbooks using fresh seasonal ingredients. Now he's earning a name for his presentations from the likes of *Bon Appétit* magazine, which named this eatery one of the best neighborhood restaurants in the East. Asian-style tuna stacked on a sesame rice cake and topped with warm crab salad is typical of his style. Moderate.

C. R. Sparks (603-647-7275; www .crsparks.com), 18 Kilton Rd., Bedford. Open Mon.–Thu. 11:30–3 and 4:30–9:30; Fri. and Sat. until 10:30, Sun. 4–8. Warm woods, comfortable booths, an open concept, and an exhibition-style kitchen form the centerpiece of this restaurant dedicated to casual gourmet dining. Locals regard it as the best stop in town for roast beef and steak. Also has function facilities.

Fratello's (603-624-2022; www .fratellos.com), 155 Dow St., Manchester. Open for lunch weekdays 11:30–2; for dinner Mon.–Sat. from 4:30, and Sun. from noon. Located in an old mill building, Fratello's is one more entry on the city's Italian dining scene. The restaurant offers a good, moderately priced menu with steaks, seafood, Italian specialties, and major desserts.

Gauchos Churrascaria (603-669-9460), 62 Lowell St., Manchester. Open Tue.–Sat. 4–10 PM, Sun. noon–9. This fun, Brazilian-style eatery offers the best high-protein diet around, starting with a salad bar and followed by round after round of pork, beef, lamb, and chicken served at your table and dexterously sliced from skewers by waiters who know what they're doing. Side dishes include black beans, fried plantains, and rice. The restaurant's new location in an old, brick-walled livery stable is both handsome and appropriate. Fixed price $19.95. The front room offers a pastry bar with Starbucks coffee.

Loafers American Restaurant (603-890-6363; www.loafersnh.com), 43 Pelham Rd., Salem. Open daily for lunch and dinner. Interesting menu with moderately prices in an attractive, "doggy-themed" setting.

Michael Timothy's (603-595-9334), 212 Main St., Nashua. Open daily for dinner, lunch (except Sat.), and Sun. jazz brunch. Jazz bar open from 4 PM. White tablecloths, Tuscan colors, and fresh flowers set the tone for this long-standing Nashua favorite (opened in 1995). The wood-grilled pizza is high-style and delicious—for instance, carmelized onion and crispy bacon with duck confit ($21)—as are such other dinner entrées as the sautéed veal scaloppine with half-dried tomatoes, leeks, white wine, and prosciutto-wrapped baked asparagus ($22).

Richard's Bistro (603-644-1180), 36 Lowell St., Manchester. Open Mon.–Sat. 11:30–2:30 for lunch, 4–10 for dinner; Sun. 10–2 and 4–9. Just off Elm Street in downtown Manchester, this attractively mellow, French-style restaurant is good for unusual soups and salads at lunch and for Sunday brunch dishes like salmon hash and poached eggs topped with horseradish dill cream, or a frittata of fresh vegetables baked with feta. Dinner entrées might include pecan-dusted chicken breast with kiwi, mango, and sweet potato garnished with raspberries, and charbroiled filet mignon with shiitake mushrooms and focaccia potatoes.

For dessert try the raspberry trifle or one of Richard's famous pastries. A number of wines are available by the glass, and the wine list is respectable.

Starfish Grill (603-296-0676; www.starfishfood.com), 33 S. Commercial St., Manchester. Open Sun. 4–8, Mon.–Thu. until 8:30, Fri. and Sat. to 9:30. Whether you like your seafood raw, fried, wood grilled, or pan blackened, this is the place to get it fresh and innovatively prepared. Cotton's chef Jeffrey Paige is one of the owners of this moderately priced, attractively restored mill-house restaurant. Children's menu; tropical thirst quenchers for adults.

Surf Seafood Restaurant (603-595-9293; www.michaeltimothys.com/surf), 207 Main St., Nashua. Open Tue.–Thu. 4:30–9:30, Fri. and Sat. until 10. Michael and Sarah Buckley of Michael Timothy's Restaurant opened this seafood sister a few years ago, and it has become the place for seafood and atmosphere in the Gateway City. Green and blue hues and gossamer fabrics introduce an ocean theme, which the menu continues. Raw bar. Most entrées, including grilled miso-marinated salmon served over jasmine rice cake with seared asparagus, shiitakes, and ponzu sauce ($16), are under $20. Sarah's sautéed 2-pound lobster, flambéed with cognac, stock reductions, chive, cream, and butter, is $38.

A Taste of Europe (603-296-0292), 827 Elm St., Manchester. Open Tue.–Thu. 4–11, Fri. and Sat. until 1 AM. Tapas bar and variety of European entrées. Moderate.

Thousand Crane (603-634-0000), 1000 Elm St., Manchester. Open Mon.–Thu. 11–10, Fri. and Sat. until 11, Sun. noon–9:30. An extensive menu ranging from Japanese sushi to popular Chinese dishes. Moderate.

Tiya's Restaurant (603-669-4365), 8 Hanover St., Manchester. Open for lunch Mon.–Fri. 11–3, for dinner on Fri. and Sat. 5–10. An attractive Thai eatery right downtown at the corner of Elm and Hanover. You can get a tuna salad or Reuben, but stir-fried dishes like shrimp, scallops, sea legs, broccoli, pepper, and mushrooms are the same price. The house specialty is pad Thai: stir-fried egg, chicken, bean sprouts, and spicy sauces garnished with crushed peanuts. Moderate.

Villa Banca (603-598-0500; www .villabanca.com), 194 Main St., Nashua. Open weekdays from 11:30 AM, Sat. and Sun. from 4 PM. Traditional Italian dishes plus contemporary adaptations, with most entrées priced under $20. The former Nashua Trust Bank building makes a great backdrop; music—a piano player or strolling violinist—adds to the weekend ambiance.

EATING OUT **The Athens** (603-623-9317), 31 Central St., Manchester. Open daily for lunch and dinner. Standard Greek dishes, generous portions, moderately priced.

Black Brimmer Bar & Grill (603-669-5523; www.blackbrimmer.com), 1087 Elm St., Manchester. Open daily except Sun. and Mon., weekdays from 11:30 AM, Sat. from 5 PM, most nights until 1 AM. Wood paneling, high ceilings, and crystal chandeliers give this an old-fashioned tavern atmosphere. Good food and drinks with frequent live music. Moderate.

Chez Vachon (603-625-9660), 136 Kelly St., West Manchester (minutes from I-293). Open daily 6 AM–2 PM. A small Franco-American eatery with a big following for its salmon pie, pork pie, French crêpes, and the like.

Down 'n Dirty Bar B.Q. (603-624-2224), 168 Amory St., Manchester. Open Thu.–Sat. 11:30 AM–9 PM, Sun. 1–6 PM. Real southern pit barbecue, eat in or take out. Pulled pork, ribs, chicken, beef, catfish, and shrimp, all cooked lovingly over hickory wood. Hush puppies and pecan-topped sweet potato pie, with a little blues music for background, will have you whistling "Dixie."

The Element Lounge (603-627-1855; www.), 1055 Elm St., Manchester. Open daily except Tue. with live jazz on Thu. from 8 PM. Outside, this popular lounge features sidewalk drinks and light dining in season. Inside, there are two rooms, one with private circular booths; the other with wall-to-wall velour couches and high-definition projection TV. The only nonsmoking bar in town.

The Korean Place (603-622-9377), 110 Hanover St., Manchester. Open Wed. and Thu. 5–8:30 PM, Fri. and Sat. until 9:30. Traditional and new-style Korean cuisine reflects this city's increasingly diverse population.

Lala's Hungarian Pastry Shop (603-647-7100), 836 Elm St., Manchester. Open daily except Sun. 7–5, Wed.–Sat. until 8. Home-style restaurant with authentic Hungarian food and pastries.

Martha's Exchange and Brew Pub (603-883-8781), 185 Main St., Nashua. Open daily for lunch and dinner from 11 AM, weekend brunch 8:30–3. Large selection of beer and ale plus expected accompaniments. Well priced and popular.

Merrimack Restaurant (603-669-5222), 786 Elm St., Manchester.

Open Mon.–Sat. 7 AM–8:45 PM. The place to eat and greet for presidential primary politicians and their followers. The atmosphere looks like a faded newsreel but the food is good.

The Peddler's Daughter, 48 Main St., Nashua. Irish restaurant and pub with indoor and outdoor seating overlooking the Nashua River. Serves traditional Irish fare and a selection of draft beers, along with various homemade items. Live music venue featuring traditional Irish music and Celtic rock.

Pine Street Eatery (603-886-3501), 136 Pine St. (between Lake and Kinsley), Nashua. Open Mon.–Tue. 6 AM–7:30 PM, Wed.–Sat. 8 AM–9 PM, Sun. 6 AM–3 PM. Homey atmosphere with diner-style food and breakfast served until 3 PM. Seniors over 60 get a 15 percent discount.

Puritan BackRoom (603-669-6890; www.puritanbackroom.com), 245 Hooksett Rd., Manchester. This longtime Manchester meeting place offers a good, moderately priced menu served in a comfortable setting. Ice cream take-out in season.

Red Arrow Diner (603-626-1118), 61 Lowell St., Manchester. Open 24/7 just a block off the main drag of Elm St. A city landmark since 1922, this small, friendly diner was voted one of the top 10 diners in the country by *USA Today*. It's the kind of place with a brass hanger for your coat and a mug of coffee that's brought the moment you sit down. Specialties like meat loaf, chicken potpie, and hot sandwiches.

Shorty's Mexican Roadhouse (603-472-3656; www.shortysmex.com), 230 Rt. 101 west, Bedford; Manchester (603-625-1730), 1050 Bicentennial Dr.; and Nashua (603-882-4070), Nashua Mall, Rt. 3 to Exit 6. Open daily. This is a local favorite: a 1940s roadhouse atmosphere with southwestern and Mexican reliables like tacos, fajitas, and enchiladas; also dinner specials like chicken mole and grilled fish with salsa. Same menu, including 20 vegetarian dishes, all day.

Strange Brew Tavern (603-666-4292; www.strangebrewtavern.info), 88 Market St., Manchester. Open daily 4 PM–1 AM. The food's good but people go for the beer—the largest draft selection in town—and live nightly jazz and blues performances. Dancing.

Venetian Canal Espresso Caffé (603-627-9200), 805 Canal St., Manchester. Open Tue.–Thu. 7 AM–4 PM, Mon. and Fri. until 3 PM; Sat. 8 AM–1 PM. Soups, salads, sandwiches, pastry, and enough yummy coffee, tea, and chai drinks to float a gondola.

Ya Mamma's (603-578-9201), 75 Daniel Webster Hwy., Merrimack. Open weekdays 11:30–9, Sat. 4–10, Sun. 1–8. Extensive, moderately priced Italian menu and casual atmosphere have made this restaurant a longtime local favorite.

✳ Entertainment

✄ & **The Palace Theatre** (603-668-5588; www.palacetheatre.org), 80 Hanover St., Manchester 03101. Opened in 1915, reopened and restored in 1974, this 883-seat theater is a beauty—with small, glittering chandeliers, bright local art, and an intimate feel. In addition to a calendar of nationally known artists, the theater has its own resident company, which mounts several productions a year. During the summer there is children's programming and a July summer camp. Phone for the current program.

Stage One Productions (603-669-5511; www.stageoneproductions.net), 124 Bridge St., Manchester. Buffet dinner theater at the Chateau Restaurant (603-627-2677), 201 Hanover St., Manchester, Nov.–Apr.

&. **Verizon Wireless Arena** (603-644-5000), 832 Elm St., Manchester. The state's new 10,000-seat venue for big-time concerts, wrestling, dirt shows, figure skating, hockey, basketball, arena football, and political forums. Tickets to most events are available through Ticketmaster at 603-868-7300 or www.ticketmaster.com.

The Dana Center, St. Anselm College (603-641-7710; www.anselm .edu), 100 St. Anselm Dr., Manchester. A state-of-the-art regional performing arts center presenting a full program of nationally acclaimed theater, dance, and music.

Majestic Theatre (603-669-7469; www.majestictheatre.net), 281 Cartier St., Manchester. A full-time community theater that produces more than a dozen plays, musicals, and dinner theaters each year.

Adams Memorial Opera House (603-437-0505; www.derryarts.org), 29 W. Broadway, Derry. Built in 1904 and renovated in 2000, this theater, now on the National Historic Register, continues its tradition of hosting concerts, plays, and other arts and civic performances.

✳ Selective Shopping

ART GALLERIES **Art 3 Gallery** (603-668-9983; www.art3gallery.com), 44 W. Brook St. (off Canal), Manchester. Open Mon.–Fri. 9–3 and by appoint-

ment. Contemporary and traditional work by a range of artists.

East Colony Fine Art Gallery (603-621-7400; www.eastcolony.com), Langer Place, 55 S. Commercial St., Manchester.

E. W. Poore Gallery (603-622-3802), 531 Front St., Manchester. This well-established, well-stocked art supply store includes a gallery featuring local artists' work.

Hatfield Gallery and Frame Shop (603-627-7560), 831 Elm St., Manchester.

SPECIAL SHOPS **Absolutely New Hampshire** (603-880-3039), 113 Main St., Nashua. New Hampshire–themed marketplace featuring items made in and about the Granite State. Offers personalized service, shipping, and extended holiday hours.

The New England Sampler (603-626-4477; www.thenewengland sampler.com), 42 Hanover St., Manchester. Open Tue.–Sat. from 10 AM, Fri. and Sat. until 7 PM. In the historic opera block near the Palace Theatre, this is a friendly venue for all things New England, from information to gourmet food to pottery, gifts, books, and photography.

Splash (603-627-2088; 603-594-3107; www.splashnh.com), 977 Elm St., Manchester, and 33 Main St., Nashua. Open Mon.–Fri. 9–5, Thu. until 8, Sat. 9–3. A luxury bath showroom featuring fixtures and accessories from home and abroad.

With Heart & Hand Unique Gifts (603-625-8100; www.withheartand hand.com), 823 Elm St., Manchester. Open daily except Sun. Country and primitive Americana linens, lighting, furniture, and tableware.

MALLS Reluctantly we include directions to malls along Salem's and Manchester's "strip," because that's what many out-of-staters are here for; New Hampshire's lack of sales tax has its appeal.

Just across the Massachusetts border on Rt. 28 (Exit 1 off I-93) in Salem, **Rockingham Park Mall**, with the usual suspects including JCPenney, Filene's, and Macy's, holds sway over a host of smaller strip mall entries. In Manchester the **Mall of New Hampshire**, 1500 S. Willow St., claims the distinction of being the state's largest. **Willow Tree Mall**, 575 Willow St., and **TJ Maxx Plaza**, 933 S. Willow St., are also large.

✳ Special Events

May: **Hillsborough County Annual Sheep and Wool Festival**, New Boston.

June–mid-October: **Manchester Farmer's Market**, on Concord St. between Chestnut and Pine, next to Victory Park.

June: **Talarico Downtown Jazz & Blues Festival** (603-668-5588): music, crafts, food. **Strawberry Shortcake Festival** (603-647-7309), Valley Cemetery, Manchester. Free shortcake and guided tours with characters dressed in 1800s-era costumes.

July: **Family Outdoor Discovery Day**, Bear Brook State Park Campground.

August: **Annual Antique Dealers Show**, Manchester. **Latino Festival** (603-644-7023), Manchester. Parade, live music, dancing, ethnic foods, and crafts.

September: **Riverfest**, Manchester. Three days with fireworks, live entertainment, canoe competitions, country fair exhibits. **A Taste of Downtown** (603-645-6285) offers food from the city's best restaurants all for one ticket. **Glendi** (603-622-9113) is the largest Greek festival north of Boston, featuring Greek bands, dancing, and delicacies. **Hillsborough County Agricultural Fair** (603-674-2510), New Boston. **Hanover Street Fine Arts Fair**, Manchester. **Deerfield Fair** (603-463-7421), Deerfield.

October: **Annual Weare Craft Bazaar**, Weare. **Head of the Merrimack Regatta** (603-888-2875), Nashua.

THE CONCORD AREA

The golden dome of the state capitol building still towers above downtown Concord. Since 1819, when it was built out of local granite by convict labor, this building has been the forum for the state's legislature—now numbering 400 members—said to be the third largest deliberative body in the English-speaking world.

The Native Americans called this site Penacook, or "crooked place," for the snakelike turns the Merrimack makes here. Concord's compact downtown clusters along the western bank of the river, and it's encircled by the concrete wall of I-93 along the opposite bank.

Concord owes its prominence to two forgotten phenomena: the Middlesex Canal—opened in 1815 to connect it with Boston—and the steam railroad from Boston, completed in 1842. Today Concord remains an important transportation hub—the point at which I-89 forks off from I-93 to head northwest across New Hampshire and Vermont, ultimately linking Boston with Montreal.

Concord is really just a medium-sized town of just over 40,000 residents, and you are quickly out of it and into the countryside of East Concord at the Society for the Protection of New Hampshire Forests headquarters, or into the western countryside at Silk Farm, New Hampshire's Audubon Society.

While still very much in the Merrimack Valley, Concord, in contrast with Manchester, is just beyond southern New Hampshire's old industrial belt with its ethnic mix. Some of Concord's surrounding towns are as Yankee, and as picturesque, as any in New England.

Canterbury Shaker Village, a striking old hilltop community, is a gathering of white wooden buildings surrounded by spreading fields. Hopkinton, a proud, early-19th-century town, boasts one of New England's most classic Main Streets, and Henniker is a mill-town-turned-college-town with more to offer visitors than many resorts.

GUIDANCE **The Greater Concord Chamber of Commerce** (603-224-2508), 40 Commercial St. (just off Exit 15W, I-93), Concord 03301. Open year-round, Mon.–Fri. 8–5. Although not in the center of town, this office is well located for many tourists and visitors, and not far off the beaten path for anyone with a car. Plenty of parking by the new Concord Courtyard Marriott & Grappone Conference Center.

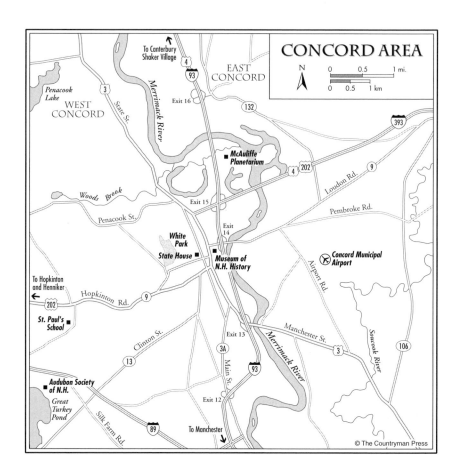

Staff are exceptionally friendly and helpful. The chamber also maintains an information kiosk downtown on State House Plaza, open weekends June–Columbus Day, depending on the availability of volunteers.

GETTING THERE *By bus:* **The Concord Bus Terminal** (603-228-3300), Stickney Ave., is served by Concord Trailways, Peter Pan Bus Lines, and Vermont Transit.

GETTING AROUND *By taxi:* **A&P Taxi** (603-224-6573), **Central Taxi** (603-224-4077). **Concord Cab Company** (603-225-4222), **Main Street Taxi** (603-226-8888). **Celebrity Express Limousine** (603-776-5775) and **Grace Limousine** (603-226-0002) offer limousine service between pickup points in Concord, Manchester, downtown Boston, and Logan International Airport.

MEDICAL EMERGENCY **Concord Hospital** (603-225-2711), 250 Pleasant St., Concord.

Henniker. West of Concord at the junction of Rts. 9/202 and 114 (take Exit 5 off I-89), "the only Henniker on earth" is a delightful college town with an outstanding small ski area, a cross-country ski center, and a number of interesting shops and restaurants. Well into the 20th century Henniker was a bustling crossroads town with a thriving inn, a number of farms, and three mills on the Contoocook River—one mill making bicycle rims; another, handles; and the third, leatherboard for shoes. Several mills, however, were destroyed by a 1936 flood, and in the 1940s **New England College** was established. With a combined student and faculty population of 1,000, the college now forms the heart of the town. The former Henniker Inn is the administration office, the art gallery next door showcases New England art, and shops and restaurants line a green strip along the Contoocook River across the street. Just across the bridge, the Simon Student Center provides a handsome venue for frequent lectures by nationally known visiting scholars and political insiders.

Hopkinton. Just west of Concord off I-89, Hopkinton village boasts a Main Street lined with picturesque churches, early white-clapboard mansions, a traditional town hall that once served as the state capitol, and the New Hampshire Antiquarian Society, an ambitiously named but excellent local museum and gallery. Beyond the village center are lovely back-road drives. Be sure to stop at Beech Hill Farm, still owned by the Kimball family nine generations after the king's grant, for Donna's home-baked coffee cake and make-your-own sundaes. Another old family property, Gould Hill Orchards, is located high enough to see Mount Washington on a clear day. It offers "pick-your-own" and a barn filled with seasonal gifts, homemade goodies, and fruit. Three miles west on Rt. 103, Contoocook village (one of three villages that form the town of Hopkinton) is host to the large annual Hopkinton Fair. The Hopkinton Town Library, just off Fountain Square on Pine Street, is a handsome shingle-style building set on a former 68-acre farm. Its screened reading porches overlook soccer and baseball fields, and the Local History Room features a dozen outstanding murals with area scenes painted by talented local artists.

* To See

MUSEUMS ♪ **Christa McAuliffe Planetarium** (603-271-STAR; www.starhop .com), 2 Institute Dr., Concord. Take I-93 Exit 15E, drive east on I-393 to Exit 1, and follow signs. The planetarium is on the campus of the New Hampshire Technical Institute. Exhibit area and gift shop open Mon.–Sat. 10–5, Sun. noon–5. $8 adults; $5 for children, college students, and seniors 62 and above. McAuliffe was a teacher at Concord High School when she was chosen from among 11,000 to be the first teacher in space. Dedicated to her memory (she died in the Challenger tragedy of 1986), this facility, with its dramatic rendition of the universe, is the most technologically advanced theater in New England, with a 40-foot dome, full-color video, surround sound system, and database of more than 110,000 stars. Although geared primarily to schoolchildren, it has a variety of programs. There are several shows daily (11 AM, 12:30 PM, 2 PM, and

CANTERBURY SHAKER VILLAGE

🌸 (603-783-9511; www.shakers.org), 288 Shaker Rd., Canterbury 03224. Open June–Oct., daily 10–5 and Fri.–Sun. in Nov. 10–4. $15 adults, $6 ages 6–17; under 6 free. Family and group discounts.

Designated as a National Historic Landmark and arguably the single most rewarding sight to see in central New Hampshire, this complex of 24 buildings set in 694 acres conjures up a unique, almost vanished way of life that produced many inventions and distinctive art, food, and music. Between the 1780s and 1990, some 2,300 Shaker men, women, and children lived in this rural community, putting their "hands to work and hearts to God." In the 1850s, when this Shaker village owned 4,000 acres with 100 buildings, it was one of 18 such American communes extending from Kentucky to Maine to

THE MEETING HOUSE AND DWELLING HOUSE AT CANTERBURY SHAKER VILLAGE

Kim Grant

3:30 PM), but advance reservations are strongly recommended since seating is limited to 92 people. Inquire about special programs and workshops; also special discount offers.

🌸 **Museum of New Hampshire History** (603-228-6688; www.nhhistory.org), 6 Eagle Square, off Main St., Concord. Follow directions to parking from I-93 Exit 14. Open Tue.–Sat. 9:30–5, until 8:30 Thu.; Sun. noon–5. Also open Mon. 9:30–5 in Dec. and July–Oct. 15. $5 adults ($4 if over age 55), $2.50 ages 6–18, under 6 free; $15 family maximum; free on Thu. evenings. Opened in 1995 by the New

Ohio. Today just six communities survive to tell their story, and Canterbury is one of just two settlements that have never been out of Shaker hands. In 1969 Eldress Bertha Lindsay (who died in 1990) had the foresight to incorporate the present buildings and property as a nonprofit museum.

The last village to assume the "Lead Ministry," Canterbury absorbed a number of brethren from other communities as they closed and so conveys a vivid sense of Shaker life from the 1880s to about the turn of the 20th century. Visitors are guided through a dozen buildings and encouraged to try the Shaker-inspired food served at the village restaurant (see *Dining Out*). You can also follow the nature trail around Turning Mill Pond, one of the eight that once powered a variety of mills on a 4,000-acre spread. The vintage-1792 Meeting House now doubles as exhibit and performance space. The Laundry is immense and fascinating, and the brightly lit sewing room is furnished with exquisitely crafted tables, and hung with the "Dorothy Cloaks" invented here, popularized by Mrs. Grover Cleveland, who wore one to her husband's inauguration in 1885. The infirmary is equally fascinating, restored to trace the evolution of medical care here. Herbs in the built-in drawers are left from the last time they were used, and the tools on the dentist chair are just as Elder Henry Blinn left them. (Also known as a cartographer and geologist, Blinn began practicing dentistry here in 1860.) In the School House it's easy to assume that the pupils are just out for recess and will be rushing back in, up the graceful staircase and into the bright, wood-paneled room that is filled with books, hung with maps. The blackboard bears a reminder written there by Sister Bertha: no one will find a spirit-real heaven, until they first create earthly heaven.

Note the many special happenings listed at the end of this chapter under Special Events.

Southbound on I-93, the village is marked from Exit 18. Northbound, use Exit 15E and follow I-393 east for 5 miles; then take Rt. 106 north for 7 miles and turn at the sign for Shaker Rd.

Hampshire Historical Society. Exhibits fill two floors of a 19th-century stone warehouse with one floor devoted to the densely packed permanent exhibit, New Hampshire Through Many Eyes. Chronological displays draw you through the state's history, from the Native Americans (in addition to an ancient dugout canoe and Indian artifacts, there is a wigwam in which youngsters can sit and hear an old Abenaki tale) to 20th-century industry. The exhibit captions tell some fascinating stories, like that of an exquisite porcupine quill belt (woven in 1763 by a young girl who had been captured by Native Americans) and of a piece of linen

MUSEUM OF NEW HAMPSHIRE HISTORY

made by Henniker's "Oceanborn Mary" (who was such a captivating baby that she charmed pirates out of capturing a ship). The collection includes the predictable Portsmouth-made highboy, Revolutionary War muskets, and, of course, a Concord Coach (3,000 were made in this town), but what's most interesting about the exhibit is its chronicle of past New Hampshire residents. You can hear Eldress Bertha Lindsay of Canterbury Shaker Village (thanks to the sound tape from Walpole resident Ken Burns's Shaker documentary) and ponder the fact that Christian Science founder Mary Baker Eddy (born in Bow, New Hampshire), poet Robert Frost, President Franklin Pierce, and *Peyton Place* author Grace Metalious are all in the same corner. The top floor, accessed through a staircase that suggests the look and view (through murals) of a White Mountains fire tower, is devoted to changing exhibits. There's no need to pay admission to access the extensive gift shop, featuring New Hampshire books and other interesting gift items related to the history of the state and beyond. The historical society's headquarters, in its original neoclassical building enhanced by Daniel Chester French's frontispiece, is nearby at 30 Park St., and contains changing exhibits and the excellent Tuck Library.

The New Hampshire Antiquarian Society (603-746-3825), Main St., Hopkinton 03229. Open year-round, Thu. and Fri. 9–4, and Sat. 9–1. On a street full of white-clapboard Colonials, this redbrick Palladian-windowed building is notable for its 1890s architecture, as well as for its genealogical materials, research library, local memorabilia, and paintings. There is an appealing shop and changing exhibits, including a popular autumn art show of exceptional regional talent. Ask for a brochure that includes a driving tour of local attractions.

HISTORIC HOMES AND SITES A leaflet describing a self-guided walking tour of Concord, *Concord on Foot*, is available from the chamber of commerce's Capital Region Visitor Center (see *Guidance*). It includes some of the following:

Benjamin Kimball House and Capitol Center for the Arts (603-225-1111), 44 S. Main St., Concord. This Romanesque Revival house was built around 1885 by Benjamin Kimball, but later became the state headquarters of the Masonic Order. Now the house and adjoining 1920s-era theater are the core of the Capitol Center for the Arts, a regional cultural art center that hosts internationally known theater troupes, dance companies, and musical acts.

The Eagle Hotel, N. Main St., Concord. For more than 135 years the Eagle Hotel was the center of Concord's social and political happenings. Andrew Jackson, Benjamin Harrison, Jefferson Davis, Charles Lindbergh, and Eleanor

Roosevelt were all guests. The hotel, now handsomely renovated as the Eagle Square Marketplace, houses mostly offices with a few shops and a restaurant.

First Church of Christ, Scientist, N. State and School streets, Concord. Mary Baker Eddy, born in nearby Bow in 1821, formulated the spiritual framework of the Christian Science faith. She contributed $100,000 toward the construction of this Concord granite building, whose steeple makes it the tallest in the city.

Kimball-Jenkins Estate (603-225-3932), 276 N. Main St., Concord. Built in 1882, this high Victorian brick-and-granite mansion has hand-carved oak woodwork, frescoed ceilings, Oriental rugs, and many original furnishings. Inspired by a directive in the late Carolyn Jenkins's will, the estate now houses two galleries and a thriving community art school.

New Hampshire Political Library (603-225-4617; www.politicallibrary.org), 20 Park St., Concord. Open Mon.–Fri. 8:30–4:30. The library houses and manages the most extensive archive of political campaign memorabilia in the country. Offering the only comprehensive collection of election campaign papers and paraphernalia from half a century of New Hampshire presidential primary history, it's a treasure trove for scholars, students, campaign managers, reporters, current candidates, future aspirants, and political pundits.

New Hampshire State House and the State House Plaza (603-271-2154), 107 N. Main St., Concord. Open year-round, weekdays for guided and self-guided tours 8–4:30. A handsome 1819 building, this is the oldest state capitol in which a legislature still meets in its original chambers. A visitors center contains

RONALD REAGAN GREETS RESIDENTS OF MILLSFIELD, NH, DURING A CAMPAIGN STOP IN 1976.

New Hampshire Political Library, Concord, NH

dioramas and changing exhibits. More than 150 portraits of past political figures are displayed, and the plaza boasts statues of several New Hampshire notables. The gift shop, located just off the lobby, offers posters, scarves, ties, books, and other items related to the state's natural resources and political history.

The Pierce Manse (603-224-5954; 603-225-2068; www.newww.com/free/pierce), 14 Penacook St. (at end of N. Main St.), Concord. Open mid-June–Labor Day, Mon.–Fri. 11–3, or by appointment. Closed holidays. $3 adults, $1 children and students. Built in 1838 and moved to its present site in 1971, this Greek Revival structure was home for Franklin and Jane Pierce from 1842 to 1848, between the time Franklin served in the U.S. Senate and was elected 14th president of the United States. Exhibits include many items owned by the Pierce family prior to 1869.

St. Paul's School (603-225-3341), 325 Pleasant St., Concord. Founded in 1855 by Dr. George Shattuck, St. Paul's is one of the country's premier preparatory schools, a 4-year boarding school with more than 500 students and 100 faculty members. Although the 2,000-acre campus is private, many of the lectures and theater and dance performances are open to the public. Exhibitions in the Tudor-style Hargate Art Center are scheduled throughout the school year, and feature a variety of works by well-known and up-and-coming professional and student artists, as well as occasional highlights from the school's collection of works. Past exhibitions have featured works by artists such as Robert Motherwell, Jacob Lawrence, Andrew Wyeth, Milton Avery, Arthur Dove, Eugene Atget, Thomas Buechner, Joyce Tenneson, and others. The school's Ohrstrom Library is also of particular interest. Designed by postmodern architect Robert Stern and opened in 1991, the building references a variety of features from other buildings on campus and offers an outstanding view of Turkey Pond from the reading room.

Upham-Walker House, (603-271-2017), 18 Park St., Concord. One of the best examples of late Federal architecture in the area, this building is open to the public by appointment and offers a glimpse into the lifestyle of successive generations of a prominent Concord family.

COVERED BRIDGES **Henniker–New England College bridge**. A single-span, 150-foot bridge across the Contoocook River on the New England College campus.

Hopkinton–Rowell bridge, West Hopkinton. Built in 1853 across the Contoocook River; rebuilt in 1997.

Hopkinton bridge, Contoocook village. No longer operating, the bridge spans the Contoocook River at Fountain Square and is said to be the oldest railroad covered bridge in the United States. The nearby depot has been recently restored.

FOR FAMILIES ✪ **New Hampshire Fish & Game Department Discovery Room** (603-271-3211), 2 Hazen Dr., Concord. Open year-round, Mon.–Fri. 8:30–4. Visit the Wild New Hampshire nature center and discover the state's wide variety of landscapes, among them a beaver pond, meadow, vernal pool, and boreal (spruce/fir) forest. Kids will enjoy the chance to get up close and personal with the life-sized replica of a moose cow and calf.

✳ To Do

BALLOONING **What's Up Ballooning** (603 428-3128), 39 Flanders Rd., Henniker. Traditional champagne balloon flights year-round.

CANOEING See *Boating* in "The Manchester/Nashua Area" for the Merrimack River Watershed Council.

In addition to the Merrimack, stretches of the Contoocook River between Henniker, Hopkinton, and Concord provide popular canoeing and kayaking. Originating in Rindge, the Contoocook flows approximately 66 miles northeast to join the Merrimack River in Penacook. The Nubanusit, Warner, and Blackwater rivers are the main tributaries. Quickwater can be found in early spring when the river is high, but by late April the river becomes flat for the summer months. Take a swim; stop for a picnic; fish for bass, pickerel, and trout; or simply enjoy the scenery and occasional wildlife.

Hannah's Paddles River Running LLC (603-753-6695), I-93, Exit 17, Rt. 4 west, 15 Hannah Dustin Dr., Concord. Offers canoe and kayak rentals and a livery service for the Merrimack and Contoocook Rivers.

Contoocook River Canoe Company (603-753-9804; www.contoocookcanoe .com), 9 Horse Hill Rd., Concord. Canoe and kayak rentals, instructions, guided tours, and shuttle service.

CAR RACING **New Hampshire International Speedway** (603-783-4931; www .nhis.com, Rt. 106, Loudon. New England's largest sports facility and home of the region's professional motor sports, this 101,000-seat complex annually attracts an estimated 400,000-plus motor-sport enthusiasts. "The Magic Mile" offers a wide range of activities, including professional and amateur motor

NEW HAMPSHIRE INTERNATIONAL SPEEDWAY

sports, bicycle racing, driving and racing schools, special performance-related activities, and even soapbox derby trials. Races include the world-class NASCAR Winston Cup series, the NASCAR Busch series, and many more. Call for current schedule.

FISHING The New Hampshire Fish and Game Department (603-271-3211), 2 Hazen Dr., Concord. A source of information about where to fish as well as how to obtain licenses. Trout fishing is particularly good in this area.

GOLF Beaver Meadow Golf Course (603-228-8954), Concord, 18 holes on the oldest course (1896) in the state. **Duston Country Club** (603-746-4234), Hopkinton, nine holes. **Loudon Country Club** (603-783-3372), Loudon, 18 holes. **Plausawa Valley Country Club** (603-224-6267), Pembroke, 18 holes. **Canterbury Woods Country Club** (603-783-9400; www.canterburywoodscc.com), 15 West Rd., Canterbury, is an 18-hole championship course.

DOWNHILL SKIING ✍ **Pat's Peak** (603-428-3245; 1-888-PATS-PEAK; www.patspeak.com), Rt. 114, Henniker. The mountain rises steeply right behind the base lodge. It's an isolated, 1,400-foot-high hump, its face streaked with expert trails and a choice of intermediate and beginner runs meandering down one shoulder, half a dozen beginner runs—served by their own lifts—down the other. Big, old fir trees are salted around the base area, and the summit and some of the intermediate trails—certainly Zephyr, the 0.25-mile-long beginner's trail off the top—convey the sense of skimming through the woods. When it comes to expert runs, Tornado and Hurricane are wide and straight, but Twister is an old-timer—narrow, twisty, and wooded. The Turbulence Terrain Park offers a changing menu of jumps, rails, and hips for snowboarders and freestyle skiers. This is a family-geared ski and snowboard area that provides a great place to learn along with some of the most accessible yet challenging skiing in southern New England. The Patenuade family, which has owned and operated the area since 1963, has spent about $4 million in the last 4 years on expanding and updating lifts, snowmaking equipment, and après-ski facilities.

PAT'S PEAK IS A FAMILY-FRIENDLY SKI AREA

Rob Bossi

Lifts: 10, including 3 double chairs and 2 triple chairs to the summit.

Trails: 22.

Snowmaking: 100 percent.

Night skiing: 19 trails, 10 lifts.

Services: Ski school, rentals, ski shop, lounge, cafeteria, child care, snowboarding.

Rates: $47 adults; $33 ages 6–17 and 65-plus on weekends; $34 and $24 mid-week; $26 and $21 for night skiing. Packages include W.O.W. (Women's Only Wednesdays, a 7-week program that includes breakfast and lunch plus weekly clinics, lessons, and video analysis), and P.O.P. (Pay One Price Saturdays, which include skiing, snowboarding, tubing, rentals, lesson tips, and entertainment for $29, 3–10 PM).

✳ Green Space

Elm Brook Park and Wildlife Management Area, off Rt. 127, West Hopkinton. Swimming and picnic areas; built and managed by the U.S. Army Corps of Engineers.

Hannah Duston Memorial, west of I-93, Exit 17 (4 miles north of Concord), Boscawen. The monument is on an island at the confluence of the Contoocook and Merrimack Rivers. It commemorates the courage of Hannah Duston, a woman taken prisoner from Haverhill, Massachusetts, during a 1696 Indian raid. She later made her escape, killing and scalping 10 of her captors (including women and children) at this spot on the river. The 35-foot-high monument, erected in 1874, depicts a busty lady with a tomahawk in one hand and what look like scalps in the other. Open all year, but the trail from the parking lot is not plowed in winter.

Silk Farm Wildlife Sanctuary (603-224-9909; www.nhaudubon.org), 3 Silk Farm Rd. (follow Audubon signs from I-89, Exit 2), Concord. Open year-round, Mon.–Fri. 9–5, Sat. from 10, and from noon on Sun. The new McLane Center, named for longtime New Hampshire legislator and environmental activist Susan McLane, is the headquarters of the Audubon Society of New Hampshire, offering an overview of Audubon centers and programs in the state. The environmentally friendly "green" building with wood pellet heating, composting toilets, and optimal solar siting has a Discovery Room with a "touch table," a research wildlife library, an aerie for spotting birds, a newly expanded hummingbird and butterfly garden, a raptor enclosure, and a gift shop with bird feeders, optics, birdseed, books, clothing, jewelry, and much more. Trails thread forests and wetlands around Great Turkey Pond and traverse orchards and fields with a variety of flora and fauna.

Society for the Protection of New Hampshire Forests Conservation Center (603-224-9945), Portsmouth St., Concord. Bring a picnic and hike along the Merrimack River on 90 acres of nature trails, or enjoy exhibits in the recently expanded and award-winning passive-solar "green" building.

⟋ **White's Park**, Liberty and School streets, Concord. In summer feed the ducks or swing on the playground; in winter sled or ice skate, just as Concord residents have done for generations. This well-kept park is located in a residential area a few blocks west of downtown.

✳ Lodging

INNS ♿ **Centennial Inn** (603-225-7102; 1-800-267-0525; www.some placesdifferent.com), 96 Pleasant St., Concord 03301. Built in 1896 as a home for the aged, this impressively turreted brick building now boasts the city's most luxurious accommodations. Converted to a hotel by Someplace(s) Different, the inn offers six individually decorated suites featuring a mix of reproduction furnishings and antiques. All have private bath; four provide whirlpool tub and private porch. Rooms include modem jack, VCR, remote-control television, and independent climate control. On the main floor, food and drink are available in the Franklin Pierce Dining Room and Dark Horse Bistro (see *Dining Out*). There are also function rooms and a paneled lounge. Single rates with complimentary continental breakfast range $139–250. Corporate and group rates are also available.

Colby Hill Inn (603-428-3281; 1-800-531-0330; www.colbyhillinn.com), just west of the village center off Western Ave., The Oaks, P.O. Box 779, Henniker 03242. Cindi and Mason Cobb's rambling 1795 farmhouse offers yesteryear charm and comfort on 6 acres just 0.5 mile from downtown Henniker. Despite the popular public dining room (see *Dining Out*), there's privacy for inn guests: a comfortable living room with hearth off by itself, and a game room. There are 10 rooms in the inn itself, 4 more in the neighboring Carriage House, 6 with working fireplace, all with phone, air-conditioning, and private bath (2 have two-person Jacuzzi). Rooms are wallpapered in flowers and furnished with antiques, with beds ranging from twins to king sized. Facilities include a pool that's sequestered behind the barn, as well as croquet and badminton; tennis is across the street. A full breakfast is served in the glass-walled dining room, overlooking birds feeding in the barnyard. It's included in the rates: $139–265.

BED & BREAKFASTS **Henniker House Bed and Breakfast** (603-428-3198; 1-866-428-3198; www.hennikerhouse.com), 2 Ramsdell Rd., P.O. Box 191, Henniker 03242. Built in 1859 on the banks of the Contoocook River, this Victorian house is comfortable and convenient, just steps away from the campus of New England College and surrounding restaurants and stores. Five bedrooms, each with private bath, cable television, WiFi access, and window air conditioners, are decorated in vintage style, three with king-sized beds. The $85–95 double rate includes a full breakfast served in the dining room solarium overlooking the river.

H. K. McDevitt Bed and Breakfast (603-746-4254), 1077 South Rd., Hopkinton 03229. Down a country road off the main street of Hopkinton village, this B&B features neighborly hospitality in an attractive reproduction saltbox home. Four guest rooms (two with private bath) offer a variety of accommodations. Innkeeper Helen McDevitt is also an accomplished craftswoman; her homemade hooked rugs and quilts are featured throughout. Rates ($70–80) include a scrumptious country breakfast.

🐾 ✿ **Lovejoy Farm** (603-783-4007; 1-888-783-4007; www.lovejoy-inn.com), 268 Lovejoy Rd., Loudon 03301. Sequestered up a back road (10 minutes' drive from I-93 and 5 miles from the Canterbury Shaker

Village, 6 from the New Hampshire International Speedway), this classic, four-square mansion looks truly grand with its attached carriage barn set against landscaped grounds and acres of surrounding woods and fields. Both the formal dining room and parlor retain their original, richly colored woodwork and the parlor, its extensive 1810 stenciling. There's also an informal sitting room/library and a large country kitchen in which the only stove is a vintage wood-and-gas Kalamazoo. Our favorite guest room, the Lovejoy Suite, is upstairs, with a working fireplace, four-poster bed, cottage furniture, and wing chairs, but there are two other smaller rooms in the main house and five more open-beamed rooms created from scratch upstairs in the barn. All rooms have private bath. The hosts are world travelers and gourmet cooks, and pride themselves on the quality of the full breakfasts included in the $112–135 double rate (can be higher during NASCAR events, Motorcycle Week, and other special occasions.) Call ahead to arrange to bring pets or children ages 8 and above. No smoking.

☃ **Meadow Farm Bed and Breakfast** (603-942-8619; www.bbonline .com/nh/meadowfarm), 454 Jenness Pond Rd., Northwood 03261. This authentic, beautifully restored 1770 New England colonial is located a few miles off Rt. 4's "Antique Alley," about halfway between Concord and Portsmouth. Surrounded by 60 acres of fields, woods, and extensive gardens (including many historic varieties of roses), the property is a short walk down a country lane to a private waterfront where guests may swim, canoe, and view the loons. In addition to three guest rooms furnished in

period antiques (one with fireplace and private bath; the other two share a bath), this home for all seasons offers several charming sitting areas, including a library with television and fireplace, a rustic screened porch furnished in twig furniture, an outdoor stone wall patio, and a large country kitchen with woodstove. Room rates, $70–90, include a full breakfast served in front of the fireplace in the paneled keeping room. There's also a cottage on the lake, available for rent by the week for $900 during the summer, or for a 3-night minimum stay during Sep. and Oct. for $150 a night. Arrange ahead to bring pets or children over 3.

Temperance Tavern (603-267-7349; 1-800-525-5673; www.temperance tavern.com), Rt. 107 (old Province Rd.), Gilmanton Four Corners, P.O. Box 369, Gilmanton 03237. You'll find all the modern amenities in this long-time stagecoach stop; otherwise, a weekend (or wedding) here, smack in the center of Gilmanton's charming historic district, is truly a trip back in time. Step into the inn's old Tap Room with its Moses Eaton stenciling and 18th-century bar, and you'll think you're in *Early American Life*. Actually, the magazine did feature several full-color pages on the inn a few years back. Over the years, this very special place has been lovingly and knowledgeably preserved, and now further enhanced by new owner Becky Ronstadt. Enjoy tea in front of an open-hearth fireplace, then climb the steep staircase (no elevator) to five well-appointed period guest rooms. All have private bath and feature antique canopy or brass beds. Two have working fireplace; others boast vaulted ceilings and fascinating histories.

Breakfasts, which are both delicious and health-conscious, are included in the $150 rate.

🍴 **Wyman Farm** (603-783-4467), Wyman Rd., Loudon 03301. Open year-round. Despite its location just a few minutes east of Concord and a 5-minute drive from Canterbury Shaker Village, the remote, storybook setting of this hilltop farm makes it feel like one of those places you could search for forever and never find. The 200-year-old "extended" Cape rambles along the very top of a hill, with lawns and fields that seem to roll away indefinitely. Expect to be greeted by Dunklee, who's the inn's model dog—literally: The golden retriever was once pictured lounging around his home turf in the Nordstrom catalog. With small-paned windows and original woodwork, the living room exudes age and comfort, and each of the three air-conditioned guest rooms has its own bath and sitting room, all furnished with carefully selected antiques. (In some cases innkeeper Judith Merrow has equipped even the bathrooms with vintage furnishings; in addition to a shower stall, one has a wooden, copper-lined tub she picked up years ago at an antiques show.) The farm has been in Merrow's family for many generations, and accommodating guests has been a tradition since 1902 when this was "Sunset Lodge" and the going rate for room and board was $5 a week. Today, with room rates ranging $65–95 (including tax), Wyman Farm remains a bargain for the genuine luxury it offers. Merrow provides a tea tray in the afternoon, and breakfast, which includes homemade breads, is cooked to order from the menu guests receive when they check in.

✳ Where to Eat

DINING OUT ♿ **Angelina's Ristorante Italiano** (603-228-3313; www.angelinasrestaurant.com), 11 Depot St., Concord. Open Mon.–Fri. for lunch 11:30–2, dinner 5–9, Sat. until 10. Exposed brick, soft pink walls, and white tablecloths make this one of the prettiest restaurants in town. Well-prepared regional Italian cuisine and decadent desserts complete the experience. Moderate.

♿ **The Barley House** (603-224-6363; www.thebarleyhouse.com), 128 N. Main St., Concord. Open Mon.–Sat. 11 AM–1 AM. Directly across Main Street from the capitol building, this watering hole for press and politicians offers billiards, darts, frequent live music performances, and a dozen micro beers on tap, plus a full menu of hearty cuisine in both the pub and more sedate dining room.

♿ **Capitol Grille** (603-228-6608; www.capitol-grille.com), 1 Eagle Square, Concord. Open daily except Mon. 11 AM–1 AM, Sun. until midnight. Located in the handsome Eagle Square shopping and office complex, this restaurant's dining room offers soft lighting and the chance for quiet conversation, while the more spirited lounge provides WiFi and big-screen plasma TV. Both have a moderately priced menu with everything from burgers to pasta, filet mignon, and swordfish.

♿ **Centennial Inn** (603-225-7102; 1-800-360-4839; www.someplaces different.com), 96 Pleasant St., Concord. Open for lunch Mon.–Fri.; dinner daily 5–9. Quiet and sedate with oak paneling and a fireplace, this inn's historic Franklin Pierce Dining Room offers a changing but always up-to-date, health-conscious menu in a late-

Victorian setting. The Dark Horse Bistro, with its ornate "staircase bar," is particularly handsome.

& **Chen Yang Li Restaurant** (603-228-8508), 520 South St., Exit 2 just off I-89 in Bow. Open Sun.–Thu. 11:30 AM–10 PM, Fri. and Sat. until 11. Extended hours in the bar. New owners have brought new style to this handy way stop built on an old mill site next to the Hampton Inn. The extensive menu features American classics and Asian specialties, including sushi, in a fine-dining atmosphere.

& **Colby Hill Inn** (603-428-3281), off Western Ave., Henniker. Open daily 5:30–8:30 PM. Candlelight makes the paneling and furniture glow, and the view of fields and gardens adds to the romantically elegant feel of this dining room. The chef's signature dish is chicken breast stuffed with lobster, leeks, and Boursin cheese, served with a supreme sauce. Leave room for dessert. Expensive.

& **The Common Man** (603-228-3463; thecman.com), 25 Water St. (Exit 13 just off I-93), Concord. Open daily for lunch from 11:30, for dinner from 5; Sun. brunch 10–2:30, dinner 2:30–close. What looks like a large green Colonial home that somehow survived the surrounding commercialization of Concord's South Main Street is actually a recently built restaurant. Post-and-beam construction provides two spacious, high-ceilinged dining rooms plus four function areas. Fireplaces and a mix of Yankee artifacts lend a cozy atmosphere. Lobster corn chowder and a deli board to make your own sandwich are among the lunch specialties; dinner entrées, including thick-cut roast prime rib, are the usual moderately priced quality fare expected from this chain of highly successful eateries.

& **Country Spirit** (603-428-7007), junction of Rts. 202/9 and 114, Henniker. Open daily 11–9, Fri. and Sat. until 10; closed Christmas and Thanksgiving. Walls are festooned with memorabilia from "the only Henniker on earth": old tools, signs, and photos. Specialties include the restaurant's own smoked meats, aged Angus sirloin, fresh seafood, and vegetarian dishes.

Crystal Quail Restaurant (603-269-4151; www.crystalquail.com), 202 Pitman Rd., Center Barnstead. Open Wed.–Sun. 5–9 PM. Reservations only. Dining in this old 18th-century post house is an experience. Service is limited to a dozen patrons per night, who are offered a "verbal menu," the better to provide what's fresh and good at the moment. Three entrées are offered, usually including chefs Harold and Cynthia Huckaby's specialty quail or pheasant. Vegetables are picked from the extensive organic garden, and vegetarian dishes can be prepared with advance notice. Needless to say, everything is made from scratch, and the desserts (Belgian gâteau au chocolat or crème caramel, for example) are exquisite. Be sure to ask for directions—there is no sign outside, and Barnstead is one of those towns webbed with back roads; even the owners admit to not knowing them all. The five-course dinner is $60 prix fixe. BYOB. No credit cards.

Daniel's (603-428-7621; www.danielsofhenniker.com), Main St., Henniker. Open daily at 11:30 AM. Friendly and attractive with a great view of the Contoocook River from the dining room and deck; there's also a brick-walled lounge. Lunch can be a Mediterranean salad (fresh greens, roast turkey, smoked ham, and imported cheeses garnished with marinated vegetables) or simply a Cajun burger. For dinner you might try chicken Contoocook—a breast of chicken baked with an apple, walnut, and sausage stuffing and glazed with maple cider sauce. Moderate.

Don Giovanni (603-226-4723; www.dongiovanni.org), 11 Depot St., Concord. Open Mon.–Sat. 11:30–2 for lunch, 5–9 for dinner, and Sun. 4–8. The china is a conversation piece, varying as it does from table to table, but all talking stops for serious eating once the food arrives. Locals love this place for everything from its Arancini (breaded and deep-fried rice balls) for $4 to its $26 veal chop stuffed with prosciutto and Fontina. Fettuccine al Quattro Formaggi (a cream sauce with Gorgonzola, Parmesan, Romano, and provolone) rivals any Alfredo dish this side of Naples. There are at least five interesting vegetable side dishes available daily, a good excuse to indulge in a post-dinner tiramisu.

55 Degrees (603-224-7192), 55 N. Main St., Concord. Open Tue.–Thu. 4–9 PM, Fri. and Sat. until 9:30. The name, inspired by the correct temperature for storing wine, reflects the level of this newly opened bistro's sophistication. The interior, with its exposed brick walls and wood floors, has been handsomely renovated. The extensive wine menu begins at $8 a glass, and the food menu, which is designed to complement the wine, features small plates, priced between $7 for a baby spinach salad with walnuts, pecorino, and honey-cider vinaigrette to $14 for a grilled beef tournedo with green bean and radish salad. Moderate to expensive, depending on your propensity for grazing.

&. **Hermanos Cocina Mexicana** (603-224-5669; www.hermanos mexican.com), 11 Hills Ave., Concord. Open daily for lunch Mon.–Sat. 11:30–2:30, dinner 5–9, Fri. and Sat. until 10. This Mexican restaurant has gotten high ratings for its authenticity and incredible margaritas since it first opened around the corner in 1984. A decade ago it expanded, and now several dining rooms on two floors are nearly always full. Live jazz Sun.–Thu. evenings.

&. **Makris Lobster & Steak House** (603-225-7665; www.eatalobster.com), Rt. 106, Concord. Open daily 11–9, Fri. and Sat. until 10; closed Mon. in fall and winter. The Makris family has been in the food business for 90 years, operating half a dozen restaurants around the city. Dozens of entrées with lobster are perennial favorites. Summer dining on the back porch patio; weekend entertainment in the lounge.

Margarita's (603-224-2821; www .margs.com), 1 Bicentennial Square, Concord. Open nightly from 4 PM. This former city jail is now a favorite (and very festive) gathering spot for locals and travelers alike. Ask for a table in one of 16 old cells for an intimate dining experience. The menu is typical Mexican fare—there are now Margarita's throughout New England, though they started here—with fajitas and margaritas as good as they get.

&. **Moritomo** (603-224-8363), Fort Eddy Plaza (Exit 14 off I-93), Concord. Open for lunch and dinner Mon.–Sat.; Sun. 2–9:30 PM. Yes, it's in a mall, but inside this Japanese restaurant there are several attractive sitting and dining choices: a Benihana-style grill, cushioned chambers for up to six, or regular tables in the main dining room; also a sushi bar and extensive menu with a variety of tempura, teriyaki, noodles, soups, and salads.

&. **The Shaker Table at Canterbury Shaker Village** (603-783-9511; www.shakers.org), 288 Shaker Rd., Canterbury. As we went to press, the Village management wasn't sure about hours or menu, but we expect this newly built facility to continue the Village's longtime culinary practice: providing creative adaptations of traditional Shaker recipes made from fresh, local ingredients. Call or check the web site for an update.

Siam Orchid (603-228-1529), 158 N. Main St., Concord. Open for lunch Mon.–Fri. 11:30–3, dinner Mon.–Fri. 5–10, Sat. to 10:30, Sun. 4–9:30. Concord's first Thai restaurant continues to draw a well-satisfied clientele. Excellent specialties and service in an attractive, well-located setting at the intersection of Main and Bridge (Centre) streets.

EATING OUT **Bagelworks** (603-226-1827), 42 N. Main St., Concord. Open Mon.–Sat. 6–6, the first Friday of the month until 8 PM. A bagel bar that also offers soups, salads, sandwiches, sweets, and more—all served with a smile.

&. **Bread and Chocolate** (603-228-3330), 29 S. Main St., Concord. Open Mon.–Wed. 7:30 AM–6 PM, Thu. and Fri. until 8, Sat. 8–4. Concord's own *konditorei*, operated by Franz and Linda Andlinger. This European-style bakery offers the best selection of breads and pastries in town, as well as *gemüttlich* atmosphere for lunch or tea. Great sandwiches and superlative pastries, plus browsing privileges and inside access to Gibson's Book Store.

Caffenio's (603-229-0020), 84 N. Main St., Concord. Open every day but Sun. 7:30–5. Live music the first Friday evening of the month. An attractive coffee bar with homemade soups, sandwiches, salads, sweets, and some Greek-inspired lunch dishes. Outside dining in-season.

&. **In a Pinch Café** (603-226-2272), 146 Pleasant St., Concord. Open Mon.–Sat. 7–3. A cheerful, informal café locally known for its gourmet sandwiches, soups, salads, and an assortment of luscious pastries. Take out or picnic inside on a snazzy, wicker-filled sunporch. No table service.

Intervale Farms Pancake House (603-428-7196), Rt. 114 and Flanders Rd. (bottom of Pat's Peak access road), Henniker. Open daily 5:30 AM–noon, on weekends until 1:30 PM. Shaped like a giant red sugar shack, this spacious, friendly, family-run restaurant is one of the very best places for breakfast in the state, featuring the farm's own homemade syrup.

The Sandwich Depot (603-228-3393), 49 Hall St., Concord. Open Mon.–Fri. 7 AM–3:30 PM, Sat. 8 AM–12:30 PM. What started as a neighborhood eatery in an abandoned train depot in 1989 now attracts those-in-the-know from Concord and towns around. Nancy Stewart is a fine but unlikely-looking poet who spends her days in ball cap and apron dishing out corned beef hash, burritos, and homemade muffins. She and her husband, Gary, are always good company, even first thing in the morning.

Susty's Café (603-942-8425), 159 First New Hampshire Turnpike (Rt. 4), Northwood. Open Mon.–Wed. 11 AM–3 PM, Thu.–Sat. until 9 PM, Sun. 8 PM. The name *Susty's* is a fusion of *sustainable sustenance* and the *Simpsons* TV show's Krusty the Clown. Such mile-a-minute witticisms and one-of-a-kind victuals from owner-chef Norma Koski have earned this novel eatery a gold plate from a Boston food critic and a full-page spread in the *New York Times Magazine*. Lavender walls adorned with stars and swirls provide the celestial atmosphere; vegetarians and beyond find the ever-changing menu equally heavenly. Check out the attached gift shop for everything from natural-fiber clothing to juggling clubs.

& **Washington Street Cafe** (603-228-2000; 603-226-2699; www .durginlane.com), 88 Washington St., Concord. Open Mon.–Fri. 7–5, Sat. until 2 PM. Deli sandwich shop that also offers take-out, catering, and outstanding Middle Eastern fare.

✳ Entertainment

✎ & **The Capitol Center for the Arts** (603-225-1111; www.ccanh .com), 44 S. Main St., Concord. Once a candidate for demolition, this one-time vaudeville venue and movie house is now the largest, and arguably best, performing arts center in the state. Over the past decade the 1,307-seat facility has been expanded, modernized, and restored. Its 1927 Egyptian-motif artwork is an outstanding example of the King Tut era of theater decoration. The center hosts a wide mix of nationally known entertainers and events, including Broadway shows; dance, music, and opera performances; pop and country

stars; family entertainment; school programs; and business conferences. Governor's Hall provides a full-service function room for up to 350 guests; the adjacent Kimball House is a Victorian mansion featuring a stately dining room and boardroom.

✎ & **Concord City Auditorium** (603-228-2793; www.concordcity auditorium.org), Prince St. (between city hall and the city library), Concord. Affectionately known as "The Audi," this 850-seat theater has been a mainstay of the capital city's community and entertainment life since 1904. In recent years an impressive group of community angels and volunteers has partnered with the city to enable the renaissance of this gilded, classically lovely venue, now host to more than 75,000 patrons and 100 musical and theatrical events per year. The reception lobby, although a new addition, features century-old stained-glass windows and period furnishings.

Capital Commons, S. Main St., Concord. Scheduled to open in late 2006, this six-story development is expected to provide a major boost to the South Main Street arts, dining, and shopping scene. Plans include room for a regional cinema center, featuring vintage, independent, and documentary films and film festivals, housed in three theaters.

✳ Selective Shopping

ANTIQUES Rt. 4 between the Epsom Circle and the Lee Rotary is widely known as **Antique Alley** (www.nh antiquealley.com). More than two dozen shops in the four towns of Chichester, Epsom, Lee, and Northwood represent more than 500 dealers; the primary customers are antiques store owners and other dealers from throughout the country. This area is just far enough off the beaten tourist path to make for exceptional pickings. Along Rt. 4 in Northwood, **Hart's Desire Antiques** (603-942-5153) has a large group shop with 150 dealers on three floors, and the **Parker-French Antique Center** (603-942-8852) represents 135 dealers. Some shops, such as **The Betty House** in Epsom (603-736-9087), specialize, this one in tools and household gadgets, while **On the Hill Collectables** (603-942-8169) in Northwood has over 200,000 vintage postcards. Other shops represent a full range of antiques, from country furniture to quilts, folk art, china, and jewelry.

Antiques & Findings (603-746-5788) and **The Covered Bridge Frame Shop & Gallery** (603-746-4996) offer sometimes rare and always interesting items within walking distance of one another on Main Street in Contoocook village.

The Brick House (877-563-2421; www.brickhouseshop.com), intersection of Rts. 107 and 140 in the historic district of Gilmanton. Open daily 10–5. What appear to be museum-quality furnishings and an ever-changing inventory of Americana are actually antique reproductions, all for sale, from the rooms of Doug Towle's imposing home.

Concord Antique Gallery, Inc. (603-225-2070), 97 Storrs St., Concord. Open Mon.–Sat. 10–6, Sun. 11–5. Just below Main Street, this popular shop offers good browsing right downtown. Two floors of merchandise from more than 125 dealers.

Henniker Kennel Company Antiques (603-428-7136), 2 Old Ireland Rd., Henniker. Deals only with antique and collectible canines.

ART GALLERIES **Anderson-Soule Gallery** (603-228-3800; www.anderson-soulegallery.com), Two Capital Plaza, Concord. Open Tue.–Sat. 10 AM–4 PM. Located in a brick courtyard just off the west side of Main St., this handsome gallery features changing exhibits with work by regionally recognized artists.

The Art Center in Hargate, St. Paul's School (603-229-4644), 325 Pleasant St., Concord. Exhibits vary throughout the school year, from student work to private collections to traveling shows by well-known contemporary artists and photographers. Gallery hours are Tue.–Sat. 10–4.

Kimball-Jenkins Estate (603-225-3932; www.kimballjenkins.com), 266 N. Main St., Concord. Open Tue. and Fri. 11–5, Wed. until 6. The longtime residence of a prominent Concord family, this estate is now home to an art school and two exhibition galleries: the Jill Coldren Wilson Gallery, which hosts historic artwork in the Victorian mansion, and another space for currently practicing artists in the nearby Carriage House Gallery.

The League of New Hampshire Craftsmen Gallery (603-224-1471) has its state headquarters/gallery at 205 North Main Street (a beige Colonial just off I-93, Exit 15) in Concord. The gallery is open weekdays and has changing shows by juried league members.

McGowan Fine Art Inc. (603-225-2515; www.mcgowanfineart.com), 10 Hills Ave., Concord. Open Mon.–Wed. 9–5, Thu. and Fri. 9–7, Sat. 10–2. Perhaps the state's premier outlet for contemporary art, this gallery features changing exhibits by the region's best-known artists.

Mill Brook Gallery & Sculpture Garden (603-226-2046; www.the millbrookgallery.com), 236 Hopkinton Rd., Rt. 202/9, Concord. Open Apr.–Dec. 23, Tue.–Sat. 11–5 ; winter hours and other times by appointment. Juried outdoor sculpture exhibit with large and small sculpture, fountains, and birdbaths displayed in seasonal gardens; rotating gallery exhibitions in a distinctive contemporary gallery on a country estate.

New England College Gallery (603-428-2329), Preston Barn, Main St., Henniker. An interesting, eclectic schedule of shows throughout the year, all of which look first-rate in this high-ceilinged exhibit space. The gallery is open Mon.–Thu. 9:30–6, Fri. and Sun. 11:30–3.

BOOKSTORES **The Book Emporium** (603-225-0555), 202 S. Main St., Concord. Open Tue.–Fri. 10–6, weekends 11–4:30. A small shop with a big, helpful attitude; 8,000 used and collectible books on site, another 8,000 in stock.

Bookland (603-224-7277), 30 N. Main St., Concord. Open Mon.–Thu. 8:30–5:30, Fri. until 8, Sat. 9–5. Lots of magazines, newspapers, and books.

& **Borders Books, Music & Café** (603-224-1255; www.bordersstores .com), 76 Fort Eddy Rd., Exit 14 off I-93, Concord. Open Mon.–Thu. 9 AM–10 PM, Fri. and Sat. until 11, and Sun. 10–8. Always busy and nearly always open, this is a great place to browse and buy. Their calendar includes frequent author visits, concerts, and special events.

✎ **Gibson's Book Store** (603-224-0562; www.gibsonsbookstore.com), 27 S. Main St., Concord. Open Mon.–Wed. 9–6, Thu. and Fri. 9–8, Sat.

9–5:30, plus expanded holiday hours. Nourish both body and soul in Michael Herrmann's friendly, well-stocked bookstore linked to a European-style bakery and café. There's a cosmopolitan selection of poetry, literary fiction, memoirs, travel, gardening, and cookbooks, plus children's story hours, book discussion groups, and frequent author signings.

Henniker Book Farm (603-428-3429), 2 Old West Hopkinton Rd. (just off Rt. 202/9), Henniker. Founder Walter Robinson recently sold this longtime "bookies" destination to Gary McGrath, but the old woodstove and more than 30,000 titles of general interest, plus Robinson's personal interests of history, literary criticism, and biography, continue to make this shop a magnet for browsing.

Old Number Six Book Depot (603-428-3334), 26 Depot Hill Rd., Henniker (up the hill from the town hall). Open daily 10–5. Boasts nearly 150,000 volumes with general and scholarly stock in all fields.

CRAFTS **Canterbury Shaker Village** (603-783-9511), Shaker Rd., Canterbury. The museum shop features Shaker crafts.

The Capitol Craftsman (603-224-6166), 16 N. Main St., Concord. Fine jewelry and handcrafts.

The Elegant Ewe (603-226-0066), 71 S. Main St., Concord. Designer yarns, rug-hooking and spinning supplies, Tuesday-night knitting clinics, quality handcrafted gifts, and the area's best selection of recorded Celtic music.

The Fiber Studio (603-428-7830; www.fiberstudio.com), 9 Foster Hill Rd. (off Rt. 202/9), Henniker. Open year-round, Tue.–Sat. 10–4, Sun. by chance. Wide selection of natural knitting and weaving yarns and spinning fibers; looms, spinning wheels, knitting machines, handwoven and knit items, workshops.

Heritage Herbs and Baskets (603-753-9005), 1 Hannah Dustin Rd., Canterbury. Open May–mid-Dec., daily 10–5:30. Herb gardens plus a charming country barn stocked with herbs, plants, handcrafted baskets, wreaths, books, and related New Hampshire crafts.

The League of New Hampshire Craftsmen (603-228-8171), 36 N. Main St., Concord. Open Mon.–Fri. 9:30–5:30, Sat. 9–5. The league's downtown shop is located in the old Phoenix Hall and has works by juried craftspeople in a range of media, including glass, pottery, jewelry, metalwork, woodwork, and fiber arts.

Mark Knipe Goldsmiths (603-224-2920), 2 Capital Plaza, Main St., Concord. Open Mon.–Thu. 10–5:30, Fri. 10–6, and Sat. 10–2. Studio and gallery with beautifully designed, custom-made jewelry.

SPECIAL SHOPS ✿ **Beech Hill Farm-stand** (603-223-0828; www .beechhillfarm.com), 107 Beech Hill Rd., Hopkinton. Open May–Aug., daily 11 AM–9 PM; until 8 PM in Sep.; 7 PM through Oct. 31. A direct descendant of the first white child born in Hopkinton, Bob Kimball and his wife, Donna, have converted their ninth-generation dairy farm into a showplace for New Hampshire products and agricultural history. There are 50-plus flavors of New Hampshire–made ice cream with make-your-own sundaes, plenty of friendly animals to pet, a garden of cut-your-own flowers,

and a barn filled with Donna's homemade goodies, as well as Kimball farm artifacts and regionally produced soaps, cheese, maple products, and decorative accessories. Kids and adults alike will enjoy navigating the 2-acre "amaizing" corn maze. With luck, you'll happen onto one of the frequent concerts, dances, or other festive gatherings in the big red barn. On a hot summer night, this place is filled with locals and visitors alike. It's not only the ice cream that gives this a real sense of New Hampshire's old-time community flavor.

Bella/The Little Hedgehog (603-746-6378, 746-5342), 390 Main St., Hopkinton village. Open Mon.–Fri. 10–6, Sat. until 5. ALSO 8 Maple St., Contoocook village. Open Tue.–Fri. 9:30–6, Sat. until 1 PM. A pair of stylish shops offering lots that's fascinating and fun, from colorful interior accents to chic clothing, playful accessories, European toys, and children's clothes. A local favorite for unique gifts.

Caring Gifts (603-228-8496), 18 N. Main St., Concord. Specializes in personalized baskets filled with everything from toys to gourmet foods.

Company C (603-226-4460), 102 Old Turnpike Rd., Concord. This brick-and-concrete warehouse hides a colorful cluster of casual contemporary furnishings, all at knockoff prices. Owner Walter Chapin is the son of a Pottery Barn founder, and his wife, Chris, has a background in fabrics. The two design the merchandise, which is manufactured offshore, then distributed to such upscale marketers as L.L. Bean and Neiman Marcus, as well as Company C's offshoot, Kate's Paperie on Prince Street in SoHo.

GOULD HILL ORCHARDS IN CONTOOCOOK

The Golden Pineapple (603-428-7982; www.thegoldenpineapple.com), off Rt. 202/9, Henniker. Open daily from 9 AM, weekends from 9:30. Since 1981, this sunny yellow shop with its way-larger-than-life wooden pineapple marker, has been a destination for unusual gifts, including Bennington pottery, Vera Bradley handbags, long-burning soy candles, regional souvenirs, and year-round Christmas wares.

Gondwana and Divine Clothing Company (603-228-1101), 13 N. Main St., Concord. Open Mon.–Wed. and Sat. 10–6, Thu.–Fri. until 7. This store recently moved down the street and doubled its size, a reflection of growing customer satisfaction with its selection of expressive clothing and decorative accessories from around the world.

Gould Hill Orchards (603-746-3811; www.gouldhill.com), 656 Gould Hill Rd., Contoocook. Open most days Aug.–Nov. 10–5. A 200-year-old family farm located high on Gould Hill with spectacular 75-mile views to the White Mountains. A nature trail winds through the orchard, and the inviting orchard store is filled with fruit (including peaches and 87 varieties of apples), baked goods, maple syrup, cider, and gifts of the season. The barn also houses The Little Nature Museum featuring displays of seashells, birds' nests, fossils, and stuffed animals.

✐ **Granite State Candy Shoppe** (603-225-2591; 1-888-225-2531), 13 Warren St., Concord. A great old-fashioned candy shop that's been in business since 1927, and a great spot for you and the kids to watch master candy craftsmen make a wide assortment of chocolates and other confections using the original copper pots and family recipes. Along with the hand-pulled crunchy nut brittle, truffles, fudge, and taffy, this newly expanded shop now offers homemade ice cream.

Henniker Pharmacy (603-428-3456), middle of Henniker. This distinctive building marks the center of Henniker in more ways than one. Pharmacist and owner Joe Clement stocks fishing gear, stationery, grocery items, wine and beer, cards, and much more. There's also a soda fountain/snack bar and, in the basement, a surprising selection of toys.

Interior Additions (603-224-3414), 38 N. Main St., Concord. Open Mon.–Sat. 10–5:30. Interesting gifts, including Simon Pearce glassware and unique finishing touches for the home.

Little River Oriental Rugs (603-225-5512), 10 N. Main St., Concord. A unique selection of rugs, plus tea, sympathy, and knowledgeable service.

❀ **L.L. Bean Factory Store** (603-225-6575), Fort Eddy Rd., Concord. Discounted clothing and outdoor gear from the well-known Maine purveyor.

Fox Country Smoke House LLC (603-783-4405; www.foxcountry smokehouse.com), 164 Briarbush Rd., Canterbury. Open daily Sep.–Christmas Eve, 10–4, Sun. noon–4; closed Mon. the rest of the year. Gift baskets of home-cured and smoked cheeses and meats in an interesting old building near Canterbury's bucolic town green.

Viking House (603-228-1198), 19 N. Main St., Concord. Open Mon.–Wed. 9–6, Thu.–Fri. 9–8, Sat. 9–5:30, and Sun. 12:30–4:30. A large selection of Norwegian sweaters, Vera Bradley products, and Scandinavian and other crystal, china, textiles, food, and gifts temptingly displayed.

✳ Special Events

June: **Garden Day**, Shaker Village, Canterbury. Herbal demonstrations, land management lectures, beekeeping.

Early June: **New Hampshire Concord Coach & Carriage Festival**, New Hampshire Technical Institute, Concord. Horse-drawn parade, rides, competitions.

End of June: **Wood Day**, with folk musicians and furniture makers demonstrating traditional techniques.

July: **Fourth Fireworks**, Memorial Field, Concord. **Strawberry Festival**, Contoocook. A 5K road race, 5-mile canoe race, parade, strawberries. **Fireman's Muster**, Pembroke. **Downtown Market Days**, Concord. Main Street closes to traffic for 3 days of entertainment, street food, and special sales. **Canterbury Fair**, Canterbury. Chicken barbecue, auction, antiques, juried crafts, Morris dancers. **Annual Bean Hole Bash weekend**, Northwood. Food, games, raffle, auction, flea market.

August: **Annual Hot Air Balloon Rally**, Drake Field, Pittsfield. Twenty balloons usually come; arts, crafts, entertainment. **Annual Northwood Community Craftsmen's Fair**, Northwood. Country fair, more than 60 craftspeople, music, food, folk dancers, flower show. **Annual New Hampshire Antiques Show**, Manchester.

Labor Day weekend: **Annual Hopkinton State Fair** (603-746-4191). **Annual Kiwanis Antique & Classic Car Show**, New Hampshire Technical Institute, Concord. **Annual Wool Day at Shaker Village**, Canterbury. Natural dyeing, rag-rug weaving, fleece-to-shawl. **NASCAR Craftsman Truck Series**, New Hampshire International Speedway, Loudon.

October: **Annual Harvest Days at Shaker Village**, Canterbury. Farm stands, produce, applesauce making, music. **Classic Car Show**, Canterbury Shaker Village. **Northern New England Sled Dog Trade Fair & Seminar**, Hopkinton Fair Grounds.

November: **Annual Holiday Craft Sale** at Shaker Village, Canterbury. Demonstrations and sales by a variety of artists and craftspeople from around the state. **Annual Gingerbread Showcase** features a landscape of edible edifices.

December: **Annual Contoocook Artisans Craft Show and Sale**, Hopkinton Town Hall.

The Lakes Region | 4

THE LAKE WINNIPESAUKEE AREA

THE WESTERN LAKES

THE LAKE WINNIPESAUKEE AREA

Winnipesaukee is one of the largest natural freshwater lakes in the country, and it's by far the largest in New Hampshire. Twenty-four miles long and varying in width from 1 to 15 miles, it harbors no fewer than 274 habitable islands and 72 square miles of very deep, spring-fed water. Ringed by mountains, it is magnificent.

It's also convenient. Sited in the very center of New Hampshire, Lake Winnipesaukee is a 90-minute drive from Boston. Not surprisingly, its shore is lined with cottages, year-round homes, condominiums, and mansions, and every property owner seems to have at least one boat. On major holiday weekends the lake is jammed with everything from sailboards to schooners, from Jet Skis to high-speed runabouts, from canoes to luxury cabin cruisers. More than 20,000 registered vessels regularly use the lake.

The message is clear. The first thing to do here is to get out on the water, and it's easy. The M/S *Mount Washington*, New Hampshire's flagship excursion boat, offers frequent daily cruises, and many marinas and outfitters rent boats, from canoes and kayaks on up.

Where you stay along Winnipesaukee's 283 miles of shoreline makes a huge difference in what you experience. Wolfeboro and Weirs Beach are, for instance, not just at opposite corners of the lake but worlds apart.

Wolfeboro, tucked in an eastern corner of Winnepesaukee and backing on Lake Wentworth, is New Hampshire's tidiest, most compact and upscale resort town, filled with small year-round shops and restaurants as well as seasonal small museums. It offers easy access to walking and cross-country ski trails as well as to boats.

Weirs Beach, on the other hand, remains a Victorian-style boardwalk, evoking the late 1800s when it was known for religious "Grove Meetings" and the large wooden hotels and gingerbread cottages that flanked its Victorian depot and docks. Fire has destroyed many buildings here, including the elaborate Weirs Hotel and the original train station, but the present depot and docks are impressive, summer home of both the M/S *Mount Washington* and the Winnipesaukee (excursion) Railroad. This remains the amusement center for the lake, one with a public beach.

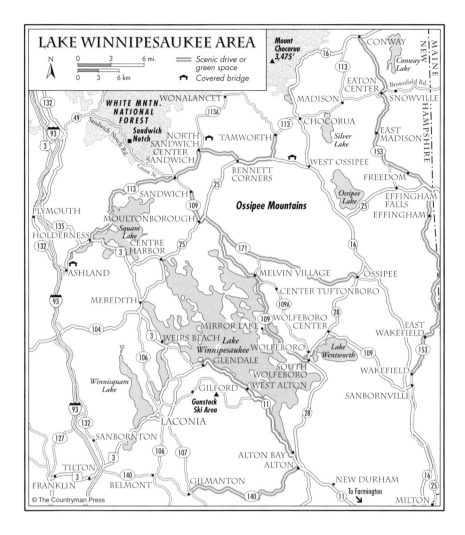

Ironically, views of and access to this lake are limited unless you are a property owner or guest at a local property. Many public beaches are restricted to local residents and guests. For more than 20 miles northwest of Wolfeboro, the lake is obscured by numerous "necks," lined with private homes. Happily, one of the more opulent old estates here, the more-than-5,000-acre Castle in the Clouds, set high on a hill in Moultonborough, is open to the public.

It's the western and southern shores of the lake—from Meredith in a north-western corner, along through Weirs Beach to Gilford on the southern shore and Alton Bay in the very southeast—that offer dramatic views of the lake and its mountains. Ellacoya State Park in Gilford is the only big public beach.

In sharp contrast to Winnipesaukee's heavy summer traffic, both on and off the water, Squam Lake is the seemingly remote and quiet haven pictured in the movie *On Golden Pond*. Just northwest of Winnipesaukee, this pristine jewel has been carefully, sensibly preserved, but it's also surprisingly visitor-friendly—on its own terms. Kayakers, canoeists, hikers, and naturalists of every ilk are welcome, as are members of Sunday open-air (Episcopal) services on Church Island.

The villages of Meredith and Center Harbor, while on Winnipesaukee, double as shopping centers for nearby Squam and for Sandwich, an exceptional hill town best known for its annual agricultural fair and as birthplace of the League of New Hampshire Craftsmen. Center Sandwich still showcases fine craftsmanship; more can be found by following its numerous and heart-stoppingly beautiful byways. Several scenic drives lead to Tamworth, the home of the Barnstormers, oldest summer theater in the country, and an equally inviting destination described in "Mount Washington Gateway Region." East of Winnipesaukee, Rt. 153 through Wakefield and Effingham is also described in that chapter.

Some visitors to the Winnipesaukee area come for the entire summer, staying in their own cottages (or mansions) or renting housekeeping cottages. Many families have owned their summer places for generations, and many renters have returned to the same cottages for the same week year after year. Indeed, while there are numerous housekeeping colonies, we have not listed many, because few of them have any weeks open for newcomers.

Winter does bring skiing, snowmobiling, and ice fishing. Gunstock offers both alpine and Nordic skiing, and there are several cross-country facilities in the region. Members of the Winnipesaukee tribe who frequented this lake and named it either "smile of the Great Spirit" or "beautiful water in a high place" (no one seems sure which) wintered over on the site that's now Weirs Beach but fanned out around the lake itself only in warm weather.

The area's mill towns are, of course, true year-round, workaday communities. Laconia, "the City on the Lakes," is by far the largest (still under 20,000 people) local community, connected to Winnipesaukee but also bordering Lake Winnisquam, and Paugus and Opechee Bays. At its core stands the tower-topped brick Belknap Mill, built in 1823 and said to be the oldest unaltered textile mill in the country. It now serves as a gallery and an entrée to the city's colorful industrial history.

Beginning in the 1840s rail lines on this western side of Winnipesaukee also invited expansion of mills in Ashland and Tilton, two towns that served as transfer points for summer visitors just as they still do as Interstate 93 exits. Ashland (Exit 24) remains an obvious dining and shopping stop en route to Squam Lake and Center Harbor, but the town of Tilton now tends

UNTITLED (POSSIBLY A VIEW OF LAKE WINNIPESAUKEE), 1853, BY BENJAMIN NUTTING
Currier Museum of Art, Manchester, New Hampshire. Gift of Barney Ebsworth in Honor of Charles E. Buckley, Director of the Currier Museum of Art, 1955–64; 1997–99

to be equated with the outlet shopping mall and commercial strip at Exit 20. The town itself is west of I-93, worth checking for its public monuments, interesting shopping, and lodging (take Exit 19).

MUST SEE AND DO Cruise Lake Winnipesaukee aboard the M/S *Mount Washington* or rent your own boat. Visit Castle in the Clouds in Moultonborough and the Science Center of New Hampshire at Squam Lake in Holderness. Sunbathe. Swim. Hike.

GUIDANCE Lakes Region Association (603-744-8664; 1-800-60-LAKES; www .lakesregion.org), P.O. Box 430, New Hampton 03256, produces *Where To in the Lakes Region*, a handy guide to towns, accommodations, and attractions, also maintains a walk-in information center on Rt. 104 just east of I-93, Exit 23, in the rear of a mustard-colored Colonial-style house. Open 8:30–4:30, later on Fri. and Sat. in summer.

Note: The following are the most active chambers. Others are included in the *Villages* descriptions. All are good for finding summer cottage rentals.

Wolfeboro Chamber of Commerce (603-569-2200; 1-800-516-5324; www .wolfeborochamber.com), Box 547 (the walk-in office is at the old railroad station, 32 Central Ave.), Wolfeboro 03894.

Meredith Area Chamber of Commerce (603-279-6121; 1-877-279-6121; www.meredithcc.org), Box 732 (office on Rt. 3 and Mill St.), Meredith 03253-0732.

Greater Laconia/Weirs Beach Chamber of Commerce (603-524-5531; 1-800-531-2347; www.laconia-weirs.org), office in the old railroad station, 11 Veterans Square, Laconia 03246. A summer information booth is maintained on Rt. 3, just south of Weirs Beach.

Squam Lakes Area Chamber of Commerce (603-968-4494; www.visitsquam .com), Box 665, Ashland 03217, and **Squam Lakes Association** (603-968-7336), Box 204, Holderness 03245. Contact this nonprofit association for hiking, boating, and wilderness information and maps.

GETTING THERE *By air:* There is regular service to airports in Manchester (see "The Manchester/Nashua Area") and Lebanon (see "Upper Valley Towns"), both of which are just a short drive via rental car from the Winnipesaukee region.

By bus: **Concord Trailways** (603-228-3300; 1-800-639-3317) provides scheduled service from Boston's Logan Airport to central and northern New Hampshire via Tilton, Laconia, New Hampton, Meredith, and Plymouth. Daily service varies.

MEDICAL EMERGENCY 911 covers this area.

Lakes Regional General Hospital (603-524-3211; 1-800-852-3311), Highland St., Laconia. Walk-in care 9 AM–9 PM; 24-hour emergency service.

Huggins Memorial Hospital (603-569-2150), S. Main St., Wolfeboro.

✳ Villages

Alton Bay. One of the lake's early tourist centers, Alton Bay's waterfront area appears little changed from the turn of the 20th century, when train passengers transferred to steamboats. Concerts are held in the bandstand, and the old railroad station is the information center. Cottages around the bay shore evoke memories of the days when summer places were small houses, not condos. The **Harold S. Gilman Museum** (603-875-2161), Rts. 11 and 140 in Alton (open 2–4 on Memorial Day as well as on Wed. and Sat. and the first Sun. in July and Aug.) is an eclectic collection of country antiques including furniture, dolls, guns, china, glass, pewter, toys, clocks, and a working Regina floor-model music box. **Alton–Lakes Region Chamber of Commerce**, Box 550 (office in the old railroad station, Rt. 11), Alton, open mid-May–Oct., issues a detailed schedule of numerous summer events, and maintains a seasonal information booth.

Ashland, the gateway town to the Squam Lakes area from I-93, is a delightfully visitor-friendly upcountry mill village. It's been this way since the 1850s, when the Boston & Montréal Railroad arrived, bringing lakes-bound visitors. The Victorian **Ashland RR Station** is now a seasonal museum (603-968-3902) open July–Labor Day, Wed. and Sat. 1–4; inquire about special excursion rides to Lakeport, Plymouth, and Lincoln. The center of town offers one of the region's most popular restaurants, The Common Man, and good shopping, ranging from Bailey's 5&10 cents store to several art and crafts galleries. The Ashland Historical Society (603-968-7716) maintains the **Whipple House Museum**, 4 Pleasant St. (open same times as the railroad station), home of a Nobel laureate (1934) for medicine, Dr. George Hoyt Whipple, featuring exhibits related to his life plus local artifacts, and the neighboring **Pauline Glidden Toy Museum**, with plenty of games, toys, and books from the mid–19th century.

Center Sandwich. This quintessential white-clapboard, green-shuttered New England village, complete with steepled churches and general store, is exceptionally visitor-friendly. You'll find an appealing café in the back of the store, fine dining and an inviting tavern in **The Corner House** up the road. Next door is the **Sandwich Historical Society** (603-284-6269), 4 Maple St. (open June–Sep., Tue.–Sat. 11–5), displaying portraits by native Albert Gallatin Hoit as well as special annual exhibits. Across the road is **Sandwich Home Industries**, founded in 1926 to promote traditional crafts, a project that evolved into the present League of New Hampshire Arts & Crafts. See *Selective Shopping* for several more shopping possibilites scattered along the back roads that web this mountainous, 100-square-mile town. Note Rt. 113A to Tamworth, described in "Mount Washington Gateway Region." Also see Sandwich Notch Rd. in *Hiking*. A century ago there were two hotels in the village itself and some 40 "guest farms" that took in summer boarders. The **Sandwich Fair**, held the 3 days of Columbus Day weekend, is the last one of the year, famed for its old-fashioned feel and for the traffic it attracts to the fairgrounds (south of the village on Rt. 109).

Center Harbor. At the head (northwestern corner) of Lake Winnipesaukee, this is the winter home of the M/S *Mount Washington*. The village is bisected by Rt. 25, but it retains its 19th-century character. The town was named for the

CENTER SANDWICH   Robert J. Kozlow

Senter family, but the *S* became a *C* somewhere along the way. Whether it's *Centre* or *Center* is still debated. The original name is preserved in its core shopping complex, Senter's Marketplace, best known for Keepsake Quilting, a mecca for quilters from the world over. Unfortunately, the village's big old 19th-century summer hotels, Senter House and the Colonial Hotel, are long gone, but the dock and a small beach survive. Note the bronze goose that's a fountain, sculpted by S. R. G. Cook, a student of Augustus Saint-Gaudens. The **Center Harbor Historical Society** (603-253-7892), Plymouth St. (Rt. 25B), maintains its collection in an 1886 schoolhouse, open Sat. 2–4 in July and Aug.

Melvin Village. The antiques center of the eastern Winnipesaukee region, the little town of Melvin Village still looks as it did in the 19th century, when many of the houses lining the Main Street were built. Some of these homes now host antiques shops, and one business repairs antique motorboats. The **Tuftonboro Historical Society** (603-544-2400), Main St. (Rt. 109), Melvin Village, open in July and Aug., Mon., Wed., and Fri. 2–4 and Sat. 10–1, displays photographs and literature relating to Lake Winnipesaukee.

Meredith. North–south Rt. 3 now runs along Meredith's waterfront, meeting Rts. 104 east and 25 at a busy junction. The village, with its shops, restaurants, and B&Bs, is actually up above, bordering Lake Waukewan. In 1818 a canal was built from the site that is now John Bond Swase Park down to Lake Winnipesaukee, a 40-foot drop that eventually powered a number of mills. Despite disastrous fires, one four-story wooden 1820s textile mill survived, functioning off and on until the 1960s, but it was largely hidden by cinder-block industrial buildings. Thanks to local developer Rusty McLear, the mill and falls have been resurrected, making this town a major destination for shops, restaurants, and four large inns, two with views of the lake and two directly on the water. The **Meredith Historical Society** (603-279-4655), 45 Main St., is open Memorial Day–Columbus Day weekend, Wed.–Sat. 11–4. Formerly the Oak Hill Church, the museum exhibits tools, costumes, photographs, "made-in-Meredith" items, and local historical information. The **Meredith Chamber of Commerce** maintains a major information center in a white cottage at 272 Daniel Webster Hwy. (Rt. 3).

Tilton is now better known for its chain stores and discount malls than its village atmosphere, but the part of town west of I-93 does boast more statues than any other American town of its size. From the interstate, you first notice the 55-foot-high, granite Tilton (actually in Northfield) arch, an exact copy of a Roman memorial built in AD 79. Beneath it is a Numidian lion carved from Scottish granite, a tribute to Charles E. Tilton, the town's wealthiest mid-19th-century citizen and a descendant of the first settler. He persuaded the town of Sanbornton Bridge to change its name to Tilton in 1869, a decision no doubt made easier by his gift of statuary. Such allegorical figures as America, Asia, and Europe can still be found around town, along with Tilton's mansion, now the library of the private preparatory Tilton School, founded in 1845. The town offers unexpectedly good lodging and shopping.

Wakefield. The sprawling town of Wakefield is composed of several villages: **Union, Brookfield, Sanbornville,** and **Wakefield Corners,** the latter now a historic district of more than two dozen mostly white-painted, 18th- and 19th-century houses and public buildings, well worth finding (it's just off Rt. 16). Stop by the **Museum of Childhood** on Mount Laurel Rd. (603-522-8073), open Memorial Day week–Labor Day, daily except Tue. 11–4, Sun. 1–4. $3 adults, $1.25 ages 9 and under. Town historian Elizabeth Banks MacRury and her late sister Marjorie Banks accumulated some 5,000 dolls and teddy bears—plus music boxes, puppets, stuffed animals, model trains, and dollhouses—in their lifetimes of collecting. When this collection outgrew their home, they bought the house next door, and eventually opened this museum with 12 rooms full of exhibits. The garage has been converted into Miss Mariah Plum's 1890 schoolroom, complete with old-fashioned desks, books, chalkboards, and the teacher herself. Sanbornville, several miles south, is the commercial center. **The Greater Wakefield Chamber of Commerce** (603-522-6106; wakefieldnh.org) furnishes maps and brochures.

✒ **Weirs Beach**, at the junction of Rts. 3 and 11B, is the attractions center of the region—the place to go for many folks, and the place to avoid for others. It is difficult to be ambivalent about two waterslides, miniature golf, a go-cart track, the country's largest arcade, and a strip of pizza parlors, fast-food spots, gift shops, and penny arcades. Right beside all of this activity is a summer religious conference center dating back to the turn of the 20th century, the wharf for the M/S *Mount Washington*, and the **Winnipesaukee Railroad**. There is also a fine public beach beside the **Endicott Rock Historical Site**, a large boulder found in 1652, when a surveying party claimed this region for the Massachusetts Bay Colony, said to be the second oldest historic landmark in the country.

Wolfeboro. Billed as "America's oldest summer resort," Wolfeboro remains a lively but low-key, old-fashioned resort village with some outstanding shops, restaurants, and museums as well as entrées to the lake and surrounding countryside. The campus of **Brewster Academy**, a private prep school, is the venue for summer music. **The Wolfeboro Historical Society** (603-569-4997), 337 S. Main St., maintains three buildings. The complex includes the restored and furnished 1778 Clark House, an 1820 one-room schoolhouse, and the replica 1862 Monitor Engine Company, complete with a restored 1872 horse-drawn, Amoskeag steam-pumper fire engine and an 1842 Monitor hand engine. **Wright Museum** (603-569-1212; www.wrightmuseum.org), 77 Center St., Wolfeboro. Open Apr.–Oct., daily 10–5, Thu. until 7, then weekends and by appointment the rest of the year. This facility is devoted to the spirit of American enterprise as it was expressed during the war years of 1939–1945. The collection includes memorabilia, artifacts, vehicles (fully operating jeeps, tanks, command cars, and half-tracks), and films from the period. Gift shop and snack bar. A 200-yard walking path connects the museum with downtown Wolfeboro.

✍ ♿ **Libby Museum** (603-569-1035), Rt. 109, 4 miles north of Wolfeboro village, is open Memorial Day–Labor Day, daily except Mon. 10–4. This natural history museum was built by a Wolfeboro native in 1912 and is now operated by the town. It has a varied collection of mounted bird, fish, and animal specimens; Native American relics, including a dugout canoe; old maps and photographs; and 18th- and 19th-century country-living artifacts. Programs include nature walks, lectures, concerts, children's programs, and art exhibits. Small fee. The **New Hampshire Antique and Classic Boat Museum** (603-596-4554), a fine collection of antique boats and related artifacts, is at 397 Center St. (Rt. 28 north). Also note the **Governor Wentworth Historic Site**, Rt. 109, the site of Royal Governor John Wentworth's summer estate. Daily late June–Labor Day (seasonal weekends before and after), 45-minute narrated tours aboard **Molly the Trolley** (603-569-1080) depart regularly from the town docks. The exceptionally helpful **Wolfeboro Chamber of Commerce** maintains an information center in the former depot at 32 Central Ave. in the middle of the village.

✳ To See

✍ **Castle in the Clouds** (603-476-2352; 1-800-729-2468; www.castlesprings .com), Rt. 171, Moultonborough. Open weekends early May–June, then daily until mid-Oct., 10–4:30. Built in 1913 at a cost of $7 million, this stone mansion complete with turrets is high on the side of the Ossipee Mountains, overlooking Lake Winnipesaukee. Part of a 5,200-acre estate constructed by eccentric multimillionaire T. G. Plant, the castle has become a family recreation area and the source of Castle Springs water. Tour the mansion, picnic, or enjoy lunch at the Carriage House.

✍ **Squam Lakes Natural Science Center** (603-968-7194; www.nhnature.org), junction of Rts. 25 and 113, Holderness. The Science Center is open May–Nov. 1, daily 9:30–4:30. This nonprofit organization features a hospitable welcome center and two well-equipped gift shops, but the emphasis remains on its walking trails with displays of live bears, deer, bobcats, foxes, owls, bald eagles (and other birds of prey), and other native wildlife. Hike through 200 acres of meadow and forest, past streams and brooks. Inquire about special summer family activities, which include live animal programs daily on thez hour 11–3 during July and Aug. The Kirkwood Gardens trail offers a display of perennials designed to attract birds and butterflies. There is also a Science Center pontoon used for Golden Pond Tours; on Sunday you can re-serve a spot on the shuttle to Church Island, site of open-air services (weather permitting)

AN EXHIBIT AT THE SQUAM LAKES NATURAL SCIENCE CENTER IN HOLDERNESS   Squam Lakes Natural Science Center

for almost a century. On rainy days the service is held at the Playhouse at Rocky-wold-Deephaven Camps, another long-standing institution.

Blink and you are through the village of Holderness, but don't miss the **Squam Lakes Association**, housed in a former motel west of the village on Rt. 3, source of information about local hikes, kayak and canoe rentals, and lakeside tenting. Also see Squam Lake tours under *Boat Excursions*.

♪ **New Hampshire Farm Museum** (603-652-7840; www.farmmuseum.org), 1305 White Mountain Hwy. (Rt. 16, Exit 18 off Spaulding Turnpike), Milton. Open May–late Oct., Wed.–Sun. 10–4. New Hampshire's rural agricultural heritage is maintained in this unusual collection of buildings, situated about midway between the Lakes region and the seacoast. The three-story Great Barn is filled with wagons and a host of other farm artifacts. The Jones Farmhouse is furnished to reflect its ownership by the Jones family from 1780 to 1900; you'll also find the adjoining Plummer Homestead, blacksmith and cobbler shops, a well-stocked country store (good for historical books, reproduction toys, and much more), and 50 acres with picnic areas and a self-guiding trail. Themed Saturday programs highlight specific traditional crafts or aspects of farming. These range from quilting and blacksmithing to rock wall building and demonstrations of horse- and mule-power. Special days are devoted to sheep, dairy animals, goats, llamas, and alpacas. Children's Day, the second Saturday in July, is geared to young children. An annual Old-time Farm Day, with many farmers, artists, and craftspeople gathered to demonstrate their skills, takes place in mid-August. $6 adults, $3 ages 3–17. See the web site for a detailed program of events. Also see *Villages* for more museums.

COVERED BRIDGES The **Grafton covered bridge** just off Rt. 3 in Ashland was built for the town by resident Milton Graton, a renowned builder and restorer of covered bridges throughout the Northeast. The **Whittier bridge** crosses the Bearcamp River, just off Rt. 16 and north of Rt. 25, in West Ossipee. The **Cold River bridge** is a little difficult to find but well worth the effort. It is located off Rt. 113A just north of North Sandwich.

SCENIC DRIVES To the east of Lake Winnipesaukee, **Rt. 153** from Sanbornville to Conway (see "Mount Washington Gateway Region") is a wandering alternative to busy Rt. 16. Another rewarding drive is **Rt. 113** east from Rt. 3 in Holderness, or **Rt. 109** north from Rt. 25 in Moultonborough. Either way you reach Sandwich Center and can opt—assuming you have a high, rugged car—for the **Sandwich Notch Road** or **Rt. 113A** to North Sandwich, Whiteface, and Wonalancet, then on to Tamworth. **Rt. 171** from Center Ossipee to Moultonborough, **Rt. 11** from Alton Bay to Glendale, and **Rt. 140** from Alton to Gilmanton are all great scenic drives.

✳ To Do

AIRPLANE RIDES **Laconia Airport** (603-524-5003), Rt. 11, Laconia, is an all-weather, paved runway facility with air-taxi operators available for charter.

Moultonboro Airport (603-476-8801), Rt. 25, Moultonborough. Sightseeing rides.

AMUSEMENT AREA ✒ **Weirs Beach**, at the junction of Rts. 3 and 11B, is the attractions center of the region, with two waterslides, miniature golf, a go-cart track, the country's largest arcade, and a strip of pizza parlors, fast-food spots, gift shops, and penny arcades. The attractions, most open weekends Memorial Day–mid-June, then daily until Labor Day, include **Surf Coaster USA** (603-366-5600; www.surfcoasterusa.com), the largest waterslide complex in the region, with seven slides, changing rooms, tidal wave pool, and lifeguards. Pay once and slide all day. Also, two 18-hole miniature golf courses (additional fee). **Weirs Beach Water Slide & Volcano Mini Golf** (603-366-5161) is a complex with a mini golf course and a variety of slides for beginners through experts. The Super Slide for experts is the longest in New England. **Funspot** (603-366-4377; www.funspotnh.com), Rt. 3, 1 mile north of Weirs Beach. Open all year and 24 hours a day, July–Labor Day: 550 games, billed as the largest complex of its type in the country. From pinball to video and driving games to simulcast golf, this has something for people of all ages, including both candlepin (a mostly New England game) and 10-pin bowling, a driving range, and miniature golf.

BICYCLING **The Cotton Valley Trail** is an evolving 12-mile rec path that begins at the Wolfeboro Depot and follows the old rail line toward Wakefield.

Mountain Sports (603-279-5540), Rts. 3 and 106, Meredith, rents mountain bikes and supplies area maps. Also see Gunstock under *Sports Park*.

BOAT EXCURSIONS **M/S** *Mount Washington* (603-366-5531; 1-888-843-6686), Lakeside Ave., Weirs Beach. Mid-May–Oct. 31. The queen of the lake and a New Hampshire landmark, special theme cruises and dinner and moonlight dancing excursions are delightful. For first-time Lakes region visitors, a ride on this famous vessel is a great introduction to Lake Winnipesaukee. Her namesake ship was a wooden side-wheeler in service from 1872–1939. She was replaced by the present steel-hulled boat, but remained in port for most of World War II, when her engines were commandeered for the war effort. In 1946 she returned to service, and in 1983 she was lengthened and changed to M/S (motor ship). Day trips 2–3 hours, $24; evening dinner/dance cruises (reservations required) $39–$49. Reduced fares and special family package fares available.

M/V *Sophie C* (603-366-5531), Lakeside Ave., Weirs Beach. Mid-June–week after Labor Day, Mon.–Sat. 11 AM and 2 PM. This is a floating U.S. post office, and her cruises wind around the islands, into coves and channels, delivering mail to residents on five islands. Some of the 2-hour cruises are with mail stops. Light refreshments available. $16 adults $16, $5 ages 4–12; under 4 free.

AT WEIRS BEACH BOARD THE M/S *MOUNT WASHINGTON* FOR A CRUISE AROUND THE LAKE

M/V _Doris E_ (603-366-5531), Lakeside Ave., Weirs Beach 03246. Departs Meredith and Weirs beaches. June–Labor Day there are three daytime cruises and one sunset cruise. Discover Meredith Bay and many islands on these 1- or 2-hour trips. $10 adults for 1-hour cruise, $16 for 2-hour, $5 ages 4–12; under 4 free.

M/V _Winnipesaukee Belle_ (603-569-3016; 1-800-451-2389), Wolfeboro. Call the Wolfeboro Inn to find out how to charter this 65-foot side paddle-wheeler based at the Wolfeboro Town Docks.

M/V _Millie B_ (603-569-1080), Wolfeboro. Half-hour boat rides in a classic 1920s motor launch departing from the Wolfeboro Town Docks; operated by the Wolfeboro Trolley Company. Daily late June–Labor Day, 10–5, weather permitting; weekends only Memorial Day–late June from 11 AM and again from post-Labor Day through the Columbus Day weekend.

Winnipesaukee Lake Tours (603-528-6900; www.winnilaketours.com), Weirs Beach boardwalk. Island and sunset cruises on the "Minni Winni" water taxi, which goes where the big boats can't, late June–Sep.

Squam Lake Tours (603-968-7577; www.squamlaketours.com), Rt. 3, Holderness. May–Oct., daily scheduled tours at 10 AM as well as 2 and 4 PM; also June–Aug., 2-hour cruises on Wed., Fri., and Sat. at 6:30 and 8 PM. Reservations suggested. See this pristine lake, the second largest in New Hampshire, aboard Captain Joe Nasser's 28-foot, canopy-top pontoon boat. He'll show you loons, Church Island, and the spot where _On Golden Pond_ was filmed. Available for charters. Joe also runs a fishing-guide service.

Golden Pond Tour (603-968-7194; www.nhnature.org) departs from the bridge at Walt's Basin, but passengers gather 15 minutes before departure at Squam Lakes Natural Science Center. Cruises are Memorial Day–foliage season at 11 AM, 1 PM, and 3 PM. Ninety-minute cruises led by naturalists in an all-weather boat to see loons, the islands, and the movie-filming location. Reservations suggested. Inquire about nature, sunset, and full-moon cruises; also a combined nature trail and lake cruise pass.

BOAT RENTALS No driver's license is required to operate a boat, but you must be 16 years old to operate one with more than 25 horsepower. There are, of course, marine patrol officers, speed limits at certain congested areas, and a number of accidents each summer. For boating regulations and education contact the New Hampshire Department of Safety's Marine Patrol Division in Gilford (603-293-2037; 1-877-642-9700). Also, keep an eye on the weather, because high winds, sudden squalls, and thunderstorms can quickly whip the lake surface into waves as rough as the ocean, an especially dangerous situation for those in small boats who have no experience in such conditions. Most towns provide public launching sites, and boat rentals are so numerous that we have given up listing them all. In Wolfeboro they include **Goodhue Hawkins Navy Yard** (603-569-2371), **Back Bay Boat 'n Sled** (603-569-3200), **Wet Wolfe Rentals** (603-569-1503), and **Wolfeboro Corinthian Yacht Club** (603-569-1234), N. Main St. In Melvin Village: the **Melvin Village Marina** (603-544-3583). In

Alton Bay: **Castle Marine** (603-875-2777), **Sun 'n' Snow Rentals** (603-387-6751), and **BaySide Inn/Lake Side Boat Rentals** (www.bayside-inn.com). In Gilford: **Fay's Boat Yard** (603-293-8000; www.faysboatyard.com) rents sailboats, pontoons, fishing boats, and canoes. In Weirs Beach: **Anchor Marine** (603-366-4311; 1-800-366-8110; www.anchormarine.net) and **Thurston's Marina** (603-366-4811; www.thurstonsmarina.com) both offer rentals. In Meredith: **Meredith Marina** (603-279-7921; www.meredithmarina.com) offers rentals, and **Sports & Marine Parafunalia** (603-279-8077) also rents Walden kayaks and water-skiing gear. **The Sailing Center on Squam Lake** (603-968-3654) in Holderness rents sailboats, sailboards, motorboats, and canoes by the half day, day, or week. Also sailing instruction.

CANOEING AND KAYAKING **Wild Meadow Canoes & Kayaks** (603-253-7536; 1-800-427-7536; www.wildmeadowcanoes.com) in Center Harbor offers rentals and sales of canoes and kayaks. For other outlets, see *Boat Rentals*, above.

Winnipesaukee Kayak (603-569-9926; www.winnikayak.com), 17 Bay St., Wolfeboro (at Back Bay Marina), offers intruction, rentals, and guided excursions.

CLIMBING **Winnipesaukee Kayak and Rock Climbing** (603-569-9926; www.winnikayak.com), 17 Bay St., Wolfeboro. Open daily 8–6. Retail sales and rentals. Customized adventure outings and activities for groups and individuals.

FISHING **Gadabout Golder Guide Service** (603-569-6426; www.gadaboutgolder.com), 79 Middleton Rd., Wolfeboro, offers guided fly-fishing trips on Winnipesaukee and nearby lakes and rivers, late Apr.–mid-Oct.

🐾 ✐ **Sumner Brook Fish Farm** (603-539-7232), Rt. 16, Ossipee. A former state fish hatchery, this is now a private business welcoming visitors to feed the fish, to catch fish (rod rentals available, also fly-fishing), or to purchase fresh or smoked fish. Fee charged, inexpensive.

Note: For advice on local fishing contact the New Hampton office of the **New Hampshire Fish and Game Department** (603-744-5470).

GOLF Most courses in this region operate mid-Apr.–Oct., weather permitting, and all offer cart rentals. **Den Brae Golf Course** (603-934-9818), 80 Prescott Rd., off Rt. 127, Sanbornton. Nine holes, driving range, full bar, and light food. **Highland Links Golf Club** (603-536-3452), Mount Prospect Rd., Holderness. Nine holes with executive par 3, pro shop, and snack bar. **Indian Mound Golf Course** (603-539-7733), off Rt. 16, Center Ossipee. Nine holes, bar, and food service. **Jack O'Lantern Resort** (603-745-3636; 1-800-227-4454), Rt. 3, Woodstock. **Kingswood Golf Course** (603-569-3569), Rt. 28, Wolfeboro. Eighteen holes, full bar, and food service. This is a busy summer place with fully stocked pro shop and driving range, so call for tee times. **Laconia Country Club** (603-524-1274), off Elm St., Laconia. Newly renovated, semiprivate 18-hole course with snack bar and beverage cart on course. Call for tee times. **Lakeview Golf Course** (603-524-2220), Ladd Hill Rd., opposite Belknap Mall, Belmont. Nine holes. Great views of the lake from this hilltop course. **Mojalaki Country Club** (603-934-3033), 321 Prospect St., off Rt. 3, Franklin. New ownership emphasizes golfing fun for the whole family. Snack bar and function room. Tee times needed, especially on weekends. **Oak Hill Golf Course** (603-279-4438), 159 Pease Rd., off Rt. 104, Meredith. Nine holes, full bar, and food service. No tee times. **Pheasant Ridge Country Club** (603-524-7808), 140 Country Club Rd., Gilford. Eighteen holes, light food, and bar service. **Province Lake Golf** (800-325-4434), Rt. 153, East Wakefield. Eighteen holes, full bar, and food service; tee-time reservations available 7 days in advance. The Maine–New Hampshire state line cuts through the course, and several holes line picturesque Province Lake. **Ragged Mountain Resort** (603-768-3600; 1-800-400-3911; www.ragged-mountainresort.com), 620 Ragged Mountain Rd., Danbury. Family-friendly, classic New England mountain golf. **Waukewan Golf Course** (603-279-6661), Waukewan Rd. off Rt. 3/25, Center Harbor. Eighteen holes, full bar, and food service, located on a wildlife sanctuary. No tee times, so plan ahead for busy weekend play. **White Mountain Country Club** (603-536-2227), 1 Country Club Dr. off Rt. 3, Ashland. Eighteen holes, full bar and food service, Stay and Play packages, tee times suggested on weekends.

HIKING Most people head for the White Mountains to hike, but the Winnipesaukee region offers a variety of trails with fewer hikers and splendid mountaintop lake views (although the peaks are not as high as those farther north). The **Squam Lakes Association**, which maintains many trails in this region, has a guidebook (see *Guidance*). We have listed only a few of the many possible trails in the region. We recommend using a guidebook, because many of these trails are traveled less and marked less than the more famous trails farther north. All times shown are for the ascent only. Hikers should carry their own water. (Also see *Green Space*.)

Sandwich Notch, from Center Sandwich to Rt. 49 in Campton. This ancient Indian trail was an important 18th- and early-19th-century route from the western White Mountains down to the lakes, and it's lined with stone walls that once marked open meadows. Once more wooded and now part of the White Mountain National Forest, this haunting, 11-mile road has been preserved as is (to widen and pave it would inevitably turn it into a heavily traveled shortcut between Winnipesaukee and Waterville Valley). Closed in winter, it remains popular with cross-country skiers and snowmobilers; in summer it's steep, rough, and slow going but passable for all but low-slung cars. It's also a popular walk, at least the 3.5 miles from Center Sandwich to **Beede Falls** (a town park). The **Wentworth Trail** to the summit of **Mount Israel** (elevation 2,620 feet), which offers fine views of the Lakes region, begins 2.6 miles from Center Sandwich. Watch for signs to Mead Base, a Boy Scout camp. The 1.6-mile-long trail usually takes 2 hours to hike. Park in the field below the camp buildings and enter the woods at a sign at the left rear of the main building. Farther along the Notch Rd. (about 3.7 miles south of the junction with Rt. 49), the 4.5-mile-long **Algonquin Trail** ascends **Sandwich Dome** (elevation 3,993 feet). It's rough but offers fine views from its rocky ledges. Hiking time is 3½ hours.

Rattlesnake is a popular short hike on Squam Lake. From Holderness go 5.7 miles north on Rt. 113, past the ROCKYWOLD-DEEPHAVEN ROAD sign. Park on the left at the base of the Mount Morgan Trail but follow the old **Bridle Trail** (across the road). It bears left at the end of a row of maples and up a wide, gradual path to the summit of **West Rattlesnake** (0.9 mile). There's an excellent view to the southwest just below the summit.

Red Hill. A fine view of Lake Winnipesaukee is the prize at the end of the **Red Hill Trail**. In Center Harbor, at the junction of Rts. 25 and 25A, take Bean Rd. for 1.4 miles, then follow Sibley Rd. (look for the FIRE TOWER sign) to a parking lot with a gate. Past the gate is a jeep road that becomes the trail. The hike is 1.7 miles and requires just over an hour. A famous Bartlett lithograph, often found in local antiques shops, shows a gathering of Native Americans on Red Hill.

Belknap Range. On the western side of the lake is a low ridge of mountains with many trails. A good starting point is the Gunstock Recreation Area on Rt. 11A in Gilford. Several trails ascend beside the ski slopes. Ask for a map at the camping area office.

Mount Major. Located just north of Alton on Rt. 11, this is everybody's favorite climb. The **Mount Major Trail** is only 1.5 miles long and requires about 1 hour 20 minutes; views across the lake are impressive. Hike on the right day and watch the M/S *Mount Washington* as she cuts through the waters of Alton Bay. Also look for Knight's Pond Conservation Area in Alton, Rines Rd. off Rt. 28 south. You'll find more than 300 acres good for fishing as well as hiking.

In the Wolfeboro area several short hiking trails are rewarding.

✔ **Abenaki Tower**, Rt. 109 in Tuftonboro. A 5-minute walk from the parking area to an 80-foot tower overlooking Lake Winnipesaukee and the Ossipee Mountains; great for short legs. In Wolfeboro itself the **Russell C. Chase Bridge Falls Path** behind the railroad station leads 0.5 mile to Wolfeboro Falls, and the **Cotton Valley Trail** stretches from the station 12 miles along the old railbed to the railroad turntable in Sanbornville. It traverses trestles and three lakes as well as woods and fields.

HORSEBACK RIDING **Gunstock Cobble Mountain Stables** (603-293-4341; 1-800-GUNSTOCK; www.gunstock.com), Rt. 11A, Gilford. Ages 8 and up can take a 1-hour trail ride through the scenic Cobble Mountain area; $40.

Pemi Valley Excursions (603-745-2744; www.i93.com/pvsr), Exit 32 off I-93, just past the Hobo RailRoad, Main St., Lincoln. Trail rides on 250 acres of old farmland, part of it along the Pemigewasset River. Group wagon rides also available.

RAILROAD EXCURSIONS ✔ **Winnipesaukee Scenic Railroad** (603-279-5253; 603-745-2135; www.hoborr.com), S. Main St., Meredith. Open weekends (except Father's Day) Memorial Day–late June; daily late June–Labor Day; and then weekends only until mid-Oct. Board from Meredith or Weirs Beach. Ride beside the lake on historic coaches of the 1920s and 1930s, or connect with the M/S *Mount Washington* for a boat ride (see *Boat Excursions*). Inquire about dinner trains featuring a Hart's hot roast turkey dinner and other special excursion rides.

Molly the Trolley (603-569-1080), Wolfeboro, offers 45-minute narrated tours of Wolfeboro, daily from 10 AM late June–Labor Day; weekends only starting at 11 AM from Memorial Day into June and again after Labor Day until mid-Oct.

SAILING **Winni Sailboarders' School & Outlet** (603-528-4110; sailboarders@ mathbox.com), 687 Union Ave., Lake Opechee, Laconia. Open daily in summer noon–7, Sun. and holidays until 5; weekends only off-season, though it's best to call ahead. Sales (and some rentals) of sailboards, sailboats, kayaks, pedal boats, wet suits, inflatables, and GPS receivers. Lessons in windsurfing, kayaking, and GPS.

SCUBA DIVING **Dive Winnipesaukee** (603-569-8080), 4 N. Main St., Wolfe-boro. Open all year. Lake and ocean diving, scuba certification programs, rentals, guided dives, charter trips.

SPORTS PARK **Gunstock** (603-293-4341; 1-800-GUNSTOCK; www.gunstock .com), Rt. 11A, Gilford. This 2,000-acre ski area is now a four-season sports park offering mountain boarding, skating, skiing, tubing, mountain biking, and horse-back riding, plus a swim pond, hiking, and camping. (Also see *Green Space*.)

✳ Winter Sports

CROSS-COUNTRY SKIING **The Nordic Skier** (603-569-3151; www.nordicskier sports.com), N. Main St., Wolfeboro. Open daily 9–5:30. Sales, rentals, and instruction for cross-country skiing, also sales and rentals of toboggans, skis, skates, and snowshoes. They schedule moonlight tours and races and maintain a 30-km trail network. Visit the shop for directions to **Abenaki Trails** (15 challenging km) or the **Sewall Woods Trails** (15 km of easy, family-geared trails); also maps or suggestions for backcountry skiing.

Gunstock Ski Area (603-293-4341; www.gunstock.com), Rt. 11A, Gilford. Tele-mark, cross-country, and downhill skiing plus snowshoeing, with full-service retail, rental, and lesson facility on 50 km of trails.

DOWNHILL SKIING **Gunstock Ski Area** (603-293-4341; 1-800-GUNSTOCK; www.gunstock.com), Rt. 11A, Gilford. The original trails in this county-operated area were designed by President Franklin D. Roosevelt's WPA in the 1930s. From the beginning it included cross-country as well as alpine trails (since then it's been almost entirely redesigned). Since 1937 it has been drawing families with intermediate-level terrain and a magnificent lake and mountain view.

Lifts: 2 quads, 2 triples, 1 double, and 2 surface lift, 1 conveyor tubing park, ter-rain park.

Trails: 50 trails, 72.5 percent intermediate.

Vertical drop: 1,400 feet.

Snowmaking: 80 percent coverage on 220 acres.

Snowboarding: All trails, terrain park, half-pipe.

Night skiing: 17 trails, 4 lifts, Thrill Hill Tubing Park and lift, Tue.–Sat.

Services: Rentals, nursery, ski school, cross-country and snowshoeing facilities.

Rates: $49 adults weekends, $39 midweek; $39/29 for teens; $29/19 per child. Special night and half-day rates.

SLEIGH RIDES **Belgian Acres Farm** (603-286-2362), 91 Clark Rd., Tilton, offers sleigh rides on 33 secluded acres.

Heritage Farm Tours (603-524-8188; www.heritagefarm.net), 16 Parker Hill Rd., Sanbornton.

SNOWMOBILING **Alpine Adventures** (603-745-9911; 1-800-SNO-TOUR; www.alpinesnowmobiling.com), 41 Main St., Rt. 112, Kancamagus Hwy., Lincoln. Guided tours, rentals, and service.

Pemi Valley Excursions (603-745-2744; www.i93.com/pvsr), Exit 32 off I-93, just past the Hobo RailRoad, Main St., Lincoln. Snowmobile, moose tours, wagon and horseback rides, depending on season.

❊ Green Space

BEACHES & **Ellacoya State Beach**, Rt. 11, Gilford. Open weekends from Memorial Day, daily mid-June–Labor Day. Fee charged. The only state beach on Lake Winnipesaukee. A 600-foot beach with refreshment stand and changing rooms; handicapped accessible. The view across the lake to the Ossipee Mountains is one of the best in the region.

Wentworth State Park and Clow Beach (603-569-3699), Rt. 109 east, Wolfeboro. Open daily mid-June–Labor Day. Fee charged. This small park on Lake Wentworth has a bathing beach, play field, changing rooms, and shaded picnic area. **Albee Beach**, Rt. 28 north on Lake Wentworth, is open mid-June–Labor Day, 9 AM–dusk. Also in Wolfeboro but on Lake Winnipesaukee, **Brewster Beach** on Clark Rd. and **Carry Beach** on Forest Rd. are both open mid-June–Labor Day, 9 AM–dusk.

OTHER **Cate Park**, Wolfeboro, on the waterfront by the town wharf. Occasional concerts and art exhibits in summer, a delightful place to relax anytime.

❧ **The Loon Center and Markus Wildlife Sanctuary** (603-476-5666), Lees Mills Rd. (Box 604), Moultonborough. The center is operated by the Loon Preservation Committee of the Audubon Society of New Hampshire. This 200-acre site has 2 miles of walking trails through the woods and down to the shore of Lake Winnipesaukee, where a loon nest can be observed. There is also a gift shop and exhibit space, but the main purpose of the facility is to research the American loon, the large waterbird whose eerie calls symbolize wilderness. Overdevelopment of New Hampshire's lakes once appeared to doom the bird, but this organization has been influential in protecting nesting sites and building public awareness of the loon's plight. The organization has accumulated some 20 years of data on the loons, which currently number about 550 birds in New Hampshire. There are programs for adults and children, and self-contained loon education kits that can be sent to schools.

New England Forestry Foundation Area (also known as the **Chamberlain-Reynolds Memorial Forest**), off College Rd. near the junction of Rts. 3 and 25B north of Meredith village, is a 200-acre conservation area on the lake with 2 miles of gentle trails and two sandy beaches with picnic tables on the shore of Squam Lake.

Ragged Island on Lake Winnipesaukee. Docking is available at the southern end of the island. Shuttle service and programs on the island are offered by the Squam Lakes Natural Science Center (see *To See*).

🐾 ✍ **Stonedam Island Wildlife Preserve** (603-279-3246), operated by the Lakes Region Conservation Trust, Box 1097, Meredith 03253. Open dawn to dusk daily from mid-May to mid-Oct. Stonedam Island is an undeveloped, 112-acre preserve in Lake Winnipesaukee. Visitors are welcome to walk the trails, relax under a tree on the shoreline, or pursue their own nature study. Private boats may dock at the 60-foot pier on the northeastern side of the island. Bring water, as none is available on the island; no pets, audio equipment, smoking, fires, or glass containers. Inquire about public water-taxi transport to the island from Wolfeboro.

Leonard Boyd Chapman Wildbird Sanctuary, Mount Isreal Rd., Sandwich. A very special 150 acres, open year-round—but you would be well advised to have four-wheel drive in winter, because it's up a steep road (off Grove St. out of Center Sandwich). There's a trail network groomed for cross-country skiing and snowshoeing, along with picnic tables. A trail leads to Eacup Lake, and in winter the ice that forms on this small pond is cleared for family skating (no hockey sticks, please).

Unsworth Wildlife Area at the Squam Lakes Conservation Society (see *To See*), Holderness. These 159 acres are webbed with trails, rich in wildlife. A canoe awaits, but you have to bring your own paddle.

Gunstock Recreation Area (603-293-4341; 1-800-GUNSTOCK; www.gunstock.com), Rt. 11A, Gilford. Operated by Belknap County, this 2,000-acre facility includes the Gunstock Ski Area and a large campground with related facilities. The 420-site campground has swimming, fishing, horseback riding, a store, and a playground. Extensive hiking trails lead to the summits of the Belknap Mountains, one of which is Gunstock. Trail maps are available. Warm-weather events include dances, craft and woodsmen's festivals, and Oktoberfest.

Also see **Sandwich Notch Road** under *Hiking*.

✳ Lodging

INNS

On Lake Winnipesaukee
♿ **The Wolfeboro Inn** (603-569-3016; 1-800-451-2389; www.wolfeboroinn.com), 90 N. Main St., Wolfeboro 03894. Open all year. This inn dates back to 1812 but now offers some the region's finest rooms and one of its better restaurants. Nine guest rooms are in the original front portion of the inn, while the modern addition, built with a contemporary design to resemble an old barn, brings the room count to 44, including some suites with four-poster beds. The country-style rooms have private bath

and king, queen, double, or twin beds, with phone, TV, and individually controlled heat and air-conditioning. The deluxe water-view rooms in the addition have decks where you can watch lake activities or catch cooling breezes. Two rooms are handicapped accessible. The center sections of the three-story addition have open areas with chairs and reading nooks. The inn has a private beach on the lake, and it's just steps to the village shops and to the dock to board the M/S *Mount Washington*. The inn has conference facilities, a large dining room (see *Dining Out*), and Wolfe's Tavern, which is located in the old portion of the inn. From $90 in winter to $305 for a suite on holiday weekends in summer. Rates include continental breakfast. Children over the age of 2 years are $15 extra. Inquire about the many packages, including spring fishing and summer water sports.

The Inns at Mill Falls are four separate well-designed inns, totaling 159 rooms, built over the past decade or so along the lake in Meredith. All share the same ownership, phone numbers (603-279-7006; 1-800-622-MILL), web site (www.millfalls.com), and address: Rt. 3, Meredith 03253. Rates range $99–359, and package plans are available for all four inns. The original **Inn at Mill Falls** is built around a tumbling waterfall and adjoins the old linen mill that's now a shopping complex. Each of the 54 rooms has New Hampshire–made maple or Shaker pine furnishings with easy chairs and desks, air-conditioning, TV, and telephone. Beds are queens, doubles, or a king, and half the rooms have views out to Meredith Bay. There is an indoor pool, a spa, a sauna, and two restaurants. The

neighboring **Chase House at Mill Falls** offers 23 rooms and 3 one-bedroom suites. Rooms feature fireplace, whirlpool spa, and private balcony overlooking the lake. There is also a function room with fireplace, patio, and panoramic view. Camp, the inn's restaurant, offers great grub and a woodsy decor (see *Dining Out*). The 24-room gleaming, white-clapboard **Inn at Bay Point**, across Rt. 3 from its sister inns, extends into Lake Winnipesaukee, resembling a ship that's just pulled into port. Amenities include a dock, sauna, and whirlpool spa area. Many rooms have lakeside balcony, fireplace, and whirlpool. All feature New Hampshire–made furnishings, including king or queen beds (some with pullout sofas) and easy chairs, desks, air-conditioning, TV, and telephone. Dine directly on the water at Lago (see *Dining Out*), or opt for a dinner for two on your balcony. The newest, most luxurious addition to the Mill Falls complex is **Church Landing**, a neo-Adirondack structure situated on a landscaped promontory overlooking the lake. Each of its 58 rooms and multiroom suites offers a gas fireplace and view of the lake. Many also have balconies, and some a two-person whirlpool tub. The property also has docking, an indoor/outdoor pool, and full-service health club and spa. The upscale log cabin decor extends into the Lakehouse Grille (see *Dining Out*).

The Lakeview Inn (603-569-1335), 120 N. Main St., Box 713, Wolfeboro 03894. Open all year. Situated on a hill on the edge of the village, this is a combination restored old inn and adjacent two-level motel. All rooms have private bath, TV, and phone; a few have a kitchenette. Beds are doubles and queens (two beds in motel units). The inn houses a good restaurant (see *Dining Out*). $60–110 for two depending on the season. Two-night minimum stay on weekends Memorial Day–Oct.

Kona Mansion (603-253-4900; www .konamansion.com), off Moultonborough Neck Rd. (turn at the blinker on Rt. 25 and follow the signs; mail: Box 458, Center Harbor 03226). Open daily Memorial Day–Columbus Day and weekends earlier and later. No expense was spared when this Tudor-style mansion was built in 1900 by Herbert Dumaresq, a onetime partner in Boston's famed Jordan Marsh department store. The elaborate painted ceiling and sumptuous dining room fireplace give the property vestiges of another time. Since 1971, the Crowley family has operated the inn, which includes 100 acres of private woodland with 15 miles of hiking trails, a nine-hole, par-3 golf course, tennis courts, extensive lawns, a private beach, and its own lakeside boat dock. There are 10 rooms with twin or one or two double beds and private bath. On the lakefront are four housekeeping cabins with 1 or 2 bedrooms and two 3-bedroom chalets. Relax in the lounge with a view across the lake to the Belknap Mountains. Breakfast and dinner are served to guests and the public. EP $69–175; MAP for two (weekly only), two-bedroom cottages are $560 per week, and A-frame chalets with two bedrooms are $795 per week. Inquire about weekly MAP rates.

On Squam Lake

The Manor on Golden Pond (603-968-3348; 1-800-545-2141; www .manorongoldenpond.com), Shepard Hill Rd. and Rt. 3 (Box T), Holderness 03245. This golden stucco mansion overlooking Squam Lake ("Golden Pond") was originally built in 1907 as a summer estate for a wealthy Englishman and his new bride, and current owners Brian and Mary Ellen Shields continue to promote this Lord of the Manse "toniness." Three of the inn's 13 hillside acres overlook the water and surrounding mountains. Inside, the rooms are a combination of old and new, with turn-of-the-20th-century leaded-glass windows and ornate woodwork partnered with whirlpool baths and updated decor. No two of the 25 guest rooms are alike, but all are furnished mostly with antiques (four-poster beds) and have private bath, telephone, and television; most have a fireplace. Eight of the rooms also have a whirlpool. Deluxe rooms have king, queen, or twin beds, ceiling fan, air-conditioning, and lake views; some have balcony. Two large common rooms have fireplaces, and there is a second-floor library. Several detached housekeeping cottages sleep two to six people. One right on the lake offers a romantic getaway with king-sized bed, fireplace, double Jacuzzi, and porch with a lake view. You'll also find tennis courts, croquet, and a private, 300-foot beach with a boat dock that offers paddleboats and canoes. Breakfast and dinner are served daily (see *Dining Out*). Rates with breakfast for two and afternoon tea range $200–450, depending on season.

Elsewhere

The 1875 Inn at Tilton (603-286-7774; www.1875inn.com), 255 Main St., Tilton. This old mill town isn't the obvious place to find a tastefully restored old inn—one that was obviously a labor of love for Joanne Oliver (owner of popular Oliver's Restaurant) and Rob Ciampa. Built in 1875 in the middle of Main Street, the three-story wooden hotel has been totally renovated. The 11 guest rooms, each with private bath, are named for a prominent visitor (Thomas Edison, Henry Ford, Mary Baker Eddy . . .) and boasts a different mix of country antiques and folk art. A second-floor library serves as a common room where a continental breakfast is served. The adjoining Tilton Historical Museum features treasures from the 2003 archaeological dig. At street level, the **Patriots Tavern** is open for all three meals, an attractive space with tables by the long, small-paned windows and by the big fieldstone fireplace. Rooms with continental breakfast run $80–150.

BED & BREAKFASTS

In the Center Harbor/Meredith area

& **The Meredith Inn** (603-279-0000; www.meredithinn.com), corner of Main and Waukewan Sts., Meredith 03253. Open all year. Innkeeper Janet Carpenter clearly knows her business, one she grew up with in Rangeley, Maine, where her parents owned the Rangeley Inn. This rambling Victorian "painted lady," the home of Meredith's leading physician for several decades, has been transformed into a charming B&B. The eight unusually spacious rooms offer a choice of twin, queen-, and king-sized beds. Each is different, but all combine real comfort and charm. They are furnished in antiques and feature luxurious linens and large, well-equipped private bath; six of the rooms have a whirlpool tub. The living room has a fireplace and is well stocked with local menus and

information. The hosts are delighted to help guests plan itineraries. It's just over 0.25 mile in one direction to downtown shopping and restaurants; 0.5 mile the other way to Lake Waukewan. Full breakfast. Nonsmoking. Children are welcome, but rooms accommodate two people only. Rates range $105–175 in low season, $125–180 Memorial Day–Oct.

Olde Orchard Inn (603-476-5004; 1-800-598-5845; www.oldeorchard inn.com), 108 Lee Rd. (R.R. Box 256), Moultonborough 03254. Open all year. Twelve acres of orchard surround this expanded Cape farmhouse, part of it brick made from clay found by the stream that bounds the property. Nine guest rooms, each with private bath and air-conditioning, are decorated in keeping with the home's early-18th-century origins. Some rooms also have fireplace and whirlpool. Innkeepers Jo and Clark Hills are full of interesting suggestions for things to do in the area, but guests with a musical bent are sometimes happy simply trying their hand at the piano and Hammond organ in the parlor. The porch offers a great view for watching the sun set behind Red Hill, and The Woodshed restaurant (see *Dining Out*) and the Loon Center (see *Green Space*) are within walking distance. High-season rates are $120–185 for two with full breakfast; lower in winter.

Tuckernuck Inn (603-279-5521; 1-888-858-5521; www.thetuckernuck inn.com), 25 Red Gate Lane, Meredith 03253. Open all year. Up the hill from Main Street, this five-room inn is within walking distance of shops, restaurants, and Lake Winnipesaukee. Owners Donna and Kim Weiland have added baths (all five guest rooms now have them) as well as stenciled walls, handcrafted quilts, and period furniture; one room has a gas fireplace. The living room has a fireplace and a huge shelf of books and games to play. $105–149 for two includes a full breakfast. Slightly lower off-season.

In Sandwich

Jonathan Beede House (603-284-7413; www.jonathanbeedehouse.com), 711 Mount Israel Rd., Center Sandwich 03227. High up on a back road, this 1787 farmhouse offers four comfortable guest rooms furnished with family antiques. Built by one of Sandwich's early settlers, it has been lovingly restored by owners Susan and John Davies. The four upstairs guest rooms share three down-the-hall baths and range from two big corner rooms to a cozy double. All have white-curtained, historic paned windows with plenty of natural light, heirloom quilts, and intriguing books. Downstairs, the formal parlor and less formal keeping room feature similar books and inviting places to read. There is also a big screened porch/sunroom overlooking the meadows; next door the **Chapman Wildbird Sanctuary** beckons you to walk, snowshoe, or cross-country ski. The house is filled with a sense of history (before the Civil War it served as a stop on the Underground Railroad) and with a warm sense of hospitality. $75–90 includes a full breakfast served in the dining room with its 18th-century fireplace and Indian shutters.

🐾 🐟 **Strathaven** (603-284-7785), Rt. 113, North Sandwich 03259. Open all year. Twenty years ago Betsy and Tony Leiper started taking in overflow guests from a local inn, and they've never stopped: Guests became friends who returned annually. Picture windows overlook beautiful grounds with extensive gardens, a trout pond for swimming or skating, and an English croquet court. Betsy is an embroidery teacher and has a flair for color. Her favorite, blue, shows up in her extensive collection of blue-and-white Meissen china in the dining room cabinet. There are four lovely rooms; two large rooms each have two double beds and a private bath, and two rooms share a bath. Many feature antiques as well as Betsy's embroidery. Tony Leiper serves as town treasurer, and leads guests on cross-country ski trails that connect the inn with Sandwich Notch. From $75 for two with full breakfast. These grandparents insist there be no extra charge for children.

On Squam Lake

The Glynn House Inn (603-968-3775; 1-800-637-9599; www.glynn house.com), 59 Highland St., Ashland 03217. Jim and Gay Dunlop are the new owners of the 1890 Queen Anne–style home and neighboring carriage house that make up this impressive B&B, set above the village. The house retains all of its handsome, original woodwork and Oriental wallpaper. Each of the 13 rooms (7 suites) is furnished to the period. Most have fireplaces and all have private bath; 9 with whirlpool. Full breakfast included. B&B $139–259 double, depending on season.

The Inn on Golden Pond (603-968-7269; www.innongoldenpond.com), Rt. 3, Box 680, Holderness 03245. Open all year. Bill and Bonnie Webb have been operating this large, cheerful, friendly B&B since 1984. While this 1870s house doesn't overlook the lake, huge picture windows in the breakfast room and living room do frame meadows and woodland, a sampling of the inn's 50 wooded acres. Most of the eight rooms (two suites) have queen-sized maple beds, and all have private bath and air-conditioning. All the rooms are furnished tastefully and comfortably "country"-style, complete with two easy chairs—a nice touch. Amenities include table tennis or darts in the separate sports shed. The living room has a fireplace, and a second common room has cable TV; there's also a small room set up for computer use with WiFi. $105–180 for two off-season; $115–190 per couple in summer and fall, includes breakfast. Single rates slightly less. Children over 10 welcome.

& **Squam Lake Inn** (603-968-4417; 1-800-839-6205; www.squamlakeinn .com), Shepard Hill Rd. and Rt. 3, P.O. Box 695, Holderness 03245. Open all year. Innkeepers Rae Andrews and Cindy Foster have breathed new life into this century-old Victorian farmhouse, making it a repeat stop for many guests who consider it one of the friendliest and most comfortable places on the lake. Each of the eight guest rooms and baths is decorated stylishly in a vintage lake theme. There are two suites with room for an extra person ($35 charge), and a lower-level room with wheelchair access. The wraparound covered porch and adjoining patio offer a wonderful spot to eat breakfast or lunch (see *Eating Out*), or relax with a book. Rates, which include gourmet breakfast, are $140–175 mid-May–Oct.; $110–130 in winter.

In Wolfeboro and vicinity
123 North Main B& B (1-800-577-9506), 123 N. Main St., Wolfeboro 03894. Open all year. This classic green-shuttered white Colonial is a handsome oasis just up the street from the bustle of Wolfeboro's shopping area. Since opening on July 4, 1997, Bob and Barbara Branscombe (the true B&B) have built their clientele via word-of-mouth by offering guests a refined yet relaxing atmosphere. The house is filled with antiques and period reproductions. The three air-conditioned guest rooms have king-sized beds, fine linens, and television. Gourmet breakfast; pastries and coffee available all day. Nonsmoking. $175–200.

Tuc' Me Inn (603-569-5702; www .tucmeinn.com), 118 N. Main St., Wolfeboro 03894. Open all year. This 19th-century inn, with screened porches, a large common room with a fireplace, TV, and guest telephone, is just two blocks from village shops and restaurants. There are seven rooms, three with private bath (the others share two full baths), with a choice of queen, double, and twin beds. New innkeepers Wes and Linda Matchett also offer a choice of three full breakfasts. $110–135 May–Oct.; $95–115 the rest of the year.

On the south shore
The Inn at Smith Cove (603-293-1111; www.innat.smithcove.com), 19 Roberts Rd., Gilford 03249. This 1890s home with a third-floor tower suite and wraparound porch is right on one of Lake Winnipesaukee's many sheltered coves. There are nine guest rooms in the inn itself, most with a water view, all with private bath (the tower suite has a Jacuzzi). The Light House in the garden is a two-level suite with a Jacuzzi; the Little House—a cabin on the cove—has a porch overlooking the water. Handy in winter to skiing at Gunstock.

$90–170 (20 percent less during low season) per couple includes a full breakfast. Ask about weekly rates for cottages.

On Winnisquam Lake

Ferry Point House (603-524-0087; www.ferrypointhouse.com), off Rt. 3 in Winnisquam (mail: 100 Lower Bay Rd., Sanbornton 03269). Open May–Nov. 1. Built in the 19th century as a summer retreat, this bracketed Victorian, with its wide parlor windows and veranda overlooking Lake Winnisquam, still fits the bill. This area is quieter than bigger Lake Winnipesaukee, with simpler pleasures such as the grassy point, across the road from the house, with a gazebo and hammock. Guests also have use of a paddleboat and rowboat. The nine rooms, all with private bath (one with a Jacuzzi), have antique high-backed beds and lovely views. Breathe deep and you can smell the lake air. Since the Damato family has published its own breakfast cookbook, be prepared for a gourmet start to your day. Try stuffed French toast, crêpes, cheese-baked apples, stuffed pears, and fresh breads and muffins. Make sure to get directions to this country location. $110–155 for two, depending on season.

Elsewhere

& **Black Swan Inn** (603-286-4524; www.blackswaninn.com), 354 W. Main St. (Exit 20 off I-93), Tilton 03276. Open all year. Dr. Sheryl Ollie offers nine guest rooms in this 1880s mill owner's mansion with its stained glass and ornate woodwork in parlors and guest rooms alike. There's a spacious, other-era feel throughout the house, furnished with a collection of European antiques. It's a comfortable, interesting place to stay. Two suites

(handicapped accessible) in the carriage house have a sitting area, bedroom, and porch with TV, air-conditioning, and a coffeemaker. In the main house rooms vary widely, with an assortment of bed arrangements, some with private and some with shared baths. Our favorite is actually up on the third floor with skylights and an amazing bird's-eye maple vanity. Children over 10 please. Full gourmet breakfast. $99–150 for two; $10 less for single.

The Wakefield Inn (603-522-8272; 1-800-245-0841; www.wakefieldinn .com), 2723 Wakefield Rd., Wakefield 03872. Open all year. A centerpiece of the historic district, this handsome, three-story 1804 Federal inn has been open to travelers in one form or another for more than a century. Now operated as a B&B, the former stage-coach stop features Indian shutters, a wraparound porch, and a three-sided fireplace in the sitting room. The seven guest rooms are reached by an unusual old spiral staircase. All the rooms, two of which are two-bedroom suites, have private bath, and the attractive furnishings feature Lou's homemade quilts. There is a large common room with a fireplace. $90–95 for two, B&B. Theme weekends; holiday and special packages available winter and spring.

COTTAGES Consult the chambers of commerce and the **Lakes Region Association** (603-744-8664; 1-800-60-LAKES; www.lakesregion.org) for cottage rentals—but we just had to mention the following:

Ames Farm Inn (603-293-4321; 603-742-3962; www.amesfarminn.com), 2800 Lake Shore Rd. (Rt. 11), Gilford 03246. Open Apr. (for fishermen) through Oct. Tradition! This 300-acre inn and cottage community has been here since 1890, having been operated by five generations of the Ames family. Needless to say, book early for the short peak season of July and August. Nineteen fully equipped housekeeping cottages are spread out on the lakefront. Each has one or two bedrooms, kitchenette, living room, and screened porch. The view across Lake Winnipesaukee stretches across the Broads for miles to the Ossipee Mountains and Mount Washington. Away from the shore are buildings with housekeeping apartments and 12 modern guest rooms with private bath. No charge to guests to launch and dock a boat. Some rental boats are available. The inn restaurant is open mid-June–Labor Day, daily 7:30 AM–2 PM. Weekly rates: apartments and small cabin, $560; housekeeping cottages and cabins, $1,100–1,200 peak season, $600 off-season. $125 per day for the private rooms.

MOTELS AND CAMPING Check the AAA and Mobil guides' motel listings if it's a motel you're after; we frankly have a hard enough time personally checking all the inns and B&Bs. Ditto for campgrounds, of which the area offers plenty.

✳ Where to Eat

DINING OUT

In Wolfeboro and vicinity

♪ **The Bittersweet Restaurant** (603-569-3636), Rt. 28 north and Allen Rd., Wolfeboro. Open Sun.–Thu. 5–9 PM, Fri. and Sat. until 10; closed Mon. Reservations recommended. Here's an 1823 barn, furnished with antiques, that has been recycled as a fine restaurant. Special-

ties include steak Diane, lobster pie, roast duck, and roast stuffed pork tenderloin. On Friday come for the all-you-can-eat fish fry.

Wolfe's Tavern & 1812 Steak House (603-569-3016; www.wolfe boroinn.com), 90 N. Main St., Wolfeboro. Open all year, 7 AM–10 PM. Located in the old section of the inn, the tavern serves a wide variety of lighter fare, from hot and cold sandwiches and salads to soups, pasta, munchies, and dinners. More than 80 brands of beer, too. The 1812 Dining Room features New England–style cuisine (prime rib and seafood) as well as daily specials and homemade desserts. Sunday brunch (10–1) is popular with guests and locals alike. Daily salad bar features more than 30 items, including a block of cheddar cheese and homemade soup and Italian bread. There are lovely views of Wolfeboro Bay and gardens.

Garwoods (603-569-7788; www .garwoodsrestaurant.com), 6 N. Main St., Wolfeboro. Open daily for lunch and dinner in summer, closed Wed. in winter. This deep, lakeside storefront that began life as a lady's clothing store in 1899 is now an attractive restaurant overlooking Wolfeboro Bay. The best seats are of course way in the back, beyond the bar (an inverted racing scull hangs above), with water views. Lunch runs from burgers to salads and pastas or the signature sandwich of grilled chicken marinated in a pineapple-teriyaki sauce; dinner features fresh daily seafood selections plus Black Angus filet mignon.

The Cider Press (603-569-2028; www.theciderpress.net), 30 Middleton Rd., Wolfeboro. Serving dinner at 5 PM. Since 1982, this has been a popular rustic spot with barnboard walls, fireplaces, antiques, candlelight dining, and a varied menu. Baby back ribs, grilled salmon, lamb chops, tempura shrimp, plus nightly blackboard specials. Entrées $12.95–19.95.

East of Suez (603-569-1648; www .eastofsuez.com), Rt. 28, South Wolfeboro. Open Memorial Day weekend–early Sep., for dinner daily except Mon. Representative Asian food of all descriptions is prepared by the Powell family. Japanese, Chinese, Philippine, Thai, Indian, and Korean specialties (all prepared with authentic ingredients and condiments), huge portions, and moderate prices make this place a dining adventure. Here for nearly 40 years, yet still something of a secret. Sushi, daily grilled seafood, and homegrown organic vegetables are featured. No alcohol is served, but you may bring your own bottle.

The Lakeview Inn (603-569-1335; www.lakeviewinn.net), 200 N. Main St., Wolfeboro. Serving dinner daily except Sun. from 5 PM. Dining is in the restored rooms of this old inn. Highly regarded locally, this restaurant has a diverse menu of American and Continental entrées, including shrimp scampi, bouillabaisse, and well-prepared veal, steaks, and chateaubriand for two. Fresh-baked breads and pastries, homemade soups. The adjacent lounge serves sandwiches, soups, salads, and lighter fare. Reservations suggested. Entrées $11.95–47.00 (for the chateaubriand).

Mise en Place (603- 569-5788), 96 Lehner St., Wolfeboro. Open daily except Sun. We haven't visited this relatively new chef-owned and -operated restaurant, but those who have say it's one of the best around for creative fine dining. We hear the room is small, however, so best to make reservations.

The William Tell Inn (603-293-8803), Rt. 11, West Alton. Open for dinner daily except Mon. during spring, summer, and fall; Sunday brunch starting at noon; call for seasonal hours. With a name from Switzerland and housed in a chalet, expect Swiss cuisine. One of the region's better restaurants, with a variety of Continental favorites served by owner-chef Peter Bossert and his wife, Susan. Wiener schnitzel, sauerbraten, venison, and cheese fondue share the menu with more conventional favorites such as filet mignon, New York sirloin, salmon, lamb, and seafood grill. The desserts feature dark Tobler chocolate imported from Switzerland. Early-bird specials Tue.– Fri., 5–6:30 PM, $9.95; entrées from $13.95.

On the west shore and northward

The Woodshed (603-476-2311; www.woodshedrestaurant.com), Lees Mill Rd., off Rt. 109, Moultonborough. Open all year, Tue.–Sun. for dinner. To operate a successful restaurant in the countryside, on a side road, off a less-than-major route, in a small, spread-out town, you must have atmosphere and good food. This place has both in abundance. What began as a small restaurant in an old farmhouse has grown into a large operation attracting the likes of Sean Penn and Michelle Pfeiffer. Dining extends into the year-round porch as well as an exquisite barn with massive hand-hewn beams and spacious loft, all decorated with antiques and collectibles. An evening could begin at the raw bar for clams and oysters or peel-and-eat shrimp and escargots.

Prime rib is the specialty, but how about a combination with king crab or lobster? After Cajun roast pork tenderloin, shrimp kebab, lamb chops, or chicken gourmet, no wonder the dessert menu begins with "We dare you." Cheesecake, a one-scoop hot chocolate sundae, or Indian pudding can complete the repast. Entrées $16–25. Reservations, particularly on summer weekends, recommended.

Abondante (603-279-7177), 30 Main St., Meredith. Open daily 5–9 PM in summer, Fri. and Sat. until 10; off-season Wed.–Sat. 5–9, Sun. 4–8; live jazz on Thu. night. An easy 2-minute hike from the Mills Falls complex, this restaurant faces Meredith's actual Main Street, as opposed to its main thoroughfare, Rt. 3. Billed as a Tuscan trattoria, Abondante boasts excellent, moderately priced Italian cuisine and a homey yet gracious atmosphere.

Canoe Restaurant and Tavern (603-253-4762; www.eatatcanoe.com), 232 Whittier Hwy. (Rt. 25), Center Harbor. Open daily for lunch 11:30–2:30, for dinner 5–9:30, 10 on Fri. and Sat. Sunday brunch 11–2. Whether you come by canoe, car, or take the valet shuttle from the Center Harbor town dock, you're likely to like this place; patrons have been praising it since its opening in 2004. Each of its five dining rooms has an outdoor theme with canoes suspended from the ceiling and hooked into rugs. One outdoor room, a screened porch overlooking woods and the lake, has space heaters to keep you toasty into fall. The extensive menu ranges from comfy (meat loaf and macaroni, $13), to Continental (osso buco, $16), to cosmopolitan (ahi tuna, $19).

Corner House Inn (603-284-6219), Rt. 109, Center Sandwich. Open daily for lunch and dinner; live music Fri. nights and for Sunday brunch. An inn for 150 years and owned by Don and Jane Brown for 20, this longtime landmark has always enjoyed a reputation for good food served with ambience in the traditional low-beamed dining room. The shellfish sauté of lobster, shrimp, and scallops in a light sherry sauce with broccoli and mushrooms ($18.95) has been a staple since 1981. Other entrées range $17.95–21.95. The upstairs pub, which features scattered couches and informal seating as well as regular tables and a semicircular bar, serves lighter fare from 4:30 PM.

The Coe House (603-253-8617; www.coehouse.com), Rt. 25B, Center Harbor. Open in-season daily from 4:30 PM; off-season Thu.–Sun. A distinctive early-19th-century mansion listed on the National Register of Historic Places. New Hampshire native Franklin Pierce once watched from its cupola as Harvard and Yale competed in a rowing race. Reservations suggested on weekends. Entrées range from a medley of fresh vegetables tossed with garlic butter pasta ($12.95) to wood-grilled western elk chop ($22.95). There are also menus to accommodate Atkins and South Beach dieters.

Camp at Mill Falls (603-279-3003; www.thecman.com), Rt. 3, in the Chase House at Mill Falls, Meredith. Dinner nightly 5–9:30. The decor is summer camp with a fieldstone fireplace and tin ceiling, appropriate in this kids'-camp-studded corner of the world. Like other members of the Common Man restaurant chain, it's a dependable bet. Moderate-priced entrées feature comfort food and range from "camp cakes" to a 20-ounce porterhouse steak—not your standard camp fare (though the s'mores for dessert may bring back memories).

The Common Man (603-536-4536; www.thecman.com), 60 Main St., Ashland. Open daily for lunch and dinner; après-ski specials 3–5 PM. Opened in 1971, this is the original, and still popular, star of a New Hampshire success story. The Great American Dining Company now operates a dozen restaurants that run north to south off I-93 from Windham to Lincoln. Here, the country decor features old posters, books, tools, and art, a comfortable feeling for relaxed dining. There is also a brick patio and lounge deck, as well as a popular menu featuring 'Sconset pie, grilled shrimp, mixed grill, hazelnut-crusted chicken, and three cuts of prime rib. Dinners include cheese, crackers, and dips; salad; fresh-baked bread; veggies; potato; and white chocolate. Most entrées under $20.

Lago at the Inn at Bay Point (603-279-2253; www.thecman.com), Exit 23 off I-93 in Meredith. Open for lunch Wed–Sat. 11:30–3; nightly for dinner 5–9, Fri. and Sat. until 9:30; Sunday brunch 10:30–2:30. In one of the newest members of the Common Man restaurant family, Lago calls on a Tuscan theme for menu and decor. Sophisticated yet rustic with dark beams and stucco walls—your villa on the lake with a great deck that could make you believe you own the water. Grilled panini, tuna white bean salad, shrimp and polenta for lunch; sea bass in parchment, osso buco, and other Italian specialties in the evening.

The Lakehouse Grille (603-279-5221; www.thecman.com), 281 Daniel Webster Hwy. (at Church Landing),

Meredith. Open for breakfast 7–10, lunch Mon.–Sat. 11:30–3, dinner from 5 daily; lounge open from 3 PM. We wonder why it's called Adirondack style since New Hampshire does it just as well, with this restaurant's elegantly casual decor a strong case in point—not that the view of Lake Winnipesaukee embraced by the White Mountains needs any enhancement. At night, the restaurant is candlelit and offers a large selection of entrées, including pan-seared Atlantic salmon and a 20-ounce "cowboy" steak.

Mame's (603-279-4631), 8 Plymouth St., Meredith. Open daily for lunch and dinner; Sunday brunch 11–2. An 1825 brick village home with barn, now with six dining rooms, Mame's offers varied and reasonably priced dining. Chicken baked in white wine with lemon and mushrooms, vegetables Alfredo, baked haddock, and roast prime rib are offered, along with nightly early-bird specials. Dinner entrées range from baked Boston scrod ($13.95) to lobster-scallop Divan ($10.50), with reef and beef at $21.95. Mud pie, liqueur parfaits, cheesecake, and more for dessert. There's also a tavern menu. Nightmare—a casserole of turkey, ham, broccoli, bacon, tomato, and mushrooms, topped with Swiss—has been a house specialty for more than 24 years ($7.75).

On Squam Lake

The Manor on Golden Pond (603-968-3348; 1-800-545-2141; www .manorongoldenpond.com), Shepard Hill Rd. and Rt. 3, Holderness. Open daily for dinner 6–9. Dining is a big deal here, as well it should be in the Manor's elegant Edwardian Van Horne Dining Room. But while the surroundings take you back in time, the food is up to the minute. The restaurant, which features what the owners call "new American cuisine," rates Four Diamonds from AAA and an award of excellence for its wine list from *Wine Spectator*. At $10–16 for appetizers and $22–40 for entrées, the prices reflect the acclaim. Reservations required.

Walter's Basin (603-968-4412; www .waltersbasin.com), 895 Rt. 3 at the bridge, Holderness. Open all year, most days from breakfast at 7 AM to late-night pub offerings. This popular restaurant cantilevered over Little Squam Lake in the middle of Holderness is easy to find, whether you arrive by land or water. Casual but polished decor offers upscale family dining with a full-time lunch menu and dinner entrées $12–26. Specialties include seafood chowder, pan-fried rainbow trout, scallop étouffée, braised lamb shank, and a Bourbon Street Grille with BBQ chicken, grilled pork chop, and bourbon demi-stuffed crab with chipotle cream sauce. The seasonal "fry shack" offers a kids' menu and built-in sandbox floor.

On Lake Winnipesaukee south
Oliver's (603-286-7379), 4 Sanborn Rd. (Rt. 3 at I-93, left off Exit 20, Tilton, handy to the outlet mall). Open daily for lunch and dinner 11–9 weekdays, 11–10 Fri. and Sat.; Sunday brunch 11–2. Reservations suggested. Locals voted this popular restaurant the most romantic in the area. There's candlelight dining in five cozy rooms, two with fireplaces. Dinner offerings include steak au poivre, veal du jour, and salmon en croute. The **Fox and Hounds Pub** serves a lighter menu until closing. Price range $7–25.

Bailey's Bubble (603-569-3612), Wolfeboro town docks. A summertime tradition for ice cream and a definite must for a visit to Wolfeboro.

Morrissey's (603-569-3662), 298 S. Main St., Wolfeboro. Open mid-May–Columbus Day for all three meals. Formerly Bailey's, this is an old favorite known for its ice cream. The Bailey family has offered casual dining in the Wolfeboro area for nearly seven decades, and the new owners continue that tradition. A full menu, from breakfast omelets and blueberry muffins to homemade clam chowder, baked Virginia ham, and barbecued stuffed chicken, keeps families happy year after year.

Caffe Salerno (569-0609; www .caffesalerno.com), 22 Glendon St., Wolfeboro. A real find a street back from the main drag by the old railroad depot. Locals know an excellent buy when they come here for Nadine's soups, salads, frittatas, grilled veggies, and daily entrées served in cozy cafeteria style. Most dinners served with two sides are under $10. Take out or eat in this friendly, casual establishment.

Strawberry Patch (603-569-5523), 50 North St., Wolfeboro. Open Mon.–Sat. 7:30–2 for breakfast and lunch, Sun. breakfast only, 7:30–1. Strawberry pancakes, shortcake, and sundaes, not to mention fresh strawberries rolled in brown sugar and sour cream. Quiche and salads, too.

Poor People's Pub (603-522-8378), Rt. 109, Sanbornville. Open for lunch and dinner. A local gathering spot with good road food: burgers, pizzas, daily specials, and subs. We can vouch for "Tramp's Treat": fresh chicken salad on a grilled roll. Beer and wine are served.

Wolfetrap Grill & Raw Bar (603-569-1047; www.wolfetrap.com), 19 Bay St., Wolfeboro. Come by car, boat, or call for shuttle service from the town docks. The sit-down component of the Wolfecatch Fish Market, this is *the* place to come for fresh lobster, shellfish, steamers, oysters, and fried clams; also hand-cut certified Angus beef. Getting there by water limo is fun too.

On Lake Winnipesaukee west
Chunky's Cinema & Pub (603-286-4444; www.chunkyscinema.com), I-93, 3 miles west of Exit 20, Tilton. Food—burgers, chicken tenders, salads, desserts, and popcorn—served alongside newly released films. Eat and watch at the same time. A great birthday party possibility; Chunky's provides all the fixin's. Open daily. Call for times.

Hart's Turkey Farm Restaurant (603-279-6212; www.hartsturkeyfarm .com), junction of Rts. 3 and 104, Meredith. Open all year at 11:15 AM for lunch and dinner. A big barn of a place serving turkey in every conceivable form, but there are also steaks, seafood, and sandwiches in this large, popular restaurant, family owned for more than 50 years. Gift shop. Moderate.

Sam & Rosie's Café and Bakery (603-253-6606), Rt. 25, Center Harbor. Open 6:30–2:45 except Sun. Sam and Rose Blake run a first-rate breakfast and lunch place, with fresh baked goods and NASCAR decor.

George's Diner (603-279-8723; www.georgesdiner.com), Plymouth St., Meredith. Open 6 AM–8 PM daily.

Breakfast daily until 2 PM. Nothing fancy, just dependably good food.

JT's Bar-B-Q and Seafood (603-366-7322), Rt. 3, Weirs Beach, Laconia. Open daily for lunch and dinner from 11 AM. Country breakfast served Sat. and Sun. 8–11. Barbecue, burgers, back ribs, and prime ribs, along with sandwiches and seafood, are available, both dine-in and take-out, at moderate prices with daily specials.

Kellerhaus (603-366-4466; 1-888-KLR-HAUS; www.kellerhaus.com), Rt. 3, just north of Weirs Beach. Known for the ice cream made here for 90 years with a view of the lake, sundaes with a dozen different toppings, an old-fashioned candy store, and waffle breakfasts weekends only May–Oct.

🦞 **Tilt'n Diner** (603-286-2204), Rt. 3 at I-93, left off Exit 20, Tilton. Another member of the Common Man family, this diner is a takeoff on the 1950s, with period menu, music, and memorabilia. Open until 9 PM for breakfast, lunch, and dinner. Nothing's expensive; everything's filling. For quick food and lots of fun, this place is just "swell!"

The Town Docks (603-279-3445), 289 Daniel Webster Hwy. (Rt. 3), Meredith. Open summer only 11–11 for ice cream. Free tie-up at the public boat docks. Ice cream all day; lobster rolls, fried clams, hot dogs, steamers, and fresh salads for most of it. Eat inside or at picnic tables or the "beach bar" overlooking the water (and just about everyone in town).

In the Sandwich/Squam Lake area
The Endeavor Café in the Sandwich General Store, Center Sandwich. Open daily for breakfast and

lunch; Sunday brunch. The back of the store is a truly pleasant space with a woodstove and easy chairs as well as tables draped in checked cloths. Order the soup you can see simmering on the stove; sandwiches, salads, and daily specials. The store also houses the Sandwich General Store (open 6 days 6:30–6:30, Sun. 7–2:30) and is a source of Sandwich Creamery ice cream. Try ginger.

Squam Lake Inn Café (603-968-4417; www.squamlakeinn.com), Rt. 3 at Shepard Hill Rd., Holderness. Open daily in summer 10 AM–2 PM. This friendly B&B now offers yummy sandwiches, soups, and salads, plus daily homemade desserts, served indoors or outside on a pleasant patio with umbrella tables. Boxed lunches, with sandwich, pickle, chips, and homemade cookie, are available for a small additional fee.

✳ Entertainment

✔ **Belknap Mill Society** (603-524-8813), Mill Plaza, Laconia 03246. Open all year. Built in 1823, this is the oldest unaltered textile mill in the country. It's now a year-round art center with art exhibits, music, lectures, and children's programs as well as many special events.

MUSIC **New Hampshire Music Festival** (603-253-4331; www.nhmf .org). For more than 50 years, this regional music institution has brought big-time classical musicians to the small towns of the New Hampshire's Lakes region. The 6-week summer season begins in early July at the Silver Cultural Arts Center at Plymouth State College. In addition to featuring world-class performers, the festival includes a preconcert lecture series,

chamber music concerts, and a children's series—more than 50 events in all. Since 2001, festival organizers have made their home at the former Red Hill Inn, a 60-acre estate in Center Harbor now in the planning stages to become a year-round center for music.

Meadowbrook Farm Summer Concert Series (603-293-4700; www .meadowbrookfarm.net). A popular summer series with lots of variety, from Meat Loaf and Bonnie Raitt to Garrison Keillor and the Boston Pops.

Great Waters Music Festival (603-569-7710; www.greatwaters.org), on the Brewster Academy campus, Wolfeboro. July–Sep., a series of performances held in an acoustically designed tent.

Wolfeboro Friends of Music (603-569-3657) sponsor a series of 10 concerts held in local churches and auditoriums Sep.–June.

SUMMER THEATER **The Lakes Region Theater** (603-279-9933), Rt. 25, Box 1607, Meredith. Professional summer-stock productions of Broadway plays presented in Inter-Lakes High School. Late June–Aug.

The Little Church Theater (603-968-2250), 40 Rt. 113 (across from the Squam Lake Science Center), Holderness. A nonprofit arts center with a variety of offerings throughout summer, including art shows, sing-alongs, puppet shows, cabaret, plays, and workshops, at mostly modest prices.

Also see the **Barnstormers** in Tamworth in "Mount Washington Gateway Region." It's New Hampshire's oldest professional theater, staging outstanding plays with Equity casts.

✳ Selective Shopping

ANTIQUES Antiques shops abound in this section of the state. We mention these few just to whet the appetite.

Burlwood Antique Center (603-279-6387), 194 Daniel Webster Hwy., junction of Rts. 3 and 104, Meredith. The largest collection of antiques in the Lakes region—175 selected dealers. Open May–Oct., daily 10–5. Furniture, jewelry, china, glass, books, the works.

Alexandria Lamp Shop (603-279-4234), 62 Main St., Meredith. Several rooms full of antique (kerosene, gas, and electric) as well as unusual fixtures and chandeliers. Also hard-to-find lamp shades, parts, and repairs.

The Glass Knob (603-253-8222), 233 Whittier Hwy. (Rt. 25), Moultonboro. Open May–Sep., daily 10–5; Oct.–Dec., Thu.–Sun. Interesting selection of vintage furniture and curiosities.

ART AND CRAFTS **Sandwich Home Industries** (603-284-6831; www.nhcrafts.org), 132 Main St., Center Sandwich. Open mid-May–mid-Oct.

LEAGUE OF NEW HAMPSHIRE CRAFTSMEN RETAIL SHOP IN CENTER SANDWICH

Courtesy of the League of NH Craftsmen

This cooperative was founded in 1926 to promote traditional crafts, eventually spawning the current League of New Hampshire Craftsmen with its stores throughout the state and its big annual August Craftsmen's Fair at Mount Sunapee. The present shop, picturesquely situated beside the town green, dates from 1934. For many years a signature item in this particular shop has been the locally made botanical lamp shades. As in other league shops, you will also find a fine selection of handmade pottery, glass, clothing, toys, ornaments, jewelry, prints, furniture, and weavings.

League of New Hampshire Craftsmen. Shops in **Center Sandwich** (603-284-6831), Main St.; **Meredith** (603-279-7920), Rt. 3; and in **Wolfeboro** (603-569-3309), 64 Center St.; are open year-round, displaying superb New Hampshire–made, juried crafts of all types including lamps, furniture, prints, carvings, textiles, pottery, and much more. Demonstration programs in July and Aug.

Cornish Hill Pottery (603-569-5626; 1-800-497-2556), 39 N. Main St., Wolfeboro, is a combination studio and showcase for Gogi Millner Adler's stunning functional and decorative pieces, all hand thrown and decorated.

Also in Wolfeboro: **The Art Place** (603-569-6159), 9 N. Main St., showcases regional, original art and limited-edition prints, as does the **Blue Shutter Gallery** (603-569-3372), 19 Lehner St. **Made on Earth** (603-569-9100), N. Main St., showcases artisans from around the earth. **Hampshire Pewter** (603-569-4944), 9 Mill St. (just off Main St.), open year-round daily except Sun., 9–5. A factory store showcasing pieces made here; factory tours are offered spring–fall.

Yikes American Craft Gallery
(603-253-4966), Rt. 25 and Main St.,
Center Harbor, and 676 Main St.,
Laconia. Open except Jan.–Apr., daily
10–6, Sun. 10–5. A zany mix of well-
chosen items representing more than
500 American craftspeople, from met-
als and clothing to toys and sculpture.

The Old Print Barn (603-279-6479),
343 Winona Rd., off Rt. 104, Meredith. Open year-round except Thanksgiving and Christmas, 10–5. One of
the largest displays of original prints
in New England, some 2,000 original
antique and contemporary works from
1600 to the present, housed in a Civil
War–era barn. We especially like the
old New Hampshire views of the lakes
and White Mountains, but you can
find etchings, lithographs, and engrav-
ings covering virtually any subject
from any continent as well as work by
locally prominent and world-famous
artists. The huge restored barn, with
its detailed, 19th-century craftsmanship, is impressive, too. Free, but it
will be hard to resist buying a print!

Oglethorpe (603-279-9909), at Mill
Falls Marketplace, Rt. 3 in Meredith,
a gallery representing work by some
300 craftspeople, including hand-
forged ironwork and handcrafted
jewelry.

Village Artists & Gallery (603-968-
4445), 51 Main St., Ashland, is a new
nonprofit cooperative representing
40 local artists, well worth checking.

Stamping Memories (603-528-0498;
www.stampingmemories.com), 45
Court St., Laconia. Open 10–5 Mon.–
Sat., later on class nights. The largest
outlet in the state for scrapbooking
supplies. Downstairs, Mike Verhoek
operates a pottery studio and showcase at the **Laconia Pottery Gallery**
(603-528-4997).

Lambert Folk Art Gallery (603-
286-4882; www.jimlambertfolkart
.com), 271 Main St., Tilton. Not the
kind of shop you might expect to find
in the middle of Tilton, but Jim Lambert points out that his whimsical creations perpetuate the town's tradition
of striking sculptures. His own folk
sculptures are the real finds here,
but many other outstanding craftspeople, most of them regional, are
represented.

BOOKS ✪ **Bayswater Book Co.**
(603-253-8858), Rt. 25 and Main St.,
Center Harbor. Open Mon.–Sat.
9:30–6, Sun. 11–4. A well-stocked
bookstore offering volumes of extra
service including kids' story hours, a
young adults' discussion group, arts
and crafts workshops, journal-writing
courses, frequent author signings, and
coffee by the pound or cup.

Innisfree Bookshop (603-279-3905),
Mill Falls Marketplace, Meredith. A
big, full-service bookstore also carrying music, toys, and cards.

The Country Bookseller (603-569-
6030; 1-800-877-READ), 23A N.
Main St., Wolfeboro. An inviting,
well-stocked independent bookstore
in the middle of the village.

Also in Wolfeboro, see **Camelot**
under *Special Stores.*

FARMS **Moulton Farm** (603-279-
3915), 18 Quarry Rd., just off Rt. 25
east of Meredith. Open May–Christmas Eve. A simply outstanding farm
stand in a great setting.

The Sandwich Creamery (603-284-
6675), Hannah Rd. off 113A, North
Sandwich. A source of ice cream (ginger is the standout flavor); also Brie
and cheddar cheeses. Also available at
the general store in Center Sandwich.

Longhaul Farm at Squam Lake (603-968-9333), Rt. 113, Holderness. Local farm products offered seasonally with a festive "Taste of the Farm" meal, including live music, presented annually in early July.

Booty Farm (603-284-7163), 610 Mount Israel Rd., Sandwich. Open year-round. The sugarhouse was billowing sweet steam when we passed. Syrup is sold year-round, along with organic produce.

Alton Farmer's Market (603-364-5279), Rt. 11, Alton Bay. Sat. 10 AM–1 PM, late June–mid-Sep.

Laconia Farmer's Market (603-267-6522), Beacon St. East. An outdoor farmer's market located in the parking lot between the mill and town hall. Open mid-June–mid-Sep., Sat. 8:30 AM–noon.

Wolfeboro Area Farmer's Market (603-323-3369), 35 Center St. Open last week in June–end of Sep., Thu. 1–5 PM. In addition to baked goods, organically grown veggies, and cut flowers, there are occasional educational events and demonstrations.

Heritage Farm Tours (603-524-8188; www.heritagefarm.net), 16 Parker Hill Rd., Sanbornton. ATV rentals, hay- and sleigh rides, petting farm, homemade ice cream, gift shop and farm stand, corn maze.

Smith Farm Stand (603-524-7673), 95 Sleeper Hill Rd., Gilford. Fifth-generation maple syrup producer boiling in 1947 sap house. Syrup available year-round.

SPECIAL STORES Keepsake Quilting and Country Pleasures (603-253-4026; 1-800-865-9458; www.keepsakequilting.com), Rt. 25, Senter's Marketplace, Center Harbor. Open daily 9–7. Mon.–Sat., Sun. until 6 in summer; closing time is an hour earlier off-season. Billed as America's largest quilt shop, this is a destination for quilters from throughout the country and even the world. Many are members, paying a nominal annual fee to display their own work here (on consignment); thousands also subscribe to the catalog, which features—as does the store—everything and anything a quilter could desire. There

KEEPSAKE QUILTING AND COUNTRY PLEASURES IN CENTER HARBOR

is nothing, however, like actually seeing and fingering the 10,000 bolts of cotton cloth in a heady range of colors and patterns. Mannequins greet patrons by the door, proffering white gloves, the better to examine both fabrics and finished quilts. Stencils, patterns, and kits are also sold.

New Hampshire Gold (603-744-6018; 1- 888-819-4255; www.nhgold.com), Exit 23 Plaza, Rt. 104, New Hampton. Maple products, bread and pancake mixes, handmade soaps, and gift baskets from a working family farm.

The Old Country Store, Rt. 25, Moultonborough. Open daily. Built as a stagecoach stop in 1781, this rambling old building offers a small museum along with enough rooms to get lost in searching for weird and wonderful gifts, books, New Hampshire–made products, and typical country store items.

Topiary at Owl's Rest Farm (603-934-3221; www.thetopiary.com), 252 Brook Rd., Sanbornton. Open by chance or appointment. Handcrafted, custom-designed silk topiaries, floral arrangements, wreaths, and swags. Twenty-seven acres with garden tours, cooking classes, and English tea by reservation.

Holderness General Store (603-968-3446; www.holdernessgeneral store.com), 863 Rt. 3, Holderness. This up-to-the-minute commissary gives a Ralph Lauren aura to the old-time, cracker barrel image of a general store. With its slatted wood ceiling and track lighting, it was an immediate hit when it opened in July 2005. The provisions go beyond the usual requirements and include such delicacies as live lobster, Asian tenderloin tips, an extensive wine (and imported

water and cocktail) selection, even a cigar humidor. Classic vestiges remain in the form of wooden vegetable boxes, a wheel of cheese with a chopping block, and a fudge bar with multiple temptations. In addition to food, there's plenty of kitchen/dining supplies for vacationers in need of housekeeping necessities nice enough to use as gifts.

Annalee Dolls (603-279-6542; 1-800-433-6557; www.annalee.com), off Rt. 3 or Rt. 104, Meredith. Open all year, daily 9–5. Dolls are for kids, of course, but these dolls are also among the more collectible items you can purchase today, so probably more golden agers stop here than children. Annalee Thorndike began making her felt dolls in 1934; now her son Chuck and daughter-in-law Karen run a major local industry employing more than 450 people, and the dolls are sold and collected nationally. For collectors, the best inventory is maintained here, including more than 1,000 different early dolls. You can see the finished pieces in the gift shop, the doll museum (open Memorial Day–mid-Oct.), and the Annalee Doll Antique and Collectible Doll Shoppe.

✒ **Camelot** (603-569-1771), 16 N. Main St., Wolfeboro. Open daily. Over more than 40 years Al Pierce has created an eclectic mix of good things that jam-pack his shop. Locals are addicted to his special cream cheddar mix, and youngsters know this as a peerless place for the kind of toys (educational and otherwise) you won't find everywhere. Cards, many books, and assorted gifts fill every inch of space remaining.

Basket World (603-366-5585), Rt. 3, Weirs Beach. Leave the kids across the street at the Funspot while you shop through this huge display of woven baskets, furniture, and other items.

chi-lin (603-527-1115; 603-279-8663), corner of Lake and Main Sts., Meredith. Terry and Suzanne Lee have filled their shop with a selection of imported and custom-made cabinets, furniture, and accessories with an Asian sensibility. They have also created an oasis off this busy shopping area, with pocket gardens for occasional tea parties. You can consult with them to implement your own design ideas.

Pepi Herrmann Crystal (603-528-1020), Lily Pond Rd., Gilford. Tue.–Sat. 9:30–5. Showroom and museum. Fine-quality, hand-cut crystal and giftware. Watch crystal cutters at work.

Country Braid House (603-286-4511; www.countrybraidhouse.com), 462 Main St., Tilton. Open Mon.–Fri. 9–5, Sat. 9–4. A workshop and showroom featuring new and antique braided and hand-hooked rugs. Custom designs and kits available.

SHOPPING COMPLEXES **Tanger Factory Outlet** (603-286-7880), Rt. 3 at I-93, left off Exit 20, Tilton. Open May–Dec. 10 AM–9 PM, Sun. 10–6; off-season closing at 6, except Fri. and Sat. when it's 8. More than 50 tax-free factory outlets include Brooks Brothers, J. Crew, Polo/Ralph Lauren, Eddie Bauer, Chuck Roast, J. Jill, Coach, Mesa, Mikasa, Harry and David, Farberware, and Black & Decker.

Mill Falls Marketplace Shops (www.millfalls.com), Rt. 3, Meredith. Open daily year-round, Mon.–Thu. 10–5:30, Fri. and Sat. until 8, Sun. until 4; nightly until 9 in summer. This remarkable restoration of an 1820s mill beside its 40-foot falls now houses 15 shops; also restrooms and an ATM.

✳ Special Events

Dozens of events are held each summer in the Winnipesaukee region, too many to list here in detail. Check with such organizations as the **Lakes Region Association** (603-744-8664), **New Hampshire Farm Museum** (603-652-7840), **Belknap Mill Society** (603-524-8813), and **Gunstock Recreation Area** (603-293-4341).

Early February: **World Championship Sled Dog Derby**, Opechee Park, Laconia. Three days of racing by colorful teams of sled dogs.

Mid-February: **Winter Carnival** (603-569-2758), Wolfeboro Lion's Club. A week of events. **Sandwich Notch Sled Dog Races**. Annual 60-mile races from Tamworth to Sandwich.

Mid-May: **Annual Winni Fishing Derby** (603-253-8689), Lake Winnipesaukee. A weekend fishing contest with cash prizes for the largest landlocked salmon or lake trout.

Early June: **Laconia Race Week** is huge, the biggest annual event in New Hampshire and the oldest motorcycle rally in the nation. In one recent year it drew some 375,000 motorcyclists over 9 days, a tradition dating back to 1916. The races are held at the New Hampshire Speedway in Loudon 10 miles away, but parades and rallies are held at Gunstock and in the Lake City itself. Two-wheeled visitors from throughout the country fill every bed for miles around. For a full schedule of events log onto www.laconiamcweek.com or call 603-366-2000. **Annual Barn Sale and Auction** (603-652-7840), New Hampshire Farm Museum, Milton. Call for a detailed schedule of many summer events.

July and August: **Alton Bay band concerts**. Several free concerts are held weekly during July and August, plus a week of events during Old Home Week in mid-August. Write the chamber of commerce for a full schedule of summer activities.

Early July: **New Hampshire Music Festival** (603-524-1000). A 6-week regional tradition, with world-class performers playing chamber and orchestral music at various venues.

Fourth of July: Regionwide celebrations with parades and fireworks, some special events, some events held the night before. Alton, Ashland, Center Harbor, Laconia, Meredith, Wolfeboro.

Mid-July: **Arts and Crafts Street Fair**, downtown Laconia.

Late July: **Annual Antiques Fair and Show** (603-539-5126), Kingswood High School, Wolfeboro. **Antique and Classic Boat Show**, Weirs Beach. **Annual Flea Market and Chicken Barbecue**, East Alton.

Early August: **Huggins Hospital Street Fair** (603-569-1043), Brewster Field, Wolfeboro. **Sandwich Old Home Days**, an entire week of very special events.

Mid-August: **Old Home Week** (603-539-6323), Freedom and Alton. **Miss Winnipesaukee Pageant** (603-366-4377), Funspot, Weirs Beach.

Late August: **Annual Lakes Region Fine Arts and Crafts Festival** (603-279-6121), Meredith. A major, juried outdoor exhibit with music, entertainment, and food.

Labor Day weekend: **Fireworks at Weirs Beach** (603-524-5531). **Lakes Region Craft Fair** (603-528-4014).

Mid-September: **New England Slalom Championships**, Back Bay, Wolfeboro (603-569-3017). **Foliage trains along Winnipesaukee**, Meredith and Weirs Beach stations (603-279-5253; www.foliagetrains .com). **Annual Mustang/All Ford Show** at the Laconia Funspot in Weirs Beach (603-753-8134). **Vintage Race Boat Regatta**, Wolfeboro Town Docks (603-569-4554). **Annual Winnipesaukee Relay Race** (603-524-5531). Teams of runners circle the lake, beginning in the Gunstock Recreation Area. **Altrusa Antique Show and Sale** at the Inter-Lakes High School, Meredith (603-279-6121). **Annual Lees Mill Steamboat Meet**, Moultonborough.

Early October: **Annual Antique and Classic Boat and Car Rendezvous**, Wolfeboro Town Docks (603-569-0087). **Annual Quilter Show** (603-524-8813), Belknap Mill Society, Laconia.

Columbus Day weekend: **Sandwich Fair** (603-284-7062; www.sandwich fairnh.com), 3 days: an old-fashioned fair with tractor pulls, ox, mule, and draft horse pulls, clogging, an antique auto parade, 4-H exhibits, fleece-to-shawl spinning, stage shows, a grand street parade, and much more.

November: **Holly Fair**, Center Harbor Congregational Church (603-253-7698; www.chcc.org) **Lakes Region Holiday Arts & Crafts Fair**, Winnipesaukee Expo Center Laconia (603-528-4014).

First weekend in December: **Annual Christmas in the Village**, Center Sandwich. Craft, bake, and book sale with the historical society decorated for Christmas.

THE WESTERN LAKES

From Lake Sunapee to Newfound Lake, this region is spotted with lakes big and small, all set in open, rolling countryside, each with a view of one of the area's three mighty mountains: Sunapee, Kearsarge, and Cardigan.

All three summits make rewarding hikes, and all the lakes offer attractive shoreline lodging as well as swimming, fishing, and boating. But this entire area is far less well known than the Winnipesaukee region, because the old hotels here were replaced with second homes instead of with the cottage colonies and motels that sprang up around Winnipesaukee. Still, these "summer people" continued to patronize summer theater, shops, ski areas, and restaurants. When lodging places began proliferating again, as they have over the past couple of decades, these amenities were all in place.

The activity is very low-key, however. The year-round hub of the area is the handsome old college town of New London, with a rambling, 18th-century inn and Colby-Sawyer College at its center and two small lakes (Little Sunapee and Pleasant) on its arms.

The region's most famous lake is Sunapee. Unusually clear (it is still a source of drinking water) and unusually high (1,100 feet), Lake Sunapee sits midway between the Connecticut River Valley and the Merrimack River Valley. Ten miles long and 3 miles wide, still sheathed almost entirely in green, it's unquestionably a special place.

Lake Sunapee, however, is a tease. Stand on the summit of Mount Sunapee (accessible by chairlift) and its 10-mile-long expanse shimmers below, seemingly inviting you to jump in. Back on level ground, though, reaching the water is elusive. You can swim at the beach in Lake Sunapee State Park, choose from two excursion boats, or rent almost any kind of boat; but no road circles the lake because, from the 1850s until the 1920s, everyone came and went by train and got around the lake itself by steamboat. The largest cluster of hotels and busiest steamboat landing was Sunapee Harbor, still the summer focal point of the lake.

Newfound Lake (8 miles west of I-93), with 22 miles of shoreline, is even more low-key than Sunapee; and Mount Cardigan looms above its western shore as Mount Sunapee does above Lake Sunapee. Both Sunapee and Newfound offer sandy state beaches, as does smaller Kezar Lake in North Sutton, off I-89, Exit 10. Other lakes accessible to guests at local inns include Little Sunapee and

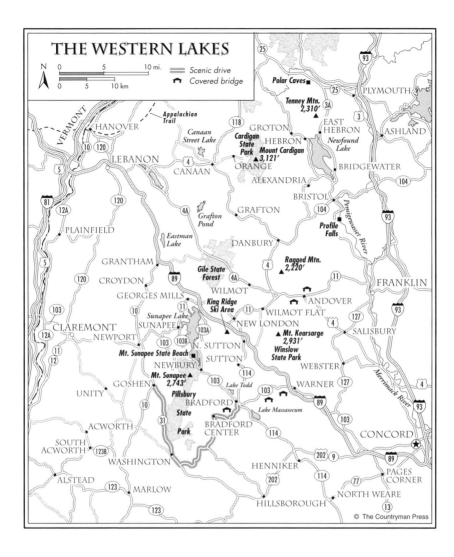

Pleasant lakes, both in New London; Lake Todd and Lake Massasecum in Bradford; Highland Lake in East Andover; and Webster Lake in Franklin.

Since its opening in 1968, I-89 has put New London and Sunapee less than 2 hours from Boston, but the increase in tourist traffic has not been dramatic. In winter, skiers tend to day-trip from Boston as well as Concord; and in summer, innkeepers complain, they whiz right on through to Vermont. Lodging prices are relatively low, even lower in the northern part of this region, which was bypassed when I-89 replaced Rt. 4 as the region's major east–west route.

In New Hampshire state promotional literature you'll find this area under "Dartmouth/Lake Sunapee," but we believe that these "Western Lakes" (west of I-93) deserve more recognition. While it is handy to the cultural happenings

A SAILOR'S PARADISE ON LAKE SUNAPEE

around the Dartmouth green, the area is equally handy to attractions in the White Mountains, the Merrimack Valley, and the Monadnock region. These Western Lakes are great spots to explore from or to just stay put.

GUIDANCE

The New London Lake Sunapee Region Chamber of Commerce (www.nhliving.com/towns/newlondon) maintains a helpful walk-in information booth in the middle of New London's Main Street, June–Labor Day, and another seasonal information booth for Sunapee in Sunapee Lower Village.

The Newport Chamber of Commerce (603-863-1510; www.newport nhchamber.org), 2 N. Main St., maintains a seasonal information booth in the center of town.

The Newfound Region Chamber of Commerce (603-744-2150; www.nhliving.com/towns/bristol) maintains a seasonal information booth on Rt. 3A at the foot of the lake.

GETTING THERE *By bus:* **Vermont Transit** (1-800-451-3292; www.greyhound .com) stops at the Gourmet Garden, 127 Main St., New London, once a day en route from Boston to White River Junction; direct service from Boston's Logan Airport.

By car: I-89 cuts diagonally across the heart of this region, putting it within 1½ hours of Boston; via I-91 it's also 2½ hours from Hartford.

By air: See *Getting There* in "Upper Valley Towns" and "The Manchester/Nashua Area."

MEDICAL EMERGENCY Dial **911**.

New London Hospital (603-526-2911), 270 County Rd., New London, has a 24-hour walk-in clinic. (Also see "Upper Valley Towns.")

✳ Villages

Andover. This is an unusually proud town, with Proctor Academy, established in 1848 (actually it moved to Wolfeboro in 1865, then back in 1875), at its core;

hence the B&Bs and unusually good dining and shopping. The **Andover Historical Society Museum**, housed in a vintage-1874, Victorian-style railroad station on Rt. 4 in the tiny village of Potter Place (open weekends Memorial Day–Columbus Day, Sat. 10–3, Sun. 1–3), is worth a stop. According to a historical marker in the nearby Rt. 11 rest area, Potter Place takes its name from Richard Potter, a 19th-century magician known throughout America. **Highland Lake** is in East Andover.

Bradford Center. Just off the main drag (Rt. 103), but it feels like a million miles away. Coming north, the turn for River Road is a left just beyond the junction of Rts. 103 and 114. You go through the Bement covered bridge, built in 1854. Continue up the hill, up and up until you come to the old hill-town crossroads. Turn left, and you will find the old schoolhouse and vintage-1838 meetinghouse with its two doors and Gothic-style tower topped with decorative wooden spikes (peculiar to New Hampshire), resembling upside-down icicles. The old graveyard is here, too. The present town hall was moved from this village down to what is now the business center of Bradford when the train arrived in the 1860s.

Hebron is a classic gathering of white-clapboard houses around a common—with bandstand, general store, post office, and handsome, two-story 1803 meetinghouse—at the northwestern corner of Newfound Lake. The Hebron Village School is housed in a churchlike building with a Gothic Revival steeple (upside-down wooden icicles again).

THE FULL MOON RISES OVER THE TOWN GREEN IN NEW LONDON
Kim Grant

New London. Sited on a ridge, good for summer views and winter skiing, New London is the home of **Colby-Sawyer College** (603-526-2010), a 4-year, coed college founded as a Baptist academy in 1837. The 80-acre campus includes the Marion G. Mugar Art Gallery, with changing exhibits by recognized artists and by college faculty and students. The **New London Historical Society Museum and Library** on Little Sunapee Road is an ambitious gathering of restored buildings, including an 1835 Cape with an attached ell and barn; also a schoolhouse, country store, and blacksmith shop on 5 acres. In 2001 the society opened the Transportation Building to house an outstanding collection of old carriages and sleighs, including an original Concord Coach. New London is also home to the Barn Playhouse, one of

New England's oldest and best summer theaters. The town's hidden gems are **Cricenti's Bog** and **Little Sunapee Lake**, site of Twin Lake Village, one of New England's most authentic and low-profile 19th-century family resorts.

Newport is an old mill town and commercial center with some elaborate 19th-century buildings like the circa-1886 **Newport Opera House** (603-863-2412) on Main Street, the scene of frequent concerts, plays, and dances. It's also the scene of the annual presentation of the Sarah Josepha Hale Medal to the likes of Arthur Miller and Arthur Schlesinger. (Hale, the town's best-known citizen, was the author of the famous children's poem "Mary Had a Little Lamb" and was instrumental in promoting Thanksgiving as a national holiday.) **The Richards Library Arts Center** (603-863-3040), 58 N. Main St., hosts continuous exhibits by local artists, including an open studio the last Thursday of the month when visitors can view and discuss weaver Patryc Wiggins's long-term Mill Tapestry Project. The handsome brick **South Congregational Church** at the other end of Main Street (it's diagonally across from the Mobil station), completed in 1823, is almost identical to the Unitarian church (1824) in Deerfield, Massachusetts. No longer an outlet for the woolen mill across the street, the **Dorr Mill Store** has become a destination for rug hookers and quilters looking for supplies.

Sunapee Harbor. In the **Sunapee Historical Society Museum**, you browse through scrapbooks filled with pictures of the village's half a dozen vanished hotels, most notably the four-story, 100-room Ben-Mere, which sat until the 1960s on a knoll in the middle of "the Harbor." Local residents worry that most of the lakeshore is now privately owned, and therefore, the Sunapee Harbor Riverway Corporation has been formed to revitalize the Harbor's adjacent waterway, which once fueled a tannery, a pulp mill, and clothespin and wooden hame (part of a harness) factories. To date the corporation has restored several buildings in Sunapee Harbor, and worked to bring in restaurants, shops, and summer entertainment.

Sutton, off I-89, Exit 10, and south on Rt. 114. **South Sutton** is a 19th-century mill-village center with a 1790s meetinghouse and a former general store—now the **Old Store Museum**, exhibiting (we're told) no fewer than 4,000 items—along with the 1863 schoolhouse. For information on visiting hours, call 603-927-4345. **North Sutton** is also an appealing village with a meetinghouse, general store, and historic marker noting the several large summer hotels that used to stand here by **Kezar Lake**. Only the annex of one (now the Follansbee Inn) survives, but Wadleigh State Beach offers access to the lake. **Muster Field Farm** conveys a sense of both the beauty and the history of the area.

Washington. A tiny gem of a village with a cluster of imposing buildings, a meetinghouse completed in 1789 (the Asher Benjamin–style steeple was added later), an 1840s Gothic-style Congregational church, and a two-story, 1830s schoolhouse—all huddled together on the northern side of the common. According to a historical marker, this is the birthplace of the Seventh-Day Adventist Church (April 1842) and also the first town in the country incorporated (December 13, 1776) as "Washington."

MUSEUMS Also see *Villages*.

Andover Historical Society Museum (603-735-5694), Rts. 4 and 11, 105 Depot St., Potter Place. This classic, authentically furnished 1874 railroad station houses local history exhibits.

& **Marion G. Mugar Art Gallery** (603-526-3000; 603-526-3661), Colby-Sawyer College, 100 Main St., New London. Open during the school year Mon.–Fri. 9–5; weekends and summer by appointment or chance. Excellent changing exhibits by recognized artists.

Mount Kearsarge Indian Museum (603-456-2600; www.indianmuseum.org), Kearsarge Mountain Rd., Warner. Open May–Oct., Mon.–Sat. 10–5, Sun. noon–5. Doors open at 10 for Special Events Days. Open Sat. and Sun. from November to the weekend before Christmas. Guided tours on the hour with last tour at 4 PM. $8.50 adults, $6.50 ages 6–12, $7.50 seniors. This is one of the most impressive displays of Native American artifacts in the Northeast. Frankly, we weren't prepared for the quantity or quality of this collection, amassed by one man, Bud Thompson, over more than 40 years. With the skill of a professional curator (he was formerly with Canterbury Shaker Village), Thompson has transformed a former riding arena into a showcase for hundreds of priceless and evocative pieces: dozens of intricate sweetgrass baskets from the Penobscot, carved ash baskets from the Passamaquoddy, intricate quillwork from the Micmac, Seneca cornhusk masks, Anasazi pottery from Chaco Canyon in New Mexico (dating from somewhere between AD 800 and 1200), Navajo Yei rugs, elaborate saddlebags beaded by the Plains Indians, cradleboards from Idaho, and much, much more.

"I don't want people bending and squinting over labels," Bud Thompson observes. Instead, guides elaborate on the various Native American pieces as well as the cultures they represent. One of the few modern pieces in this museum is an imposing, bigger-than-life statue of a Native American in full regalia, which Thompson bought many years ago at the annual League of New Hampshire Craftsmen's Fair at Mount Sunapee State Park.

"It wasn't until after I had settled on this site for the museum and positioned the statue at the entrance that its sculptor told me it was carved from a single tree he had cut from the slopes of Mount Kearsarge," Thompson relates. The museum stands at the base of Mount Kearsarge, near the entrance to Rollins State Park and its trails to the mountain's bald summit.

Sunapee Historical Society Museum (603-763-9872; soonipi@cyberportal .net), 14 Main St., Sunapee Harbor. In summer, open Tue. and Thu.–Sun. 1–4, Wed. 7–9 PM; closed Mon. In fall, open weekends until Columbus Day 1–4. A former livery stable filled with photos of Sunapee's grand old hotels and steamboats. You discover that visitors began summering on Lake Sunapee as soon as the railroad reached Newbury in 1849 and that the lake's resort development was sparked by the three Woodsum brothers from Harrison, Maine (another lake resort), who began running steamboats to meet the trains. Soon there were two competing ferry lines (one boat carried 650 passengers) serving dozens of small landings on the shore and islands.

Muster Field Farm Museum (603-927-4276; www.musterfieldfarm.com), Harvey Rd., off Keyser St., which runs along Kezar Lake from North Sutton village. Open daily. These 250 hilltop acres have been farmed since the 18th century. The original Matthew Harvey Homestead remains remarkably intact; it changed ownership only once—in the 1940s—before acquiring its current status as a nonprofit trust. On any given day visitors are welcome to stroll around, inspect a dozen and a half outbuildings like the 1881 springhouse from a long-vanished hotel in Bradford, and buy vegetables and fruit in-season. The main house, an excellent example of rural Georgian architecture, is open Sun. 1–4 during June, July, and August. During the course of the year, the farm hosts several special events—Ice Day, Harvest Day, and Farm Days, among others—designed to highlight New Hampshire's agricultural traditions. The Annual Muster Field Farm Days, the weekend before Labor Day weekend, involves more than 100 exhibitors demonstrating crafts and traditional farming methods. Admission, charged only on event days, is $4 adults, $2 teens and seniors; under 6 free.

HISTORIC HOMES Daniel Webster Homestead (603-934-5057; 603-927-4096; www.nhstateparks.org/ParksPages/DanWebster/DanielWebster.html), Flaghole Rd., marked (badly) from Rts. 11 and 127 in Franklin. This is a small, clapboard, 18th-century cabin filled with replicated furnishings. Webster (1782–1852), Dartmouth class of 1801, represented New Hampshire in Congress from 1813 to 1817 and Massachusetts in the Senate from 1827 to 1841. He was a champion of states' rights and involved in many of the major issues of his day. His legendary oratorical skills were memorialized in Stephen Vincent Benet's play *The Devil and Daniel Webster*. Webster's birthplace is open weekends and holidays Memorial Day–Labor Day, 10:30–5:30. $7 adults, $3 ages 6–17; 5 and under and NH residents 65 and over are admitted free. The Franklin Historical Society provides living history interpretation at the site on the weekends it is open.

A SCULPTURE AMONG THE FINE GARDENS IN THE FELLS STATE HISTORIC SITE IN NEWBURY

The Fells State Historic Site at the John Hay National Wildlife Refuge (603-763-4789; www.the-fells.org), Rt. 103A between Newbury and Blodgett's Landing. Open year-round dawn–dusk. House tours (11–5) on weekends and holidays, Memorial Day–Columbus Day ($5 adults, $2 ages 6–15; under 6 free). Call for a schedule of programs and workshops. The former estate of writer and diplomat John Hay, The Fells sits high above the eastern shore of Lake

Sunapee. Although the 42-room mansion is unfurnished (Teddy Roosevelt once slept here), the 800-acre property provides an example of one of New England's finest early-20th-century gardens—a delightful mix of rugged landscape, cultivated perennials, and formal terraces. Walk from the exquisite Alpine Garden 0.5 mile down along meadowlike lawn to the water. In spring the 0.5-mile walk from the parking area is magnificent with century-old stands of rhododendron and mountain laurel. In all, there are more than 5 miles of hiking paths.

The New London Historical Society (603-526-6564; 603-526-6201; www .newlondonhistoricalsociety.org), Little Sunapee Rd., New London. The society owns and maintains a village of 19th-century buildings, including a farmhouse, two barns, a schoolhouse, meetinghouse, hearse house, violin shop, blacksmith shop, and a recently constructed Transportation Building that houses the group's outstanding collection of wagons, carriages, and sleighs, including an original Concord Coach. Most of the buildings have been moved to the site, which is open for self-tours at any time. Guided tours are available on Sun. 12:30–3:30 Memorial Day–Columbus Day weekend as well as on Tue. from 12:30–3:30 during July and August—but call to see if the schedule has changed. Special events are listed on the web site.

COVERED BRIDGES **The Keniston bridge**, built in 1882, spans the Blackwater River, south of Rt. 4, 1 mile west of Andover village.

The Cilleyville bridge, now open to foot traffic only, was built across Pleasant Stream in 1887; it's now at the junction of Rts. 11 and 4A in Andover.

The Bement bridge, built in 1854, is on River Rd. in Bradford Center.

The Corbin covered bridge, rebuilt by a group of Newport citizens after being destroyed by arson in 1993, crosses the Sugar River west of Rt. 10 in North Newport.

The Warner–Dalton bridge, originally built in 1800 and rebuilt in 1963, crosses over the Warner River, south of Rt. 103 in Warner village (multiple kingpost truss).

The Warner–Waterloo bridge, rebuilt in 1972, is 2 miles west of Warner village, south of Rt. 103 (town lattice truss).

FOR FAMILIES ✄ **Ruggles Mine** (603-523-4275; www.rugglesmine.com), off Rt. 4, Grafton. Open mid-June–mid-Oct., daily 9–5; until 6 in July and August; weekends only mid-May–mid-June. Admission $15 adults, $7 ages 4–11. Children of all ages will love this place; you don't have to be a mineral buff. The eerie shape of the caves high up on Isinglass Mountain is worth the drive up the access road, and the view includes Cardigan, Kearsarge, and Ragged Mountains. Commercial production of mica in this country began here in 1803. The story goes that Sam Ruggles set his large family to work mining and hauling the mica (it was used for lamp chimneys and stove windows) to Portsmouth; from there it was shipped to relatives in England to be sold. When the demand for his product grew, these trips were made in the dead of night to protect the secrecy of the mine's location. The mine has yielded some $30 million over the years. It was last actively mined by the Bon Ami Company for feldspar, mica, and beryl from 1932 to 1959. An estimated 150 different minerals can still be found. There's a snack bar, picnic area, and a gift shop with minerals so visitors can take home a piece of the rock. Collecting is permitted.

SCENIC DRIVE Bradford Center to Washington to Sunapee. The most difficult part of this tour is finding the starting point, just west of the stoplight at the junction of Rts. 104 and 114 in Bradford. The road immediately threads a covered bridge, then climbs 2.4 miles to Bradford Center. Stop to see the original town buildings (just out of view on your left), but turn right and follow that road 1.8 miles until a sign on a tree points the way to East Washington. The route leads through the Eccardt Farm barnyard; visitors are welcome to stroll through the operating dairy farm, and to see the collection of live birds and antique farm equipment. You might also want to park your car at Island Pond and walk up the hill to the Baptist church grounds and cemetery. The old schoolhouse here, with its desks, foot organ, and vintage textbooks, is open on summer Sundays 1–3 PM. Turn north (right) on Rt. 31 into Washington, a photographer's delight with its 1787 meetinghouse, school, and Congregational church all conveniently arranged to fit into one picture. Continue north on Rt. 31 to Pillsbury State Park. Just north of Goshen village, a right brings you back to Rt. 103 and Mount Sunapee. Be sure to stop at Audrey Nelson's Used Books along the way (see *Selective Shopping*).

✳ To Do

BICYCLING The Sunapee Off-Road Bicycle Association (603-763-2303) sponsors weekly rides. Call for information.

Blackwater Ski Shop (603-735-5437), 207 Main St., Andover. For bicycle rentals and expert overnight service and repair.

Bob Skinner's Ski & Sports (603-763-2303), Rt. 103, Newbury, rents mountain bikes. Inquire about the many mapped local routes.

Outspokin Bicycle & Sport Shop (603-763-9500), junction of Rts. 103 and 103A, Newbury. Another good spot for biking gear, rentals, and information.

Village Sports (603-526-4948), 140 Main St., New London. All-season rental for bikes, kayaks, and snowshoes.

BOATING Sunapee Watersports (603-763-4030; www.sunapeewatersports .com), Sunapee Harbor. Canoes, kayaks, paddleboats, and hydro-bikes for rent from half an hour to 2 weeks.

Sargents Marine (603-763-5036), Cooper St., Sunapee. Rents canoes, boats, and motors. A great source of advice on where to fish.

Canoe put-ins can be found on Lake Sunapee; Pleasant Lake; Otter Pond in Georges Mills; Rand Pond in Goshen; Lake Todd, Blaisdell Lake, and Lake Massasecum in the Bradford area; Little Sunapee in New London; Kezar Lake in North Sutton; and Kolelemook Lake in Springfield.

Public boat launches are found in Sunapee Harbor, at Blodgett's Landing (shallow), at Sargents in Georges Mills, and at Sunapee State Park Beach.

BOAT EXCURSIONS ⚓ **M/V *Mount Sunapee II*** (603-763-4030; www.sunapee cruises.com), Sunapee Harbor. Weekends mid-May through foliage season, daily at 2 PM late June–Labor Day. $14 adults, $8 ages 3–12; 3 and under free. Hour-and-a-half narrated cruises of the lake. This is unquestionably the best way to see Lake Sunapee, complete with the captain's retelling of its history and major sights. New London's long swath of eastern shore is entirely green, with rustic cottages hidden in woods above occasional docks. In Newbury on the south, you see Blodgett's Landing, a tight cluster of gingerbread cottages descended from the tents of the 1890s Sunapee Lake Spiritualist Camp Meeting Association. All children aboard are invited to take a turn at the helm. Private and group tours also available.

M/V *Kearsarge* (603-763-5477), Sunapee Harbor. Summer months. A re-creation of a 19th-century steamer offers 1¼-hour cruises twice daily and a single dinner cruise.

FARMS, PICK-YOUR-OWN **Bartletts Blueberry Farm** (603-863-2583), 648 Bradford Rd., Newport. Blueberries mid-July–Sep.

Beaver Pond Farm (603-542-7339), 50 McDonough Rd., Newport. Open mid-July–Aug. for raspberries.

Blueberry Acres (835-2259), Derry Hill Rd., Acworth. Open 8–8 in-season.

Blue Moon Berry Farm (603-456-3822), Walden Hill, Warner. Open daily 8–5 in-season, weekends through September. Strawberries, blueberries, apples, peaches, and plums.

Huntoon Farm (603-768-5579), Huntoon Rd., Danbury. Open Memorial Day–Oct., weekends 10–5. A variety of offerings including baked goods, maple syrup, pumpkins, naturally raised beef, and fall hayrides.

King Blossom Farm (603-863-6125; www.kingblossom.com), 834 Dunbar Hill Rd., Grantham. Open daily in-season 9–6 for pick-your-own raspberries and apples.

Meadowbrook Farm/Walker's (603-7448459), 2760 Smith River Rd., Bristol. Fresh corn, tomatoes, and assorted vegetables plus maple syrup, ice cream, and cheese.

Spring Ledge Farm (603-526-6253/8483), 220 Main St., New London. Open seasonally 9–6. A succulent selection of produce and plants plus pick-your-own strawberries and flowers.

StoneField Bison Ranch (603-456-3743), 490 Pumpkin Hill Rd., Warner. Open Fri. 1–5, Sat. and Sun. 9–3. This ranch boasts the first and only certified and accredited buffalo herd in New England. Call ahead for a group tour or stop in to buy it from the source—bison steaks, burgers, and sausage.

FISHING **Dickie's** (603-938-5394; www.dickiesoutdoorsports.com), Rt. 103 in South Newbury, is a source of fishing tackle, bait, licenses, and a whole lot more. Ditto for **Sargents Marine** in Georges Mills (see *Boating*).

Lake Sunapee is good for salmon, lake trout, brook trout, smallmouth bass, pickerel, perch, sunfish, hornpout, and cusk. Otter Pond, Perkins Pond, and Baptist Pond yield bass, pickerel, and perch. Rand Pond, Croydon Pond, Long and Lempster ponds, and the Sugar River are good for trout. Pleasant Lake has salmon, trout, and bass. Inquire locally about what other lakes offer.

GOLF **Country Club of New Hampshire** (603-927-4246; www.playgolfne .com), Kearsarge Valley Rd., North Sutton 03260. Twice rated one of the top 75 public courses in the United States by *Golf Digest*. Lodging and dining adjacent; cart rentals; reservations required.

Eastman (603-863-4500; 603-863-4500; Eastman@cdredpath.com), Grantham. Public greens fee, $54 for 18 holes; $33 for 9. Cart rentals $35. Reservations required.

Newport Golf Club (603-863-7787), 112 Unity Rd., Newport. Eighteen holes; new ownership. Reservations required on weekends.

Ragged Mountain Golf Club (603-768-3600; 1-800-400-3911; www.ragged mountainresort.com), 620 Ragged Mountain Rd., Danbury. A full-service golf resort, featuring a Jeff Julian par-72, 18-hole course, and PGA pros. Lodging packages available.

Twin Lake Village Golf Course (603-526-2034), Twin Lake Village Rd., New London. Nine-hole, par-3 course by the lake.

HIKING **Mount Cardigan**. From Mount Cardigan State Park on the western side of the mountain, the **West Ridge Trail** takes you to the summit in just 1.3 miles. From Old Baldy, the principal peak, the view is of Mount Sunapee and of Mount Ascutney in Vermont. A ridge trail runs north to Firescrew Peak and south to South Peak. In all, a network of 50 miles of trails accesses the summit from various directions. Although this western ascent is the shortest and easiest, many hikers prefer the eastern climbs. You might ascend by the **Cathedral Spruce** and **Clark Trails** (2.5 miles to the summit; average time 2 hours 10 minutes, not including stops) or by the more difficult **Holt Trail** (1.9 miles to the summit, not to be attempted in wet or icy weather), and return on the **Mowglis** and **Mannin Trails** (3 miles from the summit). The Appalachian Mountain Club lodge, high on the mountain's eastern flank (posted from the village of Alexandria), is the departure point for these and other year-round ascents.

Mount Kearsarge. Despite controversy about the cell phone tower that sprouted recently on top of this peak, the view remains one of the most spectacular in New England, especially for people familiar enough with the landscape to know what they're looking at. The sweep is from Mount Sunapee on the southwest to Moosilauke (the westernmost of the White Mountain peaks), to the Sandwich and Ossipee ranges and Mount Washington. Serious hikers prefer the 2-mile

VIEW OF LAKE SUNAPEE FROM THE SUMMIT OF MOUNT SUNAPEE

ascent from Winslow State Park on the northern side of the mountain to the mere 0.5-mile saunter up from Rollins State Park. The **Northside Trail** to the summit begins in the southeastern corner of the picnic area, climbs through birch and spruce into fir, and emerges onto smooth ledges, then barren rocks. Round-trip time on the Northside Trail averages 1½ hours each way, or you can do it in 20 minutes from the other side. Either way, it's a lot of bang for the buck and a favorite hang-gliding spot.

Mount Sunapee. In winter you can opt for the chairlift, but the most popular hiking trail up is the **Andrew Brook Trail** (1.8 miles to Lake Solitude) from a marked trailhead 1.2 miles up Mountain Road, which is off Rt. 103 roughly 1 mile south of Newbury. The most ambitious approach to Mount Sunapee is along the 47-mile **Monadnock–Sunapee Trail**, which begins atop Mount Monadnock. The last and perhaps the most rewarding stretch of this trail is from Pillsbury State Park, which offers primitive camping and its own 20-mile system of trails.

SKINDIVING **LaPorte's Skindiving Shop** (603-763-5353), 1053 Rt. 103, Newbury. Equipment for sale, plus lessons, rentals, and light salvage work.

SWIMMING **Sunapee State Park Beach** (603-263-4642), Rt. 103, 3 miles west of Newbury. Open weekends mid-May–mid-June and Labor Day–mid-Oct., daily in between. Fee. A 900-foot stretch of smooth sand backed by shaded grass, picnic tables, a snack bar, and bathhouse.

Wellington State Park (603-744-2197), Rt. 3A, 4 miles north of Bristol. Open weekends from Memorial Day, daily mid-June–Labor Day. Fee. This is a beauty: a sandy, 0.5-mile-long beach on a peninsula jutting into Newfound Lake. Picnic tables are scattered along the shore, away from the bathhouse and snack bar, under pine trees.

Wadleigh State Beach (603-927-4724), on Kezar Lake, Sutton. Marked from Rt. 114. Open weekends from Memorial Day, daily mid-June–Labor Day. Fee. Smaller, less well known, and less crowded than nearby Sunapee; a pleasant beach sloping gradually to the water. Facilities include a shaded picnic area, a bathhouse, and a large playing field.

Town beaches. Many more local beaches can be accessed by guests at local inns.

TENNIS **Mountainside Racquet and Fitness Center** (603-526-9293), 31 King Hill Rd., New London. Open 6:30 AM–9 PM weekdays, 9 AM–5 PM weekends (until 1 PM in summer). Tennis, exercise machines, sauna, tanning center, and yoga classes open to the public.

Colby-Sawyer College (603-526-2010), New London. Courts (and the Sports Center with indoor swimming) are open to the public.

✳ Winter Sports

CROSS-COUNTRY SKIING **Norsk** (1-800-426-6775; www.skinorsk.com), Country Club Lane off Rt. 11 (2 miles east of I-89, Exit 11), New London. Open in-season 9–4:30. Now celebrating its 30th year, this is one of New England's most ambitious and successful cross-country centers. John Schlosser discovered the sport while attending the University of Oslo in 1972 and with his wife, Nancy, opened Norsk at the Lake Sunapee Country Club in 1976. Thanks to its unusual elevation (1,300 feet) and regular grooming, Norsk's 70 km of looped trails frequently offer the best snow conditions south of the White Mountains. A favorite 6-mile loop is to Robb's Hut, though ambitious types may prefer the 10.9-km Roller Coaster. Trails begin on the golf course, but it's possible to get quickly into the woods and stay there. Better skiers can actually access the system from the Outback parking area, 2 miles east on Rt. 11. The adjacent country-club restaurant caters to skiers. Check the web site for up-to-date trail fees. Lessons; ski and snowshoe rentals.

Eastman Cross Country Ski Center (603-863-4500; Eastman@cdredpath .com), turn right off I-89 (you can't miss the sign), Grantham. Open in-season with 30 km of groomed trails.

DOWNHILL SKIING ✿ ✎ **Ragged Mountain Ski Area** (603-768-3600; www .raggedmountainresort.com), 620 Ragged Mountain Rd., off Rt. 4, Danbury. A pleasant, intermediate mountain that's been upgraded in the past few years with snowmaking, a new lift, and a red barn look-alike base lodge with a soaring, three-sided fireplace. Still just enough off the beaten track and little known enough to be relatively uncrowded. *Lifts:* 1 six-pack, 2 triple chairs, 2 doubles, and 2 surface tows. *Trails:* 50. *Vertical drop:* 1,250 feet. *Snowmaking:* 95 percent.

&. **Mount Sunapee** (603-763-2356; snow phone, 603-763-4020; www.mount sunapee.com), Rt. 103, Newbury. With 60 trails and a vertical drop of 1,510 feet, this is a major ski area that until 1998 was operated by the state. Since then, the Muellers, who also own Mount Okemo in Vermont and Crested Butte in Colorado, have leased the ski area and spent more than $14 million, adding such amenities as a new Goosefeathers Pub in the main lodge, a PipeDragon grooming machine, and a Stimilon Approved Halfpipe and Terrain Park snowboarding facility. Nine lifts include a high-speed detachable quad, plus two other quads, as well as two triple lifts, one double, and three surface lifts. The Summit Triple Chair accesses half a dozen swooping, intermediate-to-expert runs, each at least a mile long. Off the North Peak Triple Chair, our favorite is Flying Goose—a quick, steep, and addictive run. The smaller North Peak Lodge (at the opposite end of the parking lot) and the summit cafeteria help disperse the crowds at lunchtime. When all trails are open, skiers can choose from exposures on three peaks. PSIA ski and snowboard school, and day care available. The area is home to the New England Handicapped Sports Association (NEHSA) and offers lessons, racing programs, and other services to disabled skiers. Rates: $56 weekends, $52 midweek for adults; $48 and $41 ages 13–18; $36 and $32 ages 6–12 and 70-plus. Free skiing for those 6 and under. Various specials, including a midweek Super Pass to Mount Sunapee and Okemo, are available.

MOUNT SUNAPEE'S BASE LODGE

Facilities: Ski school, ski shop, rentals, restaurant, lounge, child care, and lodging. *Rates:* $45 adults, $37 teens, $30 juniors on weekends; adults $32 midweek. A genuine family area.

Also see "The Western Whites" and "The Concord Area."

✳ Green Space

STATE PARKS Mount Cardigan State Park, off Rts. 4 and 118, 4.5 miles east of Canaan. Open mid-May–mid-Oct. This western approach to the mountain includes a picnic area sited among pines and rocks. For more about the West Ridge Trail, the shortest and easiest route to the 3,121-foot-high summit of Mount Cardigan itself, see *Hiking.*

Pillsbury State Park (603-863-2860), Rt. 31, 3.5 miles north of Washington. Open weekends from Memorial Day, daily from mid-June. Day-use and camping fees. What a gem! This 9,000-acre near wilderness was once a thriving settlement with its share of mills. Today the dams are all that survive of "Cherry Valley." Camping is restricted to 20 superb primitive sites on May Pond, and there's both stream and pond fishing. Inquire about hiking trails to nearby mountains.

Rollins State Park (603-456-3808), off Rt. 103, 4 miles north of Warner. Open weekends from Memorial Day, daily early June–Oct. A 3.5-mile road, built originally as a scenic toll road in 1874, leads to picnic sites roughly 0.5 mile below the summit. A walking trail (good for the elderly, young, or lazy) accesses the bald summit of Mount Kearsarge.

Winslow State Park (603-526-6168), off Rt. 11, 3 miles south of Wilmot. Open weekends from Memorial Day, daily from early June; fee. An auto road climbs to the 1,820-foot level of 2,937-foot Mount Kearsarge. There are picnic tables and comfort facilities, and you can inspect the cellar hole of a big 19th-century resort hotel, the Winslow House. A steep, mile-long trail leads to the summit for a 360-degree panoramic view. The park is named for Admiral John A. Winslow, commander of the sloop *Kearsarge* when she sank the Confederate gunboat Alabama in 1864.

OTHER AREAS Audubon Society of New Hampshire Paradise Point Nature Center and Hebron Marsh Wildlife Sanctuary (603-744-3516), North Shore Rd., East Hebron. This 43-acre preserve includes an extensive, rocky, and unspoiled stretch of shore on Newfound Lake. The property is webbed with trails and includes a nature center (open late June–Labor Day, 10–5 daily; also some spring and fall weekends) with hands-on and wildlife exhibits, a library, and the Nature Store. During the summer a natural history day camp and a variety of workshops and special events are also staged. Hebron Marsh is another 1.4 miles down the road toward Hebron Center (drive past the red Ash Cottage and take the next left down the dirt road; park off the road on your left by the sign). The 36-acre property includes the field directly across the road from Ash Cottage down to the Cockermouth River and the field to the southwest of the cottage. The marshes are teeming with bird life; follow signs to the observation tower.

Bradford Pines, Rt. 103, Bradford. Twelve giant white pines stand on 5 acres of preserved land.

Cricenti's Bog, Rt. 11, New London. A genuine bog with a nature trail. Wooden walkways thread a pond that's been filled with sphagnum moss and rare bog flora.

Gardner Memorial Wayside Area, Rt. 4A, Wilmot. Picnic site along a scenic brook and stone foundation.

Grafton Pond, off Rt. 4A. A 935-acre Society for the Protection of New Hampshire Forests preserve. North from Wilmot take a sharp left at the Grafton–Sullivan County line; take the first left, then an immediate right, and park at the dam site. The only amenity is a public boat ramp. The pond has a 7-mile shoreline. Good boating and fishing.

Knights Hill Nature Park, County Rd., New London. Sixty acres of fields and forest, fern gardens and a pond, a marsh, and a stream, all linked by easy trails. No dogs. Inquire at the town information booth about guided hikes.

Profile Falls, Rt. 3A, 2.5 miles south of Bristol. A popular (and dangerous) local swimming hole. This is a 40-foot falls with the profile of a man silhouetted against the water at its base.

Sculptured Rocks, west of Groton village on Sculptured Rocks Rd. The parking area is roughly a mile in (the sign may be down off-season). With grottoes formed by waterfalls, this is mermaid/merman territory. The river has carved a deep chasm through which it tumbles from pool to pool, forming a popular local swimming spot. A path, with plenty of large rocks for picnicking, follows the water down.

Also see **The Fells State Historic Site** under *Historic Homes*.

✴ Lodging

RESORTS 🐾 ♿ **Eastman** (603-863-4444; www.cdredpath.com), 18 Pioneer Point (just off I-89, Exit 13), Grantham 03753. Developed by a consortium that includes Dartmouth College and the Society for the Protection of New Hampshire Forests, this first- and second-home and condo community is scattered in clusters throughout 3,500 acres on Eastman Lake. Winter facilities include a small ski hill and an extensive ski-touring network. Summer renters can enjoy an 18-hole golf course, tennis, swimming, and boating (Sunfish, canoes, and rowboats can be rented). A restaurant, indoor pool, and recreation barn are available year-round.

Units are attractive, individually decorated condos and houses with two to four bedrooms, decks, lofts, and woodstoves. Rentals are around $550 for two bedrooms for summer weekends, slightly more in winter; $1,100-$1,200 for a whole week. Monthly rentals also available. Pets in houses only, at discretion of owner.

♿ **Ragged Mountain Resort** (603-768-3600; 1-800-400-3911; www.raggedmountainresort.com), 620 Ragged Mountain Rd., off Rt. 4, Danbury 03230. Open all year. A great family getaway for skiing or golf vacations. Eight 2-bedroom condominiums at the base of Ragged Mountain offer linens, a kitchen stocked with utensils, and cable television. Double occupancy rates start at $59. No pets.

🌸 🍴 ♿ **Twin Lake Village** (603-526-6460; www.twinlakevillage.com), 164 Twin Lake Villa Rd., New London 03257. Open just late June–Labor Day. Nothing fancy unless you count its idyllic lakeside setting, but this 1890s resort is much beloved by those who stay here. Many families have been coming for generations. Opened by Henry Kidder in 1897, it is presently owned and managed by three generations of Kidders and accommodates 160 guests among the rambling Villa and a number of Victorian houses scattered throughout surrounding trees. Sited on Little Lake Sunapee, it has a private beach and a boathouse with canoes, rowboats, and kayaks. A nine-hole golf course stretches from the rocker-lined veranda (note the untraditional rocker colors) down to the lake. All three daily meals and old-fashioned evening entertainment—maybe a suppertime picnic on Mount Kearsarge, or bingo—are included in the weekly $420–950 per-person rates.

INNS

In the Lake Sunapee area

Back Side Inn (603-863-5161; www.bsideinn.com), 1171 Brook Rd., Goshen 03752. Open year-round. Still off the beaten track in the land o' Goshen, this onetime family farm first opened its doors to overnight guests as a hunting lodge in the 1920s. More than 80 years later, the inn retains its getaway feeling. Six fresh, pretty guest rooms with private bath plus two double suites with shared bath are set amid 120 acres of hiking trails along

the backside of Mount Sunapee. No matter the season, there is plenty to do with Sunapee's mountain and lake nearby. Afterward, relax in an outdoor hot tub or warm up in the cozy living room with fieldstone fireplace. Across the road is a favorite shopping/browsing spot in the region: Nelson Crafts, Antique Collectibles, and Used Books. $99 per double room and $169 for three-to-four person suite includes a full breakfast. The BYOB restaurant provides dinner and Sunday gourmet brunch. No smoking.

Candlelite Inn (603-938-5571; 1-888-812-5571; www.candleliteinn.com), 5 Greenhouse Lane, Bradford 03221. Built in 1897 as a guest house, this inn had different names and owners for nearly a century before Les and Marilyn Gordon took over in 1993. The Gordons have added much pampering to the late-Victorian structure. The inn offers six pretty pastel guest rooms, each with queen bed and private bath (some with claw-foot tubs), where you can rest up for a scrumptious, multicourse breakfast that includes dessert. Rates range $95–140, the latter for a mini suite with access to the gazebolike porch. Contact them for a calendar of special weekend activities. Nonsmoking.

♿ **Colonial Farm Inn** (603-526-6121; 1-800-805-8504), Rt. 11, New London 03257. This inn, a previous favorite, is undergoing renovation. The new owners were unable to provide specific information about lodging or dining at the time of publication.

🐾 🍴 ♿ **Dexter's Inn** (603-763-5571; 1-800-232-5571; www.dextersnh.com), Stagecoach Rd., Sunapee 03782. Open year-round. This hilltop house dates in part from 1801, but its present look is 1930s, when it became a summer home for an adviser to Herbert Hoover. In 1948 Dexter and Janelle Richards purchased the home and transformed it into Dexter's Inn, an après-ski getaway for guests coming to the newly opened Mount Sunapee Ski Resort. Recently New Hampshire native Emily Augustine returned from New York with her husband, John, to purchase it from longtime owners. With John's business background and Emily's experience as a caterer, wedding planner, and special-events impresario, the Augustines have found the perfect home for hosting weddings, reunions, sporting events, and business retreats. A pool is set in the extensive, beautifully landscaped backyard, which also offers croquet, lawn games, and three all-weather tennis courts. Fields across the road, in front of the house, slope toward Lake Sunapee in the distance. You can also see the lake from porch rockers and from many of the 17 guest rooms (each individually decorated, all with private bath). The best views are from the annex (there are 2 rooms with wheelchair access here) across the road. There's also a great view from the cozy dining room. Common spaces include a formal living room; a pubby, pine-paneled library/lounge; and a kids' playroom with videos, games, toys, and stuffed animals. Altogether, this has the look and feel of a casual, unpretentious country club. Rates per double per night range, depending on season, $130–175 and include a full breakfast. Pets are permitted in the annex at $10 per day. The Holly House Cottage, with a living room with fireplace, a kitchen, and two bedrooms, is $300–400 per night for up to six people. A two-bedroom, one-bath efficiency condo, $200–300 per night, sleeps up to six. Discounts for longer stays.

The Follansbee Inn on Kezar Lake (603-927-4221; 1-800-626-4221; www.follansbeeinn.com), Rt. 114, P.O. Box 92, North Sutton 03260. Open year-round. Located in a small town center that time seems to have forgotten, this inn takes you back to the days of picnics, farm stands, band concerts, and idling on a porch filled with wicker and flowers. The low-beamed living room is friendly; the airy dining rooms are comfortably furnished with antiques. On the upper floors the 18 guest rooms (all with private bath) are divided by wide halls, and books are scattered around. There is plenty of lounging and reading space. The white, green-trimmed structure was built originally as an annex for the huge but long-gone Follansbee Inn that once stood across the street. The property abuts Kezar Lake, and guests can swim or boat from the inn dock; for those more comfortable with a lifeguard on duty, Wadleigh State Beach is just down the road. Many guests also discover the joys of the 3-mile walk, bike, or jog around the lake. In winter there's cross-country skiing out the back door, and the Muster Field Farm Museum, with its charming summertime farm stand, is just up the road. The $110–190 per-couple rate includes breakfast. No smoking, and no children under age 10.

Hide-Away Inn (603-526-4861; 1-800-457-0589; www.hideawayinn .net), Twin Lake Villa Rd., P.O. Box 1249, New London 03257. Go to the end of the country lane, then keep going to find this quiet lodge, originally built in 1901, then rebuilt in the 1930s as a retreat for author Grace Litchfield. Each of the six guest rooms (one a two-room suite) has a private bath, canopy bed, and beaded paneling. Two have fireplace. Oregon spruce paneling and another huge stone fireplace in the lobby add to the rustic ambience. A full breakfast, beginning with a fresh fruit and pastry cart, is included in the $79–180 (depending on season) rate. Children 10 and older are welcome. Nonsmoking.

☞ **The Inn at Pleasant Lake** (603-526-6271; 1-800-626-4907; www.innatpleasantlake.com), 853 Pleasant St., P.O. Box 1030, New London 03257. Open except for parts of Apr. and Nov. This was one of many farms in this area that began taking in boarders in the 1880s. Guests came from New York and Boston, and strangers were expected to bring letters of introduction. These days innkeepers Linda and Brian MacKenzie (Brian is a graduate of the Culinary Institute of America) are applying their talents to the place, offering such amenities as afternoon tea and elegant gourmet dining. Each of the 10 comfortable guest rooms has a view of Mount Kearsarge, the lake, or woodlands, and all have private bath. The lake just across the road provides a place to swim and fish; the inn offers two canoes and a rowboat for boating. The dining room overlooking the lake is the setting for full breakfasts (included, along with tea, in the $110–175 room rate), and prix fixe, five-course dinners for guests and public (see *Dining Out*).

☞ **The Inn at Sunapee** (603-763-4444; 1-800-327-2466; www.innatsunapee.com), 125 Burkehaven Hill Rd., Sunapee 03782. Originally built in 1875 as a dairy farm, this sunny yellow farmhouse has been an inn since the Gardner family began taking in summer folks in the 1920s. When the Harrimans purchased the property, they added an Asian flair, thanks to 25 years in the Far East. The setting above Lake Sunapee is both lovely and convenient. It also offers tennis and swimming, bay windows to take in the view, and a lounge with a massive fieldstone fireplace. Sixteen rooms, five of them suites, all with private bath, range from $90 for a single to $175 for a family suite; $20 per extra person. Children are welcome. A full country breakfast, served in the dining room, comes with your room. Dinner (the menu has echoes of both New England and Asia—clam chowder to spring rolls) is provided for an extra charge, primarily for guests of the inn.

☞ ♿ **New London Inn** (603-526-2791; outside New Hampshire, 1-800-526-2791; www.newlondoninn.net), P.O. Box 8, 353 Main Street, New London 03257. Built originally in 1792, this large (24 guest rooms) inn sits in the middle of New London, next to Colby-Sawyer College. It's always busy, but guests can usually find quiet space in a corner of the large, graciously furnished living room. The New London Barn Playhouse is just down Main Street, which is lined with attractive shops and eateries. Stroll around town or simply rock an hour away, watching the activity from the inn's second-story gallery porch. Since the Boston–Montreal bus stops at the pharmacy practically across the street, this is one place, theoretically at least, you can get to without a car. Rooms are attractive, freshly painted and papered, and furnished in real and reproduction antiques. All have private bath. $100–140 per room, depending on season; two rooms with king beds and Jacuzzi rent for $175. Room rates include breakfast gift cards to Jack's Coffee restaurant Nov.–May, and a full gourmet breakfast served on site June–Oct. Dinner (not included) is available in the dining room (see *Dining Out*).

Potter Place Inn (603-735-5141; (www.potterplaceinn.com), 88 Depot St., junction of Rts. 4 and 11, Andover 03216. Best known for its restaurant (see *Dining Out*), this inn offers two upstairs guest rooms with queen-sized bed and private bath for those nights when you'd rather end a good meal dreaming than driving home. The fanciful Potter Place Depot, once a bustling railway stop and now the home of the Andover Historical Society, is just down the road. A continental breakfast is included in the $85 double-occupancy room rate.

The Rosewood Country Inn (603-938-5253; www.rosewoodcountryinn .com), 67 Pleasant View Rd., Bradford 03221. Pretty in pink—or make that rose—this inn lives up to its name, beginning with the outside shutters. Both the color and the flower continue to make their spirit felt in the decor of 11 well-kept guest rooms and baths, each furnished in a mix of old and new. Inviting common rooms and sunny porches take advantage of the inn's peaceful garden setting on a dozen stone-walled acres once walked by the likes of Gloria Swanson, Jack London, Charlie Chaplin, and Mary Pickford. Three-course "candlelight and crystal" breakfasts are included in the $119–239 room

rate(rising to $289 mid-Sep.–Oct. and on Valentine's Day weekend). Children, over 12 only, are $25 a night.

In Danbury
♪ **The Inn at Danbury** (603-768-3318; 1-866-DANBURY), 67 Rt. 104, Danbury 03230. With Ragged Mountain just 5 miles away, this Bavarian-flavored getaway is geared to skiers and great for groups and families, children over 5. Fourteen individually decorated guest rooms with private bath. Rates, which range $89–155 on weekends (double occupancy), include a full breakfast in the Alphorn Bistro (see *Dining Out*), access to the inn's heated, indoor pool, and use of the hot tub (adults only). There's a higher charge during some holidays; packages available.

On Newfound Lake
The Inn on Newfound Lake (603-744-9111), 1030 Mayhew Turnpike, Rt. 3A, Bridgewater 03222. Open year-round. Although thoroughly rehabbed, this 1840s inn still looks its age with a full veranda overlooking spectacular sunsets on the state's fourth largest lake. Across the road,

THE ROSEWOOD COUNTRY INN IN BRADFORD

there's a 300-foot sandy beach and a dock. Inside, the main inn has 19 attractive guest rooms, 11 with private bath, and the adjoining Elmwood Cottage offers 12 more rooms, each with bath. There are comfortable parlors in each facility. The dining room in the main inn is a favorite spot for tourists and locals alike (see *Dining Out*). Rooms are $135–150 double occupancy mid-May–Oct. 25, $105–125 the rest of the year, continental breakfast included.

BED & BREAKFASTS

In the Lake Sunapee area
The Blue Acorn Inn (603-863-1144; www.blueacorninn.com), 21 Sleeper Rd., Sunapee 03782. This 1847 farmhouse offers five individually decorated rooms just minutes from Mount Sunapee and a host of outdoor activities. Stay & ski packages, with full breakfast, range $111–149 midweek, $125.50–163.50 on weekends.

✍ **Blue Goose Inn** (603-763-5519; www.bluegooseinn.com), 24 Rt. 103B, P.O. Box 2117, Mount Sunapee 03255-2117. A 19th-century farmhouse in the shadow of Mount Sunapee, this country B&B has a wraparound porch as well as an enclosed sunporch overlooking 3.5 acres of lawn and woods. Just out the door, the old Newport-to-Claremont railroad bed is now a trail for hiking, biking, cross-country skiing, snowshoeing, and snowmobiling. Rates for the five guest rooms, each with private bath and queen-sized and/or single beds, are $95 per double with full country breakfast; extra person (children welcome), $20. Nonsmoking.

Dragonflies (603-927-4053; www.dragonfliesbnb.com), 9 Keyser St., P.O. Box 3, North Sutton 03260. The street side of this charming home faces the town's old-timey general store; the back of the house has a wide view of Lake Kezar; and inside Christine and Iain Gilmour offer the warm hospitality they became known for when they operated their AAA Three Diamond establishment in Scituate, Massachusetts. Since moving to North Sutton in 2000, the Gilmours have downsized, offering just two guest rooms, both with queen-sized bed, private bath, and views of the 175-acre lake. Weeknight room rates begin at $85, weekends at $110, and include a full breakfast served outside on the deck or inside by the woodstove. A large selection of mostly classical music helps soothe you into the day, while a a trip in the Gilmours' two kayaks helps keep the stress at bay.

Maple Hill Farm (603-526-2248; 1-800-231-8637; www.maplehillfarm .com), 200 Newport Rd., New London 03257. Just off I-89, this capacious old farmhouse takes in boarders, as it did in the 19th century. An informal, comfortable place, it has a six-person spa on the deck, and an indoor basketball court that doubles as a dance floor in the barn. There are also barnyard animals, including chickens that yield those fresh eggs for breakfast. Winter weekends tend to be booked by the groups lucky enough to know about this place, but there is always plenty of space midweek. Acreage extends back through meadows to Little Sunapee Lake, where a canoe and rowboat await guests. There are 10 guest rooms, 6 with private bath, in the main house where, depending on season, rates run $75–125 and include a choice of four breakfasts. Or you can book a three-bedroom, four-and-a-half-bath lakefront home of

SHAKER MEETING HOUSE BED AND BREAKFAST IN NEW LONDON

your own for $2,700 a week or $450 a night. It's fully furnished with fireplace, spa, steam shower, and wet bar. Inquire about ski-and-stay packages. Nonsmoking.

🐾 🕊 **Mountain Lake Inn** (1-800-662-6005; www.mountainlake.com), 2871 Rt. 114, P.O. Box 443, Bradford 03221. Currier and Ives ambience in a rambling combination of a 1760 colonial and a 1930s addition on 170 acres of woods and lakefront. The inn, halfway between the Pat's Peak and Mount Sunapee ski areas, has nine guest rooms, which rent for $85 double occupancy ($70 single). Each has a private bath; all have a view either of woods or of Lake Massasecum across the road. There is also a one-bedroom, fair-weather cabin with its own living room, kitchenette, and screened porch for $600 per week. Full country breakfast included with all accommodations. Pets welcome ($25 charge) with prior notice.

Shaker Meeting House Bed and Breakfast (603-763-3122; www.shakermeetinghousecom), 1502 King Hill Rd., New London 03257. The Shaker tradition of innovation lives on in this brand-new Moses Johnson–style meetinghouse, built in 2000 as a B&B. After retiring from his job with the Defense Department in New Jersey, John Chowanski and his family moved to New London with the idea of re-creating the hospitality once espoused in the Shaker villages of nearby Enfield and Canterbury. Four guest rooms are furnished in historically correct "retiring room" style, though enhanced by the addition of private baths. Breakfast—"plain, simple, wholesome, and natural"—is served in an authentically detailed dining room with a lovely view of King Ridge Mountain. Rooms are $90. Active or retired military personnel receive a 10 percent discount. No pets or smoking. Children over 10 welcome.

🕊 **Take-It-For-Granite Farm Bed & Breakfast** (603-526-6376; www.granitebb.com), Campground Rd., Wilmot Flat 03287. Innkeepers Craig and Lindy Heim moved from Tennessee in the mid-1990s when they found their New England dream home on 10 rolling acres surrounded by fieldstone walls. Once they fixed it up, they decided to share the rambling 1840s farmhouse with guests. Four bedroom suites (each with its own bath) are all very separate and private. Three have air-conditioning; two, a fireplace. Common areas include a paneled library, two sitting rooms, and a handsome patio with a view of Mount Kearsarge and the Heims' own pond and resident ducks. An ample continental breakfast is included in the $100–140 room rate. Children 5 years and older are $20 more. Nonsmoking.

BED & BREAKFASTS **Turtle Pond Farm** (603-456-2738; 1-877-861-8623; www.turtlepondfarm.com), 4 Bean Rd., Warner 03278. Innkeepers Debbie and Walt Bury offer four private cottages on 16 acres of fields, ponds, and woods, just 3 miles from Interstate 89. Each has its own porch, bath, and TV/VCR. Rates range $100–115, depending on season, and include a hearty country breakfast in the main house. En route you can stop by the barn to visit the Burys' llama, goat, sheep, and angora rabbits. The box and painted turtles, for which the place was named, are more likely found outside. Cross-country skiing, snowshoeing, and hiking are right out the door.

🐾 **The Village House at Sutton Mills Bed & Breakfast** (603-927-4765; www.villagehousebnb.com), 14 Grist Mill Rd., Sutton Mills 03221. Outside, Marilyn and Jack Paige's 1857 Victorian house sits neat as a bandbox atop a granite-stepped slope; inside, her stenciled floorcloths and his hand-wrought iron beds add a

unique touch to the three stylishly furnished guest rooms. Each has its own bath, one a claw-foot tub. Downtown Sutton Mills is both a minute and a century away, with a quaint and quiet Main Street that boasts a town hall and library. In winter guests can cross-country ski from the door. Jack has his shop open early evenings and on weekends all year. Rates—$90 for a double or single during high season; $75 a single the rest of the year—include a full country breakfast. Children 3 years and older welcome.

In the Highland Lake area
🛶 **The Andover Arms** (603-735-5953), P.O. Box 256, Village Center, Andover 03216. Hooked and needlepoint rugs, quilts, cannonball beds, and vintage wallpapers make this sprawling 1850s guest house seem like a step back in time. In summer it caters to academics attending conferences on the nearby Proctor Academy campus. In winter it's a haven for skiers. One bedroom on the second floor has its own bath; four others share. There is a two-bedroom suite with an additional bath on the third floor. Most rooms rent for $54 and include a continental breakfast.

🌸 🛶 **Highland Lake Inn** (603-735-6426; www.highlandlakeinn.com), 32 Maple St., East Andover 03231. Open year-round. You'll know the day's a sunny one when innkeeper Steve Hodges greets you in the yellow entrance parlor of this bright and beckoning B&B. The lovely old property, which dates from 1767, retains 7 of its original acres and abuts a nature preserve. Each of the 10 guest rooms has its own bath; 2 have fireplaces. Located on a country lane, this inn is charmingly remote, yet central enough to take advantage of the area's four-season activities. A full country breakfast, overlooking the lawn and lake, is included in the $100–145 double-occupancy rate. $30 per additional person.

Inn at Ragged Edge Farm (603-735-6484; www.raggededgefarm.com), 318 New Canada Rd., Wilmot 03287. Although most of this rambling and eclectic inn was built in the late 20th century, its core is still apparent in the paneled keeping room of the original 18th-century Cape. Outside on the 50 acres surrounding this remote hostelry, there's croquet, tennis, volleyball, a pond, even miniature horses. Inside there's a swimming pool, a bar, and a great room with television, puzzles, games, and wireless Internet access. The 14 guest rooms, three of them suites, offer your choice of king, queen, or twin beds. One has a fireplace and a marble bath with freestanding tub and crystal chandelier. With Ragged Mountain ski area just 10 minutes away, this is a great place for families who enjoy summer and winter sports. Rates $95–225 with all-you-can-eat breakfast.

In the Newfound Lake area

Bridgewater Mountain Bed and Breakfast (603-968-3966; www.bridgewatermountain.com), 984 Bridgewater Hill Rd., Bridgewater 03264-5809. Once a working farm, this was Tom and Virginia Slayton's family vacation home for 60 years before they redesigned it in 2003 to accommodate guests. Each of the three guest rooms has a private bath, queen- or king-sized bed, air-conditioning, wireless Internet connection, and views of flowers, fields, mountains, and woods. The Loft also includes a kitchen, living room with futon, and separate entrance. The downstairs common area features a fireplaced living room and reading space, as well as a wicker-filled back porch and breakfast area. Rates, $95–145, include a full breakfast with organic produce in-season.

Coppertoppe Lodge and Retreat Center (603-744-3636; www.coppertoppe.com), 8 Range Rd., Hebron 03241. The view from this highly unusual, circa-1999 home is staggering, a cascade of forested mountains descending to the blue waters of Newfound Lake. Bill Powers and Sheila Oranch offer three guest rooms, each with private bath, cable TV, phone, Ethernet access, and balcony. The top-of-the-line Garnet Room also boasts a four-poster bed, fireplace, large whirlpool bath, and separate shower. Rooms run $145—275; $30 charge per person for more than two in a room. Expect Sheila to ask your breakfast preferences when you make your reservation. As Bill says, they want to make their guests feel special.

♧ **Henry Whipple House Bed and Breakfast** (603-744-6157), 75 Summer St. (5.6 miles from I-93, Exit 23), Bristol 03222. Solidly built and elaborately embellished, this turreted Queen Anne–style inn was originally built in 1902 for the town's mill owner. Today it offers six unusually spacious guest rooms, two with working fireplace, all with private bath and cable television. A first-floor room is especially designed for elderly and handicapped guests. There are also two carriage house suites big enough for families; these have self-catering kitchens. Newfound Lake is nearby, as are both Ragged and Tenney mountains. Rooms ($85 double, $70 single) include a gourmet breakfast with home-baked goodies; carriage house suites (without breakfast) are $100 double, $25 additional for children over 12; also weekly rates.

Meadow Wind Bed and Breakfast (603-744-9532; www.meadowwind.bed andbreakfast.com), 41 North Shore Rd., Hebron. Across the road from the Audubon Society Marsh Wildlife Sanctuary and on the edge of the Hebron historic district, this 1820s farmhouse is the perfect setting for bird-watching or a Sunday-afternoon band concert. In summer you can hike from the back door, or kayak and swim in the Cockermouth River. In winter there are groomed trails for snowshoeing, cross-country skiing, and snowmobiling; a hot tub in the barn. Tenney Mountain Ski Area is 10 minutes; Ragged Mountain, 20 minutes, by car. The five rooms, including two suites, are attractively furnished with top-of-the-line mattresses and a mix of antiques. The common room has a woodstove and satellite TV. Rates are $65 for a small room in the old servants' quarters to $150 for a large room with king-sized four-poster bed. Breakfast is served in the dining room or on one of three porches overlooking extensive vegetable and flower gardens.

Pleasant View Bed & Breakfast (603-744-5547; www.pleasantview bandb.net), 22 Hemp Hill Rd., R.R. 1, Box 498, Bristol 03222. A big old white farmhouse with a wide-open view of Mount Cardigan. The home has been in the business of putting up guests since around the turn of the last century, when two men came over the hill from Dartmouth and asked if they could stay overnight. New owner

Heidi Milbrand offers six recently renovated guest rooms, all with private bath. The $95 rate (May–Nov.; $90 in winter) includes a full country breakfast. Mount Cardigan's hiking trails begin 20 minutes away by car; Newfound Lake is just a mile.

Elsewhere

🐾 ✍ **The Maria Atwood Inn** (603-934-3666; www.atwoodinn.com), 71 Hill Rd., Rt. 3A, Franklin 03235. The first time we visited this inn, three women from Florida had just checked into a trio of rooms, each one of which drew more oohs and aahs than the last. Innkeepers Sandi and Fred Hoffmeister bought this well-preserved, elegant 1830 brick Federal home in 1997, then turned it into a charming B&B with seven romantic, antiques-filled guest rooms, each with private bath, four with working fireplace. Two years later, lightning struck, literally, topped off with hurricane floods while the roof was being repaired. But the Hoffmeisters made lemonade from their troubles, transforming their third floor into two post-and-beam family guest rooms. A full breakfast is served in the library; snacks and beverages are always available. Rates are $75 for a single, $100 double. Well-behaved children are encouraged to bring their parents; those under 12 stay free. Nonsmoking.

RENTAL COTTAGES The New London and the Newfound Region Chambers of Commerce (see *Guidance*) can direct you to local Realtors specializing in cottage rentals.

OTHER LODGING AMC Cardigan Mountain Lodge (603-466-2727; www.outdoors.org), 774 Shem Valley Rd., Alexandria (mail: R.F.D. 1, Bristol

03222). The Appalachian Mountain Club, founded in 1876 to blaze hiking trails through the White Mountains, maintains a number of no-frills, outdoors-oriented huts, lodges, and family camps in New Hampshire. This newly renovated facility is one of the most interesting, providing full-service overnight lodging in 13 shared bunk rooms and 2 private rooms with private bath, plus three meals daily mid-June–late Oct.; bed with full use of kitchen year-round. Perched high on the eastern side of Mount Cardigan, it offers access to literally dozens of trails to the top. Many of the lower trails are used by cross-country skiers and snowshoers in winter. Rates for the lodge, a rustic high cabin near the summit, and campsites are available and vary by season, meal plan, and number of people. Call or check the web site for current information. Summer at Cardigan includes volunteer-led hikes, swimming, and Sunday barbecues.

The Harbor House (603-763-3323; www.theharborhouse.com), 13 Maple St., P.O. Box 765, Sunapee 03782. Your home away from home can be an 11-room, 5-bath restored Victorian summer "cottage" that sleeps 18 people and sits just 500 feet from Sunapee Harbor. The whole house is $600 per night, 2-night minimum, or, depending on availability, you can rent by the room, starting at $150. Midweek packages and specials. Smoke-free.

Soo Nipi Lodge (603-863-7509; 1-800-760-8477; www.soo-nipi-lodge .com), 5 Schoolhouse Rd., P.O. Box 652, Newport 03773. Part of a classic 1761 colonial homestead, this onetime dairy barn was converted more than a decade ago into a handsome 4,000-square-foot group retreat space. Five bedrooms and baths house up to 20 guests. A large common area includes kitchen, dining, living room, and more intimate spaces. The sunroom with floor-to-ceiling windows offers breathtaking mountain views. Ideal for craft groups, skiers, or family reunions. The lodge rents for $800 a night, 2-night minimum.

Sunapee Harbor Cottages (603-763-5052; www.sunapeeharbor cottages.com), 4 Lake Ave., Sunapee Harbor 03782. Times change, as these charming cottages, rebuilt in 2002 on the site of the old Whispering Pines Cabins Resort, testify. Six cottages, delightfully decorated in true cottage style with work by local artisans, offer the only waterfront lodging on the lake. They sleep up to seven, and vary in size and price ($200–400). Amenities include wireless Internet service, babysitting services, pet care, catered meals, pontoon boat rental, massage therapy, and more.

✳ Where to Eat
DINING OUT

In the Lake Sunapee area
Alphorn Bistro (603-768-3318; www.innatdanbury.com), 67 Rt. 104, Danbury. Open Wed.–Sat. 5–8:30 PM. The annual "Best of the Wurst" festival is a good description of this restaurant's exuberantly Bavarian atmosphere. The owners, Netherlands-born Alexandra and chef Robert Graf, have created a yearlong Oktoberfest, complete with dirndl-clad waitresses, blue-and-white-checked tablecloths, an extensive beer list, and a menu of German and other European specialties. Entrées range $14–21.

Bellissima Brick Oven Trattoria (603-763-3290), 976 Rt. 103, Newbury Harbor Plaza, Newbury. Open Sun.–Thu. 11:30–9, Fri. and Sat. until 9:30. Tuscan colors and an expansive view of Lake Sunapee just across the road make this restaurant one of the area's favorites. The brick oven provides excellent gourmet pizza; the grill, entrées such as Tuscan pork served with a tomato, white bean, and herb pepperonata for $12.95. A variety of Italian-inspired appetizers, salads, soups, panini, and pasta round out the moderately priced menu.

Café Andre (603-863-1842), Rt. 103 just west of the Mount Sunapee traffic circle, Sunapee. Open daily, except Tue., 4 PM–1 AM. Reservations recommended. Chef Andre Woldkowski's long history in the restaurant business dates to working at his family's establishment while he was growing up in Poland. Before opening his own place with partner Mary Stillwell in December 2001, he worked for a decade— winters at restaurants in Vermont, summers on Block Island. He describes his menus as intercontinental. One offers formal dining choices: escargots, tournedos of beef, duck, and other classics. The other is served at the more casual pub. The dining room has white tablecloths, soft lighting, and a display of local art. Moderate to expensive.

The Flying Goose Brew Pub & Grille (603-526-6899; www.flying goose.com), 40 Andover Rd. (Rts. 11 and 114), New London. Open for lunch and dinner daily, 11:30–9; Sun. until 8. Same ownership as the Millstone Restaurant (below) but a more casual atmosphere. This 195-seat restaurant has become a widely prized, nonsmoking acoustic venue for musicians, offering seasonal Thursday-night concerts with locally and sometimes nationally known rock, folk, blues, country, jazz, and swing stylists (call for current schedule). It features 14 handcrafted ales and homemade root beer on tap, as well as a large menu that includes daily specials and burgers, sandwiches, ribs, superb soups, pastas, deep fries, and a variety of entrées, $9.95–19.95.

The Hide-Away Inn (603-526-4861; 1-800-457-0589; www.hideawayinn .net), Twin Lake Villa Rd., New London. Open for dinner daily Mother's Day–Labor Day; Thu.–Sat. the rest of the year. Rustic, Oregon-sprucepaneled getaway, just 3 minutes from Main Street. Hard to find but worth it; ask directions. Lori Freeman's the chef, her husband, Michael, the wine savant who has compiled one of the best cellars in the state. The menu specializes in seafood—seared scallops with seasonally changing sauces, lobster cakes, pecan-encrusted trout— but also offers interesting variations on beef and poultry standards. In summer there are dinner and theater specials in conjunction with the New London Barn Playhouse. Entrées $14.95–25.95.

The Inn at Pleasant Lake (603-526-6271; 1-800-626-4907), 853 Pleasant St., New London. Fixed-price ($52), five-course gourmet dinner at 6:15, Wed.–Sun. in summer; to Sat. in winter. Candlelight, classical music, and fine cuisine prepared by a graduate of the Culinary Institute of America who lovingly describes the menu while serving cocktails and canapés on the glassed-in porch. Dinner too is a ceremony, including an entremezzo course of, say, fresh citrus sections with a splash of sherry. Follow that with rack of lamb with roasted garlic rosemary demiglaze or mahimahi served with an exotic mushroom salad and yellow pepper oil; then perhaps a rosette of white chocolate mousse in a lace cookie cup with a trio of sauces. Star billing is shared with a view of the lake. Half-portion, half-price children's servings. Reservations required.

&. **La Meridiana** (603-526-2033), Rt. 11, Wilmot. Open for dinner nightly from 5 ; Sun. 3–7 PM. This is the favorite restaurant of local children's author Tomie dePaola, who based one of his books on an Italian legend he learned here. He's not alone in considering it one of the best restaurants and best values in central New Hampshire. The menu, like the owner-chef, is northern Italian, and the specialties are tender scaloppine and bistecca. Pastas and pastries are outstanding, too, and everything is moderately priced, even the wine list. Fresh salmon fillet baked in parchment paper with herbs is $13.95. There are always a number of daily specials.

&. **Millstone Restaurant** (603-526-4201), Newport Rd., New London. Open for lunch and dinner daily. A veteran of the area restaurant scene claims this is where he goes when he doesn't want to be disappointed. Entrées, ranging from Maine crab pie to Jaeger schnitzel, are creative and consistently good. Original art, warm colors, plants, and nice light shining through French doors and skylights lend a note of relaxed gentility to this bistro and wine bar. Entrées, several in both petite and regular serving sizes, range from $9.95 for a petite-sized angelhair pasta with shrimp and garlic to $29.95 for New Zealand rack of lamb.

The New London Inn Dining Room (603-526-2791; 1-800-526-2791), Main St., New London. Open Tue.–Sun. 5–9 PM. Sunday brunch is served 10–2 in summer only. This 1792 farmhouse with its extended ell has long been the heart of this handsome town. In the dining room, floor-to-ceiling windows overlook the town green. For a delicious taste of nouveau New England, try a cup of lobster bisque served with shiitake mushrooms and bacon. The seasonally changing menu is prepared by native New London chef Jarod Rockwell, who moved back home after learning his trade in Colorado. Entrées range from $15 for fresh chèvre ravioli to $23 for grilled New York sirloin served with horseradish potato puree, garlic broccoli rabe, and roasted shallots.

The Old Courthouse (603-863-8360), 30 Main St., Newport. An 1820s courthouse hidden behind the Victorian building that's better known as The Opera House. Open Wed.–Sun. for lunch and dinner; Sunday brunch 9:30–2. Reservations suggested. The menu changes weekly, but chef Red Blackington gets dependably rave reviews from patrons. The soups on a late-summer day included corn and wild rice with smoked sausage; "main events" included grilled lamb chops with pear and kiwi salsa, penne pasta with salmon and peas in dill cream, and a 10-ounce sirloin with red wine mushroom sauce. $14.95–17.95.

Potter Place Inn (603-735-5141); (www.potterplaceinn.com), 88 Depot St., Rt. 4/11, Andover. Open Tue.–Sat. from 5:30 PM. Long a favorite dining-out place for Proctor Academy faculty and students, this charming restaurant also attracts folks from around the area. Chef-owners Melba and Giovanni Leopardi offer daily specials that take advantage of their "fresh, fresh" ingredients. Homemade pastas, house-cured salmon, carpaccio Cipriani, grilled veal chops, venison; sometimes even ostrich! The award-winning wine list boasts more than 130 selections, and the small, intimate dining rooms provide a suitable ambience to enjoy them. Entrées $18–28.

& **Traditions Restaurant at Lake Sunapee Country Club** (603-526-6040), Rt. 11 and Country Club Lane, New London. In summer open every day for lunch and dinner; Nov.–May, open Fri.–Sun. for lunch, Thu.–Sat. for dinner. The attractive dining room has views of the fairway where members of this private golf course can work up an appetite. Entrées $16–27. Certified Angus beef a specialty.

In the Newfound Lake area
& **The Homestead** (603-744-2022; www.homesteadnh.com), Rt. 104, Bristol. Dinner daily from 4:30; Sunday brunch 11–2. Closed Mon. between Columbus Day and Memorial Day. This handsome old 1788 roadside Colonial, now painted pale yellow with dark green shutters and awnings, has been a restaurant since 1978. It offers a series of dining rooms ranging from traditional to glass to stone walled. The menu boasts a variety of American and Continental dishes, with more than 40 entrées priced from $12.95 for vegetarian ravioli to $22.95 for 18 ounces of roast prime rib.

& **Pasquaney Restaurant in The Inn on Newfound Lake** (603-744-9111), 103 Mayhew Turnpike, Rt. 3A, Bridgewater. Serves dinner Wed.–Sun., plus Sunday brunch 10–2. The traditional old hotel dining room has

been deftly updated with forest-green walls, white wainscoting, and flowery chintz window swags. There's also patio dining overlooking the lake. The seasonal menu includes coconut shrimp with marmalade dipping sauce as an appetizer. Entrées range from $14 for garden pasta with fresh summer vegetables to $30 for a grilled beef tenderloin with portobello mushrooms, blue cheese butter, mashed red skin potatoes, and onion fries. The **Wild Hare Tavern** serves a lighter menu along with drinks.

EATING OUT

In the Lake Sunapee area
The Anchorage at Sunapee Harbor (603-763-3334). Open mid-May–mid-Oct. for lunch and dinner 11:30–9. Jeffrey and Rose Follansbee renovated this Lake Sunapee tradition a few years back and jazzed up what was a basic menu to include specialty sandwiches and broiled as well as fried fish and seafood. They added even more jazz with live entertainment and dancing. The spot is unbeatable.

Bradford Junction Restaurant and Bakery (603-938-2424), Rt. 114, Bradford. Open daily 6 AM–2:30 PM. A remnant of the area's railroad days, this dinerlike restaurant was once a depot, and is still the showcase for an elaborate model train that tracks the perimeter of the cheery dining room. Homemade bread, muffins, soups; pot roast for $4.75, baked haddock for $4.45. The village gathering place.

& **Eagle Tavern & Grill** (603-865-2900; www.eagletavern.net), 58/64 Main St., Newport. Open Mon.–Sat. 11:30–9, Sun. from 11; bar open later. This handsome brick building dates from 1825 when it was built as a hotel to serve the new courthouse (now also a restaurant; see *Dining Out*). Newly rehabbed from top to bottom, it now serves patrons of events at the neighboring Opera House (a Victorian-era courthouse building) and also as a great road-food stop for travelers on Rt. 11/103 cutting across from I-89 to the Connecticut River Valley. Downstairs is no-smoking and a family dining atmosphere; upstairs is a tavern. The house specials include pot roast rigatoni and New England baked beans plus po'boys and a variety of sandwiches and burgers; also seafoods and steaks, all reasonably priced. Frequent live entertainment plus sports bar with discounted drinks on game nights.

The College Cafe (603-526-7186), 420 Main St., New London. Open Mon.–Sat. 7:30–7:30. A popular all-day spot just across the street from Colby-Sawyer College, featuring primarily a breakfast and lunch menu with fresh-baked pastries, salads, burgers, focaccio, and panini.

Jack's Coffee of New London (603-526-8003; www.jackscoffee.com), 180 Main St., New London. Open daily 7 AM–5 PM; dinner Tue.–Sat. 5:30–9 PM. Coffee, chow, and couches, plus WiFi Internet access, make this a definite New London "hot spot." During the day, expect casual fare—homemade soups, gourmet sandwiches, and fruit smoothies. At night, the restaurant trends upscale with linens, candlelight, and entrées ranging from $13.75 for fresh-cut fettuccine tossed with a wild mushroom ragu to $19.95 for a pecan-crusted pork chop served with jambalaya and sautéed kale.

MacKenna's Restaurant (603-526-9511), New London Shopping Center, New London. Open for breakfast, lunch, and dinner. Every town should have a place like this: clean, friendly, fast, and inexpensive. Homemade soups, great sandwiches on homemade bread (chicken salad is exceptional), steak dinners, and broiled or fried seafood and chicken; children's plates.

Marzelli's Deli (763-2222), 888 Rt. 103, Newbury Harbor. Open 7–7 daily. Lou and Mary Marzelli operate a New York–style Italian deli with meats, cheeses, gelati, pastries, homemade cannoli, espresso, beer, and wine. View of the lake from outside tables.

Murphy's Grille, Mount Sunapee (603-763-3113), 1407 Rt. 103, Newbury. Open daily for lunch and dinner. Casual family-style dining with a nice deck, game room, and reasonably priced burgers, sandwiches, pasta, and entrées. The prime rib's a specialty.

Peter Christian's Tavern (603-526-4042), Main St., New London. Pubby and popular. It's wise to come early or late since there's frequently a line and you can't make reservations. With the Barn Playhouse just down the street, there's always a crowd before a play. The menu, 11:30 AM–9 PM, stays the same: victuals like a cheese-and-meat board (plenty for two), or a hefty sandwich like Peter's Russian Mistress (open-faced turkey, bacon, Swiss cheese, spinach, tomato, Russian dressing). Dinner specials include white pesto lasagna and hearty beef stew, with prices generally under $10.

Rosarita's Mexican Cantina (603-863-1302), 8 Airport Rd. (off Rt. 10), Newport. Open for lunch and dinner most days, but call ahead. Dan Lloyd is from San Diego and knows what Mexican food should taste like. He and wife Kathy Walsh (from Long Island) make just about all the Mexican dishes you expect to find—from scratch. There's also a full bar. **The Sweet Shoppe** (603-763-4261, 36 River Rd., Sunapee Harbor. Open daily 8 AM–10 PM, Father's Day–Labor Day, then good-weather weekends through Columbus Day. All description of sweets—gelati, candy, fudge, pastries—as well as sandwiches.

Wildberry Bagel Co. (603-526-2244), 217 Main St., New London. Open 6 AM–3 PM daily. A bagel bar plus. Large selection of bagels, sandwiches, salads, and soups in a fresh, friendly atmosphere.

Elsewhere
The Foothills Restaurant (603-456-2140), Main St., Warner. Open daily except Mon., 6 AM–2 PM. For tourists, a pleasant pit stop in a picture-perfect small town just off I-89. For locals, this is the place to come to see everyone they know, even at 6 AM! Weekdays and weekends, folks from Warner and surrounding towns flock here for homemade breakfasts (huge pancake platters; great corned beef hash; toasted, buttered muffins) that are better than home since someone else does the cooking. Lace curtains, fast friendly service, daily baked specials, and a front porch with rocking chairs in case there's a wait.

✳ Entertainment

Newport Opera House (603-863-1212; www.newportoperahouse.com), 26 Main St., Newport. Rebuilt in 1886 after a fire, this majestic building boasts "the finest acoustics and largest stage north of Boston." It hosts a variety of live productions.

MUSIC **Summer band concerts**. Springfield band concert series held weekly in Sunapee Harbor. Concerts

at New London's Mary D. Haddard Memorial Bandstand on Sargent Common, New London; call the chamber of commerce for details. Concerts on Newbury Common on Thursday at 7 PM, June–Aug. Newport Band concerts every Sunday evening on the common late June–Aug. Held in the Opera House in case of rain. Summer music at Mount Sunapee.

THEATER ♪ **New London Barn Playhouse** (603-526-6710; 603-526-4631), Main St., New London. One of New England's oldest and best summer-stock theaters, featuring dramatic, musical, and children's productions. June–Labor Day.

✳ Selective Shopping

ANTIQUES **Kearsarge Lodge Antiques** (603-927-4594), Kearsarge Valley Rd., Wilmot. Open daily at 10; closed Mon. in winter. This long shingle-style lodge houses multiple antiques dealers specializing in Americana, primitives, folk art, sporting, and painted, rustic, garden, and architectural items, along with some new, mostly Adirondack-style furniture.

Prospect Hill Antiques (603-763-9676), Prospect Hill Rd., Georges Mills. The selection is immense, and the quality outstanding. If you are searching for an armoire or an end table, a desk or a stool, this barn, filled with more than 1,000 pieces of furniture and hundreds of collectibles, is worth checking.

Antiquing in the Lake Sunapee–New London Region. A map/guide to local antiques dealers is available at local information booths and from the New London Chamber of Commerce.

CRAFTS **Braided Rug Shop** (603-863-1139; www.braidedrugshop.com), P.O. Box 2154, Mount Sunapee. Braiding woolen fabric and supplies, plus rugs and novelty items made to order. Instructions for groups and individuals.

Carroll Studio (603-456-3947), 237 E. Main St. (Rt. 103), Warner. Open Sat. and Sun. 10–5, most other days by chance or appointment. A unique shop with original affordable art, mostly to do with nature, by all members of the Carroll family, including prizewinning author-illustrator-naturalist David Carroll.

The Dorr Mill Store (603-863-1197; www.dorrmillstore.com), Rt. 11/103, Guild (between Newport and Sunapee). Open Mon.–Sat. 9–5; also Sun. at holiday time. No longer an outlet for the woolen mill across the street, but a very special place that actually draws bus tours from as far away as Montreal for its line of 100 percent wool used for hooking, braiding, and quilting. Bolts of fabrics, including woolens still made at the mill, but a wider selection; also classic clothing: Woolrich, Pendleton, and others. Specializing in sweaters, woolens.

Hodgepodge Handicrafts & Ransom's Furniture (603-863-1470), 59 Belknap Ave., Newport. Open Mon.–Sat. 9–5. Specializing in spinning and knitting supplies, including spinning wheels, homespun yarns, and even a selection of hand-knit wearables.

LaBelle Cool Warm Hats (603-456-2516; www.coolwarmhats.com), 355 Kearsarge Mountain Rd., Warner. Call for times. Handmade Polarfleece hats and handmade fiber pins.

Farmer's Market
Newport Farmer's Market (603-863-3837) on the common, N. Main St. Newport. Mid-June–Oct., Thu. 3–6.

SPECIAL SHOPS **Artisan's Workshop** (603-526-4227; 1-800-457-7242), 186 Main St., New London. A small but full shop displaying an exceptional selection of handwrought jewelry, plus pottery, prints, paintings, wooden-ware, glass, cards, books, and much more in the front rooms of the old inn that now houses Peter Christian's Tavern. Frequent summer demonstrations, special exhibits, concerts.

Audrey Nelson's Used Books (603-863-4394), 1170 Brook Rd., Goshen (Brook Rd. begins just a mile from the rotary at Sunapee State Park). Open May–Oct., Fri.–Sun. 10–4. "My work is all the things I love to do," says Nelson, whose work includes photography, painting, gardening, and an almost organic bookstore well worth a detour off the beaten path. The shop offers 80,000 carefully selected hard- and softcover books, including some fine first editions and a wide variety of general and scholarly stock.

Brickstone (603-863-6760), 82 Oak St. (0.25 mile north of the town common off Rt. 10), Newport. Hours vary. A 200-year-old farmhouse with seven rooms of unique gifts and collectibles.

C. B. Coburn Fine Gifts & Candy (603-526-6010), 374 Main St., New London. Open Mon.–Sat. 9:30–5:30, Sun. 11–4. Whether you're looking for brand-name cookware, bath accessories, or New England pottery, this shop sells a mix of gifts and gourmet items, from children's author Tomie dePaola's collection of books (he's a local) to fresh fudge made daily.

MAIN STREET BOOKENDS IN WARNER

Lee a. Booker

⌀ **Main Street BookEnds** (603-456-2700), 16 E. Main St., Warner. Open daily 9–6, Fri. until 8. This combination bookstore, art gallery, and community heartbeat has a wonderful selection of books, cards, and CDs of local interest, with a big, inviting children's section nationally recognized by *Yankee Magazine*. Also changing art exhibits, fun and savvy staff, and an amazing array of literary, historical, musical, political, and community programs.

⌀ **Morgan Hill Bookstore** (603-526-5850), 170 Main St., New London. A spacious full-service bookstore with a unique, inviting children's area set up like a barn. Specializes in fine fiction and travel; also cards and CDs. Special programs, including signings and talks by area authors.

Vessels and Jewels, 180 Main St., New London (adjacent to Jack's Coffee). Open daily except Tue. 10–6, Sat. until 8, Sun. until 3. A funky mix of handmade lamp shades, work by local artists and craftsmen, along with a make-your-own bead shop.

Wingdoodle (603-456-3515; www.wingdoodle.com), 19 E. Main St., Warner. Open Wed.–Fri. 10–5, Sat. 10–4, Sun. 12–3. A colorful and creative center offering classes and gifts for all ages. Original artwork, cards, stickers, rubber stamps, journals, toys, puppets, and more.

Woodsum Gallery, (603-456-2576; www.woodsumgallery.com), 31 River Rd., Sunapee Harbor. Open daily. Specializing in art of the region with original paintings, hand-pulled prints, photography, pottery, and art supplies.

FACTORY OUTLETS **Mesa International Factory Outlet** (603-526-4497), 135 Elkins Rd. (off Rt. 11), Elkins. Mon.–Sat. 10–5, Sun. 11–4. Bright, colorful glassware and hand-painted dinnerware designed by New Hampshire artists and manufactured around the globe. Worth checking.

✳ **Special Events**

Note: The following entries represent a fraction of summer happenings in this region; check local listings.

June: Annual **Inn Tour** of the Sunapee region.

July: **New London Garden Club Annual Antiques Show**. **Hebron Fair**.

August: **New London Hospital Fair**. Annual **League of New Hampshire Craftsmen's Fair**, Mount Sunapee State Park. The biggest event of the year by far. The country's oldest and still one of its best craft fairs: a 9-day gathering of more than 500 juried artisans. Music, an art exhibit, a wide variety of craft

Courtesy of the League of New Hampshire Craftsmen

A METALSMITH DENMONSTRATES HOW
SPOONS ARE MADE AT THE ANNUAL
LEAGUE OF NEW HAMPSHIRE
CRAFTSMEN'S FAIR

demonstrations, and workshops are included in the admissions ticket, good for 2 days—the time you need to take in the full range of exhibits, try your own hand at crafting something, and see the featured demonstrations that vary with the theme of the day. **Old Home Day**, Sutton. **Annual Lake Sunapee Antique Boat Show and Parade. Alexandria Fair. Muster Field Farm Days**, North Sutton village, offers more than 100 demonstrations of colonial skills, a Grand Parade, and a roast beef dinner the last weekend of the month, the same weekend as the decades-young **Annual Apple Pie Craft Fair** in Newport.

September: **Mount Sunapee Triathlon. Danbury Grange Fair**.

Columbus Day weekend: **Warner Fall Foliage Festival**. Crafts, parades, food, entertainment, and traditional small-town hospitality.

The Connecticut River Valley

LOWER CONNECTICUT RIVER TOWNS

UPPER VALLEY TOWNS

LOWER COHASE

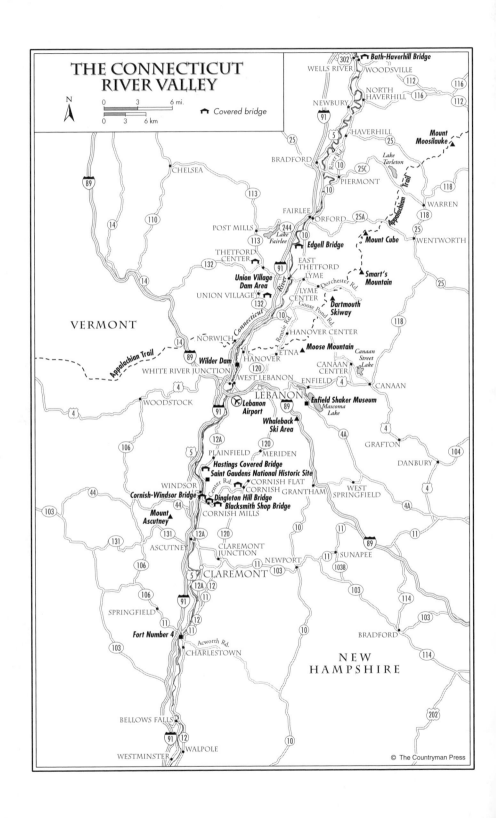

THE CONNECTICUT RIVER VALLEY

N

0   3   6 mi.
0   3   6 km

🏠 Covered bridge

VERMONT

NEW HAMPSHIRE

Bath-Haverhill Bridge
WELLS RIVER · WOODSVILLE
302
112
116
NORTH HAVERHILL
116
112
NEWBURY
91
5
HAVERHILL
25
Mount Moosilauke
BRADFORD
River Rd.
10
25C
Lake Tarleton
Appalachian Trail
118
PIERMONT
10
WARREN
FAIRLEE
ORFORD
25A
118
Mount Cube
25
POST MILLS
244
10
WENTWORTH
113
Lake Fairlee
Edgell Bridge
THETFORD CENTER
132
91
EAST THETFORD
LYME
Smart's Mountain
25
UNION VILLAGE
Union Village Dam Area
Dorchester Rd.
LYME CENTER
Dartmouth Skiway
118
UNION VILLAGE
132
Goose Pond Rd.
10
Connecticut River
HANOVER CENTER
14
NORWICH
ETNA
Moose Mountain
Canaan Street Lake
Rennie Rd.
89
Wilder Dam
HANOVER
CANAAN CENTER
WHITE RIVER JUNCTION
120
WEST LEBANON
ENFIELD
4
CANAAN
Appalachian Trail
4
LEBANON
Enfield Shaker Museum
Mascoma Lake
WOODSTOCK
✈ Lebanon Airport
91
Whaleback Ski Area
4
4
GRAFTON
106
12A
120
104
PLAINFIELD
MERIDEN
DANBURY
5
Hastings Covered Bridge
Saint Gaudens National Historic Site
CORNISH FLAT
WEST SPRINGFIELD
WINDSOR
Center Rd.
CORNISH
GRANTHAM
4A
44
Cornish-Windsor Bridge
Dingleton Hill Bridge
Blacksmith Shop Bridge
103
44
CORNISH MILLS
Mount Ascutney
10
11
11
131
131
12A
11
89
ASCUTNEY
CLAREMONT JUNCTION
SUNAPEE
106
NEWPORT
11
103B
5
CLAREMONT
11
103
103
12A
12
114
106
11
103
91
11
12
SPRINGFIELD
11
10
BRADFORD
114
Fort Number 4
Acworth Rd.
103
CHARLESTOWN
NEW HAMPSHIRE
114
202
BELLOWS FALLS
91
12
10
WESTMINSTER
WALPOLE

© The Countryman Press

INTRODUCTION

The Connecticut River flows 410 miles from its high source on the New Hampshire–Quebec border to Long Island Sound in the state of Connecticut. What concerns us here are its 270 miles as a boundary—and bond—between the states of New Hampshire and Vermont. Defying state lines, it forms one of New England's most beautiful and distinctive regions, shaped by a shared history.

Judging from 138 archaeological sites along this stretch of the river, its banks have been peopled for many thousands of years. Evidence of sizable Western Abenaki villages have been found at Newbury (Vt.), at Claremont, and at the Great Falls at present-day Bellows Falls (Vt.). Unfortunately, these tribes, along with those throughout the "New World," were decimated by disease contracted from English traders.

By the late 17th century English settlements had spread from the mouth of the Connecticut up to Deerfield, Ma., just below the present N.H./Vt. border. In 1704 Deerfield was attacked by French and Indians, who killed 40 villagers and carried off more than 100 as captives to St. Francis, a full 300 miles to the northwest. This was one in a series of bloody incidents dryly dismissed in elementary schools as "the French and Indian Wars."

Recent and ongoing scholarship is deepening our sense of relationships among Frenchmen, Western Abenaki tribespeople, and Englishmen during the first half of the 18th century. By 1700 many settlers had adopted the canoe as a standard mode of travel and, according to Dartmouth professor Colin G. Calloway in *Dawnland Encounters*, in 1704 New Hampshire passed a law requiring all householders to keep "one good pair of snow shoes and moqueshens" (moccasins). Settlers and Abenaki traded with each other. Beaver remained the prime source of revenue for the settlers, and the Indians were becoming increasingly dependent on manufactured goods and alcohol. Both at Fort Dummer—built in 1724 in what, at the time, was Massachusetts (now Vernon, Vt.)—and at the Fort at Number 4, built 50 miles upriver in 1743 in present Charlestown, N.H., settlers and Indians lived side by side.

Unfortunately, during this period former friends and neighbors also frequently faced each other in battles to the death. At the reconstructed Fort at No. 4 you learn that five adults and three children were abducted by a band of Abenaki in 1754 (all survived), and that in 1759 Major Robert Rodgers and his

Rangers retaliated for the many raids from the Indian village of St. Francis (near Montreal) by killing many more than 100 residents, including many women and children. The suffering of "Rodgers's Rangers" on their winter return home is legendary. A historic marker on Rt. 10 in Haverhill offers a sobering description.

After the 1763 Peace of Paris, France withdrew its claims to New France and English settlers surged up the Connecticut River, naming their new communities for their old towns in Connecticut and Massachusetts: Walpole, Plainfield, Lebanon, Haverhill, Windsor, Norwich, and more.

This was, however, no-man's-land.

In 1749 New Hampshire governor Benning Wenworth had begun granting land on both sides of the river (present-day Vermont was known as "The New Hampshire Grants"), a policy that New York's Governor George Clinton refused to recognize. In 1777, when Vermont declared itself a republic, 16 towns on the New Hampshire side opted to join it. In December 1778, at a meeting in Cornish, N.H., towns from both sides of the river voted to form their own state of "New Connecticut," but neither burgeoning state was about to lose so rich a region. In 1779 New Hampshire claimed all Vermont.

In 1781 delegates form both sides of the river met in Charlestown and agreed to stick together. Vermont's Governor Chittendon wrote to General Washington, asking to be admitted to the Union, incorporating towns contested both by New Hampshire and New York. Washington replied: Yes but without the contested baggage.

In 1782 New Hampshire sent 1,000 soldiers to enforce their jurisdiction and not long thereafter Washington asked Vermont to give in, and, it did. Needless to say, the River towns were unhappy about this verdict.

The valley itself prospered in the late 18th and early 19th centuries, as evidenced by the exquisite Federal-era (1790s–1830s) meetinghouses and mansions still to be seen in river towns from Walpole north to Haverhill. With Dartmouth College (established 1769) at its heart and rich floodplain farmland stretching its length, this valley differed far more dramatically than today from the unsettled mountainous regions walling it in on either side.

The river remained the valley's highway in the early 19th century. A transportation canal was built to circumvent the Great Falls at present-day Bellows Falls, and Samuel Morey of Orford built a steamboat in 1793. Unfortunately Robert Fulton scooped his invention, but the upshot was increased river transport—at least until the 1840s, when railroads changed everything.

"It is an extraordinary era in which we live," Daniel Webster remarked in 1847, watching the first train roll into Lebanon, N.H., the first rail link between the Connecticut River and the Atlantic. "It is altogether new," he continued. "The world has seen nothing like it before."

In this "anything's possible" era, the valley boomed. At the Robbins, Kendall & Lawrence Armory in Windsor, gun makers developed machines to do the repetitive tasks required to produce each part of a gun. This meant that for the first time an army could buy a shipment of guns and know that if one was damaged, it could be repaired with similar parts. In the vintage 1846 armory, now the American Precision Museum, you learn that this novel production of "interchangeable parts" became known as the "American System" of precision manufacturing. Springfield too became known for precision tool making. This area is still known as "Precision Valley."

In places the railroad totally transformed the landscape, creating towns where there had been none, shifting populations from high old town centers like Rockingham and Walpole to the riverside. This shift was most dramatic in the town of Hartford, where White River Junction became the hub of north–south and east–west rail traffic.

The river itself was put to new uses. It became sluiceway down which logs were floated from the northern forest to paper mills in Bellows Falls and farther downriver. Its falls had long powered small mills, but now a series of hydro dams were constructed, including the massive dam between Barnet, Vt. and Monroe, N.H., in 1930. This flooded several communities to create both Comerford Reservoir—and the visual illusion that the Connecticut River stops there. At present 16 dams stagger the river's flow between the Second Connecticut Lake above Pittsburg, N.H., and Enfield, Ct., harnessing the river to provide power for much of the Northeast. By the 1950s the river was compared to an open sewer and towns turned their backs to it, depositing refuse along its banks.

Still, beyond towns, the river slid by fields of corn and meadows filled with cows. In 1952 the nonprofit Connecticut River Watershed Council was founded to "promote and protect wise use of the Connecticut Valley's resources." Thanks to the 1970s Clean Water Act and to acquisitions, green-ups, and cleanups by numerous conservation groups, the river itself began to enjoy a genuine renewal. Visitors and residents alike discovered its beauty; campsites for canoeists were

A FARM IN THE CONNECTICUT RIVER VALLEY

Kim Grant

spaced along the shore. At present kayaks as well as canoes can be rented along several stretches.

The cultural fabric of towns on either side of the river has remained close knit and, although many bridges were destroyed by the hurricane of 1927, the 21 that survive include the longest covered bridge in the United States (connecting Windsor and Cornish). It's only because tourism promotional budgets are financed by individual state taxes that this stretch of the river valley itself has not, until recently, been recognized as a destination by either New Hampshire or Vermont.

Happily, a respected nonprofit, bistate group, the Connecticut River Joint Commissions—founded in 1989 to foster bistate cooperation and represent 53 riverfront towns—has stepped into this breach, with dramatic results. It has now spawned the Connecticut River Scenic Byway Council dedicated to, among other things, creating an infrastructure to identify appropriate places in which to promote tourism and the cultural heritage.

At this writing seven "waypoint" information centers are salted along the river. Those in Bellows Falls, White River Junction, Wells River, Haverhill, Lancaster, St. Johnsbury, and Colebrook are serving visitors well, and in the process reestablishing the Connecticut to its rightful place as the centerpiece of a genuine region. Similar centers in Claremont and Windsor are gearing up and another, in Brattleboro, awaits funds for remodeling. Their work has been enhanced by the federally funded Silvio O. Conte National Fish and Wildlife Refuge, which seeks to preserve the quality of the natural environment within the entire Connecticut River watershed. For a sense of wildlife and habitat in this area, stop by the Montshire Museum in Norwich, Vt. (the name melds both states).

In 2005 the Connecticut River corridor officially became "the Connecticut River National Scenic Byway." We are proud to note that for the past 20 years both our *New Hampshire* and *Vermont Explorer's Guide*s have included an Upper Valley section describing both sides of the river. Our 2006 editions expand this coverage to include the Lower Connecticut Valley and the Lower Cohase Region on the north. Just above this area the valley widens and two dams have impounded Comerford Lake and the Moore Reservoir, breaking the continuity of the river. Here our "Connecticut River Valley" chapter ends, but we continue to describe the glorious landscape as the valley once more narrows and the river is banked in meadows with views (best from the Vermont side) of the White Mountains towering in the east. This is one of the most beautiful stretches along the entire length of the river in "The Great North Woods" chapters.

Visually visitors see a river, not state lines. Interstate 91 on the Vermont side has backroaded Rt. 5, as it has Rt. 10 on the New Hampshire side. Even more backroaded and beautiful are the roads marked from Rt. 10 and 12A along the New Hampshire bank. Within each chapter prime sights to see shift from one side of the river to the other; the same holds true for places to eat, stay, hike, and generally explore this very distinctive region. Of course in this book we focus in more detail on New Hampshire, while in the latest edition of our Vermont Explorer's Guide the focus is more detailed on that state.

GUIDANCE **www.ctrivertravel.net**, an excellent, noncommercial web site covering the entire stretch of the Connecticut shared by Vermont and New

Hampshire, is maintained by the **Connecticut River Byway Council**. Also look for "waypoint" information centers serving both sides of the river, described under *Guidance* in ensuing chapters.

Helpful pamphlet guides available from the Connecticut River Joint Commissions (603-826-4800; www.ctrivertravel.net) include:

Boating on the Connecticut River in Vermont and New Hampshire (a map/guide).

Explorations Along the Connecticut River Byway of New Hampshire and Vermont (a map/guide).

Connecticut River Heritage Trail (a 77-mile driving/biking tour for the historically and architecturally minded).

Connecticut River Birding Trail map/guides (two) to the Northern Section and Upper Valley.

Recommended reading:

Proud to Live Here in the Connecticut River Valley of Vermont and New Hampshire by Richard J. Ewald with Adair D. Mulligan, published by the Connecticut River Joint Commissions (www.crjc.org).

Confluence, A River, Politics & the Fate of All Humanity by Nathaniel Tripp (Steerforth Press, Hanover).

This American River: Five Centuries of Writing About the Connecticut by Walter Wetherell (University Press of New England, Hanover).

LOWER CONNECTICUT RIVER TOWNS

Along the 410-mile length of the Connecticut River, few communities are as closely linked historically—yet so different entirely—as Walpole, N.H. and Bellows Falls, Vt.

Walpole's village is a white wooden New England classic, graced by fine old churches and dozens of mansions, some dating from the late 18th century, more from the early and mid–19th century, when it was a popular summer haven with several large inns. In the 20th century James Michener came here to research the opening chapter of *Hawaii*—the one about the New England–born missionaries and their families. Current creative residents include filmmaker Ken Burns.

Bellows Falls is named for Walpole's founder, Colonel Benjamin Bellows, who owned land on both sides of this 56-foot drop in the river. Technically a mill village within the town of Rockingham, it boomed in the late 19th century as a paper-making and rail center. It's currently enjoying a renaissance as an art center as well as a departure point for the Green Mountain Railroad's excursion trains. Walpole too is stirring after a quiet half century. The old hotels went the way of train service from Boston, around the time that residents voted to reroute the state highway away from the village down to the river's edge. Many visitors now come looking for the café and restaurant at Burdick's Chocolates and are entranced by the village. Walpole also offers several pleasant places to stay.

Visitors are drawn to Charlestown by its reconstructed French and Indian Wars–era fort, and again find much more. This is one of the valley's oldest communities, chartered by the Massachusetts Bay Colony in 1753 as "No. 4" and again in 1753 by New Hampshire, which changed the name. Its entire, 200-foot-wide Main Street is a National Historic District, lined with handsome buildings reflecting seemingly every architectural style from Federal to Richardsonian Romanesque. It also offers good food and lodging.

Claremont is a once-proud mill city, and its magnificent mills are currently undergoing a major renovation; the city, seemingly caught in a time warp, awaits rejuvenation. In the meantime the Opera House offers a schedule of live performances. Pleasant Street, the main shopping drag, is a good bet for reasonably priced antiques.

GUIDANCE **Great Falls Regional Chamber of Commerce** (802-463-4280; www.gfree.org). We can't say enough for this beautiful visitors center, sited down on Depot St. near the Amtak station in Bellows Falls, Vt., open daily 10–4. Outstanding historical displays trace the area's history; chamber staff offer practical information covering both sides of the river.

Greater Claremont Chamber of Commerce (603-543-1296; chamber@ adelphia.net), Moody Building, 24 Tremont Square, Claremont, is open weekdays 8:30–4:30. It's housed in in the city's central, most distinctive building. Pick up a walking guide. No public restrooms. A new "waypoint" visitors center on North St. (Rt. 11/103) offers restrooms but minimal visitors info and no visitors staffing.

GETTING THERE *By car:* From New York: I-91 to Vt. Exit 5. From Boston, take Rt. 12 west to 140 to 12, or I-89 to Rts. 11 and 11/103.

By train: **Amtrak** (1-800-872-7245; www.amtrak.com) stops in Bellows Falls, Vt. and in Claremont, N.H.

MEDICAL EMERGENCY **The Valley Regional Hospital** (603-542-1822), 243 Elm St., Claremont, 24-hour emergency service. **911** also serves this area.

✳ Communities

Listed from south to north.

Walpole (populaton: 3,594). A particularly handsome village set high above Rt. 12, with a handsome Congregational church and white-clapboard houses, some dating from the 1790s but more from the early and mid–19th century when Walpole was a popular summer haven with three large inns. Louisa May Alcott summered here, and Emily Dickinson visited. Current residents include filmmaker Ken Burns and chocolate maker Lawrence Burdick. **The Walpole Historical Society** (603-756-3308; open June–Sep., Wed. and Sat. 2–4) displays a significant collection of paintings, photographs, furniture, and other local memorabilia. It's housed on three floors of the tower-topped Academy Building in the middle of the village and includes a large research library. Walpole's big hotels have vanished, but a vintage golf course remains. The town is undergoing a renaissance with Burdick's Bistro and Café and the Walpole Inn now offering destination dining.

Bellows Falls, Vt. (population: 3,165). Viewed from above the dam at Bellows Falls, the Connecticut River resembles a glassy, narrow lake. The view from below the village, however, is very different. Instead of thundering falls, what you usually see is a power station between two narrow water channels and several bridges. The Bellows Falls Canal Co. was the first in the country to obtain a charter, and it was an amazing feat easing flatboats through a series of locks, substantially expanding navigation up the Connecticut. The creation of the canal also formed the island separating the village from the Connecticut River, which for much of the year is now reduced to a modest cascade, dropping through the 0.5-mile gorge beneath the dam. It's on the island that the 1920s railroad station stands, serving Amtrak and the Green Mountain Flyer.

In 1869 William Russell developed the novel idea of making paper from wood pulp, using logs floated down from both sides of the river. He went on to found International Paper. The canal was put to work powering mills, and it still powers turbines generating electricity.

Despite major fires, much of the village architecture dates from the 1890s, the period depicted in a building-sized mural just south of the square. Rockingham Town Hall, with its Florentine-style tower, includes the town-owned New Falls Cinema and Fletcher's Drug, the bus stop. The surrounding square is lined with a lively mix of shops and restaurants.

Bellows Falls is also known as the home of Hetty Green (1835–1916), who parlayed a substantial inheritance into a $100 million fortune; she was called the Witch of Wall Street, to which she traveled by day coach, looking like a bag lady in threadbare bombazine. The **Bellows Falls Historical Society** (802-463-4270) in the **Rockingham Free Library and Museum**, Westminster St., is open summer Fri. 2–4 or by appointment. The **Adams Grist Mill** (open July–Oct., Sat. and Sun. 1–4) ground grain from 1831 until 1961; the old machinery is all in place.

Charlestown (population: 4,929), was a stockaded outpost during the French and Indian Wars. Its Main Street was laid out in 1763, 200 feet wide and a mile long, with more than five dozen structures that now comprise a national historic district; 10 buildings predate 1800. Note the 1840s Congregational church; the former Charlestown Inn (1817), now a commercial building; the vintage-1800 Stephen Hassam House, built by the great-grandfather of impressionist painter Childe Hassam; and the Foundation for Biblical Research, housed in a 1770s mansion. Historic Charlestown Walkabout, a nominally priced guide, is available in most town stores. Also see **The Fort at No. 4** under *To See.*

Claremont (population: 13,344) Massive textile mills and machine shops line the Sugar River as it drops 300 feet from the city's compact core around Tremont Square. At this writing the mills are being rehabbed. Tremont Square retains some magnificent 1890s buildings, notably the massive Italian Renaissance Revival–style city hall with its magnificent and well-used second-floor **Opera House**, and the Moody Building, built originally as a hotel in 1892. Adjoining Pleasant Street is now lined with antiques shops. The mammoth brick **Monadnock Mills** on Water Street (off Broad and Main) on the Sugar River are among the best-preserved small 19th-century urban mills in New Hampshire; note the 1840s gambrel-roofed brick Sunapee Mill across the river and the small brick overseers' cottages (also 1840s) on Crescent Street. The railroad was an essential contributor to Claremont's industrial and cultural heyday. It remains an Amtrak stop. The **Claremont Historical Society** (603-543-1400), 26 Mulberry St., is open seasonally. A walking tour is available from the chamber of commerce. **West Claremont** (3 miles west on Rt. 103) is a vanished village graced by New Hampshire's oldest Episcopal and Catholic churches. It seems that the Catholic priest who founded St. Mary's parish in 1824 was the son of the Episcopal rector who built St. John's across the street. Both buildings are interesting architecturally. The only sign of the congregations that both men taught and served is the West Part Burying Ground adjoining the churches.

Listed from south to north.

HISTORIC SITES Rockingham Meeting House. Vermont's oldest unchanged public building is off Rt. 103 between Chester and Bellows Falls, and open Memorial Day–Columbus Day, 10–4. Built as a combination church and town hall in 1787, this Federal-style structure stands quietly above its graveyard. It's striking inside and out. Inside, "pigpen"-style pews each accommodate 10 to 15 people, some with their backs to the minister. The old burying ground is filled with thin old markers bearing readable epitaphs.

✦ **Fort at Number 4** (603-826-5700; www.fortat4.com), Rt. 11, 1 mile north of Charlestown village. Open June–late Oct., 10–5. $8 adults, $6 seniors, $5 children. This living history museum, set in 20 acres on the Connecticut River, conjures an otherwise almost forgotten chapter in New England history. The stockaded village exactly replicates the way the settlement looked in the 1740s. It served first as a trading post in which Natives and newcomers lived together peaceably until the outbreak of the French and Indian Wars. A full 50 miles north of any other town on the Connecticut River, the original fort fell once but then withstood repeated attacks. The complex includes the Great Hall, cow barns, and furnished living quarters; there is also an audiovisual program, and costumed interpreters prepare meals, perform chores, and staff a blacksmith forge. Inquire about frequent battle reenactments and special programs for children throughout summer. A small museum displays authentic local Native American artifacts, and the gift store carries historical books for all ages.

The American Precision Museum (802-674-5781; www.americanprecision .org), 1961 S. Main St., Windsor, Vt. Open Memorial Day–Nov. 1, 10–5 daily; $6 adults, $4 seniors, $4 over 6; $18 per family. Billed as the largest collection of historically significant machine tools in the country, housed in the 1846 Robbins,

CLAREMONT

Christina Tree

Kendall & Lawrence Armory, itself a national historic landmark, said to be the "birthplace of this country's modern system of industrial design and production." At the 1851 Great Exposition in London the firm displayed the manner in which it used interchangeable parts to assemble rifles. The British army ordered 25,000 rifles on the spot and bought 138 gun-making machines. The idea of using interchangeable parts was a significant breakthrough and became known as "the American System." Special exhibits can be excellent.

Old Constitution House (802-674-6628; www.historicvermont.org), N. Main St., Windsor, Vt. Open mid-May–mid-Oct., Wed.–Sun. 11–5. Nominal admission. This is Elijah West's tavern (but not in its original location), where delegates gathered on July 2, 1777, to adopt Vermont's constitution, America's first to prohibit slavery, establish universal voting rights for all males, and authorize a public school system. Excellent first-floor displays trace the history of the formation of the Republic of Vermont; upstairs is the town's collection of antiques, prints, documents, tools and cooking utensils, tableware, toys, and early fabrics. Special exhibits vary each year. A path out the back door leads to Lake Runnemede.

FOR FAMILIES ✿ **Family Fun Play Zone** (603-542-9351), Rt. 12, Charlestown. Open Apr.–Oct., varying hours. Kid heaven: go-carts, a mini railroad, a driving range, also an 18-hole golf course.

✳ To Do

BOATING ✿ **North Star Livery** (603-542-6929; www.kayak-canoe.com), Rt. 12A in Cornish, will shuttle patrons to put-ins either 3 or 12 miles above the Cornish–Windsor covered bridge. Roughly half of North Star's patrons camp, either at **Wilgus State Park** (802-674-5422) or at another site in Windsor, Vt. North Star itself is New England's most picturesque canoe livery: The check-in desk in the barn of a working farm, redolent of bales of hay, and owner John Hammond may well be out front shoeing horses; the canoes and kayaks are stacked behind the farmhouse. Six-person rafts are also available. Full-day, half-day, and multiday trips are offered. With over 90 boats, including 30 kayaks, this is the largest and oldest commercial rental service on the Connecticut River.

RENT A CANOE FROM NORTH STAR LIVERY IN CORNISH AND FLOAT DOWN THE CONNECTICUT RIVER

Christina Tree

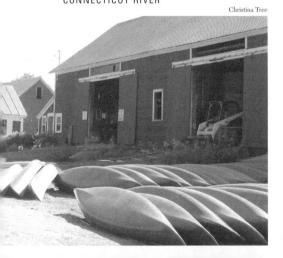

Boat access to the Connecticut River

Herrick's Cove. Picnic area, boat landing, and bird sanctuary, a good picnic spot off Rt. 5 (above I-91, Exit 6) in Rockingham, above Bellows Falls, Vt.

Hoyt's Landing Off Rt. 11 and I-91 Exit 7 in Springfield, Vt., a landing, also good for fishing.

Ashley Ferry Boat Landing. Off River Road (parallel to Rt. 11/12), about 2 miles south of Claremont. A boat landing and park at a bend in the river. Also see "The Upper Valley."

CAR RACING **Claremont Speedway** (603-543-3160), Bowker St., 4 miles east of I-91, Claremont. May–Sep., racing Sat. 7:30 PM.

HANG GLIDING **Morningside Recreation Area** (603-542-4416; www.fly morningside.com), Rt. 12 in Claremont, is the site of events on weekends. Lessons in hang gliding and paragliding are offered along with a repair service, sales, swimming, and hiking.

Ascutney Mountain Resort (802-484-7771; 1-800-243-0011), Rt. 44, Brownsville, Vt. Summer.

GOLF **Hooper Golf Club** (603-756-4020) Prospect Hill, Walpole, offers nine holes and a clubhouse serving lunch.

RAILROAD EXCURSIONS ✍ **Trains Around Vermont** (802-463-3069; 1-800-707-3530; www.rails-vt.com), 54 Depot St., Bellows Falls. Round-trips on the **Green Mountain Flyer** are available Tue.–Sun. in summer; daily during foliage season. This 13-mile (one-way) route follows the Connecticut River past covered bridges, then heads up the Williams River and through wooded rock cuts, which include the spectacular Brockway Mills gorge. Inquire about special runs. **The White River Flyer**. Based in the same handsome 1920s railroad station that serves Amtrak, this excursion is operated by the Green Mountain Railroad; rolling stock includes some turn-of-the-20th-century cars.

SPECIAL PROGRAMS **Great River Arts** (802-463-3330; www.greatriverarts .org), 33 Bridge St., Bellows Falls, Vt. Founded in Walpole, N.H., but now head-quartered in nearby Bellows Falls, Vt., this nonprofit institute offers a variety of first-class literary and visual arts workshops and programs in venues on both sides of the river.

✳ Winter Sports

CROSS COUNTRY SKIING **Ascutney Mountain Resort** (802-484-7771; 1-800-243-0011), Rt. 44, Brownsville, Vt. A touring center with instruction, rentals, 32 km of trails.

The Chase House (603-675-5391) Rt. 12A, Cornish, maintainss cross-country and snowshoeing trails open to the public. Sleigh rides are also offered.

DOWNHILL SKIING ✍ **Ascutney Mountain Resort** (802-484-7771; 1-800-243-0011; www.ascutney.com), Rt. 44, Brownsville (I-91, Exit 8 or 9), Vt. A family-geared, self-contained resort. Facilities include a 215-unit condo hotel, a sports center with indoor and outdoor pools, weight and racquetball rooms, a full restaurant, and a base lodge. Owners Steve and Susan Plausteiner have increased snowmaking and added the North Peak Area, substantially increasing expert trails, served by a new mile-long quad chair. *Trails:* 56. Lifts: 6. *Vertical drop:* 1,800 feet. *Snowmaking:* 95 percent. *For children:* Nursery/child care from 6 weeks. *Features:* Nine double-diamond advanced trails, expert tree skiing, a terrain park, a tubing slope, and a separate lift-served Learning Park. *Rates:* $56 adults weekend, $42 seniors/juniors; $54/$38 midweek. Half-day tickets are offered.

Arrowhead Recreation Area (603-542-2416; www.arrowheadnh.com) is a family ski hill. Adult all-day tickets are $7, night skiing $5; ages 7–12, $5 and $3.50. Free for ages 6 and under.

Also see **Mount Sunapee** in "Western Lakes."

✳ Lodging

RESORT ✿ **Ascutney Mountain Resort** (802-484-7711; 1-800-243-0011; www.ascutney.com), Rt. 44, Brownsville, VT 05037. A contemporary, 215-unit wooden condo-hotel and flanking condominiums at the base of Mount Ascutney. Accommodations range from standard hotel rooms to three-bedroom units with kitchen, fireplace, and deck, all nicely furnished with reproduction antiques. Facilities include the full-service **Harvest Inn Restaurant** and a sports center with Olympic-sized indoor and outdoor pools, tennis, mountain biking, and a choice of "Vermont Summer Adventures." In winter there are both alpine and cross-country trails; facilities include indoor and outdoor pools and an extensive summer adventure program for kids. Rooms $119, condo units $179–259 in summer and fall, more in winter (but nobody pays the rack rate); 2-night rates from $109 per night. Inquire about package rates.

INNS

Listed from south to north.

✿ **The Inn at Valley Farms** (603-756-2855; 1-877-327-2855; www.innatvalleyfarms.com), 633 Wentworth Rd., Walpole 03608. While it's off the beaten track, this inn is a true destination. As if the bucolic setting (105 acres bordering an apple orchard) weren't enough, this circa-1774 treasure, hidden up the hill from Walpole village, also offers exceptionally handsome, antiques-filled guest rooms along with lovely common rooms, including a formal parlor and dining room, and a sunroom overlooking a lovely perennial garden. Upstairs in the main house there is a two-bedroom suite with bath, along with two other bedrooms, each with four-poster bed, private bath, phone, and dataport. Niceties include fresh flowers, plush robes, and Burdick chocolate good-night treats. Family travelers can choose one of two cottages, each with three bedrooms, kitchen, and living area. Innkeeper Jacqueline Caserta is a serious organic farmer/gardener; uses fresh eggs as well as her organic vegetable harvest creatively to make a breakfast that's both good and good for you. Rates for the inn are $139–175, double occupancy, with full breakfast. Cottages, which sleep six, are $175 for two, plus $15 per person under 12; $29 per person over 12. A basket of homemade breads and muffins is delivered each morning to your door.

The Walpole Inn (603-756-3320; www.walpoleinn.com), R.R. 1, Box 762, 297 Main St., Walpole 03608. Originally this distinguished Colonial was home to Colonel Benjamin Bellows, commander of Fort Number 3, a strategic garrison along the Connecticut River during the French and Indian Wars. Now, in another life, it offers a restaurant that's among the best in the area (see *Dining Out*) and eight quietly elegant guest rooms, each furnished in chic understatement with a pencil-post, queen-sized bed and simple, tailored linens. Four have walk-in shower; the others feature luxurious soaking tub with shower. You can choose among chess in the paneled parlor, tennis on the grounds, or golf at the nearby Hooper Golf Course. A full breakfast comes with an artist's view of meadows and hills, and is included in the $135–165 rate.

Rochambeau Lodge at Alyson's Orchard (603-756-9800; 1-800-756-0549; www.alysonsorchard.com), P.O. Box 562, Wentworth Rd., Walpole 03608. Rustic paneling and a sauna give this renovated barn, set amid acres of working apple orchard, a casual feel. Eight bedrooms, four with twin beds, two with bunks, and two with double beds, share two and a half baths. A large common area with laundry, fully equipped kitchen, living room, and a long, inviting dining table make this the ideal setting for a reunion of family or friends. The Caleb Foster Farmhouse next door adds three more bedrooms and additional kitchen and common areas. Along with pumpkin fields and 30,000 apple trees, the property features miles of trails for cross-country skiing or hiking, and there are several spring-fed ponds suitable for swimming, canoeing, and fishing. The Orchard Room across the road is available for wedding receptions and conferences. To rent the lodge for a minimum 2-night stay is $1,300; $1,800 per week. The house is $1,000 for 2 nights; $1,500 for a week. Meals, prepared by a prizewinning chef, can be provided with advance notice.

Dutch Treat (603-826-5565; www.thedutchtreat.com), P.O. Box 1004, Charlestown 03603. Open year-round. Formerly Maple Hedge, this handsome, 1820s Main Street house has been completely refurbished by Dob and Eric Lutze, natives of Holland who have also lived in Canada, England, and Austria and speak French and German. There's a Dutch theme to guest rooms with names like the Tulip Suite (our favorite) and the Delft Room, both big sunny guest rooms in the front of the house. Smaller rooms—the Lace Maker (honoring the Dutch painter Vermeer), the twin-bedded Tasman Room (named for a Dutch explorer who discovered New Zealand and Tasmania), and the Generals Room (with a picture of a forefather who fought under both Napoleon and Wellington)—are also inviting. The sunny, square dining room is elegant. There's a big comfortable parlor, wicker on the porch, and an outdoor hot tub. Dob and Eric are delighted to help guests explore the best of the area.

🦞 ✎ **Goddard Mansion** (603-543-0603; 1-800-736-0603; www.goddardmansion.com), 25 Hillstead Rd., Claremont 03743. A grand, pillared and paneled, turn-of-the-20th-century mansion set on a knoll overlooking Mount Ascutney and tiers of smaller hills. Built in 1905 as a summer home by the president of International Shoe, it has an airy, easy elegance offering 10 guest rooms. Debbie Albee has created an unusually welcoming retreat here with a splendid library, tasteful living room (featuring a 5.5-foot fireplace) and an attractive upstairs reading and writing room. Despite the grandeur of the house, small children are welcome. $85–155.

∞ **Chase House** (603-675-5391;866-401-9455; www.chasehouse.com), 1001 Rt. 12A, Cornish. This classic Federal mansion, begun around 1775, was moved back from the banks of the Connecticut River in the mid-1940s to make way for the Sullivan County Railroad. Salmon Portland Chase, born here in 1808, is remembered as Lincoln's secretary of the treasury, the namesake of the Chase Manhattan Bank, and the man on the $10,000 bill. Previous owners restored the house and added another vintage-1810 building (from Vermont) onto the back, creating a large "rafter room" designed to accommodate weddings and functions, now the specialty of the house. There are 10 guest rooms accommodating 26 people. Amenities include a hot tub, sauna, and exercise room. Current owners Paul and Terry Toms have created extensive hiking, snowshoeing, and cross-country trails on the 160-acre property, which includes frontage (across the railroad tracks) on the river. $150–225 per couple B&B.

∞ **Juniper Hill Inn** (802-674-5273; 1-800-359-2541; www.juniperhill inn.com), 153 Pembroke Rd., Windsor, Vt. 05069. This 28-room, turn-of-the-20th-century mansion, with a view of Mount Ascutney and the valley, has been beautifully renovated. Teddy Roosevelt, we were told, once spent the night in the comfortable room we occupied, one of the two rooms set off in a quiet wing of the house, beyond a second living room (with TV) and above a classic "gentlemen's library." There's a hearth in the huge main hall, in the parlors, and in the library. Of the 16 guest rooms, 11 have working fireplace. Inn guests gather for meals in the formal dining room. $115–225 per room, full breakfast included.

✳ Where to Eat

DINING OUT ⅄ **The Walpole Inn** (603-756-3320; www.walpoleinn.com), 297 Main St., Walpole. Open Tue.–Sun. for dinner 5–9, Fri. and Sat. until 9:30. Bar and lounge open from 4 PM. The menu changes weekly. The dining room, overlooking a painterly scene of rolling meadows, is simple but elegant with celery-toned paneling, exposed brick, white linen, and appealing art. Favorite menu items include pan-seared halibut with cucumber and heirloom tomato salad ($25), and a grilled Black Angus strip steak with caramelized onions, melted Gorgonzola cheese, and whipped red potatoes for the same price. Reservations recommended.

⅄ **Burdick's Bistro and Café** (603-756-2882; www.burdickchocolate .com), 47 Main St. (next to the post office), Walpole. Open Tue.–Sat. 11:30–2:30 for lunch; 5:30–9 for dinner; Sunday brunch 10–2. Also open Tue.–Sat. 7 AM–9 PM and Sun. and Mon. until 6 PM for drinks and dessert. Chocolatier extraordinaire Larry Burdick and his friend, filmmaker Ken Burns, have transformed the town's former IGA into a *très* chic dining spot. Like the decor, the menu, much of which changes daily, is understated but close to perfect. Lunch features soups, pâtés, gravlax, salads, and omelets. On a summer day we discovered how good a salad of goat cheese with red and orange beets, walnuts, and greens can be. It came with French bread and oil and a pot of tea with lemon. Dinner might be pan-roasted chicken garnished with lemon and olive oil and served with straw potatoes; or maybe a slow-roasted pork loin served with fennel over white beans. The bread is crusty; the wine list, top-notch; the chocolate desserts, to die for. Dinner entrées are $10.50–24.50; for two, figure $50 with wine.

Oona's (802-463-9830), 15 Rockingham St., Bellows Falls, Vt. Open Mon.–Sat. for lunch and dinner, tapas and music Wed. (no cover). Oona Madden's storefront restaurant is the heart of the new Bellows Falls. It's colorful and comfortable, with an eclectic menu that changes daily, moderate at lunch and upscale at dinner. It might include pan-seared lamb chops with an orange-brandy demiglaze, and a creamy barley risotto with shiitake and portobello mushrooms, sea scallops, cheddar, crisp bok choy, and beets. Dinner entrées $14.50–25.50. More music is now staged a couple of doors down at The Windham (a defunct hotel), for which Oona's offers a bar service and light fare. Call for a schedule of events and nightly specials.

Bistro Nouveau (603-542-8000; www.bistronouveau.com), 266 Washington St., Claremont. Housed in a former pizza hut on the Rt. 103/11 strip east of town (westbound lane). Open Tue.–Sat. for lunch and dinner.

Despite its unprepossessing exterior and location, this is an attractive restaurant with outstanding food at reasonable prices. Chef-owner Doug Langevin, who is Claremont born and raised but a graduate of Johnson & Wales, prides himself on his "from scratch" kitchen. Entrées might included bourbon mustard-glazed salmon and chicken saltimbocca. "Lite Fare" options might include a slow-roasted half rack of ribs and grilled Black Angus burger. Dinner entrées $15–22.

EATING OUT

Listed from south to north.

Stuart & John's Sugar House and Pancake Restaurant (603-399-4486), junction of Rts. 12 and 63 (entrance is Rt. 63), Westmoreland Depot. Open weekends (7–3) in spring (Feb.–Apr.) and fall (Sep.–Nov.). Stuart Adams

SUMPTUOUS CHOCOLATES FOR SALE AT BURDICK'S BISTRO & CAFÉ IN WALPOLE

and John Matthews have been serving up pancakes and all the fixings in their Sugar House (it now seats 98) for more than 30 years. Plenty of people drive up from Boston to sample their four different kinds of pancakes and several grades of syrup. Belgian waffles are another specialty, and of course there's sausage and bacon—but no eggs. That's where Ellie (mother of Stuart), who orchestrates this venture, draws the line. This is also one of the area's few surviving dairy farms, and sugaring is a big part of what keeps it going. Some 7,000 taps yield an aver-

OUTSIDE THE CHARLESTOWN HERITAGE DINER, A WOODEN STATUE COMMEMORATING THE PEACEFUL COEXISTENCE OF NATIVE AMERICANS AND WHITE SETTLERS
Christina Tree

age of 2,000 gallons a year, The family farm spreads across a rise above the Connecticut River. Ellie Stuart sells syrup year-round from the house beside the sugar house.

Murray's, Walpole village. Open daily 6 AM–3 PM. Walpole's longtime local hangout, this is the kind of place where everyone looks up when a stranger walks in. But that's okay; the food is great. On a summer day the pepper pot soup and fresh fruit cocktail were splendid.

&. **Walpole Village Tavern Restaurant & Bar** (603-756-3703), 10 Westminster St., Walpole village. Open Mon.–Sat. 11 AM–9 PM. Closed Sun. The menu offers the usual suspects— soups, salads, sandwiches, burgers, and fish-and-chip baskets—along with steaks and seafood. There's also a kid's menu and full bar.

Charlestown Heritage Diner (603-826-3110), 122 Main St., Charlestown. Open daily 6 AM–2 PM; Sunday, when it's 8–11:30 AM, features a buffet. Also Wed.–Sat. 4–8 PM for fresh seafood and beef specialties. This authentic 1920s Worcester diner is attached to an 1820s brick building that expands its space (there are two small dining rooms in the older building), offering a choice of atmospheres but the same blackboard menu. There's also a tavern upstairs—and the liquor license extends to the diner. The breakfast menu is huge, while "The Live Free or Die Burger" with multiple toppings in a lunch specialty.

Charlestown House of Pizza (603-836-3700), Main St., Charlestown. Open daily 10:30 AM–9 PM, Fri. and Sat. until 10. A cut above your usual pizza place, a variety of pastas, grinders, and a really good Greek salad.

Daddypops Tumble-Inn Diner
(603-542-0074), Tremont Square next
to the Moody Building, Claremont.
Open 5:30 AM–2 PM. A genuine classic
1941 Worcester diner (#778), with
blue tile, a counter, and booths, that
has received a new lease on life from
owner Debbie Carter. It's a local
hangout: The bottomless cup of coffee is 75¢, and the menu includes
scrapple and corned beef hash. Fries
are homemade. Admittedly the
"turkey soup" we had here on our last
visit tasted more like corned beef, but
it hit the spot and the coffee was
good.

China Delight (603-542-0021), 38
Opera House Square, Claremont.
Open 11–9, 9:30 Fri. and Sat. The
restaurant's new quarters are spiffy
and the food is good. No MSG.

Café Cubana (603-542-0900), 50
Pleasant St., Claremont. The bright
spot along Claremont's main drag,
open 8–6 for coffee, light food, and
Internet access, also for frequent special events such as "Chicago Speak-
easy Party" with jazz and dancing.

Farro's Deli (603-543-6700), 162
Washington St. (Rt. 103/11), Claremont. Clean, friendly with excellent
sandwiches, soups, and salads, a great
variety of healthy drinks, house-made
cookies.

SNACKS ♿ **Burdick's Bistro and
Café** (603-756-2882; www.burdick
chocolate.com), 47 Main St. (next to
the post office), Walpole. Aside from
making and selling some of the world's
best chocolates, Burdick operates a
café (his others are in Northampton
and Cambridge, Ma.) good for teas,
coffees, and varied sinful snacks.

Walpole Grocery (603-756-9098), 47
Main St. Open Mon.–Sat. 8–8, Sun.

10–5. A few doors down from Burdick's, this upscale little market offers
fabulous breads, local cheeses, and a
deli—a good picnic source.

✳ Entertainment

Claremont Opera House (603-542-
4433), Opera House Square, Claremont. A restored Gilded Age theater,
the scene of frequent concerts, plays,
and live performances.

New Falls Cinema (802-463-4766),
The Square, Bellows Falls. First-run
films.

Walpole Unitarian Church (802-
257-0182; shouston@sover.net). Contra dancing 7:30–11 PM every third
Saturday. There's a class for beginners
at 7. Admission is $5–7.

Walpole Common. Free Sun. concerts 7–8:30 PM during July and
August.

✳ Selective Shopping

ANTIQUES Claremont has become an
antiques center in recent years as
empty stores along Pleasant Street
have filled with dealers.

ART GALLERIES **Spheris Gallery of
Fine Art** (603-756-9617; www.spheris
gallery.com), 59 The Square, Bellows
Falls, Vt. Once a fixture in Walpole
village, this standout gallery has
moved across the river but still features local artists with big-time names.
Owner Cynthia Reeves was instrumental in founding Great River Arts.

Gallery on the Square (603-543-
0001), 34 Opera House Square,
Claremont. Open Tue.–Sat. 10–4.
Paintings, prints, sculptures, photography, and wood turning by local
artists and artisans.

BOOKSTORES **Village Square Booksellers** (802-463-9404; www .villagesquarebooks.com), 32 The Square, Bellows Falls, Vt. Open Mon.–Sat. 9–6, Fri. until 7, and Sun. 10–3. Patricia Fowler's independent, full-service bookstore offers poetry readings and other special programs, and also features local photography by Alan Fowler and changing work by local artists.

Ray Boas, Bookseller (603-756-9900; www.rayboasbookseller.com), 44 Elm St., Walpole. Open most days but best to call ahead if you're traveling a distance. More than 13,000 titles with an emphasis on nonfiction in a lovely old Colonial home. Decorative arts and antiques a specialty.

FOOD AND FARM STANDS **Alyson's Orchard** (603-756-9800; 1-800-856-0549; www.alysonsorchard.com), Wentworth Rd., Walpole. Some 28,000 trees cover this beautiful hilltop overlooking the Connecticut River Valley. Heritage-variety apples, peaches, pears, blueberries, raspberries, hops, and firewood are available at the farm stand in-season.

Boggy Meadow Farm (1-877-541-3953; www.boggymeadowfarm.com), 13 Boggy Meadow Lane, Walpole; location marked from Rt. 12. The 620-acre Boggy Meadow Farm has been in the Cabot family since 1820, but Powell Cabot has been producing Fanny Mason Farmstead Swiss Cheese for less than a decade. Call ahead to make sure the retail shop and cheese plant are open for tours, which frequently include a hayride. The drive along the river to the shop is a treat in itself, and the Fanny Mason cheeses are the true farmstead

variety, all made with raw milk and vegetable rennet that pasteurizes naturally during the 60-day curing process.

Allen Brothers Farms & Orchards (802-722-3395), 6–23 Rt. 5, 2 miles south of Bellows Falls, Vt. Open year-round, daily, 6 AM–9 PM. Offers pick-your-own apples and potatoes in-season, also sells vegetables, plants and seeds, honey, syrup, and Vermont gifts.

North Country Smokehouse (603-543-3016; 1-800-258-4303), Claremont. Follow signs for the airport; it's across the way on a site established by Mike Satzow's grandfather in 1917. Delis throughout the Northeast carry North Country meats: hams, turkey, bacon, smoked goose and Peking duck, sausages, and more. Inquire about the catalog.

Claremont Farmer's Market (603-542-8687), Broad Street Park, downtown Claremont. Mid-June–Oct., Thur. 4–7. Locally grown vegetables, homemade baked goods and crafts, live music in the evening.

Also see **Stuart & John's Sugar House** under *Eating Out*.

SPECIAL STORES **Burdick's Bistro and Café** (603-756-2882; www .burdickchocolate.com), 47 Main St. (next to the post office), Walpole. Exquisite, hand-cut chocolates made from French Valrhona chocolate without extracts or flavorings are crafted in the small shop and shipped to the best Manhattan restaurants and customers throughout the country. We can attest to the quality of the mocha square and white pepper truffle. Burdick's signature is a chocolate mouse, handmade with toasted almond ears. Combined with the excellent bistro

Christina Tree

THE CLAREMONT FARMERS MARKET IS A POPULAR STOP IN BROAD STREET PARK EVERY THURSDAY FROM SUMMER TO FALL

and bakery (see *Dining Out*), this is a must-stop.

Ruggles & Hunt (603-756-9607; www.rugglesandhunt.com), 8 Westminster St., Walpole. Open Mon.–Sat. 11–6. An urbane country store (in this case, the oxymoron is accurate) offering colorful and unusual gifts, household furnishings, and men's, women's, and children's clothing and accessories from around the world.

Sam's Outdoor Outfitters (802-463-3500; www.samsoutdoor.com), 78 The Square, Bellows Falls, Vt., bills itself as "the biggest little store in the world." A branch of the Brattleboro store but still big.

✳ Special Events

See **The Fort at No. 4** (*To See*) for ongoing special events.

July: **Charlestown Yard Sale Day**, from 8 AM on the third Saturday; more than 150 yard sales in town, church breakfasts.

UPPER VALLEY TOWNS

The Upper Valley ignores state lines to form one of New England's most rewarding and distinctive regions.

Upper Valley is a name coined in the 1950s by a local daily, *The Valley News*, to define its two-state circulation area. The label has stuck, interestingly enough, to the group of towns that back in the 1770s tried to form the state of "New Connecticut." The Dartmouth-based, pro–New Connecticut party was, however, thwarted (see the introduction to "Connecticut River Valley").

In 1769 Eleazar Wheelock had moved his Indian school—which had been funded through appeals made by Mohegan preacher Samson Occum in England and Scotland to "spread Christian knowledge among the Savages"—from Lebanon, Ct., to Hanover, N.H. Initially Dartmouth College recruited Indian students, many from St. Francis, but the school also served white students and the percentage of Indians quickly dwindled.

The valley itself prospered in the late 18th and early 19th centuries, as evidenced by the exquisite Federal-era meetinghouses and mansions still salted throughout this area. The river was the area's only highway in the 18th and early 19th centuries and was still a popular steamboat route in the years before the Civil War.

The Upper Valley phonebook includes towns on both sides of the river, and Hanover's Dresden School District reaches into Vermont (this was the first bistate school district in the United States). Several Independence Day parades start in one state and finish across the bridge in the other. The Montshire Museum, founded in Hanover but now in Norwich, Vt., combines both states in its very name.

Dartmouth College in Hanover remains the cultural center of the Upper Valley. With the nearby Dartmouth-Hitchcock medical complex and West Lebanon shopping strip, this area forms the region's hub, handy to the highways radiating, the way rail lines once did, from White River Junction, Vt. North and south of the Hanover area, old river towns drowse and the river roads are well worth finding.

GUIDANCE **White River Welcome Center** (802-281-5050) in the railroad station in White River Junction, Vt. Open daily 9–5. This waypoint center staffed

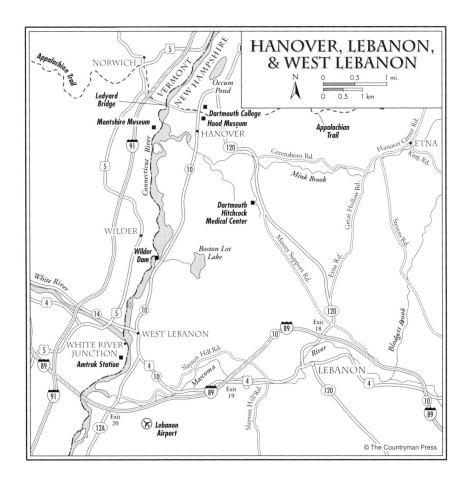

by the Hartford (Vt.) Chamber of Commerce offers friendly, knowledgeable advice and restrooms; it adjoins an evolving New England Transportation Institute and Museum. Also see www.ctrivertravel.com.

Hanover Chamber of Commerce (603-643-3115; www.hanoverchamber.org), 126 Nugget Building, Main St., maintains a seasonal (early June–Sep.) information booth (603-643-3512) on the Dartmouth green, staffed by helpful Dartmouth students and alums.

The Greater Lebanon Chamber of Commerce (603-448-1203; www .lebanonchamber.com), 1 School St. (next to the post office) is open weekdays 9–5 and maintains a seasonal information center across the street in Colburn Park (8:30–4:40).

GETTING THERE *By car:* Interstates 91 and 89 intersect in the White River Junction (Vt.)–Lebanon (New Hampshire) area, where they also meet Rt. 5 north and south on the Vermont side; Rt. 4, the main east–west highway through central Vermont; and Rt. 10, the river road on the New Hampshire side.

By bus: White River Junction, Vt., is a hub for **Vermont Transit** (1-800-552-8737; www.vermonttransit.com) with express service to Boston. **Dartmouth Coach** (1-800-637-0123; www.concordtrailways.com) offers aggressively competitive service from Boston and Logan Airport to Hanover.

By air: The **Lebanon Regional Airport** (603-298-8878), West Lebanon (marked from the junction of I-89 and Rt. 10), has frequent service to New York's LaGuardia Airport via US Airways Express, which also serves Philadelphia. Rental cars are available from Avis, Hertz, and Alamo; the airport is also served by **Big Yellow Taxi** (603-643-8294).

By train: **Amtrak** (1-800-872-7245) serves White River Junction, Vt., en route to and from New York/Washington and Essex Junction, Vt. Connecting bus service to Montreal.

MEDICAL EMERGENCY **Dartmouth-Hitchcock Medical Center** (603-650-5000) off Rt. 120 between Hanover and Lebanon is generally considered the best hospital in northern New England.

Call **911**.

✳ Communities

Listed from south to north.

Cornish. In the 1880s these riverside hills were far more open, mowed by thousands of sheep, but the wool bubble had already burst and farms were selling cheap. Many were bought by artists and writers, friends of sculptor **Augustus Saint-Gaudens** whose home is now a National Historic Site. By the turn of the 20th century 40 families had bought old farms or built homes in Cornish and neighboring Plainfield. This "Cornish Colony" included artists, writers, and other creative and wealthy bohemians, prominent in their own right. It also included artist Ellen Wilson, whose husband, President Woodrow Wilson, spent a portion of the summers of 1914 and 1915 here at the home of writer Winston Churchill (note the historic marker near the Plainfield–Cornish line). Best remembered of the artists is Maxfield Parrish (1870–1966), in whose honor 11 miles of Rt. 12A in Cornish and Plainfield has recently been named the Maxfield Parrish Highway.

Plainfield. A one-street village, Plainfield still clings to the memory of onetime resident Maxfield Parrish. In the 1920s Parrish painted a stage set in the **Plainfield Town Hall** picturing Mount Ascutney and the river in the deep blues for which he is famous (open Sun.). Stop by the vintage-1798 building to see if it's open. You might also want to follow **River Road,** where you'll find produce at local farms.

Lebanon (population: 14,000). As near to the junction of I-91 and I-89 as it can be while still on the New Hampshire (no-sales-tax) side of the Connecticut River, "West Leb" is the shopping center of the Upper Valley. The strip of malls is a good bet for most basics, and the **Powerhouse Mall** (north of I-89) offers some pleasant surprises. Positioned between the Connecticut River and Mascoma Lake, with old mills lining the Mascoma River, Lebanon itself—once you find it (east on Rt. 4)—is a city with a small-town feel. The common is circled by handsome buildings—a vintage-1828 church, substantial homes, and public buildings, including an opera house—and is the site of summer band concerts. Shops and restaurants are found along adjoining traffic-free streets.

Canaan Center is a classic hill town: a proud, old agricultural community left high and dry when the railroad came through in the 1860s and the town's business shifted to the area (now the village of Canaan) 3 miles down the road, around the depot. Like Old Deerfield Village in Massachusetts, the houses here—a few 18th-century homes and the rest built before 1850—line a single street, and over the years the community itself has become known as **Canaan Street**. Its unusual beauty—and that of its lake—was recognized early on; the train to Canaan soon began bringing summer tourists, hotels opened to accommodate them, and an elaborate pier was built. The **Canaan Historic Museum** (open July–Oct., Sat. 1–4 PM) displays souvenir dishes with CANAAN STREET and color pictures printed on them.

Hanover is synonymous with Ivy League **Dartmouth College** (www .dartmouth.edu), chartered in 1769 and one of the most prestigious colleges in the country. Dartmouth's student population averages 4,300 undergraduate men and women and 600 graduate students. Its handsome buildings frame three sides of an elm- and maple-lined green, and the fourth side includes a large inn, an arts center, and an outstanding art museum. The information booth on the green is the starting point for historical and architectural tours of the campus. **Baker Memorial Library**, a 1920s version of Philadelphia's Independence Hall, dominates the northern side of the green. Visitors are welcome to see a set of murals, *The Epic of American Civilization*, by José Clemente Orozco, painted between 1932 and 1934 while he was teaching at Dartmouth. (Some alumni once demanded these be removed or covered because of the Mexican artist's left-wing politics.) In the Treasure Room (near the western stair hall on the main floor), Daniel Webster's copies of the double elephant folio first edition of John Audubon's *Birds of America* are permanently displayed. The **Hopkins Center for the Arts** (603-646-2422) was designed by Wallace Harrison a few years before he designed New York's Lincoln Center (which it resembles). It contains three theaters, a recital hall, and art galleries for permanent and year-round programs of plays, concerts, and films. It's also home base for the Dartmouth Symphony Orchestra. **Dartmouth Row**, a file of four striking, white Colonial buildings on the rise along the eastern side of the green, represents all there was to Dartmouth College until 1845. You might also want to find Webster Cottage, maintained as a museum by the Hanover Historical Society, and the vintage-1843 **Shattuck Observatory** (open weekdays 8:30–4:40, also Tue. and Thu. evening by reservation: 603-646-2034).

Lyme is known for its splendid **Congregational church**, completed in 1812, a Federal-style meetinghouse complete with Palladian window, an unusual tower (three cubical stages and an octagonal dome), and no fewer than 27 numbered horse stalls. The gathering of buildings, including the inn, fine old houses, and general stores, is one of New Hampshire's most stately. Take **River Road** north by old farms and cemeteries, through an 1880s covered bridge.

Orford is known for its **Ridge Houses**, a center-of-town lineup of seven houses so strikingly handsome that Charles Bulfinch has been (erroneously) credited as their architect. They were built instead by skilled local craftsmen using designs from Connecticut Valley architect Asher Benjamin's do-it-yourself guide to Federal styles, *The Country Builder's Apprentice*. These houses testify to the prosperity of this valley in the post–Revolutionary War era. Each was built by an Orford resident—with money earned in Orford—between 1773 and 1839. The best remembered of the residents is Samuel Morey. While all his neighbors were in church one Sunday morning in 1793, Morey gave the country's first little steam-powered paddle-wheeler a successful test run on the river. Sam kept tinkering with the boat and in 1797 came up with a side-wheeler, but at this point Robert Fulton, who had encouraged Morey to talk freely with him and demonstrate the invention, went into the steamboating business, using a boat clearly patterned after Morey's. It's said that an embittered Morey sank his boat across the river in the Vermont lake that now bears his name. He also heated and lighted his house with gas, and in 1826 he patented a gas-powered internal combustion engine. The **Samuel Morey House** is the oldest of the seven, a centerpiece for the others.

✳ Must-See

The Vermont Instiute of Natural Science/Vermont Raptor Center (802-FLY-5000; www.vinsweb.org), Rt. 4, Quechee, Vt. Open daily year-round, Mon.–Sat. 10–4, until 5:30 in summer; $8 adults, $7.20 seniors, $6.50 children. A beloved institution, VINS is a living museum devoted to birds of prey, located just west of Quechee Gorge. Resident rators include bald eagles, peregrine falcons, snowy owls, and hawks that have been injured. They are displayed in large

THE GREAT STONE DWELLING AT ENFIELD SHAKER VILLAGE

Christina Tree

Hood Museum of Art, Dartmouth College (603-646-2808; www.hoodmuseum
.dartmouth.edu), on the Dartmouth Green, Hanover. Closed Mon.; open
Tue.–Sat., 10–5, Wed. until 9; Sun. noon–5 Free. An outstanding collection of
world-class art from almost every geographical area of the world and historical period. Featuring ninth-century Assyrian reliefs from the Palace of
Ashurnarsipal II at Nimrod (present day Iraq), European Old Master prints
and painting, two centuries of American paintings, portraits, drawings, and
watercolors; American decorative arts; ancient and Asian objects; traditional and contemporary African, Oceanic, and Native American collections,
cutting-edge contemporary art; stunning set of murals by Jose Clemente
Orozco. Two floors of galleries, permanent collections, traveling exhibitions.
Explore on your own or arrange for a tour by calling (603) 646-1469. Hood
Museum of Art Shop has something for all ages and budgets.

DARTMOUTH ROW BY ANN FRANCES RAY, CA. 1840, COURTESY OF THE HOOD
MUSEUM OF ART

Hood Museum of Art

outdoor enclosures. There are outdoor interpretive exhibits, nature trails, and a
nature shop. Inquire about naturalist walks and flight programs.

HISTORIC SITES Enfield Shaker Museum (603-632-4346; www.shaker
museum.org), Rt. 4A, Lower Shaker Village, Enfield, marked from I-89, Exit 17.
Open Memorial Day–Oct., Mon.–Sat. 10–5, Sun. noon–5; Nov.–mid-May open
weekends, closing at 4. $7 adults, $6 seniors, $3 ages 10–18. The Shaker commu-
nity, founded in 1793 in this "Chosen Vale" between Mount Assurance and Mascoma Lake, prospered through the 19th century, and 13 buildings survive. In

The Saint-Gaudens National Historic Site (603-675-2175; www.nps.gov/saga), Rt. 12A, Cornish. Grounds open daily, dawn–dusk. Buildings open 9–4:30 daily late May–Oct. $5 adults (good for a week); free under age 17. This glorious property with a view of Mount Ascutney includes the sculptor's summer home and studio, sculpture court, and formal gardens, which he developed and occupied between 1885 and his death in 1907. Augustus Saint-Gaudens (1848–1907) is remembered primarily for public pieces: the Shaw memorial on Boston Common, the statue of Admiral Farragut in New York's Madison Square, the equestrian statue of General William T. Sherman at the Fifth Avenue entrance to Central Park, and the *Standing Lincoln* in Chicago's Lincoln Park. He was also the first sculptor to design an American coin (the $10 and $20 gold pieces of 1907). His home, Aspet, is furnished much as it was when he lived there. A visitor center features a 28-minute film about the artist and his work. Augustus Saint-Gaudens loved the Ravine Trail, a 0.25-mile cart path to Blow-Me-Up Brook, now marked for visitors, and other walks laid out through the woodlands and wetlands of the Blow-

VIEW OF MOUNT ASCUTNEY FROM THE HOUSE AND GARDENS OF THE SAINT-GAUDENS NATIONAL HISTORIC SITE

U.S. Department of the Interior, National Park Service, Saint-Gaudens National Historic Site, Cornish, NH

U.S. Department of the Interior, National Park Service, Saint-Gaudens National Historic Site, Cornish, NH

THE ADAMS MEMORIAL AT THE SAINT-GAUDENS NATIONAL HISTORIC SITE, COMMISSIONED BY HISTORIAN HENRY ADAMS FOR THE GRAVESITE OF HIS WIFE, MARION HOOPER ADAMS

Me-Down Natural Area. Saint-Gaudens was the center of the "Cornish Colony," a group of poets, artists, landscape artists, actors, architects, and writers who included Ethel Barrymore, Charles Dana Gibson, Finley Peter Dunne, and Maxfield Parrish; President Woodrow Wilson's wife was drawn into this circle, and the president summered at a nearby home from 1913 to 1915. *Note:* Bring a picnic lunch for Sunday-afternoon chamber music concerts, at 2 PM in July and August.

1927 the complex was sold to the Catholic order of La Salette, which added a basilica-shaped chapel. In the 1980s the order sold the buildings to developers, and the Great Stone Dwelling—said to be the largest Shaker dwelling anywhere—was restored as an inn but has since been occupied by the museum and its gift shop. Note the single stone commemorating the resting place of 330 Shakers. You might want to climb the dirt road that begins next to the stone shop; it's a steep 0.5-mile walk to the holy Feast Ground of the Shakers of Chosen Vale. Inquire about special events. The La Salette brothers still maintain a shrine and center (603-632-4301) here.

✐ **Montshire Museum of Science** (802-649-2200; www.montshire.org), 1 Montshire Rd., Norwich, Vt. Open daily 10–5 except Thanksgiving, Christmas, and New Year's Day; $7.50 adults, $6.50 ages 3–17. Use of the trails is free. Few cities have a science museum of this quality. Happily this hands-on science center is on 110 trail-webbed acres beside the Connecticut River. The name derives from Ver*mont* and New Hamp*shire*, and the focus is on demystifying natural phenomena in the world in general and in the Upper Valley in particular. River exhibits include an elaborate 2.5-acre Science Park: Water bubbles from a 7-foot Barre granite boulder, and from this "headwater" a 250-foot "rill" flows downhill, snaking over a series of terraces, inviting you to manipulate dams and sluices to change its flow and direction (visitors are advised to bring towels). You can also shape fountains, cast shadows to tell time, and push a button to identify the call of birds and insects within actual hearing. Note Ed Kahn's *Wind Wall*, a billboard-sized sheet attached to the museum's tower, composed of thousands of silver flutter disks that shimmer in the breeze, resembling patterns on a pond riffled by wind.

Inside the museum a new, federally funded wing focuses on this stretch of the Silvio O. Conte National Fish and Wildlife Refuge; exhibits include a giant moose and tanks of gleaming local fish. Still, some of our favorite exhibits are in the original museum: the fog machine up in the tower, the see-through beehive, exhibits illustrating which vegetables and fruits float, and the physics of bubbles. There are also astounding displays on moths, insects, and birds. Most exhibits, even the boa constrictors (at designated times), are "hands-on." While there's a corner for toddlers, an outside playground, and many demonstrations geared to youngsters, this is as stimulating a place for adults as for their offspring. The gift shop alone is worth stopping for. Inquire about guided hikes, special events, and exhibits. In summer and fall the excursion train **White River Flyer** (1-800-707-3530) offers round-trip excursions from Union Depot in White River Junction, Vt., up along the Connecticut River to the museum.

THE CORNISH–WINDSOR COVERED BRIDGE WITH MOUNT ASCUTNEY IN THE BACKGROUND

Webster Cottage (603-646-3371), N. Main St., Hanover (two blocks north of the green). Memorial Day–Columbus Day, Wed., Sat., and Sun. 2:30–4:30 and by appointment. Built in 1780 as the home of Abigail Wheelock (daughter of Dartmouth founder Eleazar Wheelock), it was also the senior-year (1801) residence of Daniel Webster and birthplace in 1822 of Henry Fowle Durant, founder of Wellesley College. Maintained as a museum by the Hanover Historical Society.

COVERED BRIDGES At 460 feet the **Cornish–Windsor covered bridge**, Rt. 12A, said to be the country's longest covered bridge, is certainly the most photographed in New England. A lattice truss design, built in 1866, it was rebuilt in 1989. There are also three more covered bridges in Cornish, all dating from the early 1880s: Two span Mill Brook—one in Cornish City and the other in Cornish Mills between Rt.s 12A and 120—and the third spans Blow-Me-Down Brook (off Rt. 12A). On the Meriden road in Plainfield another 1880s, 85-foot bridge spans Bloods Brook. Near the Lyme–Orford line the **Lyme–Edgell bridge** (154 feet long) spans Clay Brook (off Rt. 10).

✳ To Do

AIR RIDES **Post Mills Airport** (802-333-9254), West Fairlee, Vt. Mid-May–mid-Nov., Brian Boland offers morning and sunset balloon rides (he spends the other 6 months in New Zealand). On the summer evening we tried it, the balloon hovered above hidden pockets in the hills, and we saw a herd of what looked like brown and white goats that, on closer inspection, proved to be deer (yes, some were white!). After an hour or so we settled down gently in a farmyard and broke out the champagne. Boland builds as well as flies hot air balloons and maintains a private museum of balloons and airships. He also maintains rustic cabins on the premises for patrons ($50 per night) and offers packages in

conjunction with nearby **Silver Maple Lodge** (1-800-666-1946; www.silver
maplelodge.com), which includes the balloon rides on its web site.

BICYCLING Given its unusually flat and scenic roads and well-spaced inns, this
area is beloved by bicyclists. Search out the river roads (for some reason they're
not marked on the official New Hampshire highway map): from Rt. 12A (just
north of the Saint-Gaudens site) on through Plainfield until it rejoins Rt. 12A;
from Rt. 10 north of Hanover (just north of the Chieftain Motel) through Lyme,
rejoining Rt. 10 in Orford. A classic, 36-mile loop is Hanover to Orford on Rt. 10
and back on the river road. The loop to Lyme and back is 22 miles. For inn-to-
inn guided tours in this area, contact **Bike Vermont** (802-457-3553; 1-800-257-
2226; www.bikevermont.com). The Sugar River Trail, a multiuse recreational
path, follows the Sugar River east from Charlestown to Newport. Inquire about
the evolving Northern Rail Trail along the Mascoma.

BOATING With its usually placid water and scenery, the Connecticut River
through much of the Upper Valley is ideal for easygoing canoeists. The Connecticut River Joint Commissions (603-826-4800; www.ctrivertravel.net) has
published a useful *Boating on the Connecticut River* guide. Information on
primitve campsites along this stretch of the river can be found on the web site
maintained by the Upper Valley Land Trust (www.uvlt.org).

The most frequently photographed reach of the Upper Connecticut is the 3
miles above the Cornish–Windsor covered bridge, set against the dramatic lone
peak of Mount Ascutney. This is part of a popular 12-mile paddle that begins
just below Sumner Falls, 0.5 mile of rolling water and jagged rock worth men-
tioning because it's so deceptive and so deadly.

✍ **North Star Livery** (603-542-6929; www.kayak-canoe.com), 58 Bridge St.,
White River Junction.,Vt. With over 90 boats, including 30 kayaks, this is the
largest and oldest commercial rental service on the Connecticut River. For more,
see the description of its home base in Cornish ("Lower Connecticut").

The Ledyard Canoe Club (603-643-6709), Hanover, is billed as the oldest
canoe club in America. It's named for a 1773 Dartmouth dropout who felled a
pine tree, hollowed it out, and took off downriver (with a copy of Ovid), ending
up at Hartford, 100 miles and several major waterfalls downstream. Hidden on
the riverbank north of the Ledyard Bridge, down beyond Dartmouth's slick new
rowing center, Ledyard is a mellow, friendly, student-run place. The canoeing
and kayaking center for the 40 river miles above Wilder Dam, it offers kayaking
clinics as well as canoe and kayak rentals. No shuttle service.

Fairlee Marine (802-333-9745), Rt. 5 in Fairlee, Vt., rents pontoons, canoes,
and rowboats, and small motors for use on the Connecticut and two local lakes.

FISHING You can eat the fish you catch in the Connecticut River—it yields
brown and rainbow trout above Orford. There's a boat launch on the Vermont
side at the Wilder Dam, another just north of Hanover, and another across the
river in North Thetford, Vt. Lake Mascoma (look for boat launches along Rt. 4A
in Enfield) and Post Pond in Lyme are other popular angling spots.

Lyme Angler (603-643-6447; www.lymeangler.com), 8 S. Main St., Hanover. This is an Orvis outfitter and guide service offering a "Fly-Fishing School." Guided trips, fly-tying classes, rental equipment, and a shop selling fishing clothing and gear.

GOLF **Hanover Country Club** (603-646-2000), Rope Ferry Rd., off Rt. 10, Hanover. Open May–Oct. Founded in 1899, an 18-hole facility with 4 practice holes, pro shop, and PGA instructors. **Carter Golf Club** (603-448-4483), Rt. 4, Lebanon. Nine holes, par 36. **Lake Morey Country Club** (802-333-4800; 1-800-423-1211), Fairlee, Vt. Eighteen holes. **Windsor Country Club** (802-674-6491), Windsor, Vt. Nine holes, par 34, no lessons. **Fore-U Driving Range** (603-298-9702), Rt. 12A, West Lebanon. Buckets of balls to hit off mats or grass; 18-hole miniature golf course.

HEALTH CLUBS **CCBA (Carter-Witherell Center)** (603-448-6477), 1 Taylor St., Lebanon. Nonmembers can purchase day passes to use the facilities of this community health center: $12 adults, $5 children (for use of pool only). Includes use of pool, whirlpool, and saunas; exercise and weight room; tennis and basketball courts; and child care. Call for hours.

River Valley Club (603-643-7720), Centerra Marketplace, Rt. 120, Lebanon. Open daily, 24 hours. $20 per day. Offers day spa services to nonmembers in its luxurious facility: massages, herbal wraps, facials, hydrotherapy, and more. Call for rates. Also included is same-day use of all facilities, including indoor and outdoor pools, whirlpool and sauna, exercise and weight room, fitness classes, and child care. A climbing wall, hair salon, and café lounge are also part of the complex.

HIKING **The Appalachian Trail** crosses the Connecticut River over the Ledyard Bridge and runs right through Hanover on its way to Mount Katahdin in Maine; note the marker embedded in the sidewalk in front of the Hanover Inn. Follow the white blazes down South Main Street to find where the trail reenters the woods just past the Hanover Food Co-op.

Short hikes in the Hanover area itself abound; a map of area trails is available from the Hanover Chamber of Commerce. Inquire locally or pick up the *Dartmouth Outing Guide*, published by the Dartmouth Outing Club. Suggested hikes include **Balch Hill Summit** north of town, the **Mink Brook Trail** off S. Main St., **Smarts Mountain** in Lyme, **Mount Cube** in Orford, and **Moose Mountain** (another section of the AT) in Etna. The westernmost peak in the White Mountains range, 4,802-foot-high Mount Moosilauke, is 50 miles north of Hanover, visible from much of the Upper Valley.

RAILROAD EXCURSION ♪ **Trains Around Vermont** (802-463-3069; 1-800-707-3530; www.rails-vt.com), Union Depot, White River Junction, Vt. Take a round trip along the Connecticut River to the Montshire Museum on the White River Flyer.

OUTDOOR ADVENTURE ❧ **Dartmouth Outdoor Rentals** (603-646-1747), in the basement of Robinson Hall, on the Dartmouth green, Hanover. Open Mon.–Fri., 7:30–noon. The country's oldest collegiate outing club rents a full line of outdoor equipment to the general public: mountain bikes and helmets, in-line skates, telemark and cross-country skis, snowshoes, rock climbing equipment, and a full line of camping gear. The scruffy, student-run rental office can be hard to reach, but keep trying.

SWIMMING Ask locally about swimming holes in the Connecticut River and public swimming in Lake Mascoma in Enfield.

Canaan Street Lake offers a small town beach on Canaan St.

✍ **Storrs Pond Recreation Area** (603-643-2134), off Rt. 10 north of Hanover (Reservoir Rd., then left). Open June–Labor Day, 10–8. Bathhouse with showers and lockers, lifeguards at both the (unheated) Olympic-sized pool and 15-acre pond. Fee for nonmembers.

❧ ✍ **Treasure Island** (802-333-9615), on Lake Fairlee, Thetford, Vt. This fabulous town swimming area is on Rt. 244 (follow Rt. 113 north of town). Open late June–Labor Day, 10–8 weekends, noon–8 weekdays. Sand beach, picnic tables, playground, tennis. Nominal admission.

Union Village Dam Recreation Area (802-649-1606), Thetford, Vt. Open Memorial Day–mid-Sep.; five swimming areas along the Ompompanoosuc River. Also has walking and cross-country skiing trails, picnic tables, and grills.

✳ Winter Sports

CROSS-COUNTRY SKIING **Dartmouth Cross Country Ski Center** (603-643-6534), Rope Ferry Rd. (off Rt. 10 just before the country club), Hanover. Open in season, Mon.–Fri. 9–7, weekends 9–7. Twenty-five km of trails through Storrs Pond and Oak Hill areas; rentals, lessons, waxing clinics. The center is on the lower level of the Outing Club House.

Lake Morey Inn Resort (802-333-4800; 1-800-423-1211), Fairlee, Vt. Turns the golf course into a touring center in winter; rentals, instruction.

DOWNHILL SKIING ✍ **Dartmouth Skiway** (603-795-2143; www.skiway.dart mouth.edu), Lyme Center, an amenity for families as well as the college, with a snazzy 16,000-square-foot timber base lodge. Open 9–4 daily; rentals and ski school. *Trails:* 32. *Lifts:* 1 quad chair, 1 double chair, a beginners' J-bar. *Vertical drop:* 968 feet. *Snowmaking:* 65 percent. *Rates:* $38 adults, $25 juniors on weekends; $26 and $18 weekdays; also half-day, senior, military, and more rates.

Whaleback Mountain (603-448-1489; www.whaleback.com), I-89 Exit 16. Zero Gravity Skate Park open year-round, winter hours with skiing/snowboarding: weekdays 12 noon–9, Sat. 9–9., Sun. 9–4:30. This beloved family mountain, just off I-89, is now an "action sports center." Reopened under new, local ownership in 2006, it offers 35 trails served by a double chair and 4 surface lifts (with 80 percent snowmaking) and night skiing. What's new: a renovated baselodge, indoor and outdoor skate parks and seasonal mountain biking. Planned: a water ramp, BMX track and paint ball. Staff is headed by two-time Olympian Evan Dybvig and it's all about teaching action sports. Weekday ski/snowboard rates: $25 adult, $20 at night skating, $12.

ICE SKATING **Occom Pond**, next to the country club, Hanover. Kept plowed and planed, lighted evenings until 10 unless unsafe for skating; warming hut.

Ascutney Mountain Resort (802-484-7771), Rt. 44, Brownsville, Vt. Lighted skating rink with rental skates.

✳ Green Space

Pine Park, just north of the Dartmouth campus between the Hanover Country Club and the Connecticut River, Hanover. Take N. Main St. to Rope Ferry Rd. Park at the trail sign above the clubhouse. These tall pines along the river are one of the beauty spots of the valley. The 125-year-old trees were saved from the Diamond Match Company in 1900 by a group of local citizens. The walk is 1.5 miles.

Rinker Tract, Rt. 10, 2.5 miles north of Hanover. This is an 18-acre knoll with a pond at the bottom of the hill below the Chieftain Motel. The loop trail is marked by blue blazes.

The city of Lebanon maintains several wooded parks for which trail maps are available from the recreation department, just inside the door of city hall (on the common). These include **Farnum Hill**, an 820-acre property with a ridge trail commanding some magnificent views. On the Connecticut River, **Chambers Park** (just off Rt. 10) offers trails through riverbank terrace, upland forest, and open field. The 286-acre **Boston Lot** lies between the river and the city reservoir, with trails good for hiking, biking, and cross-country skiing, and with picnic tables on the northern edge of the reservoir. **Goodwin Park**, adjoining Storrs Hill Ski Area, offers a 1.5-mile exercise trail.

✳ Lodging

HOTELS 🐾 ✍ ♿ **The Hanover Inn** (603-643-4300; 1-800-443-7024; www .hanoverinn.com), corner of Maine and South Wheelock sts., Hanover 03755. This is the Ritz of the North Country. It overlooks the Dartmouth green and exudes a distinctly tweedy elegance. Guest rooms are each individually and deftly decorated, and the junior suites—with canopy beds, eiderdown quilts, armchairs, a silent valet, couch, and vanity—are pamperingly luxurious. A four-story, 92-room, neo-Georgian building owned and operated by Dartmouth College, the "inn" traces itself back to 1780 when the college's steward, General Ebenezer Brewster, turned his home into a tavern. Brewster's son parlayed this enterprise into the Dartmouth Hotel, which continued to thrive until 1887, when it burned to the ground. The present building dates in part from this era but has lost its Victorian lines through successive renovations and expansions. It remains, however, the heart of Hanover. In summer the front terrace is crowded with faculty, visitors, and residents enjoying a light lunch or beer. Year-round the lobby, the porch rocking chairs, and the Hayward Lounge (a comfortable sitting room with claw-foot sofas and flowery armchairs, dignified portraits, and a frequently lit hearth) are popular spots for friends to meet. Roughly half the inn's guests are Dartmouth related. Both Zins Wine Bistro and the more formal Daniel Webster Room (see *Dining Out*) draw patrons from throughout the Upper Valley. Rates range from $260 for a standard room to $310 for a junior suite, no charge for children under age 12; senior citizens' discount; honeymoon, ski, golf, and seasonal packages. Handicapped accessible and pets accepted.

The Hotel Coolidge (802-295-3118; 1-800-622-1124; www.hotel coolidge.com), White River Junction, VT 05001, is one of the last of the old railroad hotels. It's located in a railroad town that's undergoing a small renaissance with some good shopping and dining. All 30 elevator-served guest rooms have private bath, phone, and TV. Some back rooms are dark, but others are quite roomy and attractive, and the family suites (two rooms connected by a bath) are a real bargain. We'd request Room 100, or a similar suite. The hotel sits across from the Amtrak station and next to the Briggs Opera House. Local buses to Hanover and Lebanon stop at the door, and rental cars can be arranged. Search out the splendid Peter Michael Gish murals in the Vermont Room, painted in 1950 in exchange for room and board while the artist was studying with Paul Sample at Dartmouth. Owner-manager David Briggs, a seventh-generation Vermonter, takes his role as innkeeper seriously and will arrange for special needs. $79–129 per room double. Under 17 free.

INNS ⅙ ⊙ **Home Hill Country Inn** (603-675-6165; www.home hillinn.com), River Rd., Plainfield 03781. Built in 1818, this is one of those magnificent, four-square mansions spaced along the Connecticut River (see the introduction to this chapter); it sits at the end of a 3.5-mile road, surrounded by 25 acres. Innkeepers Victoria and Stephane de Roure have renovated the main house to offer three elegant guest rooms and a two-room suite; there are also six "country French" guest rooms in the Carriage House. A small cottage, La Piscine, with a bedroom and sitting room, is beside the pool. $195–425 per couple includes breakfast and afternoon refreshments. Add a 15 percent service fee. A 2-night package including two chef's tasting menus with pairings is $1,279–1,735. Beautiful as it is, this inn is all about outstanding food; check *Dining Out*.

Moose Mountain Lodge (603-643-3529; www.themoosemountain lodge.com), P.O. Box 272, Moose Mountain Highway, Etna 03750. Closed Mon. and Tue., also Nov.–Dec. 25 and late Mar.–mid-June. Just 7 miles from the Dartmouth green, the feel is remote, and the view, quite possibly the most spectacular of any inn in New England. The design is "classic lodge," built from stones and logs cleared from these hills, walled in pine. The roomy back porch (filled with flowers in summer) is like a balcony seat above the valley, commanding a view of Vermont mountains from Ascutney to Sugarbush, with Killington off across lower hills, center stage. This is also the view from the sitting room, with its window seats, baby grand piano, and massive stone fireplace.

Kay Shumway

MOOSE MOUNTAIN LODGE IN ETNA

Upstairs the 12 rooms are small but inviting (with spruce log bedsteads made by Kay Shumway herself), and the 5 shared baths are immaculate. Kay is justly famed as a cook and, increasingly, as a cookbook author. As she continues to prepare feasts for the groups of hikers (the inn is just off the Appalachian Trail), bikers, and cross-country skiers, her fare is evolving with many creative vegetarian dishes. Kay and Peter Shumway have been innkeepers here since 1975 and still welcome each new guest with enthusiasm and interest. The 350 acres include a deep pond, ample woods, meadows, and access to 50 miles of dependably snowy cross-country ski trails. $220 per couple in winter, $200 in summer includes breakfast and dinner; $55 under age 14. No smoking.

🐾 Norwich Inn (802-649-1143; www.norwichinn.com), 325 Main St., Norwich, VT 05055. Just across the river from Hanover and less formal and less expensive than the Hanover Inn, this is very much a gathering place for Dartmouth parents, faculty, and students. The present three-story, tower-topped inn dates from 1889 (when its predecessor burned). Since acquiring it in 1991, innkeepers Sally and Tim Wilson have steadily worked to restore its high-Victorian look inside and out. The 27 rooms are divided among the main building, the Vestry, and a backyard motel. All rooms have private bath, telephone, and cable TV. Sally has redecorated with a sure touch, adding Victorian antiques but not cluttering either the guest or public rooms. A brewpub, Jasper Murdock's Alehouse, features 15 varieties of inn-made brew (see *Eating Out*). The dining rooms are open for breakfast, lunch, and dinner. Rates run from $69 in the off-season in the motel and $109 in the inn to $149 for a two-bedroom suite in the Vestry. All three meals are served but not included. Dogs are permitted in one twin-bedded room in the motel.

Alden Country Inn (603-795-2222; 1-800-794-2296; www.aldencountry inn.com), On The Common, Lyme 03768. Dating back to 1809, this substantial inn stands at the head of a classic common, offering three daily meals as well as 15 guest rooms (on the top two floors). All have private bath, phone, and air-conditioning. Frank and Darlene Godoy have renovated rooms; high-speed wireless access is available throughout. $130–195 in summer and fall, from $95 in winter, includes a full breakfast. Two-night stay required on weekends.

BED & BREAKFASTS

Listed from south to north.

Shaker Hill B&B (603-632-4519; www.shakerhill.com), 259 Shaker Hill, Enfield 03748. This is a gem, a big, airy white house with a wraparound porch, much expanded from the Jewett Farmhouse that forms its core. It was here in the 1790s that the first group of Shakers lived before building their village (presently preserved in part as a museum). The four guest rooms are decorated with taste; all have private bath, wide floorboards, and air-conditioning as well as computer access. A sitting room has a TV and is well stocked with games and books. It's just a few miles down to Mascoma Lake, with summer swimming, and the 23-acre grounds include gardens and ski/walking trails. $80–95 with a full breakfast and afternoon snacks. Innkeepers Nancy and Allen Smith are knowledgeable and helpful about the surrounding area.

The Trumbull House (603-643-2370; 1-800-651-5141; www.trumbellhouse.com), 40 Etna Rd., Hanover 03755. Four miles east of Dartmouth College, Hillary Pridgen offers four bright and spacious, tastefully decorated guest rooms in her gracious house. There's also a suite and a guest cottage. Amenities include private baths, down comforters, cable TV, and Internet access. The suite has a king-sized bed, a sitting area with TV/VCR, a trundle bed, and two baths, one

with a Jacuzzi tub. $145–290 includes a full breakfast—guests choose from a menu that includes scrambled eggs with smoked salmon and a portobello mushroom and Brie omelet. The 16 country acres include a swimming pond, hiking trails, and cross-country ski trails. Guests enjoy access to the River Valley Club.

☃ ✔ Norwich Bed and Breakfast at Shear Luck Farm (802-649-3800; www.norwichbnb.com), 229 Bradley Hill Rd., Norwich, VT 05055. A newly renovated, 125-year old farmhouse on Bradley Hill offers two guest rooms, one of them a suite, both with king bed and private bath. Just 4 miles from Dartmouth College, this 20-acre farm offers sheep, chickens, and mountain views. $100–180 includes breakfast; dinner on request.

Breakfast on the Connecticut (603-353-4444; 1-888-353-4440; www.breakfastonthect.com), 651 River Rd., Lyme 03768. This 1990s B&B is off on its own 23 wooded acres, right on the Connecticut River, with a private dock. Guest rooms are curiously designed, with whirlpool tubs in the rooms themselves. There are also gas fireplaces and skylights; many rooms have river views. They are divided between the main house and a 12-sided "barn," connected by an enclosed passageway, which also connects with a whirlpool tub in a gazebo. Innkeepers Donna and John Anderson have softened the feel. $85–175 per night for rooms, $160–225 for suites. Inquire about the cottage. Rates include breakfast.

White Goose Inn (603-353-4812; 1-800-358-4267; www.whitegooseinn.com), Rt. 10, P.O. Box 17, Orford 03777. This is as an exceptionally handsome 1830s brick house—fourchimneyed and green-shuttered, with the original 1766 clapboard home now an el at the back. Marshall and Renee Ivey have lightened and brightened this inn, expanding the common spaces. There are eight antiques-furnished guest rooms with private bath and two that share. $89 (shared bath)–149 includes a full breakfast. Inquire about floorcloth workshops. Guests can take advantage of Peyton Place (see *Dining Out*), housed in the neighboring Federal-era tavern, one of the best places to dine in the Upper Valley.

∞ **Dowd's Country Inn** (603-795-4712; 1-800-482-4712), Lyme 03768. On Lyme's classic common, geared to groups and weddings. You'll find a large living room, a meeting space, a small dining room, a cheery breakfast room, and 23 guest rooms. The presidential suite can accommodate a family of five. Rooms $125–175 in-season, double occupancy, includes breakfast and afternoon tea. Dinner by arrangement.

✳ Where to Eat

DINING OUT **Peyton Place** (603-353-9100; www.peytonplacerestaurant .com), Rt. 10, Orford. Open for dinner Wed.–Sun. 5:30–10:30; in the off-season, Fri.–Sun. Reservations a must. Destination dining, this restaurant (named for owners Jim, Heidi, Sophie, and Shamus Peyton) is housed in a 1773 tavern with a genuine old pub room (and a genuinely interesting pub menu) as well as more formal dining rooms. Dinner entrées might range from house-made vegetarian ravioli, Asian shrimp stir-fry, and steak fritters to rack of lamb with wild mushrooms. Ice creams and sorbets are handmade as well. Wine and

spirits are served. The pub menu might include house-made duck and chorizo dumplings and quesadillas with tortillas made in-house as well. Dinner entrées $15.50–26.50. Inquire about cooking classes.

Home Hill Country Inn (603-675-6165), River Rd., Plainfield. Open for dinner Tue.–Sun. in summer and fall, Wed.–Sun. in winter. Reservations a must. A four-square 1820s mansion set in its grounds down by the river, this is the valley's priciest and most elegant dining destination. Guests tend to enjoy a drink in a plush armchair before sitting down to a linen-dressed table in one of the low-ceilinged dining rooms. The menu reflects the French accent of chef-owners Victoria and Stephane de Roure. Victoria is actually English-born but has trained at the Ritz Escoffier in Paris. Stephane, from the south of France, who has owned patisseries in San Diego, carefully selects wine and oversees management of the restaurant. Dinner might begin with braised escargots or an asparagus-hazelnut tart with herbed goat cheese; you might then dine on roasted and braised milk-fed veal with morels, peas, and onions, followed by a frozen banana soufflé or tarte au chocolat with burnt orange ice cream. Appetizers $14–16; entrées $34–38; desserts: $14. Prix fixe tasting menu $89, with wine pairings $154. (Also see *Lodging*.)

Canoe Club Bistro and Music (603-643-9660; www.canoeclub.us), 27 S. Main St., Hanover. Open daily for lunch and dinner with light fare between meals (2–5) and late-night menus Thu.–Sat. Reservations suggested for dinner. Acoustic music nightly, also Sunday jazz brunch. "Sensational" is the way local residents describe this attractive addition to Hanover's dining options. The lunch may include wild mushroom stroganoff, pulled pork quesadilla, and warm smoked sausage with port-braised cabbage, a grilled baguette, and ale mustard. The dinner menu might include house-made ravioli (ingredients change daily) and Vermont lamb with Swiss chard, sun-dried tomato pesto, parsnips, sweet potatoes, and brussels sprout leaves. Dinner entrées $15–25.

Hanover Inn (603-643-4300; 1-800-443-7024), Dartmouth green, Hanover. **The Daniel Webster Room** is a large, formal dining room (open daily for all three meals), with terrace dining overlooking the Dartmouth green in summer. Executive chef Michael Gray has put this spot on New England's culinary map. Dinner might commence with country pâté with fruit chutney. Entrées might include martini-marinated grilled venison leg with whipped potatoes ($28) and roast rack of lamb ($30), as well as vegetarian timbale with grilled portobello, white beans, and pesto ($19.50). **Zins Wine Bistro** offers a wine-bar atmosphere and a moderately priced menu featuring pastas, flatbreads, burgers, and dinner plates ranging from salads to a grilled T-bone.

Three Tomatoes Trattoria (603-448-1711), 1 Court St., Lebanon. Open for lunch Mon.–Fri. 11:30–2, and nightly for dinner. A trendy trattoria with a sleek decor, a wood-fired oven and grill, and a reasonably priced menu: plenty of pasta creations like penne con carciofi—sautéed mushrooms, spinach, roasted garlic, and olive oil tossed with penne ziti regate. There are also grilled dishes like pollo cacciatora alla gorgolia—boneless chicken topped with tomato basil sauce, mozzarella, and Romano cheese, and served with linguine—and no less than 16 very different pizzas from the wood-fired oven. Wine and beer are served. Dinner entrées $10.95–17.75.

☞ **Como Va** (802-280-1956), 1 S. Main St., White River Junction, Vt. Open Tue.–Sat. for lunch and dinner. This appealing trattoria is a popular addition to the valley. You might begin with carpaccio or mussels simmered with toasted garlic, fennel, sweet tomatoes, and vermouth, and proceed to "pasta your way," combining a choice of pastas with a choice of fillings and sauces ($13.95 adults, $7.95 children). The long list of entrées ranges from classic eggplant Parmesan to herb-roasted lamb chops and rosemary skewered Gulf shrimp. Entrées $13.95–28.95. Regional Italian wines are featured.

The Tip Top Café (803-295-3312; www.tiptopcafe.com), 85 N. Main St., White River Junction, Vt. Chef-owner Eric Harting (creator of the Perfect Pear) now presides in this glass-fronted bistro on the ground floor of a former commercial bakery. The decor is spare and arty with changing art and brown paper instead of tablecloths. Lunches include soups, salads, and unusual sandwiches such as balsamic figs with spinach and Gorgonzola on rosemary focaccia. Dinner might begin with artichoke fritters with lemon jalapeño preserve. Entrées might include sesame-crusted talapia with mango salsa and mixed greens. Lunch $6–10, dinner entrées $10–18.

Carpenter and Main (802-649-2922; www.carpenterandmain.com), Main St., Norwich, Vt. Open for dinner except Tue. and Wed.; tavern from 5:30, dining room from 6; reservations a must. Chef-owner Peter Ireland is known for vegetarian dishes complementing staples like bouillabaisse and roast pork loin. A fall trio of vegetables, all presented with their tops on, comprised baby pumpkin filled with sage cream and Gruyère, zucchini stuffed with creamy polenta, and sweet onion filled with barley. Try the house pâté for starters. Entrées $18–26; moderately priced tavern menu.

Norwich Inn (802-649-1143; www .norwichinn.com), 325 Main St., Norwich, Vt. Open for breakfast, lunch, and dinner, also Sunday brunch but closed Mon. Across the river from Hanover, the dining room in this classic inn is popular with Dartmouth faculty and local residents, good for vegetarian as well as wide variety of entrées ($16.95–20.95). Jasper Murdock's Alehouse (see *Eating Out*), also on the premises, is beloved for its handcrafted brews (sold only here) as well as for its atmosphere and pub food.

Simon Pearce (802-295-1470), The Mill, Quechee, Vt. Open daily for lunch and dinner (reserve). Let's face it—this is the one place no visitor to the Upper Valley wants to miss. It's frequently crowded and touristy, but a special place with delicious food. Housed in a mill that once formed the centerpiece for a village, with views of the waterfall. The tableware features handblown, hand-finished glass designed and blown in the mill and sold in the adjoining gift shop. At lunch try the shepherd's pie or coho salmon smoked here at the mill. Dinner entrées $20–38.

Alden Country Inn (603-795-2222; 1-800-794-2296; www.aldencountry inn.com), On The Common, Lyme. Open for dinner nightly and for Sun-

day brunch. The 1809 dining room is fairly formal, with an à la carte menu that changes seasonally. Entrées might range from vegetarian ravioli ($12.95) to an 8-ounce filet mignon served with mushroom and caramelized onion risotto cake, grilled marinated portobello, fried leeks, and roasted shallot demiglaze ($29.95). A moderately priced menu is also offered in the informal **Stagecoach Tavern**.

EATING OUT **Windsor Station Restaurant** (802-674-2052), Depot Avenue, Windsor, Vt. Open daily for lunch and dinner. Windsor's original railroad station is plusher than ever with gleaming woods and brass, velvet, and railroadiana. Lunch can be a burger, but the large dinner menu includes veal Oscar and prime rib; a children's menu is offered.

Riverside Grill (603-448-2571), Rt. 4 just off I-89 in Enfield. The sign is visible from the interstate and a good road-food stop. Things can get a bit greasy, but our chicken salad and BLT were fine and the freshly squeezed lemonade alone is worth stopping for. It's been owned by the Laware family for 50 years, and the dining room with blue booths doesn't look like it's changed in the past 30. The dinner menu features fried seafood and classics like ham steak, and liver, bacon, and onions. Beer and wine served.

Three Tomatoes Trattoria. See *Dining Out*. This spot is also excellent for lunch.

Salt Hill Pub (603-448-4532), 2 West Park, on the mall, Lebanon. Weekdays 8:30 AM "till late," Sat. from 11 AM, Sun. noon–9. Soups, salads, sandwiches, and burgers plus hand-battered onion rings. At dinner, bangers and mash, fish-and-chips,

Irish country pie. A cross between a café and Irish pub atmosphere with music Tue. and Thu.–Sat. evenings.

Gusanoz (603-448-1408; www .gusanoz.com), 410 Miracle Mile, Lebanon. Open Mon.–Sat. 11–10, Sun. 10–3. The Upper Valley's hottest Mexican restaurant is squirreled away in a Lebanon mini-mall (off I-89, Exit 19; look for a movie theater and the DMV). Maria Limon and Nick Yager have already tripled their seating in answer to demand since their 2005 opening. Specialties include chicken mole, carnitas, tamales and pork asado, staples of Limon's girlhood in Durango, Mexico. On Sunday there's a dazzling "all you can eat" brunch— the only problem may be getting in.

✿ **Lui, Lui** (603-298-7070), Power-house Mall, West Lebanon. Open daily for lunch straight through dinner until 9:30. The former boiler house for the brick mill complex makes a multitiered, attractive setting for this popular, informal Italian restaurant. Pastas, salads, calzones, and specialty pizzas fill the bill of fare.

The Seven Barrel Brewery (603-298-5566), in the shopping center off Airport Rd., I-89, Exit 20. Open daily for lunch and dinner until 10 PM, drinks until 1 AM. A large, attractive brewpub with burgers and pub fare (mulligan stew, shepherd's pie, bangers and mash, and cock-a-leekie pie). Worth finding.

✿ **West Lebanon fast-food strip**, Rt. 12A just south of I-89, Exit 20, is lined with representatives of every major fast-food chain in New England—a godsend to families with cars full of kids.

Four Aces Diner (603-298-6827), 23 Bridge St., West Lebanon. Open

5 AM–3 PM and 5–8 PM; Sun. 7 AM–3 PM. A classic Worcester diner is hidden beneath the unremarkable red-sided exterior. Good, reliable food, fountain drinks, and homemade pie served at booths with jukeboxes.

Yama Restaurant (603-298-5477), 96 Main St., West Lebanon. Open Tue.–Sat. (until 10 PM) for lunch and dinner; Sun. from 3 PM. The fare is essentially Korean and terrific, if you like a large choice of udon noodle, miso, seaweed, and spicy soups, as well as house specials like "Yukye-jang," which turned out to be shredded beef and vegetables in a spicy broth with side dishes of pickled cucumber and sweet but firm baked beans. There are also donburi, tempura, and teriyaki dishes, and a reasonably priced sushi bar (served with miso soup). Wine and beer.

✿ ♿ **Jesse's** (603-643-4111), Rt. 120, Hanover. Open for lunch and dinner daily, this steak and seafood tavern has long been a mainstay for Upper Valley diners. Daily fish and shellfish specials, three salad bars, burgers, and prime rib. The atmosphere varies from Victorian to Adirondack to Greenhouse but is comfortable for all ages throughout.

❀ ✿ **Lou's Restaurant and Bakery** (603-643-3321), 30 S. Main St., Hanover. Open for breakfast weekdays from 6 AM, Sat. from 7, and Sun. from 8. Lunch Mon.–Sat. until 3 PM. Since 1947 this has been a student and local hangout and it's great: a long Formica counter, tables and booths, fast, friendly service, good soups, sandwiches, and daily specials, and irresistible peanut butter cookies at the register.

Murphy's on the Green (603-643-4075), 11 S. Main St., Hanover. A traditional college rathskeller with a dark, pubby atmosphere and a wide-ranging beer list; burgers, soups, sandwiches, and more. Smoking is permitted in the bar/TV area; it can be crowded and noisy, but the food and service are reliable.

♥ ♪ **Molly's** (603-643-2570), 43 Main St., Hanover. Open daily for lunch and dinner. The greenhouse up front shelters a big, inviting bar that encourages single dining. The menu is immense and reasonably priced: big salads, enchiladas, elaborate burgers at lunch, pasta to steak at dinner.

Mai Thai Cuisine (603-643-9980), 40 S. Main St., Hanover. Open Mon.–Sat. for lunch 11:30–3; for dinner Mon.–Thu. 5–10, until 11 on Fri. and Sat. Traditional Thai cuisine in a pleasant atmosphere.

Rosey's Coffee and Tea (603-643-5282), 15 Lebanon St., Hanover. Open weekdays 7:30 AM–6:30 PM, from 8:30 Sat.; Sun. 10–5. This stylish café downstairs from Rosey Jeke's clothing store offers great coffee, baked goods, gourmet sandwiches, desserts, and a pleasant place to linger. A bit pricey, but good.

Jasper Murdock's Alehouse (802-649-1143) in the Norwich Inn, Main St., Norwich, Vt. Open 5:30–9 PM daily. The house brew comes in 15 varieties; we favor the Whistling Pig Red Ale. A comfortable, green-walled room popular with locals, the Alehouse serves a pub menu that includes Maine crabcakes and a house-smoked brisket sandwich.

♪ **Fairlee Diner** (802-333-3569), Rt. 5, Fairlee, Vt. Closed Tue., otherwise 5:30 AM–2 PM; Thu. until 7 PM and Fri. 8 PM. Turn left (north) on Rt. 5 if you are coming off I-91. This is a classic wooden diner built in the 1930s (across the road from where it stands), with wooden booths, worn-shiny wooden stool tops, and good food. The mashed potato doughnuts are special, and both the soup and the pie are dependably good. Daily specials.

✳ **Entertainment**

MUSIC AND THEATER Hopkins Center (box office: 603-646-2422; www.hop.Dartmouth.edu), on the Dartmouth green, Hanover. Sponsors some 150 musical and 20 theater productions per year, plus 200 films, all open to the public.

Lebanon Opera House (603-448-2498), in town hall, Coburn Park. This 800-seat, turn-of-the-20th-century theater hosts frequent concerts, lectures, and summer performances by the North Country Community Players.

♪ **Northern Stage** (802-296-7000; www.northernstage.org), Briggs Opera House, White River Junction, Vt. Semiprofessional community theater offers high-quality productions year-round. Special children's theater classes and summer arts education classes.

Opera North (603-448-0400; www.operanorth.org), Lebanon Opera House, 20 Park Square. Excellent, semiprofessional summer performances feature visiting soloists from major opera companies.

For music, also see **Canoe Club** under *Dining Out* and **Salt Hill Pub** under *Eating Out*.

FILM ♪ **Fairlee Drive-In** (802-333-9192), Rt. 5, Fairlee, Vt. Summer only; check local papers for listings. This is a beloved icon, the last of the valley's seasonal drive-ins. It's attached to the Fairlee Motel and has a famously good snack bar featuring "thunderburgers," made from beef on the family's farm across the river in Piermont. The gates open at 7; films begin at dusk.

Dartmouth Film Society at the Hopkins Center (603-646-2576). Frequent showings of classic, contemporary, and experimental films in two theaters.

Nugget Theaters (603-643-2769), S. Main St., Hanover. Four current films nightly, surround sound.

Sony Theatres (603-448-6660), Miracle Mile Shopping Center, Lebanon. Six first-run films nightly.

✻ Selective Shopping

Colonial Antique Markets (603-298-8132; 603-298-7712), Colonial Plaza, Rt. 12A, West Lebanon. Open 9–5 daily, year-round. This looks like nothing from the outside because it's all basement level: dozens of dealers with art, antiques, collectibles, jewelry, clothing, books, tools, and fun old stuff. It's easy to find once you know it's there: Exit 20 off I-89 and follow signs for the airport (it's next to the highway); as soon as you turn onto Airport Rd., take a quick left into Colonial Plaza. The unpromising entrance is around the corner of the brick building on your left, across from the Seven Barrel Brewery.

Quechee Gorge Antiques Mall (802-295-1550), Rt. 4 in Quechee, Vt., with 450 dealers, offers the largest selection on the Vermont side of the river.

William Smith (603-675-2549) holds antiques auctions at the Plainfield Auction Gallery, Rt. 12A in Plainfield, year-round.

ART GALLERIES AND CRAFTS CENTERS AVA Gallery (603-448-3117), 11 Bank St. (Rt. 4 just west of Coburn Park), Lebanon. Open Tue.–Sat. 11–5. From its Hanover beginnings, the Alliance for the Visual Arts has grown to fill a sunny, former mill building. The Soho-style (and -quality) gallery mounts frequent exhibits of arts and crafts. Classes and workshops are also offered.

Dana Robes Wood Craftsmen, Inc. (603-632-5377; 1-800-632-5377; www.danadrobes.com), Lower Shaker Village, Rt. 4A, Enfield. Showroom open weekdays 8–5. Meticulously crafted, traditional, Shaker-design and other sparely lined furniture, each piece signed by the craftsman who created it. Products, made on the premises, custom-designed cupboards, tables, armoires, and beds. Beside the woodworking/display shop stands a replica of the classic 1793 Shaker Meeting House that stood here until 1903, when it became a private home in Cornish. Inquire about year-round workshops in woodworking and furniture building.

League of New Hampshire Craftsmen (603-643-5050), 13 Lebanon St., Hanover. Closed Sun. Next to Ben & Jerry's; a wide selection of local and regional crafts pieces. Craft classes offered.

Long River Studios (603-795-4909), 1 Main St., Lyme. Open Mon.–Sat. 10–5. A regional cooperative with a wide selection of art in many media, also cards, books, pottery, clothing, jewelry and more.

Simon Pearce Glass (802-674-6280), Rt. 5 north of Windsor, Vt. Open daily 9–5. Pearce operated his own glassworks in Ireland before moving to Vermont in 1981. Here he acquired the venerable Downer's Mill in Quechee and harnessed the dam's hydropower for the glass furnace (see *Dining Out*). In 1993 he opened this new, visitor-friendly glass factory featuring a catwalk that overlooks the gallery where glass is blown and shaped. Of course, there's a big showroom/shop featuring seconds as well as first-quality glass and pottery.

BOOKSTORES Dartmouth Bookstore (603-643-3616; 1-800-624-8800), 33 S. Main St., Hanover. Open Mon.–Sat. One of the largest bookstores in northern New England.

The Norwich Bookstore (802-649-1114), Main St., Norwich, Vt., next to the post offiice. This is a light, airy store with well-selected titles and comfortable places to sit. The staff is very knowledgeable. Frequent readings, and a good children's section.

Borders Books Music & Café (603-298-9963), Wal-Mart Plaza, West Lebanon.

SPECIAL SHOPPING CENTERS Centerra Marketplace, Rt. 120, Lebanon. Anchored by the co-op grocery store, this complex also features a trendy restaurant.

Powerhouse Mall, Rt. 10, West Lebanon. Open Mon.–Fri. 10–9; Sat. 10–6; Sun. noon–5. A total of 40 stores are in this unusual complex, which combines an old brick electric powerhouse, a large, new but mill-style, two-story arcade, and several older buildings moved from other places, all offering a genuine variety of small specialty stores. Anchored by **Eastern Mountain Sports** (603-298-7716) and **L.L. Bean** (603-298-6975) featuring sporting gear, other noteworthy

shops include the **Anichini Outlet Store** (603-298-8656; www.anichini .com; open 10–8 except Sun., when it's noon–5. featuring the Tunbridge, Vt.–based company's nationally lauded line of antique and fine linens at substantial savings; and a surprising choice of women's clothing stores.

SPECIAL SHOPS King Arthur Flour Baker's Store (802-649-3361; www .kingarthurflour.com), Rt. 5, Norwich, Vt. Open Mon.–Sat. 8:30–6, Sun. until 4. Home as well as prime outlet for the country's oldest family-owned flour company (since 1790), this store draws serious bakers and would-be bakers from throughout several time zones. The vast post-and-beam building itself is a marvel, its shelves stocked with every conceivable kind of flour, baking ingredient, and a selection of equipment and cookbooks, not to mention bread and pastries made in the adjacent bakery (with a glass connector allowing visitors to watch the hands and skills of the bakers). Next door too is the Baking Education Center, offering baking classes ranging from beginner to expert, from making piecrust to braided breads and elegant pastries.

Dan & Whit's General Store (802-649-1602), Main St., Norwich, Vt. This quintessential Vermont country store justifies a trip across the river. Hardware, groceries, housewares, boots and clothing, farm and garden supplies, and a great community bulletin board: If they don't have it, you don't need it.

Dartmouth Co-op (603-643-3100), 25 S. Main St., Hanover. Incorporated in 1919 and now owned by Dartmouth alumni, a source of sports clothes and of course an extensive line of Dartmouthiana: T-shirts, sweats, boxers, mugs, cushions.

Pompanoosuc Mills (802-785-4851; www.pompy.com), Rt. 5, East Thetford, Vt. Dartmouth graduate Dwight Sargeant began building furniture in this riverside house, a cottage industry that has evolved into a riverside factory with showrooms throughout New England. Some seconds. Open daily until 6 PM, Sun. noon–5. Note the branch on Lebanon St. in Hanover.

FOOD AND FARMS

In Plainfield on River Road

Edgewater Farm (603-298-5764) offers pick-your-own strawberries and raspberries; there are also greenhouses with bedding plants, and a farm stand on Rt. 12A. Also on River Road, **Riverview Farms** (603-298-8519) offers apples, pumpkins, and cider pressing and hayrides in fall. **McNamara Dairy** (603-298-MOOO) sells its own glass-bottled milk and eggnog.

MAPLE SUGARING Mid-Feb.–early April, the following local sugarhouses welcome visitors to watch them "boil off" and sample the new syrup. Most also sell their own syrup year-round. **Brokenridge Farm** (603-542-8781), Rt. 120, Cornish. Sap is gathered with horses on weekends; sugar-on-snow, tours.

Orford has the biggest local concentration of maple-syruping operations, including: **Gerald and Toni Pease** (603-353-9070), Pease's Scenic Hwy., off Rt. 25A. Draft horse with wagon or sleigh. Gale and Peter Thompson (son of a former governor) operate a traditional sugarhouse and serve pancake breakfasts at **Mount Cube Farm**

(603-353-4709), Rt. 25A. There's also **Sunday Mountain Maple Products** (603-353-4883), Rt. 25A.

✳ Special Events

For details about any of these events, phone the town clerk, listed with information.

Mid-February: **Dartmouth Winter Carnival**, Hanover. Thu.–Sun. Ice sculptures, sports events, ski jumping.

Early March: **Meriden Wild Game Dinner**, Kimball Union Academy's Miller Student Center. Usually a Saturday. At this benefit for the Meriden Volunteer Fire Department, bear, raccoon, and boar are usually on the menu.

Mid-May: **Dartmouth Pow-Wow**, Hanover. A gathering of Native American craftspeople and dancers on the second Saturday of May; sponsored by Native Americans at Dartmouth (603-646-2110) and the Native American Studies Program (603-646-3530).

Memorial Day: **Muster Day**, Hanover Center. Recitation of the Gettysburg Address and Dr. Seuss prayer by children of the third grade on the site of Hanover's pre-Revolutionary musters.

Third weekend in June: **Quechee Balloon Festival and Crafts Fair** (802-295-7900), Quechee, Vt. Some 20 hot-air balloons gather, offering rides at dawn and dusk; barbecue, skydiving, crafts, food booths. **Summer Strawberry Festival**, Plainfield Historical Society Clubhouse, Rt. 12A, Plainfield. **Lyme Summer Suppers and Horse Sheds Crafts Festivals**, Lyme Congregational Church horse sheds, Lyme. Beginning the last Wednesday in June, then every other week for four Wednesdays. The crafts festivals begin at 1 PM and the suppers, also at the church, begin at 6 PM.

Fourth of July: **Independence Day Open Fields Circus**, Thetford, Vt. A takeoff on a real circus, by the Parish Players. **Fourth of July celebration**, Plainfield. Community breakfast, footraces, parade, firemen's roast beef dinner. Lebanon stages the largest fireworks display in the area.

Mid-July: **Hanover Street Fest** (603-643-3115), Hanover. Street bazaar, hay-wagon rides, fireworks, entertainment. **Norwich (Vt.) Fair**. Mix of old-time country fair and honky-tonk carnival. Lobster dinner, parade, ox pulling. Late July: **Hanover Center Fair**, Hanover. Friday-night games, dancing, food; Saturday starts with a children's costume parade, ox pulling, food, games. **Connecticut Valley Fair**, Bradford, Vt. Ox and horse pulling, sheep show, midway, demolition derby. **La Salette Fair** (603-632-4301), at the La Salette Shrine, Rt. 4A, Enfield. Usually a midway with rides, flea market, crafts booths. **Cracker-Barrel Bazaar**, Newbury, Vt. Big old-time fiddlers' contest, antiques show, quilt show, sheepdog trials, church suppers.

Early August: **Canaan Old Home Day**, Canaan. Dances, parade, booths, suppers. **North Haverhill**

Fair. Horse show and pulling, evening live entertainment, midway. **Thetford Hill Fair**, Thetford Hill, Vt. Small but special: a rummage sale, food and plant booths, barbecue.

Mid-August: **Cornish Fair**. Horse and ox pulling, agricultural exhibits, ham and bean suppers, a Saturday woodsmen's field day.

Late August: **Quechee Scottish Festival**, Quechee, Vt. Sheepdog trials, Highland dancing, piping, Highland "games," ladies' rolling-pin toss, more.

Mid-October: **Horse Sheds Crafts Fair**, at the Lyme Congregational Church, Lyme. Saturday of Columbus Day weekend 10 AM–4 PM; also a **Fall Festival** lunch at the church.

Late November: **Bradford United Church of Christ Wild Game Supper**, Bradford, Vt. The Saturday before Thanksgiving this town nearly doubles its population as hungry visitors pour into the church to feast on 2,800 pounds of buffalo, venison, moose, pheasant, coon, rabbit, wild boar, and bear.

Mid-December–Christmas: **Christmas Pageants** in Norwich and Lyme. **Revels North**, in the Hopkins Center. Song and dance. **Christmas Illuminations**, at the La Salette Shrine, Rt. 4A, Enfield.

LOWER COHASE

C *ohase* is an Abenaki word meaning "wide valley." That's according to the chamber of commerce by that name that now embraces this gloriously little touristed 15-mile stretch of the Connecticut north of the Upper Valley.

Its southernmost towns are sleepy Piermont, N.H. and (relatively) bustling Bradford, Vt., built on terraced land at the confluence of the Waits River and the Connecticut. Bradford is a 19th-century mill village producing plows, paper, and James Wilson, an ingenious farmer who made America's first geographic globes. Handsome Low's Grist Mill survives across from the falls, now housing a popular restaurant, and a golf course spreads below the business block across the floodplain. From Bradford the view across the river encompasses Mount Moosilauke, easternmost of the White Mountains.

Moving upriver, Haverhill and Newbury, Vt., two of northern New England's most handsome and historic towns, face each other across the river.

Haverhill is immense, comprising seven very distinct villages, including classic examples of both Federal-era and railroad villages. Thanks to a fertile floodplain, this is an old and prosperous farming community, even now. Haverill Corner was founded in 1763 at the western terminus of the Coos Turnpike that wound its way up the Baker Valley and over the mountains from Plymouth. It became the Grafton County seat in 1773; a graceful 19th-century courthouse has recently been restored as a performance and information center. The village itself is a gem: a grouping of Federal-era and Greek Revival homes and public buildings around a double, white-fenced common.

Just north of Haverill Corner (but south of the junction of Rts. 10 and 25) a sign points the way down through a cornfield and along the river to the site of the Bedell Bridge. Built in 1866, this was one of the largest surviving examples of a two-span covered bridge, until it was destroyed by a violent September windstorm in 1979. The site is still worth finding because it's a peaceful riverside spot, ideal for a picnic.

In North Haverhill you come unexpectedly to a lineup of modern county buildings—the courthouse, a county home, and a jail—and then you are in downtown Woodsville, a 19th-century rail hub with an ornate 1890s brick Opera Block and three-story, mustard-colored railroad station. The Haverhill–Bath covered bridge, built in 1829 and billed as the oldest covered bridge in New England, is just beyond the railroad underpass (Rt. 135 north).

Newbury is one of Vermont's oldest towns, founded in 1761 by Jacob Bailey, a Revolutionary war general still remembered as the force behind the Bailey-Hazen road, conceived as an invasion route to northwest to Canada. It was abandoned two-thirds of the way along, but after the Revolution it served as a prime settlement route. A plaque at the northern end of the business block in Wells River (a village in Newbury) notes the beginning of the trail, while another in Hazen's Notch marks its terminus. Newbury was the site of a Native American village for many thousands of years, and its mineral springs drew travelers as early as 1800. Wells River marked the head of navigation on the Connecticut through the 1830s. In the 1840s river traffic was upstaged by the railroad, which transformed Woodsville.

GUIDANCE **Lower Cohase Regional Chamber of Commerce** (866-526-4273; 802-222-5631; www.cohase.org), P.O. Box 209, Bradford, VT 05033, publishes a helpful map/guide and maintains a seasonal welcome center in Wells River, Vt., just west of the bridge on Rt. 302.

Alumni Hall (603-989-5500), Court St., Haverhill Corner. Open mid-June–mid-Oct., 10–4. Built gracefully in brick in 1846 as the Grafton County courthouse, later part of Haverhill Academy and recently restored as a venue for performances, art shows, and the like and as a Connecticut River Scenic Byway interpretive center. Cultural map/guides and books published by the Joint River Commissions are featured, along with local info.

✷ To Do

BICYCLING Given the beauty of the landscape and the little-trafficked, level nature of Rt. 10 and of this stretch of Rt. 5, the appeal to bicyclists is obvious. Less obvious are the long-distance routes that draw serious cyclists up over the White Mountains on Rts. 116 and 25. At the **North Haverhill Inn and Bicycle Shop** (603-787-6480), 2531 Dartmouth College Hwy. (Rt. 10), Tom and Noreen Bourassa offer a full-service bike shop and four rooms ($77 with breakfast) catering to cyclists (noncyclists also welcome).

BOATING **Hemlock Pete's Canes & Kayaks** (603-667-5112; www.hpcanoes .blizland.net), Rt. 10, North Haverhill. Scott Edwards teaches at the local high school and actually makes as well as rents canoes and kayaks; guided tours, too. His shop is the barn beside Union House B&B (stay 2 nights and get a free rental), across from the fairgrounds.

GOLF **Bradford Golf Club** (802-222-5207), Bradford, Vt. Nine holes down by the river. **Blackmount Country Club** (603-787-6564; www.blackmountcountry club.com), 400 Clark Rd., North Haverhill. Cart rentals, driving range, practice green, A par-36, nine-hole golf course.

THE CONNECTICUT RIVER VALLEY

SWIMMING **Lake Tarleton State Park**, Rt. 25C in Piermont, Warren, and Benton. More than 5,000 acres surrounding Lake Tarleton, smaller Lakes Katherine and Constance, and much of Lake Armington are now public land divided between White Mountain National Forest conservation trusts and a state park featuring the sand beach on Lake Tarleton (part of a onetime resort). The property was slated for major development in 1994 when preservation forces, spearheaded by the Trust for Public Land, raised more than $7 million to preserve this magnificent woodland with its views of Mount Moosilauke. The lake is stocked with trout and also beautiful for canoeing and kayaking (public boat launch). Hiking trails are taking shape, including a connector to the Appalchian Trail, which passes through the property 0.5 mile from the lake.

✳ Lodging

☾ ♿ **Piermont Inn** (603-272-4820), 1 Old Church St., Piermont 03779. A 1790s stagecoach stop with six rooms, four in the adjacent carriage house (only the two in the inn are available year-round), all with private bath. The two in the main house are outstanding rooms, both carved from the tavern's original ballroom, high ceilinged and spacious, with writing desks and appropriate antiques. The carriage house rooms are simple but cheery; one is handicapped accessible. Common space includes a living room with a fireplace, TV, wing chairs, and a nifty grandfather clock. Charlie and Karen Brown are longtime Piermont residents who enjoy tuning guests in to the many ways of exploring this upper (less touristed) part of the valley, especially canoeing the river. Rooms in the main house are $135, and in the carriage house $95, full breakfast included.

🐾 **The Gibson House** (603-989-3125; www.gibsonhousebb.com), R.R. 1, Box 193, Haverhill 03765. Open June–Oct. New innkeepers Susie Klein and Marty Cohen have kept this amazing place exactly as Artist Keita Colton restored it. One of the valley's finest Greek Revival homes, it was built in 1850 on the green in Haverhill Corners and at one point was a stagecoach inn. The seven guest rooms, especially the four big second-floor rooms, are artistic creations, each very different from the next. Taj North is the most opulent and exotic with its faux balcony, rich colors, and glowing stained-glass moon. We enjoyed the golden, Asian-themed Bamboo Room, but our favorite is the Seashore Room, with its quilts and colors (twin beds), overlooking the garden. While the house fronts on Rt. 10, the 50-foot-long sunny back porch with wicker seats and swing takes full advantage of the splendid view west across the terraced garden and the Connecticut River. A full breakfast is served, weather permitting, in the fanciful dining room or on the first-floor screened porch. $125–175 includes a full breakfast.

🍑 **Peach Brook Inn** (802-866-3389), Doe Hill, off Rt. 5, South Newbury, VT 05051. Joyce Emery has opened her spacious 1837 home with its splendid view of the Connecticut River. What a special place! Common space includes two nicely furnished parlors with exposed beams and a fireplace, an open kitchen, and a screened porch with a view of Mount Moosilauke across the river. The house is on a country lane in the almost vanished village of South Newbury, once connected to Haverhill, N.H., across the river by a long-gone covered bridge. Plenty of farm animals are within walking distance. There are three comfortable guest rooms; $65 with shared bath, $80 with private, including full breakfast. No smoking. No children under 10, please; under 18 are $10.

☙ Union House Bed & Breakfast (603-080-5931; www.unionhouse bandb.com), 1260 Dartmouth College Hwy. (Rt. 10), North Haverhill 03774. Susan Brown welcomes guests to the oldest house in Haverhill, formerly a stagecoach stop and tavern. What's offered is the former Hired Man's Room with a separate entrance and full bath. It's an attaractive, air-conditioned room with a queen-sized bed. Guests are welcome to use the indoor Endless Pool. Brown is a longtime valley resident and a font of advice on where to eat and what to see and do. $85 per night ($5 discount for cash).

The Hayloft Inn at Blackmount (603-787-2367; prfctlie@earthlink .net), 440 Clark Pond Rd., North Haverhill 03774. The plain exterior of this house belies its airy, open post-and-beam interior. Innkeeper Joyce Read is a native of Plainfield, where her mother modeled a couple of times as a young girl for painter Maxfield Parrish. Read has been collecting the artist's distinctive prints all her life and displays them in a special gallery room. There are two bright, tastefully furnished guest rooms with private bath, as well as a two-room suite (one with two double beds and one with twins, sharing both a bath

and sitting area). A hearty breakfast is served at 8 AM. The Blackmount Country Club is next door. $75 for rooms; $125 for suites.

✳ Where to Eat

DINING OUT The Perfect Pear Café (802-222-5912; www.theperfect pearcafe.com), the Bradford Mill, Main St., Bradford, Vt. Open for lunch Tue.–Sat. 11:30–2, dinner 5–8:45. Jan.–Apr., closed for dinner Mon.–Wed. Dinner reservations recommended. Adam Coulter, formerly at the Norwich Inn, is now chef-owner. This remains a charming bistro, housed in a historic brick mill by a falls, especially appealing in summer when there's dining on the flower-decked patio overlooking the Waits River, churning along because the big falls are just across the road. Lunch is reasonably priced with choices like Gorgonzola and candied walnut salad with maple balsamic vinaigrette, and a lamb and rosemary sausage sandwich on whole grain with honey mustard. Dinner might begin with crispy pork dumplings and feature crabmeat-stuffed rainbow trout with a pesto cream, or pork tenderloin served with polenta, as well as vegetarian choices like truffled cannellini bean ravioli with a shiitake Marsala sauce and braised greens. Dinner entrées $12.95–18.95.

⚓ Warners Gallery Restaurant (802-429-2120), just off I-91, Exit 17, on Rt. 302, Wells River, Vt. Open Tue.–Thu. 5–8:30 PM, Fri. and Sat. 5–9, Sun. 11–8. A dependable (90 percent of the time) all-American family restaurant with some atmosphere. Entrées usually include twin stuffed lobster tails, a fisherman's platter, baked stuffed shrimp, and roast prime beef au jus. There's a children's menu, and Sunday brunch (11–2) is billed as "best in the Northeast." Dinner entrées $13–24. Full liquor license.

EATING OUT Note: For lunch in Bradford/Piermont check, **Perfect Pear** under *Dining Out.*

☙ **Colatina Exit** (802-222-9008), Main St., Bradford,Vt. Open daily 5–9 PM; weekends until 10:30. Carol Meagher's Vermont trattoria has been here more than 30 years but recently doubled in size, added a wood-fired pizza oven, and expanded its to-go menu. We still like the original dining room best: candles in Chianti bottles, Italian scenes on the walls, checked (green in summer, red in winter) tablecloths, and a few tables in back with a view of the river. The big menu offers plenty of antipasto and insalata choices and traditional Italian dishes like "lasagna classico" and veal parmigiano; also some nice surprises like grilled chicken portofino (with sautéed portobello mushrooms and fresh spinach in a red Marsala marinara sauce) and wood-roasted scallops carbonara (with spinach and smoked bacon). Plenty of pizza choices and calzones. There's also an upstairs pub with river views.

Bliss Village Store and Deli (802-222-4617), Main St., Bradford, Vt. Housed in a former 19th-century hotel, this is a classic general store but with Crock-Pots full of soup, chili, or stew-fried chicken and a deli with daily specials; tables are in the back—including a booth with the best river view in town.

Newbury Village Store (802-866-5681), 4991 Rt. 5, Newbury, Vt. Open 6 AM–8 PM weekdays, Sat. 7–8, Sun. 8–6. This is the new breed of nouvelle general store. Gary and Maggie Hatch have added comfortable seating near the periodicals and expanded the deli to feature sandwiches named for local landmarks like "The Oxbow" ("basil herb roasted turkey breast with Vermont cheddar, ripe tomatoes, leaf lettuce and the house garlic cream cheese spread on multi grain bread"). There's also a hummus wrap and "The Flatlander" ("shaved black pastrami warmed and piled high on rye and pumpernickel swirl bread, topped with swiss cheese and deli mustard"). There are staple groceries, also a selection of wine and Vermont products. Locals tells us these are the best sandwiches around. There are tables in the back, overlooking the river.

Happy Hours Restaurant (802-757-3466), Rt. 5, Wells River, Vt. Open daily 11:30–8, later in summer. This large, pine-paneled family restaurant in the middle of town has been lightened and brightened in recent years and hums with a sense of friendly service and satisfied patrons. Most entrées include the salad bar—and servings are generous. We couldn't finish a tender sirloin topped with red wine mushroom sauce, with baked potato and good coleslaw (a $12.99 special). Dinner entrées $11.99–22.99.

Shiloh's (802-222-5666), 142 Main St., Bradford, Vt. Open 6–2. The usual sandwiches, soups, wraps, and burgers, but the beef and as many ingredients as possible are local.

☙ **P&H Truck Stop** (802-429-2141), just off I-91 Exit 17 on Rt. 302, Wells River, Vt. Now open just 6 AM–10 PM for hot meals but still 24 hours for to-go premade sandwiches, pies, and the like. Dozens of rigs are usually parked outside on one side, with a broad range of license plates on cars in the other lot. This is a classic truck stop with speedy service, friendly waitresses, and heaping portions at amazing prices. Plus which the bread is homemade; ATM and phone are available (cell phones don't tend to work around here, and pay phones are scarce).

The Little Chef (747-8088), 19 Central St., Woodsville. Open Tue.–Sat. 8–8; Sun. 8–noon (breakfast only). A good breakfast and lunch stop with a big menu and reasonable prices. The dinner menu is basic and reasonably priced (meat loaf for $7.99, veal Parmesan for $11.99); no liquor license.

ICE CREAM **Mountain Scoops**, Rt. 10, North Haverhill. Open Memorial Day–Columbus Day, 11–9. This colorful stand in the middle of town is the source of Rhonda Abrams's homemade ice cream.

✳ Entertainment

Middle Earth Music Hall (828-4748; www.middle-earth-music.com), 134 Main St., Bradford, Vt. It's all about music, nightly. Check out the web site for current schedule: jazz, blues, honkytonk, open mike.

Old Church Community Theater (802-222-3322), 137 Main St., Bradford, Vt. (call Paul Hunt: 802-222-4254).

Alumni Hall (603-989-5500), Court St., Haverhill Corner. Open mid-June–mid-Oct., 10–4. Built gracefully in brick in 1846 as the Grafton County courthouse, later part of Haverhill Academy and recently restored as a venue for concerts and other per-

formances, art shows, and the like. Call for current schedule.

✳ Selective Shopping

Woodsville Bookstore (603-747-3811), 91 Central St., Woodsville. Dave Major's friendly, well-stocked bookstore is an unexpected find here, the best for many miles around. One room of new, one of used books.

Copeland Furniture (802-222-5300; www.copelandfurniture.com), 64 Main St., Bradford, Vt. Open Mon.–Fri. 10 AM–6 PM, Sat. 9 AM–5 PM. Contemporary, cleanly lined, locally made furniture in native hardwoods displayed in the handsome showroom in the converted 19th-century brick mill across from Bradford Falls. Seconds.

Farm-Way, Inc. (1-800-222-9316), Rt. 25, Bradford, Vt. One mile east of I-91, Exit 16. Open Mon.–Sat. until 8 PM. Billed as "complete outfitters for man and beast," this is a phenomenon: a family-run source of work boots and rugged clothing that now includes a stock of more than two million products spread over 5 acres: tack, furniture, pet supplies, syrup, whatever. Recently expanded: Shoes and boots remain a specialty, from size 4E to 16; 25,000 shoes, boots, clogs, sandals, and sneakers in stock; also kayaks, sporting equipment, furnishings, and gifts.

Round Barn Shoppe (603-272-9026), 430 Rt. 10, Piermont. Open May 2–Christmas, Thu.–Mon. 9–5; Jan.–May 1, Fri.–Sun. This 1990s post-and-beam round barn replicates the authentic 1906 barn across the road. It houses a shop selling New England products ranging from baskets and dolls to local dairy milk and fresh pies. Some 300 New England craftsmen and 100 small manufacturers are represented.

4 Corners Farm (802-866-3342), just off Rt. 5, South Newbury, Vt. Bob and Kim Gray sell their own produce and flowers. An exceptionally pretty farm, just off but up above the highway, known for strawberries, PYO vegetables.

Windy Ridge Orchard (787-6377), Rt. 116, North Haverhill. Open daily Labor Day–Thanksgiving, 9–6; weekends Thanksgiving–Christmas, 9–4. Pick your own apples and pumpkins, farm animals, kids' corral playground, nature trails, picnic tables, Cider House Café, gift shop. Apple picking begins in mid-August and lasts through mid-October depending on the variety. There are 3,500 apple trees on 20 acres, overlooking the valley and Green Mountains. There's also a Christmas tree plantation—and you can cut your own trees.

❋ Special Events

Note: Farmer's markets are held in Woodsville on Wednesdays.

July: **4th of July Parade and celebration in Woodsville and Wells River**: marching bands, floats, horses, chicken barbecue, dancing, fireworks. **Connecticut Valley Fair** (*mid-month*), Bradford. **Cracker Barrel Bazaar** (*third or final weekend*), Newbury, includes plenty of fiddling (802-866-5521). The **North Haverhill (N.H.) Fair** (*last weekend*) is an old-style fair with ox and tractor pulls, pig races, and more.

September: **Whole Hog Blues & BBQ Festival** (*last weekend*). Blues music by leading bands, roast pig cook-off, arts and crafts.

November: **Annual Wild Game Supper** (*Sat. before Thanksgiving*), Bradford (802-222-4721)—hungry visitors pour into the Congregational church for this feast.

The White Mountains 6

WHITE MOUNTAIN NATIONAL FOREST

THE WESTERN WHITES

MOUNT WASHINGTON AND ITS VALLEYS

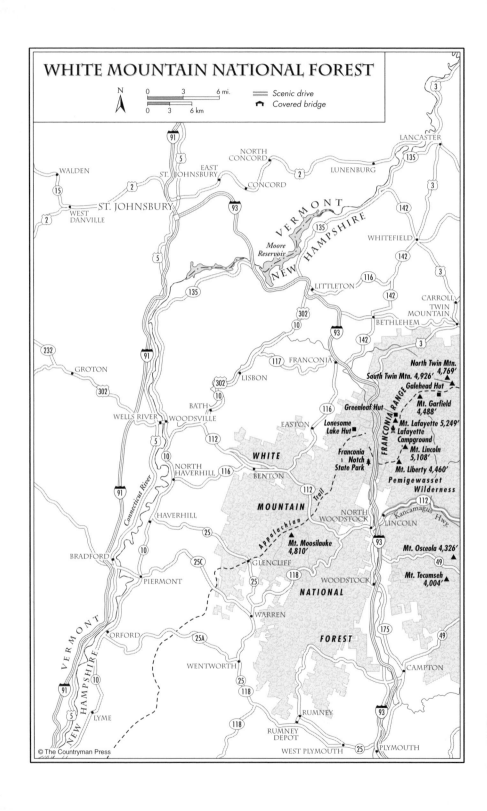

WHITE MOUNTAIN NATIONAL FOREST

N

0   3   6 mi.

0   3   6 km

Scenic drive

Covered bridge

LANCASTER

WALDEN

NORTH CONCORD

LUNENBURG

135

3

EAST ST. JOHNSBURY

CONCORD

15

ST. JOHNSBURY

2

WEST DANVILLE

93

VERMONT

135

142

WHITEFIELD

Moore Reservoir

NEW HAMPSHIRE

142

3

135

LITTLETON

116

142

CARROLL TWIN MOUNTAIN

232

302

10

BETHLEHEM

142

3

GROTON

91

117

FRANCONIA

3

302

LISBON

North Twin Mtn. 4,769'

South Twin Mtn. 4,926'

Galehead Hut

FRANCONIA RANGE

10

BATH

116

Greenleaf Hut

Mt. Garfield 4,488'

WELLS RIVER

WOODSVILLE

EASTON

Lonesome Lake Hut

Mt. Lafayette 5,249'

Lafayette Campground

112

WHITE

Franconia Notch State Park

Mt. Lincoln 5,108'

10

NORTH HAVERHILL

116

BENTON

Mt. Liberty 4,460'

Pemigewasset Wilderness

Connecticut River

MOUNTAIN

112

Appalachian Trail

NORTH WOODSTOCK

Kancamagus Hwy.

112

HAVERHILL

25

LINCOLN

BRADFORD

10

Mt. Moosilauke 4,810'

93

Mt. Osceola 4,326'

49

PIERMONT

GLENCLIFF

118

WOODSTOCK

Mt. Tecumseh 4,004'

NATIONAL

25

ORFORD

25A

WARREN

175

FOREST

CAMPTON

91

WENTWORTH

25

49

NEW HAMPSHIRE

10

118

93

LYME

RUMNEY

118

RUMNEY DEPOT

25

© The Countryman Press

WEST PLYMOUTH

PLYMOUTH

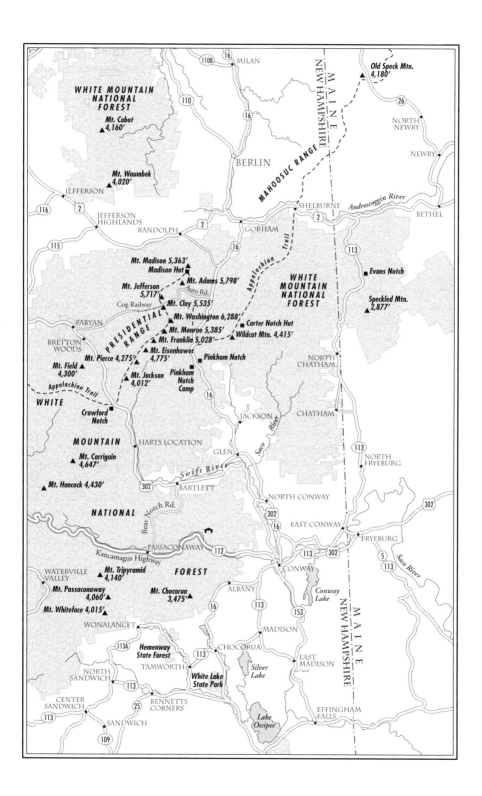

INTRODUCTION

Part of the Appalachian Mountain Range that runs from Maine to Georgia, New England's highest mountains march in a ragged line, heading diagonally northeast across New Hampshire, beginning near the Connecticut River with Mount Moosilauke and extending into Maine. They consist of several ranges among which the best known are the Presidentials, with each peak named for a different president and the highest of all for George Washington. As mountains go, these granite crags and domes are old, rounded by glaciers and "notched" with high passes. The most famous of these notches are Franconia, Crawford, and Pinkham.

In the 18th century several hardy innkeepers opened taverns in Franconia and Crawford Notches. Landscape artists W. H. Bartlett, Benjamin Champney, and Thomas Cole painted this landscape in the 1820s. Thoreau, Emerson, Hawthorne, and Whittier touted the White Mountains through prose and poetry in the 1830s. Starr King's *The Great White Hills*, first serialized in the *Boston Transcript*, brought them local city dwellers in droves, and after the Civil War steam trains linked the White Mountains with every major city in the East. Dozens of mammoth hotels dotted the entire region.

The hotels were patronized by the era's wealthy class, many of whom were also touring the Swiss Alps. It's worth noting that the Cog Railroad—"the Railway to the Moon"—was built up the western flank of Mount Washington in 1869, predating any Swiss cogs. The Appalachian Mountain Club (AMC) "high huts," patterned on Alpine facilities, opened in 1888.

The AMC was founded in 1876 by Boston-based hotel patrons to blaze and map hiking trails through the White Mountains. Inevitably their interest in the beauty of the mountains put them on a collision course with the timber companies, which built extensive rail networks through the region to harvest the dense stands of mountain trees. Their clear-cutting technique left the steep mountain slopes denuded, leading to massive erosion and downstream flooding. The limbs and branches left behind in the woods quickly dried and fueled huge forest fires that threatened the uncut areas. The Society for the Protection of New Hampshire Forests was created as a spin-off from the AMC to energize support for the first national forest east of the Mississippi. The White Mountain National Forest was created by the Weeks Act in 1911.

Like the forests, tourism in the White Mountains proved resilient. World War I, income tax, and the invention of the reasonably priced Model T combined to doom the grand summer hotels, yet as these languished motor courts mushroomed in the 1920s and '30s, serving middle-class families out for a tour in their new cars. From Boston they traveled up Rt. 3 through Franconia Notch (designated as a state park to frame the Old Man of the Mountains in 1928), on up Rt. 3 to Twin Mountain and down along Rt. 302 through Crawford Notch on the other side of Mount Washington, down to North Conway and back down Rt. 16.

Some of the country's first roadside attractions—the Cog Railway and Carriage Road up Mount Washington, Flume Gorge in Franconia Notch, and Lost River Gorge in Kinsman Notch—already lined this route. Gradually these were augmented by many more attractions, ranging from Clark's Trading Post in the 1920s and the state-funded Cannon Mountain Aerial Tramway in 1938 (conceived as a summer as well as winter operation from the beginning), later by StoryLand, Six Gun City, and Santa's Village. Over the years motels replaced motor courts; beginning in the mid-1980s, the few surviving grand hotels again came into vogue, along with inns and bed & breakfasts. Hiking, which had never ceased to attract enthusiasts, continues to thrive with an expanded AMC support system of shuttles and lodges. Both rock climbing and mountain biking in the WMNF draw athletes from throughout the country.

The White Mountains were also a proving ground for the American ski industry. In February 1905 Norman Libby of Bridgton, Maine, made the first recorded descent on skis down Mount Washington's western slopes, and a Forest Service trail from Tuckerman's Ravine (a high snow bowl on the eastern slopes of Mount Washington) drew pioneer skiers. In the 1930s the new sport exploded in popularity: Peckett's-on-Sugar-Hill claims "the country's first ski school," but several ski schools quickly followed in the town of Jackson. Acclaimed Austrian ski instructor Hannes Schneider established his famous ski school in North Conway, attracting hundreds of patrons who arrived every weekend on the "snow train" from Boston.

In the 1960s and '70s a new phenomenon was added to the region's half dozen "Ski areas": condo-based resorts such as Loon and Waterville Valley, evolving along with the transformation of Rt. 3 into I-93. In the 1970s the interstate brought this Western Whites region an hour closer to Boston, making it more accessible than the Mount Washington Valley, where similar condo clusters have since also turned several of the region's oldest ski areas into "ski resorts." Snowmobiling, tubing, and cross-country skiing have all contributed to their winter appeal for families.

School vacation periods aside, White Mountain ski areas tend to be relatively empty midweek. Summer and fall by contrast bring a steady stream of visitors. Tourists tend to follow the same route popularized in the 1930s, but now—since the opening of the east–west Kancamagus Highway through the heart of the White Mountain National Forest in 1959—it's a loop, "the White Mountain Trail," one of the country's national scenic byways. It continues to access a record number of attractions, both natural and human-made.

WHITE MOUNTAIN NATIONAL FOREST (WMNF)

The 800,000-acre White Mountain National Forest (WMNF) is the largest in the East. Its core 7,000 acres was created by the Weeks Act of 1911. Many forms of recreation—hiking, biking, fishing, camping, cross-country skiing, and snowmobiling—are permitted within this vast, mountainous, and heavily wooded domain. It attracts more than six million visitors annually, but a national park it isn't. Recreation aside, its mission is to conserve wildlife habitat, water, timber, and wilderness. Timber harvesting occurs on roughly 0.05 percent of the entire forest at any given time, with approximately 29 million board feet of timber harvested annually. More than half of the forest is unavailable for harvesting, including 114,000 acres of congressionally designated wilderness.

GUIDANCE **The White Mountains Gateway Visitors Center** in Lincoln (603-745-8720;1-800-346-3687; www.visitwhitemountains.com), just off I-93, Exit 32, includes an authentic post-and-beam barn housing a major WMNF information center. It features interactive displays about wildlife-watching and the history of the White Mountain National Forest. Rangers staff a desk (603-745-3816) stocked with hiking, biking, and cross-country maps, also information about biking trails, fishing, and camping. This is also a source of the parking passes now required within the forest (see *Parking*). The center is open daily year-round 8:30–5, July–Labor Day until 6. This is a great location, handy both to the east–west 34.5-mile-long Kancamagus National Scenic Byway through the heart of the national forest, and to Franconia Notch with its many trails just to the north.

The national forest website is: **www.fs.fed.us/r9/white**. Information is also available from:

WMNF headquarters (603-528-8721), 719 Main St., Laconia 03247. Contact them, especially in the off-season, for details of campgrounds, fishing, hiking, or other activities.

WMNF Saco Ranger Station (603-447-5448) 33 Kangamagus Hwy., just off Rt. 16, Conway. End of May–mid-Oct., open 7 days a week 8–5. Mid-Oct.–end of May, open daily 8–4:30. Rangers dispense timely information about camping, hiking, and biking. Maps, guides, and nature books are sold.

The following ranger stations are open varying hours, depending on the season:

WMNF Androscoggin Ranger Station (603-466-2713), 300 Glen Rd., Gorham.

WMNF Ammonoosuc Ranger Station (603-869-2626), 660 Trudeau Rd., off Rt. 302, Bethlehem.

WMNF Evans Notch District (207-824-2134), 18 Mayville Rd., Bethel, Me.

WMNF Pemigewasset/Ammonoosuc Ranger District (603-536-1310), Rt. 175, Plymouth.

AMC Pinkham Notch Camp (603-466-2725; www.outdoors.org), Rt. 16, Pinkham Notch, and the **AMC Highland Center Lodge at Crawford Notch** (603-466-2727; www.outdoors.org), Rt. 302, Crawford Notch. Center for hiking and camping information as well as lodging in Crawford Notch.

PARKING The **White Mountain National Forest Recreation Pass**. All unattended vehicles parked on national forest land are required—where sign-posted—to display a parking pass: $3 a day at the site, $20 annual pass, $5 good for 7 consecutive days, free for Golden Eagle National Park pass holders

CAMPGROUNDS The WMNF operates 23 campgrounds ranging in size from 7 to 176 sites. No electrical, water, or sewer connections, no camp stores, no playgrounds. Toilets, water, tables, and fireplaces are provided. The sites were designed for tent camping, although trailers and RVs can be accommodated. Most of the campgrounds are open mid-May–mid-Oct., with a few opening earlier and closing later; several are open all winter, though the roads are not plowed. The daily fees range $18–20 per site, first-come, first-served basis.

For some, where indicated below, reservations (1-877-444-6777; www.reserveusa.com) are accepted. The reservation service operates Mar.–Sep. (Mon.–Fri. noon–9 PM, weekends noon–5 PM) and costs $9 in addition to the camping fee. Reservations may be made 120 days before arrival, but 10 days before arrival is the minimum time.

Not to confuse things, **Pro-Sport Inc.** (1-888-CAMPS NH) also maintains a web site listing campgrounds and offers to make reservations.

KATE IMBRIE SETS OUT THE INFO NEEDS AT THE WHITE MOUNTAINS GATEWAY VISITORS CENTER'S HELPFUL RANGER STATION.

Christina Tree

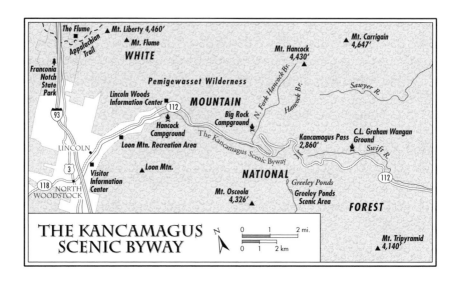

THE KANCAMAGUS
SCENIC BYWAY

The six campgrounds along the **Kancamagus Highway** are among the most popular in the White Mountain National Forest (see Scenic Drive); of these, and only Covered Bridge Campground near Conway takes reservations.

Elsewhere in the Western Whites

Campton Family (Exit 28 off I-93; reservations accepted), **Russell Pond** (Tripoli Rd., Campton), Waterville (I-93, Exit 28; reservations accepted): **Wildwood** on Rt. 112, west of Lincoln, open mid-Apr.–early Dec., 26 sites, good fishing.

In or near Crawford Notch: Just south of Twin Mountain, off Rt. 302, reservations are accepted at **Sugarloaf I Campground and Sugarloaf II**; **Zealand Campground** is first come, first served.

In Pinkham Notch: **Dolly Copp Campground** has 176 sites.

Near Conway: **White Ledge**, Rt. 16, Albany; 28 sites; reservations accepted.

In Evans Notch on the Maine–New Hampshire border (Rt. 113 south of Rt. 2): there are five campgrounds: **Basin** (21 sites), **Cold River** (14 sites), **Crocker Pond** (7 sites), and **Hastings** (24 sites) all accept reservations; **Wild River** is first come, first served.

Backcountry camping is permitted in many areas of the WMNF but generally not within 200 feet of trails, lakes, or streams or within 0.25 mile of roads, most designated campsites or huts, at certain trailheads, or along certain trails. There are also many designated backcountry camping sites, some with shelters, others with tent platforms. The WMNF promotes a carry-in, carry-out, low-impact, leave-no-trace policy for backcountry hikers and campers; fires are prohibited in many areas, and the use of portable cooking stoves is encouraged, if not required. Restricted-use areas, which help protect the backcountry from overuse, are located in many parts of the forest. See www.fs.fed.us/r9/white for a copy of

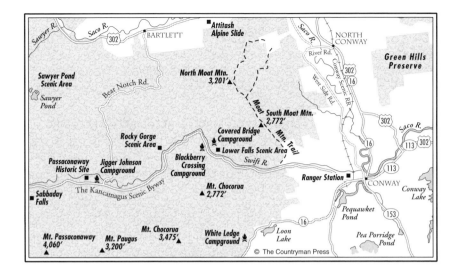

White Mountain National Forest Backcountry Camping Rules or check out one of the Forest Service's ranger stations listed above.

FISHING The WMNF publishes a comprehensive guide to trout fishing in the forest. More than 30 pond sites are listed, plus suggestions for stream fishing. A New Hampshire fishing license is required. A map showing "Fishing Opportunities on the White Mountain National Forest" can be downloaded from the WMNF web site.

HIKING The WMNF is crisscrossed with 1,200 miles of hiking trails, some short and quite easy, others longer, and many challenging even for the most experienced backcountry traveler. A long, difficult section of the Appalachian Trail crosses the forest from the southwest to the northeast corner. The weather on the high mountains of the Presidential and Franconia Ranges can approach winter conditions in any month of the year, so hikers should be well prepared with extra food and proper clothing. Bring your own drinking water since *Giardia*, a waterborne intestinal bacterium, is found throughout the mountains. Although trails are well marked, a good map or guide is essential. We recommend the *AMC White Mountain Guide* (27th edition) and waterproof detailed maps published by the Appalachian Mountain Club, available locally and at www .outdoors.org.

Note the option of bunking down along hiking trails through the Presidentials, the highest of the White Mountains, in AMC huts. See *Applachain Mountain Club* in "What's Where."

WINTER USE **Cross-country and snowshoe** trail maps are available at the nearest ranger stations. In the Western Whites: **Lincoln Woods Trails** at the western end of the Kanc. **Beaver Brook Loops**, a system of 3 loops in Twin

Mountain–Franconia. **Greeley Ponds Trail**, accessible from the Kanc and from Waterville Valley. **Smarts Brook Trail** off Rt. 49 in Waterville Valley.

Elsewhere: **Connie's Way** in Pinkham Notch. **Hayes Copp**, parking at Dolly Copp Campground. **Spruce Goose**, from Zealand parking area.

Downhill skiing is available at Tuckerman's Ravine. For details see "Mount Washington and Its Valleys."

Snowmobiling. Large portions of the WMNF are off-limits to snowmobiling, trail bikes, and off-road vehicles. For details contact the Trails Bureau, New Hampshire Division of Parks and Recreation (603-271-3254; www.nhtrails.org).

SCENIC DRIVE Kancamagus National Scenic Byway (Rt. 112). The 34.5-mile paved highway is open all year, weather conditions permitting, but there are no motorist services on the road. Named for a local 17th-century American Indian chief, the highway was opened in 1959 but not fully paved until 1964. More than 750,000 vehicles travel this route, declared a National Scenic Byway in 1996, every year. On the western side of the mountains, the road begins on Rt. 112 just beyond Loon Mountain Resort (I-93, Exit 32). Stop at the White Mountains Gateway Visitors Center to pick up detailed hiking directions. Beginning at the eastern end on Rt. 16, just south of Conway village, look for the Saco Ranger Station. Both are comprehensive information centers, open daily year-round.

Note: The following descriptions are listed from west to east—Lincoln to Conway.

5 miles east of I-93, Exit 32 in Lincoln: **The Lincoln Woods Information Center** is a log cabin ranger station staffed year-round. Stop and walk at least as far as the middle of the suspenion bridge across the Pemigewasset River, frequently a rushing torrent. From here the **Lincoln Woods Trail** follows an old logging railbed along the East Branch of the Pemi (a popular cross-country ski trail in

LOWER FALLS SCENIC AREA

William Davis

winter), and the **Black Pond Trail** leads to a trout pond. The **Hancock Campground** (50 sites, 35 suitable for RVs) is also here. This marks the southern edge of the Pemigewasset Wilderness, one of the largest wilderness areas in the eastern United States.

7 miles east is the **Big Rock Campground** (28 sites).

9 miles east you'll find the trailhead for the **Greeley Ponds Scenic Area**. Both ponds are good trout-fishing and picnicking spots. Hardy hikers and cross-country skiers continue into Waterville Valley.

Here the highway begins a long climb to **Kancamagus Pass** (2,860 feet), the highest point on this route, where

William Davis

SABBADAY FALLS

there are several scenic lookouts. As you traverse the pass, you leave the valley of the Pemigewasset behind and cross over into the Swift River watershed.

C. L. Graham Wangan Ground is a picnic spot (a *wangan* was a logging company store) near picturesque **Lily Pond**.

Turn off for **Sabbaday Falls**. The falls are a very pleasant 10-minute hike from the highway. If you have time for only one stop along the Kanc, this is it. The trail is easy, and the falls flow through a gap between towering rock walls. Resist the temptation to swim in the pothole below; there is no swimming allowed here.

The **Russell Colbath House Historic Site** is another rewarding stop. The 1831 restored farm house (open daily mid-June–Labor Day, weekends Memorial Day–Columbus Day) is the only homestead remaining and, along with a small nearby cemetery, is all that's left of a once prosperous farming and logging community. The house, furnished with period antiques, is now a museum. A costumed National Forest Service volunteer tells visitors the story of the last resident, Passaconaway's postmistress Ruth Russell Colbath. In 1891 her husband, Thomas Colbath, left the house saying he would be back "in a little while." She never saw him again but kept a light burning in a window to guide him home every night until her death in 1930. Three years later, Thomas turned up and, after trying unsuccessfully to inherit her estate, disappeared again. A Colonial-style post-and-beam barn was recently constructed at the site. It has toilets and picnic tables and is used for ranger lectures and special events. **The Rail 'n' River Trail**, a 0.5-mile interpretive loop from this visitors center, is surprisingly varied. Just east is the Jigger Johnson Campground (74 sites).

12 miles from Rt. 16 **Bear Notch Road** (not maintained in winter) diverges right for Bartlett and Rt. 302. This 9.3-mile paved road has several impressive overlooks on its northern end.

About 1.5 miles east is the **Champney Falls Trail** (3.8 miles, 3½ hours) to Mount Chocorua. The falls are an easy 3-mile round trip on the lower section of the trail. They are named for Benjamin Champney, founder of the White Mountain School of Painting, who worked in this region of the mountains for more than 60 years.

About 9 miles from Rt. 16 is the **Rocky Gorge Scenic Area**, an interesting geological site where the rushing river has washed its way through the rocks. The footbridge leads to Falls Pond. Barrier-free restrooms, drinking water, and picnic tables are found at the scenic area.

Six miles from Rt. 16: Dugway Road diverges right, through the **Albany Covered Bridge** to the WMNF **Covered Bridge Campground** (49 sites, reservations accepted). The Albany covered bridge itself was built in 1858 and renovated in 1970; it is 136 feet long. Near the bridge the **Boulder Loop Nature Trail** (3.1 miles; allow 2 hours) leaves Dugway Road and ascends rocky ledges, offering views up and down the river valley. An informative leaflet, keyed to numbered stations, is available at the Saco Ranger Station. Across the valley is Mount Chocorua, and to its right are Paugus and Passaconaway, named, like the byway itself, for Native American chiefs who once lived in this region. Dugway Road can be followed east to a junction with the West Side Road, just north of Conway village. Midway along this route, the road passes the trailhead for **South Moat Mountain** (elevation 2,772 feet), one of our favorite hikes. The 2.3-mile trail (2 hours) offers magnificent views in all directions from its open, rocky summit. En route, in-season, can be seen lady's slippers and wild blueberries. This trail follows the long ridge to **North Moat Mountain**, then down to **Diana's Baths** and the River Road, a total hike of 9.3 miles requiring about 6 hours to the WMNF Covered Bridge Campground. Opposite the junction of the Kancamagus Byway and Dugway Road is the **Blackberry Crossing Campground** (26 sites, open year-round; walk-in only in winter), and 0.5 mile west is the **Lower Falls Scenic Area**, which has restrooms, drinking water, and picnic tables. On a summer weekend afternoon you will be amazed at how many people can squeeze onto the rocks at this popular swimming hole. This is not a wilderness experience, but what a treat for people who spend most of their lives in the city!

Continuing east, the road closely parallels the winding, rocky Swift River, offering views across the rushing water to South Moat Mountain.

Also see scenic drives through **Crawford**, **Pinkham**, and **Evans Notches** in "Mount Washington and Its Valleys."

ROCKY GORGE SCENIC AREA

William Davis

THE WESTERN WHITES

INCLUDING THE WATERVILLE VALLEY REGION AND LINCOLN AND NORTH WOODSTOCK

The heart of the Western Whites is Franconia Notch, a high pass between the granite walls of Cannon Mountain and Mount Lafayette. Here I-93 narrows and traffic slows as it enters Franconia Notch State Park. This "Franconia Notch Parkway" accesses easy strolls into the dramatic Flume Gorge, and the Basin, to the aerial tram to the top of Cannon Mountain and the beach at Echo Lake. Trails also lead to AMC huts and represent some of the White Mountains' most rewarding day hikes.

A footpath from Franconia Notch to the top of Mount Lafayette is said to have been blazed as early as 1825, the year the area's first hotel opened. By the 1880s it was served by a narrow-gauge railroad transporting patrons to several hotels here, including the 400-room Profile House. The nearby villages of Franconia, Bethlehem, and North Woodstock also had more than their share of the White Mountains' best 19th-century summer hotels.

The area's steep, heavily wooded mountains were as enticing to loggers as to tourists. While early conservationists fought to preserve the "notches" and "gorges," lumber companies built wilderness railways and employed small armies of men to clear-cut vast tracts. Legendary lumberman James E. Henry transformed the little outpost of Lincoln, with 110 residents in 1890, into a booming logging center of 1,278 by 1910. His J. E. Henry Company owned 115,000 acres of virgin timber along the East Branch of the Pemigewasset River, reducing much of it to pulp.

Ultimately the tourists won out over the loggers. The Society for the Protection of New Hampshire Forests (SPNHF) was formed, an outgrowth of the Appalachian Mountain Club (AMC), specifically to work for the passage of the 1911 Weeks Act, enabling legislation to found White Mountain National Forest.

This Pemigewasset ("Pemi") River area became part of the White Mountain National Forest in the mid-1930s. In 1959 a 35-mile east–west forest road through its heart, climbing to almost 3,000 feet on the flank of Mount Kancamagus, was

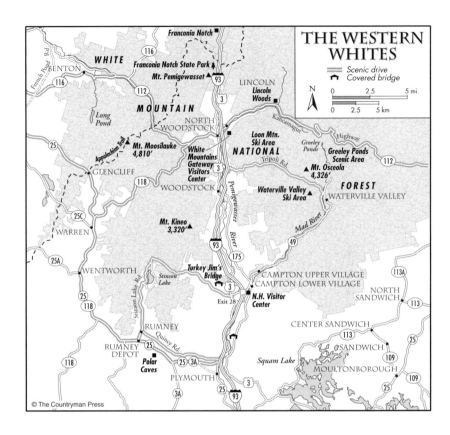

THE WESTERN WHITES

Scenic drive
Covered bridge

© The Countryman Press

opened as a scenic highway. It offers the national forest's most popular campsites and many hiking trails as well as several historic sites.

The Pemi was still being logged in 1923 when Sherman Adams came to Lincoln to work for the Parker-Young Co., J. E. Henry's successor. Over the next 20 years Adams came to know the valley intimately, and when he returned to Lincoln in the 1960s after having served as New Hampshire's governor and President Eisenhower's chief of staff, he opened Loon Mountain Ski Area.

In that same month another public figure—young ex-Olympic skier Tom Corcoran—opened another ski area less than a dozen miles away (as the crow flies) in Waterville Valley. Up in Franconia Notch, state-run Cannon Mountain's aerial tramway and steep slopes had been attracting skiers since 1938, but these newcomers both represented something novel—rather than being just "ski areas," both were "ski resorts," spawning new communities.

Dictated by both the personalities of their founders and the lay of their land, Loon Mountain and Waterville Valley have, however, developed differently. Conservative Adams saw his business as running a ski area and left condominium development to others. Corcoran, fresh from Aspen, planned a self-contained, Rockies-style resort from the start. Loon's facilities, moreover, lined a narrow shelf of land above the Pemigewasset River on the edge of a mill town, whereas Waterville was in an isolated valley with two ski hills facing each other across 500 acres just waiting to be filled.

Loon Mountain and Waterville Valley are now both owned by California-based Booth Creek and, thanks to their abundance of attractive, family-geared lodging, are as busy in summer as winter. Local summer-only family-geared attractions, most predating the region's ski era, increase the appeal of this region.

The "beaten track" through the Western Whites remains delightfully narrow. The quiet old resort villages of Bethlehem, Franconia, and Sugar Hill have changed little in many decades thanks to the persistence of locals and new arrivals who have worked side by side to preserve the area's heritage, and the Ammonoosuc Valley retains its distinctively remote feel. Farther south, the Baker River Valley offers another little-traveled, scenic byway through the mountains.

The full magnificence of the mountains themselves can only be appreciated by climbing (or riding) to their summits, but the beauty of their high, narrow notches and hidden valleys is accessible to all.

GUIDANCE **The White Mountains Gateway Visitors Center** (603-745-8720; 1-800-346-3687; www.visitthewhitemountains.com). Open 8:30–5 daily, until 6 in summer. A walk-in facility (just off I-93, Exit 32, on the Lincoln–North Wood-stock line) with restrooms, features displays on the history and nature of the area and has recently expanded to include a Forest Service information center, an outstanding source of lodging, dining, and general information for this entire area.

Ski New Hampshire Association (1-800-887-5464; www.ski.nh.com), based at the White Mountains Visitors Center in Lincoln (see above), is an information source for all the state's major ski areas.

Note: Chambers of commerce are also listed under *Guidance* within the three sections of this chapter, "The Waterville Valley Region," "Lincoln and North Woodstock" (covering the Loon Mountain area), and "Franconia and North of the Notches."

Waterville Valley itself is a 10-mile-deep cul-de-sac cut by one of New England's many Mad Rivers and circled by majestic mountains, many of them more than 4,000 feet tall.

In 1835 city folk began flocking to the town's sole lodging establishment for rest and relaxation, and by 1868 the green-shuttered inn was consistently booked. Families were attracted to the area to pursue more strenuous activities like hiking but also devoted themselves to prayer and Bible study in this inspiring wilderness. The original visitors and their progeny found the valley addictive and, in 1919, purchased the inn when it came up for sale. So principled were they that in 1928 they donated all but a few hundred of their 26,000 acres to the White Mountain National Forest. These same families founded and filled the ski clubs that fueled the inn's winter economy, beginning in 1935 when a few trails were etched on Snow's Mountain. In 1937 the Civilian Conservation Corps (CCC) cut a precipitous 1.5-mile trail down the southern shoulder of Mount Tecumseh, across the valley from Snow's.

Tom Corcoran, a prep school student from Exeter, dreamed of skiing the treacherous Tecumseh Trail and arrived at Waterville Valley in 1949 to pursue his goal. Corcoran continued downhill racing with Dartmouth's ski team, then the U.S. Olympic ski team, and headed west to work for the Aspen Corporation, for which he conducted a feasibility study that led to the acquisition of Buttermilk Mountain. By 1965, when Corcoran was ready to buy his own ski mountain, the Waterville Valley Inn was up for sale along with 425 acres—virtually all the town that wasn't in the national forest.

Corcoran's Waterville Valley—complete with four chairlifts, a T-bar, even some snowmaking—opened for Christmas 1966. The inn burned that first season, but two new ski lodges were ready the following year, as were some condominiums, then as new to the eastern ski scene as snowmaking.

Over the years Tom Corcoran developed Mount Tecumseh into a major ski mountain, and added five condo-style lodges and more than 500 condominiums, a pond, a sports center, a nine-hole golf course, and a year-round skating rink. Finally, at the center of the resort, he built a "Town Square": three interconnected, clapboard buildings 4½ stories high with traditional saltbox lines, softened by modern touches like an occasional round window and 100 dormers, a variation on the lines of an old White Mountain hotel.

In 1995 Waterville Valley Ski Area was acquired by S-K-I, New England's largest ski conglomerate, and the organization expanded the resort's snowmaking capabilities. By 1997 still another group of owners had assumed control of the resort, and year-round this area continues to be an outstanding, self-contained, family-geared resort.

The neighboring village of Campton offers a few friendly bed & breakfasts and restaurants. You'll find a surprisingly youthful atmosphere in nearby Plymouth, thanks to Plymouth State University. The number and variety of hikes and scenic drives in this area keep area residents and tourists alike active throughout the year.

GUIDANCE **Waterville Valley Region Chamber of Commerce** (603-726-3804; 1-800-237-2307), just off I-93, Exit 28, in Campton. Open 9–5 daily. Restrooms, brochures, and phones. Here you can purchase snowmobile licenses and activity-specific guidebooks from the helpful staff.

GETTING THERE *By bus:* **Concord Trailways** (603-228-3300; 1-800-639-3317; www.concordtrailways.com) from Boston's Logan Airport stops in Plymouth Chase Street Market at 83 Main St. Check with lodging to arrange local transportation.

By car: I-93 to Exit 28, then 11 miles up Rt. 49.

GETTING AROUND **The Shuttle Connection in Lincoln** (603-745-3140; 1-800-545-3140; www.theshuttleconnection.com) provides a 24-hour service among attractions, ski areas, airports, and bus terminals.

MEDICAL EMERGENCY Dial **911**.

Plymouth Regional Clinic (603-536-4467), 258 Highland St. in Plymouth, offers limited service weekdays.

✳ Towns and Villages

Plymouth (population: 6,200). From I-93, what you see of Plymouth are the high-rise dorms of Plymouth State University, a clue to the existence of shops and restaurants catering to the needs of 4,000 students. What you don't see from the highway is the region's appealing old commercial center. Its mills have produced mattresses, gloves, and shoe trees as well as lumber. The long-vanished Pemigewasset House, built by the president of the Boston, Concord & Montréal Railroad, was favored by Nathaniel Hawthorne, who was living in Plymouth before his death in 1864. Today the college campus forms the centerpiece for the town, and some good restaurants can be found within walking distance.

Rumney (population: 1,474). A picture-perfect village with a classic common, Rumney is in the Baker Valley, just far enough off the beaten path to preserve its tranquility. The Mary Baker Eddy House, Quincy Bog, the Town Pound, and Stinson Lake are all described under *Scenic Drives.*

Warren (population: 904). A white-clapboard village at the base of Mount Moosilauke, Warren has had more than its share of monuments. First there was the massive Morse Museum, built in the 1920s by a Warren native who made a fortune making shoes in Lowell, Massachusetts. It displayed exotica from his travels, as well as the world's largest private shoe collection. The Morse Museum was closed several years ago (even the mummies were sold off), but the Redstone Rocket booster with USA emblazoned on its side still towers bizarrely over the common. A local restaurant owner, we're told, brought it back from Huntsville, Alabama, and tried to give it to Derry, New Hampshire (home of astronaut Alan Shepard), which refused to take it. Warren, we understand, remains divided on whether it belongs there or not; the VFW post keeps it painted. Ask directions to the Dartmouth Outing Club cabin. From the cabin a former carriage road (to a former summit hotel) is one among a choice of hiking trails to the summit. Warren is so off the beaten path that's it's useful to note it offers two eateries— The Garlic Glove and Calamity Jane's—and a B&B.

Wentworth (population: 793). A picturesque, white wooden village with a triangular common, set above the Baker River.

✳ To See

COVERED BRIDGES **Blair bridge**. The easiest way to find this bridge is from I-93, Exit 27; at the bottom of the exit ramp, follow Blair Rd. to the blinking light, then go straight across.

Turkey Jim's bridge. At I-93, Exit 28, follow Rt. 49 west. After about 0.5 mile (as you cross over the metal bridge), look for a sign on your right for Branch Brook Campground. You must drive into the campground to see the bridge.

Bump bridge. At I-93, Exit 28, follow Rt. 49 east for about 0.5 mile. Turn right at the traffic lights and go over the dam. Turn right again onto Rt. 175 south. After 3 or 4 miles, you come to a sharp left turn; bear to the left and stay straight, down the dirt road. Take the first right, and the covered bridge is about 0.5 mile on your left.

FOR FAMILIES ✔ **Polar Caves** (603-536-1888; www.polarcaves.com), Rt. 25, 4 miles west of Plymouth. Open early May–mid-Oct., 9–5. Discovered by neighborhood children around 1900 and opened as a commercial attraction in 1922, this is an extensive property with a series of caves connected by passageways and walkways, with taped commentaries at stations along the way. The name refers to the cold air rising from the first "ice" cave, where the temperature in August averages 55 degrees. There's much here to learn about minerals and geology, much that's just fun. Added in 2005: a new cave, a mining sluice, and an extensive rock garden with contrasting hot and cool sections and formations for kids to crawl through. The complex includes picnic tables and a snack bar. $12 adult, $9.50 ages 4–9.

Also see **Waterville Valley Resort** for summer activities.

SCENIC DRIVES **Rumney Loop**. The easiest way to begin is from Rts. 25/3A west of Plymouth. Take Airport Rd., then go left on Quincy Rd. The sign for **Quincy Bog** (603-786-9465) should be just beyond Quincy State Forest, but if the sign is down, look for stone pillars flanking a small road to the right. One-tenth of a mile down this road look for a left leading to the bog entrance, from which you can access trails and a viewing deck. This 40-acre peat bog is a place to find frogs in April and May, to see bog plant blooms in May and June, to hunt for salamanders and newts, and to bird-watch. The nature center here is open mid-June–mid-Aug. En route to the bog you pass the old **Rumney Town Pound**, an unusual, natural animal pen formed by gigantic boulders. Continue into Rumney, and then head out Main Street and follow it past the **Mary Baker Eddy House** (603-786-9943), home of the founder of Christian Science in the early 1860s (open May–Oct., Tue.–Sat. 10–5). Continue along isolated **Stinson**

Lake, good fishing (trout, perch, pickerel) year-round. **Stinson Mountain Trail** is marked, beginning with a dirt road, then a left through the woods and a right at the brook, up through spruce and fir to the summit ledges. Great views. Continue east on this road out to West Campton and I-93, Exit 28.

The Baker River Valley. The Baker River charts a natural path from the base of Mount Moosilauke southeast through hilly woodland to the Pemigewasset River. It was known as the Asquamchumauke River until 1712, when a group of soldiers headed by Captain Thomas Baker of Northampton, Massachusetts, defeated a band of local Native Americans on the site that's presently Plymouth. Today Rt. 25 shadows the river, beginning as a commercial strip west of Plymouth but quickly improving. You pass the Polar Caves, Rumney, and continue on through Wentworth and Warren. To return to Waterville Valley, take mountainous Rt. 118 east to North Woodstock, then I-93 from Exit 32 to Exit 28.

Tripoli Road (closed in winter). A shortcut from Waterville Valley to I-93 north: roughly 10 miles, paved and unpaved, up through Thornton Gap (a high pass between Mount Osceola and Mount Tecumseh) and over a high shoulder of 4,326-foot Mount Osceola. Begin on West Branch Road (a left before the Osceola Library); cross the one-lane bridge and turn right into the national forest. Note the Mount Osceola Trail 3 miles up the road. Continue through the Thornton Gap. Note trailheads for the Mount Tecumseh and East Pond trails.

Sandwich Notch Road (closed in winter). A steep, roughly 10-mile dirt road from Center Sandwich to Waterville, built 1 rod wide for $300 by the town of Sandwich in the late 18th century. Best attempted in a high, preferably four-wheel-drive vehicle. Be prepared to make way for any vehicle coming from the opposite direction. The road follows the Bearcamp River; stone walls tell of long-vanished farms. Center Sandwich offers a crafts center, museum, and dining (see "The Lake Winnipesaukee Area").

✳ To Do

BICYCLING See **Waterville Valley Resort** for bike rentals and lift-assisted mountain biking on Snow's Mountain, also cross-country trails and logging roads. Mountain bike clinics, special events.

BOATING **Ski Fanatics** (603-726-4327), Rt. 49 in Campton, rents kayaks and offers shuttle service 6 miles or farther up the Pemigewasset so you can paddle back down.

Also see **Waterville Valley Resort**.

FISHING Stream fishing was one of the first lures of visitors to this valley, and the fish are still biting in Russell Pond (Tripoli Rd.) and all along the Mad River, stocked with trout each spring. Campton Pond (at the lights) is a popular fishing hole.

FITNESS CENTER See **Waterville Valley Resort**.

GOLF **Owl's Nest** (1-888-OWL-NEST; www.owlsnestgold.com), Rt. 49, 1 mile west of Exit 28 off I-93, Campton. A par-72 championship, 18-hole course with four sets of tees on each hole, accommodating all skill levels. Restaurant (see *Dining Out*) and lounge.

Waterville Valley Resort (see the box) offers a nine-hole golf course, newly designed for 2006.

Sugar Shack Golf Range (603-726-8978), Rt. 175, Compton. A multipurpose activity center.

HIKING **Mount Osceola**. A 7-mile (round trip), 4½-hour hike beginning on Tripoli Road. The Tripoli Road crests at the 2,300-foot-high Thornton Gap; the Mount Osceola Trail begins some 200 yards beyond. Follow an old tractor road up through many switchbacks and along Breadtray Ridge, then across a brook, up log steps, by another ridge to the summit ledges. This is the highest of the mountains circling Waterville Valley, and the view is spectacular.

Greeley Ponds Trail begins at the end of the old truck road, which is a left off Livermore Road, just past the clearing known as Depot Camp. The trail crosses a wooden footbridge and follows the course of the river to Greeley Ponds between Mounts Osceola and Kancamagus. It's a gradual grade all the way to the upper pond and continues as a gradual ascent to the Kancamagus Highway.

Welch Mountain. Open ledge walking at a surprisingly low elevation overlooking the Mad River Valley. It's a challenging 4-mile, round-trip hike but well worth the sweat. According to local hiking guru Steve Smith, the broad sheets of granite offer views and blueberries in abundance. The panorama from the open summit includes Sandwich Mountain, Mount Tripyramid, Mount Tecumseh, and Mount Moosilauke. You can extend the hike into a loop by continuing over the slightly higher **Dickey Mountain** and its fine north viewpoint (the ledges on this hike may be slippery when wet). The trailhead for this loop is on Orris Road, off Upper Mad River Road between Campton and Waterville Valley.

Also see **Waterville Valley Resort**.

HORSEBACK RIDING **Rocky Ridge Ranch** (603-726-8067), just off I-93, exit 28 (south of the information center). Trail rides offered year-round for beginners and intermediates, as is a 2-hour "adventure ride."

ROCK CLIMBING The most popular spot for rock climbing is the area around Buffalo Road, accessible from I-93 by taking Exit 26 and driving about 8 miles on Rt. 25 until you reach Stinson Lake Road—essentially the town center of Rumney. From there, drive about a mile to a parking lot on the right. The Meadows, the cliffs you'll be scaling, lie directly above this parking area.

SWIMMING On Rt. 49 look for **Smarts Brook Trail**—an easy mile's hike over logging and dirt roads to a swimming hole among the pools of a mountain brook.

Also see **Waterville Valley Resort**.

❋ Winter Sports

DOWNHILL SKIING Waterville Valley (see the box) is the big draw.

✰ **Tenney Mountain** (603-536-4125; 1-888-TENNEY2; www.tenneymtn.com), 151 Tenney Mountain Hwy., Plymouth. This locally popular family mountain delivers affordable family skiing and snowboarding—lots of variety plus a terrain park. *Vertical drop:* 1,450 feet. *Skiable terrain:* 110 acres. *Snowmaking:* 85 percent. *Trails and glades:* 45 (15 percent novice, 54 percent intermediate, 31 percent expert). *Lifts:* 5. *Lift tickets:* Weekends: $35 adults, less for juniors and teens.

❋ Lodging

LODGES

In Waterville Valley

❧ ✰ **Snowy Owl Inn** (603-236-8383; 1-800-766-9969; www.snowyowlinn .com), 4 Village Rd., Waterville Valley 03215. An attractive lodge with a central, three-story fieldstone hearth and a surrounding atrium supported by single log posts; there's a cupola you can sit in. A case can be made that this is the most innlike and romantic of the Waterville Valley lodges, but it's also a good place for families, thanks to the lower-level game rooms adjoining a pleasant breakfast room. There are indoor and outdoor pools as well. Of the 85 rooms, more than half have a wet bar, fridge, and whirlpool tub, and all have voice mail, dataports, and satellite television. A two-bedroom suite offers its own gas log fieldstone fireplace. Rates include a breakfast buffet. Check out the new **Owl's Roost Pub** and **Owl's Landing Restaurant**. $80–120 in summer, $100–195 for rooms, more for condo-style studios and suites per night, depending on room and season.

❧ ✰ **The Golden Eagle** (603-236-4551; 1-800-703-2453; www.golden eaglelodge.com), 6 Snow's Brook Rd., Waterville Valley 03215. Architect Graham Gund's imprint is all over this resort outpost. He first designed the Waterville Valley Town Square, then added this fieldstone- and shingle-sided hotel. Both are a tribute to another era. With its sloping roofs and tall towers, the exterior of the Golden Eagle suggests a monumental, 19th-century mountain lodge, but the inside is totally in tune with today. Amenities include an indoor pool, whirlpools, and saunas. Roughly 90

THE GOLDEN EAGLE AT WATERVILLE VALLEY

Kim Grant

WATERVILLE VALLEY RESORT

(1-800-GO-VALLEY; 1-800-468-2553; www.waterville.com), 1 Ski Area Rd., P.O. Box 540, Waterville Valley 03215.

YEAR-ROUND

FITNESS CENTER **White Mountain Athletic Club** (603-236-8303), Valley Rd. Indoor tennis, racquetball, and squash courts, 25-meter indoor and outdoor swimming pools, jogging track, fitness evaluation facilities, Nautilus exercise equipment, aerobics, whirlpools, saunas and steam rooms, tanning booths, massage service, restaurant/lounge, and game room.

SUMMER

BOATING **Corcoran's Pond at Waterville Valley Resort** (603-236-4666). Paddleboat, canoe, and kayak rentals on 6 acres.

GOLF **Waterville Valley Resort** (603-236-4805). A nine-hole "executive" course; rental carts, new design for 2006.

MOUNTAIN BIKING **Adventure Center** (603-236-4666). Daily July–Labor Day, weekends from Memorial Day and until Columbus Day. Lift-assisted biking to the 2,090-foot summit of Snow's Mountain. Rentals throughout the season.

SCREAMING DOWN MOUNTAIN BIKE TRAILS AT WATERVILLE VALLEY

SKATING **Boarding at the Super Park**. An outdoor skate park featuring a 10-foot-high half-pipe and street court, along with an outdoor dirt BMX track. Lessons, equipment rentals. Part of the Adventure Center (see above). Inquire about skate camp.

SWIMMING **Corcoran's Pond**, with a sandy beach, is Waterville Valley Resort's principal summer swimming area.

White Mountain Athletic Club, Waterville Valley, offers an indoor pool. Several lodges also offer indoor pools.

✐ **Waterville Valley Tennis Center** (603-236-4840). Eighteen outdoor clay courts, two indoor courts at the White Mountain Athletic Club; clinics, round robins. A junior tennis program for children 18 and under includes private lessons, drill sessions, and round robins.

WINTER

DOWNHLL SKIING ✐ **Waterville Valley** (603-236-8311; snow report, 603-236-4144; 1-800-468-2553). It's just a 7-minute ride to the summit of Mount Tecumseh on the high-speed detachable quad, and the way down is via a choice of long, wide cruising trails like Upper Bobby's Run and Tippecanoe. Mogul lovers will find plenty to please them on True Grit and Ciao, and beginners have their own area served by the Lower Meadows Double. Glades and terrain features all over the mountain; Little Slammer and Exhibition Park feature a street hubba and superpipe.

Lifts: 2 high-speed detachable quad lifts, 2 triples, 3 doubles, 5 surface.

Trails and glades: 52 on Mount Tecumseh.

Vertical drop: 2,020 feet.

Snowmaking: 100 percent.

Facilities: Include the inviting Schwendi Hutte near the top of Mount Tecumseh, Sunnyside Lodge (a midmountain oasis with a hearth cafeteria, good soups, and deli sandwiches), the Base Lodge Cafeteria, and T-Bars Bar and Grill.

Ski school: Specializes in clinics for all ages and all abilities, also private lessons for all.

For children: There is a nursery for children from age 6 weeks. Kids Kamps for ages 3–12. Small children have their own hill, with its own lift and terrain garden. Also evening children's programs.

Lift tickets: $49 adults, $39 teens, $29 ages 6–12.   *(Continued on next page)*

(Continued from previous page)

CROSS-COUNTRY SKIING **The Nordic/Adventure Center at Waterville Valley** (603-236-4666; 1-800-468-2553; www.waterville.com), in Town Square, Waterville Valley. Ski school, warming and waxing areas, rentals. More than 100 km through the valley and surrounding national forest; 70 km groomed for classical and skating; 35 additional kilometers marked. When all else fails you can count on a 2.5-km loop covered by snowmaking. Bull Hill is now closed. The center's location in Town Square has its pros and cons: easy access but too many condos to go by before you get up into the woods. On the other hand, you can drive to the edge of the White Mountain National Forest and ski directly off into the woods. Inquire about conditions on the Greeley Ponds Trail. Open daily 8:30–4. Skating as well as classic lessons are offered; also moonlight guided tours, weekly races, and telemark clinics. $15–17 adults, $11–13 ages 6–12, $11–13 seniors.

ICE SKATING **Waterville Valley Ice Arena** (603-236-4813; www.waterville valley.org). A covered, hockey-sized ice-skating rink maintained throughout the year in Town Square. Complete with skate rentals, maintenance, and repairs.

SLEIGH RIDES Throughout the winter, horse-drawn sleigh rides depart afternoons and evenings from **Town Square**, Waterville Valley.

ANYONE CAN LEARN TO SKI AT WATERVILLE VALLEY'S SKI SCHOOL

of the one- and two-bedroom condo suites (all have a kitchen and eating area) are available for rent at $123–288, including resort fee; inquire about the many special packages.

☞ **Black Bear Lodge** (603-236-4501; 1-800-349-2327; www.black-bear-lodge.com), 3 Village Rd., Waterville Valley 03215. This comfortable and well-laid-out condo hotel, a 3-minute walk from Town Square, offers 107 one-bedroom or loft suites that sleep four to six people. Each suite has a kitchen, a dining area, a sitting area with queen-sized bed and cable TV, and a separate bedroom; indoor/outdoor pool, outdoor whirlpool, sauna, steam room, game room, and children's cinema on the lower level. Christmas Eve–Apr. $110–250. Resort fee, additional.

☀ ☞ **Best Western Silver Fox Inn** (603-236-3699; 1-888-236-3699; www.silverfoxinn.com), 14 Snow's Brook Rd., Waterville Valley 03215. If you're looking for a room rather than a suite, this is a lower-cost alternative. All 32 guest rooms are air-conditioned, with two double beds or one queen. Breakfast, afternoon wine and cheese, and free shuttle service are included. Summer rates $110–120.

☀ ☞ **Valley Inn** (603-236-8336; 1-800-343-0969; www.valleyinn.com), Tecumseh Rd., Waterville Valley 03215. An attractive, 52-room lodge with an indoor/outdoor pool, whirlpool, saunas, exercise room, game room; the only valley lodging with its own dining room. All rooms have TV and phone, and some have kitchen unit, fireplace, sauna, or whirlpool bath. In summer, from $64 for a standard room to $225 for a suite with a deck, kitchen facilities, fireplace, and whirlpool bath.

In Campton

Note that the village of Campton is just off I-93, 10 miles west of Waterville Valley.

☀ ☞ **The Mountain-Fare Inn** (603-726-4283; www.mountainfareinn.com; mtnfareinn@cyberportal.net), 5 Old Waterville Rd., Campton 03223. Susan and Nick Preston run this B&B as smoothly as they do the slopes at Waterville Valley. Both high-powered coaches of competitive skiers (including U.S. ski team members), the Prestons spend their off-slope time managing one of the most classic ski lodges around. Their 1840s village home and carriage house annex offer 10 sunny guest rooms, many with wide-pine floors and all furnished with bright fabrics and country antiques. All but one have a private bath. Common space includes an old-fashioned living room, a great game room with pool table, television, card tables, and woodstove, and a place to store and tune skis. There's also a sauna. Guests sit down together (or separately) to breakfast in the pleasant dining room where a very full, buffet-style breakfast is set out. $95–140 high-season doubles; $75–135 low-season doubles. A great place for a family reunion.

The Sunny Grange B&B (603-726-5555; 1-877-726-5553; www.sunnygrange.com), 134 Rt. 175, Campton 03223. Situated at the intersection with Mad River Road on a triangular piece of land, this lovely yellow farmhouse built in 1811 is tastefully decorated, inviting, and relaxed. There are five rooms with private bath and access to the common areas that include fireplaces and gas-fired stoves. Two rooms are 2-room suites with fireplace, Jacuzzis, and sitting areas. Each room has telephone, air-conditioning, and TV/VCR combination. A full country breakfast is included in $95–150, depending on the room and season.

🐾 ✍ **The Campton Inn** (603-726-4449; 1-888-511-0790; peter@evp creative.com), Rt. 175 and Owl St., Campton 03223. A vintage-1835 multi-gabled village house offers a large living room with a woodstove and piano, and a pleasant screened porch. Five guest rooms, one with private bath, some designed for families. $60–90.

Elsewhere

🐾 ✍ **The Common Man Inn** (603-536-2200; 1-866-843-2626; www.the cmaninn.com), Main St., turn right off I-93 Exit 26 in Plymouth. (Mail: P.O. Box 581, Ashland 03217). A great new lodging option: an 1890s birch mill converted with the sure touch that marks everything this locally based group touches. Each of the 37 themed rooms is different; all are equipped with wireless access, some with lofts, fireplace, deck, and Jacuzzi. From $99 for a queen-bedded room in low season to $199 for an Adirondack-style "camp" suite with all the bells and whistles in high season. Inquire about packages. Amenities include a restaurant, tavern, and full-service spa.

Federal House Inn (603-536-4644; 1-866-536-4644; www.federalhouse innnh.com), junction of Rts. 27 and 25, Plymouth 03264. This classic vintage-1825 brick home has been expanded and renovated to hold two attractive guest rooms and three suites. Common space includes a library and living room with fireplace; amenities include an outside hot tub. Handy to Tenney Mountain. $99–180 includes a full breakfast.

Warren Village Inn (603-764-5600; www.warrenvillageinn.com), 254 Rt. 25, S. Main St., Warren 03279. In all honesty we didn't get to Warren on this update swing, but we applaud anyone who dares open a B&B in such an out-of-the-way place. This is a great old Victorian house; the five rooms are each $89 with private bath.

Deep River Motor Inn (603-536-2155; 1-800-445-6809; www.deep rivermotorinn.com), 166 Highland St., Plymouth 03264. The 21 units in this tidy, family-run motel range from standard motel rooms with two double beds, cable TV, and air-conditioning to seasonal cottage units with kitchens. From $55 (for a standard unit for a couple and two children) to $125; cottages $135–165.

🐾 ✍ **Hilltop Acres** (603-764-5896), East Side and Buffalo Rd., Wentworth 03282. Open May–Oct. A pleasant old farmhouse with a large, pine-paneled rec room containing an antique piano, cable television, fireplace, and plenty of books. Rooms with private bath run $100; also, two traditional housekeeping cottages with fireplace and screened porch ($125 per night, $750 per week). Pets and children are permitted in the cottages. Room rates include breakfast.

CONDOMINIUMS Some 500 condominiums are scattered in clusters between the ski slopes and Town Square, but most are not in the rental pool. Also see www.waterville.com.

✍ **Village Condominiums** (603-236-8301; 1-800-532-6630; www.village condo.com) rents roughly a dozen condos that it manages. Quality is uniformly high, but since these units lack the indoor pools and game rooms enjoyed by lodge guests, it's important to make sure rentals include access to the nearby White Mountain Athletic Club. Rates are $125–302.50 (plus tax and a 15 percent service charge and resort fee) for a two-bedroom condo; a five-bedroom unit runs $245–600.

Waterville Condo (603-236-4101; 1-800-556-6522; www.resortcondos .com). Rents some 40 condo units within the resort area.

Waterville Valley Town Square 1-888-462-9887; www.townsquare condos.com), P.O. Box 344, Waterville Valley 03215, rents 32 units on upper floors of Town Square itself. Handy to shops and the touring/Adventure Center, but access involves elevator plus step—complicated when you're toting ski gear. $171–281 in summer/fall.

Also see the **Black Bear** and the **Golden Eagle**. Both are condo hotels with efficiency units.

CAMPGROUNDS **White Mountain National Forest**. In the WMNF section of this chapter check the **Campton**, **Russell Pond**, **and Waterville** sites.

Branch Brook Campground in Campton (603-726-7001) and **Goose Hollow Campground** in Waterville Valley (603-726-2000) are privately owned alternatives.

✳ Where to Eat

DINING OUT **William Tell** (603-726-3618), Rt. 49, Thornton. Open for dinner in winter and summer seasons except Wed.; also for Sunday brunch noon–3. The pretty stucco-and-timber exterior of this long-standing local favorite is a tip-off for the menu inside. Tried-and-true Swiss and German specialties like Wiener schnitzel and veal geschnetzeltes Zurichoise

(thinly sliced veal sautéed with mushroom brandy cream sauce), prepared by Swiss native Franz Dubach. There's also a less expensive menu featuring bratwurst, osso buco, and "pastetli William Tell" (puff pastry filled with veal dumplings, vegetables, and rosti potato). Dinner entrées run $12.95 for sautéed seasonal vegetables served with barley risotto, to $22.50 for Zurcher Ratsherren Topf (charbroiled filet mignon, veal, and pork tenderloin, served with the house butter, tomato, and mushroom sauce.) Reservations recommended.

Foster's Steakhouse (603-536-2764; www.thecman.com), I-93, exit 26, 231 Main St., Plymouth. Open daily 5–9, also Sunday brunch 10–2. Housed in a former birch mill, part of the Common Man family of restaurants. Great atmosphere, dependable fare ranging from cedar-planked haddock and lobster crabcakes to a 20-ounce bone-in rib-eye steak with carmelized onions and sautéed mushrooms. Entrées $15.95–21.95.

The Sunset Room at Owl's Nest Golf Club (603-726-3076, ext. 215), junction of Rt. 49 and Owl St., Campton. Open daily for lunch and dinner. We've heard rave reviews for this attractive dining room with its views west over the mountains. The menu might include PEI mussels in a cilantro-Dijon cream sauce, baby back ribs, and espresso-rubbed rib-eye steak. Entrées $15–21; "small plates" also available.

Wild Coyote Grill (603-236-4919; www.wildcoyotegrill.com), Rt. 49, above the White Mountain Athletic Club in Waterville Valley. Dinner daily 5:30 PM–close. Casually elegant. Starters include fried calamari and sesame-seared tuna. Entrées might range from soba noodles with vegetables, tofu, and Thai peanut sauce ($12.50) to seared red deer medallions seared with fine herbs and blackberry brandy demiglaze, served with organic red rice. Entrées $12.50–18.99.

♪ **Diamonds' Edge North** (603-236-2006; www.diamondsedge.com/north.html), Town Square. Open daily for dinner, the upscale option in Town Square. A wide-ranging menu featuring pastas and steaks (entrées $11–22) with a "lighter fare" (burgers and sandwiches) and a Young Adult's Menu also available.

EATING OUT

In Waterville Valley
♪ **Latitudes Café** (603-236-4646), Town Square. Lunch and dinner served daily 11:30–9. Closed Apr. and May. A cheerful, reasonably priced café with booths, brew on tap.

Jugtown Sandwich Shop and Ice Cream Parlor (603-236-3669), the heart of Town Square. Open daily 9 AM–4 PM. An extensive deli featuring specialty sandwiches. There are some tables, but in warm-weather months you just step outside with salads and sandwiches to the tables in the square. Fresh bagels and breads baked daily. Sandwiches are served through late afternoon; ice cream all evening.

Waterville Valley Coffee Emporium (603-236-4021), Town Square. Open daily 6:30 AM–6 PM. Enjoy cappuccinos, lattes, smoothies, chai, breakfast waffles and omelets, afternoon tea, homemade pastries, and other treats while overlooking the pond and mountains.

In Campton
🍲 **Mad River Tavern & Restaurant** (603-726-4290), Rt. 49 (just off I-93,

Exit 28). Closed Tue., otherwise open for dinner, lunch on weekends. Serving Fri. and Sat. until 11 PM. A homey atmosphere with an overstuffed couch, blackboard specials, and a large, varied menu. There's a wide choice of pastas and breads as well as fish. We recommend the veal Oscar, lightly breaded and topped with lobster, asparagus, and béarnaise sauce. Burgers, sandwiches, salads, beer, and wine are also served. Appetizers $2–10; pasta $7–14; entrées $11–18. Lunch $4–7.

♪ **Sunset Grill** (603-726-3108), corner of Rts. 3 and 49. Open daily except Mon. 11:30 AM–10 PM, Sunday brunch 9–2. A funky, friendly roadhouse with good food: a wide selection of pastas and house specials ranging from calves' liver to buffalo steak; also burgers, chili, and Cajun dishes. Sunday brunch is a specialty, featuring lobster omelets and crêpes Florentine. Fifty brands of bottled beer. "Kids Menu."

Mischievous Moose Deli (603-726-1700), Rt. 49, Campton Corners (Exit 28 off I-93). Open daily 8–4. A good deli strategically positioned across from the local tourist information center, just off I-93. Freshly made soups, salads (chef's, tossed, and spinach), and hefty sandwiches stuffed with a variety of luncheon meats, cheeses, and veggies on rye, white, and wheat bread, bulky rolls, or tortilla wraps slathered with Boursin-style garlic-herb cheese. Daily Moose Blue Plate specials.

In Plymouth
Biederman's Deli and Pub (603-536-3354), 83 Main St., under Chase Street Market. Open for lunch and dinner daily. A brick-walled, pubby spot claiming 180,000 combinations using Boars Head meats and cheeses;

also deli salads and bag lunches, a wide selection of beers. Inquire about comedy nights and live bands.

♪ **The Main Street Station** (603-536-7577), 105 Main St. Open Wed.–Sat. 7 AM–9 PM, Sun. 8–2, Mon. 7–2. A classic diner car on Plymouth's tightly packed Main Street. A big menu includes international dishes, fish, salads, and sandwiches—but don't look for diner standards unless you're interested in New England–style desserts like blueberry pie, strawberry shortcake, or apple crisp. Breakfasts are a gut-busting affair of eggs in all forms, pancakes, waffles, and French toast; kids are well catered to with a special menu; wine and beer with dinner.

Italian Farmhouse (603-536-4536), 331 Rt. 3, 2 miles south of Plymouth. It's also 4 miles north of I-93 exit 24. Open for dinner nightly. Another Common Man creation, an old farmhouse now a local favorite featuring fresh-baked Italian bread, fried calamari, stuffed veal and brick-oven pizza.

The Country Cow Restaurant at Blair Bridge (603-536-1331), off I-93, Exit 27. Blair Rd., Campton. Lunch daily, dinner except Tue., Sunday brunch. Karaoke Thu. at 9. Chef owned, cheerful, reasonably priced pastas, salads, steaks, lighter items like a veggie bowl and burgers. Full liquor.

George's Seafood & B-B-Que (603-536-6330), 588 Tenney Mountain Hwy., Plymouth. Open for lunch and dinner. Steak and pasta as well as a variety of fresh seafood and ribs. Beer and wine, reasonable prices.

✳ Entertainment

Plymouth Theater (603-536-1089), 39 S. Main St., Plymouth. A 1930s movie palace that's recently been restored; screens a broad assortment of films.

Silver Cultural Arts Center at Plymouth State University (603-535-ARTS; 1-800-779-3869; www .plymouth.edu/cac), Main and Court sts., Plymouth. A series of concerts, theater, and live performances are staged Sep.–May.

✳ Selective Shopping

CRAFTS SHOPS **Shanware Pottery** (603-786-9835), Rt. 25, Rumney. A working studio in a rustic barn features distinctive, functional stoneware pottery and porcelain: mugs, casseroles, chimes, dinnerware, lamps, and distinctive, doughnut-shaped wine casks, among many other items.

SPECIAL SHOPS

In Waterville Valley Town Square

Dreams and Visions (603-236-2020), 6 Village Rd. Books and gifts.

♪ **Bookmonger and Toad Hall** (603-236-4544). Toys and games for children of all ages, paperbacks, games, CDs, magazines, general titles.

✳ Special Events

Easter Sunday: **Sunrise service** on Mount Tecumseh.

Fourth of July: **Parade and fireworks** at Waterville Valley.

August: **Plymouth State Fair**, Plymouth.

September: **Waterville Valley Labor Day End of Summer Bash**.

Columbus Day weekend: **Fall Foliage Festival** at Waterville Valley.

November: **Ski trails open** mid-month at Waterville Valley; **tree lighting** Thanksgiving weekend.

North Woodstock is a sleepy village. Lincoln, a mile east, is one of New Hampshire's liveliest resort towns. Until relatively recently, the opposite was true. Around the turn of the 20th century, Lincoln boomed into existence as a company town with a company-owned school, store, hotel, hospital, and housing for hundreds of workers, all built by the legendary lumber baron J. E. Henry. It remained a smoke-belching "mill town" well into the 1970s.

North Woodstock, set against two dramatic notches—Kinsman and Franconia—boasted half a dozen large hotels, among them the Deer Park, accommodating 250 guests. Today Deer Park is still a familiar name, but only as one of the dozen major condominium complexes that have recently become synonymous with this area. With Loon Mountain as its centerpiece, the Lincoln-Woodstock area can now accommodate 18,000 visitors.

Loon Mountain was opened by former New Hampshire governor Sherman Adams (see "The Western Whites" introduction) in 1966 with a gondola, two chairlifts, an octagonal base lodge, and the then unheard-of policy of limiting lift-ticket sales. In 1973, I-93 reached Lincoln, depositing skiers 3 miles from the lifts. But it wasn't until the early 1980s that the town of Lincoln itself began to boom.

Three things happened at that time: All the land owned by the paper mill, which had closed in 1979, became available; Loon itself had grown into a substantial ski area; and a real estate boom was sweeping New Hampshire's lakes and mountains. Just south of Franconia Notch and surrounded by national forest, Lincoln was a developer's dream: relatively cheap land with no zoning.

A heady few years ensued, and eventually zoning kicked in. Under ownership by Booth Creek, Loon Mountain has secured permitting needed to expand. "Lincoln Peak," phase 1 of South Mountain, is slated to open in December 2007. Lincoln's housing units (condos count) now number 3,600; 2,415 of them seasonal.

Summer is busier than winter, given the natural and family attractions—such as the **Annual New Hampshire Highland Games**, where thousands of people turn Scottish for this annual salute to tartan, haggis, and bagpipes—as well as hiking, camping, and touring. In winter Loon is the only big draw. It's maxed out on weekends and school vacations, but otherwise quiet. There's also skiing and snowshoeing off the Kancamagus.

GUIDANCE **White Mountains Gateway Visitors Center** (1-800-346-3687; www.visitwhitemountains.com). Open daily 8:30–5, later in summer; just off I-93 Exit 32. This is one of New England's outstanding visitors centers, recently expanded to include superb displays on the area's resort history, the logging era, and the White Mountain National Forest. The tourism side is also staffed and helpful. Note the diorama of the entire White Mountains region.

Lincoln-Woodstock Chamber of Commerce (603-745-6621; 1-800-227-4191; www.mountaincountry.com) publishes a helpful brochure.

GETTING THERE *By bus:* **Concord Trailways** (603-228-3300; 1-800-639-3317; www.concordtrailways.com) provides daily service to and from Concord, Manchester, and Boston, stopping at Munce's Convenience (603-745-3195), Lincoln.

GETTING AROUND Shuttle service within Lincoln makes coming by bus a viable option, especially during ski season when the Loon Mountain Shuttle serves most inns and condo complexes around town.

The Shuttle Connection (603-745-3140; 1-800-648-4947; www.theshuttle connection.com) requires 24-hour advance notice for Manchester and Logan Airport, serves local destinations year-round.

WHEN TO COME Summer, fall weekends, and winter weekends are all busy. Come midweek in late September or early October, and also midweek during ski season.

MEDICAL EMERGENCY Call **911**. **Lin-Wood Medical Center** (603-745-8136), Lincoln.

✷ For Families

AERIAL RIDES See the **Loon Mountain Gondola Ride** in the box, and "Franconia" for **Cannon Mountain's** aerial tramway.

✔ **Indian Head**. Like the vanished Old Man of the Mountain, this craggy profile on Mount Pemigewasset, visible from Rt. 3, is an old local landmark. It is best seen from the Rt. 3 parking lot of the Indian Head Resort. The summit is accessible via the Mount Pemigewasset Trail, which starts off the Franconia Notch Recreation Trail just north of the Flume Visitors Center.

✔ **Clark's Trading Post** (603-745-8913; www.clarkstradingpost.com), Rt. 3, Lincoln. Open daily July–Labor Day, 9:30–6; weekends Memorial Day–June and Sep.–mid-Oct. One of the country's oldest theme parks, begun in the 1920s as a sled dog ranch (Florence Clark was the first woman to reach the summit of Mount Washington by dogsled). Still owned and managed by the Clark family, known for trained bear shows (three times daily in July and August), also featuring a steam train and variety of steam-powered contractions, a haunted house, Avery's old-time garage and the 1890s fire station, a photo parlor, bumper boats, Merlin's Mystical Mansion, and variety show. $12 adults, $3 ages 6 and up,; under 3 free.

✔ ♿ **Lost River Reservation** (603-745-8031; www.findlostriver.com), Rt. 112, 7 miles west of North Woodstock. July–Aug. 9–6; May and June plus Sep.–mid-Oct., 9–5. This was the first acquisition of the Society for the Protection of New Hampshire Forests, purchased from a local timber company in 1912. The Nature

THE ANNUAL NEW HAMPSHIRE HIGHLAND GAMES AT LOON MOUNTAIN

Garden here is said to feature more than 300 varieties of native plants, and the glacial meltwater gorge is spectacular. Boardwalks thread a series of basins and caves, past rock formations with names like Guillotine Rock and Hall of Ships. Now maintained by the White Mountains Attractions, the complex includes a snack bar and gift shop. You can also pan for gemstones at the Lost River Mining Co. $11 adults, $7 children; ages 3 and under free.

✍ **Hobo Railroad** (603-745-2135; www.hoborr.com), Hobo Junction (just east of I-93), Rt. 112, Lincoln. Open Memorial Day–Halloween, daily July–Labor Day, otherwise weekends, and again on weekends from Thanksgiving to Christmas. A 15-mile round-trip excursion along the Pemigewasset River in "dining coaches" with velour seats and tables. Optional lunch and snacks. $10 adults, $8 ages 6–12.

✍ **Hobo Hills Adventure Golf** (603-745-2125), Rt. 112, Lincoln. Late May–mid-Oct. Three acres of greens and putts through caves and waterfalls. $7.50 adults, $6.50 ages 4–12.

✍ **White Mountain Motorsports Park** (603-745-6727; www.whitemountain motorsports.com), Rt. 3, Woodstock. Open late Apr.–mid-Oct. A 0.25-mile asphalt track with stock-car races every Saturday night at 6 PM. $9 adult, $2 children, $20 family pass.

✍ **The Whale's Tale Waterpark** (603-745-8810; www.whalestalewaterpark.net), Rt. 3, Lincoln. Open daily late June–Labor Day 10–6; weekends from Memorial Day. A 17-acre water park with a wave pool, speed and curvy slides, wading pool for small children, tube rentals. Rates are $25 per day, including tubes. Children under 3 and adults over 65, free.

Also see the **Loon Mountain Park** box.

✳ To Do

BICYCLING **The Franconia Notch Recreation Trail** is a favorite route that runs 9 miles one way from the Flume Visitor Center to the trailhead for the Skookumchuck Trail on Rt. 3. Note: Rentals are available at Loon Mountain, which offers a shuttle to Echo Lake, where you can pick up the bike path.

MOUNTAIN BIKERS WILL FIND MILES OF EXCELLENT CYCLING AT LOON MOUNTAIN BIKE CENTER (SEE SIDEBAR, PAGE 344)

Biking trail maps of the WMNF are available at the White Mountains Gateway Visitors Center.

Loon Mountain Bike Center. See the Loon Mountain box.

BOATING **Outback Kayak** (603-745-2002; www.outbackkayak.com), Main St., North Woodstock, rents kayaks and offers shuttles to upper (more rapids) and lower (easy) sections of the Pemi.

Kim Grant

THE PEMIGEWASSET RIVER

CAMPING For a list of public campgrounds along the Kancamagus Highway, see "White Mountain National Forest."

FISHING The free Freshwater Fishing Guide is available at local information centers. Anglers frequent the East Branch of the Pemi, Russell Pond, and many mountain streams.

GOLF Jack O'Lantern Country Club (603-745-3636), Rt. 3, Woodstock. Eighteen-hole, par-70 course, instruction, rental clubs, golf carts, and pull carts. Also see the four golf courses described in "Franconia."

HIKING Note: **Mountain Wanderer Map & Bookstore** (603-745-2594), 57 Rt. 112 in the middle of Lincoln is a prime source of local hiking suggestions as well as maps and books. Owner Steve Smith edits the AMC's *White Mountain Guide*; and his own latest book is *Wandering Through the White Mountains*.

Mount Moosilauke. The **Benton Trail** ascends the northwest flank of Mount Moosilauke at a steady, moderate grade. The trail begins in a parking area off Tunnel Brook Road; take Rt. 112 west from North Woodstock about 10 miles and drive 3 miles south on Tunnel Brook Road. Other trails, the most popular being the **George Brook Trail**, begin at the Dartmouth Outing Club's **Ravine Lodge** (603-764-5858). Our favorite description of the view from the 4,802-foot summit is credited to clergyman and author Dr. Washington Gladden: "I give my preference to Moosilauke over every mountain whose top I have climbed. The view from Washington is vast, but vague; the view from Lafayette is notable, but it shows little of the sweet restfulness of the Connecticut Valley; on Moosilauke we get all forms of grandeur and all types of beauty."

For trails off the Kancagmagus Scenic Byway, (see "The White Mountains National Forest.")

Greeley Ponds. This easy trail is 4.5 miles round trip, beginning on the Kancamagus Highway, 9 miles east of Lincoln. As local hiking guru Steve Smith describes it: The trail climbs gradually to the high point of Mad River Notch, then dips down to Upper Greeley Pond, a deep tarn hemmed in by the cliff-studded slopes of Mount Osceola's East Peak and Mount Kancamagus. Half a mile farther you reach the south shore of boggy Lower Greeley Pond, where you can look north into the cleft of the notch.

Lincoln Woods Trail begins in the parking lot of the Lincoln Woods information center (warm drinks, restrooms, trail maps) on the Kancamagus Highway just east of Lincoln. The trail crosses the East Branch of the Pemigewasset via a suspension bridge and follows the river along the bed of the old logging railroad. It accesses several other relatively short trails leading to Black Pond and Franconia Falls, connecting with the **Wilderness Trail**, which in turn accesses several trails through the Pemigewasset Wilderness.

HORSEBACK RIDING **Pemi Valley Excursions** (603-745-2744), Rt. 112, Lincoln. One- and two-hour trail rides geared to all levels of ability, also wagon rides along the Pemigewasset River and through woods and meadows. Must be 8 years old. Wagon rides also offered.

Also see the **Loon Mountain Resort** box.

MOOSE-WATCHING Look for moose along Rt. 118 and the Kancamagus Scenic Byway (see *Scenic Drives*).

PICNICKING *Note:* See the Kancagmagus Highway. Also:

Beaver Pond, Rt. 112 west from North Woodstock in Kinsman Notch, beyond Lost River. A beautiful pond with a rock promontory for picnicking or sunning and a view of Mount Blue.

ROCK CLIMBING **Pemi Valley Rock Gym** (603-745-9800), Main St., Rt. 3 at Alpine Village, North Woodstock. Twenty-foot-high indoor rock climbing wall with beginner to advanced routes.

Also see the **Loon Mountain** box.

SCENIC DRIVES **Kancamagus National Scenic Byway** (Rt. 112). The 34.5-mile paved "Kanc" is open all year, weather conditions permitting. It's detailed in "White Mountain National Forest," but you might want to stop at the **White Mountains Gateway Visitors Center** in Lincoln or at the **Lincoln Woods** information center/warming hut staffed year-round by national forest rangers. Pick up a map and guide to the highway and detailed sheets on specific trails and campgrounds.

Franconia Notch Parkway with its many natural attractions is the area's other prime scenic drive. See "Franconia."

Kinsman Notch. Rt. 112 west from North Woodstock is less traveled but as beautiful as the Kancamagus, climbing quickly into Kinsman Notch—past **Lost River** and **Beaver Pond**—crossing the Appalachian Trail. You can continue on by the Wildwood Campground to Mount Moosilauke or cut up Rt. 116 to

Easton, Sugar Hill, and Franconia, and back down through Franconia Notch. Another option is to take the dirt Long Pond Road off Rt. 116 beyond Kinsman Notch, through the national forest to Long Pond, where there is a boat launch and, we're told, good fishing; also picnic sites. You can return to Rt. 116 or continue on to Rt. 25.

Tripoli Road. Pronounced *triple eye*, this shortcut from I-93 (Exit 31, Woodstock) to Waterville Valley accesses a number of hiking trails and campsites. It is also a fine foliage-season loop, returning to Woodstock via Rts. 49 and 175.

Rt. 118 west from North Woodstock climbs steeply through the national forest (there's a panoramic view near the top of the road), then down into the Baker River Valley. You may want to stop at the **Polar Caves** in Plymouth and cut back up I-93; or take Rt. 25 to Haverhill with its handsome old village center (just south of the junction of Rts. 25 and 10), returning via Rts. 116 and 112 through Kinsman Notch.

SWIMMING *Swimming holes:* The **Lady's Bathtub**, in the Pemigewasset River, Lincoln. Deep and fringed with a little sand, accessible through the parking lot at Riverfront Condos. In North Woodstock the **Cascades** is a favorite dunking spot in the Pemi, especially good for small children, accessible from the park right behind Main Street. Other spots on the Pemi can be found along Rt. 175 in Woodstock. One is just across from the Tripoli Road–I-93 interchange.

Also see the **Whale's Tale Waterpark** under *For Families* and the **Loon Mountain** box.

TENNIS **Indian Head Resort** (603-745-8000). Outdoor tennis courts.
The Mountain Club Fitness Center (603-745-8111). Loon Mountain also offers outdoor courts.

❋ Winter Sports

CROSS-COUNTRY SKIING **Lincoln Woods Trail**. Off the Kancamagus just west of Lincoln, an inviting warming hut (warm drinks, restrooms) staffed by national forest rangers marks the entrance to an extensive trail system; the first 3 miles are groomed on both sides of the river.

Stop by the White Mountain Natinal Forest desk in the White Mountains Attractions Visitors Center (see *Guidance*) and pick up detailed maps to and advice about trail networks farther along the "Kanc." These include the Lower and Upper Nanamocomuck Ski Trails, the Oliverian/Downes Brook Ski Trail, and the Greeley Ponds Trail.

Also see the **Loon Mountain** box.

DOWNHILL SKIING See the **Loon Mountain** box.

SNOWMOBILING Trail maps available locally detail the extensive local system. Guided tours are offered by **Alpine Adventures** (603-745-9911) and **Pemi Valley Excursions** (603-745-2744) **Outback Kayak** (see *Boating*) also offers rentals.

LOON MOUNTAIN SKI AND RECREATION PARK
(603-745-8111; 1-800-229-LOON; www.loonmtn.com), Rt. 112, 2 miles east of I-93, Exit 32. Activities are offered late June–Memorial Day, from 9:30 AM. Year-round facilities include the The Mountain Club on Loon, The Mountain Club Fitness Center, and Viaggio Spa.

IN SUMMER
✦ **Aerial Ride Loon Mountain Gondola Skyride** (603-745-8111). Mid-June–Columbus Day, 9–4:30. Ride in a four-passenger, enclosed gondola to the summit, where there's an observation tower and summit cafeteria. Here, too, a stairway leads through boulders and into glacially carved caves, on to hiking trails. On summer Sundays there's a nondenominational service at the summit, followed by a pancake breakfast. $10.50 adults, $6.50 ages 6–12. Under 6 free if accompanied by an adult.

✦ **Loon Mountain Bike Center** (603-745-8111), Lincoln. Open Memorial Day–late Oct., offering mountain bike rentals and guided group tours. Shuttle service is offered to Echo Lake in Franconia Notch State Park. The 9-mile bike trail back through Franconia Park and then a few more miles to Loon is generally gently downhill. Serious bicyclists will also find guidance about trails accessible from the Kancamagus Highway. Mountain bikers should check out Snow's Mountain at Waterville Valley.

✦ **Horseback Riding Loon Mountain** (603-745-8111). Year-round trail rides offered for beginners and intermediates, also private lessons. Must be 8 years old.

RIDE HORSEBACK YEAR-ROUND AT LOON MOUNTAIN

SKI CLASS AT LOON MOUNTAIN

SWIMMING **The Mountain Club Fitness Center at Loon Mountain** (603-745-8111), Rt. 112, Lincoln. Open 7 AM–10 PM daily. Indoor lap pool, outdoor pool in summer. Full spa service.

IN WINTER

DOWNHILL SKIING Known for long cruising trails and easy access, Loon is a nicely designed mountain, with dozens of intermediate trails streaking its face and a choice of steeply pitched trails, served by their own high-altitude East Basin high-speed detachable chair on North Peak. Beginners have the Little Sister chair and slope to themselves, then graduate to a choice of equally isolated (from hot-rod skiers) runs in the West Basin.

The only hitch is that the main base area and West Basin are separated by a long, string-bean-shaped parking lot. The lay of the land dictates the strung-out shape of Loon's base facilities—along a narrow shelf above the Pemigewasset River, which in turn has cut this steep Upper Pemi Valley.

For snowboarders there's Little Sister, a first-of-its-kind Burton Progression Park.

Lifts: 4-passenger gondola, 2 high-speed detachable quads, 1 triple, 3 double chairs, and 2 surface lifts.

Trails: 45 with 20 percent easiest, 64 percent more difficult, 16 percent most difficult (22 miles total).

(Continued on next page)

(Continued from previous page)

Vertical drop: 2,100 feet (base 950 feet; summit 3,050 feet).

Snowmaking: 99 percent.

Facilities: 2 base lodges, 3 lounges, 2 rental shops, summit, terrain parks, Superpipe (400 feet), tubing, indoor climbing wall, cafeteria, and midmountain lodge (Camp 3) at the base of North Peak. Slope-side lodging at the 234-room Mountain Club includes condo units, indoor pool, game rooms, and restaurants; ice skating, cross-country skiing.

Ski and snowboard school: 170 full- and part-time instructors, modified ATM system, freestyle, mountain challenge, and NASTAR race course.

For children: Loon Mountain Nursery for ages 6 weeks–6 years; K. Boo Bear Camp (3-year-olds), Knder Bear Camp (4–6).

Lift tickets: Weekends $61 adult, $51 teens, $39 ages 6–12; weekdays: $54 adult, $44 teens, $34 youths; multiday rates.

CROSS-COUNTRY SKIING Thirty-five km of trails, some winding partway up the mountain, others following the riverbed. Rentals, instruction, special events. $14 adults, $9 juniors and seniors.

ICE SKATING Lighted rink near the main base lodge; rentals available.

✳ Lodging

CONDO-STYLE RESORTS

In Lincoln

✍ ♿ **The Mountain Club on Loon** (603-745-2244; 1-800-229-7829; www .mountainclubonloon.com), 90 Loon Mountain Rd., Lincoln 03251. Forget the hassles of parking a mile away and lugging your gear to the slope. Any time of year, this is your best bet if you want to take full advantage of what Loon Mountain Resort offers. The condo hotel has 117 rooms with king beds (from $99), studio family rooms with cooking facilities (from $135), and 117 "suites"—two rooms with cooking facilities, dining, and lounging space (from $202). Facilities include a formal restaurant, informal tavern dining, and room service. A complete fitness center—including indoor/outdoor pool, Jacuzzis, saunas, and steam rooms—plus a full-service spa add to the luxury. Packages are available throughout the year.

🍴 ✍ **Lodge at Lincoln Station** (603-745-3441; 1-800-654-6188), P.O. Box 906, Lincoln 03251. Midway between town and mountain, with studios, one-bedrooms, and loft suites overlooking the river (be sure to request one) and a central "Great Room" with a hearth; also indoor and outdoor pools, a Jacuzzi, saunas, game room, and tennis courts. Rates in-season $109–119 for a hotel room, $119–129 for a studio, $139–149 for a loft for two people.

☞ **The Village of Loon Mountain** (603-745-3401; www.villageofloon .com), 94 Loon Mountain Rd., Lincoln 03251. Of the 650 units here, just 93 are in the rental pool. Positioned directly across the road from Loon Mountain, nicely designed to blend into the hillside. Amenities include two indoor pools, 12 outdoor tennis courts (2 are flooded to form a skating rink in winter), a kids' game room with arcade, and table tennis. One-, two-, and three-bedroom units from $135–175 in summer, 2-night minimum.

INN **The Woodstock Inn** (603-745-3951; 1-800-321-3985; www.wood stockinnnh.com), P.O. Box 118, Main St. (Rt. 3), North Woodstock 03262. Known for its microbrewery and its formal (on the glassed-in front porch) and informal dining (in Woodstock Station out back; see *Where to Eat*), this long-popular establishment also offers 24 antiques-furnished rooms (22 with private bath) in the main inn and in three additional Victorian houses, Riverside and The Deachman House. All rooms have a phone and color TV; some have Jacuzzi, fireplace, and air-conditioning. $43–129 per couple. Children free in the same room with parents but charged for breakfast.

BED & BREAKFAST ☙ **Wilderness Inn** (603-745-3890; 1-888-777-7813; www.thewildernessinn.com) Rt. 3 and Courtney Rd., North Woodstock 03262. For couples, singles, and families alike, this classic 1912 bungalow-style house on the edge of the village, and within earshot of the Lost River, is

one of the most charming places to stay in the White Mountains. It has evolved and continues to evolve under longtime owners Rosanna and Michael Yarnell. Half a dozen years ago the couple and their children spent a year traveling around the world. Many rooms now reflect those travels. We particularly like the small New Zealand Room (good for a single or loving couple), the French Room with its impressive four-poster and whirlpool tub, and the colorful Caribbean Cottage with its queen sleigh bed, whirlpool tub, and gas fireplace. Breakfast, served on the enclosed sunporch and open to the public (8–10) is well known locally (see *Eating Out*). All eight guest rooms ($65–175) have private bath and TV. The cottage ($110–175) has air-conditioning and a deck. Prices include breakfast.

MOTELS ☞ **Indian Head Resort** (603-745-8000; 1-800-343-8000; www .indianheadresort.com), Lincoln 03251. First opened in the 1920s, gradually evolving to its present 90 motel rooms, cabins (with fireplaces; closed in winter), as well as bungalows. Indoor and outdoor heated pools, tennis courts, game room, coffee shop, Laundromat, and dining room. Inquire about children's entertainment and special children's activities. $135–165 per room in summer; $89–149 bungalows and cabins.

Woodward's Resort (603-745-8141; 1-800-635-8968; www.woodwards resort.com), Rt. 3, R.R. 1, Box 107, Lincoln 03251. An 85-room complex that has grown gradually over the past 48 years, this resort is now open year-round and carefully managed by the Woodward family. Rooms are clean but plain, though extras like refrigerators and coffeemakers make you feel right at home. Recreational facilities include indoor and outdoor pools, an indoor racquetball court, a tennis court (you can rent racquets), and a pond used for winter ice skating (management provides skates). In summer there are also lawn games. The **Colonial Dining Room** serves breakfast daily, and dinner is served nightly in the **Open Hearth Dining Room**; there's also a lounge. $85–125 per room.

✒ **Franconia Notch Motel** (603-745-2229; 1-800-323-7829; www .franconianotch.com), 572 U.S. Rt. 3, Lincoln 03251. The nicest kind of family-run motel: 6 two-room cottages (summer only) and 12 standard motel units, backing on the Pemigewasset River where picnic tables and grills are in place. Franconia Notch State Park is 0.5 mile up the road. Each unit is different; most have twin beds. Board games and morning coffee are available. In-season rates are $59–79 per couple; off-season is a bargain starting at $32.

Kancmagus Motor Lodge (603-745-3365; 1-800-346-4205; www .kancmotorlodge.com), Rt. 112, Lincoln. Family owned, with a nice feel to its 34 rooms with queen or two double beds, air-conditioning, steam showers and baths; some have balcony or sleeper sofa. Amenities include an indoor pool, a game room, a locally liked restaurant (Brittany's), serving breakfast and dinner (see *Eating Out*), and a sports bar. $69–119 per room in summer.

❋ **Where to Eat**

DINING OUT ✒ **Gypsy Café** (603-745-4395), 117 Main St. (Rt. 112),

Lincoln. Open except Mon. and Tue. for lunch (11–4) and dinner (5–9). Fully licensed. Reservations suggested. Chef-owner Peter Johnson has established a stellar reputation for his varied menu. We can strongly recommend the Gypsey Niçoise salad (grilled yellowfin tuna on greens with grilled asparagus, $10.95), but skip the curried shrimp. The bottom line is that we plan to return every time we are in town. Lunch options include panini and grilled sandwiches as well as daily-made soups. Dinner choices range from vegetarian pasta ($13.95) to cassis duck and a Mediterranean lamb plate ($17.95). Lighter meals, burgers included, are also available at dinner. The Cuban flan (rich and creamy with a caramel topping) is a standout. The "Kids Menu" includes pizza and quesadillas. This is a 10-table dining room, backed by an attractive (smoke-free) bar specializing in margaritas.

The Common Man (603-745-3463; www.thecman.com), at the corner of Pollard Rd. and Main St., Lincoln. Open nightly except Thanksgiving and Christmas. The winning formula here is a limited menu stressing simplicity and fresh ingredients, from pasta primavera ($11.95), to lobster and rock crab cakes ($15.95), to prime rib ($13.95) and filet mignon ($16.95). There's a great new grill menu to boot. This place, with its huge fireplace and the coziest lounge around, consistently rates rave reviews. Entrées $12–20.

✒ **Seasons on Loon** (603-745-6281), in the Mountain Club on Loon Mountain. Open daily for all three meals. A relaxed ambience with a slightly upscale menu featuring memorable appetizers and entrées. Lunch features appetizers like lump crab-cakes as well as sandwiches. House specialties at dinner include roast rack of lamb and pan-seared duck breast. Entrées $16–30. Kids have a special menu.

Clement Room Grill at the Woodstock Inn (603-745-3951; www.woodstockinnnh.com), Main St. (Rt. 3), North Woodstock. Open nightly 5:30–9:30. A glassed-in porch set crisply with white linen tablecloths and fine china is the location for fine dining. The à la carte menu includes appetizers like ostrich quesadilla and pan-fried ravioli with red pepper pesto; entrées range from chicken dishes ($12.95 up) to fillet Barcelona: a 9-ounce center-cut fillet butterflied and stuffed with sautéed scallops and crab and topped with hollandaise sauce ($23.95).

✔ Gordi's Fish and Steak House (603-745-6635), Rt. 112, Lincoln. Dinner is served daily 4–10 PM. The decor is glitzy Victorian mixed with photos of ski heroes past and present (the owners include two past members of Olympic ski teams). There are nightly specials like blackened tuna, stuffed pork with apple gravy, or salmon en papillote; standard menu items include fish-and-chips and other seafood. Beef lovers are well served with prime rib, filet mignon, or New York sirloin. Lighter meals include chicken done up a number of ways as well as pasta dishes—and you can also make a meal of the salad bar. Entrées $7.95 for pasta to 29.95 for surf and turf.

Café Lafayette Dinner Train (603-745-3500; www.nhdinnertrain.com), Rt. 112, North Woodstock. Late June–Oct.: Departures Tue., Thu., Sat., and Sun. at 6 in summer, at 5 in fall. Weekends in spring. A vintage-train ride. Rolling stock includes a restored 1924 coach with brass and stained glass, a tri-level 1952 domed observation car, and a 1953 café coach. Tables are geared to four; there's a surcharge for a private table for two (when seated with a guest, you are both on the same side of the table). Tickets include a 2-hour ride and five-course meal. The typical menu might open with pâté, then proceed through sorbet to a choice of chicken, salmon, or pork dishes; dessert but not wine is included. $60–70 adults, $40–60 ages 6–11. Reservations recommended.

EATING OUT ✿ ✔ Woodstock Station (603-745-3951; www.woodstockinnnh.com), at the Woodstock Inn, Main St. (Rt. 3), North Woodstock. This railroad station was built in the late 1800s in Lincoln and continued to serve visitors—including skiers bound for Cannon Mountain—into the 1930s and 1940s. In 1984 it was sawed in half and moved to its present location at the rear of the Woodstock Inn. The old freight room is now the bar, and the passenger waiting room is the lower dining room. This large, eclectically furnished space, which now includes the Woodstock Inn brewery, is one of the liveliest dining spots in the North Country, and the menu boasts—count 'em—148 items: everything from frogs' legs to Peking ravioli, quesadillas and nachos and burritos (lots of Mexican), a wide choice of original sandwiches, pastas, baked scrod, ribs, and burgers. The children's menu includes a $2 hot dog. Beverages fill four more pages of the menu and include a wide variety of imported and microbrewed beers.

Texas Toast Eatery (745-9977), Village Shops, Rt. 112, Lincoln. Open daily for breakfast and lunch (7–2). Hidden away in the Villages Shops (former Mill Marketplace), this pleasant café specializes in freshly made New England and southern comfort food prepared from scratch.

Brittany's Café (603-745-4899), Rt. 112, Lincoln. Open daily for breakast and dinner. This pleasant riverside dining room in the Kancamagus Motor Lodge is worth finding: good food, reasonable prices. The signature dish is grilled balsamic chicken blue ($12.95), but the choice is wide. The adjoining sports bar and pub, **CJ's Penalty Box,** is a popular gathering spot.

✔ **Peg's—A Family Restaurant** (603-745-2740), Main St., North Woodstock. Open daily for breakfast and lunch. Roll up your sleeves alongside loggers and other local denizens in this plainly furnished but friendly room for rib-sticking breakfasts of eggs and steak, omelets, pancakes, and Belgian waffles. On a budget? Keep an eye out for the 99¢ breakfast specials. New England favorites like hot meat loaf, turkey, and roast beef sandwiches—not to mention burgers, hot dogs, western and eastern sandwiches—are all served with a smile and words of wisdom. Look for daily specials like American chop suey (macaroni, beef, and tomato sauce baked together) or liver and onions served with mashed potatoes. Breakfast 90¢–$5.95. Lunch $2.25–7.25.

🍴 ✔ **Truants Taverne** (603-745-2239), Main St., North Woodstock. Open daily 11:30 AM–10 PM. Hung over the river in a back-behind kind of space, part of an old mill yard. Polished pine tables and a large menu that's fun to read. For lunch choose from a wide selection of cleverly named burgers as well as soups, sandwiches on house-made honey wheat bread, and salads. Longtime Truants chef John Marro prides himself on fresh seafood and on using Black Angus beef. You'll also find Mexican dishes and a wide selection of beers. A good place.

Chieng Gardens (603-745-8612), Lincoln Square, Main St., Lincoln. A better-than-average Chinese restaurant with a large, reasonably priced menu and the best view (upstairs, facing the mountains) of any restaurant in Lincoln.

For breakfast

Wilderness Inn and Café (603-745-3890), Rt. 3 and Courtney Rd., North Woodstock. Serving mid-Feb.–mid-Sep. 8–10 AM. A short walk from downtown to a pleasant, hospitable guest house serving freshly ground coffee, homemade muffins, selected hot crêpes, and multiple choices of pancakes, eggs, and omelets. Reservations appreciated.

The Woodstock Inn (603-745-3951; www.woodstockinnnh.com), Main St. (Rt. 3), North Woodstock. A wide range of waffles, omelets, and other memorable breakfast fare—like homemade red-flannel hash with poached egg and home fries, bagels and lox, and huevos rancheros.

Also see **Texas Toast** and **Peg's**, above.

✳ Entertainment

✔ **North Country Center for the Arts** (603-745-2141), The Mill at Loon Mountain. Shows July and Aug. Tue.–Sat., at 7:30 PM and Sun. at 2 PM; musicals, comedy, classics, children's theater on Wed. at 11 AM.

Lincoln Cinemas 4 (603-745-6238), Lincoln Center North, Main St., Lincoln. Four screens.

Summer band concerts. Regularly on the common in North Woodstock.

Loon Mountain Music Series (603-745-8111). The North Country Chamber Players perform at the Governor's Lodge during summer months.

✳ Selective Shopping

BOOKSTORES **Innisfree Bookshop** (603-745-6107), Lincoln Square, Main St. (Rt. 112), Lincoln. The region's full-service bookstore, specializing in New England titles, White Mountain guides and trail maps, ski titles, field guides, and children's books and educational toys.

Mountain Wanderer Map and Bookstore (603-745-2594; www .mountainwanderer.com), Main St., Lincoln. Not your ordinary bookstore, this is a prime source of hiking and New England maps and guides to outdoor recreation, travel, and natural history; also USGS topographic maps, compasses, and White Mountain gifts. Owner Steve Smith is himself an avid hiker, snowshoer, and expert on area trails, the author of *Wandering Through the White Mountains*, and *Snowshoe Hikes in the White Mountains*; coauthor of *The White Mountains* and *The 4,000 Footers of the White Mountains*.

SPORTING GOODS **Lahout's Country Clothing and Ski Shop, Inc.**, Main St., Lincoln. Open daily. A branch of the Littleton store opened in 1922 and was billed as "the oldest continually operated ski shop in New England." Operated by the three sons of the original Lahout and dedicated to

"beating anyone's price," this is one of the best places in the North Country to shop for ski gear, sturdy footwear, long johns, et cetera.

Rodgers Ski Outlet, Main St., Lincoln. Open daily 7 AM–9 PM. "La who?" the competition may well ask if you mention Lahout's. More than 1,500 pairs of skis in stock at any time; tune-ups, rentals, repairs are the specialties. Billed as "northern New England's largest volume ski shop."

OTHER **Village Shops**, Rt. 112, Lincoln. Several shops and restaurants in a complex incorporating three turn-of-the-20th-century mill buildings.

Pinestead Quilts (603-745-8640), Main St., Lincoln. An unusual selection of locally made quilts, machine-pieced but with hand-tied, traditional designs. From $65 for quilted wraps to $650 for king-sized quilts.

✳ Special Events

January: **Independence Day Weekend** at Loon Mountain, "celebrating Loon's independence from nature."

March: **Spring Fling** at Loon Mountain.

June: **Old New England Days** in North Woodstock: antique cars, yard sales, live music.

July: **Fourth of July celebration**, Lincoln-Woodstock.

Labor Day: **Rubber Ducky Regatta** in North Woodstock.

September: **The Annual New Hampshire Highland Games** in Lincoln is a huge celebration of all things Scottish.

October: **Oktoberfest** at Loon Mountain.

November: **Turkey Triathlon**.

FRANCONIA AND NORTH OF THE NOTCHES

Wrapped in forest and dominated by granite White Mountain peaks, the Franconia-Bethlehem area seems to be the distilled essence of northern New Hampshire. Northwest of this high, wooded country, the landscape changes suddenly, flattening around Littleton, the shopping town for this region. For views of both the Green Mountains and the White Mountains, follow this Ammonoosuc Valley south to Lisbon and Bath, then back up to Sugar Hill and Franconia on memorable back roads.

The town of Franconia alone packs into its 65 square miles more splendid scenic vistas and unusual natural attractions than many states can boast. Curiously, while annual visitors to Franconia Notch are said to outnumber New Hampshire residents, relatively few stray into the delightful neighboring valley, which seems happily trapped in a 1950s time warp.

Franconia and its small satellite towns of Sugar Hill and Easton have been catering to visitors for more than 150 years. Travelers were first attracted to Franconia Notch by its convenience as a north–south route through the mountains, but they were invariably impressed by the scenery. Not long after the War of Independence, a few inns and taverns appeared.

In the mid-19th century the railroad arrived, inaugurating a grand resort era. Such literary notables as Nathaniel Hawthorne, Washington Irving, John Greenleaf Whittier, and Henry Wadsworth Longfellow were all Franconia summer visitors whose enthusiastic accounts of the region fanned its fame. Hawthorne wrote a story about the (former) Old Man of the Mountain, "The Great Stone Face."

One of the most celebrated hotels in America in its day, and a symbol of the White Mountains' golden age, the 400-room Profile House stood in the heart of Franconia Notch. Besides elegant service in a rustic setting, the hotel offered its guests a superb view of the Old Man. An institution for 70 years, Profile House burned down in 1923. Its site is now part of Franconia Notch State Park.

Grand hotels also appeared in Bethlehem, known for its pollen-free air. It became headquarters for the National Hay Fever Relief Association, which was founded here in the 1920s. At one time Bethlehem had 30 hotels ranging from

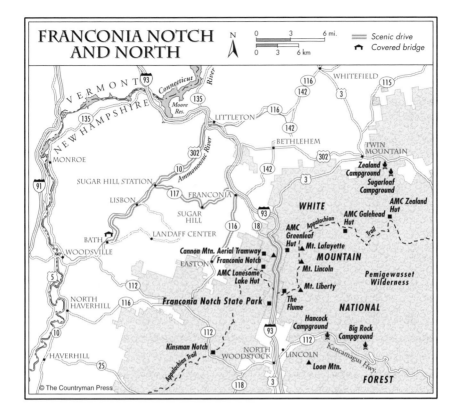

FRANCONIA NOTCH AND NORTH

simple to large and luxurious indeed. A 2-mile-long boardwalk invited guests to stroll.

Although many once-famous grand hotels closed their doors in the 1920s and 1930s, a few lasted until the 1950s, when railroad service to the White Mountains ended—and with it a resort way of life. A few traces of Bethlehem's glory days remain, such as the impressive fieldstone-and-shingle clubhouse (formerly The Casino) of the Maplewood Golf Course.

As the summer resort scene began to fade in the White Mountains, a winter season commenced. Americans discovered skiing. The Franconia area can claim a number of skiing firsts, among them the nation's first ski school (which opened at Peckett's-on-Sugar-Hill in 1929) and this country's first aerial tramway (constructed in 1938), which ran to the summit of the state-owned Cannon Mountain. Cannon also hosted America's first racing trail in the 1920s and its first World Cup race in the 1960s. The New England Ski Museum is now sited beside Cannon's tramway base station.

In 1945 a flamboyant Austrian aristocrat, Baron Hugo Von Pantz, founded Mittersill, a Tyrolean-style resort adjacent to Cannon. The baron's resort attracted high-society types from New York and Boston, and, for a time, Franconia was the New England equivalent of Aspen or St. Moritz.

Times change. The current ski crowds head for Loon Mountain and Waterville

Valley. Cannon still has its following, though, and the area offers extensive cross-country skiing. Some of New Hampshire's most pleasant inns and bed & breakfasts are scattered throughout the folds of the valleys and gentler hills north and west of Franconia Notch.

GUIDANCE **Franconia Notch Chamber of Commerce** (603-823-5661; 1-800-603-237-9007; www.franconia
notch.org), Box 780, Main St., Franconia 03580. A downtown information booth is open mid-May–Oct., 10–5; another is open summer weekends at the Cannon Mountain tramway base station.

Bethlehem Historical Museum and Information Center (603-869-3409; 1-888-845-1957; www.bethlehemwhitemtns.com), P.O. Box 748, Bethlehem 03547. Open Memorial Day–Labor Day, 11–4. A walk-in information center (junction of Rts. 302 and 142) in the middle of the village displays souvenirs from the town's many vanished hotels.

Littleton Area Chamber of Commerce (603-444-6561; www.littletonarea
chamber.com), 111 Main St., Box 105, Littleton 03561. Look for the well-stocked walk-in information center in Thayer's Hotel. Open May–Oct. daily, otherwise weekdays.

Lisbon Chamber of Commerce (603-8386673), 6 South Main St., Lisbon 03585. Open weekdays.

The White Mountains Gateway Visitors Center (see "Lincoln and North Woodstock") also covers this entire area.

Getting There

By bus: **Concord Trailways** (800-639-3317; www.concordtrailways.com) has daily service from Boston to Franconia and Littleton.

By car: From north or south, take I-93 to Franconia Notch Parkway (Rt. 3). Rt. 302 is the major east–west route, running from I-91 at Wells River, Vt., to Littleton and east through Bethlehem.

Medical Emergency

Call **911**. **Littleton Hospital** (603-444-9000), 600 St. Johnsbury Rd., Littleton at Exit 43 off I-93.

✷ Villages

Bath (population: 922). The village of Bath itself is known for its vintage-**1832 covered bridge** and for the neighboring 1804 **Old Brick Store**, billed as the country's oldest general store. A shorter covered bridge can be found on Rt. 112, spanning a branch of the Ammonoosuc River in the village of Swiftwater. **Upper Bath Village**, a few miles north of the store and covered bridge on Rt. 302, is a striking cluster of Federal-era brick homes set against surrounding fields.

Bethlehem (population: 2,294). Sited at 1,426 feet above sea level, "the highest township east of the Mississippi River," Bethlehem became a haven for hay fever sufferers early in the 1800s. Guests first came by stages from Concord; later there were three stations in town, with as many as 10 trains a day depositing guests at a total of 30 lodging establishments. Why the town's name was changed from Lloyd Hills to Bethlehem remains a bit of a mystery, though the moniker acquired new meaning beginning in 1919 with the founding of the Bethlehem Hebrew Congregation. During the 20th century the surviving hotels filled all summer with Hasidic Jews, most from Brooklyn. The hotels have now all but disappeared, but several large 19th-century summer "cottages" are now inns. The village itself is once more a cluster of interesting shops and restaurants, its art deco movie theater restored as an art house and venue for live performances. The Rocks Estate is a year-round resource.

Franconia (population: 978). Named in 1782 for its resemblance to Germany's Franconia's Alps and best known for its notch, mountains, and other dramatic natural features. The village itself clusters in the Gale River Valley west of Cannon Mountain. In the early 19th century a rich vein of iron ore was mined here; the **Franconia Iron Furnace**, just south of the junction of Rts. 116 and 117 (with interpretive panels), evokes the era. The **Franconia Heritage Museum** (603-823-5000; www.franconiaheritage.org), 553 Main St., is open year-round, Thu., Sun., and holiday weekends 1–4. Franconia College, a liberal institution of the 1960s that was housed in the old Forest Hill Hotel, has long since closed, but many of its graduates live on in the immediate area. Robert Frost also lived here. For more on Franconia resort history, see the chapter introduction.

Landaff (population: 374). Set well back into the hills east of Rt. 302, accessible from the village of Bath, this is one of New Hampshire's most-photographed old hill towns. In Landaff Center the town hall commands a superb view of the hamlet, whose population hovers around 300 souls—give or take a few summer people. You can't help wondering what it would be if Dartmouth College had been sited here the way Governor John Wentworth suggested in 1770.

Sugar Hill (population: 580). New Hampshire's youngest town, part of Lisbon—some 10 miles away and a very different community—until 1962. Set high on a ridge with views to Franconia Ridge and the Presidentials, this cluster of homes, inns, and churches is one of the state's prettiest communities. **Sugar Hill Historical Museum** (603-823-5336; www.franconianotch.org), Main St. (Rt. 117), Sugar Hill is an interesting little local museum with changing exhibits about aspects of the town from its pioneer settlement in 1780 until the present. Open July–mid-Oct., Thu., Fri., and Sat. 1–4.

Lisbon (population: 1,587). An Ammonoosuc River town centered on woodworking mills, a nontouristy " small town with a big heart." You'll also find a small golf course, a couple of places to stay and to eat, and a big Memorial Day Weekend Lilac Festival, honoring the state flower.

Littleton (population: 6,086). The spirited hub of this corner of New Hamsphire, Littleton is enjoying a downtown renaissance, its Main Street lined with interesting shops and a burgeoning riverwalk just behind Main Street (and parking). Here the vintage 1797 **Littleton Gristmill** (603-444-3971; 1-888-284-7478; www.littletongristmill.com), 18 Mill St., is open year-round. Powered by the Ammonoosuc River, it turns out organic grains for pancake, muffin, and waffle

Christina Tree

MAIN STREET, LITTLETON

mixes. The **Littleton Historical Society** (603-444-6435), 1 Cottage St. (open July–Sep., Wed. 1:30–4:30; call for off-season hours) holds a large collection of local items including stereoscopic slides developed and produced by the famous Kilburn Brothers of Littleton. Free admission.

✴ Must See

The Rocks Estate (603-444-6228; www.therocks.org), Rt. 302, R.F.D. 1, Bethlehem 03574. Owned by the Society for the Protection of New Hampshire Forests (SPNHF), this estate with huge barns is the northern headquarters for the state's largest and most active conservation organization. The estate's 1,200 acres are managed as a tree farm by the SPNHF; a large area is reserved as a Christmas tree plantation. Trees are sold during the annual Christmas tree celebration in December. Several nearby inns offer special package plans for lodging, meals, and a Christmas tree. Various conservation and family programs are held through the year, plus a self-guided nature trail that's great for snowshoeing, though a bit narrow and steep for cross-country skiing.

✐ **Bretzfelder Park** (603-444-6228; 603-869-2683; www.therocks.org), Prospect St., Bethlehem. Owned by the SPNHF, this 77-acre site is managed as a community park, with various summer programs plus picnic tables, fishing, and a guided nature trail.

MUSEUMS AND HISTORIC SITES **The Robert Frost Place** (603-823-5510; www.thefrostplace.org), Box 74, Ridge Rd., off Rt. 116, Franconia. Open Memorial Day–Columbus Day, Wed.–Mon. 1–5 (but check; also inquire about evening poetry readings). Frost's home from 1915 to 1920, now a town-run museum on a "road less traveled by," attracts international visitors. Each year a resident poet spends the summer on the property imbibing views of the same unfolding hills

FRANCONIA NOTCH STATE PARK

(603-823-8800; www.franconianotchstatepark.com). This 6,440-acre park lies between the Franconia and Kinsman mountain ranges in a 0.5-mile-wide high pass, or notch, that contains many of the White Mountains' most notable natural sights. Long used by the Pemigewasset tribe and discovered by white settlers before the Revolution, it remains the quickest route from northern Vermont and points west to Concord and Boston. It's currently a 10-mile-long segment of I-93 that's blessedly scaled back here to two lanes, the Franconia Notch Parkway, funneling traffic through with minimum scenic and environmental impact.

Franconia Notch was a major summer destination for a century. The present park includes the site of the former 400-room Profile House, named for the nearby "Old Man of the Mountain" stone profile. The hotel burned down in 1923, and the entire notch came up for sale for $400,000. It would have been acquired by logging interests had not the Society for the Protection of New England Forests (SPNHF) raised half the sale price and a Boston philanthropist supplied another $100,000. The remaining $100,000 was raised by women's clubs, schoolchildren, and small donors; the reservation became public in 1928. It is surrounded by the White Mountain National Forest, with trails maintained by the WMNF and Appalachian Mountain Club (AMC). Unfortunately the Old Man who saved the notch crumbled and fell in 2003.

The principal sights of the notch are all within the park and easily accessible from the parkway. Also see *Hiking*.

SITES ARE LISTED FROM SOUTH TO NORTH.

THE GILMAN VISITORS CENTER AT THE FLUME GORGE Exit 34A, open May–late Oct., 9–5, until 5:30 in July and Aug. Sited at the entrance to the Flume, this center provides information and shows a free 15-minute film about the park. It also has a snack bar, restrooms, and souvenir shop. Displays include a vintage-1874 Abbot & Downing 21-passenger (plus 9 on top) Concord Coach, which carried the mail from Plymouth to the Profile House until 1911.

✐ THE FLUME GORGE (www.flumegorge.com). See above. $8 adults, $5 ages 6–12; 5 and under free. A sheer-sided 700-foot-long, deep and narrow gorge—no more than 20 feet wide but up to 90 feet high—through which Flume Brook flows. It was discovered in 1808 by an avid local fisherman, 93-year-old "Aunt Jess" Guernsey. A system of staircases and boardwalks was constructed in the 19th century; now an updated network takes visitors

(Continued on next page)

through the Flume to Ridge Path, which leads to Liberty Cascade and on to **Sentinel Pine covered bridge**, overlooking a clear mountain pool. The Wildwood Path loops past giant boulders brought down by the glaciers and returns to the Flume entrance. Note also the **Flume covered bridge** here.

THE BASIN. A pull-off is marked from the parkway both northbound and southbound. From the parking lot a paved path leads to Cascade Brook and a deep glacial pothole or natural pool almost 30 feet in diameter created over the eons by the churning action of water rushing down from the nearby waterfall. Follow marked trails to Cascade Brook and Kinsman Falls.

BOISE ROCK. A marked northbound pullout. There's a spring right by the parking lot, and a short trail leads to this huge glacial boulder. Picnic tables offer views of the Cannon Cliffs and the rock climbers scaling them.

LAFAYETTE CAMPGROUND (603-823-9513). Southbound access only. Ninety-seven campsites, $19–24 each, can be reserved 3 days in advance.

PROFILE LAKE was named for its site below the former Old Man of the Mountain. No swimming, but these headwaters of the Pemigewasset River are open to fly-fishing and said to be good for brook trout.

EXIT 34B

CANNON MOUNTAIN. Parkway Exit 34B. Besides operating during ski season, the tram runs late May–Columbus Day, when autumn colors are usually at or near peak. A round-trip tram ticket is $10 adults, $6 ages 6–12; free 5 and under. One-way tickets are $8 and $6. One of New Hampshire's most popular ski areas and the site of America's first aerial tramway. The present tramway, which replaced the 1938 original in 1980, carries 80 passengers to the summit of the 4,180-foot-high mountain, where there is an observation

CANNON MOUNTAIN TRAMWAY IN FRANCONIA NOTCH STATE PARK

(Continued on next page)

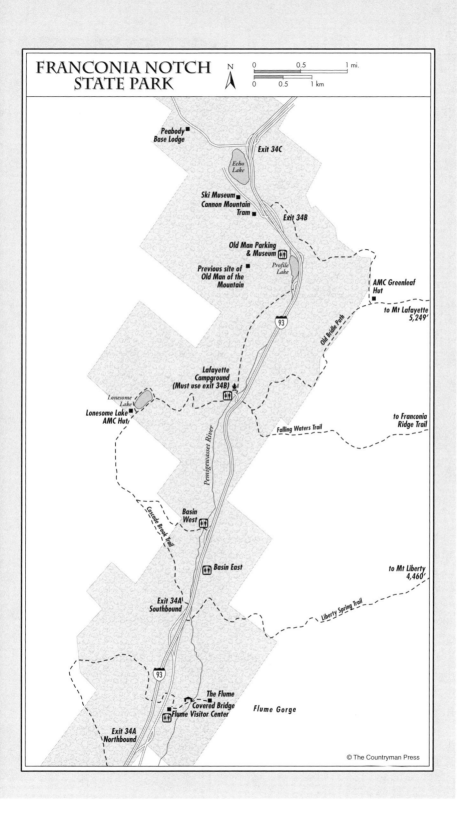

FRANCONIA NOTCH STATE PARK

N

0   0.5   1 mi.

0   0.5   1 km

Peabody Base Lodge

Exit 34C

Echo Lake

Ski Museum
Cannon Mountain
Tram

Exit 34B

Old Man Parking
& Museum

Previous site of
Old Man of the
Mountain

Profile Lake

AMC Greenleaf Hut

to Mt Lafayette
5,249'

93

Old Bridle Path

Lafayette
Campground
(Must use exit 34B)

Lonesome Lake

Lonesome Lake
AMC Hut

to Franconia
Ridge Trail

Falling Waters Trail

Pemigewasset River

Cascade Brook Trail

Basin West

Basin East

to Mt Liberty
4,460'

Exit 34A
Southbound

Liberty Spring Trail

93

The Flume
Covered Bridge
Flume Visitor Center

Flume Gorge

Exit 34A
Northbound

© The Countryman Press

tower and the panoramic Rim Trail. For winter information, see *Down-hill Skiing*.

NEW ENGLAND SKI MUSEUM (603-823-7177; 1-800-639-4181; www.skimuseum.org), Exit 34B off the Franconia Notch Parkway, beside the Cannon Mountain tram, Franconia. Open Dec.–Mar., Fri.–Tue. noon–5; every day Memorial Day–Columbus Day. Free. This popular museum relates the history of New England skiing with a combination of permanent and changing exhibits of skis, clothing, and equipment dating from the 19th century to the present, along with vintage still photos and film.

Courtesy of the New England Ski Museum

A VINTAGE POSTER AT THE NEW ENGLAND SKI MUSEUM

THE OLD MAN OF THE MOUNTAIN MUSEUM AND HISTORIC SITE. In 2003 the famous 40-foot-high rock formation high above Profile Lake—the state's official symbol—fell down. Too beloved to be forgotten, it is now

and fields of lupine that inspired New England's best-known poet. The 1859 farmhouse and barn are the site of frequent poetry readings and workshops. The home contains rare editions of Frost's books, photos, and memorabilia, and a 20-minute slide presentation depicts his life and work in Franconia. A 0.5-mile nature trail behind the house is posted with 16 Frost poems. Admission $4 adults, $3 seniors, $2 ages 7–12.

SCENIC DRIVES **The Franconia Notch Parkway**, the 10-mile segment of I-93 that's been downsized through Franconia Notch State Park (see the box), is one of the state's most scenic corridors.

Rt. 117 from Franconia village. This road winds steeply uphill to Sugar Hill. Take the short Sunset Hill Road for breathtaking mountain views, then continue down to Lisbon on Rt. 302/10 and turn north beside the Ammonoosuc River to Littleton, or turn south through Lisbon village to Bath, with its old country store and covered bridge.

memorialized in a small museum while fund-raising is undertaken for a more fitting memorial. There is also an ice cream stand here.

EXIT 34C
SWIMMING/BOATING AT ECHO LAKE BEACH at the base of Cannon Mountain in Franconia State Park. Open June–Labor Day, 10–5:30. $3 adults, $1 ages 12 and under. At this 28-acre lake (elevation 1,931 feet), the mirror-like surface perfectly reflects Mount Lafayette and Cannon Mountain. There are picnic tables, a swimming beach, a snack bar, changing facilities, a boat-launching area, **canoe and paddleboat rentals** ($10 per hour), and 10 sites for RV hookups.

BALD MOUNTAIN and **Artists Bluff**. See *Hiking*.

PICNICKING AT SUNSET BRIDGE. Turn left instead of right at the stop sign and head over the bridge to the Governor Gallen Memorial area parking lot. Walk out onto the bridge for great views.

RECREATION TRAIL. This 8.9-mile walking/biking/cross-country ski and snowmobiling trail begins at the Flume and runs uphill to Cannon, then on 2 more miles to Rt. 3. Most people begin at the northern end, as it slopes gently downhill the whole way. See *Bicycling* in this section and in "Lincoln and North Woodstock" for bike rentals and shuttle service.

Rt. 116 follows the valley between Franconia and Easton. Old farms and mountain scenery.

Rt. 142, the quick, old way from the middle of Franconia to the middle of Bethlehem, is steep, woodsy, and scenic, much better the long way around via I-93 and 302.

❋ To Do

AERIAL TRAM RIDES **Cannon Mountain Aerial Tramway**. See the Franconia State Park box.

BICYCLING **Franconia Notch Recreation Trail**. An 8.9-mile-long bicycle/walking path, used in winter as a cross-country ski trail and snowmobile corridor, traverses the notch. **Franconia Sports Shop** (603-823-5241; www.franconia sports.com), Main St., Franconia. Offers half- to 5-day mountain bike rentals.

FISHING **Profile Lake**. See the Franconia State Park box. Franconia Sports Shop (see above) sells fishing licenses.

Golf Bethlehem Country Club (603-869-5745), Main St. (Rt. 302), Bethlehem. This par-70, Donald Ross–designed course in Bethlehem offers 18 pristine holes of golf; cart and club rentals are available. Check with your accommodation about package rates.

Lisbon Village Country Club (603-838-6004), Bishop Rd.,off Rt. 302, Lisbon. Nine holes.

Maplewood Country Club and Hotel (603-869-3335; 1-877-869-3335; www .maplewoodgolfresort.com), Main St. (Rt. 302), Bethlehem. An attractive, Donald Ross–designed 18-hole layout with a grand clubhouse, this par-72 course offers a challenge to all players. There's a pro shop, driving range, and unique par-6 hole. The course is so popular on weekends that carts are required of all players to speed up play.

Sunset Hill Golf Course (603-823-5522), Sugar Hill. Recently rescued by townsfolk from outside developers, this short nine-hole par-33 course sits atop Sunset Hill and gives players dramatic mountain views.

GLIDING **Franconia Inn** (603-823-5542; 1-800-473-5299; www.franconiainn .com; info@franconiainn.com), 1300 Easton Rd., Franconia 03580. Open mid-May–mid-Oct., daily except Wed. 9–5:45. Soar with an FAA-certified glider pilot for a sublime view of some of the continent's most sublime scenery. Fifteen-, 25-, or 35-minute rides range $60–100.

HIKING Franconia Notch offers some of the most rewarding short hikes in the White Mountains. They include:

Artist's Bluff and **Bald Mountain**. Both trails begin at the Echo Lake parking lot in Franconia Notch State Park (I-93, Exit 34C). Favored by 19th-century guests at the notch's former hotels, Bald Mountain is a short but rocky ascent with sweeping views. First you follow an old carriage road to a saddle between two summits, then branch left to Bald Mountain, right to Artist's Bluff. You should investigate both. The round trip is 1 or 1.8 miles.

Basin–Cascades Trail. Start at **the Basin** (see the Franconia Notch State Park box) and ascend along Cascade Brook leading to the Cascade Brook Trail.

✎ **Lonesome Lake Trail**. From Lafayette Place on Rt. 3 in Franconia Notch, an old bridle path leads to a 14-acre lake that sits at an elevation of 2,734 feet and is warm enough in summer for swimming. The Appalachian Mountain Club's Lonesome Lake Hut offers overnight lodging and a variety of family-geared programs. Contact the AMC Pinkham Notch Camp (603-466-2727).

Mount Lafayette via the Old Bridle Path. This is a full day's hike, and you should pick up a detailed map before attempting it. After 2.9 miles you reach the AMC Greenleaf Hut (for lodging, phone 603-466-2727); the summit—with magnificent views—is another 1.1 miles. If the weather is good and your energy high, continue along the **Franconia Ridge Trail** south over Mount Lincoln to Little Haystack. This narrow, rocky route is spectacular, but there are steep

drops on both sides of the trail. At Little Haystack turn right (west) onto the
Falling Waters Trail. This trail passes more waterfalls in 2.8 miles than any
other trail in the mountains; it ends back at Lafayette Place.

Also note the **Rim Trail** from the Cannon Mountain Aerial Tramway.

Two **Appalachian Mountain Club high-mountain huts** (603-466-2727; www
.outdoors.org) are accessible from Franconia Notch. The 1.7-mile trail to **Lonesome Lake Hut**, sited at an elevation of 2,760 on a flank of Cannon Mountain,
and the 2.5-mile hike to **Greenleaf Hut** at 4,200 feet on Mount Lafayette both
begin here. Lonesome Lake is an easy hike for children, and there is swimming
and fishing in the lake. This hut is open on a self-service basis (use of kitchen
facilities) Jan.–late May and mid Oct.–Dec.; Greenleaf is open self-service mid-
to late May. Both are staffed June–mid-Oct., serving breakfast and dinner, furnishing pillows and wool blankets for their 48 bunks. For more about the AMC
see "What's Where."

HORSEBACK RIDING **Franconia Inn** (603-823-5542), Rt. 116, Franconia.

SWIMMING See the Franocnia Notch State Park box for details about **Echo
Lake Beach**.

✳ Winter Sports

CROSS-COUNTRY SKIING **Franconia Village Cross Country Ski Center**
(603-823-8078; 1-800-473-5299; www.franconiainn.com), Franconia Inn, Easton
Valley Rd. (Rt.116). This is the most extensive and best-maintained system in the
region, with 65 kilometers of tracked trails. Most are singletracks, winding
through woods and across meadows in this 1,100-foot-high valley. The full-service ski shop offers rentals (skates and snowshoes, too) and lessons. On weekends
and holidays lunch is available at the inn. Trail passes: $10 adults, $7 juniors.

Sunset Hill House Touring Center (603-823-5522; 1-800-SUN-HILL), Sunset Hill Rd., Sugar Hill. Trails are tracked on the neighboring golf course and
out across meadows. No ski shop.

In the White Mountain National Forest
For detailed trail maps, check with the **White Mountain Visitors Center** in
Lincoln.

Lafayette Trails, Rt. 3, Franconia Notch. The **Notchway Trail** is the old Rt. 3
roadbed, accessed from Rt. 141 just east of I-93, Exit 36. It's identified by a
metal sign with a skier symbol. The trail is 2.1 miles; side loops include the short
Bog Trail, the more difficult **Scarface Trail** (1.2 miles), and the **Bickford
Trail** (0.3 mile).

The Pemi Trail, Franconia Notch. Just over 6 miles long, this trail extends from
Profile Lake to the Flume parking lot and is open to cross-country skiers, snow-
shoers, and hikers. It can also be accessed from the Echo Lake, tramway, and
Flume parking areas. Pick up a map at the information booth at the Cannon
Mountain base lodge in Franconia Notch.

Beaver Brook Cross Country Trails begin at the Beaver Brook Wayside on Rt. 3 between Twin Mountain and Franconia Notch. The **Beaver Loop** is 2.3 km, Badger is a more difficult 3.1 km, and **Moose Watch** is classified as "most difficult," a total of 8.6 km with some spectacular views. These trails are ungroomed and not regularly patrolled, so be sure not to ski alone.

DOWNHILL SKIING Cannon Mountain (603-823-7771; 1-800-237-9007; www .cannonmt.com), Franconia Parkway, Exit 34B, Franconia. State-owned Cannon Mountain boasts some of the toughest trails in the East. It was the site of America's first racing trail in the 1920s, of its first aerial tramway in the '30s, and of its first World Cup race in the '60s—a clue, perhaps, to how Franconia's Bode Miller is now officially recognized as the most talented skier in the world, winning the 2005 World Cup for the United States (our first in 22 years) in Switzerland. While its image remains "The Mountain That'll Burn Your Boots Off!," in reality many trails here have been softened—broadened and smoothed as well as carpeted with snowmaking.

Vertical drop: A whopping 2,146 feet.

Lifts: The present 80-passenger aerial tram dates from the 1980s. Lifts also include 2 regular-speed and 1 high-speed quad chairs, 3 triple chairs, wonder carpet, and rope tow.

Snowmaking: 97 percent.

Trails: 55. In addition to runs in Franconia Notch itself, more than a dozen intermediate and beginner runs meander down the mountain's gentler northern face to the Peabody Slopes base area. The only trails still "au naturel" are Taft Slalom (a remnant of that 1920s racing trail) and the Hardscrabbles—both of which command their own followings.

LOWER SKI SLOPES OF CANNON MOUNTAIN RISE BEHIND ECHO LAKE

Kim Grant

Features: Brookside Learning Center at the Peabody Slopes offers separate beginners' trails and several adult learning programs, a children's program for ages 3–13, and day care for those 6 weeks and up.

Facilities: Cafeteria and retail shop at the base of the tramway. The tram is a great start for intermediate and expert skiers/riders. The Peabody Base Area also offers a ski shop, rentals, cafeteria, lounge, first aid, and deli.

Lift tickets: $49 adults, $38 ages 6–17, and, $29 over 65 on weekends and holidays; $38 adults, $25 juniors and seniors midweek/nonholiday.

SNOWMOBILING In Franconia Notch the bike path serves in winter as a corridor connector for the 100-mile network of snowmobile trails in this area. For maps and other information, contact **Twin Mountain Snowmobile Club**, Box 179, Twin Mountain 03595; the **Trails Bureau** (603-271-3254, option 4); the **New Hampshire Division of Parks and Recreation** (603-271-2006); or the **New Hampshire Snowmobile Association** (603-224-8906), Box 38, Concord 03301. (Also see "Crawford Notch and Bretton Woods.")

✳ Lodging

INNS

In Franconia/Sugar Hill

&♿ **Franconia Inn** (603-823-5542; 1-800-473-5299; www.franconiainn .com; info@franconiainn.com), 1300 Easton Rd., Franconia 03580. The grande dame of the notch region, this inn makes sure you stay busy with four clay tennis courts, a heated swimming pool, guided horseback tours, bicycles, a croquet court, and a glider port, all on 107 acres in the heart of the Easton Valley. There's even a swimming hole. In winter the inn's well-groomed cross-country trail system with touring center is a big draw. Founded just after the Civil War, the inn has 34 guest rooms (including wheelchair-accessible accommodations on the first floor), all furnished in traditional style. Common areas include an inviting oak-paneled library, a spacious living room with a fireplace, and two porches to catch sunrise and sunset. Two candlelit dining rooms provide casually elegant dining and spectacular views (see *Dining Out*). Down-

stairs there's a family-sized hot tub and the Rathskeller Lounge. $125–235 B&B, $200–285 MAP, more for suites, less for longer stays and midweek. Package plans are also available.

⊗ **Sunset Hill House** (603-823-5522; 1-800-SUN-HILL; www.sunset hillhouse.com), Sunset Hill Rd., Sugar Hill 03586. Open all year. You can see forever in two directions, the White Mountains to the east and the Green Mountains to the west, from this 1880s-era property. Located atop a 1,700-foot ridge, the inn was originally built as the annex for one of the area's grand hotels. Although the main house is now gone, this 21-room inn with its own 7-room annex remains, and has been completely renovated and remodeled. All of the traditionally furnished guest rooms come with comforters and coordinated fabrics, antique and reproduction furniture, and private baths. There are also two 2-room Jacuzzi and fireplace suites, and 5 other rooms with a choice of gas fireplace or Jacuzzi. All rooms have a phone, and local calls are free. Common areas include a TV room, a small bar, a heated pool, and a nine-hole golf course across the street. $100–379 B&B; rooms average $160. Add $45 per person for dinner (see *Dining Out*).

Lovett's Inn (603-823-7761; 1-800-356-3802; www.lovettsinn.com), by Lafayette Brook, Rt. 18, Franconia 03580. A tradition in these parts and still one of New Hampshire's outstanding inns, Lovett's was built in 1794 and is listed on the National Register of Historic Places. For the past 80 years it has operated as an inn, securing a reputation with generations of guests for its warm hospitality, fine views, and excellent food (see *Dining Out*). Innkeepers Jim and Jan Freitas have upgraded all five rooms and suites in the original inn with antiques and renovated baths, CD player, and hair dryers. Our favorite is the Nicholas Powers Room, which has great views of Cannon Mountain as well as a single whirlpool tub ($175 B&B, $245 MAP). An additional 14 fireplaced cottages are scattered around the grounds and are well appointed. Larger cottages include the Stonyhill Suite with a double whirlpool tub, and the roomy Stonyhill Cottage ($435) with three bedrooms, a living room, fireplace, TV, and porch. There is also an outdoor pool and spa. Rooms range $115–225, suites and cottages $135–235; dinner is an additional $40 per person. Rates increase during fall foliage season and decrease in winter.

Sugar Hill Inn (603-823-5621; 1-800-548-4748); www.sugarhillinn.com, Rt. 117, Franconia 03580. This rambling 1789 white-clapboard farmhouse, set on 16 acres of manicured lawns, gardens, and woodland, captures the essence of gracious but unpretentious New England hospitality. Judy and Orlo Coots are your hospitable hosts. Orlo serves as chef and Judy offers massage and facials. The nine airy guest rooms and six cottage suites feature stenciled walls, handmade quilts, candlewick bedspreads, and a variety of antiques. Fireplaces in several of the rooms add ambience, and there's a great porch to enjoy the mountain views. Rooms range $115–290, cottages and suites $225–380, including full breakfast and tea depending on time of year. Dinner is by reservation (see *Dining Out*).

B&BS ❅ ✎ **The Hilltop Inn** (603-823-5695; 1-800-770-5695; www.hilltopinn.com), 1348 Main St., Sugar Hill 03586. Mike and Meri Hern chuckle when reminded that they are now senior innkeepers in these parts. Drawn to Franconia by progressive Franconia College (opened in the 1960s, closed in 1978), they pride themselves on the warmth and informality of this expansive 1895 Victorian B&B atop Sugar Hill. The six guest rooms with full baths are furnished with period antiques. Beds are fitted with handmade quilts and English flannel sheets. On a winter morning we found it difficult to leave the breakfast table with its view of the lively bird feeder, after consuming too many strips of perfectly crisped bacon, along with quiche and a full fruit plate. The woodstove with its ring of rockers is another sticking point, as is the deck, especially if there's a sunset. Mike and Meri are, however, full of suggestions to get you out hiking or skiing and are well versed in area shops and restaurants. Pets are welcome for $10; two

150-pound Golden Maremma dogs are in residence. Rates run $90–120 per room; $125–195 during foliage season. Children are $35 in the same room as their parents.

🐾 **Foxglove, A Country Inn** (603-823-8840; 1-888-343-2220; www .foxgloveinn.com), Rt. 117 (at Lovers Lane), Sugar Hill 03585. This inn, once a favorite for its gorgeous gardens and painstakingly perfect decor, has had its recent ups and downs. Now new innkeeper Suzanne Atrat, a trained chef from California, has drawn on the area's old Hollywood aura (Bette Davis retired in Sugar Hill) for inspiration. Ms. Davis has her own room with bath named for her, and Spencer Tracy and Katherine Hepburn claim a two-bedroom suite with small sitting area and shared bath. There are two additional rooms, each with private bath, in the main house; also two cottage units with fireplace, deck, air-conditioning, and private bath. Rates range $110–175, depending on season, and include a gourmet breakfast served on the slate-floored patio overlooking the gardens or in the formal dining room. Small pets accepted in cottages only.

🐾 ♂ **The Homestead** (603-823-5564; 1-800-823-5564; www.thehome stead1802.com), on Rt. 117, Sugar Hill 03586. Sitting at the corner of Rt. 117 and Sunset Hill Rd., the Home-stead is the matriarch of Sugar Hill lodging: It's been run exclusively as an inn by the same family for seven generations, making it one of the oldest family-run inns in the United States. Your hosts, the Hayward family, offer 20 rooms, each reflecting the past with vintage furnishings as well as the slight inconvenience of shared (spank-ing clean) bathrooms. Each room has

its own sink and mirror. Rooms in the neighboring Family Cottage, more-over, all have private bath. The dining room, where you're served a hearty breakfast with maple syrup from the farm, is pine paneled with old hand-hewn beams and family collections of china, glass, and silver. Antique fur-niture, books, and photographs fill the common rooms, making the atmosphere throughout pure, authen-tic nostalgia. Cross-country skiing is free, and downhill skiing packages are available. This is one of the few places in the area to offer single rates ($60–70). Double rates are $80–95 with shared bath, $95–130 with pri-vate, slightly more in foliage season, full breakfast included. Children 6 and under are free; $10 for pets. Inquire about packages.

Bungay Jar (603-823-7775; 1-800-421-0701; www.bungayjar.com), P.O. Box 15, Easton Valley Rd., Franconia 03580. Tucked in the woods and sur-rounded by a brook, a lily pond, and amazing gardens, this whimsical inn—named for a wind that blows down through the mountains—makes you feel as if you've just stumbled onto a fairy-tale cottage. Actually, it's an enlarged 19th-century barn relocated from upstate New York in the 1960s. About 25 years ago, the onetime resi-dence was reborn as a B&B, now owned by Neil Blair and Jeffry Burr. While parts of the inn's eclectic col-lection of furnishings, accessories, and reclaimed architectural elements were inherited from previous owners, Blair and Burr have added new touches to complement the original rustic elegance. Eight rooms, all with private bath, prove that opposites attract. Sleigh beds are paired with skylights; gunstock beams with Benny

Goodman's old bathtub. Throughout the seasons, you can feel the power of nature vibrating from every corner here. The onetime hayloft, now a two-story living/dining room with fireplace, overlooks the Kinsman Range. So do many of the rooms, including two new suites, a glowing yellow one named Sunflower, along with the soft, serenely green Fiddlehead. Both boast Jacuzzi tub and gas fireplace, as does the ground-floor Garden Suite with French doors leading to a private porch next to the garden. Rates— $140–185 per room in low season, $190–215 during fall foliage and holidays—include afternoon tea, homemade snacks, complimentary beverages, a full country breakfast, luxury bedding, and access to a private, two-person sauna. There's a 2-night minimum stay during foliage season and weekends. Subtract 15 percent for midweek.

🐾 🐈 ♪ **Kinsman Lodge** (603-823-5686; 1-866-KINSMAN; www.kinsmanlodge.com), 2165 Easton Rd. (Rt. 116), Franconia 03580. An 1850s lodge that's been in Sue's family since 1910. The nine bedrooms are bright and comfortable, sharing two full baths and one half-bath. There's a large, cheerful old-fashioned dining room, as well as a room with TV and gas fireplace and another with a wood-burning hearth. In summer there are also the rocking chairs on the front porch. $45–60 single, $75 double, $100 for three, full breakfast included. Pets and kids are graciously welcomed.

In Bethlehem

INNS Adair (603-444-2600; 1-888-444-2600; www.adairinn.com), 80 Guider Lane at the junction of I-93 and Rt. 302, Bethlehem 03574. A grand house in the truest sense, Adair exudes serenity. You're instantly seduced by the winding approach through rolling lawns and landscaped gardens, just off (but out of earshot of) I-93. Double front doors open onto a large center hall with a wide stairway leading to two floors with nine luxurious guest rooms. All have private bath (three have two-person tubs, and one has a whirlpool bath) with king or queen beds and are furnished with antiques or reproductions. Note the original artwork. Back downstairs, there are comfortable dining and living rooms with fireplaces. Across the lawn, a fully equipped private cottage provides an additional guest retreat. In the basement's granite-walled common area, there's a grand old pool table and lots of cozy couches and recliners on which to snuggle. The Rocks Estate with its wooded nature trails, good for cross-country skiing, is just down the road. Innkeeper Betsy Young provides afternoon tea and a full breakfast, included in the room rate: $175–345 summer and fall, $140–295 in winter and spring, depending on accommo-

ADAIR IN BETHLEHEM

Christina Tree

dations. Dining available in-season at Tim-Bir Alley (see *Dining Out*).

✍ ⅃ **Wayside Inn** (603-869-3364; 1-800-448-9557; www.thewaysideinn .com), 3738 Main St. (Rt. 302), Bethlehem 03574. Longtime Swiss innkeepers Victor and Kathe Hofmann have preserved this friendly old inn, which dates in part to 1825. They offer 14 guest rooms furnished with traditional New England country pieces, and a dozen additional motel rooms with balcony, cable TV, refrigerator, and air-conditioning. There's a sandy beach by the river. Room rates of $119–139 in high season, $89–99 in low season, include a full breakfast. Also see the Riverview Restaurant in *Dining Out*. Check, however, as the inn is for sale at this writing.

B&BS ✍ **The Balmoral** (603-869-3169; 1-800-898-8980; www.the balmoral.com), 2533 Main St., Bethlehem 03574. Adjacent to the Maplewood Golf Course, innkeepers Mark and Elizabeth Morrison, who trace their lineage to original Bethlehem settlers, focus on attending to their guests' needs in their Federalperiod manse rather than expanding their bed count. Guests can choose among three guest rooms, all with private bath, TV/VCR, and dining table. Breakfast is served in the dining room or in your room. There's an extensive library. $110 per couple. Children are welcomed, though there is a $20-per-day fee.

❀ **The Mulburn Inn** (603-869-3389; 1-800-457-9440; www.mulburninn .com), 2370 Main St., Bethlehem 03574. Innkeepers Christina Ferraro and Alecia Loveless purchased this stately mansion in 1998 and spent many hours renovating it to provide

comfortable and affordable bed & breakfast accommodations. Built in 1908 as a summer home for a member of the Woolworth family, the house boasts imported bathroom fixtures, Italian tile fireplaces, stainedglass windows, and much handcarved woodwork. Seven guest rooms, each with private bath, are furnished in period style. Large wraparound porches, fireplaced common rooms, and a shared Jacuzzi invite relaxing. $99–165, full breakfast included. Pets accepted for an additional $25.

In Littleton
INNS ❀ **The Beal House Inn & Restaurant** (603-444-2661; www .bealhouseinn.com), 2 W. Main St., Littleton 03561. Mrs. Beal first opened her home, built in 1833, to the public 60 years ago. Current innkeepers Jose and Catherine Pawelek (from Argentina and Holland, respectively) have introduced many amenities in guest rooms: gas fireplaces, CD players, and a sitting area with lovingly restored antiques and quirky decor. Two common rooms with fireplaces offer books, television, and movies. In back a deck overlooks a fern-filled hillside. Check to see if ownership has changed, and be aware that the inn is on a busy street, so noise from traffic may filter into your room. The restaurant (see *Dining Out*), a destination in its own right, is in a separate wing. Rooms are $115–165, suites $165–245 with a threecourse breakfast. Extra guests $25–40; well-behaved dogs are $25–35.

✍ **Thayer's Inn** (603-444-6469; 1-800-634-8179; www.thayersinn.com), 136 Main St., Littleton 03561. Open year-round. Located on busy Main Street, this classic, white-pillared,

Christina Tree

THAYER'S INN IN LITTLETON

Greek Revival structure has been a beacon to weary travelers since it opened in 1843. Most of the 40 rooms have private bath, TV, and telephone, and all are air-conditioned. Since each room is individually furnished, guests are invited to select their favorite on arrival. The two-bedroom suites are great for families. From $60 per couple, per room, through $100 for family suites, continental breakfast included.

In Lisbon

The Ammonoosuc Inn (603-838-6118; 1-888-546-6118; www.amm inn.com), 641 Bishop Rd., Lisbon 03585. Open year-round. A 19th-century expanded farmhouse set on a knoll, across the Ammonoosuc River from Rt. 302, surrounded by the nine holes of the Lisbon Village Country Club. In 2005 new owners included French-trained chef Karen Melanie,

and the focus here is on Melanie's Bistro (see *Dining Out*). The nine rooms are country comfortable—certainly not worth the rack rate $175–200 B&B, but check out golf and dining packages.

Blueberry Farm Bed and Breakfast (603-838-5983), www.blueberry farmbnb.com), 445 Rt. 302, Lisbon 03585. Margaret McKenna welcomes guests to the family's cheerful 1850 farmhouse, set on a hill above Rt. 302 west of town, with views of the Ammonoosuc River. The country kitchen with its vintage Glenwood woodstove forms the center of the house. There are two downstairs guest rooms with private bath (one with a Jacuzzi) and two on the second floor. $75–85 includes a full breakfast. Amenities include a pool. The McKennas annually harvest 1,200 bushels (four varieties) of blueberries between July and September.

MOTELS 🐾 🐾 🐾 **Gale River** (603-823-5655; 1-800-255-7989; www .galerivermotel.comt), Rt. 18, Franconia 03580. Now run by Kevin Johnson, the tidy Gale River Motel has 10 rooms and two cottages. Amenities include in-room coffeemaker, refrigerator, TV, and telephone, plus a heated outdoor pool, whirlpool, and hot tub. Rates for a double, $55–110. Cottages, which sleep six, are $130–160, with a 3-night minimum stay. Summer weekly cottage rental, $750. Children under 15 are free, but pets are $10 per night. In winter just four units are open for nightly rentals, as skiers routinely rent the rest by the season.

🐾 **Stonybrook Motel** (603-823-5800; 1-800-722-3552; www.stonybrook motel. com), 1098 Profile Rd. (Rt. 18),

Franconia 03480. Tom and Pauline Palmer are the new owners of this attractive combination five-room lodge and 18-unit motel minutes from Cannon Mountain. Amenities include indoor and outdoor pools. There's also a trout pond, a game room and fireplace in the lodge, and a streamside picnic area with grills. Doubles run $80 in upstairs rooms, with incredible mountain views. Motel rooms with cable TV, fridge, phone, and two double beds are $75–100. More in foliage season.

♨ ♂ **Eastgate Motor Inn** (603-444-3971; www.easstgatemotorinn.com), Exit 41 off I-93 to Rt. 302, Littleton 03561. An easy on-the-highway location, standard motel rooms with a surprisingly good restaurant (see *Eating Out*) and reasonable rates. In summer $69.70–79.70.

CAMPGROUNDS WMNF campgrounds along Rt. 302, east of Twin Mountain; all can be reserved by calling 603-271-3618 or 1-800-280-2267; www.reserveamerica com.

Sugarloaf I and II have 62 sites, and **Zealand** has 11 sites.

Lafayette Campground (603-823-5563), a popular state park facility just off the parkway in the heart of Franconia Notch, has 97 wooded tent sites available on a first-come, first-served basis. A central lodge has showers and a small store with hiking and camping supplies.

Echo Lake in Franconia Notch also has 10 sites for RV hookups.

Local private campgrounds include **Fransted Family Campground** (603-823-5675; www.franstedcampground.com), Rt. 18, Franconia, with 65 wooded tent sites and 26 trailer sites; and **Apple Hill Campground**

(603-869-2238; 1-800-284-2238), Rt. 142 North, Bethlehem, with 45 tent sites, 20 trailer hookups, a store, and a bathhouse.

✳ Where to Eat

In Franconia/Sugar Hill

♂ ♿ **Franconia Inn** (603-823-5542; 1-800-473-5299; www.franconiainn .com; info@franconiainn.com), 1300 Easton Rd. Breakfast 7–10, dinner nightly 5:30–9. Long considered the local restaurant for elegant dining and special occasions, the Franconia Inn's two handsome candle- and hearth-lit dining rooms offer black-tie service and a mountain view. Cocktails are served in the cozy, paneled basement-level **Rathskeller Lounge**. Despite the elegant surroundings, children are warmly welcomed by the kid-oriented menu featuring a "mega-grilled" cheese sandwich and baked crispy chicken nuggets. And the kids can spend their (or your) quarters in the video game room while waiting for their meal. Entrées might include pork Wellington in a puff pastry, pan-roasted lamb, and roasted LIsland half duck served with almond cherry wild rice and kirsch. Appetizers such as lobster bisque (made with fresh lobster meat, sherry, and local dairy cream) and a vegetarian napoleon run $5–8; entrées, $20–27. Full liquor.

Lovett's by Lafayette Brook (603-823-7761; 1-800-356-3802; www .lovettsinn.com), Profile Rd., Franconia. Dinner 5:30–9; reservations suggested. You can quaff predinner cocktails in the cozy lounge, then retire to one of three connecting open-beamed rooms to savor a memorable meal. Entrées may include veal scallops sautéed in lemon herb sauce, pan-seared rainbow trout with lemon caper butter, and sliced tenderloin in a red wine shallot sauce. Full liquor. Entrées $11–25.

Sugar Hill Inn (603-823-5621; 1-800-548-4748; www.sugarhillinn.com), Rt. 117, Franconia. Dinner, by reservation only, is served nightly during foliage season; seating between 6 and 8. Open the same hours on weekends

🦞 🍴 ♿ **Polly's Pancake Parlor** (603-823-5575; 1-800-432-8972; www.pollyspancakeparlor.com), 672 Rt. 117, Sugar Hill. Open from the second Sun. in May to mid-Oct., daily 7 AM–3 PM. A restaurant operated by members of the same family since 1938, this modest 1830s former carriage house overlooks the majestic Kinsman mountain range and serves standard lunch fare, but is widely known for its legendary pancakes (buckwheat, cornmeal, oatmeal, buttermilk, and whole wheat), waffles, and French toast drizzled with the locally harvested maple syrup—the sugar in Sugar Hill. Thanks to Americana-themed restaurant guides and cultural detectives such as Charles Kuralt, Polly's has gained a national reputation for providing diners a glimpse into a passing era. Walls are decorated with antique tools found in family and neighbors' sheds as well as portraits of the family who have owned this farm, one way or another, since 1819. Expect fresh food and snappy service—just don't expect to be served one minute after the restaurant closes for the afternoon (and, believe us, it sure is disappointing to find a CLOSED sign and an empty parking lot at 3:05 PM). On the other hand, don't be discouraged by a line. It's worth waiting. Prices range $5–25.

POLLY'S PANCAKE PARLOR IN SUGAR HILL, FAMILY-OWNED SINCE 1938

Christina Tree

and holiday periods the rest of the year. Traditional but memorable four-course dinners might feature grilled tuna steak with crispy shrimp, lemon cream, and caviar, or roast Cornish game hen with figs, pine nuts, and sweet balsamic glaze. $37 for a three-course or $40 for a four-course meal. Full liquor license.

Sunset Hill House (603-823-5522; 1-800-SUN-HILL; www.sunsethill house.com), Sunset Hill Rd., Sugar Hill. Dining by reservation only, 5:30–9:30; also a lighter menu served daily in the tavern. Dine bathed in the sunset's afterglow as well as the glow of the candlelight and warmed by the fireplace in this nicely renovated old inn dining room with a spectacular view of the Presidential Range. The menu rotates seasonally. Enjoy distinctive appetizers like a crêpe filled with roasted red pepper asparagus in avocado cream sherry sauce. Specialties include vegetable-stuffed portobello mushrooms and duck Bombay: a half duckling lightly smoked, then roasted with almonds, smoked bacon, and mango-brandy sauce. Entrées $22–36.

In Bethlehem

Tim-Bir Alley (603-444-6142), 80 Guider Lane at Adair Country Inn. Dinner Wed.–Sun. 5:30–9, by reservation only. Chefs Timothy and Biruta Carr offer fine North Country dining at this intimate gourmet restaurant, serving an eclectic menu that changes weekly and features unique appetizers like pork-scallion dumplings with spicy peanut sauce or sautéed shrimp on noodles with pine nut pudding and plum-ginger sauce. Entrées might include sautéed sea scallops on scallion noodle pudding with soy-ginger vinaigrette; grilled quail on roasted

pear risotto with tangerine, fig, and balsamic glaze; or tournedos of beef on roasted onion mashed potatoes with smoked bacon, Gorgonzola, and Cabernet-thyme sauce. End your meal with homemade desserts like a white chocolate, coconut and ricotta strudel with dark chocolate sauce and mango-coconut compote. The chefs take great care to ensure that each meal looks as great as it tastes. Entrées $19.95–28.95.

&. **Cold Mountain Café** (603-869-2500), 2015 Main St. Open Mon.–Sat. for lunch 11–3:30, dinner 5:30–9, 9:30 weekends. Credit cards and reservations are not accepted. A laid-back ambience and eclectic blackboard menu attract devotees to this attractive small café (36 patrons max) in a row of shops. Run since the winter of 2000 by ex–New Yorker Jack Foley, Cold Mountain offers soups, salads, and sandwiches to eat in or take out at lunch. The menu becomes more ambitious at dinner, with items like sun-dried tomato and mascarpone ravioli served with polenta, chicken with tamari and Thai basil, or baked salmon with tamari-ginger glaze. Wine and beer are served. Dinner entrées $11.95–16.95.

Lloyd Hills (603-869-2141), Main St. Open Sat. and Sun. 8 AM–9 PM, Mon.–Fri. from 11 AM. Lloyd Hills serves a wide-ranging menu featuring hefty breakfasts; soups, salads, and sandwiches at lunch, with a few pasta dishes thrown in for good measure. But the dinner menu really allows the kitchen to shine, taking simple ingredients and whipping them into surprising meals that are for the most part French and Mediterranean in character. Chicken Piccata, scallops Valencia, and sirloin and scampi are a few examples of what you might find on the menu. And it wouldn't be a New England dining experience if you didn't finish your meal with a thick ice cream frappe drink. FYI, *Lloyd Hills* was Bethlehem's original name. Dinner entrées $12.95–14.25.

✧ & **The Riverview Restaurant at the Wayside Inn** (603-869-3364; 1-800-448-9557; www.thewaysideinn .com; info@thewaysideinn.com), Rt. 302 at Pierce Bridge. Open nightly except Mon., spring–fall; Fri. and Sat. in winter 6–9 PM. Victor and Kathe Hofmann, the European owners of this dining room at the Wayside Inn, emphasize Continental cuisine served

COLD MOUNTAIN CAFÉ IN BETHLEHEM IS A COZY SPOT FOR SOUP AND A SANDWICH
Christina Tree

on tables draped with red-checked cloth bathed in candlelight, casting a warm glow on diners. Swiss specialties are served nightly, and fondue is always popular in ski season. Kids relate to the simple meals like the grilled cheese sandwiches and spaghetti and meatballs. Appetizers $4.59–6.25, entrées $10.95–19.95.

In Littleton
✧ **Grand Depot Café** (603-444-5303), 62 Cottage St. Lunch is served Mon.–Fri. 11–2, dinner 5–9. Casual but gracious, this restaurant is fast becoming a favorite with locals and visitors alike. Kudos include the *Wine Spectator* Award of Excellence; the chef trained in New York and Paris. Rack of lamb, escargots, and pâté as well as great desserts are among the grown-up specialties, but kids can order burgers or pasta from the children's menu. Entrées $16–26.

Beal House Inn & Restaurant (603-444-2661; www.bealhouseinn .com), 2 W. Main St. Open Wed.–Sun. year-round. The owner-chef's country gourmet menu emphasizes wood-grilled items, fresh seafood, rustic breads, and made-from-scratch desserts, served in two intimate dining rooms that make an attractive setting. More than 250 martinis are available at the bar. Tasty appetizers like crunchy, fried coconut shrimp or wood-grilled duck breast leave the taste buds wanting more and are promptly rewarded by ambitious mains like snapper with Barbados rum and bananas, lamb shank over mashed sweet potatoes, chicken with Gorgonzola cream sauce, or seafood ravioli with curry, raisins, and apple, all served with house salad, home-made bread, and oven-roasted veg-etables. Desserts run the gamut from flourless chocolate cake with crème Anglaise and warm bittersweet chocolate sauce to raspberry charlotte and a classic French tarte tatin served with ice cream and warm ginger-caramel sauce. There's a good wine list with some reserve wines as well as a full bar. Appetizers range $6–8; entrées are $14–26, and desserts $5–6.

In Lisbon
Melanie's Bistro at the Ammonoosuc Inn (603-838-6118; www.ammonoosucinn.com), 641 Bishop Rd. Open (except Tue.) for lunch and dinner. Marked from Rt. 302. New in 2005, and we have not had a chance to personally review it. Classically trained chef-owner Karen Melanie presides in the kitchen of this attractive country inn dining room. The à la carte menu is intriguing with appetizers like wild mushroom and asparagus strudel served warm over baby organic greens ($8), pastas that include penne à la vodka ($14), and entrées ranging from walnut-crusted chicken breast ($16) to baby New Zealand lamb chops grilled with tomato Provençal, a risotto cake, and creamed spinach ($27).

EATING OUT

In Franconia
Above the Notch View Restaurant and Tavern (603-823-8077), 729 Main St. at the Cannon Mountain View Motor Lodge. Open Wed.–Sun. for breakfast and lunch; Sat. and Sun. for dinner, but check. Hours vary summer to winter and in between. The local choice for breakfast (the menu includes specialty omelets) and for lunchtime burgers, sandwiches, and pizzas. The dinner menu includes pastas and shrimp dishes, also chicken and chorizo sausage with tomato and

fresh basil, served over linguine in a creamy Alfredo sauce.

Dutch Treat Restaurant (603-823-8851), Main St. Open 7 AM–9 PM. A local standby. The dining room features Italian entrées; the adjoining sports lounge serves homemade pizza and screens sporting events and classic movies on its giant TV screen. Service was glacial on our last visit, but food and atmosphere were fine.

♂ ₺ **Franconia Village House Restaurant** (603-823-5405), 651 Main St. Open daily for dinner year-round; lunch and weekend breakfasts July–Oct. Mixed reviews. Family-style fare: soups, fish, fresh pasta.

In Bethlehem
♂ **Rosa Flamingo's** (603-869-3111), Main St. Dinner nightly from 5. Lunch Fri.–Sun. Bar menu 4–11. A peppy Italian menu includes standards like lasagna Bolognese, eggplant parmigiana, steaks, chops, and chicken. Locally famed for its pizza. Vegetarians are also catered to with tofu and bean ravioli or penne with a tomato cream sauce. Choose from an impressive selection of beers, too (including several locally brewed ales), or from the outstanding wine list; if you smoke, hit the cigar lounge downstairs for a stogie from the Dominican Republic or Honduras. There's a children's menu featuring chicken parmigiana, barbecued ribs, chicken fingers, and ravioli.

In Littleton
♠ ♂ **Italian Oasis & Brewpub** (603-444-6995) 106 Main St., across from Thayer's Inn. Open daily 11:30 AM–midnight. A casual, fun place, if a tad smoky for our taste. A wide variety of menu items, along with ales and stouts. Menu items include Steak Your Claim,

Man O'Cotti, and an It's Greek to Me pizza. Kids' and take-out menus.

Littleton Diner (603-444-3994; www .littletondiner.com), 145 Main St. Open daily 6 AM–8 PM in winter, until 9 in summer. No credit cards. This vintage-1930s parlor-car diner sits staunchly on Main Street thumbing its weathered nose at the fast-food outlets down the road. Admittedly, food may come a bit slowly, but portions are large and there are genuine daily specials like meat loaf, pot roast, clam chowder, and roast pork dinner. Breakfast is served all day, your coffee cup is bottomless, the pies are a specialty, and—contrary to popular myth—the diner is entirely void of noxious cigarette smoke. Prices are reasonable.

Miller's Fare (603-444-2146), 16 Mill St. Open daily (except Mon.) for lunch. Perfect for grabbing a quick bite after visiting the Littleton Gristmill, the Miller's Fare offers gourmet lunches and high-quality Italian coffee. During warm weather, eat on the deck while listening to the burbling Ammonoosuc River and down sandwiches dressed with the likes of sundried tomato and thyme dressing, lemon parsley mustard, or olive goat cheese. Sumptuous soups like roasted garlic and butternut squash or shrimp and lobster chowder are paired with upscale salads like curried couscous with tomato, capers, and currants or wild rice salad with apples, parsley, and walnuts. Vegetarians are accommodated, and the dessert and coffee menus keep you lingering longer. All the bread is organic and supplied by the neighboring gristmill.

The Clamshell (603-444-6445; 603-444-6501), Dells Rd. Open weekdays 11:30–4 and 5–9, Fri. and Sat. until 10; Sun. noon–9. Later hours in the tavern. Just off I-93's Exit 42, this is a popular seafood restaurant serving lobster, steaks, and prime rib; also sandwiches and a salad bar. At dinner most broiled or fried seafood dishes and house specialties are under $15, but for surf and turf or Alaskan king crab you can hit $25.

Eastgate (603-444-3971), off I-93 at Exit 41 on Rt. 302. Open nightly 5–9 for dinner. Well known locally as a good restaurant and good value. A wide choice of seafood, pasta, chicken, and beef, most entrées less than $15, also a kids/"small appetite" menu. Make a road-food note!

The Coffee Pot (603-444-5722), 30 Main St. Open weekdays 6:30 AM– 4 PM, Sat. until 2, Sun. noon. Jim and Jean McKenna have a loyal following for their reasonably priced breakfast (all day, every day) specials, which include chef's hash, designer omelets, and Belgian waffles. Half a sandwich and a cup of soup is still $3.65, with pickles and chips.

Topic of the Town (603-444-6721), Main St. Open Mon.–Wed. for breakfast and lunch 5 AM–2 PM; Thu. 5 AM–7:30 PM; Fri. and Sat. 5 AM–8 PM; and Sun. 6 AM–noon. Locals gather here to discuss the events of the day and to enjoy simple food at modest prices. Friday night hosts the famous fish fry with free second helping.

In Lisbon

Ammonoosuc Pub at the Ammonoosuc Inn (see *Dining Out*). Open Tue.–Sat., 5–9:30. Local brews are on tap, and the moderately priced menu features wild mushroom, asparagus, and goat cheese strudel; poached salmon; as well as burgers and sandwiches. Inquire about live music.

SNACKS

In Littleton

Bishop's Homemade Ice Cream Shoppe (603-444-6039), 183 Cottage St. (off Rt. 302). Open mid-Apr.–mid-Oct., noon–10. A destination in its own right, simply the best ice cream around. Try Bishop's Bash. Also flavored yogurts and sorbet, all made here. Eat inside or out.

The Maia Papaya (603-869-9900), 2015 Main St., next to the post office. An attractive café featuring espresso shakes, latte, boutique sodas, Bishop's ice cream, bagels, biscotti, locally made pastries, and great smoothies.

Chutters (603-444-5787; www .chutter.com), 43 Main St., Littleton. The longest candy counter in the world, according to the *Guinness Book of Records*.

✳ Entertainment

North Country Chamber Players (603-444-0309), Sugar Hill. Mid July–mid Aug., Sat. at 7 PM at the Sugar Hill Meeting House; Sun. 3 PM at various locations.

Colonial Theater (603-444-5907; www.bethlehemcolonial.org), 2050 Main St. (Rt. 302), Bethlehem. Open May–Oct. Billed as "oldest theatre in the U.S.!", this restored art deco facility shows art films and stages live performances, movies nightly at 7:30.

Jax Jr. (603-5907), Main St., Littleton. First-run films.

Also see the **Weathervane Theatre** in "Northern White Mountains" and **North Country Center for the Arts** in "Lincoln and North Woodstock."

THE COLONIAL THEATER IN BETHLEHEM IS SAID TO BE THE OLDEST THEATER IN THE U.S.

Christina Tree

Christina Tree

THE LEAGUE OF N.H. CRAFTSMEN SHOP IN LITTLETON SELLS CRAFTS FROM LOCAL ARTISANS

✳ Selective Shopping

In Bath

The Brick Store (1-800-964-2074; www.thebrickstore.com), Rt. 302 in the village. Open year-round, daily until 9 PM. Billed as "America's oldest continuously operated General Store," the Brick Store is tourist-geared with fudge, cheese, doughnuts, and much more.

In Bethlehem

Bethlehem Flower Farm (603-869-3131), Rt. 302. Open Wed.–Sun., Memorial Day–Labor Day. More than 10,000 daylilies grow in the fields, with the best array in early August during the farm's annual festival. The gift barn offers lots of gardening accessories, as well as a café for lunch and afternoon tea.

Women's Rural Economic Network (WREN) Gallery and Ovation, 2013 Main St. Fine art and crafts by more than 100 local craftspeople.

Antique Stores: Bethlehem Village is all about antiques. We counted half a dozen varied stores within a mile.

In Franconia/Sugar Hill

Franconia Marketplace, Main St., Franconia. This complex in the heart of town houses the **Quality Bakery/**

Grateful Bread (603-823-5228), which makes whole-grain and organic breads; and **Garnet Hill** (603-823-5917), known for flannel sheets and housewares.

Sugar Hill Sampler (603-823-8478) Rt. 117, Sugar Hill. Open mid-May–Christmas. A 1780s barn with a folksy pioneer museum and a large selection of candies, cheese, crafts, and antiques.

Harmans Cheese and Country Store (603-823-8000; www.harmans cheese.com), Rt. 117, Sugar Hill. The specialty is well-aged cheddar, but the store also stocks maple sugar products and gourmet items.

In Littleton

Littleton Stamp and Coin Company (603-444-5386), 253 Union St. A local business with a national reputation for selling and buying stamps and coins.

The Village Bookstore (603-444-5263), Main St. Open daily. The largest and most complete bookstore (and one of the state's best) north of the mountains. Also a superb selection of cards and educational toys.

League of N.H. Craftsmen (604-444-1099), 81 Main St. One of less than a dozen outlets for New Hampshire's premier crafts group: fine furniture and furnishings, glass, clothing, art, and more.

Tannery Marketplace (603-444-1200), 111 Saranac St., behind the Littleton Diner by the Ammonoosuc River. A former tannery, now housing salvage, antiques, and artists' studios.

Lahout's: **Main Store** (603-444-5838), 127 Union St., **Discount Warehouse** (603-444-0328), and **Northface Patagonia** (603-444-0915). Herbert Lahout, a Lebanese immigrant, opened its first store in Littleton's Grange Hall in 1920. Originally a dry goods and grocery store, it was gradually expanded by the next generation to serve the needs of skiers at Cannon Mountain. Now with four stores in Lincoln, Lahout's claims to be "the oldest ski shop in America." It's good for a full range of clothing, especially sporting.

FotoFactory (603-444-5600), 53 Main St. An outstanding photo shop. We stopped by to get a passport photo and walked out with a first-rate digital camera and a sense of how to use it.

✳ Special Events

February: **Forest Festival** (603-444-6228; www.therocks.org), the Rocks Estate, Rt. 302, Bethlehem. A mid-February day in the woods with logging demonstrations plus snowshoeing and cross-country skiing. **Frostbite Follies**. A weeklong series of events around Franconia and Littleton includes sleigh rides, ski movies, broom hockey, ski races, community suppers.

April: **Maple Season Tours** (603-444-6228; www.therocks.org), the Rocks Estate, Rt. 302, Bethlehem. Early-April weekend features a workshop about maple trees; also learn about gathering sap and boiling it down to make maple syrup.

Late May: **Lilac Time Festival** (603-838-6673): A down-home festival honoring the state flower; highlights include a golf tournament, parade, pancake breakfast, bands, and a dance.

June: **Wildflower Festival** (603-444-6228; www.therocks.org), the Rocks Estate, Rt. 302, Bethlehem. Guided walks, workshops, demonstrations, and a children's walk on a Sunday in

early June. **Fields of Lupine Festival** (603-823-5661; 1-800-237-9007), Franconia and Sugar Hill. Arts and crafts, inn tours, and concerts revolving around breathtaking hillside displays of blossoming lupine.

July: **North Country Chamber Players**, Sugar Hill. Classical concerts Saturday at 8 PM in the Sugar Hill Meeting House.

August: **Day Lily Festival**, Bethlehem. **Horse Show**, Mittersill Resort, Franconia.

September: **Franconia Scramble**, Franconia. A 6.2-mile footrace over Franconia roads. **New England Boiled Dinner**, the Town House, Franconia. Corned beef and all the fixings. **Annual Antique Show and Sale**, Sugar Hill Meeting House. Selected dealers of antiques and collectibles.

October: **Quilt Festival**, Franconia. **Durrell Methodist Church Bazaar**, Franconia, Saturday of Columbus Day weekend. **Crafts Fair**, elementary school, Bethlehem, Sunday of Columbus Day weekend. **The Halloween Tradition** (603-444-6228; www.therocks.org), the Rocks Estate, Rt. 302, Bethlehem. Ghosts and goblins haunt the estate in a program cosponsored by local Boy and Girl Scouts; also apple bobbing, pumpkin carving, and ghost stories told around the fire.

Early December: **Oh! Christmas Tree** (603-444-6228; www.therocks .org), the Rocks Estate, Rt. 302, Bethlehem, weekends. Celebrate Christmas with wreath making, ornament making, and a hay-wagon tour of the Christmas tree plantation. Pick your own tree to cut. Tree sales daily in December.

MOUNT WASHINGTON
AND ITS VALLEYS

INCLUDING MOUNT WASHINGTON GATEWAY REGION, NORTH CONWAY AREA, JACKSON AND PINKHAM NOTCH, CRAWFORD NOTCH, AND BRETTON WOODS

L iterally the high point of New England, Mount Washington has been New Hampshire's top tourist attraction for more than 150 years—despite its frequent cloud crown and temperatures more typical of a mountain three times its 6,299-foot height.

Improbably, its first recorded ascent was in June 1642 by Darby Field of Dover, assisted by Indian guides—only one of whom reluctantly accompanied him all the way to the summit. Local tribes revered the mountain as the seat of the Great Spirit.

Clearly visible from Portland, Maine (more than 60 miles to the east), Mount Washington is the central, pyramid-shaped summit in the White Mountains' Presidential Range, so called because each of its peaks is named for a different president. In 1819 legendary father-and-son innkeepers Abel and Ethan Crawford cut a bridle path (now named for the Crawford family, it's America's oldest continually used hiking trail) up the western side of the mountain, building a log cabin for patrons to rest up before venturing above tree line.

Artists and writers were among early patrons, and their work spread the mountains' fame. Dozens of mammoth hotels soon dotted the immediate area, some accommodating 500 or more guests. Hotel owners bought farms to raise their own produce, generated their own lights and power, built ponds, hiking trails, golf courses, and tennis courts, and maintained post offices. Atop Mount Washington itself a rude shelter was built soon after the bridle path opened and the first hotel, the Summit House, opened in 1852.

"We used to average 100 dinners a day . . . One noon there were representatives of 13 different nations as guests at dinner," its proprietor wrote. A rival, Tip-Top House, opened the next year. In 1861 stages began hauling tourists on the 8-mile-long Mount Washington Carriage Road up the mountain's eastern

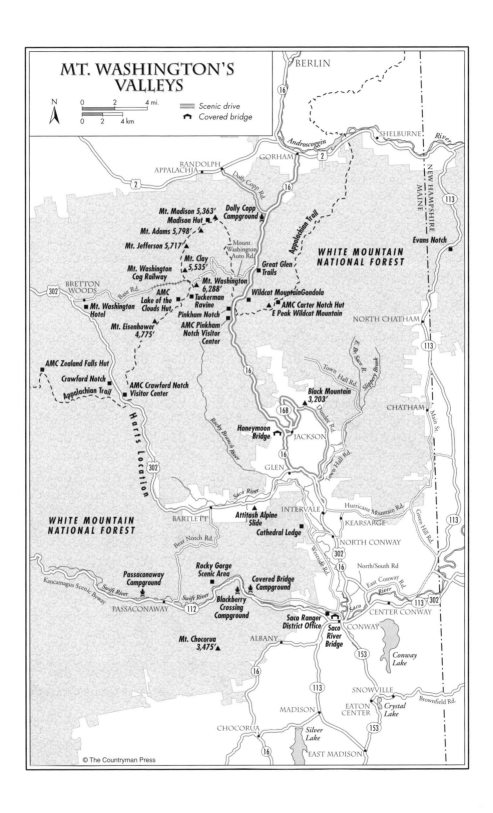

MT. WASHINGTON'S VALLEYS

N

0   2   4 mi.
0   2   4 km

▧ Scenic drive
⌂ Covered bridge

BERLIN

16

Androscoggin

SHELBURNE

River

GORHAM

2

RANDOLPH
APPALACHIA

Dolly Copp Rd.

16

NEW HAMPSHIRE
MAINE

113

2

Mt. Madison 5,363'
Madison Hut

Dolly Copp
Campground

Appalachian Trail

WHITE MOUNTAIN
NATIONAL FOREST

Evans Notch

Mt. Adams 5,798'

Mt. Jefferson 5,717'

Mount
Washington
Auto Rd.

Mt. Clay
5,535'

Great Glen
Trails

Mt. Washington
Cog Railway

BRETTON
WOODS

302

Base Rd.

Mt. Washington
6,288'

AMC
Lake of the
Clouds Hut

Tuckerman
Ravine

Wildcat Mountain Gondola

AMC Carter Notch Hut
E Peak Wildcat Mountain

NORTH CHATHAM

Mt. Washington
Hotel

Pinkham Notch

Mt. Eisenhower
4,775'

AMC Pinkham
Notch Visitor
Center

E. Br. Saco R.

Slippery Brook

AMC Zealand Falls Hut

Crawford Notch

Appalachian Trail

AMC Crawford Notch
Visitor Center

Town Hall Rd.

Black Mountain
3,203'

CHATHAM

113

Main St.

Harts Location

302

16

Rocky Branch River

16B

Honeymoon
Bridge

JACKSON

Dundee Rd.

Town Hall Rd.

16

GLEN

Saco River

INTERVALE

Hurricane Mountain Rd.

Green Hill Rd.

113

WHITE MOUNTAIN
NATIONAL FOREST

BARTLETT

Attitash Alpine
Slide

Cathedral Ledge

KEARSARGE

NORTH CONWAY

302

16

Bear Notch Rd.

North/South Rd.

Westside Rd.

Rocky Gorge
Scenic Area

Passaconaway
Campground

Kancamagus Scenic Byway

Swift River

112

Swift River

Covered Bridge
Campground

Blackberry
Crossing
Campground

East Conway Rd.

River

113 302

CENTER CONWAY

PASSACONAWAY

Saco Ranger
District Office

Saco
River
Bridge

CONWAY

Saco

Mt. Chocorua
3,475'

ALBANY

153

Conway
Lake

16

113

SNOWVILLE

Brownfield Rd.

MADISON

EATON
CENTER

Crystal
Lake

153

CHOCORUA

Silver
Lake

16

EAST MADISON

© The Countryman Press

slopes; by 1869 the Mount Washington Cog Railway ("the world's first mountain-climbing cog railway") began transporting travelers from the mountain's western base (by then named Crawford Notch). Tradition has it that showman Phineas Taylor Barnum stood atop an observation tower on Mount Washington and, surveying the vista from the Canadian border to the Atlantic, observed the view to be "the second greatest show on earth."

By 1876 it was possible to buy a 3-day $17 excursion that included a night at a hotel in Crawford Notch, a transfer to the Cog Railway to ride up Mount Washington, a night in a summit hotel, and then a carriage ride down the eastern side of the mountain to connect with a stage for a trip back to the railroad line.

The year 1876 saw the founding of the Appalachian Mountain Club (the AMC), which has cut, mapped, and maintained hundreds of miles of hiking trails through the White Mountains, erecting a series of eight "high huts," each a day's hike apart. While it's no longer possible to spend the night in a hotel atop Mount Washington, it is highly recommended to do so at the AMC's Mizpah Spring Hut off the Crawford Path or at the Lake of the Clouds Hut above tree line on Mount Washington. The AMC also maintains hiker-geared lodging in Pinkham and Crawford notches.

Unfortunately, most of the area's old hotels have gone the way of the railways. Happily, the cog railway recently also began operating in winter—but only halfway up the mountain. And the still-grand Mount Washington in Bretton Woods is now open year-round, complemented by its own major ski area as well as cross-country trails. The smaller but still elegant Wentworth and the Eagle Mountain House in Jackson are also handy to both alpine and Nordic trails.

MOUNT WASHINGTON

Virginia Moore, Mount Washington Observatory

Roughly the same number of visitors can be accommodated in the Mount Washington Valley today as in the 1890s.

So what and where exactly is the Mount Washington Valley? The promotional name was coined in the 1960s by a Boston publicist and the managers of its then three ski areas (Wildcat, Back, and Cranmore) specifically for the North Conway–Jackson area, which was known until then as the Eastern Slopes. It has since been expanded to apply to 28 towns surrounding Mount Washington, an area that now includes no less than seven alpine ski areas, six Nordic centers, 200 miles of snowmobiling trails, and, in summer, 12 "family attractions," 10 golf courses, hundreds of miles of hiking and biking trails, 7,500 beds, more than 75 restaurants, and some 200 shops, boutiques, and outlet stores.

Within this chapter we have divided the Mount Washington Valley into five distinct sections. We begin with Mount Washington itself, and an overview of how to explore it. Next comes the Mount Washington Gateway Region, a beautiful area frequently overlooked by travelers rushing up Rt. 16 to North Conway, the area's busiest and best-known village. "Jackson and Pinkham Notch" describes the distinctly 19th-century-style resort village with its many appealing lodging options and dramatic high pass that's become a year-round center for outdoor enthusiasts at the eastern base of Mount Washington. Finally, "Crawford Notch and Bretton Woods" details sights in the magnificent mountain corridor with its grand old hotel to the west of Mount Washington.

WHEN TO GO The Mount Washington Valley is quieter in winter (with the exception of school vacations at Christmas and Presidents' Week) than summer, especially midweek when genuine bargains are available when combined with downhill skiing. Memorial Day–Labor Day it's consistently busy, and you really don't want to be here in spring (Mud Season) unless you're skiing up in Tuckerman Ravine. Fall foliage season (the peak is early October) is predictably busy and expensive. November offers plenty of special promotions and incentives to do your holiday shopping here. Snow, however, rarely arrives before Christmas. March can be quite wonderful—off-season prices and plenty of snow—but check conditions before booking.

MOUNT WASHINGTON HIKING GUIDANCE **The Appaclachian Mountain Club** (www.outdoors.org) maintains two major visitors centers. **Pinkham Notch Visitor Center** at the eastern base of Mount Washington and Highland Center at Crawford Notch at the western base. Phone 603-466-2725 for weather, trail, or general information; 603-466-2727 for overnight or workshop reservations and either facility. Both serve as the information hubs for hiking throughout the Presidential Range. The AMC also operates hiker's shuttles and maintains a system of eight huts, with the Lake of the Clouds on Mount Washington itself.

WMNF Androscoggin Ranger Station (603-466-2713), Rt. 16, Gorham. Open daily.

The Mount Washington Observatory website (www.mountwashington.org) offers current information about what's open and happening on the summit.

A MOUNTAIN VIEW FROM ONE OF THE
AMC'S HIGH MOUNTAIN HUTS

GETTING THERE Daily **Concord Trailways** bus service (603-228-3300; 1-800-639-3317; www.concordtrailways.com) stops daily at the AMC Pinkham Notch Visitors Center en route from Logan Airport and Boston and to Berlin, N.H.

GETTING AROUND The AMC Hiker Shuttle operates June–mid-Oct., 8 AM–4 PM. It consists of two vans, one based at the Pinkham Notch Visitors Center, the second at the Highland Center. By changing at these transfer points, it's possible to reach all the area's major trailheads. It's suggested that you spot your car and take a van to the trailhead from which you intend to walk out.

&. **Mount Washington State Park**, on the summit of the mountain, is open daily Memorial Day–Columbus Day. Although most of Mount Washington is part of the White Mountain National Forest, there are several other owners. The state of New Hampshire operates the Sherman Adams Summit Building, named for the former New Hampshire governor who was the chief of staff for President Eisenhower. This contemporary, two-story, curved building sits into the northeastern side of the mountain, offering sweeping views. Park facilities include a gift shop, snack bar, post office, restrooms (all handicapped accessible), and a pack room for hikers. The old Tip-Top House, originally built as a summit hotel in 1853, has been restored and is open daily (free) as a reminder of the past. Other summit buildings include the transmitter and generator facilities of Channel 8, WMTW-TV, which provides transmitter service for radio stations and relays for state and federal government agencies.

Mount Washington Museum, on the summit. Open daily when the building is open. Located one flight below the main building, the museum is operated by the Mount Washington Observatory and offers historical exhibits and a wealth of scientific information on the meteorology, geology, botany, and biology of the mountain. A small gift shop helps support the activities of the observatory. Fee charged.

Mount Washington Observatory (603-356-8345; www.mountwashington.org), on the summit. Closed to the public, but members may tour the facility. There are, in fact, 4,000 members in 48 states and nine foreign countries. With membership ($40 per year, $65 for a family) comes the thick quarterly bulletin *Windswept* and the right to participate in workshops in subjects ranging from history and photography to geology. This private, nonprofit institution occupies a section of the Sherman Adams Summit Building and is staffed all year by crews of two to three people who rotate each week. Weather observations are taken every 3 hours, providing a lengthy record of data that extends back to the 1930s, when the institution was formed. The staff endured the highest wind ever recorded on earth, 231 miles per hour, in April 1934. The original building was the old Stage Office, a replica of which is on the summit. Various ongoing research projects study the effects of icing, aspects of atmospheric physics, and related subjects. The observatory has conducted research for a variety of commercial, institutional, and governmental organizations. Facilities include crew quarters, a weather-instrument room, a radio room, a photography darkroom, and a library. The staffers provide live morning weather reports on several area radio stations, including WMWV 93.5 FM in Conway.

✳ To Do

✐ **Mount Washington Cog Railway** (603-846-5404; www.thecog.com). $57 adults, $37 children; reservations recommended), off Rt. 302, Bretton Woods 03589. See "Crawford Notch and Bretton Woods."

Mount Washington Auto (Carriage) Road (603-466-2222; 603-466-3988; www.mt-washington.com), Rt. 16, is open year-round. See "Jackson and Pinkham Notch."

HIKING Mount Washington is crisscrossed with trails, but there are two popular routes. The **Tuckerman Ravine Trail** (4.1 miles, 4½ hours) begins at the AMC Pinkham Notch Camp on Rt. 16. It is nearly a graded path most of the first 2.5 miles as it approaches the ravine; then it climbs steeply up the ravine's headwall and reaches the summit cone for the final ascent to the top. The ravine area has open-sided shelters for up to 86 people, and each person has to carry up everything needed for an overnight stay. (Register at the AMC Pinkham Notch Camp; no reservations.) This is the trail used by spring skiers, and it can be walked as far as the ravine by anyone in reasonably good condition. The beginning of the trail is an easy 0.5-mile walk on a graded path to the pretty Crystal Cascade.

On the western side of Mount Washington is the **Ammonoosuc Ravine Trail** (in combination with Crawford Path, 3.86 miles, 4½ hours). It begins at the Cog Railway Base Station, located off Rt. 302 north of Crawford Notch. About 2.5 miles from the start is the AMC Lake of the Clouds Hut, one of the best areas to view the alpine flowers, near the junction with popular Crawford Path. This trail is 8.2 miles long and requires 6 hours to reach the summit of Mount Washington. It begins just above Crawford Notch and crosses a new, specially designed suspension bridge. After 2.7 miles comes the cutoff for the AMC Mizpah Spring Hut.

In the vicinity of the AMC Pinkham Visitors Center, many short hiking trails are suitable for family groups. Ask for suggestions and directions at the camp.

A few words of caution about hiking on Mount Washington and the Presidential Range. Most of these trails end up above tree line and should be attempted only by properly equipped hikers. Winter weather conditions can occur above tree line any month of the year. Annually some 50,000 hikers safely reach the summit, many in winter, but hiking is a self-reliant activity; even fair-weather, summer hikers are warned to climb well prepared, with extra clothing and food in addition to maps and a compass. Most of the trails to the summits are 4 to 5 miles in length and require 4 or 5 hours to reach the top. Although these trails are not exceptionally long, there is an elevation gain of some 4,000 feet, a distance that becomes painfully evident to those who are not in reasonably good physical condition. Western hikers, used to the higher Rockies, soon appreciate the ruggedness and the elevation change when climbing this mountain. About 100 people have died on the slopes of the mountain, some from falls while hiking, rock or ice climbing, or skiing; but others have died in summer when they were caught unprepared by rapidly changing weather conditions. Since the weather can be most severe above tree line, cautious hikers will assess the weather conditions when reaching that point on a climb. The AMC (603-466-2725) provides daily weather information. Also call 603-466-5252 for recorded weather information.

Since AMC staffers often volunteer for mountain rescues, they are careful to give considered advice to beginning and more experienced hikers. The *AMC White Mountain Guide* has the most comprehensive trail information available for hikers, but also see Daniel Doan and Ruth Doan MacDougall's *50 Hikes in the White Mountains* (Backcountry Guides).

SKIING **Tuckerman Ravine** (call the Appalachian Mountain Club, 603-466-2727), off Rt. 16, Pinkham Notch. Spring skiing has become an annual rite for many skiers, and there is nowhere better than the steep slopes of Tuckerman Ravine. There are no lifts, so you have to walk more than 3 miles to reach the headwall of this cirque, a little valley carved out of the eastern side of Mount Washington by glaciers during the Ice Age. Winds blow snow from the mountain into the ravine, where it settles to a depth of 75 feet or more. When snow has melted from traditional ski slopes, it remains in the ravine; skiers by the thousands walk the 2.4-mile trail from the AMC Pinkham Notch Visitors Center to Hermit Lake, then on up to the floor of the bowl. The headwall is another 800 feet up. Skiing begins in early April, and we have seen some diehards skiing the small patches of snow remaining in the ravine in June.

Early in the season, when there is plenty of snow, the steep John Sherburne Ski Trail provides a brisk run from the ravine back to Pinkham Notch Camp. Spring sun warms the air, and many people ski in short-sleeved shirts and shorts, risking sunburn and bruises if they fall. Skiing here is for experts, since a fall on the 35- to 55-degree slopes means a long, dangerous slide to the bottom of the ravine. A volunteer ski patrol is on duty, and WMNF rangers patrol the ravine to watch for avalanches. The three-sided Hermit Lake shelters offer sleeping-bag accommodations for 86 hardy backpackers, who must carry everything up to the site for overnight stays. Winter-use-only (Nov.–Mar.) tent platforms are also available in the ravine. Register for shelters or tent platforms through the AMC Pinkham Notch Camp (603-466-2727, no reservations; first-come, first-served only).

SCENIC DRIVE **Mount Washington Loop**. One of the region's most popular drives is the 86-mile loop around the march of mountains named for Presidents Pierce, Eisenhower, Franklin, Monroe, Clay, Jefferson, Adams, and Madison, as well as Washington. If you begin in Glen (junction of Rts. 16 and 302), your route will take you up through Pinkham Notch, past the Auto Road and through Gorham, and then back along Rt. 2 with splendid views south to the Presidentials. Follow Rt. 116 through "the Meadows" to Twin Mountain and south on Rt. 302, by the Mount Washington Cog Railroad and the Mount Washington Hotel set against the backdrop of Mount Washington itself, on down through Crawford Notch and back through Bartlett to Glen. Of course this ring around the mountains really makes no sense unless you take one (or both) routes to the summit and stop frequently along the way.

✳ Hiker's Lodging

✍ ⅙ **Appalachian Mountain Club** (603-466-2727; www.outdoors.org) offers full-service year-round lodging and meals with discounts for its members in **Joe Dodge Lodge** in Pinkham Notch ($56–76 per adult, $37–43 per child with breakfast and dinner) and at the more luxurious new **Highland Center** in Crawford Notch ($60–129 per adult, $44–49 per child or $30–35 in the neighboring **Shapleigh Bunk House**) or $48–59 per adult in the eight high huts in the Presidential Range, all accessible only by walking. Theoretically you can spend 9 days hiking from one to the next, but in practice patrons usually just spend a night at one or two. June–mid-Sep. all but Carter Notch Hut are "full service," meaning you supply your sheets (or sleeping bag) and towels; they provide meals, bunks, blankets, and educational programs. Nonmember rates are $74–96 per adult, $45–53 per child for the night's stay with dinner and breakfast (taxes included; less if you stay 3 days). Four huts continue to offer full service through mid-Oct., and Mizpah remains open almost to Halloween. Three huts— Carter Notch, Zealand Falls, and Lonesome Lake—are also open in winter on a self-serve basis ($28 per person).

MEALTIME AT THE AMC'S GREENLEAF HUT

AMC

We know **Mizpah Spring Hut** better than the others, but all share the following essentials: Bunks are stacked (at Mizpah it's six to a room), equipped with three army blankets, a mattress and a bare pillow. The two baths are dorm-style. Everything is immaculate, maintained by the youthful crew who also cook the gargantuan meals. Common space is attractive and well stocked with books, but the big draw here is your fellow hikers, who represent a span of ages and, usually, several European countries. It's the kind of place that draws people together. Frequently a naturalist leads an after-dinner hike. Breakfasts tend to feature fresh-baked breads and crispy bacon.

From Mizpah you can hike west to Zealand Falls Hut (popular with families because it's an easy hike in from Rt. 302), on to Galehead Hut on Garfield Ridge, Greenleaf Hut on the western flank of Mount Lafayette, and Lonesome Lake Hut, also popular with families because it's an easy hour's hike up from Franconia Notch. North of Mizpah is Lake of the Clouds (busy because it's right below Mount Washington's summit and favored by Boy Scout troops). Next comes Madison Spring, the most rugged of the huts, set above the sheer walls of Madison Gulf. Carter Notch Hut (open year-round on a self-service basis), the easternmost hut, lies in a sheltered divide between Wildcat Mountain and Carter Dome. We cheated by taking the Wildcat Mountain Gondola up and walking in from there. For a description of lodging at Joe Dodge Lodge, see "Jackson and Pinkham Notch," and for details about the Highland Center see "Crawford Notch and Bretton Woods." *Note:* While all three meals are open to visitors at the Pinkham Notch Visitors Center and at the Highland Center, hikers are not invited to drop in for meals at the high huts.

✷ Special Events

June: Two big races up the 7.6 mile-Mount Washington Auto Road from Route 16 in Pinkham Notch to the summit: *Third Saturday:* The **Mount Washington Footrace** (www.gsrs.com; 603-863-2537) was first held in 1936 and has been held consecutively since 1966; it's limited by lottery to 1,000 participants. *Fourth Saturday:* **Mount Washington Auto Hill Climb** (www.mt-washington.com; 603-466-3988), Mount Washington Auto Road, Pinkham Notch. First held in 1904, it's America's oldest motor-sport event.

Mid-September: **Mount Washington Bike Race** (www.mt-washington.com; 603-466-3988), Mount Washington Auto Road, Pinkham Notch. This event attracts some of the top U.S. racers.

Just off the beaten path, betwixt and between more high-profile destinations, this area offers an increasingly rare combination: beauty, hospitality, and peace. Flanking Rt. 16, just south of the Mount Washington Valley and north of Lake Winnipesaukee, this is a hilly, wooded region, spotted with small lakes—White Lake, Chocorua Lake, and Silver Lake, not to mention Ossipee, Silver, Purity, and Crystal. Its villages include picture-perfect Tamworth, Eaton Center, and Freedom.

GETTING THERE Rt. 16 is the high road from I-95 at Portsmouth to the Mount Washington Valley. Also see Rt. 153 (see *Scenic Drives*). Rt. 25 runs east to Portland and west to Lake Winnipesaukee and I-93.

✳ To See

VILLAGES Tamworth. Settled in 1771, the town of Tamworth (population 2,550) encompasses the villages of Wonalancet, Chocorua, Whittier, Tamworth Village, South Tamworth, Pequawket, and Bennett Corners. The view of compact Tamworth Village, a crossroads community with its steepled church backed by the Ossipee range and set in open fields, graces the cover of this book. Look closely and you will see the Victorian-style Tamworth Inn across from the venerable Barnstormers Summer Playhouse at its center, and the Remick Country Doctor Museum (free, open year-round). In one short block there is also a substantial library, general store (alias Remicks), and the "The Other Store." Inquire in the library about cross-country ski and walking trails. Head west on Cleveland Road to see Ordination Rock, north on Rt. 113A to Wonalancet, east on 113 to Chocorua (and Rt. 16), and south on 113 to Whittier (named for the poet John Greenleaf Whittier, who frequented the area). The town's many distinguished second-home owners included two-term president Grover Cleveland, whose son Francis moved here to stay, founding the Barnstormers in 1931. In the era when the train stopped at Depot Street, this was also a winter resort with skiing (there was a rope tow) and dogsledding, based at the famous Chinook Kennels in Wonalancet. It's still as pleasant a place to come in winter (Wonalancet is a genuine snow pocket) as summer. The **Tamworth Historical Society** (603-323-2900) is open by appointment.

Chocorua sits astride busy Rt. 16. It's named for its Matterhorn-like

TAMWORTH

Christina Tree

mountain, visible from the highway, across Chocorua Lake. The view from Rt. 16 across the waterfall and its millpond is another photo op.

Eaton Center. Its population is a third what it was in the 1850s, but this remains an idyllic village with a classic 1870s white, steepled church seemingly posing by **Crystal Lake**. The Eaton Center Village Store (groceries and small coffee shop) serves as the source of all local information.

Freedom (population 1361). Another picture-perfect village with a flagpole and a fountain. Moulton Brook flows by and behind Main Street, foxgloves bloom behind picket fences, and both the church and town hall are white with green trim. The Allard House and Works Museum (open in July and Aug., Sat. 10–noon, Sun. 2–4) is worth checking out, depicting life in this small mill town at its most prosperous.

MUSEUM **Remick Country Doctor Museum and Farm** (603-323-7591; 1-800-686-6117; www.remickmuseum.org), 58 Cleveland Hill Rd., Tamworth. Open year-round Mon.–Fri. 10–4; extended hours in summer. Free. On the edge of the village, this exceptional little museum depicts the life of a country doctor through the past century. Remicks have been active in Tamworth since the 1790s; between 1894 and 1993 two members of the family (father and son) served the medical needs of the town and outlying farms. The Remicks themselves farmed (their Hillsdale Farm's barn and stable are part of the museum) and lived frugally, judging from the vintage 1930s–1950s furnishing in the house, which doubled as doctor's office. The **Capt. Enoch Remick House**, also in the village and slightly grander, is also open on special occasions—which occur at least once a month, year-round: They include a farm fest and fishing derby (at the farm pond), an ox pull, a traditional tea, and so on. Just one of four surviving farms in Tamworth, this one happens to be in the middle of the village.

GLACIAL ERRATICS "It is a folk saying that God created the world in six days and spent the seventh throwing rocks at New Hampshire," Keith Henney wrote in *The Early Days of Eaton*. Two famous examples of these "rocks" are:

Ordination Rock, Cleveland Hill Rd., Tamworth (a few miles west of the village). A curiosity, this cenotaph perched atop a giant boulder commemorates the ordination of Tamworth's first minister in 1792. A plaque, recalling that HE CAME INTO THE WILDERNESS AND LEFT IT A FRUITFUL FIELD, gives details of his tenure.

Madison Boulder Natural Area, on a dirt side road off Rt. 113, Madison. Open all year, although access is limited to walking in winter. Just a big rock but amazing to see. During the Ice Age, this massive chunk was plucked off a mountaintop and carried along by a glacier until it reached this spot. Some three stories high and more than 80 feet long, it is one of the largest glacial erratics in the world and has been designated a national natural landmark. No facilities and no fees.

SCENIC DRIVES **The Chinook Trail**. On the late-fall morning we drove this stretch of Rt. 113A, it was magical! Turn north at the four corners in Tamworth Village, heading through woods for several miles. Note the turnoff for Hemenway State Forest and the firehouse that's the only clue that you have entered

Wonalancet. Look for the monument in front of **Chinook Kennels**, named for its most famous resident, born in 1917 and sire of the still-famous breed (now around 500 dogs). Chinook himself served as lead dog on Admiral Byrd's expeditions to Antarctica, but the monument is for all dogs who did so. For many years these kennels were a big attraction; dogsleds met the trains. Traveling this direction it's easy to miss the **Wonalancet Chapel**, at the bend in the road as the countryside opens up around you (look back for the best view; it's a classic chapel in the middle of nowhere, a favorite for weddings). It's a glorious 10 miles from here to Sandwich, through the tiny village of Whiteface (note the swimming hole by the bridge), and on down to North Sandwich.

Rt. 153 from Wakefield through the Effinghams and Freedom to Eaton Center. This route begins in the Lake Winnipesaukee area, but we think it belongs here because you tend to be heading north on it, into the Mount Washington Valley. Frequently we begin looking for road food at this point, so it's good to know about the **Poor People's Pub** in Sanbornville. It's less than a mile east of Rt. 16 (at the junction of Rts. 109 and 153), open daily for lunch and dinner, a local gathering spot that's a good bet for a sandwich or full meal. Note the cheerful **Choo-Chew Café** (good for breakfast and light lunches, open 7–2) by the tracks in this railroad-era village. You might also want to stop by Lovell Lake, just up Rt. 109, with a town beach.

Sanbornville is one of several villages in the town of Wakefield. Heading north up Rt. 153 (note Toad Hollow, a small gem store with plenty to please crystal lovers and rockhounds), you soon come to the old town center with its impressive lineup of early-19th-century houses, including the Wakefield Inn. At 2784 Wakefield Road you might want to check out the **Museum of Childhood** (603-522-8073, open mid-May–Labor Day, 11–4, Sun. 1–4; closed Tue.; $3 adults, $1.25 ages 9 and under). Elizabeth MacRury offers 12 rooms filled with 5,000 dolls and 57 dollhouses of varying ages.

Continue up Rt. 153 to Province Lake with its narrow ribbon of sand between the road and the lake (you won't be the first to wade in) and a view of mountains to the west. Here too is the entrance to the **Province Lake Golf** (800-325-4434) with 18 holes. Technically, you are in Parsonfield, Maine. Bill Taylor in **Ye Olde Sale Shoppe** in Taylor City, South Effingham (the next village), tells you that the state line runs almost down the middle of his shop, every inch of which is crammed with possible purchases. Effingham Center is definitely in New Hampshire, with surprisingly substantial buildings for its size. Continuing north, your head also swivels at the sight of **Squire Lord's Mansion**, a three-story unmistakable Federal mansion with a large cupola in the middle of nowhere (please drive on; it's a private home). In **Effingham Falls** you cross Rt. 25, the high road west to Portland (44 miles) and east to Ossipee Lake (6 miles). You begin to see antiques stores (we browsed through **Brown's Chicken Coop Antiques** and picked up a map/guide to several shops in this area).

Be sure to detour the mile or so into the village of **Freedom**, a real beauty, with an attractive B&B. Continue on through **East Madison** to **Eaton Center**, or turn west on Rt. 113 to **Chocorua** and **Tamworth**.

THE BALD SUMMIT OF MOUNT CHOCORUA AFFORDS SPECTACULAR VIEWS OF THE
WHITE MOUNTAINS

MOUNT CHOCORUA

This distinctive peaked mountain gets its name from a prophet of the
Pequawket Indians who refused to leave the graves of his ancestors in
Tamworth when his tribe fled to Canada. He lived amicably among the settlers and left his son in the care of a local farm family while he journeyed to
visit his tribesmen. When he returned, his child was dead. Chocorua refused
to believe the farmer's story that the boy had mistakenly eaten poison meant
for a fox. In retaliation he killed the farmer's wife and children. The husband
tracked him to the summit of this mountain and shot him, but not before
Chocorua laid a curse on the settlers who, according to legend, soon fell
sick; then their crops died, and the settlement was abandoned. Cattle continued to die in this area, it seems, until a University of New Hampshire professor tested the local streams and discovered that they contained muriate
of lime, palatable to humans but not livestock.

✳ To Do

HIKING **Mount Chocorua** is only 3,475 feet high, but its rugged, treeless summit makes it a popular destination, and there are many trails to its summit. The
Piper Trail begins on Rt. 16 at a restaurant-campground parking lot (fee charged
for parking) a few miles north of **Chocorua Lake**. The well-trod trail is 4.5 miles
long and requires about 3½ hours hiking time. The **Liberty Trail** begins on Paugus Mill Rd., which is off Rt. 113A, southwest of the mountain. Some 3.9 miles
long, requiring about 3 hours and 20 minutes, this oldest trail on the mountain
passes the Jim Liberty cabin, a mountainside cabin with bunks (there for anyone
willing to use it). The **Champney Falls Trail** ascends the mountain from the

Kancamagus Highway. West of Chocorua are Mounts Paugus, Passaconaway, and Whiteface, all of which can be climbed from a parking lot off Ferncroft Rd., in Wonalancet on Rt. 113A.

Foss Mountain. From Eaton Center head west on Brownfield Road and right on Stuart Road, then take the first right and look for trailhead parking. Not particularly high but with a bald summit offering a 360-degree view: the full march of the Presidentials to the northwest and nearer, the Moat Mountains, Chocorua, and, to the southwest, the Ossipee Range.

HORSEBACK RIDING **Happiness Farm** (603-539-1702; www.happinessfarm .com), Freedom. Trail rides and riding lessons.

SWIMMING **White Lake State Park**, Rt. 16, Tamworth. Open late May–mid-Oct. Here is a sandy beach and campground. Rental boats and good trout fishing. The 1.5-mile trail around the lake takes you through a large stand of tall pitch pines, a national natural landmark. Fee charged.

Chocorua Lake, Rt. 16, Tamworth. Just north of Chocorua village, this location offers perhaps the most photographed scene in the country: rugged Mount Chocorua viewed across its namesake lake. Most of the lakeshore has been preserved for its scenic beauty, and nary a summer cottage disturbs the pristine character of the place. At the northern end of the lake, adjacent to the highway, is a popular swimming area and a place to launch a canoe or sailboard, but public facilities are minimal.

✳ Winter Sports

CROSS-COUNTRY SKIING In Tamworth inquire about the local trail along the Swift River, and see **Hemenway State Forest** under *Green Space*.

King Pine (see *Downhill Skiing*) also offers a 20-km groomed trail network throughout the Purity Spring property and Hoyt Audubon Sanctuary. Lessons, rentals.

DOWNHILL SKIING ✍ **King Pine Ski Area** (603-367-8896; www.kingpine.com), Rt. 153, East Madison. Dating back to the 1930s as a ski area, operated since 1952 by the Hoyt family and part of the Purity Spring Resort complex, this is a fine family ski area with snowmaking, night skiing, nursery, ski school, equipment rentals, two triple and one double chairlift, a tubing park, and 17 trails. $36 adults on weekends, $24 juniors and seniors; $28 adults midweek, $18 juniors and seniors; less on certain days and with lodging packages.

ICE SKATING **King Pine Ski Area Skating Arena** (see *Downhill Skiing*) is open to the public.

SLEIGH RIDES **Happiness Farm** (603-539-1702; www.happinessfarm.com), 98 Bennett Rd., Freedom. Sleigh rides are a specialty, with cider and cocoa in the warm barn after.

✹ Green Space

Hemenway State Forest, Rt. 113A, Tamworth. There are two trails here: a short, self-guided nature trail, and a longer trail with a spur to the Great Hill fire tower offering views of the southern White Mountains. Brochures for both trails can usually be found in the box a few yards up each trail. Note Duck Pond near the parking area, good for a dip. In winter this is a popular, dependably snowy bet for cross-country skiing.

✹ Lodging

RESORT ♪ **Purity Spring Resort** (603-367-8896; 1-800-373-3754; www .purityspring.com), Rt. 153, East Madison 03849. Open year-round. Off by itself southwest of the Conways, this low-key, affordable, 1,000-acre, family-geared resort has been run by the Hoyt family since 1870. In summer most guests stay a week, taking advantage of activities and of sports facilities that include canoes, rowboats, and waterskiing on Purity Lake as well as tennis, volleyball, and arts-and-crafts programs. The inn van delivers guests to trailheads for guided hikes, to rivers for a canoe trips, and to North Conway for a play. In winter the draw is King Pine Ski Area, also part of the resort. Some 75 country-style rooms are divided among 10 buildings, ranging from remodeled farmhouses and barns (several are suited to family groups) to six condominiums at King Pine and the sleek Mill Building, which also houses the indoor pool, hot tub, and fitness center. Rates are $40–135 per person depending on season and meal plan. Winter ski packages include skiing at King Pine Ski Area.

INNS ♪ **Snowvillage Inn** (603-447-2818; 1-800-447-4345; www.snow villageinn.com), Snowville 03832 Open year-round. With rolling lawns and towering iris and lupine in spring and summer; year-round there is a heart-stopping view of Mount Washington and the Presidential Range set off across the valley. Built as a summer home in 1912, the 18-room inn, a lively blend of New England charm and alpine flair, is perched 1,000 feet up Foss Mountain east of Eaton Center. New innkeepers Karen and Bern Galat have preserved the inn's special character. The guest rooms—each named for an author and all furnished with antiques—are scattered throughout three buildings: the main inn, the Carriage House, and the Chimney House. The latter provides fireplaces in the rooms, and all rooms have private bath. Each building also has a guest living room with books and games; the main inn has a large brick fireplace and spacious porch. You can cross-country ski on a 15-km groomed course, or snowshoe on Foss Mountain. A four-course candlelight dinner is served in a chaletlike dining room (see *Dining Out*). B&B rates are $109–214 per room. The inn is also now home to the White Mountain Cooking School; special packages include "Cook n' Ski," chocolate cooking, and vegetarian cooking weekends.

The Tamworth Inn (603-323-7721; 1-800-642-7352; www.tamworth.com), Main St., Tamworth 03886. Open all year. In the center of the village, this rambling Victorian-style inn, dating in part from 1833, backs on lawns that sweep down to the Swift River. Summer guests enjoy the heated outdoor pool and strolling across the street to the Barnstormers summer theater. There are 16 individually decorated rooms, including 7 suites, all with private bath, 3 with Jacuzzi, 2 with fireplace. Beds range from twins to king sized. The inn is popular locally for dinner (see *Dining Out*), and its tavern is a good bet for lighter fare. A full country breakfast is served, as is afternoon tea. The $115–300 rates include staff gratuities. Summer theater packages include room, dinner, and tickets to the Barnstormers.

✒ **Rockhouse Mountain Farm Inn** (603-447-2880), off Rt. 153, Eaton Center 03832. Open mid-June–Oct. Since 1946 members of the Edge family have shared with guests their 450 acres of fields, forest, and assorted animals, as well as a private beach and boats on Crystal Lake. Guests often help with haying or feeding the animals or gathering fresh vegetables from the garden for the evening meal. There are 18 rooms, 8 with private bath; the rest share one bath for every 2 rooms. Breakfast and dinner are served daily, and children are fed early. The single-entrée meals, which vary over the course of the summer, include roasts, homemade breads and cakes, and farm-picked vegetables and salads. Fresh eggs, milk, and cream come from the resident animals. There are weekly steak roasts, riverside picnics, and chicken barbecues. Most guests are families who stay for a week (Sat.–Sat.); some have been enjoying the Edges' easy hospitality for generations. $68 MAP per person 12 and up; reduced rates for younger children.

Bed and Breakfast (603-323-7440; 1-800-628-6944; www.riverbendinn .com), Rt. 16, Chocorua 03817. Open all year. Up a long driveway and facing the Chocorua River behind it, this 10-room inn is Yankee plain on the outside—but inside, it's wonderful to behold. Innkeepers Craig Cox and Jerry Weiss have traveled widely in Asia and decorated the inn, which has won interior design awards, with art work they acquired. We were particularly impressed by a statue of the South Indian god of doorways that graces a living room with persimmon-colored walls. Six rooms have private bath, the others semiprivate facilities. Each has a different decor but all have mahogany beds and Oriental rugs, equipped with robes, hair dryer, air conditioner, cable TV, and high speed Internet access. The two common rooms both have fireplace; there is also a small guest kitchen, and decks overlooking the river. The $89–219 room rate includes a full breakfast, served on a riverside deck or in a sunny patio room with linen-covered tables and a massive antique candelabra. Our breakfast began with gingered melon and apple coffee cake, followed by blueberry pancakes with local maple syrup. Our hosts were full of suggestions about antiques shops and peaceful places to snowshoe or cross-country ski.

The Inn at Crystal Lake (603-447-2120; 1-800-343-7336; www.inna tcrystallake.com), Rt. 153, Eaton Center 03832. Open all year. This distinctive four-story, triple-porched (one on top of another) Greek Revival building overlooks Crystal Lake. Built in 1884 as a private home, it became an inn almost immediately, then a private school. Happily, it's now an inn again. Bobby Barker and Tim Ostendorf are opera and classical music buffs with a large collection of recordings and videos. They offer 11 rooms, all with private bath, phone, cable TV/VCR, and most with air-conditioning. There is ample common space, plus the cheery, funkily decorated Palmer House Pub in the rear (see *Dining Out*). Guests may use Crystal Lake for swimming. Rates $109–239 double, including full country breakfast. No smoking. Children over 8 please.

⊙ **Lake View Cottage** (603-367-9182; 1-800-982-0418; www.lakeviewcottage.com). Open year-round. This spacious, very Victorian "painted lady" is sited on a knoll overlooking Silver Lake. It was built by Becky Knowles's grandfather, namesake of Grampa David's Room, a first-floor gem with a fireplace, canopy bed, antique furnishings, a Jacuzzi in the bathroom, and a porch overlooking the lake. Grampa Earle's Room, named for the grandfather who built a (long-gone) hotel on Mount Chocorua, is also a beauty, and even Helen's, the most modest of the five guest rooms, is unusually appealing. Becky and husband David Coogan renovated and opened the family home as a B&B in 2000. In summer guests can swim, fish, and boat from the dock and are supplied with towels for the beach. In winter there's similar access to NH Snowmobile Corridor 19. A full breakfast is served at a central table in front of the fire. Small weddings in the Rose Garden can be arranged. $125–195 includes a full breakfast.

Freedom House Bed and Breakfast (603-539-4815), 17 Old Portland Rd., Freedom 03836. Open all year. Located by a millpond in a quiet village, this 140-year-old house is decorated in country Victorian style. Four rooms sleep two to three each and share two full baths. Guests can relax on two porches or in the parlor or library. Innkeepers Patrick Miele and John Immediato also run an antiques shop in the adjoining barn. Full breakfast and four o'clock tea. $60–80 single or $75–90 double occupancy. A nonsmoking inn. There is a minimum 2-night stay on weekends June–Oct.

🐾 **The Lazy Dog Inn** (603-323-8350; 1-888-323-8350; www.lazydoginn.com), 201 Rt. 16, Chocorua 03817. Innkeepers Steven and Lauren Sousa describe their inn as "A truly dog friendly bed and breakfast." They're not exaggerating. You get the message as soon as you pull up in front of the mid-19th-century former farmhouse, which is decorated with banners bearing the images of happy dogs of different breeds. WIPE YOUR PAWS! a sign by the front door advises. "We wanted to make this the kind of B&B we were always looking for when we traveled with our dog but couldn't find," Lauren says. There are seven guest rooms, four with private bath and three sharing a full bath and a half-bath. All are cozily furnished and decorated with dog-themed pictures, quilts, knick-knacks, and framed sayings like LOVE IS A FOUR-LEGGED WORD. There is no restriction on the number of dogs accommodated or their size; all breeds are welcome. Dogs can sleep in the same room as their owners but can't be left alone in a room. A former barn has been converted into a climate-controlled "Doggie Lodge," a canine day care center with fenced-in play areas, toys and agility equipment, and piped-in soothing music. (The building also has a smaller exercise room for two-legged guests.) There is also a large outdoor fenced dog run. A full country breakfast is served to dog owners, and there is always a "bottomless jar" of dog treats in the kitchen. Rates are $95–190 double occupancy with one dog. Additional persons or dogs are $25 each.

The Wakefield Inn (603-522-8272; 1-800-245-0841; www.wakefieldinn .com), 2723 Wakefield Rd., Wakefield 03872. Open all year. Lin and John Koch are the innkeepers at this centerpiece of the historic district. A former stagecoach stop, this handsome three-story is now a B&B, featuring Indian shutters, a wraparound porch, and a three-sided fireplace in the sitting room. The seven guest rooms are reached by an unusual old spiral staircase. All the rooms, two of which are two-bedroom suites, have private bath, and the attractive furnishings feature Lin's stenciling and quilts. There is a large common room with a fireplace. $90–95 for two, B&B. Theme weekends; holiday and special packages available winter and spring.

CAMPING *Note:* There are also several private campgrounds in this area.

White Lake State Park (603-323-7350; www.nhparks.state.nh.us), Rt. 16, West Ossipee. Open mid-May–Columbus Day. There are 200 campsites here, and the trick is to get one of the couple of dozen with a water view. No pets permitted. $19–27 per night for two adults and dependent children. Facilities include a camp store, showers, ice, and firewood. No hookups. The lake offers swimming, canoeing, and a 2-mile walking trail. Reservations accepted after Jan. 1: 603-271-3628.

✳ Where to Eat

DINING OUT Snowvillage Inn (603-447-2818; 1-800-447-4345; www .snowvillageinn.com), Snowville. Open for dinner year-round. The cheery, wood-paneled and -beamed, alpine-style dining room features spectacular long views across the valley to the Presidentials—and the food is exceptional. You might begin with beef carpaccio drizzed with roasted garlic and topped with roasted shallots, then dine on salmon baklava (topped with Brie and wrapped in phyllo); rack of venison; or pork tenderloin with ginger cranberry jam. Entrées $17.95–33.95.

The Brass Heart Inn (603-323-7766;1-800-833-9509; www.thebrass inn.com), off Rt. 113, Chocorua. Call for reservations. The dining room is decorated in attractive wine and ocher colors and has a fine local reputation. Entrées change frequently but might include roast Peking duck, torta rustico, and rack of lamb. Entrées, including a house salad, warm bread, and a seasonable vegetable, are $14–25. Full liquor license.

The Tamworth Inn (603-323-7721; www.tamworth.com), Main St., Tamworth. Open all year for dinner, nightly in summer, but just Thu.–Sun. off-season. This old inn's attractive dining room includes a sunporch (overlooking the back lawn) and has an ever-changing menu that might range from eggplant pesto to grilled pork loin medallions with a cider, port, and cranberry glaze; from spiced pumpkin pancakes to grilled 8-ounce beef tenderloin topped with a Merlot au jus and served with whipped red bliss potatoes and Gorgonzola crackers. Entrées $15–25. Lighter fare is served in the pub.

Inn at Crystal Lake and Palmer House Pub (603-447-2120; www .innatcrystallake.com). Open Wed.– Sun. from 5 PM. The pub is fun, featuring a walnut bar from Boston's Ritz-Carlton and a light menu that includes every imaginable cocktail as well as short ribs and shepherd's pie. The small, comfy, more formal dining room showcases creations by chef Trevor Tasker, entrées such as scallops pan-seared and served with a lobster-scented vodka sauce, long-grain and wild rice, and grilled asparagus spears, or grilled herb-crusted sirloin with roasted garlic mashed potaoes, sautéed carrots and green beans. Entrées $17–24.

EATING OUT Whittier House (603-539-4513), Rt. 116 near the junction

THE OTHER STORE, HOME OF DALEY CAFÉ

Christina Tree

with Rt. 25, West Ossipee. Open daily for lunch and dinner, weekdays until 9, weekends until 10; Sunday brunch from 7:30 AM. A big, ornate Victorian house, this has been the site of a tavern since 1784; its 19th-century counterpart was frequented by poet John Greenleaf Whittier. Inside it's surprisingly spacious and informal, obviously a local favorite. The menu is large, featuring a choice of "great grazables," "substantial salads," and "full plate offerings" ranging from fish, through some tempting vegetarian dishes like Popeye Pie (fresh spinach with almonds, walnuts, and mushrooms topped with puff pastry), to roast prime rib. We can recommend the beef tips. Dinner entrées $12–29. Most entrées are $16 or less and include a big salad bar. There is also an unusual choice of beers.

The Yankee Smokehouse (603-539-7427), junction of Rts. 16 and 25, West Ossipee. An authentic open-pit barbecue and plenty of it. Beef and pork barbecue and other sandwiches. Full dinners, including combination plates with barbecued chicken, beef, pork, and baby back ribs. Wine and pitchers of beer.

Daley Café at The Other Store (603-323-8872), Tamworth Village. Open daily for breakfast and lunch, a dependable oasis with a counter, a few tables, and a seasonal deck overlooking the Swift River (in summer inquire about pretheater dinner). The walls are hung with art, and flowers bloom above the small, open grill. There's a soup of the day (the tomato is freshly made, studded with real tomatoes), good sandwiches, pie and ice cream (paper plates and cups). Browse through the store's stationery, cards, and gifts while you wait or pick up some hardware—a large part of what this place is about. There is a good selection of books about Tamworth and the area. Owner Kate Thompson explains that this became known as "the other store" during the many years that it served as an annex to Remick's, as the general store was long known.

Rosie's Restaurant (603-323-8611), 1547 White Mountain Hwy. (Rt. 16), Tamworth. Near White Lake State Park, a local gathering spot year-round for breakfast, also open for lunch, take-out, and ice cream in warm-weather months.

The Chequers Villa (603-323-8686), Rt. 113, south of Tamworth Village. Lunch on weekends, dinners nightly. Reasonably priced pizza, soups, and salads with atmosphere.

Jake's (603-539-2805), Rt. 16, West Ossipee. Open daily 11–9. Fried fish and seafood platters, pasta; a family restaurant that can be packed in summer.

Eaton Village Store (603-447-2403), Eaton Center. Open weekdays 6–6, Sat. 7–5, Sun. 7–7. The heart of Eaton Center, a combination post office, grocery store, and restaurant with a counter and tables for breakfast and lunch; breakfast only on Sunday.

Tamworth Village Store (603-323-8050). Open daily, formerly Remicks and now under the same ownership as the Chocorua General Store. Pizza is served, and there is an extensive deli department.

☀ Entertainment

The Barnstormers (603-323-8500), Tamworth. One of the country's oldest professional summer theaters, founded in 1930 by Francis Cleveland, son of the president. The theater stages outstanding plays in July and August with an Equity cast. Musicals, some popular plays, and other lesser-known offerings. Dinner theater packages are available with the Tamworth Inn.

The Arts Council of Tamworth (603-323-8693) presents monthly (except summer) performances—from string quartets to vaudeville—in the Tamworth-Sandwich area, mainly at the Barnstormers Theater.

Contra dances are held Sat. night (usually 7 PM) in the Tamworth Town House. Participants are invited to come early to learn the evening's dance.

Concerts by the River are held every summer Sun., 3–5 PM, on the deck beside the Swift River, at The Other Store in Tamworth Village (see *Eating Out*).

☀ Selective Shopping

Chocorua Village Pottery (603-323-7182), 118 Deer Hill Rd. (Rt. 113). Open daily but off-season only Thu.–Sun. 10–5. Myles Grinstead produces a variety of functional tableware and much more. Worth checking.

☀ Special Events

Third Saturday of February: Annual **dogsled races** from Sandwich to Tamworth.

Fourth of July: The **parade** in Tamworth is big.

August: **Old Home Days** in Freedom; **Tamworth History Day**.

Also see *Entertainment* and special events sponsored by the Remick Country Doctor Museum and Farm (www.remickmuseum.org; 1-800-686-6117) in Tamworth Village.

The town of Conway comprises the villages of Conway, Intervale, and North, East, Center, and South Conway. It is North Conway, however, that dominates the community and region. A summer haven for more than 150 years and one of the country's first ski destinations, it's now a major shopping mecca, with some 200 shops and factory outlets. It represents the White Mountains' largest concentration of inns, motels, and restaurants.

Early in the 19th century travelers began finding their way to this sleepy farming community in the broad Saco River Valley, the obvious staging ground for "adventure travel" into New England's highest mountains, which rise dramatically just a few miles to the north. By 1825 Conway had five inns, and by the 1850s hotels were sprouting on and around Mount Washington itself. Then in the 1870s rail service reached North Conway and was extended up through Crawford Notch. The town's status as the heart of the White Mountains was secured.

North Conway's most striking building remains its ornate, twin-towered rail station, built in 1874 to serve formally dressed ladies and gentlemen arriving to pass summer weeks and months at literally dozens of local hotels.

The trains were still running in the 1930s when New Englanders "discovered" skiing. In 1938 Harvey Gibson, an enterprising North Conway businessman, designed and built the ground-hugging "Skimobile" to ferry skiers up the slopes of Mount Cranmore. A year later he brought famed Austrian instructor Hannes Schneider to town to teach folks how to ski down. Winter visitors came by ski train, found lodging in the village, and walked to the mountain.

The Skimobile is gone, but Mount Cranmore remains a popular family resort for boarding and tubing as well as skiing. North Conway's ski allure now includes extensive trails at Attitash a few minutes' drive (if you know the shortcut) northwest of the village. Inns are also connected by more than 60 km of cross-country trails.

North Conway's popularity caters to a mix of hikers and climbers, skiers and families here to see the White Mountains' attractions both natural and human-made (Storyland, Heritage New Hampshire, water slides), and to shop.

As late as the 1930s, the strip along Rt. 16 south of North Conway village was a dirt road; but it was the only area left for development, and business began to establish itself there. With no zoning, commercial enterprises began to line the strip, slowly at first; then in the 1980s the factory outlet craze hit, and North Conway became one of the major shopping destinations in New England.

In summer the Conway Scenic Railroad now runs excursion trains south along the Saco to Conway and north over scary Frankenstein's Trestle into Crawford Notch. But while this is one of the few resort areas in northern New England that you can actually reach by bus—a service particularly popular with hikers from other countries—virtually everyone now arrives by car.

On weekends in foliage season and the days just before Christmas traffic can be stop-and-go on Rt. 16 for several miles north and south of the village, especially in the afternoon.

A north–south bypass paralleling to the east the most traffic-clogged stretch of Rt. 16 was built a few years ago and is much appreciated by local residents.

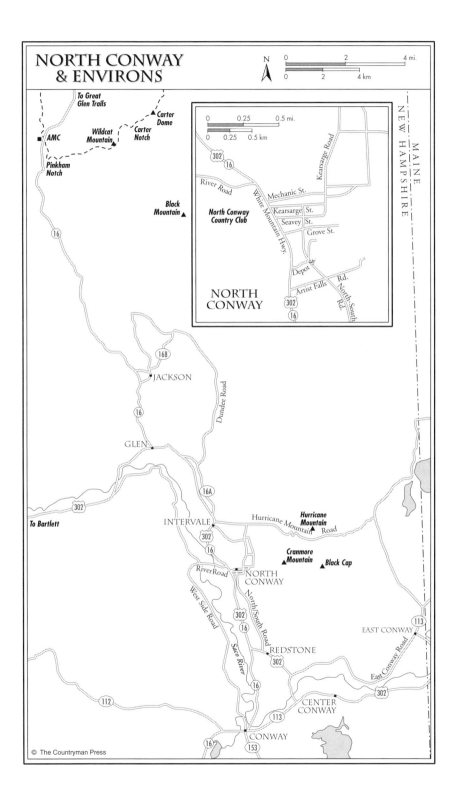

NORTH CONWAY & ENVIRONS

N

| 0 | | 2 | | 4 mi. |

| 0 | | 2 | | 4 km |

To Great
Glen Trails

Carter
Dome

AMC

Wildcat
Mountain

Carter
Notch

Pinkham
Notch

16

Black
Mountain

NORTH CONWAY

| 0 | 0.25 | 0.5 mi. |

| 0 | 0.25 | 0.5 km |

302

16

River Road

White Mountain Hwy.

Mechanic St.

Kearsarge St.

Seavey St.

Grove St.

North Conway
Country Club

Kearsarge Road

Depot St.

Artist Falls Rd.

North-South Rd.

302

16

MAINE

NEW HAMPSHIRE

16B

JACKSON

16

GLEN

Dundee Road

302

To Bartlett

16A

INTERVALE

302

16

RiverRoad

West Side Road

Saco River

North South Road

302

16

NORTH
CONWAY

Hurricane Mountain Road

Hurricane
Mountain

Cranmore
Mountain

Black Cap

EAST CONWAY

113

East Conway Road

REDSTONE

302

16

112

113

16

153

CONWAY

CENTER
CONWAY

302

© The Countryman Press

It isn't advertised or signposted from the highway, however, and many visitors spend days in North Conway without knowing it exists.

Shopping aside, North Conway is a bustling village with plenty of inns and restaurants—also a hub for biking, climbing, canoeing, kayaking—great for families. North Conway is what you make of it.

GUIDANCE **Mount Washington Valley Chamber of Commerce & Visitors Bureau** (603-356-3171; 1-800-367-3364; www.mountwashingtonvalley.org), Box 2300, North Conway 03860-2300. Free vacation guide, visitors information, and central reservation service for more than 90 varied properties throughout the area. It maintains a walk-in information center on Rt. 16 (Main St./White Mountain Hwy.) in North Conway village, open daily in summer and fall foliage season, weekends all year. A kiosk with reservations phone outside the information booth is open 24 hours.

White Mountain National Forest Saco Ranger Station (603-447-5448), on the Kancamagus Highway just west of Rt. 16 in Conway. Open year-round from 8 AM, until 5 PM in summer, 4:30 in winter. Pick up maps and information on activities ranging from wildlife-watching to mineral collecting.

State of New Hampshire Information Center, Rt. 16, Intervale, 3 miles north of North Conway at a "scenic vista" of Mount Washington. Restrooms, telephones, and well-stocked brochure racks. Open all year.

Conway Village Chamber of Commerce (603-447-2639; www.conway chamber.com), junction of Rt. 16 and W. Main St. at the southern end of Conway village. Open daily in summer, weekends in winter.

See *Guidance* within each section of this chapter for other chambers of commerce.

GETTING THERE *By car:* Rt. 16 is the way from Boston and places south. In Conway it joins Rt. 302, the high road from Portland, Maine (just 62 miles to the east). Also see *Scenic Drives* in "Mount Washington Gateway Region" for details about **Rt. 153**, a variation on Rt. 16.

To access the **north–south bypass paralleling Rt. 16** to the east, take a right onto Rt. 302 (Eastman Rd.) at the traffic light at the intersection of Rts. 16 and 302. At the next light take a left onto the bypass, which is signposted to North Conway village. Settlers Green and other shopping plazas can be accessed at the rear from the byway, and most of the side streets on the east side of Main St. (Mount Washington Hwy.) in the heart of the village connect to it. Coming from the north on Rt. 16, take a left onto Mechanic St. and then the first right onto North-South Rd. The **West Side Rd.**, the alternate and scenic route that also avoids the lights and traffic on Rt. 16, begins in Conway as Washington St., a left at the first light (junction of Rts. 16 and 153). Pass the two covered bridges, and at the fork bear right.

By bus: **Concord Trailways** (603-228-3300; 1-800-639-3317; www.concord trailways.com) provides scheduled service from Boston and its Logan Airport via Manchester, Concord, and Meredith.

Memorial Hospital (603-356-5461), Rt. 16, north of North Conway village. As you might imagine, this facility has extensive experience in treating skiing injuries!

North Conway ambulance: 603-356-6911. Conway ambulance: 603-447-5522.

✳ To See

Mount Washington Weather Discovery Center (603-356-2137; 1-800-706-0432; www.mountwashington.org), 2779 Main St. (Rt. 16). Open daily 10–5 through Oct.; closed Wed. and Thu. off-season. Free admission. At this writing the center is tricky to find, but well worth it: It's housed in a brick building adjacent to the Citizens Bank, across from the Eastern Slope Inn on the northern edge of North Conway village. This is an extensive and fascinating museum in which you can experience what it sounded and felt like to be on top of Mount Washington in the highest winds (231 miles per hour) ever recorded. A variety of hands-on exhibits illustrate the workings of weather. It's the public outreach center for the world-famous summit observatory (see "Mount Washington").

FOR FAMILIES ✐ ♿ **Heritage New Hampshire** (603-383-9776; www.heritage nh.com), Rt. 16, Box 1776, Glen 03838. Open Memorial Day–Father's Day, weekends 9–5; through Labor Day, open daily; then weekends again Labor Day–mid-Oct. Heritage New Hampshire evokes the history of this state as you travel from England on a 17th-century vessel, visit past personalities such as Daniel Webster, and reenter modern times on a train ride through Crawford Notch. Designed around an 1,800-foot walkway, which is handicapped accessible, this attraction is a 300-year review of New Hampshire history through photographs, dioramas, rides, and talking mannequins. This is a fine introduction to the state's past. Allow 2 hours. $11 adults, $5 ages 4–12; under 4 free.

✐ **Story Land** (603-383-4293; www.storylandnh.com), Rt. 16, Box 1776, Glen 03838. Open daily 10–5 Memorial Day–Labor Day, weekends 9–6; Labor Day–Columbus Day, weekends 10–5. Created some 50 years ago and regularly expanded, Story Land is organized around well-known fairy tales and children's stories. Sixteen rides range from a pirate ship, railroad, and antique autos to an African safari, bamboo chutes flume, and Dr. Geyser's remarkable raft ride. Cinderella, the Old Woman Who Lived in a Shoe, the Three Little Pigs, and the Billy Goats Gruff are all here, along with Heidi of the Alps, farm animals to pet and feed, and dozens

CHILDREN ADORE THE RIDES AND FAIRY-TALE CHARACTERS AT STORY LAND

of other favorites. There is a restaurant, gift shop, and free parking. Admission for those 4 and up is $22, which covers all rides.

✏ **Hartmann Model Railroad and Toy Museum** (603-356-9922; www .hartmannrr.com), Town Hall Rd. at Rts. 16/302, Intervale. An extensive American and European model-train layout, plus the Brass Caboose hobby shop. There is also a new café and crafts shop. Open daily, 10–5 except major holidays. Admission is $6 adults, $5 seniors, $4 ages 5–13.

Also see **Santa's Village** under in "Northern White Mountains," plus **Wildcat Mountain Gondola Ride** and the **Mount Washington Auto Road** in "Jackson and Pinkham Notch," and the **Mount Washington Cog Railway** in "Crawford Notch and Bretton Woods."

HISTORICAL SOCIETY **Conway Historical Society** (603-447-5551; 1-800-447-5551; www.conwayhistory.org), the Eastman-Lord House, 100 Main St., Conway. Open Memorial Day–Labor Day, Wed. 2–4 PM, Thu. 6–8 PM. Donation. The Eastman-Lord House features a Victorian parlor and 1940s kitchen, plus local memorabilia and special exhibits, including paintings by 19th-century White Mountain artist Benjamin Champney.

COVERED BRIDGES **Saco River Bridge**, on Washington St. (turn west at the Rt. 16 lights, junction of Rts. 16 and 153) in Conway village. Bear right at the fork to see this two-span bridge, originally built in 1890, rebuilt a century later. If you bear left (instead) at the fork, you come to the **Swift River bridge**. No longer used for traffic, this 144-foot, 1869 bridge has been restored (after being threatened with demolition) with picnic tables at its entrance, by the river. Covered-bridge buffs may also want to head out 9 miles east from Conway on the Kancamagus Highway and turn north at the sign to find the **Albany covered bridge** across the Swift River, dating from 1858. The **Bartlett covered bridge** on Rt. 302, 4.5 miles east of Bartlett village, is also the real thing despite its use as a gift shop. It has been closed to traffic since 1939.

SCENIC DRIVES **West Side Road**, running north from the Conway village traffic lights to River Road in North Conway, is not only a scenic road that passes two covered bridges, working farms, and mountain views, but also a way to avoid much of the Rt. 16 traffic snarl between Conway and North Conway. In Conway it begins as Washington Street, a left at the first light (junction of Rts. 16 and 153). Pass the two covered bridges, and at the fork bear right (a left would lead eventually to the Albany covered bridge on the Kancamagus Highway). At the intersection with River Road, a right brings you quickly into North Conway village at the north end of Main Street. Turn left for Echo Lake State Park, Cathedral Ledge, Diana's Baths, and Humphrey's Ledge, and then continue along the Saco River to join Rt. 302 just east of Attitash ski resort in Glen.

Hurricane Mountain Road and Evans Notch. For a satisfying day's loop turn east off Rt. 16 onto Hurricane Mountain Road. It begins in Intervale, 3 miles north of North Conway (just north of the scenic vista turnout). Not for the fainthearted, the road climbs and twists across a mountain ridge to connect with north–south Green Hill Road. Turn south (right) if you want the short loop back through East Conway and Redstone to North Conway. Turn north (left) to link up with Rt. 113, in tiny Stow, Me., and equally rural Chatham, N.H. (population 274), surrounded by the national forest. Rt. 113 north is not maintained in winter, but it is a smoothly graded road through Evans Notch—one of the lesser known of the White Mountain passes but featuring four campgrounds, many hiking trails, and good fishing along the Wild River. In North Chatham look for the **Chester East-man Homestead** (603-694-3388; www.cehfarm.com), site of seasonal special events—a maple-sugaring day in March, spring plowing in April, a fall harvest day, a logging day in November, and ice harvesting in January—as well as hayrides by reservation. Rt. 113 connects with Rt. 2 in Gilead, Me. Turn west (left) to head back through Shelburne and Gorham and back down through Pinkham Notch.

Cathedral Ledge. A winding, two-lane 1.7-mile-long road leads to the top of Cathedral Ledge with its fabulous view of the valley—an obvious place for a picnic. From the lights at the north end of North Conway village take River Road 1.4 miles to the marked turnoff.

Bear Notch Road. Closed to vehicles in winter, this road through the White Mountain National Forest is a popular shortcut from the Kancamagus Highway to Crawford Notch (totally avoiding North Conway). It's also a beautiful woods road, however, and a good place to spot wildlife. From Conway head west on "the Kanc" (Rt. 110) to the turnoff near Jigger Johnson Campground. It meets up with Rt. 302 in Bartlett village.

✸ To Do

✔ **Conway Scenic Railroad** (603-356-5251; 1-800-232-5251; www.conway scenic.com), North Conway village. Runs weekends mid-Apr.–Memorial Day, daily late June–fourth Sat. in Oct. The splendid Victorian North Conway depot, serving passengers 1874–1961, stood boarded and derelict for a dozen years until this excursion train company restored and reopened it as a base for its two trains and three different excursions: the Valley Train south to Conway (11 miles, 1 hour), and north to Bartlett (21 miles, 1¼ hours), and the spectacular North Conway through Crawford Notch trip (50 miles, 5 hours). The latter trip traverses the most spectacular rail route in the Northeast (reservations a must). Inquire about the special foliage runs (5-plus hours) all the way through Crawford Notch to Fabyan Station. Lunch and dinner are served in a refurbished steel dining car (see *Dining Out*). The in-service rolling stock includes steam and diesel engines as well as vintage passenger cars and a parlor observation car. Historic buildings include the large turntable, roundhouse, freight house, and the old depot, which has a gift shop and

TAKE A TRIP ON THE CONWAY SCENIC RAILROAD

exhibits. Rates are $10 for an adult coach ticket from North Conway to Conway; $20 for a first-class parlor ticket from North Conway to Bartlett; $35 to Crawford Notch; and for a dome-car trip to Fabyan Station, $54. Children's fares are less; trips with meals included cost considerably more.

BIKING **Bike the Whites** (1-800-448-3534; www.bikethewhites.com). This is a self-guided inn-to-inn biking package with your luggage transported; rentals are available. The distance is 20 miles per day over back roads. The three lodging places are the 1785 Inn in North Conway, Snowvillage Inn in Snowville, and the Tamworth Inn in Tamworth. Rates are $279 or $379 depending on time of year. Bicycles can be rented at an additional charge.

Mountain bike rentals are easy to come by at North Conway sports stores, and bicycle routes abound. We can recommend the ride to and around Echo Lake State Park and on up or down the West Side Road. At Attitash mountain bikers are welcome on ski trails. The Conway Town Trail (marked in yellow) is a designated recreation trail for mountain biking, running 4 miles along the river. Begin on East Conway Road off Rt. 302 in Redstone. Turn right immediately after the Conway Police Station onto Meeting House Hill Road for the parking lot. Also see Whitaker Woods under *Green Space*.

CANOEING AND KAYAKING The Saco is a popular canoeing river. Many people like to put in where River Road crosses the river (turn west at the traffic lights at the northern edge of North Conway village), then paddle about 8 miles downstream to the Conway village covered bridge. In summer the river is wide and slow, except for light rapids between the Swift River covered bridge and the Conway (second) covered bridge. Take out after the second bridge at Davis Park.

Saco Bound (603-447-2177; www.sacobound.com), Rt. 302, Center Conway. Rentals, sales, instruction, canoe camping, shuttle service, and guided trips. They also maintain a seasonal information and sales and rental shop on Main St., North Conway. Inquire about whitewater rafting and guided flatwater kayaking tours from their (seasonal) base in Errol (see "Northern White Mountains").

Rentals are also available at **Northern Extremes Canoe & Kayak** (1-877-722-6748; www.nothernextremes.com) with outlets on Main St., North Conway (603-356-4718). **Saco Canoe Rental** (603-447-2737) in Conway and **Saco Valley Canoe** (603-447-2444; 1-800-447-2460) in Center Conway also offer canoe rentals.

FISHING Brook and brown trout, lake trout, bass, and salmon are the target fish for anglers in this area. Try your luck in the Saco, Cold, or swift Rivers; Conway Lake, the area's largest, is managed for landlocked salmon (the access is off Mill Street in Center Conway). Mountain Pond in Chatham (see *Scenic Drives*) is favored for brook trout. Fishing licenses are required.

North Country Angler (603-356-6000; www.northcountryangler.com), 2888 White Mountain Hwy. (Rt. 16), North Conway village. Specialists in trout and Atlantic salmon fishing, they sell equipment and clothes and offer local fishing information, a professional fly-tying school, guiding, and multiday fly-fishing instruction programs.

FOR FAMILIES ✒ **Attitash Alpine Slide and Waterslides** (603-374-2368; www.attitash.com), Rt. 302, Bartlett. Open late May–mid-June and Labor Day–early Oct., weekends 10–5; late June–Labor Day, open daily 10–6. A day pass (also good for the skate park, climbing wall, and mountain biking) is $29 for people over 48 inches, $13 for those shorter. Great fun for the kids and adults too. The Alpine Slide includes a ride to the top of the mountain on the ski lift, then a slide down a curving, bowed, 0.75-mile chute on a self-controlled sled. Then cool off in the Aquaboggin Waterslide.

✒ **Pirate's Cove Adventure Golf** (603-356-8807; www.piratescove.net/ location16), Rt. 16, North Conway. Open May–mid-Oct. Eighteen-hole miniature golf with plenty of challenges for young and old. Rates are $7.50 or $12 for adults, $6.50 or $11 for children, depending on courses played.

GOLF **North Conway Country Club** (603-356-9391, pro shop), in the center of the village, North Conway. Eighteen holes.

The White Mountain Hotel and Country Club (603-356-2140; www .whitemountainhotel.com), on the West Side Road. Hale's Location has a nine-hole course.

HIKING **Black Cap Mountain Path** (2.4 miles round trip). Highly recommended for young and/or lazy hikers. The trailhead is on Hurricane Mountain Road, 3.7 miles east of Rt. 16. The trail is through the spruce and beech forest of The Nature Conservancy's Green Hills Preserve to the rocky summit of Black Cap for views north and west to the high peaks of the White Mountains.

Mount Kearsarge North Trail (3.1 miles one way, 2¼ hours). Mount Kearsarge (elevation 3,268 feet) is just north of North Conway, and this hike has been popular since the turn of the 20th century. At Intervale, north of North Conway village, Hurricane Mountain Road diverges east. Follow this road for 1.5 miles to the trailhead. From the summit fire tower there are views across the Saco River Valley to the Moat Range and north to Mount Washington and the Presidential Range.

Also see *Green Space*.

HORSEBACK AND HORSE-DRAWN RIDES **Farm by the River Stables** (603-356-6640; 888-414-8353),2555 West Side Rd., North Conway. Year-round horseback rides offered daily, ponies for small children. Geared to novices. $40 per hour. Also wagon rides and sleigh rides ($15 per person). Also see *Lodging*.

Attitash (603-374-2368; www.attitash.com) offers guided horseback tours along the Saco River in summer.

Darby Field Inn (see *Lodging*) offers sleigh and carriage rides.

ROCK CLIMBING **Cathedral Ledge** is famous for its many challenging routes, and from the base you can observe climbers inching up its cracks and sheer faces. If you'd like to join the climbers, contact **Eastern Mountain Sports Climbing School** (603-356-5433; www.emsclimb.com) or **International Mountain Equipment Climbing School** (603-356-7064; www.ime-usa.com). **Cranmore Sports Center** (603-356-6301; www.cranmore.com) has an indoor climbing wall and offers instruction programs. If you are already an experienced climber, pick up Ed Webster's *Rock Climbs in the White Mountains of New Hampshire*, published by Mountain Imagery.

SWIMMING **Echo Lake State Park**, Old West Side Rd., North Conway. Set against the backdrop of White Horse Ledge, this lovely lake offers a sandy beach, picnic area, and changing rooms. Nominal parking fee.

Diana's Baths. Lucy Brook cascades through a series of inviting (if chilly) granite basins below the waterfalls (swimming above is prohibited, because water there is piped into the public water supply). From North Conway follow River Road to the turnoff for Cathedral Ledge. A marked, 0.5-mile path leads from the parking lot.

Davis Park, Washington St., Conway. A great swimming beach with picnic tables next to the Saco River covered bridge, plus tennis and basketball courts.

Conway Lake, Center Conway. This is the area's largest lake, and the beach is public.

Saco River at Hussey Field, River Rd., North Conway. Turn onto Weston River Road at the light and park by the first bridge. This is a popular swimming hole, minutes from the middle of the village.

❋ Winter Sports

CROSS-COUNTRY SKIING **Mount Washington Valley Ski Touring and Snowshoe Center** (603-356-9920; www.crosscountryskinh.com). More than 60 km of groomed trails through the valley, connecting inns. Rentals and information at Ragged Mountain Equipment, Rt. 16/302 in Intervale.

Bear Notch Ski Touring Center (603-374-2277; www.bearnotchski .com), Rt. 302, Bartlett. This is a favorite with everyone who tries it: 60 km of wooded, groomed trails with warming stations (snacks) and picnic tables; ski school, guided snowshoe and moonlight tours.

Also see the **Jackson Ski Touring Foundation** (wwww.jacksonxc.org), the region's most extensive network, and **Great Glen Trails Outdoor Center** (www.greatglentrails.com) in "Jackson and Pinkham Notch," and the **Bretton Woods Touring Center** in "Crawford Notch."

DOWNHILL SKIING AND SNOWBOARDING ⚓ **Attitash** (603-374-2368; snow phone, 1-877-677-SNOW; lodging, 1-888-554-1900; 1-800-223-SNOW; www .attitash.com), Rt. 302, Bartlett. Boasting New Hampshire's most powerful snow-making system, this two-mountain ski area has profited from extensive upgrading in recent years. With its 143-room **Grand Summit Hotel** and 60-acre Attitash

AERIAL VIEW OF ATTITASH

Mountain Village, it offers the advantages of a reasonably priced self-contained resort within easy striking distance of both Crawford and Pinkham notches and North Conway.

Lifts: 12: 3 quads (2 high-speed), 3 triples, 3 doubles, 3 surface.

Trails: 70 trails and glades: 20 percent novice, 47 percent intermediate, 33 percent advanced.

Vertical drop: 1,750 feet at Attitash, 1,450 feet at Bear Peak. Snowmaking: 98 percent coverage.

Snowboarding: Terrain garden and 500-foot half-pipe.

Cross-country skiing: Guided snowshoeing and cross-country tours; see Bear Notch Center, above.

Facilities: Base lodges with children's services. Three pubs and two cafeterias. Package plans include skiing, lessons, and lodging at the slope-side Grand Summit Resort Hotel and at Attitash Mountain Village with condos for 2 to 14 people, indoor pool, outdoor ice rink.

Lift tickets: Sat. and holidays: $59 adults, $49 juniors, $ 39 seniors; Sun.–Fri.: $55 adults, $45 juniors, $29 seniors.

✎ **Cranmore Mountain Resort** (800-SUN-N-SKI; slope-side lodging package information, 1-800-786-6754, ext. 331; www.cranmore.com), Skimobile Rd., North Conway. A granddaddy among New England ski areas and still a favorite for its in-town location, sunny and moderate slopes, and night skiing. This is a great family mountain with lift-serviced snow tubing, a relaxed place for anyone to learn to ski or snowboard. The sports center at the bottom is big, tubing is allotted its own space and lift, and a fast quad chair has replaced the beloved old

Skimobile. Inquire about the Mountain Meister racing series, billed as the largest citizens' racing program in the country, with as many as 800 racers in 15-person teams in two runs competing against each other and against the clock.

Lifts: 9: 1 express quad, 1 triple, 3 doubles, 3 surface, Magic Carpet.

Trails and glades: 40, plus a tubing center with 8 lift-service lanes.

CRANMORE MOUNTAIN RESORT IS A FAVORITE FAMILY SKI DESTINATION

Vertical drop: 1,200 feet.

Snowmaking: 100 percent.

Snowboarding: All trails plus a mini half-pipe and 2 terrain parks.

Facilities: Base lodges with children's center and services; Meister Hut Summit Restaurant; Cranmore Sports Center with indoor tennis courts, pool, exercise equipment, climbing wall; slope-side condos.

Lift tickets: One price any day: $42 adults, $32 teens, $22 youths. With "Add-a-Day," daily rates are $29 adults, $24 teens, $19 youths.

Also see Wildcat Mountain and Black Mountain in Downhill Skiing in "Jackson and Pinkham Notch," and Bretton Woods in "Crawford Notch."

ICE CLIMBING North Conway is a world-class center for ice climbing, said to offer more businesses geared to technical climbing than anywhere else in the country. Foremost is the **International Mountain Equipment Climbing School** (www.ime-usa.com; 603-356-7064), sponsor of the annual February Ice Fest, a series of shows, demonstrations, and clinics.

ICE SKATING The setting and price are hard to beat: **Schouler Park** in the center of North Conway in front of the train station is free. The **Ham Ice Arena** (603-447-5886), 87 W. Main St., Conway, is open year-round, featuring a 16-speaker sound system for music, rentals, and a café.

SLEIGH RIDES **The Darby Field Inn** (603-447-2181), off Bald Hill Rd. in Conway, offers sleigh rides through its high woods with views of Mount Washington.

The Chester Eastman Homestead (603-694-3388), North Chatham, offers sleigh rides by reservation throughout winter. The 12-person sled is drawn by two Percheron draft horses. Rides are 20 minutes, followed by popcorn and cocoa at the farm.

Farm by the River B&B (see *Horseback Riding*) also offers sleigh rides.

SNOWMOBILING Corridor 19, one of the state's main snowmbole corridors, crosses Rt. 16 right in North Conway, also accessed from **Bear Notch Trails** (rentals). **Northern Extremes** (603-356-4718) and **Alpine Adventures** (603-374-2344) offer guided tours geared to all abilities.

SNOWSHOEING Snowshoe rentals are available from **Eastern Mountain Sports** (603-356-5433) and **Ragged Mountain Equipment** (603-356-9920). **Animal Tracking Tours** at Attitash depart from the conservation center at Thorn Pond; rentals available.

✳ Green Space

Echo Lake State Park (603-356-2672), off River Rd., 2 miles west of Rt. 16 in North Conway. Open weekends beginning Memorial Day, then daily late June–Labor Day. A swim beach with picnic tables and bathhouse plus dramatic views across the lake to White Horse (can you see the horse?) Ledge and a 1.7-mile road to the top of 1,150-foot Cathedral Ledge, good for broad views across the valley of the Saco. This is a favorite ascent for rock climbers and a nesting place for rare peregrine falcons, which can sometimes be seen soaring on the updrafts.

Whitaker Woods, Kearsarge Rd., North Conway. North of North Conway village on the east side of Rts. 16/302. A wooded, town-owned conservation area with trails for walking, mountain biking, or winter cross-country skiing.

Diana's Baths, River Rd., 2.2 miles west of North Conway. Watch for a dirt road on your left and park beside the road; it's a short walk to the stream. No swimming above the falls, since this is a public water supply. Lucy Brook has eroded and sculpted the rocks in this beautiful place. Moat Mountain Trail (4.2 miles, 3½ hours) leads to the summit of North Moat Mountain (elevation 3,201 feet).

Green Hills Preserve, North Conway. Access from Thompson Rd. with a designated parking area. This is a 2,822-acre preserve belonging to The Nature Conservancy, New Hampshire Chapter. It's home to several rare and endangered plants and a high-elevation stand of red pine. Half a dozen options include the Peaked Mountain Trail (2.1 miles, 1,739 feet) and Middle Mountain Trail (2 miles, 1,857 feet, with excellent views to the south, east, and west).

✳ Lodging

INNS **The Darby Field Inn and Restaurant** (603-447-2181; outside New Hampshire, 1-800-426-4147; www.darbyfield.com), 185 Chase Hill Rd., Albany 03818. Open all year. Operated by Marc and Maria Donaldson since 1979, the place is named for that intrepid first climber of Mount Washington, whose summit and other high peaks can be seen from the inn. Set on a secluded hilltop—well south of North Conway, with Abenaki Road (summer only) leading directly down to the Kancamagus Highway—the inn is surrounded by landscaped grounds and woods that include 15 km of cross-country trails. In recent years the Donaldsons have positioned the inn as a romantic getaway. All 13 rooms have private bath; 6 suites now feature Jacuzzi, gas fireplace, TV/VCR, and a balcony with views north to the Presidentials. Rooms vary, and the key factor, to our thinking, is the views: Room 11 on the third floor is small and old-fashioned but has a fireplace and a great view, while Room 12 has all the bells and whistles plus view. The common room has a fireplace; there's also a small pub with a woodstove. Dinner (see *Dining Out*) is served by reservation. In summer there's a pool. B&B $110–280, MAP $180–350 (add 12 percent for service), depending on the season and accommodations. Ask about packages and midweek specials.

✔ **The 1785 Inn** (603-356-9025; 1-800-421-1785; www.the1785inn.com), Rt. 16 (mail: Box 1785, North Conway 03860), Intervale. Open all year. The vista from the living room and many guest rooms in this genuine 1785 house are across the Saco River intervale to Mount Washington. Built by a Revolutionary War veteran when there was still plenty of space to choose from, it sits on a knoll with its dining room and guest living rooms, each with a large fireplace, facing the panorama. The inn's 17 rooms, 12 with private bath, have king-sized and double beds. Rooms are comfortably furnished, and some have two beds. Room 5 is a beauty; we also like 7 and 17. You'll definitely want a quiet room in the back of the inn as opposed to one on Rt. 16. The dining room is considered one of the best restaurants in the valley (see *Dining Out*). There is a swimming pool, and many trails are handy for walking in summer or cross-country skiing. Longtime innkeepers Becky and Charlie Millar charge $69–219 per couple, including a full breakfast.

The New England Inn and Resort (603-356-5541; outside New Hampshire, 1-800-826-3466; www.new englandinn.com), Rt. 16A, Box 100, Intervale 03845. Open all year. This is a valley landmark, dating back in part to 1809. We found rooms in the old main inn looking a bit tired, but the classic clapboard cabins with fireplaces are still attractive. Also nice is the most recent addition, the Lodge, a two-story North Woods–style log structure across the road from the inn. Rooms are named for woodland animals and feature Jacuzzi. Facilities include a restaurant and **Tuckerman's Tavern**, and an outdoor swimming pool. Inn rooms $69–130; cottages, cabins, and cottage suites $159–260; Lodge $99–175.

BED & BREAKFASTS ✔ **The Buttonwood Inn** (603-356-2625; 1-800-258-2625; www.buttonwoodinn.com), Mount Surprise Rd., Box 1817, North Conway 03860. At this writing the 10 guest rooms include 8 suites, 1 with a two-person Jacuzzi and 2 with gas fireplace; all have private bath. Just minutes from Mount Cranmore and Rt. 16 shopping, the 1820s farmhouse sits at the end of a road. Innkeepers Elizabeth and Jeffrey Richards have retained its country atmosphere with wide-pine floors, Shaker furniture, quilts, and period stenciling. There are two common rooms, one downstairs with a fireplace and games, and an outdoor swimming pool surrounded by gardens. In winter you can cross-country ski from the door. The breakfast menu changes daily and includes options such as "Peachy Keen Pancake" (made with tender peaches caramelized overnight) and rhubarb coffeecake. $95–255 for two, depending on the season and accommodations. Seasonal packages also available.

✔ **Cranmore Inn** (603-356-5502; outside New Hampshire, 1-800-526-5502; www.cranmoreinn.com), Kearsarge St., Box 1349, North Conway 03860. Open all year. Opened more than 130 years ago, this is the oldest continuously operating inn in the valley. Christopher and Virginia Kanzler have preserved the old-style feel in 18 rooms. Fourteen have private bath; beds are mostly queens, and some rooms have two beds. There are 2 one-bedrooms and 1 two-bedroom unit with kitchens. Country decor includes matching bedspreads and curtains, stenciled wallpaper, and antique bed frames. Seasonal drinks are served in the afternoon. The common room is cozy, with a fireplace and a piano; there is a separate TV room. You'll also find a pool and lawn games, and guests can pay a nominal fee to use the nearby Mount Cranmore Recreation Center. Just minutes from Main Street's shops and restaurants but in a quiet area. No smoking. $59–159 with full breakfast, depending on season and accommodations. Children under 4 free; for those 4 years and older, pay $1 per year to age 12.

Victorian Harvest Inn (603-356-3548; outside New Hampshire, 1-800-642-0749; www.victorianharvestinn .com), Locust Lane, Box 1763, North Conway 03860. New owners Nelson and Tana Hall have completely redecorated the inn, filling it with antiques and artwork they have collected. Since the ambience is now more eclectic than Victorian, they plan to eventually rename it The Red Elephant, while retaining the same phone numbers and web site. Whatever the name, this is a special place on a quiet side street above the clutter along Rts. 16/302. Painted a sunny yellow, it has views across the valley from most of its eight well-furnished, air-conditioned rooms, the largest with a gas fireplace and two-person

Jacuzzi tub. All rooms have private bath, four have king bed, three have queen, and one has a double bed. There's a swimming pool, a library with bay window, television, films, and books. Full breakfast. No smoking. Because the decor includes so many breakable objects, children under 13 are discouraged. $100–240.

✔ **The Farm by the River B&B with Stables** (603-356-2694; 1-888-414-8353; www.farmbytheriver.com), 2555 West Side Rd., North Conway 03860. Open all year. Built in 1785 on a land grant from King George III, this picturesque, three-story farmhouse and barn is part of a still-active farm. Surrounded by 70 acres with mountain views and Saco River frontage, the onetime boardinghouse is now an inn where guests return year after year, often to the same room they had the previous season. Each of the 10 rooms, all named for former guests, is decorated in country style with antiques, quilts, and Oriental rugs. Some have king-sized bed and two-person Jacuzzi bath and fireplace, and there are a couple of two-room suites, perfect for families. Innkeepers Rick and Charlene Browne-Davis provide horseback riding all year, as well as fall foliage wagon rides, Victorian carriage rides, and sleigh rides in winter. Snowshoes are provided for guest use on the property. Walk to the Saco for swimming and fly-fishing. Rick is a justice of the peace and small, off-season weddings are possible. $90–190 double includes a full patio or fireside breakfast.

✔ **Cranmore Mountain Lodge** (603-356-2044; 1-800-356-3596; www .cml1.com), Kearsarge Rd., North Conway 03860. Open all year. Babe Ruth's daughter once owned the place, and if it's not taken you can ask for the Babe's old room (Room 2, with his original furniture). The main inn has 15 rooms (some are family suites). Next door in the barn are 3 family suites and 4 loft rooms, all with antiques, private bath, air-conditioning, and TV. There's also a two-story town house that sleeps up to nine, with a full kitchen, dining room, living room, cable TV, and deck/patio. The lower section of the barn is a 22-bed dorm. Outside is a heated year-round pool and hot tub, regulation tennis court, and hard-surface basketball court. $59–299.

☀ ✎ **Spruce Moose Lodge** (603-356-6239; 1-800-600-6239; www .sprucemooselodge.com, Seavey St., North Conway 03860. Open all year. Formerly Sunnyside Inn, this gabled house on a quiet street near Mount Cranmore is an easy walk to Main Street. Nine rooms, all with private bath and air-conditioning, fireplace in the common or "great" room. Full breakfast. Rates in the main house $59–159, depending on season and accommodations. All rates include breakfast. There are also three pet- and family-friendly cottages with gas fireplace and full kitchen, and two suites with fireplace and Jacuzzi. $129–245.

✎ **Mountain Valley Manner** (603-447-3988; www.mvmbandb.com), West Side Rd., Box 1649, Conway 03818. Open all year. In Conway village this inn is just across the street from the Swift River covered bridge and only a short walk to swimming and tennis at Davis Park. Built in 1885, it's furnished primarily with antiques and floral accents. There are four guest rooms, all with air-conditioning and private bath. Beds are

king, queen, and twins. One room is a suite with a king. Full breakfast and afternoon tea. $75–135. Ask about special packages.

♿ **Cabernet Inn** (603-356-4704; 1-800-866-4704; www.cabernetinn .com), Rt. 16 (mail: Box 38, Intervale 03845). Begin with an 1840 house, raise it 13 feet, totally renovate and update it, and you have this striking inn just south of the intervale. Innkeepers Bruce and Jessica Zarenko offer 11 guest rooms, all with queen beds, air-conditioning, private phone, and bath. Two rooms have fireplace and Jacuzzi; 2 with wood-burning fireplace open onto a back deck. One, with a private entrance, is totally handicapped accessible right down to the roll-in shower. There's a formal living room on the entry levels as well as a comfortable downstairs den with a 10-foot-high hearth, TV/VCR, fridge, and board games. As with all properties on Rt. 16, we suggest you request a quiet back room with a view. The inn is on the valley's cross-country trail system. No children under 12, please. $90–225 includes a full breakfast.

✎ **Nereledge Inn** (603-356-2831; www.nereledgeinn.com), River Rd., North Conway 03860. Open all year. Nicely old-fashioned, in a quiet setting by a swimming hole in the Saco River and with a view of Cathedral Ledge, but steps from the summer playhouse and a short walk to the village. There are 11 cheerful but unfussy guest rooms (5 with private bath, 1 with a half-bath). Two adjoining rooms can be converted to a family suite. Guests have use of two comfortable sitting rooms, one with a woodstove, and the other with dartboard, TV, and fireplace. This inn appeals to active people: Many of the guests are hikers, rock climbers, and cross-country skiers. Innkeepers Laura Glassover and Steve Hartmann include a full breakfast in the rates: $65–251. The innkeepers have small children (so this is a place you might not want to come to escape your own); children $1 per year to age 16. No smoking.

The Kearsarge Inn (800-637-0087; www.kearsargeinn.com), 42 Seavey St., North Conway. In the heart of the village, this is a "modern rendition" of a famous 19th-century inn with 15 rooms and suites with antiques and reproductions of period furnishings and such contemporary amenities as gas fireplaces and Jacuzzis. Children of any age are welcome in suites but have to be 12 or older to stay in the main inn. $79–265 depending on season and type of unit. Ask about golf and other packages.

Glen Oaks Inn(603-356-9772; 1-800-448-3534; www.forest-inn.com), Rt. 16A, Box 37, Intervale 03854. Open all year. Formerly the Forest Inn (hence the web address), this inn has been welcoming guests for more than a century. Its 11 rooms are decorated in country Victorian style with queen beds, private baths, and air-conditioning; three have a fireplace. In the neighboring stone cottage 3 more rooms each has a fireplace and one, a whirlpool tub. Innkeepers Linda Trask and Mitch Scher serve a full breakfast and afternoon refreshments. There's an outdoor pool; hiking and cross-country ski trails are out the door. Inn rooms $95–165, cottage rooms $120–195.

Covered Bridge House B&B (603-383-9109; 1-800-232-9109; www.coveredridgehouse.com), Rt. 302, Glen 03838. Open all year. Six

fresh and pretty guest rooms (four with private bath, most with in-room air-conditioning) in a Colonial Revival home on the Saco River. Two rooms share a bath. Innkeepers Dan and Nancy Wanek also own the Covered Bridge Gift Shoppe, housed in the neighboring 1850s covered bridge. There's a swimming hole out back, plus tubing and fishing on the river. $64–119 includes a full breakfast.

MOTOR INNS *Note:* Half a dozen large contemporary motor inns account for about two-thirds of the lodging options in the Conway area. For the real old-timers, see Mount Washington Resort in "Crawford Notch and Bretton Woods" and the Wentworth Hotel and Eagle Mountain House in "Jackson and Pinkham Notch."

Red Jacket Mountain View (1-800-RJACKET; www.redjacket mountainview.com), Rts. 16/302, North Conway 03860-2000. Set in 40 acres atop Sunset Hill, above the main drag, this 163-room facility has a lot going for it. The property began as a railroad baron's summer estate and has evolved into a sprawling motor-inn-style resort over the past 30 years. The 151 rooms in the main building have all the basic amenities plus the view; 12 units are two-bedroom town houses. The lounge and **Champney's** (the restaurant named for the 19th-century artist whose painting hangs there) are at the core of the building, and the large, attractive lobby with its formal front desk is a source of information about frequent special happenings. In summer a daily children's program is offered. Year-round themed packages are a house specialty: November shopping, Christmas, mystery and Valentine's weekends, and more. Some rooms include lofts or bunks for families and others, Jacuzzis. $99–299 for rooms, $229–359 for town houses. Meal plan packages available.

✱ ♿ **The White Mountain Hotel and Resort** (603-356-7100; 1-800-533-6301; www.whitemountainhotel .com), West Side Rd. at Hale's Location, Box 1828, North Conway 03860. This is a 1990s motor inn with expansive grounds that include a nine-hole golf course and large condo development, near the base of Cathedral and White Horse Ledges. The 80 rooms (they include 13 suites and 2 handicapped-accessible rooms) are furnished in reproduction antiques, all with air-conditioning, TV, telephone, and views off across the valley to Mount Cranmore. The dining room, open to the public, serves three meals daily (see *Dining Out*). Amenities include an Irish pub, restaurant and lounge, all-season outdoor pool and Jacuzzi, sauna, fitness center, and tennis court. The entire hotel is non-smoking. $99–269 per room depending on season and accommodations; MAP, golf, and other special plans available; breakfast is included midweek off-season.

✱ **Grand Summit Resort Hotel and Conference Center** (603-374-1900; 1-888-554-1900; www.attitash .com), Rt. 302 at Attitash, Bartlett 03812. Located at the base of Attitash, a contemporary condominium resort with 143 guest rooms ranging from units with two queen-sized beds to three-bedroom suites. Most have a full kitchen and dining area. There's a health club, year-round outdoor pool, whirlpool spa, arcade, a full-service restaurant, lounge, and on-site day care. $89–429.

The Green Granite Inn & Conference Center (603-356-6901; 1-800-468-3666; www.greengranite.com), Rt. 16 in the outlet shopping strip. The 91 rooms and suites are big, some with two-person whirlpool tubs and private patios. Facilities include indoor and outdoor pools, a fitness center, a playground and children's activity programs, and a lobby lounge with a fieldstone fireplace. Complaint: Our "smoke-free" room smelled of smoke. $79–185 includes a full breakfast buffet.

Hostelling International White Mountains (603-447-1001), Washington St., Conway. Reserve. Check-in is between 5 and 10 PM. A couple of blocks from the bus stop, an old farmhouse now serves as a busy hostel, accommodating more than 40 people. There are four private rooms; the remainder are dorm style, all with shared baths. The kitchen is fully equipped, and linens are provided. Clunker bikes are also available for patrons to get around and to trailheads. Private rooms are $51, dorms $21 for HI members and $24 for nonmembers.

✳ **Where to Eat**

DINING OUT *Note:* Also see **Snowvillage Inn** (www.snowvillageinn .com) in the Mount Washington Gateway section of this chapter. Many North Conway village innkeepers recommend this as the area's best dining.

Coyote Rose (603-356-7673), White Mountain Hwy. (Rt. 16). Open daily at 5 PM; serving lunch on weekends (but check); closed Wed. off-season.

Reservations advised. Kate and Peter Willis specialize in southwestern spices, turning a former service station into (no pun) one of the hottest dining spots in the valley. Guests usually begin by choosing which of 25 tequilas should go into their margarita. While deciding on a main course there are small tortillas, corn bread, and salsa to sample. Entrées usually include wild boar, ostrich, venison, and (Maine) buffalo. We settled for the smoked duck breast with a prickly pear glaze. Entrées $15–35.

The Darby Field Inn and Restaurant (603-447-2181; outside New Hampshire, 1-800-426-4147; www .darbyfield.com), Bald Hill Rd., Conway. Dinner served weekends 6–9 PM, midweek depending on season; reservations required. Chefs vary but the candlelight dining, pleasant dining room, and superlative view of the Presidentials in the distance are constants. The menu always includes half a dozen choices, which usually range from a vegetarian special and the fish of the day to rack of lamb or beef tenderloin tips. There are always seafood, pasta, and vegetarian specials. Entrées $18–24.

Moat Mountain Smokehouse and Brewing Co. (603-356-6381; www .moatmountain.com), 3378 White Mountain Hwy. (Rt. 16), North Conway. Open daily for lunch and dinner. A restaurant specializing in its own microbrew and southern fare like cornmeal-crusted catfish, St. Louis ribs, and a family-style barbecue dinner with generous platters of ribs, brisket, chicken, skillet corn bread, bowls of slaw, garlic mashed potatoes, and, naturally, black beans and rice. Of course you can also get by with a wood-grilled pizza, smokehouse sandwich, or burger, but don't pass up the brew. We lunched sumptuously in a mural-walled room with a view of Moat Mountain. Entrées $9.95–29.95.

♪ **Bellini's Tuscan Steakhouse and Pizzeria** (603-356-7000; www .bellinis.com), White Mountain Hwy. (Rt. 16), North Conway. Open daily. The Marcello family has more than 50 years' experience in the Italian food business, and they use all of their talents in this large and colorful new restaurant in the Willow Place shopping plaza. The pasta is imported, but everything else is freshly prepared. All the well-known southern and northern Italian specialties are offered here, including 20 different kinds of pasta and braciola (sirloin rolled and stuffed with prosciutto, stuffing, garlic, and mozzarella), along with baked minestrone soup. Save room for gelato, canneloni, and tiramisu. Portions are large, but there's a children's menu. Entrées average $16–24.

The 1785 Inn (603-356-9025; 1-800-421-1785; www.the1785inn.com), Rt. 16 at the Intervale. Breakfast weekdays 8–9:30; weekends and holidays 7–10. Open nightly for dinner at 5; also lunch during the cross-country season. Dependably outstanding. There are more appetizers than you'll find at many restaurants, and among the entrées are such memorable dishes as veal and shrimp in a rum cream sauce with artichoke hearts, sherried rabbit, raspberry duckling, and rack of lamb. The wine list includes some 200 labels. There's a fireplace and, if you request the right table, a view of the intervale and Mount Washington. Entrées $17.85–29.85.

♨ ♂ **The Red Parka Pub** (603-383-4344; www.redparkapub.com), Rt. 302, Glen. Open daily 4–10 PM. A favorite with the locals and for après-ski, this is a traditional ski tavern, with skis dating back to the 1930s adorning the walls and ceilings. The mottos is: "Still crazy after all these years!" Outdoor dining on the patio. Famous for hand-cut steak and prime rib, the Red Parka Pub also features baked seafood, barbecued spareribs, and varied chicken dishes. Entrées $12.50–23.95. An extensive salad bar rounds out the meal; special kids' menu.

Stonehurst Manor (603-356-3113; 1-800-525-9100 www.stonehurst manor.com), Rt. 16, North Conway. Breakfast 8–10, dining nightly 5:30–10; reservations suggested. Eat indoors surrounded by elaborate woodwork and stained-glass windows, or outside on the screened patio. In addition to a full menu of classic Continental favorites, offerings include gourmet pizza baked in a wood-fired stone oven, and stuffed pork loin with red pepper port wine sauce. Entrées average $16.75–28.75. Thursday night is special with "candlelight dinner for two"—a bargain at $25.

♂ **The Ledges at the White Mountain Hotel and Resort** (603-356-7100; 1-800-533-6301; www.white mountainhotel.com), West Side Rd. at Hale's Location, North Conway. Breakfast 7–10; lunch 11:30–2 daily except Sunday, when there's brunch 10:30–2; dinner is served nightly from 5:30 in a large, nicely tiered dining room with views across the valley to Mount Cranmore. The Friday seafood buffet is legendary, featuring a raw bar, seafood pastas, and fish fried and poached as well as the night's specials, salads, and chowders. Sunday brunch is another event. The dinner menu ranges from Tuscan vegetable pie to rack of lamb, veal Oscar, duckling, and filet mignon. Varied appetizers, salads, and desserts. Children's menu. Entrées ($19–28) include bread, vegetables, and salad. Pianist nightly in-season.

♂ **Conway Scenic Railroad** (603-356-5251; www.conwayscenic.com), North Conway. Lunch (11:30 AM and 1:30 PM) and dinner (6 PM) are served weekends beginning late June, daily except Mon. July 4–Sep., then a reduced schedule again until foliage season (Sep. 10–Oct. 20), when lunch is served daily, dinner Thu.–Sat.; obviously, it's a good idea to check. The venue is the refurbished, steel-exterior, oak-interior, 47-seat dining car *Chocorua*. The luncheon menu features soup or salad and a choice of entrées. With lunch, the fare for a 55-minute trip to Conway is $25.95 per adult; the 1¼-hour trip to Bartlett runs $34.95 per adult. "Sunset" dinner trips to Bartlett, where the dining car is transformed into a deluxe restaurant with white linens and china, include an elegant four-course meal: $52.50 per adult. Inquire about the children's menu and rates. Reservations strongly recommended for dinner. Full liquor license.

EATING OUT

In Conway village
♨ ♂ **Horsefeathers** (603-356-2687; www.horsefeathers.com), Main St. Open daily 11:30 AM–11:30 PM. The best-known hangout and an all-around good bet for a reasonably priced meal in an attractive setting in the middle of the village. The menu is

large and varied; the day's from-scratch soup may be curried crab and asparagus. Designer sandwiches like black pastrami with roasted peppers. Salads, pastas, fish-and-chips, plenty of desserts, fully licensed. Kids' menu.

Hooligan's (603-356-6110), Kearsage St. This popular restaurant has a local reputation for offering good value in a convivial atmosphere. It's noted for appetizers such as shrimp tempura and crab-stuffed mushrooms. Entrées are $9.95–21.95 and include surf and turf, Alaska king crab legs, and pork loin Dijon. There is no smoking in the dining room, but it's allowed in the adjoining (and usually lively) bar area.

Bangkok Café (603-356-5566) 2729 White Mountain Hwy. (Main St.). Open for lunch and dinner. Closed Tue. This pleasant small restaurant has an extensive menu that's mostly Thai but includes some classic Chinese dishes. It gets consistent raves from Asian-food aficionados. Appetizers are $3.95–9.95, entrées $18.95–19.95. Beer and wine are available.

✔ **Shalimar** (603-356-0123), 27 Seavey St. Open for lunch and dinner. Closed Mon. off-season. A popular Indian restaurant featuring a wide selection of vegetarian dishes as well as chicken, lamb, beef, and shrimp dishes. There's also a children's menu that includes chicken fingers and cheese ravioli. Wine and beer served.

Flatbread Company (603-356-4470; www.flatbread.net), Eastern Slope Inn, 2760 Main St. Open lunch through dinner. A pleasant new restaurant hidden away in the back of the hotel, featuring the distinctive pizza developed by the Vermont-based American Flatbread Company, made from 100 percent organically

grown wheat and springwater, baked in a special wood-fired clay oven. Sun-dried tomatoes, fresh herbs, goat cheese, and olive oil figure in most of the toppings.

Decades (603-356-7080; 800-637-0087), 32 Seavey St. Known primarily as a steak house, although seafood is also a specialty. The grilled filet mignon is topped by crispy fried onions and served with vegetables and veal demiglaze. Deep fried jumbo shrimp and fresh haddock come with apple cabbage coleslaw. For some mysterious reason an antique motorcycle is the centerpiece of the dining room. Entrées $16.95–25.95.

South of the village

✔ **Muddy Moose Restaurant & Pub** (603-356-7696), Rt. 16, North Conway, in "the Strip" south of the village. Open for lunch and dinner. This is a zany, fun place, both in decor and in menu options like buffalo burgers (the real thing), spicy venison sausage (served with mushrooms, scallions, peppers, and penne pasta), and wild boar Marsala. You can also have a plain old burger, spareribs, or baked haddock. In summer there's a nice deck.

In Conway

Chinook Café (603-447-6300), Rt. 16. One of the valley's semi-hidden gems, well known to locals. Open daily 7–4; closing Sun. at 3. Owner Laurel Tessier is a well-known chef who also caters and offers cooking classes. Breakfast on a freshly made bagel with caper and dill cream cheese, red onions, and tomatoes, served with sweet tomato home fries—or try polenta and goat cheese, served piping hot with a red bell pepper marmalade.

Lunch on a curried chicken salad sandwich on sesame whole wheat, on chickpea latkes, or on white bean and portobello bruschette. The atmosphere is that of a colorful coffeehouse. There's also a bakery.

✧ **Café Noche** (603-447-5050), 147 Main St. (Rt. 16). Open daily 11:30 AM–9 PM. The best Mexican restaurant in the North Country, plenty of atmosphere and all the classics, as hot as you like. Mexican beer and mean margaritas. Children's menu.

North of Conway village
✧ **Delaney's Hole in the Wall** (603-356-7776), Rt. 16, just 1 mile north of North Conway village. Open 11:30 AM–11 PM. A friendly, informal place, good for panhandle chicken, a portobello wrap, or baby back ribs. Fully licensed. Kids' menu.

✧ **Glen Junction** (603-383-9660; www.glenjunction.com), Rt. 302, Glen. Open daily 7–3; breakfast served all day. Designer omelets, specialty sandwiches, apple pie and ice cream. Kids (and adults) are fascinated with the two large-scale model trains that circle the dining rooms on tracks near the ceiling.

COFFEE HOUSES North Conway village has more than its share of cafés, but in the course of researching this guide we have watched several come and go. One, however, stands out and seems as firmly entrenched as its building.

The Met (603-356-2332; www.metropolitancoffeehouse.com) is housed in a former bank building in the middle of the village, 2680 White Mountain Hwy. Open 8 AM–10 PM. Walls are hung with local art (for sale); WiFi.

✳ **Entertainment**

✧ **Arts Jubilee** (603-356-9393) offers summer musical performances, weekly afternoon children's programs, and a fall art show. Thursday-night free outdoor concerts in Schouler Park.

✧ **Mount Washington Valley Theatre Company** (603-356-5776), Eastern Slope Playhouse, Main St., North Conway. Season: late June–Labor Day. Curtain at 8 PM, $24 tickets, good old chestnuts like *The Music Man* and *A Chorus Line*. Children's theater Friday mornings at 10 and 11:30.

M&D Theatre Productions (603-356-4449; www.md-productions.org), Willow Place Mall, present plays and other live entertainment with proceeds benefiting local nonprofits.

Majestic Theater (603-447-5030; www.hometowntheatre.com), Rt. 16, Conway village, is a classic 1930s art deco movie hall with first-run movies on two screens.

The Red Parka Pub (see *Eating Out*) is good for après-ski and for music on summer weekends.

✳ **Selective Shopping**

Rt. 16 from the traffic lights in Conway village north through North Conway may be motorist's hell (with more traffic lights than the rest of northern New Hampshire combined) but it's shopper's heaven, with more than 200 specialty shops and outlets offering substantial savings, further sweetened by New Hampshire's zero sales tax. The outlet boom hit in the 1980s, and most of the leading manufacturers have opened stores here. The largest concentration, with more than 40 stores, is the **Settlers Green Outlet Village** (Adidas, April Cornell, Banana Republic, The Gap, et cetera).

The **L.L. Bean Center** is, of course, anchored by its namesake store but also includes a number of others—including our favorite, **Chuck Roast**, featuring locally well-made Polartec fleece clothing. The **Tanger Red Barn** factory outlet is another smaller complex that includes Corning Revere, Danskin, and Swank; others are strung along Rt. 16 (anglers should search out the **Orvis Factory Outlet** near the entrance to Settlers Green). A longtime favorite is **Yield House**, at the southern end of the Rt. 16 strip, offering reproduction finished and unfinished furniture and kits. Also see *Sporting Goods*, below.

ANTIQUES SHOPS **Richard M. Plusch Antiques & Appraisals** (603-356-3333; 603-383-9222), 2584 Main St., North Conway. Period furniture and accessories, glass, sterling, Oriental porcelains, rugs, jewelry, paintings, and prints. Open daily 10–5 in summer, rest of year Sat. 10–5, Sun. noon–5 or by appointment. Pick up the free map/guide to area antiques shops and the directory of New Hampshire antiques dealers, which covers the state.

ARTS AND CRAFTS **League of New Hampshire Craftsmen** (603-356-2441), North Conway village. Quality handmade crafts including pottery, jewelry, clothing, and furnishings. Open all year.
Handcrafters Barn (603-356-8996), Rt. 16, North Conway. Open all year. Works by some 250 artisans as well as specialty foods, furniture, garden, and bath items.

GENERAL STORES **Zeb's** (603-356-9294; www.zebs.com), Main St., North Conway village. Ye olde tyme

Christina Tree

ROUTE 16, NORTH CONWAY'S MAIN SHOPPING HUB

tourist-geared general store with a 67-foot-long candy counter, boasting a large stock of New England products.

5&10 Cents Store, Main St., North Conway village. This is the real thing: the local five and dime under the same family ownership since 1931. Children's books, toys, cards, stationery, and friendly old-timers at the checkout counter.

SPECIALTY SHOPS **White Birch Booksellers** (603-356-3200; www.whitebirchbooks.com), Rt. 16 just south of the village, is an attractive full-service independent bookstore, well stocked with everything from children's to travel books with plenty in between. There is a particularly good selection of books about New Hampshire and by local writers; also about hiking, mountain climbing, and other forms of outdoor adventure.

Peter Limmer and Sons (603-356-5378), Rt. 16A, Box 88, Intervale 03845. Closed Sun. If anything is a craft item, it is a pair of handmade mountain boots created by the third generation of the Limmer family. The boots are expensive, and you may wait a year or more to have a pair custom-made to fit your feet. Still, "Limmers" have gone from Mount Washington to Mount Everest, and many hikers wouldn't enter the woods without a pair. You'll also find street and golf shoes.

SPORTING GOODS This is New England's prime center for mountaineering equipment.

Eastern Mountain Sports (603-356-5433; www.emsonline.com) occupies much of the ground floor in the Eastern Slope Inn, North Conway village, with a full line of skis plus hiking and climbing equipment. Inquire about their climbing school.

Joe Jones Ski & Sport (603-356-6474; www.joejonessports.com), Rt. 16 at the northern end of North Conway village, good for rentals as well as sales.

Ragged Mountain Equipment, Inc. (603-356-3042; 1-877-772-4433; www.raggedmountain.com), Rts. 16/302, Intervale. Here you'll find cross-country and snowshoe rentals in winter, plus a full line of equipment that varies with the season. Inquire about free ski and snowshoe tours in winter, naturalist-led walks and hikes in summer.

Wild Things (603-356-9453; www.wildthingsgear.com), 1618 Mount Washington Hwy. (Rt. 16), North Conway. Open Sun.–Thu. 10–5, Fri.–Sat. 10–7. Mountaineering equipment, climbing gear, backpacks, cold-weather clothing.

✳ Special Events

We have primarily listed annual events but not specific dates, since the exact dates change each year.

Contact the Mount Washington Valley Chamber of Commerce (www.mt washingtoncvalley.org) for details. Cranmore is often the host for professional tennis tournaments, and world-class skiing races are often held at valley ski areas.

March: **Maple Sunday** at the Chester Eastman Homestead, North Chatham (603-694-3388).

July–Labor Day: **Arts Jubilee**. Free outdoor concerts in Schouler Park, at the gazebo, and at the fire station in Conway village.

Fourth of July: **Carnival**, North Conway. Fireworks and parade.

Early September: **World Mud Bowl**, North Conway. Some people enjoy this annual football game, played in knee-deep mud. At least local charities benefit from the proceeds.

Mid-September: **Bark in the Park Expo**, billed as New England's largest pet expo, benefits the Conway Area Humane Society.

Late September: **Fall on the Farm**, Chester Eastman Homestead, North Chatham (603-694-3388).

First week in October: **Fryeburg Fair**, Fryeburg, Maine. This is a large agricultural fair, with horse and cattle pulling, livestock exhibits and judging, midway, and pari-mutuel harness racing. Just across the border from the Mount Washington Valley, this annual fair attracts a huge crowd in the middle of foliage season.

November: The **Harvest to Holidays Annual Promotion** is a big deal because this is such an obvious place to shop at what otherwise is low season for local shops and restaurants. Lodging and dining bargains, shopping coupons, and special events.

Pinkham Notch is a high, steep-walled pass between the eastern slopes of the Presidential Range and neighboring mountains. Here Rt. 16 threads a 5,600-acre section of the White Mountain National Forest that includes Tuckerman Ravine, famous for spring skiing, adjacent Huntington Ravine, known for winter ice climbing, and the Great Gulf Wilderness, a larger glacial valley surrounded by the state's highest peaks.

Of course you see little of all this if you stick to Rt. 16. You shouldn't. More than any other place in New England, Pinkham Notch has become the place ordinary folk come—year-round—to tune in to and engage with New England's highest mountains in all their splendor.

Back in 1861 the 8-mile "Carriage" (now "Auto") Road, billed as "America's first man-made attraction," opened the way for anyone to ride to the summit of Mount Washington, and it remains the route that most visitors take to the top. The hiking hub of the White Mountains, the Appalachian Mountain Club (AMC)'s Pinkham Notch Visitors Center, is just down the road, a place to learn about hiking trails and outdoor skills, to hear a free lecture, or to catch the "hiker's shuttle" that circles the base of Mount Washington, stopping at trailheads. At Wildcat Mountain a four-person gondola hoists passengers to the 4,062-foot summit, from which you can walk a ridge portion of the Appalachian Trail. Great Glen Trails Outdoor Center at the base of the Auto Road offers miles of winter cross-country ski trails that turn into mountain bike trails (rentals available), as well as opportunities for novices to try their hand at fishing or paddling.

Pinkham Notch, moreover, offers year-round access to its spectacular heights. In winter SnowCoaches carry visitors (weather permitting) up the Auto Road, and the AMC Visitors Center is the venue for workshops in winter sports and skills. Wildcat Ski Area offers some of New England's longest and most satisfying trails and boasts eye-level views from its slopes of spectacular Tuckerman Ravine, which becomes a ski mecca in its own right come April and May. Great Glen also draws cross-country skiers and snowshoers.

Just south of Pinkham Notch, Jackson is cradled in the high, horseshoe-shaped Wildcat River Valley. From Rt. 16, the first entrance to the village is through a covered bridge; beyond is a steepled church shouldering the shingled library and the imposing Wentworth Resort Hotel with its adjacent 18-hole golf course. Follow the stream uphill and you come to another nicely restored 19th-century survivor, the Eagle Mountain House. At the top of "the Loop" you'll find Whitneys Inn and Black Mountain, New England's only surviving ski hill (and there were many) to be opened behind an inn.

An incubator for alpine skiing in the 1930s (there were also rope tows behind the Wildcat Tavern and Thorn Hill), Jackson is better known today as a cross-country ski destination. The nonprofit Jackson Ski Touring Foundation, founded in 1972 when that sport too was in its infancy, presently maintains a 154-km trail system.

Thanks to careful zoning and a strong community spirit, the atmosphere in Jackson is relaxing for guests and residents alike. As a group, its inns and restaurants are as nice as can be found anywhere.

GUIDANCE **Jackson Area Chamber of Commerce** (603-383-9356; 1-800-866-3334; www.jacksonnh.com), Box 304, Jackson village 03846. Information and reservation system.

The Appalachian Mountain Club Pinkham Notch Visitors Center (603-466-2721; www.outdoors.org) is a departure point for hiking and other ways of tuning in to this naturally spectacular area. Check out the daily weather information (ext. 773). Also see *To Do*.

Mount Washington Valley Chamber of Commerce and Visitors Bureau (603-356-3171; 1-800-367-3364; www.mtwashingtonvalley.org), Box 2300, North Conway 03860.

GETTING THERE **Concord Trailways** (www.concordtrailways.com) offers daily bus service (603-228-3300; 1-800-639-3317) from Boston and Logan Airport, with a flag stop on Rt. 16 in Jackson and at the Appalachian Mountain Club's Pinkham Notch Camp.

GETTING AROUND The **AMC Hiker Shuttle** (603-466-2721) operates June–mid-Oct., 8–4, based at the Pinkham Notch Visitors Center and serving trailheads throughout the White Mountains. For details, see "Mount Washington."

✳ To See

SCENIC DRIVES **Pinkham Notch Scenic Area**, Rt. 16, between Jackson and Gorham. Approaching from the Jackson end of the notch, Rt. 16 begins a long, gradual ascent, passing the beginnings of several hiking trails and a few pullouts adjacent to the Ellis River. Watch the ridge of the mountains on the western side, and gradually the huge Glen Boulder becomes silhouetted against the sky. This erratic was dragged to this seemingly precarious spot eons ago by a glacier. Situated at an elevation of about 3,700 feet, the boulder is a 1.5-mile, 2-hour hike from the highway, a short but steep climb to tree line. At the top of the notch, the mountainside drops steeply to the east and allows a panoramic view south down the Ellis River Valley toward Conway and Mount Chocorua. Across this valley rises the long ridge of Wildcat Mountain. Just ahead is a parking lot for Glen Ellis Falls, one of the picturesque highlights of the notch. To see the falls, cross under the highway by the short tunnel, then walk 0.2 mile down a short trail to the base of the falls.

North along Rt. 16, as the highway skirts along the side of Mount Washington, are the AMC Pinkham Notch Visitors Center, then Wildcat Mountain (with summer and fall mountain gondola rides) and the Mount Washington Auto Road at the Glen. Here is one of the most magnificent views in all the mountains. At left can be seen the summit of Mount Washington, although it doesn't appear to be the highest spot around. Rising clockwise above the Great Gulf—another glacial valley—are Mounts Clay, Jefferson, Adams (the state's second highest peak), and Madison. Rt. 16 continues north to Gorham, passing en route the WMNF Dolly Copp Campground and the entrance to Pinkham B (Dolly Copp) Road, which connects to Rt. 2 at Randolph. Just north of Pinkham Notch, several hiking trails

THE MOUNT WASHINGTON AUTO ROAD

MOUNT WASHINGTON AUTO ROAD

603-466-3988; www.mt-washington.com), Rt. 16, Pinkham Notch, Box 278, Gorham 03518. Open daily, weather permitting, early May–mid-Oct., 7:30–6 most of the summer, with shorter hours earlier and later in the season. The Mount Washington Carriage Road opened in 1861, and for its first 50 years a 12-person wagon pulled by six horses carried passengers to the summit. The advent of the Cog Railroad cut into business, but with the advent of the motorcar its popularity revived. The first motorized ascent in 1899 was by F. O. Stanley of Stanley Steamer fame. The 8-mile, graded road climbs steadily, without steep pitches but with an average grade of 12 percent, from the Glen to the summit. Although the road is narrow in spots and skirts some steep slopes, it has a remarkable safety record and annually carries some 100,000 visitors. En route there are many places to pull off and enjoy the view, and the road is crossed by several hiking trails. Inquire about annual foot, bicycle, and auto races. Most (but not all) passenger cars are permitted to make the climb to the summit. A 1½-hour guided tour in chauffeur-driven vans, called stages to keep alive a historical tradition, is also offered. A base building, serving both the Auto Road and Great Glen Trails, includes a cafeteria. Passenger-car rates: $20 for car and driver, $7 each additional passenger, $5 ages 5–12, includes an audio tour in English, French, or German. Guided tour: $22 adults, $20 seniors, $10 ages 5–12. $8 for motorcycle and driver. In winter the SnowCoaches, a van especially designed for the ascent, transports you up the Auto Road to just above tree line, with a view down into the Great Gulf Wilderness ($40 per adult, $25 per child).

head east into the Carter Range. One, the Nineteen Mile Brook Trail (3.8 miles, 2½ hours), leads to the AMC Carter Notch Hut, another full-service facility. It is also open on a self-service, caretaker basis in winter.

Jackson Loop. This 5-mile circuit drive begins in Jackson village. Follow Rt. 16B at the schoolhouse, up the hill, and past farms and views across the valley to Whitney's; then turn left for a couple of miles to Carter Notch Road, where you turn left again, past the Eagle Mountain House and Jackson Falls, before reaching the village. For a variation on this drive, turn right at Whitney's, and right again at Black Mountain onto Dundee Road, which changes to gravel now and again as it passes abandoned farms and mountain scenery en route to Intervale at Rt. 16A. Turn right and pick up Thorn Hill Road to return to Jackson.

✳ To Do

The Appalachian Mountain Club Pinkham Notch Visitors Center (603-466-2727; www.outdoors.org). Opened in 1920 and expanded several times since, this complex (alias Pinkham Notch Camp) is the North Country headquarters for an organization of some 90,000 members (the main office is in Boston). Members receive the AMC's several publications and discounts on its many books, maps, hikes and workshops, and accommodations, which include a variety of family "camps" (inquire about **Cold River Camp** in Chatham) and **Joe Dodge Lodge** as well as at their eight high huts, each spaced a day's hike apart in the White Mountains (see *Hiker's Lodging* in "Mount Washington"). Everyone is, however, welcome to use AMC facilities and to participate in their programs. With its trained staff and large membership, the AMC is one of New England's strongest conservation voices, promoting the protection and enjoyment of the mountains, rivers, and trails throughout the Northeast.

In the **visitors center** a diorama of the Presidential Range presents an overview of the area's hiking trails. The center also sells hiking guidebooks and maps and posts the day's weather and trail conditions. Three daily meals (see *Eating Out*) are served up in the big open-timbered dining hall, which is also the venue for year-round free evening lectures on a broad range of topics (including slide shows on exploring the world's backcountry). In the neighboring Joe Dodge Lodge you'll find year-round workshops on outdoor skills, ranging from hiking, skiing, snowshoeing, woods crafts, and canoeing to bird study, photography, art, and writing. These vary in length from a few hours to a few days. This is also pickup point for the **Hiker Shuttle** (see *Getting Around*).

Note: Because AMC staffers often volunteer for mountain rescues, they are careful to give considered advice to hikers. The *AMC White Mountain Guide* has the most comprehensive trail information available for hikers, but also see Daniel Doan and Ruth Doan MacDougall's *50 Hikes in the White Mountains*.

AERIAL LIFT Wildcat Mountain Gondola Ride (603-466-3326; www.ski wildcat.com), Rt. 16, Pinkham Notch. During summer months Wildcat's quad chair is replaced by a gondola that hoists visitors to the summit, with a viewing platform of Mount Washington and a trail along the ridge.

GOLF **Wentworth Resort Golf Club** (603-383-9641; www.thewentworth.com), Jackson village. Eighteen holes, with pro shop, club and cart rentals, full lunch available. Call for tee times.

Eagle Mountain House (603-383-9111; 1-800-966-5779; www.eaglemt.com), Carter Notch Road, Jackson. Nine holes, full hotel facilities.

FISHING **Great Glen Outdoor Center** (603-466-2333; www.greatglentrails .com) offers an introduction, based at its pond; also guided canoe, driftboat, and wading trips to North Country waters. Open daily 9–5.

HIKING Mount Washington is crisscrossed with trails, but by far the most popular is the **Tuckerman Ravine Trail** (see "Mount Washington"), beginning at the AMC Pinkham Notch Camp on Rt. 16. We also recommend **Eagle Mountain Path** (1 mile, 50 minutes) beginning behind the Eagle Mountain House (see *Lodging*) in Jackson. **Black Mountain Ski Trail** (1.7 miles, 1¾ hours) begins on Carter Notch Road, 3.7 miles from the village. It leads to a cabin and a knob that offers a fine view of Mount Washington. **North Doublehead**, via the Doublehead Ski Trail, begins on Dundee Road, 2.9 miles from the village, and follows an old ski trail to the WMNF Doublehead cabin on the wooded summit. A path leads to a good view east, and by using the Old Path and the New Path, you can make a round-trip hike from Dundee Road over both North and South Doublehead and back to the road. To North Doublehead, 1.8 miles and 1¾ hours; a round trip to both summits is about 4.3 miles and 4 hours. **Rocky Branch Trail** makes a loop from Jericho Road off Rt. 302 in Glen to Rt. 16 north of Dana Place. We suggest walking the Jericho Road end (turn off 302 in Glen and follow the road about 4.3 miles to the trailhead), which follows the brook for a couple of miles to a shelter. Allow 2 hours to make the round trip on a smooth trail. The Rocky Branch is one of the better trout-fishing brooks, and in spring it is prime wildflower country (look but don't pick!).

Note: The Jackson Area Chamber of Commerce and Mount Washington Valley Visitors Bureau both publish folders describing short walks in and around the village. Also: Although some cross-country trails are suitable for hiking, many of them are on private land and not open to the public except during the ski season.

HORSEBACK RIDING **Black Mountain Stables** (603-383-4491), Rt. 16B. Memorial Day–Halloween. Trail rides geared to novices depart five times daily. $40 for the hour ride.

MASSAGE AND YOGA Finding a local massage therapist is not a problem. According to Shana Myers, the first in Jackson a dozen years ago, there are 35 in the Mount Washington Valley. Note the full-service spas at the Thorn Hill Inn and Christmas Farm Inn and Carriage House Spa. Myers operates Balance Works Wellness Center, Rt. 16 across from the covered bridge. Inquire about joining a regularly scheduled yoga class. Contact her at Moondance Massage (603-383-9377; www.moondancemassage.info).

MOUNTAIN BIKING **Great Glen Trails Outdoor Center** (603-466-2333; www .greatglentrails.com), Rt. 16, Pinkham Notch. In summer the 25-mile network of cross-country trails is smoothly graded, perfect for beginning to intermediate bikers and their families. Rentals include a special attachment that turns an adult bike into a tandem bike so small children can ride too. Inquire about biking workshops.

SWIMMING ✍ At **Jackson Falls**, above Jackson village, the mountain-cool Wildcat River tumbles over rocky outcrops, forming several glorious swimming holes. **Rocky Branch Brook**, just off Rt. 302 in Glen, is another favorite spot. Watch for Jericho Road; follow it to the Rocky Branch Trailhead and walk about 50 yards back along the river toward Rt. 302.

✳ Winter Sports

CROSS-COUNTRY SKIING ✍ **Jackson Ski Touring Foundation** (603-383-9355; 1-800-927-6697; www.jackonxc.org), Rt. 16A, Jackson. This nonprofit organization promotes the sport of cross-country skiing and maintains some 154 km— that's 66 miles—of groomed (doubletrack) trails, the most extensive in the East. The trails range in elevation from 755 feet to 4,000 feet and from easy to difficult, so be sure to consult the map before heading off. The popular **Ellis River Trail** heads from the center north to Dana Place Inn and loops back through the woods. Our favorite is the **East Pasture Loop** with great views down Ellis River Trail. Conditions permitting, you can link to this circuit from the Black Mountain chairlift. Expert backcountry skiers (again, conditions permitting) can also access the **Wildcat Valley Trail**, dropping down into the valley from the top of the Wildcat quad chair to that summit. The touring foundation's center is on the golf course in the middle of the village and includes a retail and rental shop, also changing rooms with showers. It sponsors guided tours, clinics, and races. Trail fees and memberships pay for trail maintenance and improvements. $15 adult trail fee, $8 ages 10–15. Rental pulks are available to pull small children behind.

Great Glen Trails Outdoor Center (603-466-2333; www.greatglentrails.com), Rt. 16, Pinkham Notch, Gorham 03581. Open daily 9–5. Located near the base of the Mount Washington Auto Road, this is a four-season recreational park with ski trails used for hiking or mountain biking in warmer weather. There are 40 km of wide trails, some groomed specifically for skate skiing, diagonal stride, or snowshoeing, plus miles of backcountry trails. Heated yurts with sundecks are spaced along the trail. A lodge at the base of the Auto Road offers a choice of dining as well as retail, plus rentals. Lessons and guided tours are offered. Experienced snowshoers, skiers, and telemarkers inquire about taking the SnowCoaches 4 miles up the Auto Road and skiing down. Adult ski passes are $15; $10 ages 5–12 and 62-plus. Seniors over 70 ski free. Mountain biking is $8 all day.

AMC Pinkham Notch Visitors Center (603-466-2727; www.outdoors.org). Many miles of ungroomed cross-country trails are found in Pinkham Notch. Ask advice at the AMC Visitors Center and pick up a copy of the AMC Winter Trails map detailing cross-country and snowshoeing trails in the area.

Also see **Bear Notch** in "North Conway Area."

www.skiwildcat.com), Rt. 16, Pinkham Notch, Jackson. North-facing Wildcat gets and holds snow, and its 2,112-foot vertical drop makes for some of the longest continuous runs in the East. It faces Mount Washington's eastern slopes across Pinkham Notch, with spectacular views of Tuckerman Ravine. Surrounded by national forest, it retains a "pure" feeling and enjoys a dedicated following. Lifts and grooming are thoroughly up to date. The Wildcat Trail, cut by the Civilian Conservation Corps in 1933, was ranked among the toughest racing trails in the United States, but Wildcat the ski area didn't open until 1957.

It was founded by a small group of former ski racers who cut fall-line black diamonds. While it continues to appeal to expert skiers (many regulars know off-piste routes down), it also offers "Polecat," a 2.75-mile run from the summit, gently canted in such a way as to nudge even the most nervous novice into step with gravity and that soaring sense of what it means to ski. It's also a favorite with telemarkers and skiers of every level. Longtime legendery manager Stan Judge designed several other intermediate trails, noteworthy for the way they curve naturally with the contours of the mountain, a rarity among modern ski trails. Wildcat can be windy and cold, but trails seem designed to maximize shelter—and come March they are glorious.

POWDER SKIING AT WILDCAT MOUNTAIN

Brooks Dodge–Wildcat Mountain

Lifts: 1 high-speed detachable quad, 3 triple chairs.

Trails: 47 on 225 acres, including glades, bumps, and backcountry tree skiing.

Vertical drop: 2,112 feet.

Snowmaking: 90 percent coverage.

Facilties: Base lodge with ski shop, rentals, lockers, pub and snack bar, ski school.

For children: Lion's Den Kids' Ski & Snowboard School (ages 5–12), Lion Cubs ski & snow-play program (ages 3–5), Lion Cubs Nursery Sitting Service (ages 2 months–5 years).

Lift tickets: Weekend and holiday: $55 adults, $42 teens/seniors, $25 juniors. Additional days $25. Specials: Wed., two ski or ride for the price of one; Thu., $45 for women.

✎ **Black Mountain** (603-383-4490; 1-800-698-4490; snow phone: 603-475-4669; www.blackmt.com), Rt. 16B, Jackson. A historic New Hampshire ski area, dating from the 1930s when Bill Whitney fashioned a rope tow with shovel handles. Now a haven for families in search of a small, quiet mountain. Trails off the 3,303-foot-high summit include several double diamonds.

Lifts: Double and triple chairlifts and a T-bar.

Trails: 40 trails and glades on 143 acres.

Vertical drop: 1,100 feet.

Snowmaking: 95 percent snowmaking.

Facilities: Base lodge with ski and snowboard school, rentals, and a connection (conditions permitting) to Jackson's 154 km of cross-country trails. Dining and lodging at the base in Whitneys' Inn, also slope-side condominiums.

For children: Kids' programs and child care.

Lift tickets: $32 adults, $20 ages 24 and under on weekends; $24 adults, $22 juniors midweek; $17 seniors.

Also see Attitash Ski Area in the "North Conway Area," and Tuckerman Ravine in "Mount Washington."

ICE SKATING ✍ A town-maintained ice-skating rink is located in the center of the village across from the grammar school, and **Nestlenook Farm** (see below) has skating for a fee.

SLEIGH RIDES ✍ **Nestlenook Farm** (603-383-9443; www.nestlenookfarm.com), Dinsmore Rd., Jackson village. Daily except Wed. Sleigh rides last 25 minutes and take you through the woods beside the Ellis River in a 25-person rustic sleigh or a smaller Austrian-built model. Oil lamps light the trails at night. Wheels are added for summer rides.

WINTER WORKSHOPS **The AMC Pinkham Notch Visitor Center** (603-466-2727; www.outdoors.org) and Joe Dodge Lodge serve as a base for midweek and weekend workshops in cross-country skiing, telemarking, snowshoeing, winter camping, ice climbing, tracking, winter photography, and more.

✻ Lodging

RESORTS ⟁ **Wentworth Resort Hotel** (603-383-9700; 1-800-637-0013; www.thewentworth.com), Jackson village 03846. Dating back to the 1860s and accommodating 400 people at its height as a self-contained summer resort (with its own farm, electric plant, greenhouse, orchestra, and golf course), the 55-room Wentworth has been reborn as a smaller, friendly, comfortable, but still-grand hotel. Over the past dozen years Swiss-born and -trained owner-manager Fritz Koeppel has been transforming rooms one by one, adding bells and whistles like Jacuzzis, hot tubs, and gas fireplaces as well as air-conditioning and discreetly hidden cable TVs, furnishing each in a different combination of reproduction antiques. Guest rooms are divided among the handsome three-story main building and several adjoining, neighboring annexes. In summer the long porch is lined with

Kim Grant

A SNOW-COVERED GAZEBO AT THE WENTWORTH RESORT HOTEL IN JACKSON

wicker rockers, decked in flowers, shaded by green-and-white-striped awnings. Guests can take a dip in the heated pool or walk to the river for a dip in the cool mountain water of the Wildcat River. The Wentworth's golf course is 18 holes; its clubhouse doubles as the winter lodge for the Jackson Ski Touring Foundation. Guests can also walk to tennis and to several lunch options "downtown." Breakfast and dinner are served in the hotel dining room, and food is very much a part of the experience here (see *Dining Out*). Rooms are $185–355, but there are special packages. At this writing, midweek in late autumn gets a couple not only a room but also full breakfast and a five-course candlelit dinner. Inquire about renting one of the 14 two- and three-room condominiums that adjoin the property, overlooking the golf course.

✍ **Eagle Mountain House** (603-383-9111; 1-800-966-5779; www.eaglemt .com), Carter Notch Rd., Jackson 03846. Open all year. Another among the few surviving Victorian White

Mountain hotels. The flavor is graciously vintage, and the essentials are up to date. All 93 completely renovated rooms, including 30 suites, have private bath, phone, and cable TV. Most rooms have queen beds and are furnished in a country style. There is a nine-hole golf course, lighted tennis courts, health club, and heated pool. Winter guests can link directly with the Jackson Touring Foundation's extensive trail system. Unwind in the Eagle Landing Lounge, where lunch is served. Breakfast, Sunday brunch, and dinner are served in Highfields, the inn's dining room (see *Dining Out*). $79–209 per room, depending on season and accommodations; also B&B, MAP, and a variety of package plans, especially in ski season. Children 17 and under stay free in the same room with parents.

🐾 **Whitneys' Inn** (603-383-8916; 1-800-677-5737; www.whitneysinn .com), Rt. 16B, Jackson 03846. With Black Mountain (one of the state's oldest ski areas) just behind the inn, this was one of the first ski inns, but its top-of-the-valley location is great other seasons as well. It was looking really down at the heels for a while, but recent renovations have improved it considerably. The 30 rooms vary widely. Some have sitting area, fireplace, and king-sized bed. There are also 8 family suites with cable TV in a separate facility, 2 cottages with fireplaces, and the four-room Brookside Cottage with fireplaces. The lounge and dining room also have fireplaces, and there is a separate common room for guests. The remodeled barn includes the venerable Shovel Handle Pub, now no longer an après-ski spot and used only as the inn dining room in ski season, as well as rec rooms for teens and younger children. In summer there are lawn games, a mountain pond and heated pool for swimming, and tennis and volleyball courts. The dinner menu (see *Dining Out*) changes seasonally. Rates are $125–295 per couple with breakfast.

INNS The Inn at Thorn Hill & Spa (603-383-4242; 603-383-6448; 1-800-289-8990; www.innatthornhill .com), Thorn Hill Rd., Jackson village 03846. Open all year. Long considered one of New Hampshire's most romantic inns, this 1895 mansion, designed by Stanford White, was completely rebuilt and upgraded after a fire in 2002 and offers "luxury with a view." Innkeepers Jim and Ibby Cooper took great pains to preserve the inn's Victorian character, retaining the gambrel roof, adding gables and a turret. The number of rooms was also increased and new spa facilities added. All 16 rooms in the main inn now have Jacuzzi tub, fireplace, TV, and traditional decor. There are 6 more rooms in the Carriage House (4 with Jacuzzi) plus 3 deluxe cottages, all with fire-

place, Jacuzzi, and outside deck and/ or screened porch. Common areas include an attractive bar and lounge that serves an à la carte menu and has a wide selection of wine by the glass. (The inn's wine cellar holds 2,500 bottles.) The main dining room seats 75 and has a view down the valley to the village and across the hills to Mount Washington. Dining nightly 6–9 (see *Dining Out*). Swim in the inn pool, have a restorative spa treatment, relax in the outdoor hot tub, or cross-country ski from the door. The village is just a short walk down the hill. No smoking. MAP $169–410 depending on season and accommodations; various package plans including ones for the spa. For B&B, deduct $35 per person.

Christmas Farm Inn & Spa (603-383-4313; 1-800-443-5837; www .christmasfarminn.com), P.O. Box CC, Rt. 16B, Jackson 03846. Among the oldest inns in Jackson, under new management Christmas Farm has added a new Carriage House annex with luxury suites, a fitness center, and an elegantly appointed full-service spa. There are now 42 guest rooms and cottages. The main inn incorporated the original 1786 farmhouse (given as a Christmas present, hence the name) and adjacent saltbox. Each has nine rooms, and there are four loft suites in the nearby old barn. A two-room log cabin, a two-room sugarhouse (it looks like a dollhouse and is popular with honeymooners), and 5 two-bedroom cottages suitable for families are also scattered around the grounds; there are also 12 suites in the Carriage House, all with king-sized bed, whirlpool tub, gas fireplace, and either private deck or patio. The restaurant and Mistletoe

Pub, both in the main building, are open to the public (see *Dining Out*). B&B rates are $163–373, double occupancy. MAP and spa packages are available.

✒ **Dana Place Inn** (603-383-6822; 1-800-537-9276; www.danaplace.com), Rt. 16, Pinkham Notch, Jackson 03846. A combination of old and new, the main inn is an old farmhouse; additions include a large heated indoor pool and Jacuzzi. An unusual amenity for an inn of this size, the pool is accessed through the cozy library. Sited on 300 acres adjoining the White Mountain National Forest, it has 34 rooms, all with private bath. Facilities include tennis courts, a natural river swimming hole, hiking trails, fishing, and cross-country skiing. The dining room is open to the public (see *Dining Out*). B&B rates range $99–-175, MAP $125–225.

✒ **Wildcat Tavern** (603-383-4245; 1-800-228-4245; www.wildcattavern .com), Jackson village 03846. Open all year. If you like to be in the middle of everything, try this old favorite, the 1930s home of the Jackson Ski School. Walk to cross-country skiing, shopping, golf, or tennis; the tavern offers folk music on weekends. Upstairs are 14 rooms, 10 with private bath. The rooms are cozy, with country furniture and some antiques, and most of them can be arranged as suites for families. A cottage in the tavern garden, the Igloo, can accommodate four people. There is also a large TV and game room and a separate living room with a fireplace. Three meals are served daily in one of the area's most popular restaurants (see *Dining Out*), and there's a tavern with a lighter—and cheaper—pub menu. B&B $129–149, double occu-

pancy. Add $35 per person for dinner. The Igloo is $350 a night with breakfast. There are also theater, tennis, and golf packages.

BED & BREAKFASTS **The Blake House** (603-383-9057; www.blake housebandb.com), Rt. 16, Jackson 03846. Open all year. Sarah Blake Maynard's father built this place as a ski cabin in the 1930s, and Sarah and Jeff Blake now offer four rooms with two shared baths. Set back from the highway and surrounded by white birches, this is a quiet, woodsy place frequented by hikers and skiers. One room has a king-sized bed, one has a double with a separate screened porch, others have twins. The guests' living room has cozy chairs, TV, VCR, books, games, and a fireplace, while the dining room features a huge window overlooking the forest and the rushing Sand Hill Brook. Breakfast is an expanded continental offering with fresh fruit and breads, hot and cold cereals, and egg dishes featuring eggs from Sarah's chickens. $50–100.

✒ **The Inn at Jackson** (603-383-4321; 1-800-289-8600; www.innat jackson.com), Jackson village 03846. Open all year. This Stanford White–designed mansion overlooks the village. New innkeepers Don and Joyce Bilger brought in professional decorators to brighten up the old inn while retaining is character. The dining room has been opened up by incorporating a former sunporch and has a panoramic view of the village and the mountains. There are 14 large, well-furnished rooms, all with private bath. Second-floor rooms are Victorian themed and have gas fireplace and tastefully recessed TV. Less expensive but quite cozy third-floor rooms are "lodge style" with wood-paneled walls. Amenities include a downstairs parlor with fireplace and overstuffed arm-chairs, a second-floor common room with Internet access, and an outdoor hot tub. Cross-country ski from the door; walk to lunch or dinner. A full breakfast is served with a choice of hot entrées. B&B $119–239. Inquire about packages.

Carter Notch Inn (603-383-9630; 1-800-794-9434; www.carternotchinn .com), Carter Notch Rd., Jackson 03846. Perched on a hillside overlook-ing the Wildcat River Valley beside Eagle Mountain House, this attractive B&B offers a wraparound front porch, a living room with a wood fire, seven air-conditioned guest rooms, and a hot tub on the back deck—not to mention plenty of old-time nostalgia. Rates are $89–229 and include a full country breakfast.

THE SNOWFLAKE INN IN JACKSON

Jackson House Bed & Breakfast (603-383-4226; 1-800-338-1268; www .jacksonhousenh.com), Box 478, Jack-son 03846. Set back from Rt. 16, this circa-1868 house was formerly an apple farm. Jane and Craig Stevenson welcome guests to share their living room with its fireplace and their sunny solarium with its bubbling hot tub. The clapboard house is bigger than it looks: nine cheerful rooms with quilts and some homemade furniture, all with private bath. Craig is a profes-sional chef, a graduate of Johnson and Wales; his breakfast specialty is baked walnut French toast. Hikers, skiers, children, and pets are all welcome. $59–159 for rooms, suite $149–259.

✿ **The Inn at Ellis River** (1-800-233-8309; www.innatellisriver.com), 17 Harriman Rd., Box 656, Jackson 03846. Open all year. Situated just off the main road by its namesake river, this is a turn-of-the-20th-century farmhouse, long geared to accommo-dating guests. There are 20 rooms with period furnishings, and all with private bath. Three rooms are family suites. Fourteen have gas fireplace, eight have two-person Jacuzzi, and all are air-conditioned. There is a heated outdoor swimming pool with adjacent sauna, and a Jacuzzi overlooking the river. You can swim or fish in the river, play volleyball, or cross-country ski from the door. A full breakfast with two hot entrées and afternoon snacks are included in the rates, $110–295. For $20 the inn will prepare a take-away "hiker's lunch" for two.

Snowflake Inn (603-383-8259;888-383-1020; www.snowflakeinnjackson .com), Main St., Jackson village 03846. Jackson's newest inn is all about romance. The 20 "suites for two" all have gas fireplace and two-person Jacuzzi. Packages include "candles and petals" (call for details) and in-room massage. The yellow-clapboard inn is in the very middle of the village, with a spacious common area and a small, jet-fed indoor pool. $165–350 depending on room and season.

Nestlenook Farm (603-383-0845; 1-800-659-9443; www.nestlenookfarm .com), Dinsmore Rd., Jackson village 03846. Open all year. Elaborately decorated, this renovated old inn is a gingerbread "Magic Kingdom" for couples only. Painted peach and green, the house is part of a million-dollar development with extensive gardens, a gazebo, a four-season pool, and a pond ("Emerald Lake") by the Ellis River. Each of the seven "guest suites" has a private bath with a Jacuzzi. Some rooms have working fireplace or parlor stove. All have queen-sized beds, many with canopies, and separate sitting room. Guests may enjoy complimentary sleigh rides and skating, and use of the inn's snowshoes and trails, which connect to the extensive Jackson trail network. B&B $125–399.

MOTEL 🐾 ♿ **The Lodge at Jackson Village** (603-383-0999; 1-800-233-5634; www.lodgeatjacksonvillage .com), Rt. 16, Jackson 03846. Open all year. Inspired by the area's Colonial architecture, this decade-old motel with award-winning gardens offers both charm and convenience. Thirty-two guest rooms with mountain views, air-conditioning, cable television, telephone, and refrigerator. There's a pretty pool and gardens, tennis courts, an outdoor hot tub, and an 18-hole golf course across the

street. $89–179 per room depending on season.

OTHER ⚓ ♿ **Appalachian Mountain Club Pinkham Notch Visitor Center** (603-466-2727; www.outdoors .org), Rt. 16, Pinkham Notch, Box 298, Gorham 03581. This is a full-service facility offering three all-you-can-eat meals, bunk beds, and shared baths. Knotty-pine-walled bunk rooms for two, three, and four people accommodate more than 100 guests in the Joe Dodge Lodge. A few family rooms have a double bed and three bunks. Handicapped accessible. Geared to outdoorspeople (hikers, skiers, and such), it is cheerful (quilts, curtains, and reading lights) and comfortable, with a library and a huge fireplace in the living room and a game room with a children's corner (educational games and nature books). The main-lodge dining area is another gathering area. Free lectures nightly after dinner in July and August and Wed. and Sat. throughout winter. Families are encouraged. Open to AMC members and the general public. Reservations are a must. $43 for nonmember adults without meals; inquire about packages. For nonmembers breakfast is $8, trail lunch $7.75, and dinner $16.75. For information about the eight full-service mountain huts (only reached by walking) maintained by the AMC in the White Mountain National Forest, see *Hiker's Lodging* in "Mount Washington."

Luxury Mountain Getaways (603-383-9101; 1-800-472-5207; www .luxurymountaingetaways.com), Rt. 16, Jackson 03846. This resort complex is a mix of condo clusters and a B&B, Nestlenook Farm, on 165 acres south of the village of Jackson. Units feature fireplace, two-person Jacuzzi, and cooking facilities (ranging from token to full); facilities include indoor pools and four-season outdoor pools, tennis, and skiing (trails connect with the Jackson Touring Foundation system). Choose units in the Victorian Village ($149–729), Nordic Village ($89–479), Nordic Highlands ($119–665), The Chateaus at Highland Ridge ($199–1,600), or Nestlenook Farm ($125–399.) Add a 12 percent "amenities fee."

CAMPGROUNDS **WMNF Dolly Copp Campground** (603-466-3984, July–Labor Day), Rt. 16, Pinkham Notch, Gorham 03581. Open mid-May–first week in Oct.; camping fee is $18. Some of the 176 sites are available through the National Recreation Reservation Service (1-877-444-6777; www.reserveusa.com). There is a $10 charge for changing or canceling reservations. The reservation service operates Mar.–Sep.

✳ Where to Eat

DINING OUT **The Thompson House Eatery** (603-383-9341), Jackson village. Lunch 11:30–3.30 (mid-May–Oct.), dinner 5:30–10. Open Thu.–Sun. for dinner only Nov.–Christmas, closed Apr.–mid-May. Reservations accepted. Owner-chef Larry Baima prepares a host of distinctive and imaginative combination sandwiches, soups, salads, and dinner entrées in a 1790 farmhouse. Try something Italian, Oriental, or traditional American, from pastas to seafood; it's all made fresh daily, to order, and can be prepared to suit dietary needs. Entrées come with salad and fresh bread, $14.95–26.95.

Patio dining in summer and a glowing woodstove in winter make this place popular with locals, too.

Inn at Thorn Hill (603-383-4242; 603-383-6448; 1-800-289-8990; www .innatthornhill.com), Thorn Hill Rd., Jackson village. Open all year. Dining by reservation nightly 6–9. The menu, characterized as New England fusion cuisine, includes an award-winning wine list and changes biweekly. You might start with peekytoe crab cakes in soy mustard or Thai coconut steamed mussels, continue on to roasted butterfish on lobster fried rice or braised pheasant with asparagus and dried cherries, and finish with sweet potato dumplings with toasted walnut sauce or roasted pear with Gorgonzola dulce ice cream. Entrées $25.95–31.95. A lighter, but equally interesting, à la carte menu is served in the lounge ($5–19).

Wentworth Resort Hotel (603-383-9700; 1-800-637-0013; www.thewent worth.com), Jackson village. Dinner served 6–9; reservations recommended. This is Four Diamond dining in an elegant 150-plus-year-old hotel dining room. (Jackets are not required, but jeans, T-shirts, and the like are considered inappropriate.) Chef Brian Gaza came to the Wentworth from the upscale Boston Harbor Hotel and knows his craft. Salad choices could be Belgian endive and caramelized pear or cucumber-wrapped field greens; appetizers include pan-roasted cranberry, pistachio, and chicken sausage or New England crab and cod cake. More than half a dozen entrée choices might include Gulf shrimp ravioli or coarse mustard and parsley rubbed tenderloin of pork. Entrées $20–29.

The extensive wine list has earned the *Wine Spectator* Award of Excellence.

Wildcat Inn and Tavern (603-383-4245; www.wildcattavern.com), Jackson village. Open all year. Three country gourmet meals are served daily in one of the area's most popular restaurants. Dinner ranges from lasagna to lobster fettuccine, crispy duck breast, and the house specialty, Tavern Steak (with béarnaise, brandy peppercorn, or garlic-herb butter). $15.95–25.95.

Whitneys' Inn (603-383-8916; 1-800-677-5737; www.whitneysinn.com), Rt. 16B, Jackson. Best known for its location at the base of Black Mountain, this old inn also has a pleasant, rustic dining room serving dinner nightly spring–fall. In winter dinner is served in the adjacent **Shovel Handle Pub**. The menu changes seasonally, but entrées ($18–29) might include marinated sirloin tips, brandy apple chicken, baked stuffed haddock, or vegetarian lasagna. There is always a children's menu.

✍ **Dana Place Inn** (603-383-6822; 1-800-537-9276; www.danaplaceinn.com), Rt. 16, Pinkham Notch, Jackson. Open year-round for breakfast 7:30–9, dinner 6–9. Elegant à la carte dining in an old inn with a contemporary twist. Signature dishes include brandied apple chicken, duckling à l'orange, and chicken topped with spinach and portobello mushrooms wrapped in puff pastry. $19.95–24.95.

Highfields Restaurant (603-383-9111; www.eaglemt.com), Eagle Mountain House, Carter Notch Rd., Jackson. A classic hotel dining room, this is also a popular restaurant. Entrées range from Downeast haddock and sautéed venison to scampi and filet mignon. $13.95–24.95 includes soup, salad, vegetables, and bread. The à la carte menu, from $5.95 for Caesar salad to $12.95 for grilled sirloin steak, is a bargain. Also a good deal is the champagne brunch served Sun. 10–1. $15.95 adults, $8.95 ages 12 and under.

Also see **Libby's Bistro**, destination dining in Gorham, in "Northern White Mountains."

EATING OUT WildCat Tavern (603-383-4245), Rt. 16A, Jackson village. The tavern itself (as opposed to the dining room) remains the town's ever-popular après-ski spot with its overstuffed couches and easy chairs by the fire as well as the long, inviting bar area. "Tavern Suppers" include baby back ribs and shepherd's pie, along with the signature 8-ounce Tavern Burger. From $7.95. Tuesday is Hoot Night when local musicians congregate.

The Shannon Door & Pub Restaurant (603-383-4211). Rt. 16, Jackson village. An Irish pub that's popular for après-ski in winter, open 4–9 for dinner, until 11 for pizza, burgers, and spirits weekdays, until midnight on weekends with live entertainment. Entrées $6.95–13.95.

Eagle's Landing (603-383-9111; www.eaglemt.com) Carter Notch Rd., Jackson. The pub at Eagle Mountain House serves light fare such as pizza and sandwiches from $6.95.

Yesterdays (603-383-4457), Main St., Jackson village. Open daily 6:15–2. Literally the heart of the village, decorated with blow-ups of vintage postcards. Breakfast all day and good for burgers and sandwiches. We lunched happily on eggplant and pepper soup with half a sandwich on crusty oat-meal bread.

The AMC Pinkham Notch Visitor Center (603-466-2727), Rt. 16, Pinkham Notch. Check to see what the evening lecture is (Wed. and Sat. in winter, Sat. in summer). The big open-timbered dining hall with its long tables is the setting for an all-you-can-eat breakfast (6:30–8), lunch (11:30–1) and dinner (6 sharp, except Fri. when it's a buffet, (6:30–8). Breakfast and dinner are ample and frequently outstanding, served family style. Lunch and snacks available too.

As You Like It Café (603-383-6425), Rt. 16A, Jackson village. Tucked into the same white-clapboard complex that houses the Jackson Chamber of Commerce, creative sandwiches

THE DISTINCTIVE EXTERIOR OF THE RAVENWOOD CURIO SHOPPE IN JACKSON VILLAGE

William Davis

on fresh-baked breads, limited eat-in, soups, coffees, great source for picnics.

✒ **The Red Fox Bar & Grille** (603-383-4949; www.recom), Rt. 16, Jackson village. Open daily for lunch and din-ner. Check out the reasonably priced Sunday jazz breakfast buffet 7:30–noon. A cheerful restaurant featuring Buffalo wings, baby back ribs, baked pesto bread, and a range of soups, sandwiches, salads, and burgers, along with moderately priced entrées, typi-cally $12.95–15.95. There are three large dining rooms, each with a dis-tinctive decor and atmosphere.

✳ Selective Shopping

Ravenwood Curio Shoppe (603-383-8026), Jackson Village. Larry Siebert took 9 years building this mul-tistory, fantastical shop on the site of a garage. He explains that the building couldn't exceed its footprint. Siebert continues to expand the sculpture garden, and the shop itself is filled with an eclectic selection of furnish-ings and gift items, all of them fairly unusual. Beware: We came away with a lamp we certainly never needed.

Jack Frost Shop (603-383-4391), Main St., Jackson. Reduced in size but still a major ski and specialty shop, in business for more than 50 years.

White Mountain Puzzles (603-383-4346; www.puzzlemaps.com), made in Jackson, are available at the chamber of commerce and at Gallery for all Seasons in the Snowflake Inn.

✳ Special Events

Winter: **Cross-country skiing**, Jack-son village. Throughout the ski sea-son, weekend citizens' races are held, and often special international events use the Jackson trails.

Late January: **New Hampshire Snow Sculpture Competition**.

March: **Great Glen to Bretton Woods Adventure**, a 50-km cross-country ski race.

Memorial Day weekend: **Wildquack River Festival**, Jackson village. Some 2,000 rubber duckies race down the river; first duck down wins $1,000. Rent your own for $5.

Early June: **Jackson Covered Bridge 10 km**, Jackson village. One of the most demanding 10K road races in New England. **Wildflower Guided Tour and Barbecue**, Jackson village. See more than 400 wildflowers and ferns and classic 18th- and 19th-century gardens, plus a chicken barbecue.

Mid-June: **Bikes Only Day**—motorcycles rule on the Mount Washington Auto Road.

Late June: **Mount Washington Auto Hill Climb**, Mount Washington Auto Road, Pinkham Notch. First held in 1904, America's oldest motor-sport event: On consecutive weekends, first runners, then autos race from the Glen to the summit over the steep, winding course. See wwww.climbto theclouds.com.

⚓ *Fourth of July:* **Family in the Park**, Jackson village. An old-fashioned Fourth of July celebration.

Mid-July: **Jackson Jazz Festival**, Black Mountain Ski Area.

Late August: **White Mountains Arts Festival** in Jackson Village. **Mount Washington Auto Road Bicycle Hillclimb**.

Early September: **Apple Days Hospitality Tour**; **Mount Washington Bike Race** (603-466-3988), Mount Washington Auto Road, Pinkham Notch. This event attracts some of the top U.S. racers.

October: **Return of the Pumpkin People** in Jackson: creative pumpkin sculptures.

November: **Traditionally Yours Holiday Celebration**.

Early December: A **Yankee swap**.

In 1771 Timothy Nash of Lancaster was tracking a moose over Cherry Mountain when he noticed a gap in the high range to the south and recalled Native American lore about a trail to the coast. Nash found his way through the "Notch" and all the way to Portsmouth, where he convinced Governor John Wentworth to grant him land at the head of the pass on condition he build a road through it. This trail was passable by 1775, and in 1790 Abel and Hannah Crawford traveled it to settle at present-day Fabyans in Bretton Woods. Two years later Hannah's father, Eleazer Rosebrook, brought his family to join them but, declaring he needed "more elbow room," Abel and his family moved 12 miles south to present-day Harts Location at the head of the notch. Both families maintained inns, and in 1819 Abel and his son Ethan Allen blazed the Crawford Path, the first footpath to the summit of Mount Washington. By 1840 summer visitors were making the trek on horseback.

Despite daunting difficulties—the gain in 1,623 feet in elevation in the 30 miles between North Conway and Fabyans and the required construction of the 80-foot-high, 500-foot-long Frankenstein Trestle and Willey Brook Bridge (100 feet high and 400 feet long)—the railroad began runs from Portland, Maine, to Fabyans in 1857. The Crawford House, opened in 1859 in Harts Location, was a prefab, cut in nearby towns and hauled overland, then assembled in 9 months on the spot, with neither pillars nor posts in its grand dining hall. In 1869 the world's first mountain-climbing cog railway opened, running from Fabyans up to the summit of Mount Washington. Eventually as many as 57 trains a day transported guests to hotels in and above Crawford Notch.

"Look at me gentlemen, . . . for I am the poor fool who built all this!" coal baron Joseph Stickney is reported to have exclaimed on the July day in 1902 when the Mount Washington Hotel first opened. It's noted that he "laughed heartily at his own folly." By and large the 200-room hotel has been lucky. Although Stickney died in 1903, it remained in his family until World War II and was then lavishly refurbished by the U.S. government for the 1944 Bretton Woods Monetary Conference, which set the gold standard and created both the World Bank and the International Monetary Fund. During the ensuing decades it had its ups and downs until its 1991 purchase on the auction block by a group of North Country businesspeople. Thanks to their commitment to preserve this grand New England resort and the area's unsurpassed scenic beauty, the hotel, now more than a century young, has reclaimed its former status as a showplace of the mountains and then some: It is now open year-round, offering some of the best downhill and cross-country skiing in New Hampshire. In addition to the Mount Washington Resort, Crawford Notch lodgings include the new Highland Center on the site of the Crawford House, and Notchland, a small but special inn, said to mark the site of Abel's tavern in Harts Location.

Impressive as they are, all the human-made attractions past and present in Crawford Notch and the valley above it are dwarfed by natural beauty, a fact recognized by the state in 1912 when Crawford Notch State Park was established, easing access to several dramatic waterfalls and panoramic views.

GUIDANCE **Appalachian Mountain Club Highland Center** (603-466-2727; www.outdoors.org), Rt. 302, Crawford Notch. Open year-round, hiking information, maps, rental equipment, and workshops. See *Hiker's Lodging*.

Twin Mountain/Bretton Woods Chamber of Commerce (1-800-245-TWIN; www.twinmountain.org) produces a brochure and operates a summer information center at the junction of Rts. 2 and 302.

GETTING AROUND **The AMC Hiker Shuttle** (www.outdoors.org) operates June–mid-Oct. serving trailheads. It's suggested that you spot your car and take a van to the trailhead from which you intend to walk out.

For sights on the top of Mount Washington, see "Mount Washington."

✳ To Do

GOLF **The Mount Washington Resort Golf Course** (603-278-GOLF; www .mtwashington.com), Rt. 302, Bretton Woods. There's much to see and tee here, starting with the original nine-hole, par-35 Mount Pleasant Course, which opened in 1895. Two decades later Scotsman Donald Ross designed and supervised the construction of a second, 18-hole, par-71 course. Both have been restored and supplemented by an 18-hole putting green, full-service golf shop, and 300-yard driving range ($5 per bucket) and practice area, all with the Presidential Range as a backdrop. A new golf clubhouse with full-service, alfresco dining to complement the hotel's architecture opened in 2003. Meanwhile, history holds forth in the men's locker room where the vintage wooden lockers boast brass nameplates to remind you that such folks as Bobby Jones, Babe Ruth, and Thomas Edison once stepped here. Plans are under way to complete an additional nine holes by 2007.

HIKING Many hiking trails cross and parallel the notch. One is the Appalachian Trail—follow it north to Maine or south to Georgia. Consult the *AMC White*

APPALACHIAN MOUNTAIN CLUB HIGHLAND CENTER

Sarah Jan Shangraw

Mount Washington Cog Railway and Ski Train (603-278-5404; 1-800-922-8825; www.thecog.com), off Rt. 302, Bretton Woods. Operates more or less year-round, depending on week and weather. Opened in 1869, this was the world's first mountain-climbing cog railway, and it remains one of the few places where you can observe steam locomotives at work. Since 2004 it has been operating during snow months about a third of the way to the summit, offering cross-country skiers, snowshoers, and alpine skiers (who exit higher up than the others) a chance to ski groomed trails down.

At one time regular trains followed a spur line to the base station, where passengers boarded the cog railway directly for the summit. So unique and ambitious was the plan to build the railroad that its promoter, Sylvester Marsh, was told he might as well "build a railway to the moon." The eight little engines that could, each made for the purpose by this railroad company, have boilers positioned at an angle because of the steep grade up the mountain. Spring through fall the 3-hour round trip, which includes a 20-minute stop at the summit, features each engine pushing a single car up, then backing down in front of the car to provide braking. Unique cogwheels fit into slots between the rails to provide traction and braking. The average grade along the 3.25-mile track is 25 percent, but at Jacob's Ladder trestle it rises to 37.5 percent. Several switches permit ascending and descending trains to pass en route. In winter months the base station, a short drive on a paved road from Rt. 302, includes a visitors center and museum, a restaurant, a gift shop, and an RV park. $57 adults $52 seniors 65 and over, $37 ages 4–12; ski train: $29 adults, $24 children; more for multiple runs and all day.

RIDE THE COG RAILWAY TO THE SUMMIT AND SKI DOWN!

Mountain Guide for details of the many trails. Below are some of our favorite, less ambitious alternatives.

Arethusa Falls Trail is a 1.5-mile, 1-hour, easy-to-moderate walk to New Hampshire's most impressive and highest waterfall, at its best in spring and early summer when water is high. The well-marked trail begins on the southern side of Rt. 302 near the eastern entrance to Crawford Notch State Park.

Mount Willard Trail begins at the AMC Crawford Notch Highland Center. An easy 1.4-mile, 1-hour walk along a former carriage road leads to rocky ledges with a truly panoramic view down through Crawford Notch. The railroad station once served the old Crawford House, one of the earliest of the old hotels. It was closed in the 1970s and finally burned.

Saco Lake Trail (0.4 mile, 15 minutes), across the street from the AMC Highland Center, the source of the river that flows through Crawford Notch, then on to Maine and the Atlantic Ocean. Behind the trail is Elephant Head, a rocky ridge shaped like a pachyderm.

Crawford Path, from Rt. 302 (opposite the Crawford House site) to Mount Washington, is the oldest hiking trail in the country, built in 1819 by the Crawford family and used as a bridle path in the 1870s. The path is a long, 8.2-mile, 6-hour walk. The **AMC Mizpah Spring Hut** is a 2.5-mile, 2-hour walk over the well-worn trail.

Ammonoosuc Ravine Trail. See "Mount Washington."

HORSEBACK RIDING **Mount Washington Resort** (603-278-1000), Rt. 302, Bretton Woods. The Mount Washington's impressive Victorian-era stables offer unusually scenic trail rides, with guided group and individual trail rides for both beginner and advanced riders. The hotel also offers a horse-drawn carriage tour of its grand grounds.

✳ Winter Sports

CROSS-COUNTRY SKIING **Bretton Woods Nordic Ski Center** (603-278-5181) at the Mount Washington Hotel, Rt. 302, Bretton Woods. A spacious, full-service center offers parking, a café, ski passes, equipment sales and rentals for the 100-km network (95 km are tracked and groomed for both skating and diagonal stride), one of the best in New England. Trails are mapped, marked, and divided into linked trail systems. The wooded, 5-mile Mountain Road trail on Mount Rosebrook can be accessed via the Bethlehem Express quad chair at Bretton Woods Ski Area. (A shuttle service operates back and forth.) There are gentler options past beaver ponds and forest glades, and several rest stops. Nordic daily trail passes are $17 adults, $10 ages 6–12 and over 65, $14 for ages 13–18. The **AMC Highland Center at Crawford Notch** (see *Hiker's Lodging*) also rents equipment as well supplying it (free) to guests. The Bretton Woods cross-country ski network can also be accessed from here.

Backcountry skiing is popular in the **Zealand Valley**, off Rt. 302 between Bretton Woods and Twin Mountain. Well-equipped and -prepared skiers can schuss from Rt. 302 some 2.5 miles into the **AMC Zealand Hut** (603-466-2727),

DOWNHILL SKIING

Bretton Woods Ski Area (603-278-5000; 1-800-232-2972; www.brettonwoods .com), Rt. 302, Bretton Woods. Although traditionally this ski area was considered more enjoyable than challenging, an aggressive expansion policy has added acres of expert terrain, including 30 acres of expert glade trails and 11 trails in Rosebrook Canyon. Arguably the state's largest ski area and one with a commanding view of Mount Washington.

Trails: 101, 63 trails and 30 glades; 31 percent novice, 41 percent intermediate, 28 percent advanced/expert. 434 aces of skiable terrain.

Summit elevation: 3,100 feet.

Vertical drop: 1,500 feet.

Snowwwmaking: 92 percent of trails; annual snowfall of 200 inches.

Lifts: 9, including 2 high-speed quads.

For children: The Hobbits; nursery for ages 2 months–5 years.

Lift tickets: $64 adults, $52 teens, $39 juniors.

Bode Miller, 2005 FIS World Cup winner, is director of skiing, a largely honorary title but he does appear here. The multitiered, post-and-beam base lodge is nicely designed, and the Top'O' Quad Restaurant offers a glorious view of Mount Washington. There's night skiing weekends and holidays on four trails. The entire mountain is open to snowboarding and the terrain park is open for snowboarding and skiing. Riders will also enjoy bumps, jumps, bowls, and glades on West Mountain and in the Rosebrook

which is open all winter on a caretaker basis. Bring your own sleeping bag and food; use their cabin and cooking facilities. Telemark ski rentals available at the Bretton Woods Ski Area (see below).

SNOWSHOEING Snowshoes can be rented at Bretton Woods Ski Area, and a new network of high-altitude trails is accessible from the Bethlehem Express Quad. You can download on the same chairlift they can take up to access the mountaintop trails. Adult snowshoe rental (ages 13–64) $15; all other ages $12. Single chairlift ride $7. Nordic trail pass required.

ICE SKATING AND SNOW TUBING Rent tubes at the Mount Washington Hotel and Resort's Outdoor Activities Center, located at the southern end of the hotel. Tube rental costs $5 per hour. Ice skating is offered on an outdoor rink located at the southern end of the hotel, adjacent to the center. Skate rentals are complimentary to resort guests and run $5 per hour to the public.

A VIEW OF MOUNT WASHINGTON FROM THE BRETTON WOODS' SKI LODGE

Canyon area! The Alpine Rental Center offers half-day, full-day, and night equipment rentals. Red Carpet Learn to Ski and Ride lift and lessons begin at $65 (ages 13 and up). Group Lessons (1½ hours) $30. Inquire about the Adaptive Skiing Program for physically and developmentally challenged individuals (603-278-3398; adaptiveprogram@brettonwoods.com).

✳ Green Space

Crawford Notch State Park (603-374-2272), Rt. 302, Harts Location, 12 miles west of Bartlett. This 5,775-acre park is surrounded by, and predates, the White Mountain National Forest. The **Willey House Snack Bar, Visitors Center and Gift Shop** (open daily, Memorial Day–Columbus Day weekend), housed in 1920s log buildings (originally a cabin colony), mark the site of an unusual mountain tragedy. In August 1826 a terrible rainstorm blew through the notch, frightening the Willey family, who operated a small inn. Hearing an avalanche sliding down the steep side of the mountain, the family and two employees ran from the inn—only to be swallowed up in the debris as the avalanche split above the inn, leaving it intact. All seven people died; the avalanche scar can still be seen on the mountain. This park was established in 1911 when the state purchased the virgin spruce forest to save it from loggers' axes. The park includes picnic tables, a waterfowl pond, and self-guided nature trail. Note the trails to Arethusa Fall (see *Hiking*); two more waterfalls, the **Silver and Flume Cascades**, can be seen from your vehicle at the top of the notch, where there is a parking lot and a scenic outlook. Also note small Saco Lake, just north of the park, headwaters for the Saco. The **Dry Diver Campground** (603-271-3628) with 36 primitive sites is open early May–early Dec. ($13 per site).

Eisenhower Memorial Wayside Park is on Rt. 302, 2 miles west of Crawford Notch. A short walk leads to a magnificent view of Mounts Eisenhower, Monroe, Washington, Jefferson, Adams, and Madison. The tracks of the Mount Washington Cog Railway can be seen ascending the side of Washington, and sometimes smoke from one of the engines is visible.

✳ Lodging

INNS **The Notchland Inn** (603-374-6131; 1-800-866-6131; www.notch land.com), Rt. 302, Harts Location 03812. Open all year. This granite mansion was built by pioneering Boston photographer Samuel Bemis in 1862. An inn since the 1920s, it's set in 100 acres of woodland, surrounded in turn by national forest, projecting a true sense of isolation. The parlor, complete with unusual hearth, was designed by Arts and Crafts pioneer Gustav Stickley, and innkeepers Ed Butler and Les Schoof have a nonfussy, though respectful, attitude about this legacy. They offer seven exceptionally attractive and spacious guest rooms and five suites with sitting rooms. All feature wood-burning fireplaces; some also have private deck, skylight, and Jacuzzi. There's a music room with piano and stereo, a library, and, for summer guests, a sunroom with wicker furniture that overlooks the pond. The Saco River flows through the property (harboring fine swimming holes), and the Davis Path up Mount Crawford begins across the road. Notchland's two Bernese mountain dogs may accompany your hike. In winter snowshoes are available at a nominal rate and trails lead into the woods. Five-course dinners, served nightly at 7, draw raves (see *Dining Out*). A room with breakfast (2-night

minimum required on many weekends) runs $195; $260 for a suite with river view; $245–310 during holiday and foliage seasons; for dinner add $35 per person; 2- to 5-night midweek packages are also available. $25 per extra person, $30 less single.

🔥 🐾 ♪ **The Bartlett Inn** (603-374-2353; 1-800-292-2353; www.bartlett inn.com), Rt. 302, Box 327, Bartlett 02812. Open all year. Just west of Bartlett village, this comfortable, simple inn appeals especially to hikers, Nordic skiers, and lovers of the outdoors. The innkeepers, Miriam Habert and Nick Jaques, are enthusiastic and knowledgeable about all kinds of outdoor recreation in the surrounding area, and they can direct guests to the best areas while they're cooking and serving the hearty breakfast that is included in room rates. Nordic skiers can ski directly from the inn onto the extensive trails of the Bear Notch cross-country ski area and return to soak in the inn's outdoor hot tub. The main inn has 6 rooms, and there are 10 rooms in attached cottages, where pets are permitted. Eleven rooms have private bath, and some have fireplace and kitchenette. $79–195 per double.

The Bernerhof (603-383-9132; 1-800-548-8007; www.bernerhofinn .com), Rt. 302, Box 240, Glen 03838.

THE AMC'S ZEALAND FALLS HUT

Open all year. Breakfast for guests, dinner for the public. George and June Phillips are the new owners of this landmark inn. They offer nine rooms including six with Jacuzzi (half of these are in the bathrooms). Oak paneling accents the **Black Bear Pub** and adjacent dining room. B&B $119–189.

AMC HIKER'S LODGING ☸ **The AMC Highland Center at Crawford Notch** (603-466-2727; www .outdoors.org). Opened in October 2003, this is the Appalachian Mountain Club's most luxurious lodge. It's constructed, as you might expect, of energy-efficient materials and in a way to maximize heat, minimize fuel. Sheathed in natural clapboard and featuring attractive common spaces with mountain views, it accommodates 122 people in 15 private and 32 "shared" rooms. First-floor rooms are in the "Hardwoods," the second are on the "Boreal" level, and the top floor are "Alpine. " An impressive array of educational and outdoor programs is offered. There's also a children's discovery room. We

visited in March and took advantage of the cross-country trails connecting with the Bretton Woods nordic system. Here, as at the Pinkham Notch Visitors Center, three very good, full meals a day are served; both wine and beer are available. This is also a year-round information center for outdoor activities. Outdoor gear, donated by L.L. Bean, is available to guests and program participants. Check the web site for current programs. $68–155 adults, $44–49 ages 15 and under, includes break-fast, dinner, and tax. In the neigh-boring (also new) **Shapleigh Bunk House** rates are $29 adult B&B, $49 with dinner. Prices quoted are for nonmembers. For membership details see *Appalachian Mountain Club* in "What's Where."

Zealand Falls Hut, an **Appalachian Mountain Club high hut** (603-466-2727; www.outdoors.org), off Rt. 302 at Zealand Rd. You must hike 2.8 miles to the hut and supply your bed-clothes and towels; meals, bunks, blankets, and educational programs

Robert S. Kozlow

THE MOUNT WASHINGTON HOTEL IS SPECTACULARLY SITUATED AT THE FOOT OF THE PRESIDENTIAL RANGE

RESORTS Lodging at the **Mount Washington Resort at Bretton Woods** (603-278-1000; 1-800-258-0330; www.mtwashington.com) includes the **Bretton Arms Country Inn**, **the Lodge at Bretton Woods**, and **Townhomes at Bretton Woods**. The mailing address is Rt. 302, Bretton Woods 03575.

✐ **The Mount Washington Hotel**. Open year-round. Think *Titanic*: This 200-room, national historic landmark rises like a white cruise ship from a landlocked green sea, backed by New England's highest, frequently snow-capped mountains. The approach is up a mile-long drive, the veranda is vast, the lobby is high and columned, the dining room and the menu are immense (see *Dining Out*). This "Grande Dame of the White Mountains" took 2 years and 250 Italian

THE MOUNT WASHINGTON RESORT GOLF COURSE

artisans to build, and its steel frame was considered state of the art when it opened in 1902. Winston Churchill and John Maynard Keynes were among the 700 delegates who gathered at the hotel for the Bretton Woods Monetary Conference of 1944. The roster of famous visitors includes Babe Ruth, Thomas Edison, Princess Margaret, and several U.S. presidents. After nearly a century, however, the hotel was showing its age, and in 1991 it was auctioned off. Luckily the group of northern New Hampshire entrepreneurs who purchased it has restored it to its previous grandeur and even winterized it.

Tours are offered several times a day, and the public is welcome to attend various lectures on White Mountain human and natural history. Families are especially welcome here, with a number of two-room suites joined by a common bath being most popular. Kids' Camp offers daily and evening programs for ages 5–12, including hikes, visits with the golf pro and the chef, crafts, and various sports. Other amenities include the granite-walled **Cave** lounge with nightly live entertainment; gift, clothing, flower, and ice cream shops; heated indoor and outdoor pools; a dozen red clay tennis courts; horseback riding; movies; guided hikes (the resort's own 1,250 acres are surrounded by 18,000 acres of White Mountain National Forest); a 27-hole golf course; and the Bretton Woods Ski Area. Its indoor pool has recently undergone a compete renovation and now features lap lanes, along with a new whirlpool. A fitness center fully equipped with Nautilus machines and a full-facility spa are scheduled for completion by the time

THE MOUNT WASHINGTON HOTEL OFFERS NUMEROUS TRAILS FOR NORDIC SKIING

this book appears. MAP rates per couple (dine at any of the resort's four dining rooms) start at $260 standard to $690 deluxe for a room; suites range $455–1,000 for a three-bedroom, one-and-a-half-bath tower affair with rooftop patio and Jacuzzi. Inquire about special-event and weekend packages. (See the introduction to this section for more about the hotel's history.)

🦴🐾 *⃝ **The Bretton Arms Country Inn** (603-278-1000; 1-800-258-0330; www .brettonarms.com), Rt. 302, Bretton Woods. A former annex of the Mount Washington Hotel, built in 1896, this is a more intimate, casual, countrylike alternative to the grandeur of the main hotel, still with facilities for a small conference, a lounge with weekend entertainment, and dining (see *Dining Out*). All 34 guest rooms were renovated in 2005 with new bedding, furniture, carpets, and window treatments. Pets are accepted in some rooms. $130 for two per night includes breakfast.

*⃝ **The Lodge at Bretton Woods**, Rt. 302, Bretton Woods. The 50 rooms are all motel style, large and pleasant with two double beds, TV, and private patio or balcony overlooking the historic Mount Washington Hotel and Presidential Range. Amenities include an indoor heated pool, Jacuzzi and sauna, and comfortable common rooms with fireplaces. The restaurant, Darby's, serves breakfast, lunch, and dinner (see *Eating Out*). $99 per night includes continental breakfast.

*⃝ **The Townhomes at Bretton Woods**, Rt. 302, Bretton Woods. A variety of one- to five-bedroom condominiums with full kitchens, laundries, and fireplaced living rooms; includes access to the health and fitness center and the resort shuttle. From $199 for one-bedroom midweek accommodations to $2,694 for a five-bedroom unit for 7 days during peak season.

are provided. In winter you must pack in your food but have full use of the kitchen, oven, stove, and cookware. Also see Mizpah Spring Hut in "Mount Washington."

CAMPGROUNDS For details about **Dry River Campground** see Crawford Notch State Park. **Crawford Notch General Store and Campground** (603-374-2779), Rt. 302 (south of Crawford Notch) in Harts Location. The store, open all year, sells gas, groceries, and hiking and camping supplies; the campground, with wooded sites, tables, fireplaces, and hot showers, is open May–Oct.

WMNF Campgrounds, near Twin Mountain off Rt. 302 on Zealand Rd. Sugarloaf I offers 29 sites and flush toilets ($18), while Sugarloaf II has 32 sites and vault toilets ($16). Both are open mid-May–mid-Oct. and can be reserved (1-877-444-6777).

✳ Where to Eat

DINING OUT **The Mount Washington Hotel Main Dining Room** (603-278-1000; 1-800-258-0330), Rt. 302, Bretton Woods. Lavish breakfast buffet ($18 adults, $10 ages 3–12; under 3 free), and a dinner menu that changes nightly. Dress for dinner in this historic room, originally designed as a circle so that no one ends up in a corner. Every night is an occasion with dancing, tuxedoed waiters, crystal chandeliers, and the full-blown elegance of another era. Prix fixe dinner, $60 adults, $20 ages 3–12; under 3 free.

Bretton Arms Dining Room and Parlor Lounge (603-278-1000), Rt. 302, Bretton Woods. Open year-round for breakfast and dinner. Casually elegant dining room. Entrées $17–31.

The Notchland Inn (603-374-6131; 1-800-866-6131; www.notchland .com), Rt. 302, Harts Location. Open Wed.–Sun. Said to be part of Abel Crawford's original tavern, this dining room was moved down the road to the Notchland Inn in the 1920s. It overlooks gardens and a pond on one side, Mount Hope on the other. Although the chef creates a new menu nightly, there's always a choice of appetizers and soups, three entrées, and three desserts. You might begin with herbed biscuits and a spicy tomato soup, then a moist crabcake, followed by braised chicken thighs with a mixed greens salad, topped off with a caramel-apple tart. Allow at least 2 hours to dine. Generally for guests, the five-course dinners are also served in a single, 7 PM seating to the public, by reservation only. Prix fixe is $40 for nonguests, $45 on Fri. and Sat. The rate for guests is $35 all evenings.

EATING OUT **Darby's Restaurant and Lounge** (603-278-1000; 1-800-258-0330), Rt. 302, Bretton Woods. Full or continental breakfast and dinner year-round. The Bretton Woods Motor Inn offers views of the Presidential Range and the Mount Washington Hotel from its 1950s–1960s diner.

Fabyan's Station Restaurant and Lounge (603-278-2222), Rt. 302 at the junction of the access road to the Cog Railway, Bretton Woods. Offers a specialized lunch and dinner menu year-round in a restored railroad station. Pub menu in the lounge.

Also see the AMC Highland Center under *Lodging* and the **Red Parka Pub** on Rt. 302 in Glen, described in "North Conway Area."

The Great North Woods

THE NORTHERN WHITE MOUNTAINS AND
NORTHERN GATEWAY REGION

THE NORTH COUNTRY AND LAKE
UMBAGOG AREA

Kim Grant

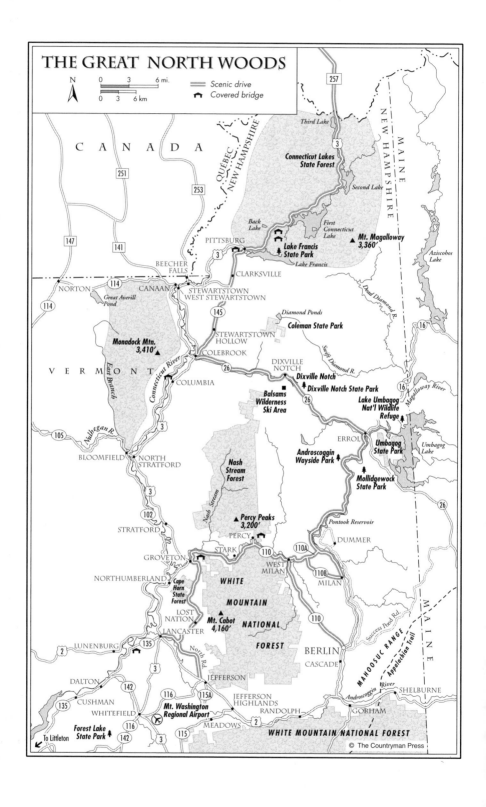

THE GREAT NORTH WOODS

N 0 3 6 mi.
0 3 6 km

Scenic drive
Covered bridge

CANADA

QUÉBEC
NEW HAMPSHIRE

MAINE

NEW HAMPSHIRE

257

251

253

147

141

Third Lake

Connecticut Lakes
State Forest

3

Second Lake

Back
Lake

First
Connecticut
Lake

Mt. Magalloway
3,360'

Aziscohos
Lake

PITTSBURG

Lake Francis
State Park

Lake Francis

BEECHER
FALLS

CLARKSVILLE

Dead Diamond R.

NORTON

114

CANAAN

STEWARTSTOWN
WEST STEWARTSTOWN

Great Averill
Pond

16

114

VERMONT

East Branch

Monadock Mtn.
3,410'

145

STEWARTSTOWN
HOLLOW

COLEBROOK

Diamond Ponds

Coleman State Park

DIXVILLE
NOTCH

Swift Diamond R.

Dixville Notch

26

Dixville Notch State Park

COLUMBIA

Connecticut River

Balsams
Wilderness
Ski Area

26

16

Lake Umbagog
Nat'l Wildlife
Refuge

Magalloway River

105

Nulhegan R.

BLOOMFIELD

NORTH
STRATFORD

3

Nash
Stream
Forest

Androscoggin
Wayside Park

ERROL

Umbagog
State Park

Umbagog
Lake

Mollidgewock
State Park

26

102

STRATFORD

Nash Stream

Percy Peaks
3,200'

Pontook Reservoir

PERCY

110A

DUMMER

GROVETON

STARK

110

NORTHUMBERLAND

Cape
Horn
State
Forest

WEST
MILAN

110B

MILAN

LOST
NATION

WHITE

Mt. Cabot
4,160'

MOUNTAIN

NATIONAL

110

Success Pond Rd.

2

LUNENBURG

135

LANCASTER

North Rd.

FOREST

BERLIN

CASCADE

MAHOOSUC RANGE

Appalachian Trail

MAINE

3

DALTON

142

116

JEFFERSON

115A

JEFFERSON
HIGHLANDS

Androscoggin River

SHELBURNE

135

CUSHMAN

WHITEFIELD

Mt. Washington
Regional Airport

RANDOLPH

GORHAM

Forest Lake
State Park

116

142

116

115

MEADOWS

2

WHITE MOUNTAIN NATIONAL FOREST

To Littleton

3

© The Countryman Press

INTRODUCTION

New Hampshire's high hat—its least populated, narrowest, northernmost region—is actually larger than Rhode Island. It roughly coincides with 1,855-square-mile Coos County (pronounced *co-hos*), an Abenaki word for which we have read several meanings, including "place of white pines" and "crooked," perhaps referring to a river bend. The *Great North Woods* designation is relatively recent, coined to underscore the contrast between this region and the more heavily touristed sections of the White Mountains directly to its south. Towns are small and widely scattered. Most attractions are natural, not human-made.

Ironically, on road maps the Great North Woods shows up as gray, in contrast with the green of the White Mountain National Forest to the south. That's because, with the exception of an 800,000-acre WMNF tract and the vast Nash Stream State Forest, it is largely privately owned by paper and timber-management companies. For a century these have permitted recreational use while managing the woods for a continuous yield. Although most woodland has been cut more than once, the overall impression is one of wilderness. Unfortunately, this system of dual use is now threatened by global economics as paper companies sell off their forests. Still, there are some positive developments, such as the 171,000 acres of formerly commercial timberland around the Connecticut River headwaters that were secured by The Nature Conservancy and recently acquired by the state.

Coos County is home to less than 33,000 people and not many less than 6,000 moose. It's an area of broad forests, remote lakes, fast-running rivers, and rugged mountains. It's also the source of two of New England's mightiest rivers, the Connecticut and the Androscoggin. Early inhabitants are said to have traveled these rivers at least 8,500 years before the first white settlers arrived and set to chopping trees. Then, for more than a century, the rivers carried timber to mills, which were positioned at their steepest drops. Log runs on the Androscoggin continued into the 1960s.

In the 1850s railroads began exporting wood products and importing summer tourists. Local farmers were encouraged to take in guests, and huge hotels sprouted in the wilderness. By the 1950s, however, when passenger service from Portland ceased, all but a handful of the big old hotels had closed and travel patterns had shifted. In subsequent decades the interstates (I-93 on the west and

I-95 on the east) steered travelers in other directions. New Hampshire's "North Country," as it's still commonly known, remained chiefly the preserve of serious outdoorsmen—with two high-profile exceptions.

Both the Balsams Grand Resort Hotel up in Dixville Notch, and the Mountain View, recently resurrected atop a ridge near Whitefield, were gracious 19th-century summer hotels that now attract guests year-round.

Less well known are the sporting camps and campgrounds at the very apex of the state. Similar to the rustic hunting and fishing lodges scattered widely across Maine's North Woods, here they cluster around lakes near the pristine source of the Connecticut River.

Camps and campgrounds are also gathered near the shore of beautiful Umbagog (*um-BAY-gog*) Lake to the east. From Umbagog the Androscoggin River flows south through a long, wooded valley, beloved by canoeists and anglers. Eventually it drops through the city of Berlin and, not far below in Gorham, turns abruptly east and heads into Maine.

Logistically (if not politically) the Great North Woods divides into a northern tier—the Connecticut Lakes, Dixville Notch, and the Umbagog Area—and a southern tier, the Connecticut and Androscoggin River valleys, including towns along the two roads linking them.

The Great North Woods will never be a tourist destination in the Mount Washington Valley sense—not unless a new interstate slashes across it, once more changing traffic patterns. The region is, however, reawakening as a destination for birders and hikers as well as hunters and fishermen. Visitor services are increasing, and many seasonal lodging places now operate year-round, thanks to snowmobilers.

The 19th-century hotels were all geared to summer use only and, while Berlin's Nansen Ski Club (founded in 1872) claims to be the country's oldest ski club, this region, unlike the White Mountains to the south, was virtually unchanged by the alpine ski boom and cross-country ski boomlet. With New England's most reliable snow cover (equaled only by Maine's less accessible North Woods and Aroostook County), it is now a mecca for snowmobilers. Far fewer in number, but growing quickly, are snowshoers. Thanks to recent advances in equipment and clothing, average folks are discovering the beauty of winter woods, empty of all but animal tracks and sparkling with sun on snow.

The animal for which this region is best known is, of course, the moose. The Great North Woods is a moose mecca. The Annual North Country Moose Festival in late August is the event of the year, and the Gorham-based Moose Tours are a big attraction.

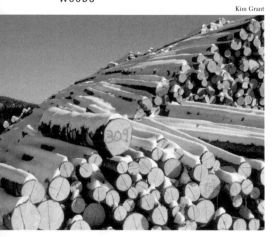

CUT LOGS FOR TIMBER, THE GREAT NORTH WOODS

Kim Grant

THE NORTHERN WHITE MOUNTAINS AND NORTHERN GATEWAY REGION

THE ANDROSCOGGIN AND CONNECTICUT RIVER VALLEYS, INCLUDING SHELBURNE, GORHAM, BERLIN, WHITEFIELD, JEFFERSON, AND LANCASTER

This easily accessible tier of the North Country is far less touristed than the landscape just to its south. It's also surprisingly varied.

The New Hampshire stretch of Rt. 2, which both defines the area's southern boundary and serves as its prime east–west highway, measures just 36 miles, but links two very different north–south corridors carved by two major rivers, the Androscoggin and the Connecticut.

The Androscoggin rises in streams above Umbagog Lake, long a mecca for birders and anglers and now both a national wildlife refuge and a state park. Nearby Errol (population: 303) serves as the hub for canoeing, fishing, and otherwise exploring both the lake and the wooded corridor along the Androscoggin as it courses south, shadowed by Rt. 16. At Berlin the river drops 200 feet in 3 miles, the obvious site for mills. By the 1890s Berlin boasted the world's largest paper mills, employing skilled workers representing no less than nine major ethnic groups. The Northern Forest Heritage Park on the northern fringe of town offers a sense of the rich past of the city and its woodlands, and also serves as departure point for river tours.

At Gorham, 6 miles south of Berlin, the Androscoggin River turns abruptly east. Gorham has been catering to tourists since 1851, when the Atlantic and St. Lawrence Railroad (now the Canadian National) began transporting them from Portland to the White Mountains via this direct, northern route, avoiding North Conway and more southerly White Mountains resorts. The old railroad station now houses a historical collection as does the neighboring library; the 1858 four-story Gorham House, while no longer a hotel, still marks the center of town.

Gorham remains a prime crossroads. Main Street is a brief stretch of Rt. 2, on its way west to Burlington,Vt., and east to Bangor, Me. Here it meets Rt. 16, running south through the White Mountains and north into the northern forest. The Appalachian Trail passes through too on its way from Georgia to Maine. This explains the choice of reasonably priced good places to eat in town as well as the unusual number of good, family-owned motels. Gorham's hidden gem is Exchange Street, an appealing mix of shops.

East of Gorham, Rt. 2 follows the Androscoggin River 10 miles to the Maine border, passing through an impressive corridor of birch trees that the town of Shelburne maintains as a memorial to their war dead. Across the river on the Maine line is Philbrook Farm, currently operated by the fourth and fifth generations of a family who responded to the state board of agriculture's 1860s pleas that local farmers take in guests.

West of Gorham, Rt. 2 traverses Randolph and Jefferson, century-old summer havens with exceptional panoramic views of the northern peaks of the Presidential Range. In Jefferson the memory of the Waumbec, one of the grandest of all the vanished White Mountain hotels, is preserved in its 18-hole golf course. The imposing 146-room Mountain View in nearby Whitefield has been luckier. After decades of decline and then closure, the 19th-century landmark is a grand resort once more. Its neighbor, the gracious old Spalding Inn, continues to thrive.

If Rt. 2 continued due west, it would run into Whitefield (Rt. 116 forms the link). Instead it angles north, following the Israel River to Lancaster seat of Coos (co-hos) County, an inviting North Country town with a classic village square surrounded by shops, homes, and churches. Note the Great North Woods Welcome Center just off Main Street.

Around the turn of the 20th century, when lumbering was at its peak in this area, it was Lancaster native John Wingate Weeks who sponsored the highly controversial bill resulting in the creation of the White Mountain National Forest. Weeks's former estate atop Mount Prospect, south of Lancaster, is now a state park, well worth a stop.

From Lancaster, Rt. 3 follows the Connecticut River north. The approach to Groveton is a tableau combining North Country history and the region's prime industry: Before the Wausau paper mill stands the Groveton covered bridge, and beside it is an old logging engine dating to the days when many miles of logging railroads webbed this area. Rising high in the background are the distinctive Percy Peaks, suggesting, perhaps, that the future of this area lies in its wilderness.

Turn east on Rt. 110 from Groveton and continue 6 miles to tiny Stark village. Here a covered bridge stands by the Union Church, both built in the 1850s. During World War II, German prisoners of war were brought to a camp here to work in the woods. To complete a loop through this region, continue east on Rt. 110, through White Mountain National Forest. It also accesses the 40,000 acres that now form Nash Stream State Forest.

GUIDANCE **Northern White Mountain Chamber of Commerce** (603-752-6060; 1-800-992-7480; www.northernwhitemtnchamber.org), 164 Main St., Box 298, Berlin 03570.

Great North Woods Gateway Welcome Center (603-788-3212; www .northerngatewaychamber.org), 25 Park St. (off Main Street between the Lancaster Motor Inn and Sullivan's Drugstore), Lancaster. Open Memorial Day weekend–Oct., 9–5; shorter hours in shoulder seasons. Off-season contact the Northern Gateway Chamber at 603-788-2530; 1-877-788-2530.

A New Hampshire Information Center, Rt. 2 in Shelburne, with restrooms and picnic tables, is open year-round, Mon.–Thu. 9 AM–8 PM, Fri. and Sat. 9–9.

WMNF Androscoggin Ranger Station (603-466-2713), 2.5 miles south of Gorham on Rt. 16. Open daily 8–4:30. Good for year-round outdoor recreation info.

Seasonal information booths can be found on the town common in **Gorham** (603-466-3103; www.gorhamnewhamsphire.com) and on the square in **Whitefield**.

GETTING THERE *By bus:* **Concord Trailways** (1-800-639-3317; www.concord trailways.com) provides scheduled service from Boston to Gorham and Berlin daily.

MEDICAL EMERGENCY **911** works throughout this area.

Androscoggin Valley Hospital (603-752-2200), 59 Page Hill Rd., Berlin.

Weeks Medical Center (603-788-4911), Middle St., Lancaster.

✳ To See

MOOSE The local "Moose Alley" is Rt. 16 north from Berlin and the length of Rt. 110. Organized **Moose Tours** (603-466-3103; 1-877-986-6673) run from Memorial Day weekend through foliage season. Nightly 2½-hour moose-viewing van tours depart at dusk from the Gorham information center at the town common, Gorham, and from the Northern Forest Heritage Park (603-752-7202), 962 Maine St., Gorham. Call for reservations.

FOR FAMILIES 🐾 **Santa's Village** (603-586-4445; www.santasvillage.com), Rt. 2, Jefferson. Open from 9:30 AM (closing time varies) Memorial Day weekend; weekends until mid-June; daily through Labor Day; weekends until Columbus Day; then weekends again, featuring Christmas lights, Thanksgiving–mid-Dec. Santa and his elves, along with the reindeer, are in residence, and you can ride the Yule Log Flume, the railroad, Ferris wheel, or roller coaster; watch the trained macaw show; see the animated Twelve Days of Christmas kiosk; and, of course, sit on Santa's lap. Food and gift shops. Admission includes unlimited rides and shows. $19.50 ages 4–adult, $17.50 seniors; ages 3 and under with an adult free as Santa's guest.

🐾 **Six Gun City** (603-586-4592; www.sixguncity.com), Rt. 2, Jefferson. Open Memorial Day weekend and weekends through mid-June, then daily through Labor Day; 9–6 in summer, 10–5 in the shoulder seasons. Over the past 50 years this family-run attraction has evolved from a few false-fronted buildings to a variety of cowboy skits and frontier shows, combined with 35 western town buildings; an outstanding horse-drawn-vehicle museum (preserving coaches from the area's many vanished inns); miniature burros and horses and other animals; 11 rides; and two waterslides plus a Gold Rush Express Ruanaway Roller Coaster. Food and gift shops. Admission includes unlimited rides and shows. $17.95 ages 4–adult; ages 3 and under free with an adult; $13.95 over age 65.

Berlin. Pick up the leaflet walking tour. As you may suspect, judging from the steep tilt of Berlin's streets, they were laid out on a map in Boston, with no thought to the actual topography. Highlights include the Holy Resurrection Church (20 Petrograd St.) on Russian Hill—which, unfortunately, is not open on a regular basis. Cathedral-sized St. Ann's Church, serving the city's dominant French Canadian population, crowns the city's central hill. The **Berlin Public Library** (603-752-5210), Main St., displays a collection of Native American stone implements, some dating back 7,000 years. Note the strong French Canadian influence here, because many residents are descended from Quebec immigrants who came to work in the woods and mills. French remains a second, and sometimes the primary, language of many people.

Weeks State Park (603-788-4004), Rt. 3, 2 miles south of Lancaster. This 420-acre mountaintop park is open year-round for outdoor recreation (the gated access road is open when either the park manager or fire lookout is on duty). In winter people walk, snowshoe, and ski the access road. The 3-mile Around the Loop Trail (rated "easy walking") is well maintained, and the 0.5-mile Nature Trail loop begins at the fire tower. The lodge/museum is usually open mid-June–Labor Day, Wed.–Sun., and weekends until Columbus Day. Not recommended for RVs, the narrow access road winds for 1.5 miles up the side of Mount Prospect, through stands of white birch and with two scenic lookouts overlooking the Connecticut River Valley. At the top is the summer home of Lancaster native John Sinclair Weeks (1860–1926) who, as a Massachusetts congressman, was responsible for the 1911 bill establishing the White Mountain National Forest and all national forests in the eastern United States.

Mount Propsect is only 2,059 feet in elevaion but, true to its name, offers a spectacular 360-degree view—from the Presidentials to the Green Mountains and the Kilkenny Range. Weeks's ancestors, who farmed on this mountain, maintained a bridle path to the summit in the early 19th century, which was improved and served a hotel built on the top of the mountain in 1883. The hotel closed, but local residents continued to come to the summit. When Weeks bought much of the mountain, he upgraded the road for motor traffic and built the 87-foot-high fieldstone Mount Prospect Tower. His fanciful 1912 summer home, Mount Prospect Lodge, is pink stucco and houses the Lancaster Historical Society's collection of local birds, as well as displays on the White Mountains and on his own fascinating life. On summer Thursdays, 7:30 PM lectures (free) are sponsored by Friends of the Park here in the Great Hall. Subjects range from nature to history, music, and art. Inquire about naturalist-led bird and flower walks.

COVERED BRIDGES Mechanic Street bridge, Lancaster, built in 1862, spans the Israel River east of Rt. 2/3.

The Mount Orne bridge crosses the Connecticut River to Lunenburg, Vt., 5 miles southwest of Lancaster off Rt. 135. Built in 1911, it's more than 266 feet long.

HISTORIC SITES AND MUSEUMS

Northern Forest Heritage Park (603-752-7202; www.northernforestheritage .org), 961 Main St., Berlin. Open May–Oct., Tue.–Sat. 11–6 and off-season for special events. Sited on 10 riverside acres on the northern fringe of the city, the park celebrates the story of the working forest and the multicultural heritage of the region. A three-story clapbard Brown Paper Company boardinghouse, built in 1853 to house incoming employees, serves as an interpretive center and Artisans Gift Shop. In the reconstructed logging camp across the street on the river, costumed interpreters reenact life in the woods circa the 1880s through the 1920s. This is also the departure point for narrated river tours (aboard a pontoon boat), describing the way the river was used to float logs down to the mills. Just above Berlin you see large pilings, once used to anchor booms that kept the logs moving swiftly to the mills. This is also the departure point for self-guided historical walking tours and for Moose Tours, with a pre-tour video on the habits and habitat of moose. The park's riverside amphitheater is the venue for a lively series of year-round events, including annual Great North Woods Lumberjack Championships in early October and periodic Lumberjack Dinners in the lumber camp cookhouse.

Northern Forest Heritage Park

The Groveton bridge, just south of the Wausau paper mill on Rt. 3, is open to foot traffic.

The Stark bridge, just off Rt. 110, east of Groveton.

HISTORICAL SOCIETIES **The Moffett House Museum** (603-752-4590), 119 High St., Berlin, open Tue.–Sat. noon–4 and Wed. evenings 6–8, is a Victorian house with exhibits on the history of Berlin and Coos County.

Gorham Historical Society (603-466-5338), Railroad St., Gorham. Open most days in July and August and weekends through foliage but dependent on volunteers. The Railroad Station Museum contains displays on local history and especially railroading, tourism, and logging, while a nearby boxcar offers more on local railroading in the area.

Jefferson Historical Society (603-586-7021), Rt. 2 east of the Waumbec Golf Course, open Memorial Day weekend–Columbus Day, Tue., Thu., and Sat., 11 AM–2 PM. Housed in St. John's Methodist Church, displays include photos of the more than a dozen summer hotels for which Jefferson was once known. The largest and most famous was the Waumbec.

Wilder-Holton House (603-788-3004), 226 Main St., Lancaster 03584. The first two-story house built in Coos County (1780), now the museum of the Lancaster Historical Society, summer Sundays but dependent on volunteers.

Groveton's Old Meeting House (603-636-2234), south of town on Rt. 3. This 1799 house with Northumberland Historical Society exhibits is open summer weekends but depends on volunteers.

THE RAILROAD STATION MUSEUM IN GORHAM

Christina Tree

SCENIC DRIVES Rt. 16 North from Berlin to Errol. The 31 miles between Berlin and Errol twist and turn with the Androscoggin River. Four miles north of Berlin look for riverside **Nansen Wayside Park** with several picnic sites and a boat launch ramp. Across the road you can see the 170-foot steel ski jump built by the Nansen Ski Club in 1936. For 50 years it was the largest ski jump in the East. North of Dummer, the **Thirteen-Mile Woods Scenic Area** is the most beautiful stretch of the river. At about the midpoint **Androscoggin Wayside Park** offers picnic tables on a bluff overlooking the river.

Pinkham B Road (formerly Dolly Copp Road) is a mostly unpaved wilderness road running from Dolly Copp Campground on Rt. 16, past the base of Mount Madison, to Rt. 2 at Randolph. Several hiking trails begin on this road. Not winter-maintained.

Jefferson Notch Road is an historic route beside the western edge of the Presidential Range. Not winter-maintained, this winding gravel road reaches the highest elevation point of any public through road in New Hampshire at Jefferson Notch (3,008 feet). Drive with care, because snow and mud remain until late in spring and ice returns early in fall; it is best used in summer. The Caps Ridge Trail, at the 7-mile point on Jefferson Notch, offers the shortest route to any of the Presidential Range peaks: 2.5 miles to Mount Jefferson. From the north, Jefferson Notch Road leaves Valley Road (which connects Routes 2 and 115) in Jefferson and runs south to the Cog Railway Base Station Road. At that intersection, paved Mount Clinton Road continues on to the Crawford House site on Rt. 302.

Shelburne's **North Road** is a winding country byway with great views of the Presidential Range across the Androscoggin River.

North Road connects Lancaster with Jefferson and offers country views of the mountains, especially Mount Cabot and the Kilkenny Wilderness Area east of Lancaster. Just south of Lancaster, **Lost Nation Road** departs from North Road and runs north to Groveton. According to one tradition, this area was named by a traveling preacher who, when he could get only one person to attend church, likened the local folks to the lost tribes of Israel. **Rt. 110 and Rt. 110A/110B** from Groveton to Milan and Berlin are picturesque in any season, but also try the secondary road that runs parallel to Rt. 110 north of the Upper Ammonoosuc River. It runs from Groveton village through Percy and Stark to rejoin Rt. 110 just west of the 110–110A intersection.

Pleasant Valley Road is a loop beginning in downtown Lancaster's Middle Street (there's only one way to turn). Take the first left (past the medical center) onto Grange Road. Follow Grange to a fork in the road and bear right onto Pleasant Valley to its junction with Garland Road. Maps are available at Lancaster Town Hall (603-788-3391).

In Vermont. From South Lancaster you might cross the Connecticut on the covered bridge (Rt. 135) into Lunenburg, a beautiful village with views east to the mountains.

Also see **Weeks State Park** under *Historic Sites and Museums*.

✳ To Do

BIKING **Moriah Sports** in Gorham sells and services bikes and steers patrons toward innumerable trails and loops. **Moose Brook State Park** in Gorham and the **Nansen Ski Club Trails** north of Berlin are popular with mountain bikers.

BIRDING **Pondicherry National Wildlife Preserve** (see *Green Space*) in Whitefield with its Big and Little Cherry Ponds and extensive wetland is well known to New England birders. More than 234 species have been recorded here. It's also a haven for buterflies, dragonflies, and moose. The adjacent grasslands around the Whitefield Airport are also a prime birding area.

Also see **Weeks State Park** under *To See*.

CANOEING AND KAYAKING The **Androscoggin River** north of Berlin is one of the state's most popular canoeing waters. Paddlers are advised to check with the *AMC River Guide* or *Canoe Camping Vermont and New Hampshire Rivers* (Countryman Press). Pick up the AMC's *Androcoggin River Map and Guide*. East of Gorham you can paddle flatwater to Bethel and on to Rumford. See the next chapter for rentals in Errol. **Wild River Adventures** (207-824-2608), based in Bethel, Me., rents canoes and kayaks, also offers shuttle and guide service, on the Androscoggin in Gorham.

The **Connecticut River** from the Columbia bridge south to Moore Dam is beautiful paddling with many put-in places. See *Connecticut River* in "What's Where."

CAR RACING **Riverside Speedway** (603-636-2005), Brown Rd. (just off Rt. 3), Groveton. Phone for the schedule of weekend races. Sited on flats along the Connecticut River with 20 acres of field (camping permitted) and a 0.25-mile track with seating for 3,500 on the front stretch and another 5,000 in the pit area.

FISHING The Androscoggin River is a source of pickerel, bass, trout, and salmon. New Hampshire fishing licenses, required for adults, are sold at many stores throughout the region. Another recommended fishing spot is South Pond Recreation Area, off Rt. 110, West Milan. It has a picnic and swimming area. The Peabody River and Moose Brook are also frequented by anglers. See Great Glen Outdoor Center in "Jackson and Pinkham Notch" for fly-fishing programs. Also see the next chapter.

GOLF **Androscoggin Valley Country Club** (603-466-9468; pro shop 603-466-2641), Rt. 2, Gorham. Eighteen holes, bar and food service.

The Waumbec Club (603-586-7777), Rt. 2, Jefferson, is an 18-hole course overlooking the Presidential Range, built to serve one of the region's largest 19th-century resort hotels. Food and beverages, also tennis, are available.

Mountain View Country Club (603-837-2100), Whitefield. Nine-hole course with a clubhouse offering tennis courts, a pool, and saunas, operated by the

Mountain View. On a clear day the summit of Mount Washington seems but a long 2-iron shot away. Collared shirts are required.

HIKING *Note:* This area offers some of New England's most spectacular hikes. Indeed, hikers represent a larger percentage of visitors here than in the Mount Washington Valley. In Gorham, Moriah Sports and several lodging places cater to through-hikers on the Appalachian Trail (it crosses Rt. 2 here). The following hikes just begin to suggest the quantity and quality of hikes accessible from this area in the Presidentials, as well as in the Moriah, Mahoosuc, and Kilkenny Ranges.

Presidential Range. The **Appalachian Mountain Club's Pinkham Notch Visitors Center** (603-466-2727; www.outdoors.org), 9 miles south of Gorham on Rt. 16, offers an overview of what's available on these northern and western slopes of the Presidential Range. If you're not familiar with the area, it's the place to begin. Since 1888 the AMC has also operated Madison Spring Hut, a full-service, summer-only facility at tree line between Mount Madison and mile-high Mount Adams.

For any White Mountain hiking, consult the *AMC White Mountain Guide* for details about trailheads, routes, distances, hiking time estimates, and special information. (Also see *50 Hikes in the White Mountains* or *50 More Hikes in New Hampshire*, both by Daniel Doan and Ruth Doan MacDougall, Countryman Press.) A map is vital here, since myriad trails interconnect on the northern side of the rugged Presidential Range peaks. There are three parking areas on Rt. 2 and another on Pinkham B (Dolly Copp) Road, connecting Routes 2 and 16, which are at the most popular trailheads for climbing the northern peaks of Madison, Adams, and Jefferson. Most of these trails lead above tree line and should be attempted only by properly equipped hikers. Winter weather conditions can occur above tree line any month of the year. Most of the trails to the summits are 4 to 5 miles in length and require 4 or 5 hours to reach the top. The lower portions of the trails pass through wooded areas along streams and are suitable for short walks.

Randolph Mountain Club (www.randolphmountainclub.org) maintains a 100-mile network of hiking trails, along with two cabins and two shelters for hikers high on the side of Mount Adams. Nominal overnight fees are charged. The cabins have cooking utensils and gas stoves in July and August, but hikers must supply their own food and bedding.

Pine Mountain is a less rigorous hike, yielding fine views of the Presidential Range. Off Pinkham B (Dolly Copp) Road (2.4 miles from Rt. 2 or 1.9 miles from Rt. 16), a private road that is open only to public foot traffic leads to the summit and connects to a loop trail. Estimated hiking time is 2 hours for a 3.4-mile round trip.

Mahoosuc Range. Stretching from Shelburne northeast to Grafton Notch in Maine, this rugged range offers some of the most difficult hiking on the Appalachian Trail (the mountains are not high, but the trails steeply ascend and descend the peaks). Many of the peaks—as well as rocky Mahoosuc Notch, where the ice stays in crevasses year-round—are most easily reached by Success

Pond Road, a logging road (sometimes rough) on the northern side of the mountains. In the middle of Berlin, turn east at the traffic lights across the river, through the log yard of the paper company, then travel up to 14 miles along the road to get to the various trailheads. Watch for logging trucks on this road. (See the *AMC White Mountain Guide* for hiking details.)

Waumbec and Starr King Mountains, north of Rt. 2 in Jefferson, are popular hikes. The climb is 3.8 miles and requires just over 3 hours to the top.

The Kilkenny District of the White Mountain National Forest is popular although the trails are not as well marked as in the mountains farther south. The Percy Peaks (2 miles, 2 hours), north of Stark, offer views across the North Country and are not likely to be crowded with other hikers. Check the *AMC White Mountain Guide* for directions to Cabot and the Percy peaks.

The Cohos Trail (www.cohostrail.org) is described in the *The Cohos Trail* by Kim Nilsen (Nicolin Fields Publishing). This new trail links existing hiking paths, railbeds, and logging roads to form a continuous trail, accessible at many points along the way, running north–south through the region beginning in Bartlett and ending at the Canadian border in Pittsburg.

SWIMMING 🐾 ♿ **Forest Lake State Beach, Dalton** (603-837-9150), on a side road off Rt. 116 south of Whitefield. Open weekends from Memorial Day, daily late June–Labor Day. One of the original state parks dating from 1935, this 50-acre site has a 200-foot-long swimming beach, a bathhouse, and picnic sites. Handicapped accessible. Free.

Libby Pool, Rt. 16, Gorham. Facilities include a bathhouse, slide, and floats, but no lifeguards. Nominal admission.

South Pond Recreation Area in the White Mountain National Forest, off Rt. 110, West Milan. Open mid-June–Labor Day, this spot offers a long, sandy beach and picnic area. Fee.

❄ Winter Sports

CROSS-COUNTRY SKIING The **Mountain View Grand Resort** (www.mountain viewgrand.com) in Whitefield offers rentals and 27 kilometers of trails for both cross-country and snowshoeing. See *Lodging*.

The **Nansen Ski Club** (603-752-7968; 603-752-1650), arguably the country's oldest ski club (in 1872, when it was founded, you had to speak Norwegian to belong), maintains 23 miles of trail north of Berlin, on the far side of the Androscoggin River from Rt. 16. Trail maps are available at the clubhouse (with a woodstove) on the Success Loop Road off the East Milan Road (look for Nansen Ski Club signs on Rt. 16).

Cross-country ski **rentals** are available at **Great Glen Trails Outdoor Center** (www.greatglentrails.com; see the "Jackson and Pinkham Notch" section), which also offers 25 kilometers of trails groomed for traditional stride and skating (8 miles south of Gorham), and at **Bretton Woods Nordic Ski Center** (www.mt .washington.com; see "Crawford Notch and Bretton Woods") with its outstanding 100-kilometer network.

SNOWSHOEING **Moriah Sports** in Gorham (see *Selective Shopping*) rents as well as sells snowshoes, publishes a guide to local trails, and offers occasional evening tours. *Snowshoe Hikes in the White Mountains* by Stephen Smith details excellent hikes in this area.

SNOWMOBILING Hundreds of miles of trails web this area, connecting with Vermont and Maine systems. New Hampshire registration is necessary (call Fish and Game: 603-271-3422). Snowmobile rentals are available at **Seven Dwarfs Motel** (603-846-5535) in Twin Mountain and at **Jefferson Notch Snowmobile Rentals** (800-345-3833) in Randolph. On the **New Hampshire Snowmobile Association** (603-224-8906) web site (www. NHSA.com), click on Coos County for the contact info for local clubs: the **Lancaster Snowdrifters**, **Presidential Range Riders** (Gorham), **White Mountain Ridge Runners** (Berlin), and **Whitefield Sno-kings**.

The nearest **alpine skiing** is less than 12 miles south of Gorham at **Wildcat Mountain** (www. skiwildcat.com; see "Jackson and Pinkham Notch") and at **Bretton Woods** (www.mtwashington.com; see "Crawford Notch and Bretton Woods"), 4 miles south of Twin Mountain.

✳ Green Space

White Mountain National Forest. For information about the sections in the Milan, Berlin, Gorham, and Shelburne areas, check with the WMNF Androscoggin Visitors Ranger Station south of Gorham on Rt. 16 (see *Guidance*).

Nash Stream State Forest (603-788-4157) is a 40,000-acre, undeveloped wilderness located in the towns of Odell, Stratford, Columbia, and Stark. Jointly managed by conservation groups and the Forest Service, it was rescued from sale to a developer back in 1988. It is open to day use for mountain biking, hunting, fishing, hiking, cross-country skiing, and snowmobiling. There is a seasonal, maintained gravel road off Rt. 110 (4 miles west of Groveton, turn north off Emerson Road).

Pondicherry National Wildlife Preserve, Airport Rd., Whitefield. This exceptional 5,500-acre preserve includes bogs (traversed by a 1.5-mile trail), fens, marshes, and Big and Little Cherry Ponds as well as streams and boreal forest. A mecca for bird-watchers, it's said to offer the greatest diversity for breeding birds in New Hampshire. Foot, canoe, and wheelchair access are planned for 2006.

Also see **Weeks State Park** under *To See* and see Milan Hill and Mollidgewock State Parks under *Campgrounds*.

✳ Lodging

RESORTS

∞ ✿ ♪ **The Spalding Inn** (603-837-2572; 1-800-368-8439; www.spalding inn.com), 199 Mountain View Rd., Whitefield 03598. Open mid-June–mid-Oct. This century-old estate—a seasonal resort since the 1920s—was once known for its lawn bowling (it hosted the U.S. singles and doubles championships). While lawn bowling is still an option, other activities include tennis, golf (next door at the

⊙ ♂ ⅃ **The Mountain View, Grand Resort and Spa** (603-837-2100; 1-866-484-3843; www.mountainviewgrand.com), Mountain View Rd., Whitefield 03598. Built originally in 1865, this was a 200-room wooden summer hotel when it closed in 1986, seemingly forever. Since 2002 when it reopened after a $20 million makeover, the resort has changed hands once more, this time expanding its acreage from 400 to its original 1,800-acre holdings. What has never changed is the spectacular panorama, which bursts on you only as you round the last curve of its driveway. The Presidentials and seemingly all of the White Mountains appear to march across the horizon. The Mountain View now offers 145 rooms with private bath, featherbed, mahogany furniture, phone with Internet hookup, individual temperature control, and oversized TV. Amenities include twice-daily housekeeping and 24-hour room service. A spa now occupies the Italian Revival–style central tower. Amenities include a 9-hole golf course (there are plans to expand to 18 holes) with a clubhouse and elaborate landscaping, including waterfalls and flower gardens; an Olympic-sized outdoor pool at the clubhouse and indoor pool in the hotel; a fitness center; and tennis. In winter there's ample cross-country skiing and connecting trails to interstate snowmmobile corridors (snowmobile rentals). Dining options range from the informal **Clubhouse Café and Grill** and **Stage Coach Tavern** to fine dining in The Maples (see *Dining Out*). Rates range through no less than seven categories of rooms, from $149–299 (low season) to $199–379 (high EP). Inquire about package plans.

THE MOUNTAIN VIEW, GRAND RESORT AND SPA

Christina Tree

Mountain View Country Club), shuffleboard, volleyball, and swimming. The rambling, brown-shingled inn offers 24 rooms (all with private bath); there are also 6 family suites (2 adjoining rooms) plus 6 attractive "guest houses" (pets permitted) with 1 to 4 bedrooms, all with private bath and kitchen or kitchenette, fireplace, and dining/living area. There are also 12 rooms, including 3 that adjoin, in the remodeled Carriage House. All rooms have a phone and are nicely furnished. Common space includes a library, sunroom (with TV and puzzle table), and children's playroom as well as the broad rocker-lined front porch with its views of the Presidential Mountains. A full breakfast and candlelight dinner are served daily (see *Dining Out*). B&B $145–159 for rooms, $129–545 for the guest houses, which innkeepers Walter and Dona Loope are currently condoing and working with a developer on plans for housing lots. Special family plan offers reasonable rates for an adjoining room and children's meals. Look for a variety of theater and golf packages.

Also see **The Balsams** in the next chapter.

BED & BREAKFASTS

Listed east to west along Rt. 2.

The Wildberry Inn (603-466-5049; www.thewildberryinn.com), 592 Rt. 2, Shelburne 03581. Innkeepers and longtime local residents Bob and Jackie Corrigan share their 1877 home and knowledge of this glorious area. The Appalachian Trail crosses their wooded back lot, beyond the stream and landscaped pond (with chairs to sit and read in). The Androscoggin River is across the road, and a canoe or kayak can be secured. The

Corrigans offer shuttle service to cross-country ski trails as well as the river. Snowmobile Trail 19 passes by the property. The house has two attractive rooms with private bath, and a portion of the 125-year-old barn has been converted into a handsome two-story suite, with cooking facilities and room for up to four people. A Palladian window offers views of the stream and pond. $89–135 per couple includes a hearty breakfast with the wildberry theme a main ingredient; from $79 off-season.

✪ **Mt. Washington B&B** (603-466-2669; 1-877-466-2399; www.mt washingtonbb.com), 421 Rt. 2, Shelburne 03581. At this classic 19th-century clapboard inn Mary Ann Mayer offers a hearty welcome and a choice of two-room suites with whirlpool tub, along with several rooms with private bath and family suites (well separated from the romantically themed rooms). The decor is a mix of antique and reproduction furniture. Rates, which include breakfast, range $130–185 for the suites, $90–130 for the rooms, a very full breakfast included.

◎ ✪ **The Jefferson Inn** (603-586-7998; 1-800-729-7908; www.jefferson inn.com), Rt. 2 (at the junction with Rt. 115A), Jefferson 03583. Open year-round. Mark and Cindy Robert and Bette Bovio have reinvigorated this fine, century-old inn with its wraparound porch and view of the Presidential Range. The 11 rooms, all with private bath, include bright, inviting doubles and family suites accommodating up to five. The Monticello is the turret room with a four-poster. Santa's Village is just down the road. A trail for nearby Starr King and Waumbec mountains leaves from the inn, which is a favorite with hikers

🏵 🏠 ✍ **Philbrook Farm Inn** (603-466-3831; www.philbrookfarminn.com), North Rd., Shelburne 03581. Open May–Oct. and Dec. 26–Mar. Back in 1861, when Susannah and Harvey Philbrook began hosting summer boarders, "guest farms" were as common as B&Bs are today. Sited as it is above a floodplain on the Androscoggin River and circled by magnificent mountains, this one prospered.

"Every generation has added a piece," notes Connie Philbrook, a member of the fourth generation to operate the inn that's now three stories high and rambles far from its original 1830s core. In the 1890s several summer "cottages" were built, each large enough to sleep a family of eight. Resort amenities now include an outdoor pool and lawn games. In winter there's snowshoeing and cross-country skiing.

While it's definitely not for the Jacuzzi set, this 18-room inn offers far more than firm mattresses and private baths. Guest rooms are comfortable as well as gracefully old-fashioned, curtained in organdy, papered in delicate flowers, and furnished with the kind of hand-me-downs for which many innkeepers would kill. The seasonal cottages range from one room to up to five bedrooms. All have a fireplace and living room.

Parlors meander on and on, and everything in them has a story. Standing lamps in the living room turn out to be muskets (one from the War of 1812, the other from the Civil War); a closet is stuffed with jigsaw puzzles cut by grandfather Augustus. Connie recounts how people laughed when her parents paneled the large, handsome dining room in pine, considered junk wood at the time. Your hosts are Connie Leger and her sister Nancy Philbrook, along with Connie's children Ann Leger and Larry Leger. This is said to be the country's oldest inn continuously operated by the same family.

Dinner is served by reservation (6:30–7:30 PM). It's hearty New England fare, usually soup and a roast with vegetables plus a relish tray (BYOB). Breakfast is memorable for the littlest, lightest of doughnuts, baked that morning by Nancy.

and bikers. Golfers will enjoy the 18-hole Waumbec Country Club course, said to be the oldest in the state. Just across the street is a wonderful old spring-fed swimming pool with a beach for children. Rates are $90–190 (high end are suites), including afternoon tea and a full breakfast.

🏠 ✍ **Applebrook B&B** (603-586-7713; 1-800-545-6504; www.applebrook.com), Rt. 115A, Box 178, Jefferson 03583. Open year-round, this rambling, pink, Victorian inn is an informal, shoes-off kind of place that caters to groups. On our last visit it was a group of guitarists and banjo

Although no longer a working farm, the property is still 1,000 acres of fields and wooded trails, surrounded by White Mountain National Forest. A time warp outside as well as in, it's a difficult place to leave.

MAP rates include a full breakfast and single-entrée New England dinner with breads and pastries baked daily. Rates per couple are $130–150 MAP, $120–140 B&B; housekeeping cottages for up to eight people are $800 a week. Single rates also available. Pets are accepted in the cottages.

HOLIDAY INN, A WATERCOLOR PAINTING OF THE PHILBROOK FARM INN BY OWNER ANN LEGER, 1986

players, but more often there are bicyclists, hikers, or skiers, and the occasional individual guest. Children are welcome. There are 12 rooms, all but the 4 on the third floor with private bath. Two suites have their own hot tub. There's an outdoor hot tub and cross-country/walking trails nearby. A full breakfast is included, and dinner is available to groups by advance reservation. The new innkeepers are Thomas and Joy McCorkhill; rates: $60 (shared bath) to $150 for the Sunset Room and Nellie's Nook, both with spas and breakfast brought to your room if desired.

Elsewhere

🐾 **Stark Village Inn** (603-636-2644), just across the covered bridge off Rt. 110, west of Milan or east of Groteton (mail: 16 Northside Rd., Stark 03582). Open summers, weekends, and vacation weeks. Beautifully positioned beside a church and a covered bridge spanning the Upper Ammonoosuc River, this restored farmhouse is furnished with antiques and comfortable furniture. It offers three rooms, two with double beds and all with private bath. A long, rambling living room overlooks the river and is filled with books and magazines. Nearby you'll find trout fishing, hiking, bicycling, cross-country skiing, skating on the river, and snowmobiling. For $50 a double room, $30 a single (tax included!), innkeeper Nancy Spaulding throws in a full breakfast.

MOTELS

In Gorham

Gorham, a former rail junction with several large hotels, is now a major highway junction with, we are told, some 600 motel rooms. We've checked out the following:

🐾 ✂ **Town and Country Motor Inn** (603-466-3315; 1-800-325-4386; www.townandcountryinn.com), 120 Rt. 2 (P.O. Box 20), Gorham 03581. East of town on the verge of the Shelburne Birches, the T&C offers 160 air-conditioned rooms with a restaurant, health club, indoor pool, whirlpool, and steam bath. It's been owned since 1956 by the Labnon family and is a favorite meeting place for area residents as well as a way stop for families and groups. Rack rates are $64–90 per couple; inquire about golf, attractions, ski, and many more packages.

Royalty Inn (603-466-3312;1-800-43-RELAX; www.royaltyinn.com), 130 Main St., Gorham 03581. Family-geared and family-run since 1956 by three generations of the King family, this middle-of-town motor inn offers indoor and outdoor heated pools, Jacuzzi and sauna, a fitness center, racquetball and basketball courts, a game room, and a restaurant. There are also 90 spacious guest rooms, some with kitchenette. $62–119, less off-season. Inquire about packages.

🐾 **Colonial Fort Inn** (603-466-2732; 1-800-470-4224; www.hikersparadise .com), 370 Main St., Gorham 03581. A motel with standard motel rooms, phone, TV, and fridge; several with whirlpool tub. Full-service restaurant, laundry room, and pool as well. Regular units are $39–95 depending on size and season. The facility also caters to groups and hikers with three apartments with kitchen: $17 per person.

In Lancaster

🐾 ✂ ♿ **Coos Motor Inn** (603-788-3079; www.coosmotorinn.com), junction of Rts. 2 and 3, also on Snowmobile Trail 5 and Main St., Lancaster 03584. An attractive 41-room motel in the middle of town. Amenities include a 24-hour Laundromat and continental breakfast; air-conditioned rooms with two double beds, phone, and cable TV. $49–79.

🐾 ✂ ♿ **Cabot Motor Inn & Restaurant** (603-788-3346; www.cabot motorinn.com), 200 Portland St., Lancaster 03584. Located a mile east of downtown Lancaster on Rt. 2, a 55-room motor inn with an indoor pool, sauna, Jacuzzi, game and fitness room, and locally popular restaurant. All rooms have phone and cable TV. $59 in the older motel building across the road, $90 in the newer building.

☙ ♿ **Lancaster Motor Inn** (603-788-4921; 1-800-834-3244; www.lancastermotorinn.com), 112 Main St., Lancaster 03584. You'll find 33 clean, comfortable, middle-of-town rooms, along with some efficiency and family units with sleep sofas. All have TV, VCR, free videos, Internet access, and phone; a continental breakfast is served. The motel caters to snow-mobilers in winter. $69 per couple, $55 single; children free under age 16, extra adult $5.

CAMPGROUNDS **White Mountains National Forest Dolly Copp Campground** (603-466-3984, July–Labor Day), off Rt. 16, just south of Gorham 03581. Open mid-May–mid-Oct. With 176 sites, many of them available through a toll-free reservation system (1-877-444-6777), this is one of the most popular camp-grounds in the WMNF, attracting reg-ulars year after year. The reservation service operates Mar.–Sep. (Mon.–Fri. noon–9, weekends noon–5). Reserva-tions are accepted, but must be made at least 7 days before arrival.

Two private campgrounds that come highly recommended are **Timber-land Camping Area** (603-466-3872) and **White Birches Mountain Camping Park** (603-466-2022), both on Rt. 2 in Shelburne.

For details on reserving sites at the the following state-operated camp-grounds, see www.nhparks.state.nh.us:

Milan Hill State Park, Rt. 110B (off Rt. 16), Milan. A small park with 24 primitive camping sites, picnic tables, and a playground. A fire tower atop the 1,737-foot-high hill offers sweep-ing views of the North Country and into Canada. Camping and day-use fees charged.

♂ **Mollidgewock State Park** (603-482-3373), Errol 03579. Open mid-May–Columbus Day. Located about 3 miles south of Errol village, in the Thirteen-Mile Woods Scenic Area. There are 42 somewhat primitive tent sites with picnic tables, fireplaces, water, and outhouses, but they are beside the river and perfect for fish-ing and canoeing. For reservations, call 603-271-3628.

☙ ♂ **Moose Brook State Park** (603-466-3860), Jimtown Rd., off Rt. 2, Gorham. Mid-May–mid-Oct. This small park has a large outdoor pool (known for its cold water), a small beach, 58 tent sites, a store, and showers. Camping and day-use fees charged.

In Vermont
Maidstone State Park (802-676-3930) in Brunswick. Open daily Memorial Day–Labor Day. Easily accessible from North Stratford. Five miles south of Bloomfield on Rt. 102, then 5 miles on a dirt road, this is a forest of maple, beech, and hemlock around a large lake, with a beach, pic-nic area, rental boats, picnic shelter, hiking trails, and 83 campsites, including 37 lean-tos.

✷ **Where to Eat**

DINING OUT **Libby's Bistro** (603-466-5330), 111 Main St., Gorham. Open Wed.–Sat. 5:30–9 PM. Closed Apr. and Nov. Reservations recom-mended. Liz Jackson's appealing bistro, a series of warmly lit rooms in the vintage-1902 former Gorham Sav-ings Bank, draws patrons from restau-rant-rich North Conway (20 miles south) as well as from throughout the North Country. The half a dozen entrées change frequently, but you might begin with a creamy mushroom soup, garnished with truffles from Umbria, and move on to moist, seared ahi tuna, crusted with sesame and served with wasabi-laced mashed potatoes and crispy, light vegetables tempura. Don't make the mistake we did of dipping too heavily into the tapenade. Leave room for the restaurant's signature flourless baby chocolate cake. Jackson's skills were honed in cooking school and prepping for Julia Child's television shows, but she likes to point out that she is cooking just down the street from a diner her grandmother opened during the Depression. Her husband, Steve, shares both the cooking and hosting. Entrées $17–23.

The Spalding Inn (603-837-2572), Mountain View Rd., Whitefield. Open mid-June–mid-Oct. Reservations. The menu changes daily. The atmosphere is causal fine dining with a wide choice of entrées, vegetarian as well as seafood, pork, beef, and chicken. Entrées $15.95–23.95.

The Maples at the Mountain View (603-837-2100), Mountain View Rd.,

THE MOONBEAM CAFÉ ON RAILROAD ST. IN GORHAM

Christina Tree

Whitefield. Ownership has changed recently, and the resort's formal dining room (formerly Juliet's) is now The Maples. It's divided into three elegant spaces with windows overlooking the mountains. At this writing chefs have been changing frequently but the latest reviews are rave.

New England Cattle Company Steakhouse (603-788-4555), 24 Main St. (Rt. 3), Lancaster. In summer open Tue.–Sun. for lunch and dinner year-round; in winter lunch is served only on weekends. This is a recent, welcome addition to the area's dining options: a sleekly decorated restaurant with a limited but tempting menu. Dinner entrée choices include fish, pork, and chicken, but the specialty is steak: The menu might include an 18-ounce Delmonico and tenderloin medallions. Entrées $15–24.

EATING OUT

In Gorham
🍴 **Wilfred's** (603-466-2380), 117 Main St. Open daily except Wed. for lunch and dinner until 9 PM. Turkey in every conceivable form is what the Piattonis have been known for through many years. Our turkey potpie turned out to be better than in a pot: a thick, tender mix of turkey, stuffing, and veggies with a light popover-type pastry on the side. There are other options on the menu. The **News Room Pub** in back is a local gathering spot.

The Moonbeam Cafe (603-466-5549), 19 Exchange St. Open Wed.–Sun., 7 AM–2 PM. The black bean and pumpkin soup is so delicious that the recipe is a secret. Breads (celery, onion, anadama, and the like) are baked daily, sandwiches tend to the unusual (like Oriental chicken salad with walnuts), and breakfast, featuring crêpes, is served all day. This is an attractive storefront space with pressed-tin walls and a mirrored credenza left over from its days as a barbershop. This is not a quick in-and-out place.

Mr. Pizza Family Restaurant & Cracker Jack Lounge (603-466-5573), Rt. 2. Open until 9 PM. This looks and feel like a chain but it isn't and, judging from the number of vehicles always parked here, it's the local hot spot. The full menu ranges from burgers, salads, and pizza to surf and turf with a choice of salads; cocktails served.

The Willow Tree Apothecary and Health Food Store (603-466-2503), 10 Exchange St., offers "healing soups" and organic sandwich wraps to go. Chef-owner Tuesday Willow is a trained herbalist, and the store also stocks herbs, spices, produce, teas, and vitamins.

The Northland Dairy Bar and Restaurant (603-752-6210), 1826 Riverside Dr., Berlin (Rt. 16, just north of the city). Popular with canoeists and hikers, this eatery features fresh seafood, sandwiches, and its own fresh-made pies and ice cream.

⚲ Grandma's Kitchen Restaurant (603-837-2527), Rt. 3 north of Whitefield. Open 6 AM–9 PM weekdays, 7–9 weekends. One of the best way stops along the entire length of Rt. 3: a screened porch, a U-shaped counter, immaculate, good for homemade chowders, open-faced sandwiches, and Grape-Nut pudding. Breakfast (served all day) includes superb omelets and steak or corned beef hash with eggs on toast. Dinner options include liver and onions and roast turkey with all the fixings ($8.95).

In Jefferson/Lancaster

Glendon's Chowder House in the Lancaster Motor Inn (603-788-4921; www.lancastermotorinn.com), 112 Main St. Hours are flaky but the seafood is excellent.

Lancaster SS Restaurant (603-788-2802), 70 Main St. Casual, family atmosphere with wooden booths, American and Chinese food. An upstairs pub has pool tables and entertainment.

Cabot Inn (603-788-3346), in the motel by that name, Rt. 2 west of downtown. Open 5 AM–8 PM. All the basics.

Common Ground Café (603-788-3773), 55 Main St. Open Sun.–Thu. 9 AM–8 PM, Fri. 9–3, closed Sat. An adjunct to Simon the Tanner sports and shoe store operated by the Twelve Tribes. Good for soups, sandwiches, and baked goods.

Water Wheel (603-586-4313), Rt. 2, Jefferson. Open daily June–Oct. 6–2, otherwise closed Tue. and Wed. Breakfast and lunch.

✳ Entertainment

Weathervane Theatre (603-837-9322; www.weathervanetheatre.org), Rt. 3, Whitefield. Open July and August. A widely respected repertory theater (since 1966), housed in a converted barn featuring old favorites, musicals, comedies, and mysteries.

St. Kieran's Community Center for the Arts (603-752-1820; 603-752-2880), 162 Madison Ave., Berlin. Plays, concerts, and other live entertainment.

Royal Cinema I & II, Green Square, Rt. 16 north of downtown Berlin, shows first-run films.

Rialto Theater (603-788-2211), 80 Main St., Lancaster. Recently restored and reopened, a classic old downtown theater showing first-run films.

✳ Selective Shopping

ANTIQUES Israel River Trading Post (603-788-2880), 69 Main St., Lancaster. Open Tue.–Sat. 10–4. Antiques, auctions.

Potato Barn Antiques (603-636-2611), Rt. 3, Northumberland, 4.5 miles north of the Lancaster Fairgrounds. Billed as the largest group shop in northern New Hampshire: two floors of vintage clothing, costume jewelry, china, and paper.

MAPLE PRODUCERS Bisson's Maple Sugar House (603-752-1298), 61 Cates Hill, accessible both from Gorham and Berlin. High on Cates Hill with panoramic views, this has been a family-operated business since 1921. The wood-fired evaporator is also used to make maple taffy, butter, and sugar.

Fuller's Sugarhouse (603-788-2719), 267 Main St., Lancaster. Open year-round. Dave and Patti Fuller operate a sugarhouse and country store selling maple products and local specialty items.

GORHAM HARDWARE & SPORTS CENTER

Christina Tree

OUTDOOR EQUIPMENT AND SPORTS STORES Moriah Sports (603-466-5050), 101 Main St., Gorham. Open daily July 4–Labor Day, otherwise closed Sun. and Mon. A popular, long-established stop on the AT as well as with savvy hikers in general. Mike Miccuci stocks a wide selection of backpacks, outdoor clothing, and gear; he sells and services bikes and offers maps and info. His selection of snowshoes (which he also rents) is wide. He publishes a brochure guide to local hiking and snowshoeing trails and offers occasional nighttime snowshoe treks. Cross-country skis are also sold. Check out the bargain basement.

Gorham Hardware & Sports Center (603-466-2312). A big, old-fashioned hardware store with plenty of things you may have forgotten if you are camping. Also a full line of sports equipment.

Emerson Outdoor Outfitters (603-636-2211; 1-866-636-2211; www.emersonoutdoors.com), Rt. 3, Groveton. Open daily 9–6, Sat. until 9. A vast, recently expanded sporting store specializing in hunting (archery, guns, and more), fishing, snowmobiling equipment, and outdoor gear as well as hardware.

Also see LL Cote (www.llcote.com), cenral supply for the Lake Umbagog area, under *Selective Shopping* in the next chapter.

OTHER Old Mill Studio (603-837-8778), on the common, Whitefield. Open Fri.–Sun. 11–5, longer in summer. Tucked into a corner of the common overlooking the river, representing well over 100 local artists, also offering classes.

Wonderland Book Store (603-466-2123), 10-A Exchange St., Gorham.

Open Mon.–Fri. 9:30–5:30, Sat. 10–4, Sun. by chance. Heather Reid's first-rate independent bookstore is a mecca for area residents and regulars. Hiking books and maps are carried; there's an entire children's room.

Artisans Store at the Northern Forest Heritage Park (603-752-7202), 961 Main St., Berlin. Open May–Oct., Tue.–Sat. 11–6 and off-season for special events. This adjunct to the museum (see *To See*) is a wide but selective representation of artisans and craftspeople of the North Country.

Gateway Gallery and Gifts (603-466-9900), 11 Exchange St., Gorham. A mix of vintage glassware and jewelry, art, and photographs by owner Carla Lapierre.

Simon the Tanner (603-788-3773), 55 Main St., Lancaster. Open the same hours as the Common Ground Café (see *Eating Out*), which it adjoins. An extensive and sophisticated shoe and casual clothing store operated by the Twelve Tribes.

Christina Tree

GATEWAY GALLERY AND GIFTS IN GORHAM

✳ Special Events

January: **Winterfest** in Berlin / Gorham. Winter activities including children's sports, a Loggers' Dinner at the Northern Forest Heritage Park, sleigh rides and more.

Third weekend in March: **New Hampshire Maple Weekend**. The area's sugar shacks hold open house.

Late May–early October: **Moose Tours** daily from Gorham Information Booth and from the Northern Forest Heritage Park in Berlin. **River Heritage Boat Tours**, daily (weather permitting) from the Heritage Park.

Last Sunday in June: **Old Time Fiddlers' Contest** (603-636-2106), Whit-

comb Field, Stark. Bring a picnic lunch and a blanket or lawn chairs, and enjoy the music of dozens of fiddlers. Food available. Admission fee.

July–August: **Weathervane Theatre** in Whitefield.

June–October: **Lancaster Farmers Market**, Saturday 9–noon. Local and organic produce, cheese, flowers, and much more.

July: **Androscoggin Source to Sea**—6 days of canoeing, kayaking, and related events.

Early August: **Old Home Days** in the tiny towns of Milan and Stewartstown.

❧ Labor Day weekend: The **Lancaster Fair** is a real old-fashioned country fair. A large midway, food, and thrill rides plus 4-H animal judging, Grange exhibits, displays of vegetables and handcrafts, and ox and horse pulling. Admission fee; children under 12 free.

Late September: **Great North Woods Lumberjack Championships**, Northern Forest Heritage Park, Berlin.

THE NORTH COUNTRY AND LAKE UMBAGOG AREA

INCLUDING CONNECTICUT LAKES, DIXVILLE NOTCH, COLEBROOK, AND ERROL

Two destinations draw travelers to the top of New Hampshire: the Connecticut Lakes in Pittsburg and the Balsams in Dixville Notch.

In all there are four Connecticut Lakes, and below them Lake Frances (created in the 1930s). Each is successively larger and lower in elevation and connected by the nascent, stream-sized Connecticut River as it begins its journey down the length of New England. The lakes are strung along some 22 miles of Rt. 3 between the village of Pittsburg and the Canadian border, the stem of a backwoods system of timber company roads.

This magnificent semi-wilderness has been known for more than a century to anglers and hunters, sustained in recent winters by snowmobilers. Now word is spreading, thanks chiefly to its reputation as a moose mecca, promoted through the colorful North Country Moose Festival, held the last weekend in August. Visitors are discovering the area's exceptional bird life, its hiking and mountain bike trails, its wilderness cross-country and snowshoeing possibilities, and the expanses of quiet water so inviting to canoeists and kayakers. Lodging options are surprisingly varied and plentiful, ranging from classic lodges like the Glen and Tall Timber Lodge through rental camps to primitive and not-so-primitive campgrounds.

This entire Connecticut Lakes area lies within Pittsburg, New Hampshire's largest and northernmost town. With more than 300 mostly wooded and watery square miles and a population of less than 1,000, Pittsburg retains a frontier atmosphere. Many residents work in the woods and spend their spare hours hunting and fishing, often displaying a spirit of independence that goes back to 1832 when portions of this town became an independent nation called the Indian Stream Republic. The name comes from a tributary of the Connecticut River, but the nation evolved when local settlers, disgruntled by boundary squabbling between Canada and the United States, solved the problem by seceding (at a town meeting) from both countries. They created their own stamps, coins, and government, but their independence lasted only a few years before the Webster-Ashburton Treaty in 1842 put the republic back in New Hampshire.

From Pittsburg two roads (Rts. 3 and 145), both exceptionally scenic, run south to bustling, friendly Colebrook, a crossroads shopping center (junction of east–west Rt. 26 from Errol as well as north–south Rt. 3 from Lancaster) for the Vermont communities of Canaan and Beecher Falls (site of Ethan Allen's huge furniture factory) as well as Columbia, Stewartstown, Errol, Pittsburg, and Dixville Notch.

Not so much a town as it is a place (since its tiny population is mostly connected with The Balsams resort), Dixville gets a moment of fame every 4 years when all 30 voters stay up past midnight to cast the first votes in the presidential election. The northernmost of New Hampshire's notches, Dixville is worth the ride just for views of this rugged, narrow pass surrounding The Balsams, the grandest of all New England's grand old hotels. It draws repeat winter- and summer-season patrons from every corner of the country, for a week at a time. It's been lucky in its ownership. In 1954, when it came up for auction, the hotel was acquired by Neil Tillotson, a descendant of Dixville Notch homesteaders. An inventor and inventive businessman, Tillotson (who died at age 102 in 2001) installed a rubber balloon factory in the former garage (still producing medical exam gloves). Even if you aren't a registered guest here, be sure to stop. The palatial resort—its dining rooms, golf courses, and 15,000-acre property webbed with hiking, mountain biking, and cross-country ski trails—welcomes visitors.

Dixville Notch lies midway between Colebrook on the Connecticut River and Umbagog Lake, long a mecca for birders and anglers and now both a national wildlife refuge and a state park. Nearby Errol (population: 303) serves as the hub for canoeing, fishing, and otherwise exploring both the lake and the wooded corridor along the Androscoggin River to the south.

GUIDANCE **North Country Chamber of Commerce** (603-237-8939; 1-800-698-8939; www.northcountrychamber.org), P.O. Box 1, Colebrook 03576. Rt. 3, 1.5 miles north of Colebrook. Open year-round weekdays 9–noon. The chamber offices are in The **Great North Woods Welcome Center**, open year round daily 9–7, weekends 8–8. This is an exceptional rest area stocked with information on the entire area, from Island Pond, Vt., on the west to Errol on the east. Other helpful web sites: www.northnh.com; www.ctrivertravel.net; www.nh connlakes.com; www.greatnorthwoods.org.

Umbagog Area Chamber of Commerce (603-482-3906; www.umbagog chambercommerce.com) is a year-round source of information with a seasonal booth that also serves the Errol area.

Note: Pick up a current local map at a local store. We bought *Connecticut Lakes Region Pittsburg, NH Road & Trail Guide*, printed in Colebrook,

Christina Tree

showing local woods roads (which change each year) and pinpointing landmarks like Magalloway Mountain and Garfield Falls. The *Colebrook Chronicle* (free) is an excellent way of tuning in to the local scene, accessible online: www.colebrookchronicle.com, and the *News and Sentinel*, Inc., keeps you up to date on all so-called happenings and upcoming events. www.colebrooknewsandsentinel.com.

GETTING AROUND *Crossing the border:* The U.S. Customs and Immigration Service maintains a point-of-entry station in Pittsburg on Rt. 3 at the international border (819-656-2261), open 24 hours, 7 days a week.

Note: Throughout this area, especially above the village of Pittsburg, moose are quite common—especially at dusk when they are least visible to vehicles. Proceed slowly.

MEDICAL EMERGENCY **911** works throughout the region.

Upper Connecticut Valley Hospital (603-237-4971), Corliss Lane (off Rt. 145), Colebrook. This little, well-equipped hospital is the health care center for a large area of northern New Hampshire, Quebec, Vermont, and Maine. At least one doctor has a private plane and makes house calls by air.

✳ To See

MOOSE

The local "Moose Alley" is Rt. 3 north from Pittsburg to the Canadian border. The annual North Country Moose Festival, held the last weekend in August, has become the region's biggest event, usually attracting more than 3,000 people, featuring a Moose Calling Contest, street fairs and dancing, barbecues, an antique car show, and a moose stew cook-off.

SCENIC DRIVES **Rt. 3 north** from Pittsburg. It's 22.5 miles from the village to the border, much of it through the Connecticut Lakes State Forest, a wooded corridor along both sides of Rt. 3, from the northern end of the First Connecticut Lake to the Canadian border. Lake Francis comes into view in the village of Pittsburg itself. Look for the turnoff for Lake Francis State Park, a right after the left

Christina Tree

turn for Back Lake. First Connecticut Lake is next, sprinkled with lodges and cabins off the shore along Rt. 3 but uninterrupted forest on the far side. Note the lakeside picnic facilities. When you next see the Connecticut River itself, just south of the Second Connecticut Lake, it is a small stream. Note the Deer Mountain Campground next on your left, and finally the Third Connecticut Lake. Even in mid-August the light is northern here, and the sky seems very close. Third

ABOUT MOOSE

Moose are the largest animal found in the wilds of New England. They grow to be 10 feet tall and average 1,000 pounds in weight. The largest member of the deer family, they have a large, protruding upper lip and a distinctive "bell" or "dewlap" dangling from their muzzle.

"Bull" (male) moose have long been prized for their antlers, which grow to a span of up to 6 feet. They are shed in January and grow again. Female moose ("cows") do not grow antlers, and their heads are lighter in color than the bull. All moose, however, are darker in spring than summer, grayer in winter.

Front hooves are longer than the rear, as are the legs, the better to cope with deep snow and water. In summer they favor wetlands and can usually be found near ponds or watery bogs. They also like salt and so tend to create and frequent "wallows," wet areas handy to road salt (the attraction of paved roads).

Moose are vegetarians, daily consuming more than 50 pounds of leaves, grass, and other greenery when they can find it. In winter their diet consists largely of bark and twigs. Mating season is mid-September until late October. Calves are born in early spring and weigh in at 30 pounds. They grow quickly but keep close to their mothers for an entire year. At best moose live 12 years.

When under attack, moose face their attacker and stand their ground—so it's natural for them to freeze when a car approaches head-on. It's best to stop and pull to the side of the road yourself.

Moose are most numerous along roads early in the morning and again at dusk. Along "Moose Alleys" such as Rt. 3 north of Pittsburg and Rt. 16 north of Berlin, it's not unusual to see a dozen within that many miles, especially as the summer wears on and the animals become accustomed to "moose-watchers." Remember, however, that moose are wild animals. Don't try to see how close you can get.

While the area's first settlers reported seeing moose aplenty, they were hunted so aggressively (the tongue and nose were particularly prized as delicacies in 19th-century Boston) that they dwindled to a dozen or so in the entire state. The current count is around 9,500. New Hampshire's annual moose hunt is 9 days, beginning the third Saturday in October.

WARNING

The state records hundreds of often deadly collisions between moose and cars or trucks. The common road sign and bumper sticker reading BRAKE FOR MOOSE means just that. Be extremely wary at dusk when vision is difficult and moose are active.

Christina Tree

A WARNING SIGN AT THE BEGINNING
OF "MOOSE ALLEY," ROUTE 3 NORTH OF
PITTSBURG

Lake is smaller than the others, with wooded mountains rolling away to the east and north.

Magnetic Hill in Chartierville, Quebec. Continue 1 mile north of the border on Rt. 3, then 0.25 mile and turn around. A sign instructs you (in French) to put your vehicle in neutral and hold on while your car is pulled backward uphill. It's one of those things that are impossible to describe.

Rt. 26 from Colebrook through Dixville Notch. Just east of Colebrook, Fish Hatchery Road departs Rt. 26 north for the Diamond Ponds and Coleman State Park. The road is paved most of the way, but several gravel side roads wind over and around the hills of East Colebrook, and one continues on to Stewartstown Hollow and Rt. 145 (see below). Rt. 26 continues to climb gradually into Dixville Notch where the castlelike Balsams Grand Hotel rises above Lake Gloriette, backed in turn by craggy Abenaki Mountain. The road continues to climb by Table Rock and crests before spiraling down between sheer mountain walls. Note the picnic area on Flume Brook and, a bit farther west, the turnoff to the picnic area at Huntington Cascades. Rt. 26 continues 5 more miles to Errol, site of Umbagog Lake State Park. Rt. 26 south through Thirteen Mile Woods and the loop back via Rt. 110 to Rt. 3 takes you through uninterrupted timberlands.

Rt. 145 between Colebrook and Pittsburg is best driven from north to south for the sweeping view from Ben Young Hill. En route to and from Pittsburg, you will cross the 45th parallel, halfway between the North Pole and the equator. Dairy farms with red barns are impressive, dotting the hillsides and views. Beaver Brook Falls, just north of Colebrook on Rt. 145, is the local Niagara, with a picnic area maintained by the Kiwanis.

HISTORICAL SOCIETIES AND MUSEUMS **Colebrook Area Historical Society** (603-237-4470), Colebrook Town Hall, 2nd floor, Bridge St. Open July and Aug., Sat. 10–2. **Pittsburg Historical Society** (603-538-6342) maintains a museum in the town hall that's open for the July 4 Moose Festival, Old Home Day in August, and 1–3 PM on Sat. in July and Aug. Town memorabilia aside, this museum displays a flag of the Indian Stream Republic and material relating to it.

In Canaan, Vt., just over the bridge from West Stewartstown, the **Alice M. Ward Memorial Library**, open daily, houses the Canaan Historical Society's fascinating changing exhibits. The lovely yellow, Greek Revival building was built as a tavern in 1846 and said to have served for a while as the northernmost U.S. stop on the Underground Railroad.

The **Poore Family Homestead Historic Farm Museum** (603-237-5500), Rt. 145 halfway between Colebrook and Pittsburg, is generally open June–Sep., weekdays 11–1, weekends 11–4, and for special events. The 1840s barn displays tools and daily household and farm equipment. The neighboring 1825 farmhouse on this 100-acre property is under restoration (suggested donation $4 per adult). Inquire about concerts and demonstrations.

COVERED BRIDGES **The Columbia bridge** crosses the Connecticut River south of Colebrook, linking Columbia village with Lemington, Vt. Pittsburg has three covered bridges: The **Pittsburg–Clarksville bridge**, 91 feet long, is off Rt. 3, 0.25 mile east of Pittsburg village; **Happy Corner bridge**, 86 feet long, is east of Rt. 3, 6 miles northeast of the village; **River Road bridge**, 57 feet long and one of the state's smallest covered bridges, is 1 mile east of Rt. 3, 7 miles northeast of the village.

✳ To Do

BIKING Request or pick up a free map/guide, *Great North Woods Bicycle Routes* (www.nhbikeped.com) from the North Country Chamber of Commerce. Actually this is a no-brainer if you want to stick to paved roads; for mountain bikers there are miles and miles of woodland roads. **Tall Timber Lodge** (603-538-6651) rents mountain bikes.

BIRDING A splendid, free *Connecticut River Birding Trail/Northern Section* map/guide is available from local lodges and by contacting the Connecticut River Birding Trail (802-291-9100, ext.107; www.birdtrail.org), 104 Railroad Row, White River Junction, VT 05001.

BOATING, INCLUDING CANOEING AND KAYAKING Several lodges keep paddleboats moored on more than one lake for use by guests. **Pathfinder Tours** (603-538-7001) based at Timberland Lodge on First Connecticut Lake rents kayaks and also offers guided tours on the lakes and the Connecticut River. **Tall Timber Lodge** rents kayaks for use on Back Lake, and **Lopstick Lodge** does the same for First Connecticut Lake. **The Balsams** offers kayak instruction on Lake Gloriette, kayaking on Mud Pond, and guided tours on Umbagog Lake.

On Lake Umbagog

Northern Waters Outfitters (603-482-3817; www.beoutside.com) in Errol village has rentals, instruction, guided trips, and other canoeing information. They also coordinate flatwater kayak trips on the Magalloway River and Lake Umbagog and offer whitewater rafting, wildlife pontoon boat cruises, and tubing.

Umbagog Outfitters (603-356-3292), Box 268, Errol 03579. Offers guided flatwater and whitewater kayak tours and instruction on Lake Umbagog and nearby rivers.

On the **Connecticut River** paddlers put in at the Vermont end of the Canaan–West Stewartstown bridge off Rt. 3. The only difficult rapids (Class II) in this area are below Columbia. They run for about 7.5 miles and cannot be navigated when the water is low. Paddlers are advised to check the *AMC River Guide: Vermont and New Hampshire* (AMC Books) and two free guides: *Explorations*

Along the Connecticut River Byway of New Hampshire and Vermont, a detailed guide available from the Connecticut River Joint Commissions (www.ctriver travel.net), and *Canoeing on the Connecticut River*. See *Connecticut River* in "What's Where."

FISHING Fishing is what this area is about: Operators of most of lodges, motels, and campgrounds depend for their livelihoods on seekers of trout and salmon. The several Connecticut Lakes; Lake Francis; Back Lake; Hall, Indian, and Perry Streams; and the Connecticut River provide miles of shoreline and hundreds of acres of world-class fishing: trophy brook trout, giant browns, and landlocked salmon for both fly- and spin-fishermen. The 2.5-mile "Trophy Stretch" of the Connecticut River (good throughout the summer because of dam releases) is fly-fishing only. The trout season opens Jan. 1 on streams and rivers, on the fourth Sat. in Apr.–Oct. 15 for lakes, but the best fishing months are May, June, and early fall. Most of the lodges provide guides, sell licenses, sell or rent tackle, rent boats, and will give fishing information. The North Country Chamber of Commerce publishes a pamphlet guide listing local ponds, rivers, and rules.

Osprey Fishing Adventures (603-922-3800; www.ospreyfishingadventures .com), P.O. Box 121, Colebrook 03576. Mid-June–Labor Day. The first fishing guide on this uppermost stretch of the Connecticut River, Ken Hastings is a biologist who teaches at Colebrook Academy in the "off-season." His 1- and 3-day fly-fishing trips use a special 14-foot, three-person MacKenzie-style driftboat and include the guide, fly-fishing instruction if requested, and lunch. Both Connecticut and Androscoggin River trips are tailored to meet clients' abilities.

Tall Timber Lodge (1-800-83-LODGE; www.talltimber.com) offers boat rentals and sells a wide selection of flies. Inquire about fly-fishing school.

Lopstick Outfitters and Guide Service (1-800-538-6659; www.lopstick.com), First Connecticut Lake, Pittsburg. Fly-fishing shop, driftboat fishing.

For fishing in the Upper Androscoggin Valley see the previous chapter. **LL Cote**, a sporting goods store in Errol, is the source of fishing tips as well as equipment for Umbagog Lake area (see *Selective Shopping*).

GOLF **Panorama Golf Course** (603-255-4961), part of the Balsams Resort, Dixville Notch. This 18-hole, par-72 course, rolling over beautiful mountain slopes, was designed by Donald Ross in 1912. The lower nine-hole Coashaukee course is great for novices. Pro shop, lessons, and cart rentals; tee times are required.

Colebrook Country Club (603-237-5566; www.colebrookcountryclub.com), Rt. 26, east of Colebrook village. A nine-hole, par-36 course that has a wide following.

HIKING **Fourth Connecticut Lake: The Source**. A small sign just north of the U.S. Customs Station marks the start of the 0.5-mile trail to the 78.1-acre watershed surrounding the pond-sized Fourth Connecticut Lake. Owned and maintained by the New Hampshire Chapter of The Nature Conservancy, it's a surprisingly rugged trail, and you should allow 2 hours to adequately enjoy the round trip. (In 2005 the trail and bridge systems around the lake were generally improved.) The first 15 minutes are the steepest and well worth the effort as you scramble back and forth along the ridge between Canadian and American rocks, with views into the Oz-like Quebec Valley that lies just north, a pastoral mix of farms and woods around the village of Chartierville. At 0.1 mile the Conservancy's trail turns south from the international boundary, and you follow it 0.1 mile to the north end of the lake. The 2.5-acre pond lies in a wooded hollow at 2,670 feet in elevation. According to The Nature Conservancy's pamphlet guide, it's a "northern acidic mountain tarn, a remnant from the post-glacial tundra ecosystem and unusual in New Hampshire." A 0.5-mile path circles the pond, and you can step back and forth across the stream that marks the first few feet of the river's 410-mile course. The actual outlet varies, determined by resident beavers. The entire loop is 1.7 miles.

Monadnock Mountain. Overlooking Colebrook from the Vermont side of the river is Monadnock Mountain, which rises steeply and offers a nice view from the summit fire tower. From Colebrook cross the Connecticut to Rt. 102 in Vermont and turn right. Park in the sand/gravel pit by the marked signs on the left. The trail leads to a former (but safe-to-climb) fire tower.

Table Rock in Dixville Notch. Take Rt. 26 east 10 miles from Colebrook. There's a trailhead parking area on the right, behind the sign ENTERING DIXVILLE NOTCH STATE PARK. This cliff is less than 10 feet wide at its narrowest point; the vertical drop is 700 feet. The view is fabulous, but be careful! The trail is step and rocky and should not be attempted when wet.

Mount Magalloway (2 miles, 1½ hours)—at 3,360 feet, the highest peak in this neck of the woods—offers access to a fire tower. From First Connecticut Lake Dam, turn right just past Coon Brook onto a gravel road and follow LOOKOUT TOWER signs. Two trails, the Coot and the Bobcat, lead to the summit. Coot is quicker, but Bobcat is less strenuous. Bobcat is the recommended way down. *Note:* Logging trucks have right of way on this road.

HUNTING Contact the listed lodges or New Hampshire Fish & Game (603-271-3211; www.wildlife.state.nh.us.

SWIMMING **First Connecticut Lake** has a sandy beach and picnic area; watch for sign on Rt. 3. On **Back Lake** a slide and sand beach are good for young children. **Garfield Falls** is also a local swimming hole. Ask locally about access to this beauty spot: a 40-foot drop in the East Branch of the Dead Diamond River with pools below.

WHITE-WATER RAFTING **Northern Waters Outfitters** (603-482-3817; www.beoutside.com), based in Errol, offers rafting on the Magalloway and Rapid Rivers to take advantage of timed releases, usually the last two weekends in July and first in August. The Magalloway is a beginner-level trip but the Rapid is advanced.

✷ Winter Sports

CROSS-COUNTRY SKIING **The Balsams Grant Resort Hotel** (1-800-255-0600; in New Hampshire, 1-800-255-0800), Rt. 26, Dixville Notch. This 95-km network is one of New England's best-kept secrets. Elevations range from 1,480 feet at Lake Gloriette in front of the hotel to 2,686 feet at the summit of Keyser Mountain. The majority of the 35 trails generally can be skied even when far more famous White Mountain touring centers are brown or icy. Most trails are doubletrack and packed for skating, but a few remain narrow and ungroomed. Our favorite is Canal Trail, a 2-km corridor between tall balsams, following the turn-of-the-20th-century canal that still channels water from Mud Pond (where there's a warming hut) to the hotel. Rentals, lessons. Trail fee; free to guests.

DOWNHILL SKIING **The Balsams Wilderness** (1-800-255-0600; in New Hampshire, 1-800-255-0800), Rt. 26, Dixville Notch. The most remote ski area in New Hampshire, with abundant natural snow, rare lift lines, and a country-club rather than commercial-ski-area feel. Geared to guests at the resort. Lifts: 4 (1 double chair, 2 triple chairs, 1 surface). Trails: 16. Vertical drop: 1,000 feet. Services: Ski school, rentals, restaurant, child care. Rates: Free to inn guests, otherwise $40 per adult on weekends, $35 weekdays; $30 per junior weekends, $25 weekdays.

SNOWMOBILING More than 200 miles of groomed trails are maintained by the **Pittsburg Ridge Runners** alone, one of a dozen North County clubs, linking with trail systems in Maine, Vermont, and Quebec. From the Pittsburg lodges and Colebrook motels, the snowmobiler can head off after breakfast and have lunch in Maine or Canada, then return to the lodge for dinner. For maps and other information, contact the New Hampshire Snowmobile Association (603-224-8906; www.nhsa.com).

Pathfinder Sno-Tours (603-538-7001) offers tours with your own or a rental snowmobile. Rentals are also offered by **Pittsburg Motor Sports** (586-7123) and **Lopstick Snowmobile Rentals**.

The Umbagog Snowmobile Association (603-482-7669; www.umbagog snowmobile.com) based in Errol maintains trails and offers maps for that area. **LL Cote** (1-800-287-7700), Main St., Errol rents as well as sells and services snowmobiles.

TRACKING **Paul Piwarunas** (603-538-0356) is one of several New Hampshire–registered guides who offers winter tracking in the Pittsburg area.

✷ Green Space

Coleman State Park (603-538-6707; off-season, 603-538-6707). Primarily in Stewartstown but accessed from Rt. 26, 12 miles east of Colebrook. Excellent trout fishing in Little Diamond Pond; small boats are permitted but speed is restricted. Pets are permitted. The park marks the terminus of the 55-mile Androscoggin Trail from Berlin.

Lake Umbagog National Wildlife Refuge (603-482-3415), Rt. 16 (5.5 miles north of Errol village), mail: P.O. Box 240, Errol 03579. Umbagog (pronounced *um-BAY-gog*) is said to mean "clear water" in the Abenaki tongue. This 10-mile-long (with more than 50 miles of shoreline and many islands) largely undeveloped lake, with some 15,000 surrounding acres now declared a national wildlife refuge, is one of the finest wild areas in New England. It's home to nesting bald eagles, sharing the skies with ospreys, loons, and varied waterfowl. Moose amble the shorelines, and the fishing is great. The northern end of the lake is the most interesting, especially in the extensive freshwater marshes where the Androscoggin and Magalloway rivers meet. Contact the refuge headquarters for detailed canoe and kayaking routes.

Umbagog Lake State Park (603-482-7795; www.nhstateparks.org), Rt. 26, south of Errol, offers boat rentals (canoes, kayaks, rowboats, and motorboats), boat launch, 35 campsites with water and electrical hookups, three cabins, and 34 remote campsites around the lake, accessible only by boat. There's a beach area for swimming. Admission $3 adults, $1 ages 6–11.

Nash Stream State Forest (603-788-4157) is a 40,000-acre, undeveloped wilderness located in the towns of Odell, Stratford, Columbia, and Stark. Jointly managed by conservation groups and the Forest Serice, it was rescued from sale to a developer back in 1988. It is open to day use for mountain biking, hunting, fishing, hiking, cross-country skiing, and snowmobiling. There is a seasonal, maintained gravel road off Rt. 110 (4 miles west of Groveton, turn north off Emerson Road).

Johnson Memorial Forest (860-642-7283). The trailhead with a user register and posted trail map is on Rt. 3, just above Pittsburg village, across from the fire/safety complex. With 2.5 miles of loop trails, this is a great place for birding.

✳ Lodging

INNS

🐾 ♂ **The Glen** (603-538-6500; 1-800-455-GLEN; www.theglen.org), First Connecticut Lake, Pittsburg 03592. Open early May–mid-Oct. Since 1962 this former private estate (vintage 1904) has been catering to hunters, anglers, and vacationers. Novices to the Great North Woods will feel at home here, thanks to longtime innkeeper Betty Falton, who is so naturally hospitable that everyone immediately feels like family— the kind of family who appreciates the area's excellent birding ("more species of birds than anywhere else in New Hampshire") and moose-watching, mountain biking, and canoeing as well as fishing. Roughly 60 percent of the patrons are, of course, here to fish (staff will serve your catch at one of the three home-cooked meals), but there's no pressure to do anything; just tuning in to the inn's 180-acre lakeside property can absorb a week. The main lodge, with its large stone fireplace and long porch, offers six rooms with twins and doubles with private bath. Seven cabins, some accommodating up to seven people, are scattered along the lake; the two up behind the lodge also have water views. Boats and motors for rent. Rates include all three

RESORT ♂ **The Balsams Grand Resort Hotel** (1-800-255-0600; in New Hampshire, 1-800-255-0800; www.the balsams.com), Rt. 26, Dixville Notch 03576. Open year-round. Set beneath the jagged peaks of Dixville Notch, this rambling hostelry is one of this country's outstanding survivors from the era of the grand resort. First opened in 1866 with 25 rooms, The Balsams now offers more than 200 guest rooms and a staff of more than 300. Under the same ownership since 1954, it saw new management take over in 2005, but initial changes are limited to more flexible dining hours, as well as increased activity and rate options.

Outside, 15,000 acres of mostly wilderness celebrate nature's grandeur; inside, refined elegance reigns. In the evening gentlemen still don jackets and ladies dresses. Even the children—of whom there are usually a number—seem to sense what's expected of them in this opulent world of intricately carved teak, ginger jars, potted palms, and endless carpeting. Youngsters find their way (via an ornate, vintage-1912 Otis elevator) to the library with its tiers of books and piles of puzzles. Some never make it to the pool tables, TV, or game rooms. For adults there is evening music in the Wilderness Lounge, the ballroom, and during dinner.

Dinner is the big event of the day. At 6 PM promptly, the leaded-glass doors of the dining room slide open and guests begin strolling in to eye samples of each dish on the menu—appetizers through desserts—all exhibited on a specially designed, two-tiered table topped by silver candelabra.

Over the last few years all guest rooms have been totally renovated, from plumbing and windows to flower-patterned wallpaper, and their number has been reduced as rooms were merged to create sitting areas and new, larger bathrooms. Closets remain deep and sizable, and the windows are still curtained in organdy, the better to let in the amazing view.

In summer there is the 18-hole, par-72 Panorama Golf Course as well as hiking, biking, tennis, boating, and swimming. The options of horseback riding, whitewater rafting, and guided kayaking as well as pontoon cruises

meals (lunches are boxed): $95–125 per person, discounts for 7 days or more; children 4–16 are one-half adult rates. Pets are permitted in the cabins.

SPORTING LODGES 🐾 ♂ **Tall Timber Lodge** (603-538-6651; 1-800-835-6343; www.talltimber.com), 609 Beach Road, Back Lake, off Rt. 3, Pittsburg 03592. Open year-round. Founded in 1946 and owned by the Caron family since 1982, this is New Hampshire's top sporting camp. With guide services, a tackle shop, and a fly-fishing school, it's a base place for novices as well as seasoned fishers.

Christina Tree

THE BALSAMS GRAND RESORT HOTEL

on nearby Lake Umbagog have recently been added. In addition, a daily summer camp and babysitting are offered.

Winter brings skiing on the resort's own 16-trail ski hill and 95 kilometers of high-elevation, dependably snow-covered trails. Snowshoeing is on an entirely separate, superb 45-km network. Snowmobilers also find direct access to the area's extensive trail system. One way or another you can steep yourself in the magnificence of these mountains.

Rates are on a per-person, per-diem basis and range $125–269, plus tax and service, depending on day and room. Summer rates include all meals; in winter, it's breakfast and dinner. Inquire about special ski and summer week packages, a new leisure plan, B&B rates from $99, and children's rates ($10 times the age of the child).

Guests are also encouraged to try kayaking (rental kayaks), mountain biking (rental mountain bikes), and sledding (rental snowmobiles). Cross-country skiing, hiking, boating, and birding venues are researched by the staff, who all seem to have the same last name. Connie ("Mom"), Judy,

Cindy, Tom, and David Caron operate the lodge and, happily, each seems to have a different area of expertise. In the lodge itself are eight air-conditioned rooms (two with private bath) that share their own upstairs common room with wet bar. The 18 two- to four-bedroom cabins, most lakefront,

Christina Tree

TALL TIMBER LODGE IN PITTSBURG

range from rustically comfortable 1940s "camps" to house-sized retreats with cathedral ceiling, stone fireplace, two-person Jacuzzi, color television, and a wall of glass overlooking the lake. Cabin and cottage rates run $105–355 in high season (Dec. 24– Mar. 12 and May 20–Columbus Day weekend), less off-season and by the week. Lodge rooms are $49–84 (single rates also available). Children under 6 are free; those 6–16 are prorated by age. The Rainbow Grille and Tavern (see *Dining Out*) is open nightly in-season, and breakfast is served daily. Inquire about a variety of packages.

🐾 🐾 **Lopstick Lodge and Cabins** (1-800-538-5569; www.lopstick.com), Rt. 3 at the First Connecticut Lake, offers a wide variety of housekeeping cabins, from vintage one- and two-bedrooms to more than a dozen built or renovated recently and featuring Jacuzzi and gas fireplace. Most overlook First Connecticut, but two are

beside Perry Stream; the most luxurious (three bedrooms) is on Back Lake. $85–300 per cabin in summer. Also see *Fishing*.

Ramblewood Cabins & Campgrounds (603-538-6948; 1-877-RAMBLEWOOD; www.ramblewood cabins.com), 59 Ramblewood Rd., Pittsburg 03492. Strung along the First Connecticut Lake (and Rt. 3), these attractive modern cabins, some Lincoln Log style and almost all log brown, appear to be unusually nicely designed and furnished, some with docks. $80–180 per couple plus $45 per additional adult in summer, slightly more in winter. Inquire about cross-country trails.

In the Lake Umbagog area
🐾 🐾 ♿ **Magalloway River Inn** (603-482-9883; www.magriverinn.com), 3331 Dam Rd. (Rt. 16), Wentworth Location, Errol 03579. Unfortunately the namesake 19th-century inn burned down in 2002, but Granite

State natives Bob and Suzanne Senter have replaced it with five cozy cabins, each with a kitchen/living room combo and sleep sofa as well as bedroom; one is handicapped accessible. $75–85 per couple, $10 per extra person, $5 per pet.

The Errol Motel (603-482-3256; www.errol-motel.com), P.O. Box 328, Rt. 26, Errol 03579. Open year-round under new ownership. There are eight recently renovated rooms and three housekeeping units. Snowmobile trails from the motel connect with all local trails; this is also a popular place for kayakers and fishermen. Rates are $50 per person, $60 per couple, $70 for three. Housekeeping units begin at $70; add $10 per person. Free wireless access and satellite TV.

Worth crossing the Connecticut River

🐾 🎣 **Quimby Country** (802-822-5533; www.quimbycountry.com), P.O. Box 20, Averill, Vt. 05901, 10 miles east of Stewartstown, N.H.). As northeast as you can get in Vermont's Northeast Kingdom. This 1,050-acre resort is a 19th-century lodge and grouping of 20 cabins overlooking 70-acre Forest Lake. It is also 0.25 mile from 1,200-acre Great Averill Pond, 4 miles from 400-acre Little Averill, and surrounded by its own woodland, which, in turn, is surrounded by more woodland, much of it now conservation land. Begun as a fishing lodge in 1894, Quimby Country evolved into a family-oriented resort under the proprietorship of Hortense Quimby, attracting a large following in the process. Fearful that the place might change when it came up for sale upon Miss Quimby's death, a number of regular guests formed a corporation

and bought it. When the place is in full operation, late June–late August, it's about families and returnees. Rates are $145–167 per adult, $65–96 per child depending on age and week, with all three meals and a supervised children's program geared to ages 6–15 that includes swimming, hiking, overnight camping, and rainy-day activities. Reasonable rates during spring fishing season (May 10–June 27), and again August 30 through foliage season when cottages are available on a housekeeping basis and it's quiet enough to hear the leaves fall. This is a great place for birders, walkers, good conversation, and family reunions.

COLEBROOK MOTELS Colebrook motels include the **Northern Comfort** (603-237-4440); the **Colebrook Country Club and Motel** (603-237-5566), which also has a dining room and a lounge; and the **Colebrook House** (603-237-5521; 1-800-626-7331), a small village hotel with motel section, lounge, and dining room.

CAMPGROUNDS **Coleman State Park** (603-237-4560) is in Stewartstown, but it is most easily reached from Rt. 26 east of Colebrook. Open May–mid-Oct. There are 30 tent-camping sites, a recreation building, and picnic tables. Fishing is good in the Diamond Ponds and surrounding streams. No reservations. Fee charged.

Lake Francis State Park (603-538-6965), off Rt. 3 on River Rd., 7 miles north of Pittsburg village. Open mid-May–Columbus Day. This small park beside the 2,000-acre, human-made lake has 40 primitive campsites, a boat-launching ramp, and a picnic area. A popular camping site for anglers and canoeists. No reservations. Fee charged.

Deer Mountain Campground (603-538-6955), Rt. 3, 5.5 miles south of the Canadian border. State run, no electricity, spring for water, earth toilets, 22 primitive sites.

🐾 🛶 **Umbagog Lake State Park** (603-482-7795), Rt. 26, Errol. Mid-May–mid-Sep. Formerly a private campground, this park now offers a store, boat rentals, showers, laundry facilities, housekeeping cabins, and 38 campsites as well as 30 primitive sites accessible only by boat (rentals available). Campers must bring tents and food; there are picnic tables and fireplaces. See **Lake Umbagog National Wildlife Refuge** under *Green Space*.

Note: There are also half a dozen private campgrounds in the area.

✳ Where to Eat

DINING OUT **The Balsams** (603-255-0800; 1-800-255-0800; www.the balsams.com), Rt. 16, Dixville Notch. Breakfast until 10, dinner until 9, Country Club Restaurant open until 7. Check the resort web site for current menus. Note that in addition to the hotel's classic dining room, Beaver Lodge offers an upscale dining option with a table d'hôte menu. For non guests, dining room reservations are requested for the $48, five-course dinner.

Quimby Country (802-822-5533; www.quimbycountry.com), P.O. Box 20, Averill, Vt., 10 miles east of Stewartstown, N.H. Open last week of June–last week in August, serving a very full breakfast ($10) and a generous delicious dinner (BYOB) featuring fresh local produce, on-premises daily baking, and a limited menu as well as weekly lobster bakes ($30 for dinner, plus gratuity).

The Glen (603-538-6500), marked from Rt. 3 on First Lake. Open mid-May–mid-Oct. By reservation, space permitting. When you call, check what's for dinner. It's a blackboard menu and includes everything from juice to dessert. $18–25 per person; add 15 percent gratuity (BYOB). See *Lodging.*

🛶 **Rainbow Grille at Tall Timber Lodge** (603-538-6651; 1-800-83-LODGE), 6091 Beach Rd., Back Lake, Pittsburg. Dinner nightly 5:30–8, Fri. and Sat. until 9. Request a table as close as you can get to windows, overlooking the lake in this lakeside lodge. The house specialty is rainbow trout encrusted with hazelnut flour, pan-fried in lemon butter; also baby back ribs and an extensive selection of Black Angus beef. Entrées $17.95–27.50, including soup or salad. Children's menu and full bar. There's also a reasonably priced tavern menu. Reservations suggested.

Sutton Place (603-237-8842), 152 Main St., Colebrook. In winter open Tue.–Sat. 5:30–9 PM.; in summer nightly. Reservations appreciated. Here's fine, intimate dining in the front rooms of a Queen Anne–style house. Chicken cordon bleu to steak au poivre, with seafood, a few Italian specialties, and a light menu with smaller portions for the diet-conscious. The specialty is lobster pie. Moderately priced; daily specials from $7.95.

🛶 **Indian Stream Eatery** (603-538-9996), Rt. 3, 2 miles south of Pittsburg village. Open daily for lunch and dinner—but check. There's a bar side and an attractive dining side. The specialty is prime rib ($19.95 for 16 ounces, $15.95 for 12 ounces) but most entrées are under $15 (with salad, starch, and rolls). The lunch menu (burgers, wraps, et cetera) is available all day, along with quesadillas and a full range of Tex-Mex.

EATING OUT 🍴 🐾 **Bessie's Diner** (603-266-3310), 166 Gale St., Canaan. Open weekdays from 6 AM, Sat. from 7, and Sun. from 8; closes at 8 every night. Admittedly we're suckers for cheap and friendly, but Vernon and Bonnie Crawford's place is so pleasant and wholesome—ditto for the food—that we can't rave enough. The menu includes burgers, 30 different kinds of sandwiches. We recommend "The Gobbler": turkey, cream cheese, cranberry, and lettuce! Open-faced bagelwiches (try the Grump-Fish), subs, and wraps. Poutines (Quebec-style french fries with gravy and cheese curds) are a specialty; a wide array of dinner choices average $6.75. Service is fast and friendly. Wine and beer. "Cow Licks," an ice cream window, operates summers.

Happy Corner Café (603-538-1144), Rt. 3 Pittsburg. Open Sun.–Thu. 6:30 AM–8 PM, Fri. and Sat. until 9 PM. Sharing the parking lot with Young's, the big supply source for this backcountry, this is a cheerful place specializing in big breakfasts—the usual choices plus biscuits with sausage, gravy, eggs, and home fries ($4.95)—soups (always French onion), sandwiches, pastas, and chicken. Wine and beer served.

Dube's Pittstop (603-538-9944), 1564 Main St., Pittsburg village. The café in this general store (with ATM) is open Mon.–Sat. 5:30 AM–2 PM, Sun.

from 6 AM (check hours; they vary with season). Burgers, omelets, and the like, but the baking is the big thing here, known locally for cookies and whoopee pies.

The Spa Restaurant (603-246-3039), West Stewartstown. Open Mon. and Tue. 3:30 AM–8 PM, Thu. until 9 PM, Fri. and Sat. until 10 PM, Sun. 5 AM–8 PM. This is a big, locally popular place with breakfast specialties that include homemade rolled crêpes ($3.95) and corned beef hash with a poached egg. The lunch and dinner menus are both large. Dinner runs from pizzas through king crab legs and lobster tail.

Wilderness Restaurant (603-237-8779), Main St., Colebrook. Open 3:30 AM–9 PM daily. All down-home cooking; lounge and entertainment on weekends.

Le Rendez Vous Café (603-237-5150), 121 Main St. (corner of Bridge). Open Tue.–Fri. 7–5:30, Sat. from 8. Parisian bakers and cut Belgian chocolates, great pastries and a café full of armchairs and inviting corners seems almost like an apparition on Colebrook's Main Street. Friday is the big bread day; choices includes French baguettes, wheat, Polish, dark rye, and fougasse (herbed), not to mention real croissants.

In Errol

Nothern Exposure (603-482-3468), junction of Rts. 16 and 26. Open weekdays 4 AM–8 PM, Sat. from 5, Sun. 6. Pub opens Thu.–Sat. at 3 PM. On a snowy Sunday in January we waited more than an hour to even place our order here—not because the staff members weren't friendly and efficient, but because this also happens to be at the junction of two major snowmobile trails. Winter weekdays and snowmobile season aside, no problem. This is a popular local gathering place any day, with a downstairs pub.

✳ Selective Shopping

Le Rendez Vous Café (see above), outstanding chocolates and munchies.

Creative Natives (603-237-5541), 117 Main St. A gallery of locally crafted items and collectibles.

The Copper Leaf Gift Shop (603-237-5318), Rt. 3 north of Colebrook. A green warehouse with a retail store showcasing gifty items from the Far East, also manufactures its own art glass.

Young's Store (603-538-6616), Rt. 3, Pittsburg. Everything you can think of needing, way beyond where you thought you'd find it: a huge store with a wide choice of meats, groceries, sporting goods, hunting and fishing licenses, boat and snowmobile registration, diesel and gas, liquor, hardware, and pizza to go.

LL Cote (603-482-7777; www.llcote.com), 25 Main St., Errol. This was the largest establishment in town even before its 2004 expansion. "Coty's" is now 50,000 square feet filled with guns, fishing tackle and flies, bows and arrows, clothing, ATVs, snowmobiles, hardware, and much more. Needless to say, this is information central for fishermen and for supplying northern forest camps and campers for hundreds of surrounding miles. Also rents canoes and kayaks; inquire about snowmobile rentals.

✳ Special Events

February: **Pittsburg-Colebrook Winter Carnival**, Kiwanis Club. Activities and events daily during the week of February school vacation.

March: **Sno-Deo** in Colebrook.

June: **Blessing of the Bikes**, Shrine of Our Lady of Grace, Rt. 3 south of Colebrook. The shrine was built some 50 years ago to serve the motoring public. The festival, held the weekend after Father's Day, attracts thousands of bicyclists and an ever-increasing number of RVs, snowmobiles, and antique cars.

Late June: **Family Fly-Fishing Weekend**, Coleman State Park (603-237-4560), Stewartstown.

Fourth of July: **Fourth of July celebrations**. Fireworks at dusk at Murphy Dam, Lake Francis, also barbecue, live music, airplane rides. Parade and barbecue in Colebook.

Late July: **Logfest** in Stewartstown (www.logfest.com).

Third Sunday of August: **Pittsburg Old Home Day**.

Last week of August: **Annual North Country Moose Festival** (603-237-8939; www.moosefestival.com), Pittsburg, Colebrook, and Errol, N.H., and Canaan, Vt. By far the biggest annual event in the North Country, this is a regionwide celebration of the popular moose with parades, barbecues, dances, auto shows, arts and crafts exhibits, and sales.

September: **Annual Fiddler's Contest**, Colebrook.

INDEX